# RAF Bomber Command Profiles

# 49 Squadron

Chris Ward

www.aviationbooks.org

This edition first published 2023 by Aviation Books Ltd., 25 Cromwell Street, Merthyr Tydfil, CF47 8RY.

Copyright 2023 © Chris Ward.

The right of Chris Ward to be identified as Author of this work is asserted by him in accordance with the Copyright, Designs and Patents Act 1988.

The original Operational Record Book of 49 Squadron RAF and the Bomber Command Night Raid Reports are Crown Copyright and stored in microfiche and digital format by the National Archives. Material is reproduced under Open Licence v. 2.0.

All rights reserved. No part of this publication may be reproduced, stored in a retrieval system, transmitted in any form or by any means, electronic, mechanical or photocopied, recorded or otherwise, without the written permission of the copyright owners.

This squadron profile has been researched, compiled and written by its author, who has made every effort to ensure the accuracy of the information contained in it. The author will not be liable for any damages caused, or alleged to be caused, by any information contained in this book. E. & O.E.

Cover design: Topics - The Creative Partnership www.topicsdesign.co.uk

Photos and captions: Clare Bennett

A CIP catalogue reference for this book is available from the British Library.

ISBN 978 1915335166

Also by Chris Ward from Bomber Command Books:

*Casualty of War: Letters Home from Flight Lieutenant Bill Astell DFC*

*Dambuster Deering: The Life and Death of an Unsung Hero*

*Dambusters : The Complete WWII History of 617 Squadron*
(with Andy Lee and Andreas Wachtel)

Other RAF Bomber Command Profiles:

*10 Squadron* (with Ian MacMillan)
*35 (Madras Presidency) Squadron*
*44 (Rhodesia) Squadron*
*50 Squadron*
*57 Squadron*
*75(NZ) Squadron* (with Chris Newey)
*83 Squadron*
*101 Squadron*
*102 Squadron*
*103 Squadron* (with David Fell)
*106 Squadron* (with Herman Bijlard)
*115 Squadron*
*138 Squadron* (with Piotr Hodyra)
*207 Squadron* (with Raymond Glynne-Owen)
*300 Squadron* (with Grzegorz Korcz)
*301, 304 and 305 Squadrons* (with Grzegorz Korcz)
*460 Squadron RAAF*
*467 Squadron RAAF*
*514 Squadron* (with Simon Hepworth)
*617 Squadron*
*619 Squadron*

# Table of Contents

| | |
|---|---|
| Introduction | 9 |
| Dedication | 11 |
| Narrative History | 12 |
| 1940 First quarter | 14 |
| April 1940 | 16 |
| May 1940 | 20 |
| June 1940 | 25 |
| July 1940 | 32 |
| August 1940 | 36 |
| September 1940 | 42 |
| October 1940 | 49 |
| November 1940 | 54 |
| December 1940 | 60 |
| January 1941 | 64 |
| February 1941 | 67 |
| March 1941 | 71 |
| April 1941 | 75 |
| May 1941 | 81 |
| June 1941 | 86 |
| July 1941 | 92 |
| August 1941 | 100 |
| September 1941 | 109 |
| October 1941 | 116 |
| November 1941 | 119 |
| December 1941 | 123 |
| January 1942 | 172 |
| February 1942 | 178 |
| March 1942 | 183 |
| April 1942 | 188 |
| May 1942 | 195 |
| June 1942 | 199 |

July 1942 ............................................................................................................................. 203

August 1942 ....................................................................................................................... 207

September 1942 ................................................................................................................. 212

October 1942 ...................................................................................................................... 219

November 1942 .................................................................................................................. 224

December 1942 ................................................................................................................... 229

January 1943 ...................................................................................................................... 232

February 1943 .................................................................................................................... 236

March 1943 ........................................................................................................................ 241

April 1943 .......................................................................................................................... 248

May 1943 ........................................................................................................................... 256

June 1943 ........................................................................................................................... 262

July 1943 ............................................................................................................................ 269

August 1943 ....................................................................................................................... 326

September 1943 ................................................................................................................. 334

October 1943 ...................................................................................................................... 340

November 1943 .................................................................................................................. 345

December 1943 ................................................................................................................... 351

January 1944 ...................................................................................................................... 355

February 1944 .................................................................................................................... 361

March 1944 ........................................................................................................................ 365

April 1944 .......................................................................................................................... 372

May 1944 ........................................................................................................................... 380

June 1944 ........................................................................................................................... 387

July 1944 ............................................................................................................................ 394

August 1944 ....................................................................................................................... 402

September 1944 ................................................................................................................. 410

October 1944 ...................................................................................................................... 417

November 1944 .................................................................................................................. 421

December 1944 ................................................................................................................... 426

January 1945 ...................................................................................................................... 431

February 1945 .................................................................................................................... 435

March 1945 ........................................................................................................................ 441

April 1945 ..................................................................................................................447
May 1945 ...................................................................................................................450
Roll of Honour ..........................................................................................................451
STATIONS ................................................................................................................472
COMMANDING OFFICERS ...................................................................................472
AIRCRAFT .................................................................................................................472
OPERATIONAL RECORD .......................................................................................473
CATEGORY OF OPERATIONS ...............................................................................473
Aircraft Histories .......................................................................................................474
Key to Abbreviations .................................................................................................484

# Introduction

RAF Bomber Command Squadron Profiles first appeared in the late nineties and proved to be very popular with enthusiasts of RAF Bomber Command during the Second World War. They became a useful research tool, particularly for those whose family members had served and were no longer around. The original purpose was to provide a point of reference for all of the gallant men and women who had fought the war, either in the air, or on the ground in a support capacity, and for whom no written history of their unit or station existed. I wanted to provide them with something they could hold up, point to and say, "this was my unit, this is what I did in the war". Many veterans were reticent to talk about their time on bombers, partly because of modesty, but perhaps mostly because the majority of those with whom they came into contact had no notion of what it was to be a "Bomber Boy", to face the prospect of death every time they took to the air, whether during training or on operations. Only those who shared the experience really understood what it was to go to war in bombers, which is why reunions were so important. As they approached the end of their lives, many veterans began to speak openly for the first time about their life in wartime Bomber Command, and most were hurt by the callous treatment they received at the hands of successive governments with regard to the lack of recognition of their contribution to victory. It is sad that this recognition in the form of a national memorial and the granting of a campaign medal came too late for the majority. Now this inspirational, noble generation, the like of which will probably never grace this earth again, has all but departed from us, and the world will be a poorer place as a result.

RAF Bomber Command Squadron Profiles are back. The basic format remains, but, where needed, additional information has been provided. Squadron Profiles do not claim to be comprehensive histories, but rather detailed overviews of the activities of the squadron. There is insufficient space to mention as many names as one would like, but all aircraft losses are accompanied by the name of the pilot. Fundamentally, the narrative section is an account of Bomber Command's war from the perspective of the bomber group under which the individual squadron served, and the deeds of the squadron are interwoven into this story. Information has been drawn from official records, such as group, squadron and station ORBs, and from the many, like myself amateur enthusiasts, who dedicate much of their time to researching individual units, and become unrivalled authorities on them. I am grateful for their generous contributions, and their names will appear in the appropriate Profiles. The statistics quoted in this series are taken from The Bomber Command War Diaries, that indispensable tome written by Martin Middlebrook and Chris Everitt, and I am indebted to Martin for his kind permission to use them.

Finally, let me apologize in advance for the inevitable errors, for no matter how hard I and other authors try to write "nothing but the truth", there is no such thing as a definitive account of history, and there will always be room for disagreement and debate. Official records are notoriously unreliable tools, and yet we have little choice but to put our faith in them. It is not my intention to misrepresent any person or Bomber Command unit, and I ask my readers to understand the enormity of the task I have undertaken. It is relatively easy to become an authority on single units or even a bomber group, but I chose to write about them all, idiot that I am, which means 128 squadrons serving operationally in Bomber Command at some time between the 3$^{rd}$ of September 1939 and the 8$^{th}$ of May 1945. I am dealing with eight bomber groups, in which some 120,000 airmen served, and I am juggling around 28,000 aircraft serial numbers, code letters and details of provenance and fate. I ask not for your sympathy, it was, after all, my choice, but rather your understanding if you should find something with which you disagree. My thanks to you, my readers, for making the original series of RAF Bomber Command Squadron Profiles so popular, and I hope you receive this new incarnation equally enthusiastically.

I am indebted to Ed Norman and "the crew", who form the committee of the 49 Squadron Association and kindly gave their approval for this new work on the squadron. All of those seriously interested in WWII RAF Bomber Command are aware of the great work of my friend and namesake, John Ward, whose book, Beware of the Dog At War, set the standard for 49 Squadron histories. John left us far too soon in December 2017 and out of respect for him, I delayed adding the 49 Squadron Profile to the series until a respectable period had passed. Now, five years on from his passing, the time is right and the approval of the committee and their willingness to help with photos and information mean that we can bring this magnificent squadron back into the limelight with a new perspective. My style differs from John's and this account of the squadron's wartime history is intended to stand alongside his and not to eclipse it. My thanks are due, as always, to my gang members, Andreas Wachtel, photo editor, Clare Bennett, Steve Smith and Greg Korcz for their unstinting support, without which my Profiles would be the poorer. Finally, my appreciation to my publisher, Simon Hepworth of Mention the War Publications, for his belief in my work, untiring efforts to promote it, and for the stress I put him through to bring my books to publication.

Chris Ward. Skegness, Lincolnshire. January 2023.

# Dedication

This wartime history of 49 Squadron is dedicated to the memory of John Ward, a close and valued friend and outstanding human being, who left us far too soon on the 5th of December 2017 at the age of 65. John's research into RAF Bomber Command in WWII and his generosity in sharing it, helped us all in our endeavours to keep alive the memory of that unique generation, and his knowledge of 49 Squadron, in particular, was encyclopaedic. Historian, author, artist musician, but above all, family man, he is missed by all who had the privilege to know him.

Rest in peace dear friend.

It is dedicated also to the memory of the 883 members of aircrew who sacrificed their lives in the service of 49 Squadron and to all of the unsung heroes, men and women, who fought their war in a variety of ways on the ground on the bomber stations which 49 Squadron called home.

# Narrative History

Formed on the 15th of April 1916, 49 Squadron began life as a training unit, until moving to France in November 1917 for day bombing and reconnaissance duties. At the conclusion of the Great War, the squadron remained in Germany as part of the force of occupation and was disbanded there on the 18th of July 1919. On the 10th of February 1936, the squadron was reformed in the light bomber role and became the first unit to receive the twin-engine Handley Page Hampden in September 1938. It was with this type that the squadron faced the impending Second World War as one of 5 Group's front-line units under the command of W/C Chick, who had been in post since the end of February.

On the day of the declaration of war, Sunday, the 3rd of September 1939, Bomber Command was represented by 3, 4 and 5 Groups as its main offensive arm, equipped respectively with Wellingtons, Whitleys and Hampdens, while 2 Group operated Blenheim light bombers. 1 Group had been sent to France with its Fairey Battles on the 1st and 2nd of September to operate as the Advanced Air Striking Force (AASF) and would remain there until the fall of France in June. 5 Group, whose Air-Officer-Commanding was Air Commodore Callaway, organised its six front-line squadrons on three stations, 44 and 50 at Waddington, 49 and 83 at Scampton and 61 and 144 at Hemswell. 49 Squadron's strength stood at twenty-four officers and 214 airmen with sixteen Hampdens I.E. (Initial Equipment) and five I.R (Immediate Reserve) and fifteen Hampdens were declared serviceable.

Notification was received at Scampton and Waddington at 17.50 to prepare nine aircraft each to attack enemy warships, which were reported to have sailed from Wilhelmshaven at 14.30. At Scampton, the crews of F/L Lerwill, F/O Learoyd and Sgt Pratt took off at 18.15 in L4036, L4040 and L4093 respectively and, according to the squadron Operations Record Book (ORB), headed for the Horns Reef lightship off the Danish port of Esbjerg. Other sources state the Schillig Roads, located off the north-western corner of Jade Bay, as the destination, some 350 miles distant, and the duration of the flights would seem to support this. Darkness fell before the formation reached the target area, and they were still forty minutes short when adverse weather conditions effectively brought an end to proceedings. They returned to Scampton at 22.30 without having sighted their quarry and would have to wait a considerable time before next venturing into battle. Two of those taking part in this operation would achieve decoration and fame in the years ahead, 49 Squadron's F/O Learoyd, and 83 Squadron's F/O Guy Gibson.

On the 14th, Air Commodore Callaway was posted to HQ 18 Group to be succeeded by Air Vice Marshal Arthur Harris, who would become a household name in the ensuing years of war. On the 29th of September, 5 Group sent eleven Hampdens from Hemswell in two sections to attack enemy warships in the Heligoland area, from which the 144 Squadron element of five failed to return. There would be a number of further small-scale forays by the group, and some of a larger-scale by other groups, during which, the Command learned some expensive but valuable lessons about daylight unescorted incursions into enemy airspace. In fact, by the outbreak of war, 4 Group alone had trained its crews to operate by night, and for the remainder of 1939 and into early 1940, 4 Group Whitleys would roam far and wide over a blacked-out Germany, conducting reconnaissance and leafleting (nickelling) sorties, which condemned the crews to trips of up to twelve hours in the extreme discomfort of unheated aircraft. Most survived and learned a great deal about how to operate and navigate by night, while the rest of the Command clung to an as yet unproved theory.

In 1919, Italian air-war strategist, General Giulio Douhet, had propounded the idea that future wars would be fought between giant armadas of self-defending bombers, flying directly over the front lines in daylight to target the economic centres of the enemy, and, thereby, destroy its will and capability to continue the fight. This theory would gain support in a number of countries, in Britain with Arthur Harris, in America with Billy Mitchell and in Germany with Walther Wever. Fortunately for the conduct of WWII, Wever would lose his life in a flying accident in 1935 and the development of the Luftwaffe be put in the hands of army minded strategists, who saw bombing as a tactical extension of artillery. This would prove to be an inspired decision in a short war, and Blitzkrieg would be highly successful in rolling up France and the Low Countries. However, an extended conflict required a strategic bomber force, and by the time Germany realized that fact, it would be too late to catch up. The main flaw in the Douhet theory concerned the suggested ability of bombers to get through in sufficient numbers in daylight to reach the target. During a shipping sweep in the Schillig Roads on the 14th of December, five of twelve Wellingtons would be lost, and twelve out of twenty-two on the 18th. This would force the air planners to take stock, and, ultimately, would lead to all but 2 Group becoming a largely nocturnal force.

49 Squadron suffered its first wartime casualties by way of a training accident involving Anson N5096, one of a number of the type on squadron strength employed for training purposes, which crashed in flames in the grounds of the Radcliffe mental hospital in Nottinghamshire on the 4th of October, killing P/O Harker and the other occupant. An even more tragic outcome attended the loss of L4034, also during training on the 23rd of November. While adopting a ZZ approach to land at Waddington in very poor visibility during a training flight, the Hampden appeared suddenly out of the gloom at around ten feet heading directly for the watchtower. In attempting to avoid it, S/L McGregor-Watt banked and flew into the side of a hangar, killing all on board and five men working inside. Acting F/L Allen arrived from 44 Squadron on the 24th and he and acting F/L Lowe were handed the acting rank of squadron leader to enable them respectively to succeed S/L McGregor-Watt and the posted-out S/L Rae as flight commanders.

On the 2nd of December, acting W/C Sheen was posted in from his command of 106 Squadron, which at this stage of the war was non-operational and performing the role of group pool training, in which it prepared new crews for squadron service. A few days later, he took over the reins of command at the departure of W/C Chick to a staff job at 40 (Maintenance) Group. Also, during the 2nd, the squadron operated for only the second time during the war to date, when dispatching three B Flight Hampdens from Scampton at 11.45 on a shipping sweep over the North Sea. Each carried four 500lb SAP (Semi-Armour-Piercing) bombs, for which the crews of F/O Mitchell and Sgts Benson and Marshall found no suitable target in deteriorating weather conditions and returned after dark at 17.07, complaining of cold. On the 3rd, P/O Peter Ward-Hunt arrived on attachment from 106 Squadron pending posting and would prove to be one of the outstanding characters in 5 Group in a career that would see him serve a number of squadrons and survive the war.

Late on the evening of the 20th, Scampton and Waddington were alerted to prepare twelve aircraft each for an operation to seek out and attack the German "pocket battleship", Deutschland, which was believed to be off the coast of Norway. Deutschland would soon be renamed Lützow, to avoid the risk to national pride should she be lost in battle while bearing the nation's name, the original Lützow having been sold to the Russians even before her superstructure had been completed. Their sister vessel, Admiral Graf Spee, had just been lost following the epic and tension-filled stand-off in Montivideo harbour, where she had sought sanctuary after the Battle of the River Plate. Wishing to avoid an unnecessary loss of life for no possible gain, Kapitän-zur-See, Hans Langsdorff, had scuttled her in the mouth of the river on the 17th of December, before committing suicide two days later. 49 Squadron briefed nine crews and 83 Squadron three, which departed Scampton at 08.00 on the 21st with W/C Sheen and S/L Allen the senior pilots on duty and W/C Sheen in overall command of the operation. They rendezvoused with the Waddington element at 08.10, before heading for the Lincolnshire coast at Skegness, which they crossed at 08.25 on course for the Lister Fjord, which feeds into the Waddensee off the western coast of the Schleswig-Holstein peninsula. They flew out at 1,000 feet beneath ten-tenths cloud, which dissipated from the mid-point of the North Sea, allowing them to climb to 8,000 feet until approaching the Danish coast, at which point the conditions deteriorated and forced them back down to 1,000 feet. Having reached the limit of their range without sighting the target, they headed back for a planned landing at Kinloss and Lossiemouth in Scotland, but in poor visibility, the Scampton contingent eventually found itself over Northumberland and put down at Acklington. L4072 ran out of fuel on approach and struck a chapel building one mile from the airfield at 16.00, before crashing with fatal consequences for two of the crew, and injuring the pilot, Sgt Marshall, and his navigator. Meanwhile, the 44 Squadron element had been intercepted by Spitfires from Drem and two shot down into the sea off Berwick, a tragic incident that cost the life of one crew member.

There would be no further operational activity for the squadron before the year ended, and after almost four months of hostilities, the tally to date stood at three operations, fifteen sorties, the loss of an Anson and a Hampden to training accidents costing six lives and a single Hampden from an operation with two fatalities.

# 1940 First quarter

The winter of 1939/40 would prove to be particularly harsh and would severely restrict opportunities to fly training and operational sorties until its grip weakened in a gradual thaw towards the end of February. The American press dubbed this period the "Phoney War", an apt description considering the reluctance of either combatant to attack the other's territory for fear of reprisals. It should be remembered that attacks on private property were still off-limits, which meant that the only legitimate targets were military ships at sea, where stray bombs could not hit land. The conditions actually seemed to worsen as the new year progressed, but, before the snow brought a complete cessation of activity, the squadron managed to get off three leafleting sorties on the 18th of January to Hannover, Bremen and Braunschweig (Brunswick), flown by the senior officers, W/C Sheen, and S/Ls Lowe and Allen in L4092, P1177 and P1174 respectively. They departed Scampton between 17.15 and 17.40 and returned some five hours later complaining of extreme cold and difficulty in dispensing the propaganda material efficiently through the flare chute.

On the 26th, the squadron moved up to Kinloss on detachment to 18 (Reconnaissance) Group of Coastal Command, from where it would provide defensive cover for large convoys from Norway, which might come under attack from German surface vessels. They would stand-by for operations whenever convoys were at sea, but not be called into action, and it was during this period on the 16th and 17th, that the armed German tanker/supply vessel, Altmark, had become cornered by elements of the Royal Navy in Jøssingfjord in south-western Norway and had been fired upon and boarded in what the Germans correctly claimed were waters belonging to neutral Norway. Altmark had famously acted as the supply vessel for the Graf Spee, which sank nine merchant ships during its highly productive campaign off Africa and in the South Atlantic between September and December 1939. The crews of the merchantmen had been picked up by Graf Spee and transferred to Altmark, and the three hundred merchant sailors found on board were liberated. Eight German sailors were killed by small arms fire during the action, and the Germans denounced the episode as a gross violation of international law and Norwegian neutrality. The Waddington, Scampton and Hemswell squadrons were put on stand-by on the 17th to attack Altmark or any naval escorts, but, in the event, the thirty-six Hampdens were not called into action. On the 18th, German naval units were reported to be icebound in the Heligoland Bight and 5 Group was put on stand-by to take advantage between the 19th and the 22nd, but again, nothing became of it.

A month had elapsed in Scotland before elements of 49 Squadron were called into action for a navigation and reconnaissance exercise on the 26th involving seven Hampdens. Each was loaded with two 500lb SAP bombs and departed Kinloss at 11.10 in two sections of three led by W/C Sheen and P/O Drakes, with S/L Allen flying independently but in close contact. They were to proceed to Kinnaird Head and conduct a square search within a radius of twenty miles and attack only submarines, should any be sighted. S/L Allen turned back at 12.10 because of an engine issue and the others returned safely between 16.00 and 16.10 with their bombs still on board. A similar training exercise on the 28th involving six aircraft under the command of F/L Mitchell proved to be equally unrewarding and it was the same story on the 2nd of March, when W/C Sheen led a formation of six.

On the 19th, 49 Squadron was ordered to return to Scampton having missed nothing of consequence during its absence, as there had been little to occupy the squadrons of Bomber Command while the ban on bombing of enemy territory held firm on both sides. Occasional leafleting sorties and sea patrols over German seaplane bases broke the monotony of training, until the gloves partially came off on the day that 49 Squadron was preparing to return to 5 Group. At dusk on the 16th, fifteen enemy bombers had carried out attacks on elements of the Royal Navy at Scapa Flow in the Orkneys, hitting HMS Norfolk and killing four of her officers. Bombs also fell close to Hatstone aerodrome and Bridge of Wraith on the road between Kirkwall and Stromness on the island of Hoy, and two cottages had been damaged, leading to the death of one civilian and injury to seven others. In retaliation for this, orders were issued on the 19th to carry out an attack on the seaplane base at Hörnum, located on the southern tip of the island of Sylt, off the western coast of the Schleswig-Holstein peninsula. 4 Group made ready thirty Whitleys, which were assigned a four-hour slot in which to carry out their attacks, to be followed by twenty 5 Group Hampdens from Waddington and Hemswell during a two-hour window later in the evening. As events were to prove, this would be an undistinguished first deliberate attack on a German land target, despite the fact that the majority of returning 4 and 5 Group crews were enthusiastic about their part in the raid and were convinced that the base had been severely damaged. It was a claim that was splashed across the front pages of the dailies, 5 Group recording that its aircraft had attacked between 23.45 and 01.50 from heights ranging from 1,000 to 10,000 feet and had delivered a total of sixteen 500 and forty-four 250 pounders along with 660 x 4lb incendiaries. The report added that the hangars had been hit several times and direct hits were observed on the living quarters and slipway. A cursory reconnaissance a day or so later failed to detect any signs of damage, which raised eyebrows in high places, and it was not possible to carry out a full reconnaissance until the 6th of April, which confirmed the worst fears. This would be the first of countless examples of overly enthusiastic claims of success by bomber crews, however, the propaganda value to the folks at home was massive. Only one aircraft failed to return, and all the Hampdens got back safely.

Serving with 49 Squadron at this stage of the war were a number of notable officers, who would progress to greater things in the future. S/L "Bob" Allen was destined to command 106 Squadron, where he would be Guy Gibson's predecessor, and F/O Laurence Deane would attain the rank of Group Captain and lead 83 Squadron in 1944. F/O Learoyd would win the Victoria Cross before the year was out, and eventually take command of 83 Squadron and eventually 44 Squadron. Canadian, F/L Nellis Timmerman became the first commanding officer of 408 (Goose) Squadron RCAF, and P/O "Penny Beauchamp joined 207 Squadron during its time with the troublesome Manchester in 1941, before, in 1944, taking command of 100 Group's 157 Squadron, with which he would become the scourge of Luftwaffe night-fighter crews while flying "Serrate" Mosquitos. Serving with him at 207 Squadron would be F/O Peter Ward-Hunt, whose operational days were to end as a flight commander under Gibson at 106 Squadron, before he was eventually posted to a staff job at Ludford Magna.

## April 1940

Squadron strength on the 1st, the day on which W/C Gillan was posted in from the Air Ministry as commanding officer elect, stood at thirty-four officers and 276 other ranks, with sixteen Hampdens I.E. That evening, the crews of F/O Forsyth, F/O White and the newly promoted F/L Timmerman departed Scampton at 22.15, 22.42 and 23.40 respectively to reconnoitre the Frisian Islands of Borkum and Norderney and Sylt further north, and all returned safely between 04.30 and 06.15 with nothing of value to report other than a dozen searchlights aimed at F/O White over Sylt. On the 5th, F/Os Burnett and Learoyd were briefed to carry out security patrols over Borkum and Norderney and reconnoitre Jade Bay and the Schillig Roads in search of capital ships. They departed Scampton at 20.05 and 20.25 respectively each loaded with six 250 pounders and returned after six hours having seen nothing of interest. The operation was repeated on the following evening by the crews of F/O Forsyth, Sgt Hills and S/L Lowe, the last mentioned with P/O Beauchamp flying as navigator. The fighter style single occupant cockpit arrangement of the Hampden dictated that second pilots gain experience by flying as many as a dozen sorties as navigator/bomb-aimer before being given command of their own crew. They took off at five-minute intervals from 19.30, and on return at 02.05, S/L Lowe and crew reported flying directly over a battleship at berth in Wilhelmshaven and being fired upon by "pom-poms", which missed.

On the 8th, W/C Gillan became the new commanding officer on the posting of W/C Sheen to 5 Group HQ. His appointment coincided with Bomber Command's first real campaign as the German invasion of Norway and Denmark on the 9th brought an end to the shadow boxing that had characterized events since September, and it was the signal for the strategic bombing war to begin hesitantly, but in earnest. It took German forces just six hours to subdue Danish resistance after sending in forces by ground, sea and air, while the Norwegians would resist for two months, supported by British and French forces. 5 Group responded by sending twenty-four Hampdens in search of enemy warships and troop transports off Bergen on the 9th, and although twelve of the force were recalled, two of the remainder claimed hits on a cruiser. F/L Timmerman and F/O Forsyth and their crews departed Scampton at 23.20 and 23.50 respectively on the 10th to join four others from 5 Group to patrol seaplane bases on Borkum and Sylt and returned at dawn with nothing to report.

Elements of the Royal Navy and the Kriegsmarine came face-to-face on the 10th and 13th, and this was followed by landings at Narvik involving British, French and Polish troops, which linked up with Norwegian forces. Bomber Command was prevented by the extreme range from directly supporting the landings and would focus instead on attacking enemy supplies of men and materials arriving by air on airfields at Oslo and Stavanger and by sea in the southern ports. On the 11th, squadrons across the Command were instructed to prepare for what would be the largest commitment of bombers since the war began. Eighty-three Wellingtons, Hampdens and Blenheims were assembled for the operation, which would take place on the following day, but in the meantime, six Hampdens were sent to Kristiansand Bay in daylight to search for shipping, including the Admiral Scheer, which was the third of the three Deutschland Class "pocket battleships", along with Graf Spee and Deutschland (Lützow). In the event, a lack of cloud cover forced them to turn back, while that night, twenty Hampdens joined a contingent of Whitleys in a shipping sweep from Kiel Bay to Oslo, and at least one ship was hit. The 49 Squadron ORB offers a confusing insight, which suggests that six of its Hampdens took off at ten-minute intervals from 22.00 on the night of the 11/12th to carry out a reconnaissance of the "Fredericia-Middelfart-Little Belt-Kattegat region off Denmark's eastern coast and deliver nickels (leaflets) to the populace. They were under strict instructions to not employ machine gun fire against land targets and inland waterways and to be west of 04.00E by dawn. Sadly, the names of the crews involved were not recorded.

At 08.20 on the 12th, seven Hampdens from 44 Squadron followed five of 50 Squadron into the air to conduct a shipping search in Kristiansand harbour, after reports of the presence in the region of the heavy cruisers, Scharnhorst and Gneisenau. The Admiral Scheer was not mentioned specifically on this occasion but was almost certainly among the capital ships gathered near the port. Four 50 Squadron Hampdens and two from 44 Squadron were hacked down by German fighters and this effectively put an end to daylight operations by all but 2 Group.

On the night of the 13/14th, 5 Group carried out the first mine-laying operation of the war, a task to which the Hampden was to prove itself eminently suited. This would represent the initial tentative steps in a new departure for Bomber Command operations, which would prove to be hugely successful, and by war's end, would have sunk or damaged more enemy vessels than the Royal Navy. The laying of parachute mines by air was given the code-name "gardening" and the entire enemy-held coastline from the Pyrenees in the south-west to the Baltic port of Königsberg in the north-east, and even the northern Italian coast, would be divided into gardens, each with a horticultural or marine biological name. The process of delivery was known as planting and the mines, themselves, were referred to as vegetables, and it would not be long before the other groups joined in to create a spiders' web of mines in chains across all of the sea-lanes employed by the enemy. There were no gardens allotted to the Kristiansand coastal region of south-western Norway at this early stage, and areas A and B were referred to in the ORBs, which would later become the Silverthorn and Hawthorn gardens off the east and west coasts respectively of Jutland. On this night, Waddington, Hemswell and Scampton provided fifteen Hampdens between them for mining duties, for which the crews of S/L Allen, F/L Mitchell and F/O Forsyth departed Scampton between 19.30 and 19.42 to operate in the sea lanes of the Skagerrak and Kattegat between the German ports and southern Norway. They were airborne for up to seven-and-a-quarter hours and it was calculated that each aircraft consumed seventy gallons of fuel per hour. Details were scant, and we are told only that the operation was carried out satisfactorily.

On the 14th, all three 5 Group operational stations were notified of further mining operations that night off Denmark, for which twenty-eight Hampdens were made ready, three of them by 49 Squadron at Scampton. The crews of S/L Lowe, F/L Mitchell and F/O Forsyth took off at five-minute intervals from 19.00 and headed for the Carrot garden in the Little Belt region of the western Baltic but ran into inhospitable weather conditions that would prevent them from fulfilling their briefs. F/L Mitchell and F/O Forsyth returned safely at around midnight, while S/L Lowe was experiencing difficulty in establishing a bearing and one provided by Hemswell proved to be inaccurate. An aerodrome was spotted as they crossed the Northumberland coast, but it could not be raised by radio or Aldis Lamp and it was only after the firing of a verey cartridge that searchlights came on to the north. Heading in that direction and running low on fuel, an engine failed and the other one began to falter, at which point the crew was given the option to bale out. None wished to do so, and S/L Lowe ordered them to gather in the compartment behind the cockpit while he prepared to force-land L4043, a precarious undertaking in a barely controllable aircraft. Unable to remain airborne any longer, S/L Lowe pulled off a tail-first landing at 00.30 on a beach near the mining village of Ryehope, situated between Seaham and Sunderland, sadly, before gunner, P/O Bryan-Smith, had fully accessed the compartment and he was killed instantly. The other occupants sustained injury but were able to extricate themselves from the wreckage. *(Co-incidentally, it would be at Ryehope on the 31st of March 1944 that F/O Cyril Barton earned a posthumous Victoria Cross, the only one gained in a Halifax, for sacrificing his life in the act of saving his crew on return from the Nuremberg disaster).*

Thirty-three Hampdens were made ready for a return to the Baltic, to the Asparagus (Great Belt) and Carrot (Little Belt) gardens on the 17th, which provided W/C Gillan with the opportunity to register his first operational sortie with the squadron. He and his crew departed Scampton at 20.05 and set course for the Carrot garden, located to the south of Denmark's Fyn Island, and was followed over the ensuing forty-nine minutes by the crews of F/O Robinson, F/L Timmerman and F/O Learoyd. They had reached Jutland's western coast by the time that F/O Forsyth took off at 23.05 bound for a reconnaissance sortie, it is believed, to the Alborg area of north-eastern Jutland, where an important aerodrome was supporting Germany's Norwegian campaign and was on Bomber Command's to-do list. The night's final take-off involved the crew of F/L Mitchell at 23.50 with a similar brief to that of F/O Forsyth, and all returned safely from their respective duties between 02.15 and 06.00.

5 Group launched a major mining effort on the 21st, detailing seventeen Hampdens each from Waddington and Scampton and a dozen from Hemswell to operate in the Baltic and the Eglantine garden in the Elbe Estuary, the vital waterway providing access to Germany's second city,

Hamburg and passage from there to the North Sea for its merchant, naval and U-Boot fleets. 49 Squadron made ready eight Hampdens, which departed Scampton between 19.00 and 20.00 with S/L Allen the senior pilot on duty and the seven-hour-plus duration of their sorties suggest that they were bound for one of the Baltic gardens, Asparagus, Carrot and Daffodil (Oresund or The Sound, located between Copenhagen and Sweden's western coast.) The 49 Squadron ORB is scant on detail, but other records tell us that the moonlight was so bright as landfall was made on Germany's western coast in the region of Sylt and Husum that it was possible for crews to map read their way across the Schleswig-Holstein peninsula. F/O Robinson and crew were coned by searchlights as they crossed Sylt and were subjected to a hostile flak reception but came through unscathed and continued on to deliver their mines as briefed. At this stage of the war, and until well into 1943, mining was conducted from low level, typically from between 500 and 800 feet, from where accuracy could be guaranteed and the greatest danger came in the form of light flak from shore and ship-based batteries. On return to Scampton at 03.15, F/O White overshot his landing in P1175 and wrote it off, happily without casualties among the crew. At debriefing, S/L Allen reported observing ten ships at anchor in the River Elbe, and one must assume that he planted his vegetable here, before continuing on to the north to the town of Schleswig, where he came upon an aerodrome with an illuminated flarepath and hangars. He joined the circuit and orbited four times to take in the details, before setting course for home with one mine still on board.

The 23rd brought further mining operations in the Baltic for twenty-seven Hampdens, eleven based at Scampton and five of which represented 49 Squadron, whose crews learned at briefing that their destinations were the previously visited Carrot garden in the Little Belt, and Hollyhock, located off Travemünde at the mouth of the waterway leading to the Hansastadt (ancient free trade city) and port of Lübeck. They departed Scampton at five-minute intervals from 19.00 with W/C Gillan and S/L Allen the senior pilots on duty and all returned to diversion airfields after round trips of up to seven-and-three-quarter hours duration. We have no insight into the conduct of their sorties, other than a report by W/C Gillan that he had instructed his rear gunner to strafe a nearby 250-ton vessel to distract its crew from observing the point of entry of the mines. The enemy responded with inaccurate tracer, and W/C Gillan landed safely at Martlesham Heath at 02.45.

Two nights later, 5 Group committed twenty-eight Hampdens to mining duties in the Forget-me-not garden, located on the approaches to Kiel Harbour, four of them to combine this with security patrols over Borkum and Sylt. The eight-strong 49 Squadron element departed Scampton between 21.05 and 21.40 with S/L Allen the senior pilot on duty and began the North Sea crossing at Skegness, before running into adverse weather conditions in the form of fog and ten-tenths cloud between sea level and 10,000 feet, which tested the crews' navigation skills as they made for the Terschelling light vessel at between 4,000 and 8,000 feet. F/O Ward-Hunt and crew turned back with an engine issue, and their early return prompted the take-off at 22.40 of F/L Timmerman as the reserve. They made landfall near the Westerhever light on the west coast of the Schleswig-Holstein peninsula, but unable to break cloud even at 1,000 feet and having to rely on navigation based on dead-reckoning and e.t.a., it proved impossible to establish a pinpoint, and all but one abandoned their sortie. Five landed at Montrose, the last of them, F/L Timmerman and crew, at 06.25, and the return of the remaining three was awaited in vain. It is believed that the crews of F/O White and P/O Benson in L4040 and P1319 respectively had been tasked with the security patrols, and the latter was shot down near Sylt by a BF109 flown by Ofw Hermann Förster of IV./JG2 in what is believed to have been the first shooting down of a Bomber Command aircraft.

The former came down further south near the Elbe estuary and neither produced a survivor. L4092 disappeared without trace with the crew of F/O Rowan-Robinson and is presumed to have crashed into the sea off Kiel.

49 Squadron had now completed its operational activity for the month in which twelve operations had been undertaken, generating forty-nine sorties for the loss of five Hampdens, three complete crews and one gunner. Five Hampdens were dispatched from Hemswell on the 30th bound for Alborg (Aalborg) aerodrome, but only one completed its sortie as briefed.

# May 1940

The squadron was in action immediately at the start of the new month, supporting mining operations in the Eglantine and Nasturtium gardens, respectively in the Elbe Estuary and at the northern end of The Sound between Denmark's Sjælland Island (Copenhagen) and Helsingborg in Sweden. At the same time, other elements of 5 Group were sent to attack the aerodrome at Ålborg (Aalborg) in northern Denmark. F/L Timmerman and W/C Gillan departed Scampton at 20.45 and 20.55 before setting course for the Elbe estuary and were followed into the air between 22.43 and 23.15 by five crews bound for the Baltic with S/Ls Allen and Lowe the senior pilots on duty. The first two-mentioned planted their vegetables as briefed in the Eglantine garden and F/L Timmerman's gunners shot down an Arado 196 floatplane, while some 160 miles to the north-east, four crews delivered their mines into the allotted location and one into an alternative.

F/L Timmerman was awarded a DFC on the 4th, and later that evening, F/Os Forsyth and Learoyd departed Scampton at 19.45 and 19.50 respectively bound for the Onion garden in Oslo harbour. They encountered a hostile reception in the form of searchlights and anti-aircraft fire, but planted their vegetables as briefed before returning safely to Kinloss after eight hours aloft. Six crews each from 49 and 83 Squadrons were briefed on the 6th to conduct mining sorties in the Hollyhock garden off Travemünde, for which the former departed Scampton between 19.45 and 20.10 with S/Ls Allen and Lowe the senior pilots on duty. They encountered adverse weather conditions, which prevented them from fulfilling their briefs and returned home between 02.00 and 04.30. The squadron was not involved in mining operations by thirty-one Hampdens in the Elbe estuary and the Baltic on the night of the 9/10th, just hours before the ill-fated Norwegian campaign became eclipsed by the advance of German forces into the Low Countries at dawn on the 10th. It was an event that signalled the beginning of the massacre of the Fairey Battle squadrons stationed in France as part of the AASF, and the Blenheims of 2 Group would also be thrust into the unequal fight against marauding BF109s, ME110s and murderous ground fire and suffer heavy losses over the succeeding weeks. On the 10th alone, twenty-four Battles and ten Blenheims were lost either during operations or destroyed on the ground and the figure for the 11th was nine and ten respectively.

Bomber Command was to play its part by attacking communications targets behind enemy lines, and in so doing, would bomb mainland Germany for the first time. The first raid of the war on a German urban target followed quickly on the 11th, for which nineteen Hampden and eighteen Whitley crews, including six of the former from 49 Squadron, were briefed. Their targets were road, rail and air communications in Mönchengladbach, a town located on the south-western edge of the industrial Ruhr Valley. The 49 Squadron element departed Scampton between 23.30 and

23.55 with S/Ls Allen and Lowe the senior pilots on duty and the newly promoted F/L Learoyd also on the order of battle, each Hampden carrying four 500 pounders, intended, according to the squadron ORB, for oil refineries. In fact, there were no such targets in Mönchengladbach and reference to H76 identifies the target as the local aerodrome. The weather conditions were perfect as they set out from Skegness via corridor G towards the enemy coast between The Hague and the Scheldt estuary, where they were greeted by intense searchlight activity. The target area was already on fire after being attacked by the Whitley element, and together with the glare from searchlights, this created challenging conditions in which to identify precise aiming points. For whatever reason, both flight commanders failed to complete their sorties as briefed, while the others successfully attacked the target and observed the burst of their bombs. L4068 was homebound across France when the starboard engine failed and it began to lose height, leaving the crew with no prospect of crossing the Channel. P/O Drakes put the Hampden down at 03.50 three miles north of the seaside resort of Le Treport and all crew members emerged unscathed from the wreckage to return quickly to the squadron.

The carnage at the battle front continued on the 12th with the destruction of fourteen Battles and twenty Blenheims and on the 14th with thirty-three Battles and fourteen Blenheims, which effectively knocked the Battle squadrons out of the fight. On the evening of the 14th, 5 Group sent twenty-two Hampdens mining in the Baltic and a further twelve to attack road and rail communications in Holland. 49 Squadron dispatched just the crew of F/O Haskins at 22.25, and they returned at 03.10 to report observing their four 500 pounders burst across railway lines five miles north-west of Deventer in north-central Holland.

Following the Luftwaffe's bombing of Rotterdam on the 15th, which caused an outcry across the world, the War Cabinet finally sanctioned operations against Germany proper, thus prompting the start of the strategic offensive for which the Command had been prepared. That night, ninety-nine assorted aircraft took off to attack sixteen industrial and railway targets in the Ruhr, while twelve Wellington crews were briefed to bomb communications in Belgium, and this was the first time that a hundred aircraft had been despatched in a single night. 5 Group detailed a dozen Hampdens from Hemswell, Scampton and Waddington, 49 Squadron briefing nine crews to attack A108, an oil refinery in Dortmund at the eastern end of the Ruhr, and three for the marshalling yards at Vohwinkel, a suburb of Wuppertal on the region's southern rim. Take-off from Scampton was spread between 20.30 and 22.50 with W/C Gillan and S/Ls Allen and Lowe the senior pilots on duty, the first two mentioned among the Dortmund-bound element. The route to Dortmund was via corridor B to the Ijmuiden area of Holland, while the Vohwinkel-bound trio headed via corridor G to the Scheldt estuary, and on arrival enjoyed mixed fortunes. W/C Gillan and S/L Allen were thwarted by the failure of their bomb release systems, which prevented them from carrying out an attack. F/L Timmerman and crew failed to locate the target and flew south to end up near Cologne, where they bombed a railway station, while F/O Burnett and crew headed north to attack a railway station and junction a mile from the town of Dorsten, which sits on the Wesel-Datteln Canal and the River Lippe on the northern edge of the Ruhr. F/L Mitchell and crew were another to fail to identify the primary target and attacked a large unidentified marshalling yard to the south, almost certainly at Schwerte. Sgt Hills and crew lost their intercom after crossing the Dutch coast and were prevented by searchlight and flak activity from identifying their target. F/O Ward-Hunt and crew attacked a marshalling yard as an alternative target a mile north-west of Lünen on the northern edge of the Ruhr and P/O Campbell and crew went for a railway junction three miles north of

Dortmund. This left just P/O Forsyth and crew to claim to have attacked the primary target, observing three bursts but no detail. Meanwhile, some twenty-five miles to the south, Sgt Pratt and crew attacked the Vohwinkel marshalling yards, before straying off course on the way home and landing on the Curragh racecourse near Dublin in the Republic of Ireland. The authorities had every right to intern them, but instead, gave them two hundred gallons of fuel and sent them on their way to Aldergrove, Belfast, whence they returned home. Neither S/L Lowe nor P/O Pinchbeck and their crews located their primary target and attacked respectively an illuminated railway siding and a railway junction north-west of Siegburg on the south-eastern outskirts of Cologne.

A major assault on Germany's oil industry was mounted on the 17th, when 5 Group detailed forty-eight Hampdens for targets in Hamburg, while twenty-four 4 Group Whitleys were assigned similar targets in Bremen and a handful of 3 Group Wellingtons went for railway installations in Cologne. As these raids were taking place over Germany, a force of forty-six Wellingtons and six Hampdens would conduct tactical operations against a road and railway junction in Belgium, through which enemy troop columns were passing on their way to the front. 49 Squadron briefed ten crews, which departed Scampton between 20.35 and 22.10 with S/Ls Allen and Lowe the senior pilots on duty. Their targets were the refineries coded A5 and A8, which, it is believed, were located on the northern bank of the River Elbe to the west of the city centre, while others from Waddington focused on A10, the Rhenania oil refinery at Harburg, situated on the southern bank. They exited the English coast over Skegness on a night of unlimited visibility enhanced by an almost full moon, which would enable them to map-read to the enemy coast via the lightship at Terschelling and the lighthouses at Westerhever and Heligoland. Those choosing to follow the course of the Elbe into the heart of the docks and industrial districts could expect an intense searchlight and flak defence from both banks of the river and a more prudent approach was from the south or the north. At this stage of the war, such details of routes, altitudes and timings were left very much to be decided at squadron level. The ORB provided no details of the bomb load, but 44 Squadron's aircraft had been loaded with 250 pounders and incendiaries. S/L Lowe and crew claimed to have set their target on fire, and this acted as a beacon to attract the rest of the squadron. P/O Pinchbeck and crew were victims of bomb-release system failure and F/O Ward-Hunt reported bombing A5. On return, crews claimed to have observed bomb bursts and fires and stated that the glow was visible from the coast at Cuxhaven, some fifty miles away to the north-west.

A similar pattern of operations against industrial targets in Germany and communications in Belgium and France would occupy the following two nights, and the need to continue supporting tactical operations would continue through to the fall of France in June. On the 18th, orders were received at Waddington and Hemswell to prepare six Hampdens each to attack road junctions and bridges in the battle area at Givet, located right on the Franco-Belgian frontier. Twenty-four hours later, seventy-eight aircraft, including thirty-six Hampdens, were poised to carry out widespread attacks on German troop communications in France and Belgium and on railway and industrial targets in Germany. The 5 Group crews were briefed for a number of oil-related targets, those at Scampton and Waddington learning that A21, a refinery at Salzbergen, was to be their target. Situated on the River Ems in the Münsterland, north of the Ruhr and ten miles from the Dutch frontier, the Wintershall refinery was, in fact, the oldest in Germany, having been established in 1860, and was one of a number now run by this company at various sites across Germany. Of the twelve Hampdens detailed by 49 Squadron, only eleven were listed in the ORB as departing Scampton, the first six between 20.28 and 21.05 with F/L Mitchell the senior pilot on duty and each carrying four 500 pounders plus small bomb containers (SBCs) of incendiaries. They formed the vanguard to set the target alight as a beacon for the remaining Scampton and Waddington crews following in their wake. The second section, led by F/L Timmerman, took off between 21.30 and 21.53 loaded with just four 500 pounders and flew out over Skegness to begin the North Sea crossing, which the Waddington crews planned to undertake in formations of three as far as the Dutch coast, before proceeding independently to the target. Bright moonlight glinted off the River Ems to aid navigation, and, by the time that the main element closed on the target, it was already on fire. Those arriving during the later stages of the attack described intense searchlight and flak activity, but only F/O Ward-Hunt's P1176 of the 49 Squadron contingent sustained damage in the form of a punctured outboard fuel tank and he and his crew landed safely at Feltwell. On return, P/O Parker and crew reported attacking railway sidings to the south of the target and F/L Mitchell conceded that his bombs had missed the aiming point and that the incendiaries had failed to release. F/L Timmerman and crew had been unable to locate the target, but on the way home, spotted four destroyers and another vessel off the southern Frisians, which they attacked with inconclusive results.

The need to hinder the enemy advance continued to draw elements of the Command's resources from strategic to tactical bombing, including, on the 20th, ninety-two aircraft to attack troops and armour that were breaking into northern France. 5 Group detailed six Hampdens each from Waddington, Hemswell and 83 Squadron at Scampton to attack road bridges over the River Oise. The focus shifted to railways in Germany on the 21st, to attempt to stem the flow of troops and armour being fed into the battle area. 5 Group contributed twenty-five Hampdens to an overall force of 124 aircraft assigned to numerous aiming points on lines to the west of Cologne from Mönchengladbach in the north to Euskirchen in the south. The 5 Group effort was to be directed at a twenty-mile stretch of track between Cologne and Düren, situated to the south-west of the Rhineland capital, and the order was to attack any trains encountered. The eight 49 Squadron participants departed Scampton between 20.40 and 21.40 with S/L Allen the senior pilot on duty and each crew sitting on four 250 pounders and SBCs of incendiaries. They set course for the Scheldt estuary, from where they continued on a south-easterly track to the target area, which lay within Cologne's western defence zone. An initial reconnaissance revealed no moving trains on the briefed stretch of line but prompted an intense and accurate searchlight and flak response. Sgt Pratt claimed a direct hit on a train a mile-and-a-half south-east of Langerwehe and Sgt Hills a very near miss on another, which was stationary at a junction further north between Mönchengladbach and Viersen. There were two major marshalling yards in Aachen, Aachen-West and Rothe-Erde in the east, and one of these was attacked by P/O Pinchbeck and crew and may have been where F/O Butler and crew claimed a direct hit on two items of rolling stock. The others attacked sections of track or roads, and all had returned safely by 03.05 to offer their impressions to the intelligence section at debriefing.

It had been intended that the target for thirty-five Hampdens on the 22nd would be the oil refinery at distant Leuna, near Merseburg, one of many similar plants situated in an arc from north to south to the west of Leipzig. In the event, unfavourable weather conditions prompted a recall, which all but W/C Watts, the commanding officer of 144 Squadron, picked up and he went on alone to bomb and damage the target. Meanwhile, 5 Group contributed a dozen Hampdens from Waddington and

83 Squadron at Scampton to attacks on railway bridges and road targets in France, Belgium and Holland. It was similar fare on the following night, when fifty Hampdens were among 122 aircraft sent to attack railway communications and trains in motion on either side of the Dutch/German frontier in the region of Aachen. 49 Squadron loaded a dozen Hampdens with four 250 pounders and a container of incendiaries each, and dispatched them from Scampton between 21.45 and 21.17 with S/L Lowe the senior pilot on duty. They flew out over Skegness in formation at between 4,000 and 6,000 feet, setting course for the Ijsselmeer above a thick layer of cloud, and some elements of the 5 Group force were fired upon by a convoy. Once darkness closed in at the Dutch coast, the formations separated, and each crew proceeded independently to their respective targets, where rain-bearing cloud, thunderstorms and poor visibility hindered the search for trains in motion. F/O Forsyth and crew had apparently been assigned to the Wintershall oil refinery at Salzbergen, but having been put off by the weather conditions, found themselves south of the Ruhr, where they attacked a train north of Grevenbroich and overshot it by one hundred yards. F/O Haskins and crew were frustrated by the failure of their bomb-release circuitry and had to bring their ordnance home, while F/O Butler and crew failed to locate a suitable target in the conditions. The others attacked railway track or marshalling yards and S/L Lowe added his load to a fire caused by someone else's incendiary bombs. On the way home, when some forty miles east of Skegness, a convoy opened up on him but missed!

Fifty-nine aircraft were made ready on the 24th for a repeat of the previous night's operations against enemy communications between Germany and the advancing battle front, for which 5 Group contributed eighteen Hampdens. With the British Expeditionary Force now trapped with its back to the Channel in a reducing pocket at Dunkerque, the relentless round of operations continued with further attacks on troop positions and communications on the 25th. 103 aircraft were involved, twenty-nine of them Hampdens, which, together with the Whitley element, would focus on road and railway links to the battle front between Düren and Aachen in Germany and near Liege in Belgium, while the Wellingtons targeted troop concentrations. 49 Squadron made ready ten Hampdens and sent them on their way from Scampton between 21.03 and 21.50 with F/Ls Timmerman, Learoyd and Mitchell the senior pilots on duty and P/O Beauchamp operating as crew captain for the first time. They followed corridor "G", the standard route for making landfall over the Scheldt estuary, before heading towards their primary targets of railways near Liege. F/O Burnett and crew attacked a railway at Visé, to the north-north-east of the city and then strafed the aerodrome at Woensdrecht on the way back to the Scheldt, while F/O Ward-hunt bombed a motorised convoy on the road between Bree and Beverlo. The others attacked sections of track or yards and P/O Drakes and crew had to evade the attentions of a fighter near Jülich before coming home safely. Absent from debriefing was the crew of F/O Butler, whose P1318 is believed to have crashed into the sea off the Belgian coast. The remains of the second pilot, P/O Bennett, and gunner, LAC Parsons, were recovered for burial, while F/O Butler and Sgt Harrison are commemorated on the Runnymede Memorial.

The evening of the 26th brought the first evacuations from the Dunkerque beaches in a heroic campaign that would last until the 3rd of June and result in the rescue of 338,000 men. Meanwhile, operations continued against enemy communications and airfields in France, Belgium, Holland and Germany, for which forty-three aircraft were detailed, twenty-one of them Hampdens. His Majesty King George VI visited Scampton on the 27th to decorate a number of 5 Group airmen, and W/C Snaith of 83 Squadron led the parade. F/L Timmerman received his DFC and His Majesty congratulated S/L Lowe and Sgt Hills on the awards of their DFC and DFM respectively on the 25th. 120 aircraft were detailed for a busy night of operations on the 27th, for which 5 Group assigned forty-nine Hampdens to a variety of targets. Twenty-four were assigned to oil refineries, one in the Altona district of Hamburg, situated on the northern bank of the Elbe to the west of the city centre, the Rhenania plant on the opposite bank in Harburg (A10) and another in Bremen. The remaining twenty-five Hampdens, including a dozen representing 49 Squadron, were to attend to communications targets, principally trains in motion in the area between Cologne and Leuven in Belgium or other targets of opportunity. They departed Scampton between 22.00 and 22.25 with S/L Allen the senior pilot on duty and set course for the Scheldt estuary on a night when weather conditions over the whole of western Europe were less than favourable for what amounted to precision attacks on specific targets. While this would restrict success, it would also result in an absence of bomber casualties. P/O Matthews and crew failed to release their bombs because of a technical issue, Sgt Haskins and P/O Drakes were unable to locate a suitable target in the conditions and F/O Learoyd and crew were thwarted by widespread smoke concealing their intended target. Frustrated by that, they set off to roam around the Ruhr region and strafe anything that attracted the gunners' attention, expending in the process some 1,100 rounds of .303 ammunition. P/O Parker and crew successfully attacked a factory, a railway junction and a train, while F/O Ward-Hunt and P/O Beauchamp dropped their bombs on Flushing aerodrome on Walcheren as they crossed the Scheldt estuary on the way home. Others found road and railway targets south of the Ruhr and in Belgium before returning home safely to conclude the month's operational activity.

During the course of May, the squadron took part in thirteen operations and dispatched ninety-eight sorties for the loss of two Hampdens and one crew.

# June 1940

The Squadron was in action on the first night of the new month, when supporting 5 Group operations against oil targets and marshalling yards in Germany. Hemswell provided twelve Hampdens for the latter, while Waddington and 49 Squadron at Scampton put up twelve each to attack the previously targeted A7 plant in Harburg and A19, a refinery at Ostermoor, a location between the western end of the Kiel Canal, and the North Bank of the River Elbe. The 49 Squadron element took off in pairs between 22.10 and 22.30 with S/L Allen the senior pilot on duty and based on the fact that the Waddington squadrons had been assigned to A19, were bound, it is believed, for A7 at Harburg. The weather conditions deteriorated as they crossed the North Sea, and low cloud and extreme darkness in the target areas combined with accurate anti-aircraft fire to frustrate the efforts of both elements. Not a single Scampton crew located and attacked the primary target, and only the crews of Sgt Haskins and F/L Mitchell found a suitable alternative, the aerodrome on the German Frisian Island of Spiekeroog, which responded with light flak. At debriefing, the Haskins crew reported four bursts on the landing ground away from the hangars.

A proposed operation by elements from Waddington and Scampton against the Ostermoor oil plant on the 2nd was cancelled in the face of an unfavourable weather forecast, and it was left to Hemswell to provide six Hampdens to attack Ruhr marshalling yards. The Dunkerque evacuations ended on the 3rd, and that night, Bomber Command launched 142 sorties, the largest number in one night to date, to target German industry, particularly oil plants at various locations between Hamburg in the north and Frankfurt in the south. 5 Group committed forty-eight Hampdens to the fray, six of them made ready by 49 Squadron and assigned to an oil-related target in Emmerich, a town situated on the North Bank of the Rhine on the frontier with Holland, north-west of the Ruhr. S/L Lowe was the senior pilot on duty as the first five crews departed Scampton between 21.40 and 21.55, leaving Sgt Haskins and crew on the ground until 22.50, and all made their way via corridor "B" to make landfall on the Dutch coast north of The Hague. S/L Lowe failed to identify the primary target and attacked a railway junction to the north of the garrison town of Münster as an alternative, while the others returned after some five hours to report fulfilling their briefs, the Haskins crew specifying an attack from 10,000 feet.

Later, on the 4th, an assessment by the government of Germany's oil industry suggested that a concerted effort against it could reduce its output by half a million tons over the summer period. In the light of the massive offensive by four-engine aircraft in 1944, this was a wildly optimistic view, and, although a sizeable proportion of the Command's effort would be directed against oil refineries and storage sites, the effect on Germany's war effort during this early stage of the war would be negligible. That night, twenty-four Hampdens were among fifty-eight aircraft returning to Germany, Scampton sending eleven from 49 Squadron back to A161, the oil depot located on the River Main in the Offenbach district to the south-east of Frankfurt city centre. Waddington and Hemswell, meanwhile, provided six Hampdens each to attack an oil production and storage plant at Mannheim some forty-five miles to the south. The 49 Squadron element departed Scampton between 21.25 and 21.53 with W/C Gillan and S/L Allen the senior pilots on duty, but soon lost the services of F/O Ward-Hunt and crew to an engine issue. The others crossed the North Sea over low cloud, which cleared shortly after entering enemy territory via the Scheldt estuary, and traversed Belgium to enter Germany over the Eifel region. As always, the squadron ORB is light on detail, but it seems that seven crews reported attacking the primary target and the three others may have done so.

5 Group stations were busy on the 5th preparing thirty-six Hampdens for an attack on A22, an oil refinery and storage facility at Schulau/Wedel, situated on the North Bank of the River Elbe a dozen miles downstream from Hamburg city centre. The Group would also be providing six Hampdens to resume the mining campaign, focusing on this night on the western Baltic. 49 Squadron stayed at home and was alerted on the 6th to make ready for operations that night, when Harburg would be the destination for eighteen Hampdens from Hemswell, Scampton and Waddington, where the previously attacked oil refinery A7 was the target. A further six Hampdens would sneak in under cover of the main event to plant mines in the Eglantine garden in the Elbe estuary. 49 Squadron briefed six crews for Harburg and five for gardening, and they departed Scampton together between 21.05 and 21.55 with S/Ls Allen and Lowe respectively the senior pilots on duty. The bombing element reached the target area to find haze and intense searchlight activity, the glare from which hampered their ability to identify the aiming point. Despite the challenges, the crews of S/L Allen, F/L Timmerman and F/O Ward-Hunt carried out an attack on A7, while P/O Campbell and crew headed north to attack the Ostermoor plant, A19. P/O Matthews and crew failed to locate the target and brought their bombs home, while P/O Murray and crew turned their attention upon a road junction to the west of Jade Bight at Neuenburg. The gardeners

fared less well in difficult conditions and only P/O Drakes and crew were able to fulfil their brief, while the others returned their mines to store.

The main battle for the next week would be the vain attempt to rescue France from impending occupation, as German ground forces consolidated their hold on the country and prepared for the assault on Paris. However, it was oil that continued to be the focus for 5 Group on the 7th, as the hectic start to the month continued with the launching of twenty-four Hampdens to attack A17, the Deutsche Erdölraffinerie, also known as Deurag, a synthetic oil refinery at Misburg, situated east-north-east of Hannover city centre, for which 83 Squadron represented Scampton. 5 Group issued orders for a number of operations on the 8th, one of them by twelve crews from 49 Squadron to attack enemy communications in the Amiens area of north-eastern France, while other elements attended to industrial targets in Germany. The 49 Squadron contingent departed Scampton in pairs at ten-minute intervals between 21.43 and 23.03 with S/Ls Allen and Lowe the senior pilots on duty. Last away were the crews of P/O Pinchbeck and P/O Parker, and it was on the point of lifting off that the latter's port engine lost power, leaving them struggling to gain sufficient height to go around. L4044 was doomed and came back to earth under some semblance of control on top of Carlton Hill, some four miles north-north-west of Lincoln. P/O Parker freed himself and with the assistance of two local farmers extricated the wireless operator from the wreckage and all four occupants survived with varying degrees of injury. Meanwhile, F/L Learoyd and crew turned back because of W/T failure, leaving the others to set course for landfall over the Scheldt estuary, from where they encountered extreme darkness, haze and poor visibility that created challenging conditions for target location. Each crew found a road or railway target to attack but were unable to determine the results of their efforts. P/O Parker was recognised for his part in the rescue of his crew member with the award of a medal that would be renamed George Cross in September.

Forty-two Hampdens were detailed for operations on the 9th, thirty-six of them to continue the previous night's assault on marshalling yards in and around the Ruhr, while 49 Squadron stayed at home. The priority on the 10th, the day on which Italy declared war on Britain and France, was to try to stem the tide of the German advance into Northern France, for which 5 Group committed twenty-nine Hampdens to attack railway yards, junctions and bridges over the River Meuse at Sedan. 49 Squadron briefed a dozen crews to attack targets at Liart and Charleville in the Grand Est region adjacent to the Belgian frontier and dispatched them from Scampton between 21.30 and 22.26 with S/L Allen the senior pilot on duty. They were routed out via corridor "G" to cross the enemy coast over the Scheldt estuary, before turning south over Belgium to the target area, where they would encounter the most challenging weather conditions of towering cloud with magnetic storms, which would compromise accurate navigation. Despite the challenges, it seems that all but one managed to find either their primary or a suitable alternative target of some description and return safely.

The need to slow the German advance demanded further attacks on communications targets in France, in response to which, 5 Group detailed thirty-six Hampdens for operations on the 11th, thirty-one of them to return to the Sedan area and five for mining duties. At the same time, eighteen Wellingtons of 3 Group were to attack the Black Forest in south-western Germany with incendiary devices known as "deckers" or "razzle" in an attempt to cause widespread fires, and thirty-six Whitleys would carry out the first attacks on Italy with a raid on Turin. Only nine would actually bomb at Turin, while the ill-conceived policy of setting fire to forests, which would be played out over the ensuing months, would prove to be a monumental waste of resources at a time when the Command had more important matters to focus on. 49 Squadron dispatched the lone crew of Sgt Pratt at 22.05 on a night when few would be successful in the face of intense darkness and haze, and they returned at 02.35 to report bomb bursts on the east side of the river near the Pont des Americains.

A reduced effort on the night of the 12th saw thirty Hampdens and eight 4 Group Whitleys detailed for a return to the same general area of north-eastern France, but further west in the Hauts-de-France region, while five other Hampdens were assigned to gardening duties. 49 Squadron briefed three crews each to attack communications targets at Fargniers, a dozen mile south of St-Quentin and Neufchatel-sur-Aisne and sent them on their way between 22.03 and 22.57 with S/L Allen the senior pilot on duty. They had been preceded into the air between 21.30 and 21.43 by six Hampdens bound for the Baltic, two, including the one occupied by S/L Lowe and crew, to mine the waters of the Wallflower garden in Kiel Harbour and four for the Radish garden in the Fehmarn Belt in Mecklenburg Bay. They lost the services of F/O Haskins to engine trouble early on and P/O Pinchbeck and crew reached the target area only to fail to locate a suitable pinpoint in the face of haze and extreme darkness. The others fulfilled their briefs and returned safely after round trips of up to seven hours. The bombing element, meanwhile, flew out over the Norfolk coast to cross the North Sea via corridor "G", where they ran into a thick bank of ten-tenths rain-bearing low cloud. They found that this extended over the Scheldt estuary all the way to the target areas and would prevent some crews from locating their briefed objective or an alternative and "Penny" Beauchamp and crew brought their bombs home. S/L Allen and crew were heading south-east when they encountered a Heinkel III, which they shot down in flames, only then to come upon a Ju86, which suffered the same fate at their hands. Continuing on, they attempted to hit cross-roads near Laon, but overshot by some fifty yards. P/O Drakes and crew attacked the primary target at Fargniers, and Sgt Cooke and crew went for a road and river junction at La Fere, while F/L Timmerman found railway sidings and F/O Burnett marshalling yards in the vicinity of Guise.

163 aircraft were prepared for operations on the 13th, their crews briefed to attack a wide variety of communications targets in France, Belgium and Holland. 5 Group called for a maximum effort from its three operational stations at Scampton, Hemswell and Waddington, and sixty-four Hampdens answered the call, a dozen of them provided by 49 Squadron. They had been briefed for a return to Fargniers, situated south of St-Quentin and north-west of Laon, where it was believed that wagons were being used to store petrol. They took off at five-minute intervals between 21.29 and 22.00 with F/Ls Learoyd and Timmerman the senior pilots on duty, each loaded with four 500 pounders. They faced moderate weather conditions over the North Sea with six-tenths cloud, which would disperse over northern France to leave haze. This was particularly thick in the Laon region, where the visibility was down to around a thousand yards under six-tenths low cloud at 1,000 feet, and the moonlight became a hindrance by reflecting off the mist. F/O Forsyth and crew were defeated by the conditions and brought their bombs home, while F/L Timmerman and crew bombed a railway station at Chaulay (untraced). The others located the primary target and carried out attacks, the manner and results of which were not recorded.

While 4 Group prepared its Whitleys to continue the losing battle to save France from occupation on the 14th, Wellingtons and Hampdens from 3 and 5 Groups were detailed to attack targets in Germany. In fact, only five Hampdens were mobilized, three at Hemswell, one from 83 Squadron at Scampton and one from 50 Squadron to represent Waddington. There were no operations for 5 Group on the 15th, the day on which the battered remnants of the Advanced Air Striking Force arrived back from France with what remained of their Fairey Battles. 12 Squadron settled in at Finningley and 142 Squadron at Waddington, both temporarily, until they could become part of the newly reconstituted 1 Group, which, after continuing briefly with Battles, would convert to Wellingtons later in the year. Adverse weather conditions on the 16th kept most of the Command on the ground that night, while 3 Group Wellingtons went to Italy, and Waddington detailed three Hampdens each from 44 and 50 Squadrons to carry out mining duties in the Radish garden in the Fehmarn Belt, between the Danish islands of Fehmarn and Lolland in Mecklenburg Bay.

Forty-six Hampdens were made ready for operations on the 17th, six from Scampton to continue the mining campaign, while a further twenty-one from there and nineteen from Waddington were assigned to attack the oil refineries coded A3, A7 and A10, respectively at Dollbergen, east of Hannover, and at Harburg on the South Bank of the Elbe and marshalling yards M107 and M434 at Coblenz and Hamm. 49 Squadron briefed a dozen crews for the Hugo Stinnes-Riebeck Öl A G (BASF) Dollbergen plant and sent ten of them on their way from Scampton between 21.15 and 21.50 with F/Ls Learoyd, Mitchell and Timmerman the senior pilots on duty, and they were followed an hour later by the crews of P/Os Beauchamp and Campbell. P/O Matthews returned early with engine trouble, leaving the others to fly out over the North Sea under a full moon and in good weather conditions with a few areas of cloud. All were subjected to intense heavy and light anti-aircraft fire as soon as they crossed the Dutch coast in the Alkmaar area, but reached the target, where eight crews carried out an attack on the primary target, while it seems that P/O Beauchamp and crew overshot Dollbergen and eventually bombed a large factory at Fallersleben some twenty miles further east. As F/L Timmerman strayed perhaps too close to Amsterdam on the way out, he spotted activity at Schiphol aerodrome and could not resist the opportunity to join the circuit, where his gunners destroyed an enemy aircraft in the act of landing. The four 500 pounders were dropped onto buildings on the north-eastern side of the airfield and P/O Campbell and crew added theirs also on the north-western corner. A reconnaissance of the Dollbergen oil plant apparently revealed extensive damage.

On the 18th, 5 Group detailed five Hampdens to seek out and destroy trains in motion north of the Ruhr in the area from Wesel on the Dutch frontier as far east as Hamm, and south of the Ruhr between Düren and Koblenz. P/O Matthews and crew took off at 21.45 and headed via the Scheldt estuary to the Mönchengladbach region, where they attacked a railway junction with indeterminate results.

On the following night, 112 aircraft from 3, 4 and 5 Groups were detailed to attack oil and railway targets between Hamburg in the north and Mannheim in the south. 5 Group contributed fifty-three Hampdens, seven of which were made ready by 49 Squadron to co-operate with others from Hemswell. Six of the 49 Squadron participants were briefed to attack H150, Handorf aerodrome, located north-east of Münster, with the purpose of dissuading the Luftwaffe from interfering with a simultaneous attack on M25A, a newly built aqueduct next to an old one (M25) carrying the Dortmund-Ems Canal over the River Ems between Gittrup and Fuestrup to the north of the city. It is believed that S/L Lowe's target was M25A, and he and his crew were last away as the 49 Squadron element departed Scampton between 21.16 and 22.55 with F/L Learoyd the senior pilot on duty among those assigned to the aerodrome. Details are scant, but it seems that the attack on the aerodrome proceeded as planned and there were claims of strikes on hangars. The ORB tells us only that S/L Lowe and crew carried out an attack.

On the 20th, 4 and 5 Groups were notified of operations in the Ruhr and in the Münsterland region to the north on the 20th, the latter responding with orders, among others, to Waddington and Scampton to prepare six Hampdens each to attack an aircraft park, K9, at Paderborn, situated some forty miles to the east of Hamm. The 49 Squadron element took off from Scampton between 21.55 and 23.00 with W/C Gillan the senior pilot on duty and set course from Skegness to cross the North Sea over ten-tenths low cloud, which cleared as they made their way eastwards over the Dutch/German frontier to be greeted by bright moonlight in the target area. Despite the favourable conditions, only the crews of W/C Gillan and P/O Drakes appear to have located the primary target to deliver their bombs on the edge of the aerodrome, while three others found alternatives including a factory at Hitzacker, south-east of Hamburg (F/O Burnett), Schiphol aerodrome (F/O Ward-Hunt) and a factory building possibly associated with the aircraft park at Göttingen (P/O Pinchbeck). P/O Matthews and crew were thwarted by cloud and returned their bombs to store.

Forty-two Hampdens were among 105 aircraft from 3, 4 and 5 Groups detailed on the 21st to carry out operations in northern and central Germany and the Ruhr in-between, for which 49 Squadron was called upon to provide just three aircraft to attack trains in motion. Their target area was north of the Ruhr, for which they departed Scampton between 22.04 and 22.20 only to lose the services of the crews of P/Os McClure and Lewis to engine issues early on. This would have been a frustration for P/O McClure, who was operating as crew captain for the first time after serving his apprenticeship under the tutelage of Sgt Hills. This left just Sgt Stretton and crew to carry the fight to the enemy, and they found a junction and train at Diepholz, located between Osnabrück to the south-west and Bremen to the North-east, but failed to score a hit on either.

Bomber Command stayed at home on the night of the 22/23rd, after forty-four consecutive nights of operations since the balloon went up in May. This was the day on which the French authorities signed the instrument of surrender at Compiegne, to leave Britain standing alone against a seemingly unconquerable enemy. Unfavourable weather conditions were to blame for the brief break in bombing operations, but orders were issued on the 23rd to resume the fight and 5 Group detailed fifty-three Hampdens for that night's activities. Thirty-eight of them from Scampton and Waddington were to attack F74, the Horten aircraft factory at Wismar on the Baltic coast, and F49, the Hamburger Flugzeugbau aircraft works belonging to Blohm & Voss at Wenzendorf, south-west of Hamburg, which was building subassemblies on a contract basis for Messerschmitt, Dornier, Heinkel, Junkers and Focke-Wulf. The Hemswell crews were briefed either for the marshalling yards at Hamm or barges in the Dortmund-Ems and Mittelland Canals north of the Ruhr. The fourteen-strong 49 Squadron contingent took off between 20.30 and 21.23 with S/L Lowe the senior pilot on duty and set course from Skegness to make landfall on the west coast of southern Jutland. Weather conditions over the Schleswig-Holstein peninsula were unfavourable and included a thunderstorm, which persuaded S/L Lowe to jettison his bombs to maintain height on reaching Flensburg on the eastern coast. Only F/L Learoyd and crew located and bombed the Horten factory, while others attacked targets of opportunity or brought their bombs home.

The squadron did not operate on the 24th, when a handful of 83 Squadron crews conducted gardening operations. On the 25th, S/L Allen and gunner, Sgt Williams, were awarded a DFC and

DFM respectively for shooting down two enemy aircraft. The squadron stayed at home again that night, while seven 83 Squadron crews were briefed to attack a variety of targets including the Korff A G oil refinery in Bremen and A8 in Hamburg. Fifteen 49 Squadron crews attended briefing on the 26th to learn that eight of them would be joining twenty-six others for attacks on marshalling yards, aerodromes and rail and canal traffic, according to the 5 Group ORB, in north-western Germany. A further seven crews were briefed for a special mining/reconnaissance operation in the Lettuce garden in the Kiel Canal, (Kaiser Wilhelm Kanal) a sixty-one-mile-long vitally important waterway that traversed the Schleswig-Holstein peninsula and provided access for U-Boots from Kiel's construction yards to the North Atlantic via the Elbe estuary at Brunsbüttel. The gardening element departed Scampton first between 21.42 and 21.55 with S/L Allen the senior pilot on duty and they were followed into the air by the bombers between 22.19 and 22.58 led by F/L Timmerman. Cloud in the Kiel Canal area prevented the crews of F/O Ward-Hunt and Sgt Hills from establishing a pinpoint and they were unsuccessful, while the others delivered their mines and S/L Lowe bombed but narrowly missed a ship in the Canal. P4305 was hit by flak and crashed into the canal, killing two members of the crew and delivering F/L Mitchell and P/O Reavell-Carter into enemy hands. *(The latter would take part in the epic Great Escape from Sagan PoW camp in March 1944. Having survived the war, he would represent Great Britain in the discus event at the 1948 London Olympic Games. Beware of the Dog at War. John Ward).* Meanwhile, the bombing element appears not to have targeted north-western Germany, but remained over the occupied countries, where aerodromes were the principal objectives.

While 49 Squadron remained on the ground on the 27th, 5 Group sent twenty-three Hampdens on mining operations and to attack an oil-tankerage site at Nyborg on the eastern coast of Denmark's Fyn Island. The Commander-in-Chief of Bomber Command, Air marshal Sir Charles Portal, visited Scampton on the 28th, while ten Hampdens were being prepared to join ten others from Waddington to operate over the southern Ruhr against the Bayer explosives and chemical works at Dormagen, located on the western side of the Rhine between Neuss to the north and Leverkusen to the south. This plant was part of the infamous I G Farben conglomerate and is believed to have been engaged in the production of poison gas, probably Zyklon B. A further four Hampdens from Scampton, two from each squadron, were to attack Handorf aerodrome as a diversion for Hemswell's attempt on the lock gates on the new Dortmund-Ems Canal aqueduct, M25A. The 49 Squadron element departed Scampton at five-minute intervals from 21.30, but no details of the crews involved or the conduct of the operation were provided by the ORB. According to the 44 Squadron account, crews crossed the Norfolk coast to follow corridor "G" in favourable weather conditions to the Scheldt estuary, and, although the ORB makes no mention, once past the Rhine, they were forced to run the gauntlet of intense searchlights and flak of all calibres, which burst at the correct level but mostly behind. The 50 Squadron participants mostly failed to identify the target, blaming industrial haze, but the 44 Squadron crews all located it and carried out their attacks in the glare of searchlights, which blinded them to the results. Two large explosions were followed by a fire and a large, low, white blanket of cloud, possibly gas, and a column of black smoke was rising through 2,000 feet as they turned away. Meanwhile, it is believed that the crews of F/Os Burnett and Forsyth took off shortly after 22.00 bound for Handorf aerodrome, and the former landed a few bombs on the western boundary.

A busy June ended on the 30th with 5 Group detailing a dozen Hampdens each from Scampton and Waddington respectively to attack an aerodrome near Dortmund and an oil refinery at Hamburg, while Hemswell attended to marshalling yards at Osnabrück and took on gardening duties. The 49 Squadron element departed Scampton between 21.07 and 23.10 with S/L Allen the senior pilot on duty and all reached the general area of the Ruhr, but only the crews of F/O Burnett, P/O Murray and Sgt Hills located and bombed the primary target. The crews of S/L Allen and Sgt Pratt found a blast furnace south of Gelsenkirchen, while others attacked a road/rail crossing at Werne in Bochum, a railway junction at Dülmen, a factory at Recklinghausen and a flare path north of Lünen.

During the course of the month the squadron took part in twenty-two operations and dispatched 170 sorties for the loss of two Hampdens and one crew.

# July 1940

Squadron strength on the 1st stood at thirty-three officers and 308 airmen with nineteen Hampdens I.E. It was left to 83 Squadron to represent Scampton on the night of the 1/2nd, when the heavy cruiser Scharnhorst was targeted at a floating dock at Kiel and F/O Guy Gibson delivered the first 2,000 pounder dropped by the RAF in anger. Six 49 Squadron crews were briefed on the 2nd for mining duties in the Baltic in Kiel Bay's Quince garden. They departed Scampton between 21.15 and 21.55 with no senior pilots on duty and each carrying two 250 pounders in addition to the mines. The crews of P/O Parker and F/Sgt Apps failed to establish a pinpoint from which to make a timed run to the drop zone, but the former and P/Os Lewis and Drakes and their crews found an aerodrome each in Denmark and Germany for their 250 pounders.

Temporary residents, 12 Squadron, moved out of Scampton with its battles on the 3rd and into a new home at Binbrook. The crews of S/Ls Allen and Lowe and P/O Matthews attended briefing later in the day to be handed the task of attacking M465, which is believed to be one of a multitude of marshalling yards in Cologne. According to the 5 Group ORB, six Scampton crews were briefed to attack a marshalling yard at Osnabrück, but as 83 Squadron remained at home on this night and could not have contributed the additional three crews, this clearly is an error. They departed Scampton between 22.00 and 22.07 and encountered ten-tenths ice-bearing cloud that topped out in the target area at 10,000 feet, which persuaded the crews of S/L Lowe and P/O Matthews to jettison their four 500 pounders, the latter south of Mönchengladbach, a short distance from the Dutch frontier on the western edge of the Ruhr. S/L Allen reported attacking the primary target and observing one burst among lights before entering cloud and losing sight of the others.

Among 5 Group operations on the 4th was a return to Kiel by a dozen Hampdens from Scampton and four from Hemswell to attack a floating dock in the Krupp-Germania shipyard at Kiel, one of which was believed to be holding the under-repair cruiser Scharnhorst. P/O Pinchbeck and crew were the sole 49 Squadron representatives and took off at 21.55 bound for what the ORB recorded as both D117 and D197. They returned seven hours later to report attacking the primary target but were too busy taking evasive action to observe the fall of their 2,000lb bomb. 5 Group continued the assaults on Scharnhorst and the embankments of the Dortmund-Ems Canal on the 5th, while 49 Squadron sent a dozen Hampdens to conduct mining sorties in the Eglantine garden in the Elbe estuary. They departed Scampton between 22.00 and 22.30 with F/L Timmerman the senior pilot on duty and returned up to seven hours later, all but two to report fulfilling their briefs.

50 Squadron was stood down from operations on the 8th while the move took place to a new home at Hatfield Woodhouse, located across the county line in Yorkshire, five miles north-east of Doncaster. This was a brand-new airfield, completed in June, and 50 Squadron would be its first resident unit. To prevent confusion with the Hatfield in Hertfordshire, which was home to the de Havilland aircraft factory, Hatfield Woodhouse would be renamed in August to become Lindholme, after a country house and hamlet on the eastern boundary of the airfield. Mining operations were the preserve of 5 Group at this stage of the war and a dozen crews were sent out each night to deliver their lethal cargos into the main shipping lanes. The next time that 49 Squadron was called into action was on the 8th, when a dozen crews were briefed for mining duties in the Baltic in the Hollyhock garden off Travemünde, the gateway to the city of Lübeck. All but one took off between 21.03 and 21.30 with S/L Lowe the senior pilot on duty, leaving P/O Lewis and crew on the ground until their departure at 21.52, way too late to make up time and they eventually turned back. The crews of Sgts Cooke and Haskell failed to establish a pinpoint in the conditions, but the latter dropped their wing-mounted 250 pounders on Kiel, while the crews of S/L Lowe attacked the Glambæk seaplane base on Fehmarn Island, Sgt Hills went for flak ships in the target area and P/O Matthews bombed Westerland aerodrome on the island of Sylt.

It was reported that the battleship Tirpitz, the sister ship of Bismarck, was at berth in Wilhelmshaven, where it had been built between 1936 and 1939 and was still in the process of being fitted out. Eleven Hampdens from Scampton and three from Hemswell were detailed to attack her on the 9th, for which the six-strong 49 Squadron element took off between 22.00 and 22.15 with W/C Gillan and S/L Allen the senior pilots on duty. Three were carrying four 250 pounders and one SBC of incendiaries and three four 500 pounders, and all reached the target area, where five crews delivered their loads onto the approximate location of the berth or the docks generally without observing bursts. Sgt Jennings and crew let theirs go onto the aerodrome on the Frisian island of Borkum. Earlier in the day, F/O Forsyth and P/O Beauchamp had been awarded a DFC.

Another busy night for 5 Group on the 13th brought further gardening operations and attention on the Dortmund-Ems Canal, while thirteen Hampdens belonging to 49 Squadron were loaded with four 500 pounders each for use against the Blohm & Voss shipyards on the southern bank of the Elbe in the Finkenwerder district of Hamburg. They departed Scampton between 21.25 and 21.55, and according to the 5 Group ORB, most were unable to locate the target in the prevailing conditions. However, the crews of S/L Allen, P/O Murray and Sgts Haskell and Cooke claimed to have attacked it without observing the results, while the crews of P/Os Drakes and Parker targeted the docks at Emden and others went for aerodromes at Stade and on Norderney and Borkum and Eelde in northern Holland. Two nights later, the crews of F/Sgt Apps and F/O Ward-Hunt took off at 21.30 and 21.40 respectively to attack the aircraft park at Paderborn situated thirty-five miles east of Hamm and north-east of the Ruhr Valley. The former managed to hit the south-western corner of the aerodrome, but the latter failed to locate it and bombed a railway junction at Goch on the way home.

The Command ordered attacks on six targets in Germany on the 18th, for which thirty-eight Hampdens and thirty 3 Group Wellingtons were detailed. Scampton was to launch seventeen aircraft, fourteen representing 49 Squadron assigned to E8, the Krupp complex in Essen and three from 83 Squadron for marshalling yards in Cologne, while Hatfield Woodhouse sent ten to target the aircraft park at Paderborn and Waddington nine to a similar objective at Eschwege, situated twenty miles east-south-east of Kassel. The name Krupp conjures up a vision of a massive factory, but this is far from what actually existed. The Krupp organisation had been the largest manufacturer of weapons in Europe since before the Great War and had a hand in all aspects of German war production from tanks to artillery and ship and U-Boot construction and was given a controlling share in all major heavy engineering companies in Germany and the Occupied Countries. It also built manufacturing sites in other parts of Germany, many situated close to concentration camps, and employed vast numbers of forced workers in all of its factories. Once known as "Die Waffenschmiede des Reichs", the weapons-forge of the realm, its manufacturing sites in Essen included among others the Friedrich Krupp steelworks, the Friedrich Krupp locomotive and general engineering works, six coal mines and ten coke-oven plants, the Altenberg zinc works, the Presswerk plastics factory and the Goldschmidt non-ferrous metals smelting plant, all situated either within or close to the four Borbeck districts in a segment radiating out from near the city centre to the Rhine-Herne Canal on the north-western boundary on the banks of the Emscher River. The steel and engineering works alone employed in the region of eighty thousand workers, and the company's sites covered an area of more than two thousand acres, of which three hundred acres were occupied by factories and workshops. All of that required massive rail and canal access in the form of marshalling yards and its own harbour, and energy from at least four nearby power stations.

The 49 Squadron contingent departed Scampton between 21.50 and 22.35 with F/Os Burnett, Haskins and Ward-Hunt the senior pilots on duty, half of them carrying six 250 pounders and one SBC of incendiaries and the others four 500 pounders. All of the ordnance reached the target area although not all the primary target as low cloud rendered it difficult to locate. On return after up to six hours aloft, the crews of F/O Burnett, P/Os McClure, Matthews, Murray and Pinchbeck and Sgt Stretton reported bombing the primary without observing the results, while F/O Ward-Hunt had gone back to the railway junction at Goch, the newly promoted F/O Beauchamp had attacked a marshalling yard in Dortmund, P/O Fox a blast furnace believed to be in the Krefeld area and F/O Haskins a searchlight battery south of Rotterdam. Two others had attacked SEMOs (self-evident military objectives) and one returned their bombs to store.

On the 20th, orders were received on 5 Group stations to prepare for a number of operations to be conducted that night, for which Hemswell would provide fifteen Hampdens for an attack on the Tirpitz and Admiral Scheer at berth in Wilhelmshaven, while Scampton took care of gardening and Waddington returned to the aircraft park at Eschwege aerodrome with eight aircraft. A dozen 49 Squadron crews learned at briefing that their destination was the Daffodil garden at the southern end of The Sound (Oresund) between Denmark's Sjælland Island (Copenhagen) and southern Sweden. They departed Scampton between 20.30 and 20.50 with S/L Lowe the senior pilot on duty and outstanding serviceability saw all reach the target area to plant their vegetables in the allotted locations, Sgt Stretton and crew also narrowly missing a ship with two wing-mounted 250 pounders. On return and flying on fumes, L4077 was crash-landed by P/O Michie at 04.35 near Hunstanton in Norfolk, and all walked away from the wreckage with minor injuries.

On the following day, 5 Group detailed a total of twenty Hampdens from its four stations and briefed their crews for an attack on the important Dornier aircraft factory located in the Hansastadt (ancient free-trade city) Wismar, on the Baltic coast. 49 Squadron remained at home on this night and also on the 22nd, when 5 Group detailed twenty-three Hampdens for a variety of targets including the Nordstern (Gelsenberg A G) synthetic oil refinery in the Horst district of Gelsenkirchen in the Ruhr and the aircraft park at Eschwege. Consequently, the crews were fully rested when orders were received on the 23rd to prepared for an operation that night against the Blohm & Voss-owned Hamburger Flugzeugbau factory at Wenzendorf. The seven-strong element departed Scampton between 21.43 and 22.08 with F/O Burnett the senior pilot on duty and each carrying either four 500 pounders or four 250 pounders and one SBC of incendiaries. Weather conditions over the North Sea were found to be challenging, with a bank of storm-bearing cloud at between 500 and 10,000 feet, and this would prevent some from locating the primary target. F/O Burnett's bombs overshot the factory and burst in a wood to the east, as did those released by P/O McClure and crew, while F/Sgt Apps and crew scored a direct hit, which produced a large explosion that was felt as well as seen. The crews of P/O Pinchbeck and Sgt Haskell attacked the alternative target, the docks at Wilhelmshaven, but were prevented by cloud from observing the results and Sgt Pratt and crew narrowly missed an aerodrome near Bremen.

On the 24th, F/L Timmerman was rested and posted to 14 O.T.U at Cottesmore in the county of Rutland for instructional duties. He would return to the operational scene with 5 Group in June 1941 as the first commanding officer of 408 (Goose) Squadron RCAF. The night of the 25/26th was a busy one for 5 Group, in which forty-one aircraft from Hemswell, Waddington and Hatfield Woodhouse were sent to attack oil refineries in the Ruhr, while Scampton's eighteen aircraft focused on the Dortmund-Ems Canal. This was an important component in the German communications system, through which raw materials were imported into the industrial Ruhr and finished products exported to wider Germany to assist the war effort. There were two stretches of the canal which featured a twin aqueduct section, the already mentioned and attacked M25 and M25A at the junction with the River Ems and another some six miles further north, near Ladbergen, which carried the waterway over the Ibbenbürener Aa River. The canal would develop a close association with 5 Group and, along with the nearby Mittelland Canal, would continue to be a target for the remainder of the war. W/C Gillan and S/L Allen were the senior pilots on duty as the nine-strong 49 Squadron element departed Scampton between 21.20 and 21.43, five bound for M25 and M25A and four to create a diversion. It is believed, that the 83 Squadron element had been assigned to the Ladbergen section and this is based on the report by one of its crews that they had bombed on the west side of a canal bridge south of Recke, which is a village on the Mittelland Canal, some dozen miles or more to the north-east of Ladbergen. W/C Gillan and crew attacked a lock system at Münster but were denied by cloud from observing the outcome, while F/Os Drakes and Haskins targeted aerodromes and Sgt Cooke an undisclosed diversionary target. This left the crews of S/L Allen and the others to focus on the aqueducts, and although bombs from four of them were observed to enter the water, no results were determined.

On the following night it was the turn of the Scampton squadrons to attack what the 5 Group ORB described as oil refineries at St Nazaire at the mouth of the Loire and Nantes situated some thirty miles upstream. The nine 49 Squadron participants departed Scampton between 21.30 and 21.53 with S/L Lowe the senior pilot on duty and set course for Z159, which was St-Nazaire aerodrome, suggesting that the target was an oil storage depot rather than a refinery. All reached the target area and delivered their four 500 pounders each, those observing the outcome reporting bomb bursts, small explosions, fire and black smoke. The squadron reserved its largest commitment of aircraft for the final operation of the month, when fifteen of its Hampdens were made ready to attack A161, the oil depot at Offenbach to the east of Frankfurt city centre, while one joined forces with an element from Hemswell to attack the Dortmund-Ems Canal at its junction with the River Ems. They took off between 21.10 and 21.45 with S/L Allen the senior pilot on duty and lost the services of F/O Ward-Hunt and crew to the failure of their intercom. Nine returning crews claimed to have bombed the primary target and reported fires and black, oily smoke, while the crews of F/O Haskins bombed an aerodrome near Spa in Belgium, F/Sgt Apps another near Liege, P/O Parker M475 (unidentified) and Sgt Unsworth a small factory in the Rhine Valley. Sgt Hopkins and crew failed to locate a suitable target and dumped their bombs in the sea.

During the course of another hectic month, the squadron took part in fifteen operations and dispatched 122 sorties for the loss of a single Hampden without casualties.

# August 1940

August's operations would follow a similar pattern to those of July as the Battle of Britain raged overhead and invasion fever increased. 5 Group divided its effort on the 2nd between the oil refinery at Misburg near Hannover for the Hemswell crews and mining for the 83 Squadron boys at Scampton. On the 3rd, while fourteen 49 Squadron crews were being briefed to attack the cruiser Gneisenau at berth in the Krupp-Germania shipyard in Kiel, a dozen of their Hampdens were being loaded with four 500 pounder and two with a 2,000 pounder each. The ORB lists only thirteen departing Scampton between 20.40 and 21.09 with the recently arrived F/O Riley the senior pilot on duty, and, according to the 5 Group ORB, none actually identified the Gneisenau, although the crews of Sgts Hills and Roberts and P/O Pinchbeck specified attacking her, while P/O Gower and Sgt Stretton were convinced that they had bombed Scharnhorst. The crews of F/O Riley, P/Os Harris and Fawcett and Sgts Hopkins and Unsworth reported targeting the shipyard generally, while those of P/O McClure and Sgt Haskell went for a mole in Kiel Bay and that of P/O Fox for Nordholz aerodrome near the coast south-west of Cuxhaven, most failing to observe the results. P4351 ran out of fuel on the way home and Sgt Unsworth ditched it at 06.40 ten miles off Skegness and within sight of the SS Sheraton, which picked them up safe and sound after an hour in the dinghy. P2112 came to grief while landing at Harlaxton near Grantham in the hands of P/O Fox, and second pilot, P/O Paramore, sustained injury that required his admission to Grantham station hospital. The ORB declared the Hampden to be a write-off, when, in fact, it was repaired and eventually found its way to 14 O.T.U.

Briefings on the 5th revealed that nine Hampdens from 83 Squadron at Scampton and eight belonging to 50 Squadron were to seek out the battleship Bismarck, which was under the final stages of fitting-out in Hamburg. 49 Squadron remained at home on this night, and on the following day received orders to prepare a dozen Hampdens for mining duties in the Tomatoes and Undergrowth gardens, respectively off Fredrikstad in Oslo Fjord and Frederikshavn in the Kattegat off northern Jutland. They departed Scampton between 21.00 and 21.13 with F/Os Beauchamp,

Drakes and Riley the senior pilots on duty and each carrying two wing-mounted 250 pounders in addition to the mine. Sgt Haskell and crew turned back within the hour because of engine trouble and at some point, P4377 disappeared into the sea with the crew of Sgt Jennings DFM never to be seen again. Of the others, F/O Riley and P/O Gower were defeated by the weather conditions in the target area and Sgt Hopkins by a technical failure, almost certainly in the release system, which left seven crews to plant their vegetables as briefed and bring their 250 pounders home. It was at this time that F/O Lewis "Bob" Hodges arrived on posting from 106 Squadron to begin his first operational tour in what would turn out to be an outstanding and varied career.

Scampton represented 5 Group on the 8th when dispatching eighteen Hampdens to attack the I G Farben synthetic oil plant at Oppau in Ludwigshafen in southern Germany. 49 Squadron made ready just six of its Hampdens, loading each with four 500 pounders and sending them on their way from Scampton between 20.56 and 21.06 with F/O Haskins the senior pilot on duty and a S/L Knowles flying with P/O Pinchbeck. In contrast to the highly detailed accounts provided by some other squadrons, the 49 Squadron ORB informs us only that the crews of P/Os Pinchbeck, Campbell and Fawcett returned between six and eight hours later to report attacking the primary target, while two others bombed aerodromes.

On the 11th, Scampton was ordered to provide nine Hampdens from each squadron to operate against A108, an oil refinery in Dortmund at the eastern end of the Ruhr and to employ "razzle" to attempt to set fire to a heavily wooded region from Cologne eastwards as far as Herborn. The 49 Squadron element departed Scampton between 21.05 and 21.35 with S/L Allen the senior pilot on duty and each loaded with four 250 pounders, one SBC of incendiaries and fifty tins of incendiary pellets. The "razzling" seemed to go well, but not so the bombing, as only the crews of Sgts Hills and Cooke positively identified the primary target, while others either bombed its approximate location or found targets of opportunity. One 83 Squadron crew returned to report a successful attack on the refinery, which resulted in a large explosion and fire. P1323 arrived in the Scampton circuit with a compromised hydraulics system courtesy of flak and was put down safely by Sgt Stretton without causing excessive additional damage and the Hampden would be returned to service. L4036, however, was brought down by flak in the target area and there were no survivors from the crew of P/O Gower. Later in the year, "razzle" would be discontinued and consigned to the "It was worth a try" file.

One of two bombing operations on the night of the 12/13th was conducted by an element from Hemswell against the previously targeted oil refinery at Salzbergen, while the almost personal association between 5 Group and the Dortmund-Ems Canal, which would extend right to the end of the war, was continued by eleven Hampdens of 49 and 83 Squadrons. It was to be a low-level attack on M25, the older branch of the twin aqueduct section at its junction with the River Ems north of Münster. The plan called for the 83 Squadron crews of F/Ls Pitcairn-Hill and Mulligan and F/O Ross and the 49 Squadron crews of P/O Matthews and F/L Learoyd to attack the target while the remaining six crews carried out diversionary activities. 49 Squadron loaded one of its aircraft with four 500 pounders, three with six 250 pounders and two with a special "NM" mine and dispatched them between 20.30 and 20.50 with S/L Lowe the senior pilot on duty. The 83 Squadron aircraft went in first and numbers 2 and 3 were shot down before P/O Matthews carried out his attack and sustained severe flak damage which knocked out an engine. Last to attack was F/L Learoyd, who would have witnessed the preceding events and knew what awaited him and his crew as they bore down on the aiming point at 150 feet into the blinding glare of searchlights and a wall of light flak. Somehow, they emerged on the other side having delivered an accurate attack and set course for home with damage to the hydraulics system but both engines running smoothly. On arrival in the circuit, F/L Learoyd circled until daylight provided better conditions for landing, which was accomplished without incident. Post-raid reconnaissance confirmed the success of the attack by the Learoyd crew, which had left the aqueduct breached, drained and unnavigable. In recognition of his gallantry, F/L Learoyd was awarded the first Victoria Cross to go to a member of Bomber Command, and F/O Matthews received a DFC, while the members of their crews were honoured with a DFM. *(F/O Garland and Sgt Grey of 12 Squadron had been awarded a VC each in May 1940, but were part of the AASF, which, at the time, was not technically part of Bomber Command.)* This would be "Babe" Learoyd's final operation with the squadron before his posting on the 15th to the Air Ministry as personal assistant to Sir Robert Brooke-Popham, who was head of the training mission to South Africa. Learoyd's absence from the squadron would be brief and he would return in September to continue his operational career.

On the 13th, all four operational stations were alerted to operations that night against Junkers aircraft factories at Dessau and Bernburg, situated some twenty miles apart in east central Germany, south of Magdeburg. Twenty-eight Hampdens set off, with 83 Squadron representing Scampton while 49 Squadron enjoyed a night off. A change of focus on the 14th would pitch 5 Group against marshalling yards in Cologne and oil production and storage facilities at Pauillac, situated on the West Bank of the Gironde River some twenty-five miles north of Bordeaux in south-western France. Bordeaux was an important port and U-Boot base on the Garonne River from where the Gironde estuary provided access to the Atlantic, in addition to which, oil facilities at Pauillac, Bec-d'Ambes and Blaye were of interest to Bomber Command, although it would be the summer of 1944 before a concerted effort was mounted against these targets. 49 Squadron detailed ten Hampdens for France, loading eight with four 250 pounders and incendiaries and two with four 500 pounders and briefed the crews to attack target Z161, which suggests that the oil facility was located on Pauillac aerodrome. They departed Scampton between 20.30 and 21.10 with no senior pilots on duty and set course for the south coast and the four-hour outward flight. Conditions in the target area were found to be excellent, which enabled most to carry out their attacks with great accuracy and claim direct hits on oil storage tanks, leaving a sea of flames that remained visible for up to 130 miles into the return flight. P2111 crashed on landing in the hands of Sgt Cooke, but the crew emerged unscathed and the Hampden would be returned to service.

The 15th was the day selected by the Luftwaffe as "Adlertag", Eagle Day, which was intended to be the opening salvo in the destruction of the RAF's ability to defend Britain. It began the most intense four weeks of the Battle of Britain, and its outcome might determine the course of the war. Bomber Command's attention switched to the Ruhr that night, when 5 Group would be operating alone, sending thirty-three Hampdens from Scampton and Hemswell to a variety of targets. 49 Squadron loaded five of its own with four 500 pounders and four with six 250 pounders plus one SBC of incendiaries and dispatched them from Scampton between 21.00 and 21.20 again with no senior pilots on duty. Their destination was A71, the Nordstern (Gelsenberg A G) synthetic oil refinery in the Horst district of Gelsenkirchen, where six crews delivered an attack, some of them observing bomb bursts and fires. Three crews found alternative targets, a factory at Mönchengladbach, the Krupp complex in Essen and a quay and jetty on the Rhine at Emmerich, and all returned safely after being airborne for between five and six-and-a-half hours.

Waddington and Hatfield Woodhouse were back in harness on the 16th, when A77, the I G Farben-owned oil refinery at Leuna, near Merseburg, was to be their target, which, as already mentioned, was one of many oil production and storage sites situated in an arc to the west of Leipzig from north of the city to the south. This would be an area of major interest to the Command from mid-1944 onwards, but that was in the distant future, when a thousand sorties might be launched in a single night, while on this night, the commitment of 150 sorties to targets in the Ruhr and eastern and southern Germany represented a major effort. 49 Squadron made ready eight Hampdens and sent them on their way from Scampton between 20.40 and 21.37 with S/L Allen the senior pilot on duty. They climbed away into a fine night with gentle moonlight to illuminate their path, but once over enemy territory, low cloud slid between them and the ground, happily, to disperse as the target area drew near. Despite the clear skies and the brightness of the moonlight, some crews experienced great difficulty in identifying the well-camouflaged complex and spent a long time searching, before either finding it or giving up. Somewhat optimistically, they had been briefed to aim for specific areas of the site, particularly the power generation and hydrogenation plants, and the crews of S/L Allen, F/O Ward-Hunt and P/O Harris all claimed to have scored hits, while Sgt Hills and crew aimed at a nearby railway junction, P/O Pinchbeck and crew at a flak battery and P/O Lewis an aerodrome at Nordhausen on the way home. P/O McClure and crew were unable to locate the primary or a suitable alternative target and brought their bombs home. P1333 failed to return home with the crew of Sgt Stretton, and news eventually came through that they had crash-landed near Breda close to the Scheldt estuary in Holland and had all been taken into captivity. At debriefings, crews from other squadrons reported bomb bursts, blue-green flames and fires, but most were too intent on evading the defences to take in the detail. The 44 Squadron crew of F/O Crossley was an exception and observed their bombs to burst near the base of chimneys and set off three explosions, followed by dense clouds of smoke and a fire that remained visible for seventy miles into the return flight.

On the 17th, Hatfield Woodhouse underwent the change of name described earlier, and would now be known as Lindholme. That night, 102 aircraft took part in wide-ranging operations, 49 Squadron preparing five for mining duties in the Eglantine garden in the Elbe estuary and three to attack the Krupp complex at Essen. They departed Scampton together between 20.10 and 20.20 with S/L Lowe the senior pilot on duty, the bombing element carrying four 500 pounders each and the gardeners two wing-mounted 250 pounders in addition to their mine. S/L Lowe and three others planted their vegetables in the briefed location, while Sgt pratt and crew realised that they had released theirs too far upriver, near Cuxhaven. Meanwhile, some two hundred miles to the south, the crews of P/O Haskins and Sgt Roberts attacked the Krupp complex, the former observing an explosion followed by a very large fire, while F/Sgt Apps and crew bombed the aerodrome on Texel as a last resort.

The German synthetic oil industry relied on two main production methods, the Bergius process, which involved the hydrogenation of highly volatile bituminous coal to manufacture high-grade petroleum products like aviation fuel, and the Fischer-Tropsch process, which produced lower-grade diesel-type fuels for vehicle, Tank, U-Boot and shipping requirements. The dual targets for forty-four Hampdens on the 21st were a ship lift at the eastern end of the Mittelland Canal at its junction with the River Elbe, and the Bergius-process Braunkohle A G (Aktien Gesellschaft or production company) synthetic oil refinery (hydrogenation plant) coded A78, both located in the same Rothensee district to the north of Magdeburg city centre. Also, on the target list and assigned to five Hampdens of 49 Squadron was M44, a second ship lift located at Hohenwarthe, close by to the north-east, which, in reality, had not been built, and as a result of the war, would not be. They departed Scampton between 20.40 and 20.55 with P/O Campbell the only commissioned pilot on duty and met with unfavourable weather conditions, including severe icing, which prevented all but P/O Campbell and crew from reaching the target area. They aimed their four 500 pounders at lock gates north of M44 before returning safely after six-and-a-half hours aloft.

Hemswell, Lindholme and Waddington received orders on the 22nd to prepare between them twenty-three Hampdens for an operation that night against an aircraft components factory (G82) in Frankfurt, while a dozen representing 49 Squadron took care of mining duties in the Artichoke garden off the Biscay port of Lorient. They departed Scampton between 21.00 and 21.20 with S/L Allen the senior pilot on duty and set course for the south coast to traverse the Channel and the Brittany region of north-western France intending to establish a pinpoint, possibly on Groix Island, from which to make a timed run to the drop zone. All but two were successful in that regard, while two found alternative locations and the crews of P/O Fawcett, F/O Burnett and F/O Haskins respectively attempted to bomb a ship and jetty in the Channel, Morlaix aerodrome near the Channel coast and a large armed trawler.

On the following night, 5 Group launched forty Hampdens to conduct mining sorties in the Jellyfish garden off the port of Brest. The seven-strong 49 Squadron element departed Scampton between 21.58 and 22.16 with S/L Lowe the senior pilot on duty and F/L Forsyth back on the order of battle after some time absent from it. They began the Channel crossing at the Dorset coast, heading for landfall on the French coast somewhere to the west of St-Malo, before arriving in the target area to find excellent conditions with bright moonlight and the defences already stirred into action by earlier arrivals. The pinpoints for the timed runs, among them Pointe-Sainte-Mathieu on the northern headland, were easily established, and the vegetables planted by five crews according to brief from between 400 and 800 feet. P/O Pinchbeck and crew suffered the frustration of a hang up and F/Sgt Apps and crew returned their mine to store after failing to complete their sortie.

In retaliation for the inadvertent bombing of London on the night of the 24/25th, the War Cabinet sanctioned the first raid of the war on Berlin by around fifty aircraft to take place on the 25th. 5 Group responded with the preparation of forty-six Hampdens for this and other operations, thirty-four from Scampton, Waddington and Lindholme to attack an electrical power station, B57, one of five serving the city, while twelve from Hemswell targeted Tempelhof aerodrome to the south. Germany's capital lay at the limit of endurance for Hampdens carrying a load of four 500 pounders and might have to rely on perfect weather conditions to complete a round trip, which for some would exceed eight hours. 49 Squadron made ready a dozen of its own and dispatched them from Scampton between 20.27 and 21.03 with W/C Gillan and S/L Allen the senior pilots on duty. They set course via the Lincolnshire coast for the target, six hundred miles away, adopting a route that would take them close to Hannover and Braunschweig, but a blanket of cloud stretching across northern Germany largely denied them a sight of the ground. The unfavourable conditions persisted in the target area, where the cloud base was down to 2,000 feet and only the crews of F/O Ward-Hunt, P/O Pinchbeck and Sgts Pratt and Hills would report attacking the primary target without observing the results. Most of the others found alternative objectives in the form of a marshalling yards, a blast furnace, a factor, a SEMO and a searchlight and flak battery, before heading home into a headwind, the very worst prospect for fuel management. Absent from debriefing was the experienced crew of F/O Fawcett, who disappeared without trace in P4416 as one of four Hampdens to run out of fuel over the North Sea, the crews of the others, happily, being picked up safe and sound. Local sources confirmed that most of the bombing had missed the city to the south and that the only building destroyed was a summerhouse, but it was an unsettling experience for the Nazi leadership and gave further lie to Göring's boast that no enemy aircraft would fly over the Reich.

Scampton remained off the order of battle on another busy night of operations on the 26th, which saw the preparation of twenty Hampdens from Hemswell and two from Waddington to attack A77, the Leuna (Merseburg) oil refinery near Liepzig, while six others from Waddington were assigned to a gas production plant in the city itself. On the 27th, Scampton was called upon to provide eight Hampdens for mining duties in the Artichoke garden off Lorient and Port-Louis, the latter situated opposite the port on the southern side of the Blavet Estuary. A further nine aircraft, all belonging to 49 Squadron, were detailed for a bombing operation against the oil facility at Bec-d'Ambes on the River Gironde, north of Bordeaux and were loaded with either four 500 pounders or four of 250lbs and incendiaries. They took off between 20.45 and 21.55 with F/O Drakes the senior pilot on duty and were followed into the air at 23.40 by the two gardeners, captained by F/Sgt Apps and F/O Riley. The ORB provided no insight into the conduct of the mining sorties, but they apparently found their target area without difficulty and delivered their single mine each as briefed. The bombers faced a four-hour outward flight to their target on the Biscay coast, which all completed, and six crews attacked the primary target, while two went for the nearby Pauillac facility and Sgt Cooke and crew returned their bombs to store. At debriefing, some crews reported bomb bursts and fires at the primary target, while both of those attacking the Pauillac site claimed a large fire. P/O Matthews had been charged with photographing the results of the operation, a new innovation, but was unsuccessful. Earlier in the day, he had been awarded a DFC.

Orders were received on all 5 Group stations on the 28th to prepared thirty Hampdens for an operation that night against the Siemens and Halske A G factory in the Siemensstadt district of Spandau, north-west of Berlin city centre. This site produced components for aero-engines and would be found after the war to have employed slave workers from concentration camps. The four 49 Squadron Hampdens were loaded with four 500 pounders each and took off from Scampton between 20.40 and 21.00 bearing aloft the crews of P/O Parker, F/O Haskins, Sgt Pratt and F/O Ward-Hunt. Some squadron ORBs provided a highly detailed account of each individual sortie on this night, while the 49 Squadron record tells us only that the crews of F/O Haskins and P/O Parker attacked the primary target, and that F/O Ward-Hunt was defeated by darkness and haze and bombed the aerodrome on Borkum on the way home. Sgt Pratt and crew located the undisclosed secondary target but failed to observe the burst of their bombs.

On the 29th, Hemswell and Waddington dispatched twenty Hampdens between them to attack the Scholven-Buer synthetic oil refinery, situated north of Gelsenkirchen city centre in the Ruhr, while Scampton remained inactive. It was Scampton's turn on the 30th to send fourteen Hampdens back to the recently attacked A78, the Bergius-process hydrogenation plant at Magdeburg, for which, according to the Form 540 of the ORB, 49 Squadron briefed ten crews and loaded their Hampdens with either four 500 pounders or four 250 pounders plus one SBC of incendiaries. Two other crews were detailed for M25, the old aqueduct of the Dortmund-Ems Canal, but the Form 541 of the

ORB lists only eleven crews in all and identifies the crew of F/O Riley as the only one assigned to M25. They departed Scampton between 20.35 and 22.30, and F/O Riley and crew are recorded as attacking M25 but failing to observe the results. Of those involved in the main event, few were able to identify the target in the conditions, and alternative recipients were found for the bomb loads as the crews made their way home. P/O Matthews reported dropping a stick of bombs from high level on A78 and the crews of P/O McClure and F/O Hodges were the only others to claim to have bombed the primary target. The crews of Sgts Hills and Roberts attacked the synthetic oil plant at Wesseling near Cologne, P/O Parker a railway junction and sidings east of Magdeburg, P/O Fox and Sgt Cooke an aerodrome at Langenhagen near Hannover, P/O Lewis a railway junction east of Nienburg and S/L Lowe brought his bombs home.

On the last night of the month, Scampton was ordered to make ready ten Hampdens and Lindholme five for a return to the Magdeburg synthetic oil plant, while fifteen from Hemswell and Waddington were assigned to two targets in Berlin. 49 Squadron briefed five crews and loaded their aircraft with four 500 pounders each and, as was standard practice at the time, sent those not involved in the night's activities to nearby Dunholme Lodge for dispersal. Sgt Roberts took off at 16.15 in P2135 with three members of ground crew on board and stalled out of a turn before crashing close to the airfield, killing all on board. Those involved in the operation departed Scampton between 20.50 and 21.00 with the newly promoted F/L Haskins the senior pilot on duty but none would be able to identify the target in conditions of nine to ten-tenths low cloud. F/L Haskins had to contend with an engine issue and bombed an aerodrome at Cloppenburg between Bremen and the Dutch frontier after abandoning his sortie, while F/O Beauchamp attacked a blast furnace near Celle, north-east of Hannover, Sgt Pratt and P/O Pinchbeck aerodromes in northern Germany and F/O Burnett brought his bombs home.

During the course of the month, the squadron took part in twenty operations and dispatched 159 sorties for the loss of six Hampdens and five crews.

## September 1940

While the Battle of Britain was reaching a crescendo overhead, and invasion fever gripped the nation, the overriding priority for the Command in September would be the destruction of the invasion craft assembling in ports along the occupied coast. That said, the new month began for 5 Group on the 1st with small-scale attacks on industrial targets in Germany, Hemswell providing six Hampdens to attack an aircraft components factory in Stuttgart, possibly the Hirth aero-engine plant in the northern suburb of Zuffenhausen, Scampton two for marshalling yards in Mannheim, and Waddington two for a hydrogenation plant at Ludwigshafen. On the following night, Scampton provided six crews from each squadron for the first of many future raids on U-Boots at berth in ports, on this occasion at Lorient, for which the 49 Squadron element took off between 20.20 and 20.30. The crews had been briefed to bomb six U-Boots moored in the harbour as the primary targets and if unable to do so, to seek out SEMOs or MOPAs (military objectives previously attacked). Each was carrying either four 500 pounders or six 250 pounders, all of which reached the target area, where F/O Drakes and crew were unsuccessful owing to an undisclosed error of judgement. The others claimed success, and according to the 83 Squadron account, eight U-Boots had been found and five of them seriously damaged.

Berlin was the destination for a dozen Hampdens on the 3rd, nine of them provided by Scampton, four belonging to 49 Squadron. The primary target was an electrical power station on the outskirts, against which 500 and 250 pounders were to be employed. The 49 Squadron quartet first flew over to the 3 Group station at Feltwell, before taking off between 20.20 and 20.25 with F/O Matthews the senior pilot on duty. Unfavourable weather conditions doomed the operation to failure and F/O Matthews and crew attacked Lastrup aerodrome some thirty miles from the Dutch frontier on the way home. The crews of P/Os Haskell and McClure also found alternative targets, respectively an aerodrome at Celle and marshalling yards in Hannover, while P/O Pinchbeck and crew returned their bombs to store.

Another distant target was posted on the 4th, for which twenty-three Hampdens were detailed and sent to Mildenhall for bombing up and launch. Crews learned at briefing that their primary target was the I G Farben-owned Wintershall synthetic oil refinery at Politz to the north of the Baltic port city of Stettin. 49 Squadron made ready five of its own for the crews of F/O Hodges, P/Os Fox and Lewis and Sgts Pratt and Unsworth, who took off between 20.07 and 20.15 for what would be an eight-hour round trip. They set course for Heligoland, to make landfall on the Danish coast north of Sylt, from where they were able to map-read their way across southern Jutland and the Baltic to the target area in favourable conditions that offered ten miles visibility. All arrived in the target area under continuing clear skies but extreme darkness, and each delivered an attack, which resulted in explosions.

In view of the lack of information recorded in the 49 Squadron ORB, and in order to better describe the operation, the following passage has been constructed from the 50 Squadron ORB. *P/O Stenner and crew identified the target straight-away, and attacked it from 10,500 feet at 23.35, observing their four 500 pounders to burst along the southern edge of the site, although they were unable to determine the effects. F/O French and crew found the searchlight and anti-aircraft fire over Denmark to be both accurate and troublesome but came through unscathed to deliver their attack from 10,000 feet at 00.27, registering three direct hits that caused explosions and white fires visible for fifteen minutes and from fifty miles away. S/L Willan and crew spent thirty minutes searching for the target, before bombing it from 7,000 feet at 00.30, and observing their four 250 pounders and incendiaries to burst on buildings at the southern extremity of the site, causing fires with white flames that remained visible for twenty miles into the return flight. P/O Banker and crew bombed the target at the same time, having adopted a slightly different outward flight that made landfall first on Terschelling. They had found a thick haze lying over Denmark, which dispersed as they neared the target area, and, having identified the refinery, they carried out a dive attack from 7,000 to 3,000 feet. The four 500 pounders were seen to fall across the centre of the complex and cause three tall chimneys to collapse, the resultant large fires remaining visible for forty miles into the return journey.*

The 5 Group ORB declared the operation to be a success and claimed that four tall chimneys had been brought down. On the way home, F/O Hodges and crew strayed off course and believing themselves to be on approach to St Eval aerodrome in Cornwall, were surprised to be fired upon by light flak. Now, critically low on fuel, F/O Hodges ordered his crew to bale out, before force-landing P1347 in a field and discovering that Sgt Wyatt was still on board having failed to hear the bale-out order. They had come down near St-Brieuc in the Brittany region of north-western France and, while their two crew mates were taken into captivity, they set off on the long journey to Spain. They were arrested by Vichy police near Marseilles but escaped from custody and made it across the Pyrenees, only to be arrested again in Spain and imprisoned. Following release, they were able to reach Gibraltar, from where they were flown home, arriving on the 31st of July 1941, whereupon "Bob" Hodges returned to 49 Squadron.

On the following day, Scampton, Hemswell and Waddington were alerted to a return to the same target that night, for which eighteen Hampdens were made ready, seven of them belonging to 49 Squadron and loaded with six 250 pounders each plus one SBC of incendiaries. Hemswell was also to provide aircraft on this night for an attack on an oil refinery in Hamburg, and to disrupt and delay the repairs to the Dortmund-Ems Canal north of Münster. The main event was launched from Marham, where the 49 Squadron element took off between 19.45 and 20.15 with F/L Haskins the senior pilot on duty, and it is believed that all reached the target area, where the crews of Sgt Cooke and F/Os Burnett, Drakes and Ward-Hunt carried out an attack, while P/O Haskell and crew bombed Rodbyhavn aerodrome on Denmark's Lolland island on the way home after failing to identify the primary target in conditions of haze and extreme darkness. P4350 did not return with the others and was duly posted missing along with the crew of F/L Haskins, of whom news eventually arrived to confirm that they had come down in the Channel, well south of track, and had been picked up from their dinghy by the enemy off Calais and taken into captivity. Had they managed to stay on course, they would easily have reached one of the many aerodromes between Yorkshire and East Anglia.

The intensive period of back-to-back operations continued on the 6th, when a dozen Hampdens were detailed, eight at Scampton and four at Hemswell, to attack an oil refinery in Dortmund, and while we are provided with the code A108, we do not know whether it referred to the Hoesch-Westfalenhütte A G, the Hoesch-Benzin GmbH or the Zeche Hansa coking plant. In addition, nine Hampdens from Waddington were sent to attack marshalling yards at Hamm, Krefeld, Trier and Mannheim. The crews of F/O Beauchamp, P/O Pinchbeck, F/O Murray and F/Sgt Apps took off between 19.30 and 19.40, each carrying six 250 pounders, one SBC of incendiaries and "razzles". Not one reached the primary target after encountering unfavourable weather conditions and the crews of F/Os Beauchamp and Murray respectively attacked SEMOs in the form of marshalling yards at Emmerich to the north of the Ruhr and a blast furnace in the vicinity of Mönchengladbach to the south. P/O Pinchbeck and F/O Murray also dispensed "razzles". As F/O Beauchamp landed, P4304 was fired upon by an enemy intruder, which missed.

The anti-invasion campaign continued on the night of the 7/8th, with operations against concentrations of barges in the occupied ports. Ninety-two aircraft were committed to the night's endeavours, most of them against barges, and they included Battles operated by a number of 1 Group squadrons. Five 49 Squadron Hampdens were among twenty-nine sent by 5 Group to Ostend, and they got away safely from Scampton between 20.15 and 20.25 with F/Os Matthews and Riley the senior pilots on duty. They set course via corridor "G" towards the mouth of the Scheldt, before turning to the west and running in on the target. A mist lay over the area, and light from a quarter moon reflected upon it to decrease visibility, but the main impediment to target identification and assessment of results was the hostility of the flak and searchlight defences.

Although the searchlight glare blinded the attacking crews, the beams did, at least, provide an indication of the whereabouts of the target, All from Scampton reported attacking as briefed, and bomb bursts and sparks were observed, but no accurate assessment of the results could be made. One 44 Squadron crews observed their bombs to fall among a concentration of around sixty barges moored on the western side of the basin, and another watched debris being flung into the air from the detonation of their bombs in the Bassin d'Evolution.

For the seventh day in a row, 49 Squadron crews were called to briefing on the 8th to learn of their part in the night's activities, which were to involve 133 aircraft attacking ports, and were told that they would be going to Hamburg in company with forty-two others to attack a specific dockyard installation located some 500 yards from the Blohm & Voss shipyards on a heading of 120° from its centre. For any unable to locate the primary target, the alternative was invasion barges in the port of Delfzijl on Holland's north-eastern coast. Seven Hampdens were loaded with either four 500 pounders or six of 250lbs plus incendiaries and dispatched from Scampton between 19.20 and 19.42. The standard route to Germany's second city involved skirting the chain of the Frisian Islands to make landfall on the Schleswig-Holstein peninsula, before running in from the north. An alternative was to pinpoint on Scharhörn island north of the mouth of the Elbe, thence to follow the river's course into the heart of the city, usually under the constant attention of searchlights and flak from both banks. In the event, six of the 49 Squadron crews located the primary target and carried out an attack on the general area, some observing bomb bursts and others not, while F/O Ward-Hunt and crew went for the alternative, where the bombs were seen to detonate but no determination of the outcome was possible.

The operation was repeated on the following night by twenty-one Hampdens, including a singleton from 49 Squadron containing the crew of Sgt Cooke. They returned at 04.10 to report that they had attacked the target but had not observed the results. The campaign against invasion craft continued on the 10th, when nine aircraft from Scampton and Lindholme were assigned to Ostend, where concentrations of craft were reported to be eight or nine deep on the eastern side of the outer harbour. Hemswell and Waddington, meanwhile, would focus their attention on Calais. Although seven 49 Squadron aircraft had been detailed, only six were listed as taking off between 19.33 and 20.20 with F/O Riley the senior pilot on duty. They reached the target to encounter seven to ten-tenths cloud that severely hampered their attempts to establish a position and the crews of F/O Riley and P/O Lewis failed to locate the target, while the others attacked but observed no results.

Following two nights at home, ten 49 Squadron crews were called to briefing on the 13th to hear that they would be returning to Ostend, while ten others from Hemswell were to be sent against Boulogne. They departed Scampton between 20.58 and 21.50 with S/L Lowe the senior pilot on duty and all reached the target to carry out an attack which resulted in many bomb bursts and fires. The Battle of Britain reached its climax on the 15th, and although skirmishes would continue into October, the decision had already been taken by Hitler to abandon Einsatz Seelöwe, Operation Sealion, and prepare instead for an assault on Russia in the coming summer. The docks at Antwerp were posted as the target for that night, for which 49 Squadron made ready eleven Hampdens, loading eight with four 250lb general purpose (GP) bombs and two 250lb anti-shipping (AS) bombs plus incendiaries and three with six 250lb GP and two 250lb AS. They departed Scampton between 22.28 and 23.25 with S/L Allen the senior pilot on duty and the newly-arrived S/L Whitehead flying with F/O Ward-Hunt and joined forces with fifteen others from 83 Squadron.

Nine of the 49 Squadron crews located and bombed the primary target, while the crews of F/O Murray and P/O Parker attacked the designated alternative, the docks at Flushing on Walcheren Island. In his book, Enemy Coast Ahead, Gibson described flying alongside a Hampden on fire and recognising it as belonging to 83 Squadron. P1355 had been hit by flak during the run-up to the target, and a fire had erupted amidships. Two crew members took to their parachutes, Gibson observing one to land in a river, while eighteen-year-old Sgt Hannah fought the fire alone with his bare hands. His heroic actions enabled P/O Connor to bring the badly damaged Hampden home to a safe landing, for which Sgt Hannah was award a VC and P/O Connor a DFC.

The 17th brought Bomber Command's greatest commitment of aircraft to date in a single night of 197, approximately two-thirds of them assigned to invasion craft in the occupied ports. 49 Squadron made ready fifteen Hampdens, eight to send against the docks at Terneuzen on the southern bank of the western Schelde opposite Walcheren Island and seven for the docks at Flushing (Vlissingen) some ten miles to the north-west on the island itself. At the same time, twenty-two other Hampdens would be targeting shipping in Antwerp harbour. The Scampton crews took off between 19.45 and 20.55 with S/L Allen the senior pilot on duty and S/L Whitehead flying on this occasion with F/L Burnett. All reached and bombed their respective targets or designated alternatives and S/L Allen and crew carried out four strafing attacks on a water power station four miles south of their primary target. P/O Lewis and crew reported a large explosion and fires following a direct hit at Terneuzen and P/O Campbell and crew bombed four trawlers in the harbour entrance but did not observe the result.

5 Group detailed thirty-seven Hampdens on the 19th to send against the Dortmund-Ems Canal and shipping and barges at Ostend and Flushing and eight for mining duties in the Deodar garden in the Gironde estuary. 49 squadron divided its strength ten/five between M25, the aqueduct and embankments of the canal and Ostend and sent them on their way from Scampton between 23.30 and 01.18 with S/L Allen the senior pilot on duty and S/L Whitehead back with F/O Ward-Hunt. They soon ran into challenging weather conditions over the North Sea, with driving rain in a band of cloud between 1,000 and 10,000 feet, and this would prevent most from fulfilling their brief. The crews of F/Os Beauchamp and Ward-Hunt and P/Os Haskell and Parker carried out attacks on M25 and M25A and Sgt Hopkins and crew bombed the docks at Ostend, while P/O Harris and crew found a SEMO, but they were the only successful sorties on an unsatisfactory night for Scampton.

Berlin had been posted as the main target for forty-five Hampdens on the 21st, but adverse weather conditions caused a cancellation and the 5 Group effort was reduced to eight Hampdens from Scampton and seven from Lindholme with Ostend as their destination and an alternative of Dunkerque. The 49 Squadron quartet took off between 23.15 and 23.22 with S/L Lowe the senior pilot on duty and, according to the ORB, the crews of F/O Drakes and S/L Lowe attacked the primary target, while the crews of Sgt Hills and P/O Lewis bombed the docks at Terneuzen. On return, the Hills and Drakes crews reported a fire visible in the region of Dunkerque, while the Lewis crew described a large explosion believed to be at Calais. On the following night, thirty Hampden crews were briefed for operations against the ports of Ostend, Boulogne, Le Havre, Flushing and Antwerp, and it was for Le Havre on the Normandy coast that the eleven 49 Squadron aircraft departed Scampton between 00.30 and 01.05 with F/Os Murray and Riley the senior pilots on duty. Each was carrying six 250lb GP bombs in the bomb bay and two wing-mounted 250lb

AS bombs, most of which would reach the primary target. P/O Fox and crew made it across the Channel with an ailing engine and dropped their load on Dunkerque docks before turning back, leaving the others to fulfil their briefs some 145 miles along the coast to the south-west. Returning crews described explosions, fires and black smoke and Sgt Pratt and crew report that a ship had blown up.

The Berlin operation was reinstated on the 23rd and a force of 129 Hampdens, Wellingtons and Whitleys assembled to attack eighteen specific targets, made up of seven railway yards, six electrical power stations, three gasworks and two aero-engine and aircraft component factories. It was unique at this stage of the war to focus the entire strength of an operation on a single city, and it was a policy, which in the years ahead, would prove that a concentration of bombing was the most effective way to achieve the desired results. 5 Group contributed forty-five Hampdens from Scampton, Hemswell, Waddington and Lindholme, just four provided by 49 Squadron for the crews of P/Os Lewis and McClure, F/O Ward-Hunt and F/L Burnett. They took off between 19.50 and 19.56, bound, it is believed for the power station B59, located in Berlin's western district of Moabit and each loaded with four 500 pounders, half with an instant fuse and the others with delay fuses of various lengths. They also carried "razzles" to dispense in the area between Bremen and Berlin, encompassing Soltau in the west through Uelzen to Buchholz in the east and Lüneberg and Celle to the south. Some probably flew out at high-level, in order to put themselves above a front that lay between the Dutch coast and a point 150 miles from Germany's Capital, but the crews of P/O Lewis and F/L Burnett ran into severe icing conditions, which persuaded the former to drop their bombs on a bridge over the Weser-Elbe Canal near Hannover and the latter on the docks at Bremen. F/O Ward-Hunt dispensed his "razzles" on the way out but lost his starboard engine twenty miles east of Celle and had to jettison the bombs. This left just P/O McClure and crew to attack the primary target without observing the results. Earlier in the day, F/L Learoyd VC had been posted back to the squadron from his post at the Air Ministry.

It was back to the anti-invasion campaign on the 24th, when 5 Group detailed thirteen Hampdens from Scampton and Hemswell to attack the harbour lock, barges and shipping at CC24, Le Havre, while ten others from Hemswell and Lindholme targeted Calais. The 49 Squadron quartet, consisting of the crews of Sgt Nichol, F/Sgt Apps, F/O Beauchamp and F/L Forsyth, took off between 00.10 and 00.18 and all reached the target to deliver their four 500 pounders each. Fires were observed, but only F/O Beauchamp and crew witnessed the detonation of their bombs. Among other targets on this night had been an electrical power station in Berlin, and B56 and B57 were briefed out as the targets for twenty-one Hampden crews on the 25th. In the event, the Lindholme element of four would be prevented from taking off because of enemy intruders operating near Bircham Newton, the forward base in use, but the nine-strong 49 Squadron element experienced no such difficulty and departed Scampton over an extended period between 18.45 and 20.01 bound for B57 with F/L Learoyd the senior pilot on duty. Sgt Cooke and crew penetrated as far as Hannover, where they attacked marshalling yards before turning for home, leaving the others to reach Berlin but not necessarily locate the primary target. The crews of Sgt Pratt and P/Os Fox, Haskell and Campbell and F/L Learoyd all reported carrying out successful attacks, while those of Sgt Hills and F/Os Riley and Drakes went for alternatives within the city in the form of marshalling yards and Tempelhof aerodrome.

On the 26th, some of what might be termed the old guard, those who had been part of the backbone of the squadron since the German advance, were posted out to 14 O.T.U at Cottesmore, where they would pass on the benefit of their skills and experience as instructors. The presence of F/L Burnett, F/O Murray DFC, P/O Pinchbeck, P/O Lewis and P/O Parker would be missed, but they would be succeeded by eager young men fed in mostly from 106 Squadron at Finningley, which had been performing the role of the group pool training unit but would now take its place in the front line as O.T.Us became responsible for training. 5 Group would divide its forces that night, sending eight Hampdens from Hemswell and four from Waddington to attack the heavy cruiser, Scharnhorst, which was at berth in the Krupp-Germania shipyard in Kiel. This magnificent vessel, which entered service in January 1939, displaced 38,700 tons fully loaded, and boasted a length of 771 feet, with an armament of nine eleven-inch guns arranged in three triple turrets. During an engagement in June 1940, in which she sank the aircraft carrier, HMS Glorious, she was damaged by a torpedo from the sinking destroyer, HMS Acasta, and would spend the next six months at Kiel under repair. Another 5 Group effort on this night involved six more Hemswell crews taking another swipe at the Dortmund-Ems Canal north of Münster, while seven from Lindholme continued the anti-invasion campaign at Calais, and Finningley took care of gardening duties.

The anti-invasion campaign continued on the 27th, when twenty-five Hampden crews were briefed at Scampton, Hemswell and Lindholme to target barges, motor torpedo boats and U-boots at Lorient, which, early in the coming year, would be the site of a massive civil engineering project to construct three huge concrete U-Boot facilities. 49 Squadron had enjoyed two nights off when eleven crews were called to briefing on the 28th to learn that six of them would be returning to M25A, the Dortmund-Ems Canal, while five would continue the anti-invasion campaign at Le Havre. The former departed Scampton between 01.04 and 01.10 with S/L Lowe the senior pilot on duty and S/L Whitehead performing the role of bomb-aimer. Those bound for the Normandy coast took off at 01.30 led by F/O Riley and both elements encountered adverse weather conditions over the North Sea and Channel in the form of ten-tenths low cloud. F/Sgt Apps and crew failed to locate Le Havre and Sgt Wright and crew attacked the docks generally, leaving the crews of F/O Riley, P/O Haskell and Sgt Nichol to locate and bomb the primary target. Meanwhile, almost five hundred miles to the north-east, none of those charged with hitting the new Dortmund-Ems Canal aqueduct was able to locate it and four found alternatives in the form of aerodromes and marshalling yards.

Tragedy struck on the 29th, when P2134 flew into high ground two miles north-east of Wigan at 23.30 during a training flight, killing the pilot, Sgt Catley, second pilot, Sgt Nichol and gunner, Sgt Hastie. The first two-mentioned had operated against Le Havre on the previous night, when Sgt Nichol had been the captain and pilot. It was a sad end to another busy month of operations, during which the threat of invasion had been banished and a long, attritional war now lay in prospect. During the course of the month, the squadron took part in twenty-two operations and dispatched 139 sorties for the loss of three Hampdens and crews.

# October 1940

Ninety-nine aircraft were detailed by the Command to open the new month's account on the 1st and Scampton was in action immediately, providing ten crews from 49 Squadron to join five from Waddington for an attack on the synthetic oil refinery at Wesseling, or to give it its full name, the Union Rheinische Braunkohlen-Kraftstoff A G, situated on the West Bank of the Rhine in the southern reaches of Cologne. They took off between 18.55 and 19.20 with F/L Learoyd the senior pilot on duty and S/L Whitehead still serving his apprenticeship as navigator/bomb-aimer. Their sortie was cut short by engine failure as they reached the Dutch coast over the Scheldt estuary and the bombs were dropped onto a row of white lights and a flashing white beacon three miles south of Ouddorp on Goeree Island. Six others located the primary target and carried out an attack, some reporting explosions and fires, while two of three new NCO crews defeated by poor visibility bombed Haamstede aerodrome on Zeeland Island and the third a similar target of opportunity on the way home towards Antwerp.

The target for nineteen crews from Hemswell, Lindholme and Waddington on the 2nd was an oil refinery in Hamburg (A8), and as often was the case at this early stage of the war, an operation might be spread over an extended period with individual squadrons deciding for themselves routes and timings. On this night, the arrival in the target area of the Waddington Hampdens would be some five hours after the Lindholme crews had attacked and two behind those from Hemswell. Barrage balloons were reported to be tethered at 6,000 feet over Wilhelmshaven, and this inconvenience had to be added to the eight to ten-tenths cloud with haze below, and the usual gauntlet of intense searchlight and flak activity on the route along the course of the Elbe south-east towards the heart of Germany's second city.

In a low-key start to the month, the Hampden brigade was employed sparingly over the ensuing nights as 2 Group took the strain, and it would be the 5th before 5 Group ventured forth again with thirty Hampdens distributed between the Nordstern oil plant at Gelsenkirchen, marshalling yards north and south of the Ruhr and gardening duties. This was the day on which Sir Charles Portal relinquished his post as Commander-in-Chief of Bomber Command and took up his new appointment as Chief of the Air Staff. He was succeeded by ACM Sir Richard Peirse, whose tenure was to be dogged by the inadequacies of the equipment available to him and the increasing and often unrealistic demands from on high. Scampton remained inactive until the 7th, when a dozen 49 Squadron crews were called to briefing, six to be assigned to mining duties in the Artichoke garden off Lorient and six divided between M116, the marshalling yards at Soest to the north of the Ruhr and M465, one of a number of large marshalling yards in Cologne. They took off together between 18.30 and 19.53 with S/L Lowe the senior pilot among the bombing element, accompanied by S/L Whitehead, and F/L Learoyd leading the gardeners. Conditions over the Biscay coast were favourable, and all of the gardeners were able to plant their vegetables in the briefed locations, three of them going on to bomb the docks at Lorient with their wing-mounted 250 pounders, while a fourth attacked a flak concentration on the way home. Conditions over Germany were less helpful and having failed to locate the Soest marshalling yards, S/L Lowe and crew bombed Texel on the way home, while the crews of Sgts Ball and Wright bombed through cloud and haze, the latter observing bursts and fires. Meanwhile, south of the Ruhr, the crews of

F/L Forsyth and Sgts Imber and Richman located M465 and delivered attacks, which resulted in bursts and fires.

Orders were received at Waddington and Scampton on the 8th to prepare for an operation that night against the Bismarck-class Battleship Tirpitz, which was in the final stages of fitting-out at a floating dock in Wilhelmshaven. The Admiralty was acutely conscious of the threat posed by Germany's mighty battleships Bismarck and Tirpitz, and there was a constant pressure on Bomber Command to deal with them before they began their careers as surface raiders. Laid down in the Kriegsmarinewerft yards in 1936, Tirpitz had been launched in the spring of 1939, and, once ready for sea trials in early 1941, she would be two thousand tons heavier than her sister ship. 83 Squadron represented Scampton, and despite a gallant effort by all involved in the face of an intense searchlight and flak defence, the attacks failed to result in damage to the vessel. On the following night, a 5 Group effort by twenty Hampdens was directed at the highly important Krupp complex in Essen. The weather conditions were unfavourable and most of the force failed to find the target under a blanket of thick, low cloud.

On the 10th, S/L Allen was posted out to HQ 7 Group pending a permanent appointment and was succeeded as a flight commander by S/L Jefferson, who had been posted in from 106 Squadron. S/L Allen's leadership qualities would see him return to operations in the coming April as the commanding officer of 106 Squadron, a post in which he would excel. The promise of bright moonlight for that night may have been a consideration in scheduling another assault on the battleship Tirpitz at Wilhelmshaven, for which thirteen Hampdens were made ready, nine at Waddington and four at Lindholme. A simultaneous operation would be conducted against the Krupp-Germania shipyard in Kiel by eleven 49 Squadron Hampdens, probably with the intention of hitting the heavy cruiser, Scharnhorst, while Hemswell attended to the mining of the Kiel Canal. They departed Scampton between 18.20 and 19.00 with S/L Jefferson the senior pilot on duty and S/L Whitehead flying with F/O Beauchamp, and should any be unable to locate the primary target, the docks at Wilhelmshaven would be their alternative. F/Sgt Apps and crew turned back early because of excessive engine vibration and bombed the seaplane base on Norderney, while the others all reached and attacked the primary target in the face of a spirited flak defence. Those observing the fall of their bombs reported explosions and fires but no detail.

49 Squadron remained on the ground on the 11th, as the pursuit of the Tirpitz continued at the hands of five Hampdens from Lindholme, while another one joined five from Hemswell to target the Blohm & Voss shipyards at Hamburg. Under cover of this, three Finningley crews would conduct mining sorties in the Eglantine garden at the mouth of the Elbe estuary. On the eastern side of the Schleswig-Holstein peninsula, a dozen Hemswell Hampdens were to attack Kiel dockyards, a few miles south of the Kiel Canal, where nine Scampton crews were to carry out mining duties in the Lettuce garden. Poor weather conditions hampered each operation, and few crews were able to carry out their brief.

The night of the 12/13th would bring the final operations against invasion craft in the occupied ports and would bring down the curtain on the operational career of the Fairey Battle. Elsewhere, sixteen crews at Scampton and two at Hemswell were briefed for an operation that night against an aluminium factory producing aircraft components in the Herringen district of Hamm, while ten crews at Waddington were informed that they would be attacking the Krupp complex at Essen.

The eleven 49 Squadron participants took off between 18.09 and 18.20 with F /L Learoyd the senior pilot on duty and S/L Whitehead flying with F/Sgt Apps. In unhelpful weather conditions, only the crews of F/Sgt Apps and Sgts Ball and Shaw succeeded in identifying the primary target and carrying out an attack with indeterminate results, while the others went for the secondary target, an electrical power station, or targets of opportunity mostly north of the Ruhr, although Sgt Wright and crew attacked the Wesseling oil refinery south of Cologne and Sgt price and crew ventured as far east as Kassel, where they bombed an aerodrome. On return, Sgt Richman overshot his landing and P2095 ended up in a hedge on the airfield boundary, fortunately without causing serious damage to either aircraft or occupants.

The Admiralty continued to obsess about the Tirpitz, in response to which, 5 Group detailed thirty-five Hampdens from Hemswell, Lindholme, Waddington and 83 Squadron at Scampton on the 13th, and briefed their crews for a return to Wilhelmshaven. Having reached the mid-point of the North Sea crossing, they ran into one of the enormous fronts that frequently barred the route into north-western Germany. Characterized by ice-bearing and storm-laden towering cumulonimbus cloud, they were a nightmare to negotiate and often too enormous to circumnavigate. The icing layer on this night extended from 6,000 to 12,000 feet, with rainstorms from 1,000 to 12,000 feet, which prevented most crews from reaching the target.

5 Group detailed twenty Hampdens on the 14th for another shot that night at H41, the Air Ministry building in Berlin's Leipzigstrasse, on a night when cities in eastern Germany were targeted by fifty aircraft from other groups. 49 Squadron contributed six Hampdens, which departed Scampton between 22.30 and 22.45 with F/O Drakes the senior pilot on duty and lost the services of F/Sgt Apps and crew to the failure of their oxygen system and Sgt Price and crew to their aircraft's sluggish performance, and they unloaded their bombs respectively on De Kooy aerodrome on the Den Helder peninsula and Emden docks. Those reaching the target area encountered up to ten-tenths cloud and haze, which required them to spend time either circling or making dummy runs from a variety of directions in order to familiarize themselves with the lay of the land and to establish the best method of attack. They had to face searchlight and flak activity, and some crews from other units also noticed a number of barrage balloons tethered at up to 15,000 feet. The crews of F/O Drakes and Sgt Shaw attacked the primary target and observed evidence of fires in the city, while the crews of Sgt Ball and Sgt Imber respectively bombed the marshalling yards, M499, and an unidentified aerodrome before returning after seven and eight-hour sorties.

Oil targets featured prominently on the 15th, when 134 aircraft were detailed for wide-ranging targets in Germany and the Channel ports, 5 Group directing the bulk of its effort of thirty-three Hampdens against oil targets in Magdeburg, principally the Rothensee plant that they had attacked last in early September. Twenty-four Hampdens were made ready at Hemswell and Waddington on the 16th for an operation that night against the oil refinery at Leuna, near Merseburg, west of Leipzig, while Scampton prepared a dozen belonging to 49 Squadron to mine the waters of the Deodar garden in the Gironde estuary and then to attack U-Boots in their base a few miles further south at Bordeaux. *(The form 541 of the 49 Squadron ORB annoyingly omits a record of participating crews who fail to return or are involved in crashes on return, detailing them only on the Form 540 summary, which denies us take-off and landing times.)* Nine crews are recorded as taking off between 18.00 and 18.45 with F/L Forsyth the senior pilot on duty, and the services of Sgt Bates and crew were lost to adverse weather conditions within three hours. On attempting to land at Abingdon, X2900 came to grief and was written off, happily without casualties among the Bates crew. P/O Haskell and crew abandoned their sortie sometime later also in the face of adverse weather conditions, while Sgt Unsworth and crew turned back after becoming concerned about their fuel situation. They chanced upon three vessels, which they attacked from 800 feet with indeterminate results. Sgt Hopkins and crew dropped their mine at 23.45 in a position indicated by the track of a vessel of some three thousand tons and picked up a flak splinter in the tail boom for their troubles. The crews of F/L Forsyth, F/O Riley, P/O Green and Sgt Ball were the others to fulfil their briefs, the last mentioned another to sustain flak damage, which left their tailplane riddled with machine-gun bullet holes and the top of a rudder shot off. L4195 had been holed in the petrol tanks and was running short of fuel when it was force-landed at 04.50 by P/O Evans at Lenham, nine miles north-west of Ashford in Kent. The rear gunner was thrown clear, and the navigator sustained a broken leg, but the wireless operator was trapped inside the wreckage and tragically perished in the ensuing fire. Thirty minutes later, P2143 crashed near Andover in Hampshire, probably as a result of empty fuel tanks, and there were no survivors from the crew of F/O Pitman. A sad night was completed by the failure to return of Sgt Imber and his crew, who, it was learned later, had lost their lives when L4129 was shot down by flak seven miles north-west of Bordeaux.

There was little activity generally on the 18th, but 5 Group detailed nineteen Hampdens from Scampton and Lindholme to target the Bismarck at berth in Hamburg. They had to battle through ice-bearing cloud over the North Sea, and on arrival over the Elbe estuary, they encountered eight to ten-tenths cloud that severely inhibited their attempts to locate the aiming point. Only eight crews were able to release their loads on estimated positions, and it was a typically indeterminate operation at this stage of the war.

The briefing of six 49 Squadron crews on the 19th came to nothing after the intended operations against the Air Ministry building in Berlin and the Aluminium works at Lünen were cancelled because of adverse weather predictions. In the event, S/L Jefferson and crew took off alone at 16.20 bound for Berlin but having assessed during the course of the outward flight that they would not reach it in the allotted time, they bombed an aerodrome at Hage (untraced). The operation was rescheduled for the following night with the Air Ministry building the primary target and the M499 marshalling yards the designated alternative. These were, of course, a euphemistic cover for an area raid on the city centre in retaliation for German attacks on British cities. According to pre-war principles, it was still morally unacceptable to specifically target civilian areas, despite the fact that the Luftwaffe had bombed Warsaw and Rotterdam indiscriminately and was currently engaged in a fifty-seven-consecutive day and night assault on London. As far as the British public was concerned, the RAF was retaliating by attacking military and war-production targets, which, in reality, was beyond its capability and it would be a further seventeen months before the pretence officially ended. Thirty Hampdens were made ready, while the Whitley boys of 4 Group were briefed to venture across the Alps into Italy and to Pilsen in Czechoslovakia. Eight 49 Squadron Hampdens apparently departed Scampton, but only five were listed on the Form 541 with take-off times between 17.05 and 20.45 and P/Os Bufton and Green the only commissioned pilots on duty. It is not known how many reached the general target area, where favourable conditions prevailed, but only Sgt Shaw and crew claimed a successful attack on the primary target and the crew of Sgt Richman on the alternative. Returning short of fuel after straying off track, P/O Green force-landed X2962 six miles south-east of Truro in Cornwall, writing off the Hampden and injuring two members of the crew. P4404 was also damaged while landing at Waddington in the hands of Sgt Shaw but would soon be back in service.

5 Group airfields were largely fogbound over the ensuing two days, and the local watering holes did good business until the 23rd, when Lindholme, Waddington and Scampton were alerted to that night's operation against the Rothensee oil refinery in Magdeburg, while Hemswell targeted the Deurag plant at Misburg near Hannover. In the event, conditions proved too testing with complete cloud cover thwarting most attempts to locate the primary targets and a variety of alternative targets of opportunity received the bombs. 49 Squadron had remained at home and its turn came on the 24th, when eight crews (seven listed) were briefed to attack A17, the Deurag oil refinery at Misburg near Hannover in company with fourteen other Hampdens. They departed Scampton between 00.10 and 01.40 with no senior pilots on duty and encountered ten-tenths low cloud over northern Germany, which prevented all but the crews of Sgts Fulton and Shaw from identifying and attacking the primary target. The others mostly found alternatives in the form of an aircraft park north of the Dümmersee, an unidentified railway station and De Kooy aerodrome on the Den Helder peninsula.

The main focus on the 25th would be Germany's oil industry and shipbuilding, and 5 Group sent out orders to Hemswell, Lindholme and Scampton to prepare eighteen Hampdens to attack the Krupp-Germania shipyard at Kiel, while Waddington took care of the gardening requirements. 49 Squadron made ready four Hampdens and sent them on their way from Scampton between 18.10 and 18.20 with S/L Jefferson the senior pilot on duty. Despite the fact that the gardeners in nearby Kiel Harbour reported clear skies over the Baltic coast, S/L Jefferson and his crew encountered a layer of ten-tenths cloud between 3,000 and 6,000 feet, which prevented them from locating the primary target. They found an alternative objective in the form of a factory north-west of the town of Schleswig, while, in contrast, the crews of Sgts Ball, Price and Richman all located the designated shipyard and delivered their bombs into the general area without determining the results.

On the following night, when a total of eighty-four aircraft were committed to operations, 5 Group detailed seventeen Hampdens from Hemswell, Scampton and Waddington for what would be the night's largest raid, against the electrical power station in the Moabit district of north-western Berlin. On the 27th, Scampton, Lindholme and Waddington were ordered to prepare for an attack that night on A10, the Harburg oil plant situated on the southern bank of the Elbe. An attack by an enemy intruder on Lindholme reduced the 50 Squadron effort to three crews, along with eight from 49 Squadron and four from Waddington. They took off between 17.40 and 17.55 with P/O Bufton the senior pilot on duty and all but one reached the target area, negotiating the searchlights that sprang into action from Elmshorn on the North Bank. The flak was fairly intense over Hamburg itself, for which a layer of cloud provided an element of protection but contributed to challenging conditions for target locating. Despite the difficulties, seven of the 49 Squadron participants managed to locate and bomb the primary target, where bursts and a large fire were observed. Sgt Bates and crew failed to identify the primary target and attacked the Hörnum seaplane base on Sylt from 11,000 feet as a last resort. P/O Bufton and crew had Skegness in sight when an intruder flown by Lt Volker of I./NJG2 fatally damaged X3027, which had to be ditched immediately. Despite the close proximity of the beach, no more than a mile away, rescue came too late and the crew was lost. The remains of three members of the crew were recovered for burial, but P/O Ballas-Anderson remained missing.

Twenty-four hours later, Hamburg hosted another visit from 5 Group, ten Hampdens from Hemswell and Lindholme assigned to the Harburg oil refinery, while ten others from Scampton and Waddington targeted dock installations. 49 Squadron was not involved on this night and was called upon on the 29th to provide just three Hampdens among twenty from Scampton, Hemswell and Lindholme for a variety of targets in Berlin, including the Danziger Strasse Gas Works situated to the north-east of the city centre. This may have been the G221 referred to in the 49 Squadron ORB as the objective for two crews, while a third was assigned to M501 marshalling yards, with an electrical power station and an oil production site at Tegel as alternatives. The crews of F/L Scoltock and Sgts Howden and Richman departed Scampton between 16.35 and 16.55 and would have to battle conditions, which, ultimately, would prevent each from reaching their planned destination. Sgt Richman and crew were actually closing on the target area when diminishing oil pressure in the port engine demanded that they jettison their load. The others failed to penetrate that far and attacked alternative targets in the form of Wilhelmshaven docks and the seaplane base on Norderney.

During the course of the month, the squadron took part in thirteen operations and dispatched ninety-four sorties for the loss of six Hampdens, three complete crews and one additional airman.

# November 1940

By the onset of November, the Battle of Britain had run its course, and the fear of invasion had been banished for the time being at least. Industrial Germany would now become the main focus of attention as the winter took hold, with oil related targets at the head of an impressive list drawn up by the Air Ministry in a new directive issued three weeks after the enthronement of C-in-C Sir Richard Peirse. 5 Group hoped soon to have a new weapon in its armoury, the Avro Manchester, a twin-engine replacement for the Hampden, which would soon be delivered to Waddington and into the hands of 207 Squadron for introduction into operational service. The squadron was reformed officially on the 1st under the command of W/C "Hettie" Hyde, who had spent August with 44 Squadron to gain operational experience. While the Manchester would prove to be hugely disappointing, its failure would force the development of its offspring, which would become the war's most successful bomber.

The trend of sending small forces to wide-ranging targets continued in November, and this diluting of the effort would render the operations ineffective and of little more than nuisance value. The first targets of the new month for 5 Group were two of Berlin's many electrical power stations, for which seventeen Hampdens were detailed from Hemswell, Lindholme and Waddington on the 1st, while Scampton and Finningley took care of mining duties in the Jellyfish garden off Brest. 49 Squadron dispatched five Hampdens from Scampton between 02.08 and 02.19 with F/L Scoltock the senior pilot on duty and all but one crew fulfilled their brief, while one returned their mine to store.

The weather continued to challenge the raid planners, and most of the Command remained on the ground for the ensuing few nights. 5 Group detailed ten Scampton Hampdens on the 3rd and briefed their crews for a raid on the Krupp-Germania shipyard at Kiel, after cancelling the participation of the Lindholme and Hemswell elements. The five 49 Squadron participants took off in very heavy rain between 01.14 and 02.02 with P/O Howell the only commissioned pilot on duty, and just five minutes after leaving the ground at 01.39, X3029 crashed four miles west of the airfield, happily without casualties among the crew of Sgt Richman. The others pressed on in unfavourable weather conditions and only the crews of P/O Howell and Sgt Unsworth delivered an attack on the primary target, while the crews of Sgts Hopkins and Price went for the designated alternative, D3, the Deutsche-Werke shipyard, before all returning to land at Leuchars in Scotland.

It was the 5th before the other groups stirred into life again, detailing ninety-seven aircraft for operations over Germany, Italy and the occupied countries. The target for eighteen Hampdens was A78, the Rothensee oil refinery at Magdeburg, while five others from Lindholme and Hemswell targeted a shipyard in Bremen and seven took care of gardening duties in the Willow garden off the Baltic port of Sassnitz on the island of Rügen. 49 Squadron made ready three Hampdens for A78 and provided the crews of Sgts Bates, Shaw and Wright with an alternative target of L40, which based on other targets with an L prefix, was an aluminium plant. They departed Scampton at 00.22, 00.24 and 01.44 respectively, and headed into severe icing conditions over the North Sea, which persuaded the Bates crew to turn back after two hours. Sgt Shaw and crew had reached the Osnabrück area when the port engine failed, and the bombs were jettisoned "live" as they began the return journey on one good engine. Sgt Wright and crew were battling the conditions as they crossed the Dutch/German frontier and struggled on as far as Cloppenburg, some forty miles north of Osnabrück, where they dropped their bombs on a searchlight and flak concentration.

The prospects for decent weather conditions were again bleak twenty-four hours later, when 5 Group dispatched twenty-five Hampdens to the twin cities of Mannheim and Ludwigshafen, which face each other from the East and West Banks respectively of the Rhine in south-central Germany. On this night, marshalling yards and or the Rhine docks appear to have been the intended targets, although the 49 Squadron record indicates that the primary target for its seven participants was C88, which is believed to be the I G Farben chemicals factory (synthetic oil) at Oppau in the northern reaches of Ludwigshafen. They departed Scampton between 01.12 and 02.37 with F/L Scoltock the senior pilot on duty and set course for the French coast. The departure of Sgt Baird and crew, more than an hour after the others, left them with little prospect of reaching the target and returning under cover of darkness, and the unpleasant weather conditions over France provided a further reason to abandon their sortie and bring their bombs home. Sgt Bowden and crew ran into severe icing conditions and dropped their bombs east of Maastricht before also turning back. According to reports from a number of squadrons, the weather relented to leave perfect conditions in the target area, while the 49 Squadron participants described cloud that prevented all but F/L Scoltock and crew from identifying and attacking the primary target with indeterminate results. P/O Green and crew dropped their bombs on the western bank of the Rhine close to C88 and also failed to observe the outcome. The crews of Sgts Phillips and Unsworth attacked the designated secondary target, Ludwigshafen's Rhine docks complex, while Sgt Ball and crew found marshalling yards in a town that they believed to be Bastogne in south-eastern Belgium.

On the 7th, 2, 3 and 5 Groups combined to send sixty-three Blenheims, Wellingtons and Hampdens to attack the Krupp works at Essen in the heart of the Ruhr, 5 Group contributing thirty aircraft, while 49 Squadron remained on the ground. Another exodus of long-serving pilots on the 8th took F/O Riley and Sgts Hills and Cooke to 14 O.T.U and they would not be the only departures to change the face of the squadron. Meanwhile, 5 Group notified its four main stations of an operation that night against the Pasing marshalling yards and engine sheds in the western suburbs of Munich, for which twenty-three Hampdens were made ready, eight of them by 49 Squadron, some fitted with long-range fuel tanks for the thirteen-hundred-mile round trip. They took off between 17.41 and 17.54 with F/O Howell the senior pilot on duty and set course for the Scheldt estuary, and it was in these early stages that Sgt Price and crew abandoned their sortie through an engine issue. After making landfall, the remaining seven flew the length of Belgium until crossing into Germany south of the Eifel region, all the way over an unbroken layer of cumulus cloud until some twenty miles from Frankfurt, where a tail wind picked them up and sped them the remaining two hundred miles to the target. Every one of the 49 squadron crews carried out an attack on the primary target, most observing bursts followed by fires.

Adverse weather conditions affected operations on the 9th and 10th, and while 49 Squadron sat out the former, tragedy struck as 83 Squadron's Sgt Garwell took off at around 01.30 as one of three crews briefed to attack U-Boots sheltering at Lorient. The Hampden swung off the runway and careered into a nissen hut, killing three occupants and injuring a fourth. X2964 caught fire, but the crew scrambled clear with just cuts and bruises. On the 10th, 49 Squadron responded to 5 Group orders to prepare twenty-eight Hampdens for a number of long-range operations that night, with destinations from Mannheim in the south to Danzig in the north-east and Merseburg, near Liepzig, in the east. Three crews at Scampton and two at Waddington were briefed to attack military objectives in distant Danzig on the Baltic coast (now Gdansk in Poland) and to dispense nickels to the natives in celebration of Polish Independence Day. This daunting task was handed to the crew of Sgt Price, who took off at 16.17 with a round trip of some sixteen hundred miles in prospect, a somewhat ambitious undertaking for a winter's night in 1940. In the event, they would be the only crew to press on to the target area, where, in the face of poor visibility, they were unable to locate either the primary or alternative targets and dropped their bombs on a railway some two-and-a-half miles away. They dispensed nickels (leaflets) over an area between Danzig and the River Vistula and were well on their way home when five other 49 Squadron crews departed Scampton between 22.57 and 00.34 bound for M70, Mannheim's Rhine docks. The crews of Sgts Bowden and Wright were soon back in the circuit after experiencing engine trouble, and another unidentified crew was dispatched as a reserve at 01.35 only also to suffer a similar fate and have to turn back. It was after they had landed that the price crew returned from their epic flight of ten hours and twenty minutes to report enduring the most difficult conditions of severe icing and a snow-covered landscape that created challenges for navigation. For their perseverance, Sgt Price would be awarded the DFM and the second pilot/navigator, P/O Reid, the DFC. The crews of P/O Green and Sgt Ball attacked the primary target and the latter landed at a neighbouring station, before flying back to Scampton later in the morning. Clearly suffering from fatigue, Sgt Ball failed to deploy the undercarriage and P2068 flopped down on its belly, fortunately without causing crew casualties or terminal damage. Less fortunate was the crew of F/O Bulmer in X2985, which was fixed by a W/T transmission at thirty miles off the Norfolk coast, before disappearing.

The last of the "Old Guard", P/O Campbell, F/Os Beauchamp, Drakes, Ward-Hunt and McClure and Sgt Unsworth were posted out to 14 O.T.U on the 12th, while F/L Forsyth moved across the tarmac to 83 Squadron in a direct swap with F/L Cooper. The 5 Group targets for eighteen aircraft that night were much closer to home and were oil refineries in the Ruhr, A80, the Krupp Treibstoffwerke at Wanne-Eickel, north-east of Gelsenkirchen for the Scampton and Lindholme crews, and A108, one of the Dortmund sites further to the east for Hemswell and Waddington. Originally detailing ten crews, only five from 49 Squadron took off between 02.10 and 02.29 with F/L Scoltock the senior pilot on duty and each carrying four 500 pounders and two of 250lb on wing racks. They ran into heavy cloud over the North Sea that extended beyond the target area, which prevented any from positively identifying the oil plant and the crews of F/L Scoltock, F/O Howell and P/O Green bombed fires and a flak concentration believed to be in close proximity to it. The crews of Sgts Hopkins and Shaw also attacked flak batteries in the Bochum area, but there was little to pass on to the intelligence section at debriefing. P/O Green had doubts about the integrity of the undercarriage and ordered his crew to bale out over Dunholme Lodge, while he landed X3001 without incident.

Seventy-two aircraft took off for various targets in Germany on the night of the 13/14th, twenty-two of them Hampdens detailed for operations over Hamburg after the Lindholme element of five had been cancelled by the station commander because of poor visibility. P/O Barlow and crew were the sole 49 Squadron representatives and took off at 01.22, only to be thwarted by adverse weather conditions in the target area, which prevented them from locating their primary objective and reduced them to bombing a flak concentration to the north of the city. Not mentioned in the 5 Group record was an operation on this night by three other 49 Squadron aircraft against A108, one of the Dortmund refineries, with the marshalling yards as the designated alternative. Sgts Bowden, Baird and Fulton departed Scampton between 00.55 and 01.10, and not one reached the target area, two returning because of engine trouble and the third due to severe icing conditions after reaching the Frisian Island of Terschelling. On the following night, the 14th, more than five hundred Luftwaffe bombers attacked the city of Coventry over a period of many hours and left the central districts in ruins and unrecognisable. While this was in progress, 5 Group dispatched seventeen Hampdens to target an oil refinery and the Blohm & Voss shipyards in Hamburg, and ten to attack an electrical power station in Berlin's south-western suburb of Wilmersdorf. 49 Squadron briefed six crews for A8 in Hamburg, with a time-on-target of 03.40 to 04.00, and designated A2, the Korff oil plant in Bremen, as the alternative, sending them on their way from Scampton between 00.10 and 00.26, each captained by an NCO pilot. The Ball brothers were operating with the squadron on this night, Peter as crew captain and Leslie as second pilot/navigator with Sgt Fulton. They began the North Sea crossing between Mablethorpe and Skegness, and for a change, the weather conditions over north-western Germany were excellent, enabling crews to pick up the targets without difficulty. All of the 49 Squadron participants reached and attacked the primary target, some observing bursts and others not and all returned safely on a night when ten failures to return represented the largest single night loss of the war to date.

The night of the 15/16th brought a two-wave attack on Hamburg separated by eight hours, for which the twenty-five-strong Hampden element took off after midnight in the second phase to target a number of aiming points including the power station at Altona on the North Bank of the Elbe to the west of the city centre. The five 49 Squadron crews were briefed to attack A366, which the ORB described as a small gas works in a populated area of the city, and each would have two

500 pounders and two SBCs of incendiaries to aim at it. As events turned out, only four actually took off between 01.14 and 02.06, after S/L Jefferson's aircraft became unserviceable at the last minute. This left F/L Cooper as the senior pilot on duty for the first time since his posting from 83 Squadron, and after facing the challenges of ice-bearing cloud at between 1,500 and 11,000 feet and driving rain during the North Sea crossing, the weather conditions over the target were favourable. P/O Green and crew attacked the primary target, while the crews of F/L Cooper and Sgt Richman bombed in its vicinity and observed an explosion and fires. Sgt Price and crew were unable to locate the aiming point, and, for whatever reason, continued on across the Schleswig-Holstein peninsula to attack the docks at Kiel. The attacks by the relatively modest number of sixty-seven aircraft produced probably the most successful raid of the war to date, after which the Hamburg authorities reported sixty-eight fires and substantial damage in the Blohm & Voss shipyard.

For the third night running, Hamburg was posted as the destination for a force from Bomber Command on the 16th, this time of 130 aircraft including thirty-four Hampdens of 5 Group. 49 Squadron briefed six crews, five for A10, one of the Harburg refineries, and one for another swipe at the gas works, A366. The Waddington crews had been among those briefed to attack the industrial areas of Veddel and Peute, located on the islands in the Elbe in the heart of the city, but the weather would have its say and most of the carefully laid plans would come to nothing. The 49 Squadron crews departed Scampton between 01.16 and 01.42 with F/O Howell the senior pilot on duty and a time-on-target of 04.25 and 05.00. They headed into a weather front over the North Sea that contained all kinds of unpleasant surprises and in the face of low cloud and severe icing conditions, the crews of Sgts Baird and Wright turned back, following in the wake of Sgt Bowden and crew, whose sortie had been curtailed by engine problems. They arrived back at Scampton at 02.08 and were airborne again in the spare aircraft by 02.30 but so far behind schedule that they would bomb the town of Neumünster, located some thirty miles north of Hamburg. The crews of F/O Howells and Sgt Hopkins were unable to identify the target and respectively bombed an unidentified marshalling yard in the city and a flak concentration in the Schillig area to the west. P/O Barlow and crew fulfilled their brief by attacking A366 and observing a fire develop, and reserved a single bomb for a searchlight concentration near the city.

On the 18th, F/L Learoyd VC joined 83 Squadron on attachment pending a permanent posting, upon which he would be granted acting squadron leader rank and installed as A Flight commander. On the 19th of December 1941, he would begin a six-month tour as commanding officer of 44 (Rhodesia) Squadron, after which, it seems that his operational career ended.

Adverse weather conditions at home and over Germany caused the cancellation of 5 Group operations on the following two nights, and, when orders were received on its stations on the 19th, they contained details of that night's long-range operations, by eight aircraft to the Skoda armaments works at Pilsen in Czechoslovakia and by thirteen to A74, a Bergius-process oil production site at Lützkendorf near Leipzig, with the nearby A77 Leuna refinery as the designated alternative. 49 Squadron briefed five crews for the latter, and three for the former and it was those bound for Czechoslovakia that departed Scampton first, between 23.10 and 23.34 with F/L Cooper the senior pilot on duty. His W/T failed almost immediately, and he returned to the circuit as the second element was taking off between 00.04 and 00.51. The weather conditions would prove to be too difficult for many of the crews to reach their assigned targets, but to their credit, the crews of P/O Green and Sgt Shaw identified and attacked the Skoda works, observing an explosion and fires and returned after nine hours aloft. Meanwhile, the crews of Sgts Ball and Bowden had located and attacked A74 and had observed an explosion and a fire, while Sgt Baird and crew had bombed A77 and a SEMO. Sgt Price and crew cut short their sortie for an undisclosed reason and bombed a flak concentration at Rheine on the way home. The return of Sgt Fulton and crew was awaited in vain, and this was particularly trying for Sgt Peter Ball, whose brother, Leslie, was on board X3024. No trace of the Hampden and its crew was ever found, and their names are perpetuated on the Runnymede Memorial.

The target for eighteen Hampdens on the 20th was much closer to home, requiring a trip to the East Bank of the Rhine at Duisburg in the Ruhr, where Germany's largest inland docks, Duisburg-Ruhrort, lay to the south of the city centre. 49 Squadron sat this one out and the entire group remained at home on the 21st. On the 22nd, AVM Sir Arthur Harris left 5 group on his appointment as second deputy to the Chief of the Air Staff, Sir Charles Portal, and he was succeeded by AVM Bottomley. Fifteen months hence to the day, Harris would return to lead the Command and rescue it from the brink of disbandment. That night, 5 Group sent seven Hampdens back to Duisburg-Ruhrort and a further fourteen to destroy hangars on Merignac aerodrome near Bordeaux. 49 Squadron contributed the two newly arrived crews of F/Os Tench and Smith to the Ruhr, sending them on their way from Scampton at 17.09 and 17.15 respectively, and would return before the Bordeaux-bound element took off. Neither had located the primary target and had delivered their bombs on last resort objectives in the Essen and Oberhausen region of the Ruhr. The second element took off between 23.35 and 00.30 on the long trip south with S/L Jefferson the senior pilot on duty, and all reached the target area, where conditions proved to be favourable. Most observed their bombs fall among hangars and other buildings and returned after nine hours aloft to report a successful night's work.

Twenty-four hours later, 5 Group sent ten Hampdens back to Duisburg-Ruhrort, while also assigning five to Gelsenkirchen. 49 Squadron sat out this night at home but was back on the order of battle on the 24th, when contributing five of eleven crews to target the Blohm & Voss shipyards at Hamburg. They departed Scampton between 01.38 and 02.53 with F/O Smith the senior pilot on duty and soon ran into six to ten-tenths cloud with tops at between 4,000 and 6,000 feet, which prevented all from identifying the primary target. The crews of Sgts Morphett, Price and Richman bombed flak concentrations in Hamburg, while F/O Smith and crew dropped four bombs each on the town of Rendsburg and the Island of Sylt. X3052 had been homebound in daylight and was approaching the North Sea coast over the Den Helder peninsula when it was confronted by three BF109s from III./JG54. Cannon shells from Lt Wubke's aircraft set the Hampden ablaze, and Sgt Phillips maintained control long enough to carry out a force-landing on the beach a dozen miles south of Den Helder, where it was consumed by fire after the occupants had scrambled clear to be taken into captivity.

On the following night, Hemswell and Lindholme joined forces to send ten Hampdens to attack the Deutsche-Werke shipyard at Kiel, where the heavy cruiser, Gneisenau, had been built between 1935 and 1938. 49 Squadron remained on the ground until the 27th, when Cologne was posted as the destination for sixty-two aircraft, which would be allotted to five separate aiming points within the city. The ten 5 Group Hampden crews were briefed to attack E10, a target described as a "land armament factory", which was, in fact, the Klöckner-Humboldt works in the Deutz district on the eastern bank of the Rhine, which manufactured aero-engines and heavy and tracked vehicles for the Wehrmacht. The five-strong 49 Squadron element departed Scampton between 02.03 and 02.23 with F/O Fisher the senior among the all-commissioned pilots and set a course to make landfall over the Scheldt estuary. Here, they found their path inland barred by a bank of towering, ice-bearing cumulonimbus cloud, extending from 6,000 up to 15,000 feet, and this would prevent any of the 49 Squadron participants from attacking the primary target. P/Os Evans and Wilson jettisoned their bombs over the North Sea, F/O Fisher attacked a flak concentration in the Cologne area, while P/Os Donaldson and Tench bombed railway lines near Arnsberg and Düren respectively.

It was an unsatisfactory way to complete a month in which the squadron had taken part in twenty operations generating eighty-five sorties for the loss of four Hampdens and three crews. Hemswell and Lindholme were the stations called upon on the 28th to provide eleven aircraft for operations against a naval store at Mannheim and the inland port on the other side of the Rhine at Ludwigshafen, while 44 Squadron sent two crews to a naval store in the port of Le Havre and 50 Squadron one to attack the Veddel and Peute industrial area in the heart of Hamburg. Le Havre was again the destination for six Hampdens on the 29th as 5 Group concluded its operations for the month.

# December 1940

The new month began for 5 Group with the receipt of instructions for a new type of operation which effectively turned Hampdens into night-fighters. *"No 49 Squadron to provide four aircraft to take part in an experiment to be carried out as to the possibility of intercepting and destroying enemy bomber aircraft over their target, by concentrating twenty Hampden aircraft in a stepped-up patrol over the area being attacked. The patrol would operate if large-scale enemy formations attacked either Coventry, Birmingham, Derby, Manchester, Sheffield, Bristol, Liverpool or Wolverhampton."* Each aircraft was to be given a sky-layer of five hundred feet, and Scampton was allotted the piece of sky between 16,000 and 20,000 feet. They would be working in co-operation with the searchlight and flak defences and must not arrive in their patrol area until "zero-hour" or remain in it once the four-hour patrol time had elapsed. Each aircraft was to carry maximum ammunition and an additional gunner to man the midships guns.

S/L Whitehead, having spent time with 49 Squadron to gain operational experience as a second pilot, was posted to RAF College, Cranwell on the 1st. During the afternoon, ten Scampton crews were briefed for an operation to be conducted that night against shipbuilding yards at Wilhelmshaven. 49 Squadron briefed five crews and dispatched them between 02.32 and 04.10 on the 2nd, intending them to return in daylight. Sgt Wright and crew turned back immediately because of W/T failure, leaving the others to press on in unfavourable weather conditions that would prevent them from fulfilling their orders. Each attacked SEMOs in the form of flak concentrations in the vicinity of Wilhelmshaven, Schillig and the Frisian Islands and none observed the results through the ten-tenths cloud.

The weather continued to be unfavourable, causing the cancellation of bombing operations planned for the 2nd, 3rd, 4th and 5th. On the 6th, ten 49 Squadron crews were among fifty-five briefed for intruder sorties over Luftwaffe bomber aerodromes in the occupied countries, while twenty others from Scampton, Hemswell and Waddington stood by for the first offensive patrols. The departure of the bombing element was spread throughout the evening between 17.15 and 01.28 and F/L Scoltock was the senior pilot on duty. F/O Matthews and crew were first away of 49 Squadron's "night-fighter" contingent at 19.20, leaving the other four to take-off between 22.16 and 23.09 and head south-west to the Bristol area, where not one would encounter an enemy aircraft but two did observe bomb bursts and fires. What became clear at debriefing was that provisions for crew comfort were seriously lacking and all complained of inadequate heating. Of the bombers, the crew of P/O Wilson turned back because of an engine issue, while the others battled the most adverse weather conditions and mostly failed to locate their assigned targets. P/O Fisher and crew attacked Vannes aerodrome, situated between Lorient and St-Nazaire on the Biscay coast, and Sgt Ball and crew a flak battery at Le Touquet south of Boulogne, but they were the only ones with something positive to pass on at debriefing. F/O Michie and crew had been the second of the bombing brigade to take-off in the early evening and were returning shortly after midnight, when X3028 crashed at 00.10 at Welton, five miles north-north-east of Lincoln, killing the pilot and two others and seriously injuring the second pilot/navigator, Sgt Barrier. Further bad news came with the failure to return of X3050 and P4404 with the crews of Sgt Greeves and Sgt Shaw respectively, and it was learned eventually that the former had been brought down by flak off Ostend and had disappeared into the North Sea. News soon came through that the latter were in enemy hands after flak damage had resulted in a force-landing some fifty miles south of Paris. A number of crew members had sustained injury requiring hospital treatment and the local civilians were asked to contact the Germans. Tragically, Sgt Shaw would be shot and killed during a failed escape bid from his PoW camp in January 1942.

On the 8th, Hemswell and Lindholme joined forces to send fourteen Hampdens to Düsseldorf to target the Mannesman Rohrenwerke, which, it is believed, was manufacturing heavy gun barrels, while nineteen aircraft from Hemswell, Scampton and Waddington were sent to patrol the skies over Oxford. The 49 Squadron element of eight took off between 18.55 and 19.24 with the newly promoted F/L Smith the senior pilot on duty and encountered very poor visibility, which restricted their ability to spot enemy aircraft or assess what was happening on the ground. A few bomb bursts and fires were observed in the direction of Reading and London, and although no enemy aircraft were seen, F/O Howell and crew watched a Wellington pass just thirty feet over their heads.

49 Squadron would not be called into action again for a week, during which period on the 10th, Scampton and Lindholme sent six Hampdens each to target the inland docks on the on the Rhine at Mannheim, while three 44 Squadron crews attended to mining duties in the Deodar garden in the Gironde estuary. It was back to security patrols for six 44 Squadron crews on the evening of the 11th, and, for the first time during this type of operation, enemy aircraft were spotted, and attempts made to engage them. A dozen Hampdens were sent to Duisburg on the 12th to attack the Ruhrort docks complex and the Thyssen steelworks and thirty were committed to a variety of objectives in Berlin on the 15th, while other elements of the Command targeted Frankfurt and Kiel.

Orders were received from 5 Group on the 16th to prepare fifty-eight Hampdens to attack various targets in Mannheim that night in two waves. At briefings, crews learned that this was to be a major operation involving two hundred aircraft under the codename, Operation Abigail Rachel, launched in retaliation for recent devastating raids on English cities, particularly Coventry and Southampton. The Abigail part of the plan called for eight of the most experienced 3 Group Wellington crews to open the attack on the centre of the city with all-incendiary loads, in order to start fires that would act as a beacon to the Rachel force following behind. As the day drew on, it became clear that the weather conditions over the bomber stations might cause problems, and the force was cut to 134 aircraft. 49 Squadron briefed ten crews, nine of which were assigned to the first wave and departed Scampton between 19.54 and 20.26, leaving F/L Scoltock and crew on the ground until their departure as part of the second wave at 22.02. According to a number of official records, twenty-nine Hampden crews had been given the Motorenwerke Mannheim in the northern outskirts of the city as their aiming point, which is curious, as the purpose of the raid was to cause as much damage as possible to the central districts in what was the first officially sanctioned area attack. The same official records suggest that some of the second wave crews were to target Mannheim's Rhine docks. The weather conditions outbound persuaded perhaps a quarter of the force to turn back, but those reaching the target area found largely clear skies and a full moon, with only a modest defence in operation. Only five of the 49 Squadron participants reported attacking the primary target and four claimed fires as a result, while the others found last resort objectives. X3063 failed to return and was believed to have crashed into the sea off the Isle of Wight, taking the crew of F/L Scoltock with it. Post-raid reconnaissance revealed that the operation had not produced the desired results, after the "pathfinder" element had missed the city centre and the subsequent bombing had been scattered. Even so, local reports provided a figure of 240 buildings either destroyed or seriously damaged, with more than a thousand people bombed out of their homes.

The weather kept 5 Group at home on the ensuing two nights, while very small forces returned to Mannheim. The teleprinters on 5 Group stations burst into life on the 19th to reveal plans to attack the Wesseling Bergius-process oil refinery, situated on the West Bank of the Rhine south of Cologne. Forty Hampdens were made ready across the group, while eight others, five from Waddington and three from Finningley, would take care of mining duties in the Jellyfish and Artichoke gardens off Brest and Lorient respectively. The 20th would mark the resurgence of 1 Group, which had been reconstituted on return from its role as the major component of the AASF in France for the first nine months of the war. The Fairey Battles of 12, 103, 142 and 150 Squadrons had been replaced, and with four squadrons of fanatical Poles added to its ranks and working towards operational status, this night would see the first six operational sorties in Wellingtons.

5 Group detailed a dozen Hampdens for Berlin on this night and thirty-one for a return to the Wesseling plant at Cologne, and it was for the former, the Schlesischer Tor railway station, southeast of Berlin's city centre, that the 49 Squadron crews of Sgt Ball, P/O Green and F/O Barlow departed Scampton between 23.24 and 23.36. Quite why they had been held back until then is unclear, particularly as the 83 Squadron element had taken off either side of 17.00. As a consequence, they and the Lindholme and Waddington crews would be under time pressure throughout, conscious that they would struggle to vacate enemy territory before the arrival of daylight. They exited the English coast at Skegness, and adopted a direct course for the target, but P/O Green and crew were forced to turn back within the hour because of an engine issue. The other two reached Berlin at around 03.30, the navigating having benefitted from clear skies most of the way, and these favourable conditions persisted over the target. Sgt Ball and crew attacked the Air

Ministry building and marshalling yards, observing one burst and a large fire, while F/O Barlow and crew dropped their bombs in the vicinity of the primary target but failed to observe the outcome. Meanwhile, the eight-strong Wesseling-bound contingent had taken off between 01.44 and 02.18 with F/Os Howell and Tench the senior pilots on duty and had encountered little opposition as they crossed enemy territory in near perfect conditions. These persisted all the way to the target, where attacks were delivered on a variety of headings from south-west to north-east, south-east to north-west and east to west and bomb bursts, explosions and fires observed.

5 Group detailed twenty-four Hampdens from Hemswell, Scampton and Lindholme for operations on the following night, when an electrical power station at Halle, situated to the north-west of Leipzig, was to be the target. 49 Squadron remained at home and would be the only 5 Group unit called into action for bombing duties on the 22nd, when A161, the Offenbach oil depot to the south-east of Frankfurt city centre and A402, the gas works, were briefed out to six and five crews respectively, with the inland docks complex as the designated alternative for all. Earlier in the day, W/C Gillen had concluded his period in command and was posted to the Air Ministry to be succeeded by the newly elevated acting W/C Jefferson, who presided over the briefing. They departed Scampton between 01.32 and 02.37 with F/L Smith the senior pilot on duty and seven crews delivered an attack through haze onto the snow-covered oil depot, one causing a large fire. P/O Wilson and crew attacked the gas works, where the incendiaries started a fire, and the remaining crews dropped their bombs on the city of Aachen (F/O Howell), a factory on the north-western outskirts of Koblenz (Sgt Price) and a train south of Bingen and factory at Reims (Sgt Richman).

Waddington would now enjoy a five-day break from operations, during which, the second wartime Christmas was observed in traditional style. In the meantime, Scampton and Finningley took care of 5 Group business on the 22nd, Hemswell on Boxing Day, before Hemswell, Scampton and Waddington were alerted on the 27th, for operations that night, Waddington for mining duties in the Lettuce garden in the Kiel Canal, while the other stations sent ten Hampdens each to attack the aerodrome at Merignac near Bordeaux. It was on this night, during training, that P4384 crashed at Abingdon in Berkshire with fatal consequences for the crew, whose names were not recorded. On the following night, 5 Group operated for the final time during the year, when sending fifteen Hampdens from Hemswell and Scampton to target U-Boots in the docks at Lorient, while Scampton and Waddington detailed seven crews between them to return to the Lettuce garden to try to redress the previous night's failure. 49 Squadron made ready four Hampdens for Lorient and three for mining and launched them together between 17.23 and 18.11, the gardeners setting course for the Lincolnshire coast a few miles north of Mablethorpe, while the bombing element headed south. Of the gardeners, Sgt Wright and crew were unable to establish a pinpoint and jettisoned their mine "safe", but the crews of F/O Howell and P/O Wilson were able to fulfil their brief and dropped their 250 pounders respectively on a railway junction at Heide on the western side of the Schleswig-Holstein peninsula, and on Heiligenhafen on the eastern seaboard. The bombing quartet, meanwhile, had encountered cloud over the Biscay coast, which prevented Sgt Morphett and crew from locating Lorient and they jettisoned their bombs, leaving the crews of Sgt Bowden and P/Os Newhouse and Mervyn-Jones to carry out an attack but not observe the outcome.

During the course of the month, the squadron took part in eleven operations and dispatched sixty-seven sorties for the loss of five Hampdens, four complete crews and three members of another. It had been a backs-to-the-wall year, and one of presenting a defiant face to an as-yet all conquering enemy. 1941 was not destined to bring more than a slight increase in effectiveness, and it would be a case of treading water for the foreseeable future. Some new aircraft were emerging to offer a degree of hope for the future, but the problems arising from pressing them too soon into service would result in a painfully slow development, and the existing types were to bear most of the burden for the next twelve months and even beyond.

# January 1941

A second successive severe winter would restrict operations at the start of the year, when most of the effort would be directed at French and German ports. The Command detailed 141 aircraft for operations on New Year's Night, with Bremen posted as the year's first target for 5 Group, which detailed ten Hampdens each from Scampton, Lindholme and Waddington. The briefings covered two targets, the Korff A.G. oil refinery, which the ORB suggested was also a depository for food stocks, and, it is believed, the Focke-Wulf aircraft factory in the south-eastern district of Hemelingen. 49 Squadron prepared ten Hampdens and sent them on their way from Scampton between 16.40 and 16.55 with the newly promoted acting S/L Tench the senior pilot on duty and the Korff refinery as their objective. As always, there would be contradictory reports concerning the weather during the outward journey, for which we have to rely on the testimony of crews from other squadrons. Some described the conditions as good, while others complained of a snowstorm over eastern England that extended as high as 11,000 feet, and severe icing as they climbed over the North Sea. A number of crews turned back, citing the weather, but it was airscrew and engine issues that persuaded the crews of Sgt Bates and P/O Newhouse to turn back. The latter would have taken off again in the spare aircraft had a heavy snowstorm not prevented them from doing so. The others reached the target area at around 19.00 and found that the cloud had built to between eight and ten-tenths, despite which, some crews from other squadrons were able to locate their aiming points, aided in part by the intensity of the flak, which was bursting at around 9,000 feet. Not one of the 49 Squadron participants positively identified the primary target, and S/L Tench and crew were among those thwarted by a layer of ten-tenths cloud at 3,000 feet. They were lucky to survive a heavy burst of flak just above them, from which a piece of shrapnel penetrated the right side of the navigator's Perspex and struck him on the right shoulder without causing injury. P/O Green and crew stooged around for ninety minutes until a large gap opened to reveal a fair-sized fire, and their bombs created two more. Sgt Morphett and crew found the primary target obscured and bombed the docks area instead, while Sgt Beckett and crew attacked a railway station in Wilhelmshaven. The others bombed in the general target area, and all returned safely, some to diversion airfields.

5 Group returned to Bremen twenty-four hours later with eight Hampdens from Hemswell and Scampton on a night of technical failures and wasted effort. On the 3rd, the new bomber station at Coningsby was declared open on a Care & Maintenance basis and would shortly welcome 106 Squadron as its first resident unit. Also, on this day, the decision was taken to draft all Rhodesian aircrew into 44 Squadron as they became available. This would lead, ultimately, to the adoption of the title, Rhodesia, to be inserted after the squadron number, once Rhodesian aircrew predominated. That night, Scampton sent fifteen Hampdens back to Bremen as part of an overall

force of seventy-one aircraft, which benefitted from improved weather conditions and inflicted further damage that was confirmed by local sources. Orders were received at Hemswell, Lindholme and Waddington on the 4th, to prepare thirty Hampdens between them for an operation that night against an unnamed Hipper class German cruiser in a dry dock at Brest. A process of elimination suggests that it was the Admiral Hipper herself, which had been raiding in the Atlantic following her part in the Norwegian campaign. Laid down in the Blohm & Voss shipyards in 1935, she had a length of 673 feet and displaced 18,500 tons, and was one of three of her design, including Prinz Eugen, which entered service in August 1940. The 5 Group contingent was part of an overall force of fifty-three aircraft, while others, four from Finningley and two from Waddington, were to take care of mining duties in the Artichoke garden off Lorient.

It was left to 49 Squadron to represent 5 Group on the 5th with a dozen Hampdens detailed for mining duties off the Biscay coast, ten in the Jellyfish garden off Brest and one each in Artichoke (Lorient) and Beech (St-Nazaire). They departed Scampton between 16.35 and 17.50 with F/L Smith the senior pilot on duty and headed for the south coast, where they encountered very poor weather conditions including icing, which persisted over the Channel. Sgt Bowden and crew were unable to break into clear air and abandoned their sortie to land at Boscombe Down. The crews of Sgt Ball and F/L Smith also failed to reach the target area and blamed the conditions for their woes, while the crews of Sgt Richman and P/O Henderson found the target area covered by ten-tenths cloud with a base at 400 feet and failed to identify a pinpoint. The crews of Sgts Bates, Beckett, Green, Morphett and Wright chanced upon gaps in the cloud, through which they were able to establish their positions and deliver their mines. The last mentioned then spotted a train travelling towards Lorient and attacked it from 200 feet, the rear gunner aiming at the driver but missing. P/O Green and crew described the weather at their target as very good and planted their vegetable without difficulty, before joining the others at St-Eval in Cornwall. Absent was the crew of Sgt Price DFM in P4322, which is believed to have crashed into the sea some ten miles south of Sidmouth in Devon with no survivors.

The naval shipbuilding yards at Wilhelmshaven and the battleship Tirpitz were posted as the targets for thirty-two aircraft on the 8th, ten provided by 5 Group from Lindholme and Waddington, while sixteen other aircraft were assigned to Emden, some forty miles to the west. Nine further Hampdens were required for mining duties in the Eglantine garden in the Elbe estuary, and these were also provided by 44 and 50 Squadrons, while 49 Squadron remained at home. The Commander-in-Chief, Sir Richard Peirse, had decided on launching one major raid each month on an important industrial city, for which Gelsenkirchen was selected on the 9th, and a force of 135 aircraft assembled. 5 Group detailed the Hemswell squadrons to take part, and the crews were briefed to aim for one of the synthetic oil plants, while four Finningley crews went mining in Kiel Bay. In the event, fewer than half of the force reached the assigned target area, and bombs were reported in various parts of Gelsenkirchen and its environs. On the following night, thirty-five Hampdens and Wellingtons were detailed to go in search of the Tirpitz again at Wilhelmshaven, and the 5 Group ORB recorded that all sixteen of the former were provided by Scampton, completely ignoring the fact that nine of them were actually launched from Waddington.

Eight 49 Squadron crews were put on stand-by late on the 11th for another shot at the Tirpitz at Wilhelmshaven and took off between 01.30 and 02.00 with S/L Tench the senior pilot on duty. He returned almost immediately because of wireless failure and after apparently fixing the issue, took off again, only for the problem to recur and put an end to his interest in proceedings. The others encountered ten-tenths cloud all the way to the target, where the crews of P/O Wilson and Sgt Ball chanced upon a sizeable gap in the cloud and were able to identify the aiming point and deliver their bombs through intense flak, but without observing the results. Four others bombed the general target area through cloud, which left the bomb load of P/O Newhouse and crew unaccounted for. It was not on board L4045 as it approached Kirton-in-Lindsey in Lincolnshire at 07.45, at which point, according to eyewitnesses, it stalled after climbing sharply to avoid houses and crashed at Northorpe, killing all on board. L4045 was known as "The Queen" and, at her end, had amassed 786 hours of operational flying. The squadron would take part in no further operational activity during January.

In recognition of his skills as a pilot and crew captain while serving with 49 Squadron, F/O Hugh Matthews DFC was posted to 207 Squadron on the 15th to fly the Manchester. While taking off from Waddington for Hamburg on the 13th of March, his aircraft was attacked by a Luftwaffe intruder and struggled into the air, only to crash at Whisby, a few miles to the west, killing twenty-three-year-old Matthews and all but one of his crew. It was the first Manchester to be lost on operations. In a directive issued on the day of his posting, the Air Ministry had decided that an all-out assault against oil related targets would eventually take its toll on the German war effort, and operations from now on would reflect this. A list of seventeen sites was drawn up, the top nine of which represented 80% of Germany's synthetic oil production, and of these, Scholven-Buer and Gelsenkirchen were in the Ruhr, Leuna, Zeitz, Böhlen and Lützkendorf were in the east near Leipzig, Magdeburg and Ruhland were north and east of Leipzig respectively and the other was at Politz close to the Baltic coast, but it would be February before Peirse was able to comply. In the meantime, a force of ninety-six aircraft was assembled that night to target the dockyards at Wilhelmshaven, for which Hemswell provided the seventeen Hampdens. Returning crews claimed many fires in the town, and local sources confirmed damage to the head post office, main police station, army barracks, dock offices and seven commercial buildings.

Waddington and Scampton detailed a further fifteen Hampdens on the 16th to return to Wilhelmshaven to target Tirpitz as part of an overall force of eighty-one aircraft, on a night when the weather conditions would prove to be inhospitable. Thereafter, twelve consecutive nights of operations were cancelled because of severe weather conditions, which rendered airfields frozen under a blanket of snow, and then left them waterlogged as a thaw set in. When operations finally resumed for 5 Group on the 29th, Wilhelmshaven, or more specifically, the Tirpitz, was posted as the target yet again, for a force this time of nine Hampdens from Lindholme and twenty-five Wellingtons. The Tirpitz remained elusive, and those locating the target area mostly bombed the town, inflicting, according to local sources, a degree of residential damage. During the course of the month, the squadron took part in just three operations and dispatched thirty sorties for the loss of a single Hampden and its crew.

# February 1941

February began as January had ended, with ports occupying the bulk of the Command's attention, although the accent shifted to those in France and Belgium. 5 Group dispatched a dozen Hampdens to attack warships in Brest on the night of the 2/3rd, and eleven more, all from Waddington, to lay mines in the Jellyfish and Artichoke gardens off Brest and Lorient twenty-four hours later.

In a new departure for night raids, the Command assigned a specific target to each of 2, 3, 4 and 5 Groups on the 4th, aerodromes for the Blenheims, French ports for 3 and 4 Groups and the Ruhr city of Düsseldorf for 5 Group. Thirty Hampdens were made ready at Scampton, Hemswell and Lindholme, while Waddington remained off the Order of Battle. Six 49 Squadron crews joined a dozen from 83 Squadron in the briefing room to be told that they were to attack a specific aiming point with no designated alternative. The 49 Squadron element departed Scampton between 17.50 and 18.00 on a night when the moon was waxing towards full and clear weather conditions prevailed up to within about ten minutes of the target, when eight to ten-tenths cloud obscured the ground. However, an intense searchlight and flak defence left them in no doubt that they were over the target, whether or not they caught a glimpse of it through small gaps in the cloud. They ran in at 8,500 to 9,500 feet and delivered their attacks either side of 20.15, most observing the fall of their bombs close to the aiming point and P/O Bowden and crew reported an exceptionally large flash from their 1,900 pounder. P4299 failed to return with the crew of Sgt Baird, and news eventually arrived via the Red Cross to confirm their survival in enemy hands.

The weather deteriorated again to keep 5 Group on the ground on the next two nights, but the Group Meteorological Section staff managed to find a window of acceptable weather across the Channel on the north-eastern coast of France on the 7th. This was sufficient to allow an operation by a dozen 49 Squadron crews and fifteen from Lindholme against shipping and dock installations at Dunkerque. The 49 Squadron element departed Scampton between 20.45 and 21.30 with S/L Tench the senior pilot on duty and all reached the French coast around ninety minutes later to find a thin layer of cloud, through which moonlight filtered to provide generally favourable conditions. A number of aircraft were held in searchlights as they approached the aiming point and intense flak was a constant danger, despite which, P/O Green and crew delivered their bombs in two passes at 10,000 feet. Sgt Ball chose a diving attack from 9,000 down to 5,000 feet and had to work hard to extricate himself from four minutes of being coned, while seven others bombed the primary target from between 4,000 and 8,000 feet. The crews of Sgts Beckett and Wright and P/O Mervyn-Jones attacked Calais as an alternative target and P/O Bowden Ostend as a last resort. At debriefing, most were able to report their bombs falling within the target area, but no details were forthcoming.

On the 8th, Hemswell and Waddington were ordered to prepare nine and six Hampdens respectively for an operation that night against a specific target in Mannheim. Most reached the target area after flying south-east across Belgium and entering Germany via Luxembourg, but two layers of cloud blotted out the ground, forcing crews to descend in an attempt to break into clear air to establish their whereabouts and all would be forced to bomb on e.t.a., on estimated positions. On the following day, twenty-three Hampdens were detailed at Hemswell and Scampton to be sent against the Tirpitz at Wilhelmshaven, but heavy cloud again ruined the operation, and only one crew claimed to have attacked the primary target.

While 5 Group conducted the two above-mentioned operations, the rest of the Command had stayed on the ground, and C-in-C Peirse had not yet implemented the January directive against Germany's synthetic oil industry. First, he would launch his monthly "big" effort against a major industrial city, and orders went out across the Command on the 10th to prepare a force, which, at take-off time, would number 222 aircraft, a record for a single target. At briefings, the crews learned that the northern city of Hannover was to be their destination, and that they were assigned to attack one of a variety of aiming points in the industrial sector. The city was a major centre of war production, the home among others to the Accumulatoren-Fabrik A G factory which manufactured lead acid batteries for U-Boots and torpedoes, the Continental tyre and rubber factory at Limmer, the Deurag-Nerag synthetic oil refinery at Misburg, the VLW (Volkswagen) metalworks, and the Maschinenfabrik Niedersachsen Hannover and Hanomag factories, which were producing guns and tracked vehicles. A second operation was also planned for this night involving forty-three aircraft in an attack on oil storage tanks in Rotterdam, and in a demonstration of the burgeoning power of the Command, the contribution by 3 Group of 119 aircraft would be the first time that any group had exceeded one hundred aircraft. Among them, as part of the Rotterdam force, would be the first three sorties by the new four-engine Short Stirling in the hands of 7 Squadron.

5 Group notified all of its operational stations to prepare for the main event, and forty-six Hampdens were made ready, a dozen of them by 49 Squadron, which departed Scampton between 22.14 and 22.55 with F/L Smith the senior pilot on duty. The weather conditions were ideal, with clear skies and bright moonlight to assist navigation and map-reading, and all of the 49 Squadron participants reached the target area, pinpointing, initially, on the Steinhuder Lake to the west, and then the Maschsee to the south of the city centre. Over the target itself, around three-tenths cloud was reported at 7,000 feet, but it would have no influence on the course of the raid, which attracted what appeared to be only a limited and inaccurate light flak defence. This emboldened crews to circle, if necessary, to establish their positions and decide on a method of attack, and, in a number of cases, to descend to a fairly low level. Some adopted a glide approach, while most favoured a higher-level attack from between 10,000 and 14,000 feet. Most of the 49 Squadron crews appear to have attacked from around 9,000 to 10,000 feet, although F/O Fisher and crew selected a dive approach to release their bombs at 5,000 feet. Night-fighters were waiting over Holland to catch the returning bombers and P/O Green and crew were in sight of the North Sea at Egmond when they were intercepted by Lt Leopold Fellerer of 5./NJG1 and shot down. X3001 crashed at 03.50 some seven miles north of Alkmaar, killing the second pilot/navigator, and delivering the three survivors into enemy hands. AD719 almost made it home and was in the Scampton circuit when an intruder flown by Oblt Kurt Hermann brought it down to crash at Sudbrooke, three miles north of Lincoln. at 06.30. Sgt Bates and his wireless operator survived with injuries, but their two crew colleagues lost their lives.

On the 11th, a force of seventy-one Hampdens, Wellingtons and Whitleys was made ready for Bremen that night, while eighteen Wellingtons and eleven Hampdens returned to Hannover. Fog over the bomber stations at home caused twenty-two returning aircraft to crash or be abandoned by their crews, three of them belonging to 5 Group, and one 83 Squadron crew died as a result.

The oil directive was finally implemented on the night of the 14/15th, when the Nordstern (Gelsenberg A G) refinery at Gelsenkirchen was earmarked for an attack by Wellingtons, while Wellingtons and Blenheims tried their hand at a similar target, the Rhein Preussen (Meerbeck) synthetic oil plant at Moers/Homberg, situated on the West Bank of the Rhine opposite Duisburg. Both of these massively important plants were vital to the German war effort and employed the Bergius process to refine high-grade petroleum products such as aviation fuel. It was on this night that 207 Squadron had hoped to launch its maiden sorties, but the modifications to the Manchesters had taken twice the time planned for, and the aircraft had not been tested. According to the 49 Squadron ORB, it launched eleven Hampdens on this night against the Homberg oil plant, while all other squadron records suggest that 5 Group did not operate. It seems certain that the 49 Squadron entries refer to the following night, when thirty-three Hampdens and thirty-seven Blenheims were sent against the Homberg plant, while seventy-three Wellingtons and Whitleys targeted the Hydrierwerke-Scholven refinery at Sterkrade-Holten.

The operation was spread over many hours, some of the 5 Group elements taking off as early as 18.00, when conditions were quite favourable, while the 49 Squadron contingent departed Scampton between 02.45 and 03.15 in rain and only broke cloud at 7,500 feet over the North Sea. Ten-tenths cloud accompanied them all the way to the target, and although the ORB records that only one crew attacked the primary target, it is not possible to deduce which one from the crew reports. A variety of last resort objectives were bombed in the Ruhr from between 5,000 and 8,500 feet, but no results were observed and the entire undertaking was a waste of resources.

S/L Lowe DFC had not been mentioned in the ORB since early October, by which time he had completed twenty-seven sorties. He is recorded in the 49 Squadron ORB as being posted to 14 O.T.U., on the 18th. On the 20th, Finningley was transferred out of 5 Group to be taken over by 7 Operational Training Group, and the evicted 106 Squadron moved south to take up residence at Coningsby. Small-scale operations against Channel and North Sea ports had occupied the week following the Homberg operation, as low cloud and rain kept Scampton effectively closed for business. It had been planned to send a minelaying force to Brest on the night of the 19/20th, with the intention of sinking a Hipper-class cruiser, should it try to venture out into open water. In the event, the operation was cancelled, but two 49 and nine 83 Squadron crews were called to briefing on the afternoon of the 21st, to be told that it was on again for that night, and that they were to join thirty-three others from 5 Group. It was recorded in the ORB as a mining operation in the Jellyfish garden, for which the crews of Sgts Richman and Lowe departed Scampton at 18.20. They were to begin the Channel crossing at the Dorset coast, but the former landed at Upper Heyford after two hours aloft as a result of W/T failure. Sgt Lowe and the rest of the force set course for the target area in predominantly favourable conditions, encountering cloud over the sea, which had dispersed to five-tenths at 2,000 feet by the time that the target area drew near. Sgt Lowe and crew undertook this part of the outward leg on auto-pilot to reach their destination and establish a pinpoint with ease in good visibility. Most employed Pointe-Saint-Mathieu on the headland west of the port, where searchlights ensnared some of the attackers and flak ships took pot-shots at them as they made their timed runs. The Lowe crew delivered their mine in a shallow dive from 2,500 down to 500 feet and returned safely after a round trip of five hours and ten minutes.

5 Group would spend the next two nights on the ground, while a small force of Wellingtons targeted enemy warships at Brest on the 22nd and the docks at Boulogne twenty-four hours later.

When orders arrived on 5 Group stations on the 24th, they signalled the introduction to operations of a new squadron and aircraft type. 207 Squadron had completed its working-up programme with the Manchester at Waddington and would contribute six of the type to this night's raid by fifty-seven aircraft on enemy warships at Brest. It had been a difficult gestation period for the squadron, and the coming operational career of the Manchester would be dogged by grounding orders caused largely by the unreliability of its Rolls-Royce Vulture engines. Despite this, and ignorant of the full extent of the problems that would occur, orders would be issued on the following day to reform 97 Squadron at Waddington as the second Manchester unit. The Manchester would bring a massive increase in bomb-carrying capacity, and on this night, each would be loaded with a dozen 500 pounders to drop on the cruiser, Admiral Hipper. They were part of an overall force of fifty-seven aircraft, eighteen of them Hampdens, while Scampton remained inactive.

Düsseldorf was posted as the target on the 25th, for which a force of eighty aircraft was assembled, Hemswell and 49 Squadron at Scampton providing the 5 Group contribution of twenty-two Hampdens. The eleven 49 Squadron crews were briefed to attack the Rhine docks and departed Scampton between 18.20 and 18.40 with S/L Tench the senior pilot on duty and lost the services of the crews of Sgts Ball and F/O Fisher to W/T failure and Sgt Richman to high oil pressure. The others encountered poor weather conditions and ten-tenths cloud over the entire Ruhr area, and this would result in only around seven bomb loads falling within the city. The 49 Squadron crews had little idea of their whereabouts as they stooged around with only searchlights, flak and an occasional barrage balloon as a reference, and delivered their bomb loads indiscriminately in the vicinity of Düsseldorf and Duisburg.

Briefings on the 26th revealed Cologne to be the target for a force of 126 aircraft, for which Hemswell, Lindholme and Scampton made ready twenty-eight Hampdens, while Waddington contributed five Manchesters and 49 Squadron stayed at home. The Admiralty continued to maintain pressure on the Command to deal with the enemy's capital ships, and it was the Tirpitz at Wilhelmshaven that featured in briefings on the 28th. 116 aircraft were made ready across the groups, a dozen of the Hampdens by 49 Squadron and eleven of them took off between 01.35 and 02.13 with S/L Smith the senior pilot on duty. Sgt Lowe and crew were delayed for an undisclosed reason until 02.40 and, unable to make up the time, bombed the docks at Emden as an alternative target. The Hampdens were carrying either two 2,000 pounders or four 500 and two 250 pounders, the majority of which would not reach the target in the face of severe icing conditions from the Dutch coast, ten-tenths cloud at heights up to 15,000 feet and extreme darkness. S/L Smith and crew were not able positively to identify Tirpitz but found the docks area close to her berth and dropped a stick across the area in the face of intense flak in barrage form. F/L Howell and crew ran in from east to west along the channel towards the Bauhafen and dropped two 2,000 pounders one-and-a-half seconds apart, of which one was seen to burst on the slipways to the west of the Bauhafen. P/O Bowden and crew made two passes and observed the bombs during the first to burst on the side of the Bauhafen close to Tirpitz. P/O Wilson and crew released a flare but could not find Tirpitz and bombed the general area as did the others from between 6,000 and 9,500 feet.

Ten months after it had begun, an assessment of the efficacy of mining operations revealed that seventeen enemy vessels had been sunk in the Baltic's Great and Little Belts and eighteen damaged. It was believed that a further eighteen had probably been sunk and it was considered safe to estimate that for every known case of a sinking or damage, another would have occurred without news of it reaching England. Among the known sinkings was that of a troopship carrying three thousand men, of whom fewer than four hundred survived. During the course of the month, 49 Squadron took part in seven operations and dispatched sixty-six sorties for the loss of three Hampdens, two complete crews and two additional airmen.

# March 1941

The new month began with a return to Cologne on the night of the 1/2nd by an initial force of 131 assorted aircraft, of which forty-four Hampdens were provided by 5 Group from its stations at Coningsby, Hemswell, Lindholme and Scampton. The crews enjoyed favourable weather conditions over the North Sea and were able firmly to establish their positions as they made landfall over the Scheldt estuary and headed across Holland. They arrived in the target area to find clear skies and easily identifiable ground features, predominantly the distinctive bends in the River Rhine, which provided most with the references they required to run in on the briefed aiming point. Bombs were delivered from a variety of altitudes up to 16,000 feet in the face of an intense defensive response, and returning crews claimed a successful operation. This was confirmed by local sources, which reported extensive damage in central districts, particularly in the docks areas on both banks of the Rhine.

The threat of adverse weather conditions caused a reduction in the 5 Group force briefed to attack the Admiral Hipper at Brest on the night of the 2/3rd, and, ultimately, it was left to eight crews from 44 Squadron to carry out the operation. A force of seventy-one aircraft was assembled later on the 3rd to send once more against Cologne, for which Coningsby and Scampton provided the 5 Group element, while Waddington made ready three Hampdens and two Manchesters for a return to the Admiral Hipper at Brest. 49 Squadron launched a dozen Hampdens between 19.10 and 19.35 with F/L Howell the senior pilot on duty and they arrived in the target area to find nine to ten-tenths ice-bearing cloud with tops at 12,000 feet and a base at around 6,000 feet. Conditions otherwise were generally fair, and the few gaps allowed crews to gain glimpses of the Rhine and the city after searching for up to thirty minutes. Even so, not all were able to positively establish themselves over the Rhineland capital, but those who could, delivered their bomb loads from an average of 9,000 feet in the face of considerable searchlight activity, but little flak. Having failed to locate the primary target, P/O Wilson and crew attacked an aerodrome in Holland from 7,000 feet on the way home, while three others bombed flak concentrations in the target area or further north near Duisburg. The consensus of returning crews was positive, when, in fact, only a few locations in the western fringes of the city had been hit.

Thereafter, the weather took a hand to keep most of the Command on the ground for the next week, and it was during this period, on the 9th, that the Air Ministry responded to the urgent and burgeoning threat posed by U-Boots, which were claiming a massive tonnage of shipping crossing the Atlantic in convoys with vital war supplies. A new Directive was issued, which would unleash a concerted campaign against this menace and its partner in crime, the Focke-Wulf Kondor long-range maritime reconnaissance bomber. These two threats were to be attacked where-ever they could be found, at sea, in their bases in the occupied ports, and at their point of manufacture in the shipyards and in the assembly and component factories. A new target list was drawn up, which was headed by Kiel, Hamburg and Vegesack (Bremen), all of which were home to U-Boot construction yards, and Bremen itself, which also boasted a Focke-Wulf aircraft factory in its south-eastern Hemelingen district. Other related targets included the diesel engine plants at Mannheim and Augsburg, aircraft factories at Dessau, and, of course, the U-Boot bases at Brest, Lorient and St Nazaire. Until otherwise instructed, this was to be the focus of Peirse's efforts, and, only occasionally, would he be able prosecute the oil campaign.

When 5 Group resumed operations on the 10th, only Hemswell and Waddington were involved in sending nineteen Hampdens back to Cologne. The new directive would be implemented first on the night of the 12/13th, at the end of a day of hectic activity across the Command, as aircraft were made ready for three major raids to be conducted that night. Eighty-eight aircraft were to attack the Blohm & Voss shipyards at Hamburg, while eighty-six other crews were briefed for the Focke-Wulf factory and the city of Bremen, and, finally, seventy-two aircraft were prepared for the long slog to Berlin to target two aiming points. 5 Group was to support the first-mentioned with forty Hampdens and four Manchesters, and the last-mentioned with thirty Hampdens, and, with the addition of a single freshman crew on gardening duties, this represented the largest effort undertaken by the group thus far in the war. The four Manchesters and three 4 Group Halifaxes at Hamburg would be the first of their type to operate over Germany. 49 Squadron briefed seven crews for Hamburg and four for Berlin and dispatched the former from Scampton between 19.15 and 19.23 with F/O Barlow the only commissioned pilot among them. They climbed away into largely clear skies and were closing on the target by the time that the Berlin-bound quartet took off between 21.45 and 22.13 with S/L Tench the senior pilot on duty and last away.

Hamburg was basking under what were described as perfect weather conditions, which allowed easy identification of the aiming point once the crews had run the usual gauntlet of intense searchlights and flak as they approached from the north and north-west. The 49 Squadron crews carried out their attacks from between 6,500 and 10,500 feet and observed bursts and fires, which remained visible for sixty miles into the return flight. With the whole of northern Germany under clear skies, those heading for Berlin also experienced no difficulty in navigating across Holland on course for the gap between Bremen and the Hannover/Braunschweig area. All identified the target area if not necessarily the designated aiming point and delivered their attacks from between 7,000 and 10,000 feet, S/L Tench and crew counting thirteen fires as they turned away. P2126 lost an engine to fuel deprivation at the English coast and P/O Mervyn-Jones put it down at Donna Nook on the Lincolnshire coast at 07.00. Local sources in Berlin reported sixty buildings damaged, mostly in southern districts, while, at Hamburg, twenty high-explosive bombs and up to four hundred incendiaries had inflicted significant damage on the Blohm & Voss U-Boot construction yards and four other shipyards. Meanwhile, Wellingtons had attacked the Focke-Wulf factory at Bremen, and a number of hits had been scored there also.

Weather conditions remained favourable as preparations were put in hand on the 13th to return to Hamburg that night with a force of 139 aircraft, including a contribution from 5 Group of thirty-four Hampdens and five Manchesters. 49 Squadron's four Hampdens took off from Scampton between 19.25 and 19.33 with F/L Howell the senior pilot on duty, and they crossed the Lincolnshire coast in the region of Skegness, before making their way independently of each other, as was the practice at this stage of the war, towards the enemy coast. Moonlight helped with identification of the aiming-point, and the bombs were released from around 10,000 feet in the face of accurate searchlights and heavy and light flak. On approach to the target, the Perspex in Sgt Morphett's rear gunner's door was shot out, but they continued on to deliver their bombs and observe three explosions on the north-western edge of the target. The general consensus among returning crews was of an effective raid, which local sources and post-raid reconnaissance confirmed had inflicted further damage on the Blohm & Voss shipyards and caused 119 fires in Hamburg generally, thirty-five of them classed as large.

A raid on the Hydrierwerke-Scholven synthetic oil refinery at Gelsenkirchen was briefed out to twenty-one Hampden crews on the 14th, as part of an overall force of 101 aircraft assigned to a number of similar targets in the city. 49 Squadron's participation was cancelled for what turned out to be the most successful attack yet on the oil industry, after some sixteen bomb loads hit the oil plant. Hemswell, Lindholme and Waddington were notified of a return to the Ruhr on the 15th, this time to attack a specific target in Düsseldorf, but 49 Squadron had to wait until the 17th for action, when it fell to Scampton and Coningsby to contribute eighteen Hampdens to a force of fifty-seven aircraft targeting shipyards in Bremen, while 2 Group Blenheims targeted Wilhelmshaven. The ten 49 Squadron participants took off between 00.30 and 01.05 with F/L Fisher the senior pilot on duty and all reached the target area to benefit from the excellent conditions, which enabled them to establish their positions for the bombing run. F/L Fisher and P/O Mervyn-Jones elected to make a glide attack from 12,000 feet and released their bombs from 8,000 and 9,000 feet respectively, the latter pinpointing on the commercial docks. Sgt Lowe and crew lost their heating while outbound and dropped their bombs at the first opportunity on the western edge of the target before heading home in great discomfort to thaw out. The Mervyn-Jones crew was approaching the Humber homebound at 2,000 feet when they were fired upon by a convoy, which managed to hit the port engine, fortunately, without causing damage.

Thirty-eight Hampdens and two Manchesters were detailed by 5 Group on the 18th for an operation that night against the Deutsche Werke U-Boot yards at Kiel, which would also involve fifty-seven Wellingtons and Whitleys. Local reports would claim this to be the heaviest raid yet on Kiel, mentioning an increase in the number of incendiaries, and confirming damage to the U-Boot yards. On the 20th, 5 Group committed forty-two Hampdens to an extensive programme of mining off the Biscay ports of Brest, Lorient and St-Nazaire, while three Manchesters and twenty-one Whitleys turned their attention upon U-Boots at the base being built on the Keroman peninsula on the southern extremity of Lorient. The first phase of the massive construction project had begun just weeks earlier, and would continue until January 1942, by which time K1, K2 and K3 would be completed and capable of sheltering thirty vessels and their crews under cover. The complex would boast a revolutionary lift system, which could raise U-Boots from the water and transport them across the facility to repair and servicing bays. The thickness of the concrete would render the structure impervious to the bombs available to Bomber Command at the time, and attacks would be directed predominantly at the town and its approaches to prevent access by road and rail, while extensive minelaying compromised access by sea.

Twelve Hampden crews were briefed to return to Lorient on the night of 21st, while a handful of others would be sent mining in the Deodar garden in the Gironde Estuary on the approaches to Bordeaux. The 49 Squadron ORB is confusing and contradictory, but it seems that six aircraft took off, three to attack U-Boots at Lorient and three for mining duties in the Gironde estuary. The crews of P/O Wilson and Sgts Merralls and Morphett departed Scampton between 18.20 and 18.25

and headed for the Dorset coast to begin the Channel crossing. They flew out over ten-tenths cloud, which had only broken slightly by the time they reached the Biscay coast. Sgt Merralls dropped a flare and established a pinpoint by its light, before delivering a stick of eight bombs across the estimated position of the docks. Sgt Morphett carried out a shallow dive to 4,000 feet and watched his stick of eight 250 pounders splash across the docks and wharf buildings. On return, X3054 crashed into high ground on Hamel Down Tor on Dartmoor, killing three of the occupants, while P/O Wilson lingered until succumbing to his injuries on the following day. Meanwhile, the gardeners had taken off between 22.35 and 22.48 led by F/L Fisher and settled in for what would be an eight-hour round-trip to the Bordeaux region. Sgt Lowe and crew claimed that the weather was bad all the way with ten-tenths cloud, while F/L Fisher described hazy conditions and P/O Bowden clear skies. All planted their vegetables as briefed, after which, F/L Fisher and crew dropped their wing bombs on an aerodrome and shot down an unidentified enemy aircraft, and F/O Bowden and crew attacked a flak position at Brest.

With the moon out of commission for a period, and weather conditions over northern Germany unfavourable, 5 Group sent thirty Hampdens to Kiel on the 23rd, while Berlin played host to a force of sixty-three Wellingtons and Whitleys. The six-strong 49 Squadron element departed Scampton between 19.09 and 19.15 with S/L Tench the senior pilot on duty and encountered heavy cloud over the North Sea, which persisted all the way to the Danish coast. The cloud began to thin sufficiently over the Schleswig-Holstein peninsula to allow the others to identify pinpoints, and, by the time that they reached the western Baltic, the horizontal visibility was adequate for their purposes. S/L Tench and crew spent ninety minutes in a vain search for the target and dropped their bombs on a searchlight and flak concentration at Bremen, setting off a large fire. Sgt Morphett and crew were defeated by low cloud and bombed an alternative target before heading home in the greatest discomfort after the heating failed. The others located and bombed the primary target, P/O Bowden and crew despite severe icing issues, and they also captured a rare target photo.

Düsseldorf was posted as one of the targets on the 27th, for which a force of thirty-nine aircraft was made ready, consisting of twenty-two Hampdens from Hemswell, Scampton and Waddington, four 207 Squadron Manchesters and thirteen Whitleys from 4 Group. The 49 Squadron element of eight took off between 19.22 and 19.41 with F/O Barlow the senior pilot on duty and all reached the target area to be greeted by the expected industrial haze and intense searchlight and flak defence. The glare of searchlights on the haze produced challenging conditions for target identification, and it took between thirty and fifty-five minutes for the 49 Squadron crews to establish their positions, assisted to some extent by the distinctive reversed S-bend in the River Rhine to the west of the city centre. By the time they released their bombs some had made up to four passes over the hostile city, and most were able to observe bursts and developing fires. No detailed assessment was possible, and an absence of post-raid reconnaissance and local reports left the crews uncertain as to the effectiveness of their work.

On the 29th, the German cruisers Scharnhorst and Gneisenau were reported to be off Brest, and 50 Squadron was ordered to dispatch six Hampdens from Lindholme to carry out a cloud-cover daylight attack, a type of operation that would come to be known as "moling". The arrival of the vessels must have been expected, because Lindholme had been standing-by at two-hours readiness for seven days when the order was received. They flew out in two vics over the Lizard, until insufficient cloud cover over the Channel forced them to turn back. That night, twenty-five

Hampdens were dispatched from Scampton, Waddington and Coningsby to mine the waters of the Jellyfish garden on the approaches to the port, while 49 Squadron remained on the ground.

Hemswell and Lindholme joined forces on the 30th to send six Hampdens each on another daylight foray, but an absence of cloud cover again forced them to turn back. That night, a force of 109 aircraft was assembled for a return to the port, and this number included fourteen Hampdens and four Manchesters representing 5 Group, while ten others from the group attended to gardening duties in the approaches. 49 Squadron loaded nine of its Hampdens with bombs and three with a mine each and sent them on their way from Scampton between 18.59 and 19.31 with no pilots on duty above flying officer rank. Sgt Ball and crew returned almost six hours after taking off, having lost the use of their W/T, but the others reached the target area and were typically at variance in their description of the conditions. P/O Henderson and crew reported them to be perfect as they released their bombs from 9,000 feet following a shallow dive, while Sgt Morphett and crew claimed that the warships were obscured by cloud and their estimated location had to be bombed from 8,500 feet. Most, however, found the target to be easily identified and attacks were carried out in the face of an intense flak defence from the vessels themselves and batteries around the port. While this was ongoing, the three gardeners sneaked in to deliver their mine each from below 1,000 feet, F/O Barlow and crew gliding down to 100 feet only to suffer the frustration of a hang-up. Returning crews were enthusiastic about the conduct of the raid, and while no hits had been achieved, no aircraft had been lost.

During the course of the month, the squadron took part in eleven operations and dispatched sixty-nine sorties for the loss of a single Hampden and crew.

# April 1941

The first week of the new month was reserved exclusively for operations on and around Brest with the intention of disabling its lodgers. Scharnhorst and Gneisenau were dubbed in the British press as Salmon & Gluckstein, in a comic reference to the country's largest tobacconist, established in 1873 by a German Jewish émigré and his English partner. The assault on Brest began with 5 Group launching a dozen Hampdens from St Eval in Cornwall for a daylight attack on the 1st, when all but one turned back in the absence of cloud, and the one that continued on failed to return. 49 and 83 Squadrons sent six Hampdens each from their Scampton base to St Eval for another attempt on the 3rd, for which the details are omitted from the ORBs of 5 Group and both squadrons. We are told only that Sgt Beckett and crew took off at 08.30 and returned at 11.15 to report that they had dive-bombed one of the cruisers from 9,000 down to 6,000 feet and that the results had been obscured by cloud. The others involved in this action had turned back in the face of insufficient cloud cover and a second attempt launched in the afternoon was also recalled. Ninety other aircraft were made ready during the course of the afternoon to return to Brest that night, while fifteen Hampdens were to sneak in under cover of the main event to mine the approaches and also the waters of the Cinnamon garden off La Rochelle. The crews of P/O Henderson and Sgts Richman and Ball took off between 18.55 and 19.05 bound for the latter and planted their vegetables in the allotted locations from 700 feet, after which, Sgt Ball and crew dropped their 250 pounders on searchlights at Lorient and Sgt Richman and crew theirs on an aerodrome at St-Nazaire. On return to St-Eval, Sgt Ball overshot the landing and P4403, in which F/L Learoyd had earned his VC, ended up in a hedge, fortunately without damage to the aircraft or its occupants.

On the 4th, Gneisenau entered a dry dock, which was to be drained on the following day for an inspection of the vessel, while 5 Group detailed eleven Hampdens and four Manchesters for yet another attempt on the enemy cruisers that night as part of a force of fifty-four aircraft. Five of the eleven participating Hampdens carried out low-level attacks, and one went in at 1,000 feet at 22.55 to score a direct hit on Scharnhorst, which was recognised in the flash as being in a dry dock precisely as depicted in the reconnaissance photos shown to the crews at briefing. The rear gunner confirmed the success, but it was impossible to determine which part of the vessel had been hit. Another of the low-level attackers was the 106 Squadron commanding officer, W/C Polglase, whose Hampden was seen to be shot down. The Continental Hotel in the town was also struck by bombs just as dinner was being served, and a number of naval officers were killed. When Gneisenau's dry dock was drained on the following day, the 5th, a single unexploded 500lb bomb was found nestling at the bottom, and the ship's captain, Kapitän-zur-See Otto Fein, decided to move his vessel out into the harbour while it was dealt with. The dock was refilled to allow Gneisenau to vacate it, and she was spotted by a reconnaissance aircraft at some point, which led to an operation being planned by Coastal Command to be carried out at first light on the 6th.

In the meantime, on the 5th, 44 and 50 Squadrons were ordered to prepare for another daylight operation to be launched from St Eval, concerning which, the 5 Group record mentioned only that the weather conditions were inhospitable with ten-tenths low cloud. By the time that they had passed south of the Isles of Scilly, they were in rain at 500 feet, and although a number of Lindholme crews reached the target, only one carried out an attack on estimated position, with no hope of hitting anything of value.

The Coastal Command operation on the 6th took place in poor weather conditions, which led to the six Beauforts becoming separated while outbound, and F/O Kenneth Campbell and his crew alone pressed home an attack, which caused damage to Gneisenau that would require six months to repair. In the face of the most concentrated anti-aircraft fire, the Beaufort stood little chance of getting away with it and was shot down without survivors. F/O Campbell was posthumously awarded a Victoria Cross for his actions.

That evening, fifteen Hampdens were made ready at Scampton for mining duties in the Jellyfish garden off Brest, while four others were to ply their trade in the Nectarine garden around the Frisian Islands. The Nectarine region encompassed the entire Frisian chain and was divided into three gardens, Nectarine I from Texel to the eastern tip of Ameland, Nectarine II, from east of Ameland to Memmert, and Nectarine III, Juist to Wangerooge, and it appears from a reference in the ORB to Borkum that this night's destination was Nectarine II. Waddington would also be sending five crews to conduct mining sorties in the Beech garden off St-Nazaire. 49 Squadron briefed seven crews for Jellyfish and sent them on their way between 19.00 and 19.15 led by S/L Smith, and they were followed into the air between 19.20 and 20.20 by five crews bound for the Frisians. P/O Bowden and crew abandoned their sortie after two members of the crew became indisposed, leaving the others to reach the target area off the Finistere coast, where, beneath the ten-tenths cloud, the visibility was good and enabled them to establish their positions and deliver their stores into the allotted locations from between 400 and 750 feet. Some then went on to bomb and strafe flak ships and searchlights before returning safely from an effective night's work. Meanwhile, some six hundred miles to the north-east, ten-tenths cloud with a base at 1,500 feet created challenging conditions for some crews, who searched for up to an hour to find their pinpoints. The mines were delivered from between 450 and 800 feet in the absence of any opposition and no suitable targets were found for the 250 pounders.

When Kiel shipyards were posted as the primary targets on the 7th, a new record force for a single target of 229 aircraft was assembled, among which were sixty Hampdens, a dozen of them representing 49 Squadron. They departed Scampton between 20.05 and 20.35 with S/L Tench the senior pilot on duty and crossed the English coast near Skegness, before setting course for Rømø Island on Denmark's western coast, where they would turn east to a position north of Flensburg to approach Kiel from the north. They encountered cloud at 6,000 feet for the first fifty miles of the North Sea crossing, and it was at this stage that they lost the services of the crews of F/L Fisher and P/O Henderson to engine trouble and a failed heating system respectively. The others benefitted from clear skies for the remainder of the outward flight and reached the enemy coast at around 10,000 feet before traversing the Schleswig-Holstein peninsula and arriving in the target area to find the defences had already been stirred into action. The bright moonlight helped to tone down the glare from dozens of searchlights, which were co-operating with medium calibre flak batteries that were hosing shells up to 12,000 feet, while heavy flak reached as high as 18,000 feet and the light stuff awaited any crew foolhardy enough to try to sneak in lower down. The 49 Squadron Hampdens bombed from an average of 9,000 feet, some after a glide approach, and noted many fires, which remained visible for up to eighty miles into the homeward leg. Returning crews were confident that the raid, which had taken place over a period of almost five hours, had struck a major blow against this important target, and this was confirmed by local reports of widespread damage to housing in the town, and to port facilities and the eastern docks area. The nightshift workers at the Germania Werft and Deutsche Werke U-Boot construction yards had been sent home, causing a number of days' loss of production.

A force of 160 aircraft was made ready during the following day to return to Kiel that night, and among them were twenty-nine Hampdens and twelve Manchesters, four of the latter belonging to 5 Group's latest addition, 97 Squadron, which would be operating for the first time. Returning crews reported a very large explosion that was followed by a column of black smoke, and they described the target area as a mass of flames as they retreated to the west. Local sources confirmed another damaging raid, which had fallen more into the town than the docks and seafront area and some eight thousand people had been bombed out of their homes.

The main operation on the 9th was to be directed at Berlin and was to be prosecuted by eighty aircraft, including twenty-four Hampdens, eleven of them provided by 49 Squadron. An additional Hampden was made ready for the freshman crew of Sgt Lamb to take mining in one of the Nectarine gardens, and all took off together between 20.23 and 20.47 with S/L Smith the senior pilot on duty. The Lamb crew planted their vegetable in the briefed location without difficulty and reported that they believed that they had shot down an enemy aircraft on the way home. Meanwhile, the others found Berlin under largely clear skies and almost perfect conditions for the accurate bombing of the briefed aiming point, the main railway station and its marshalling yards. The 49 Squadron crews carried out their attacks from between 9,000 and 14,000 feet, some after a glide approach, and large explosions were followed by burgeoning fires. They had to run the gauntlet of searchlights and flak and Sgt Pinney dived down to 2,000 feet in an effort to escape the forest of searchlights while his gunners did their best to shoot them out. They were not the only crew to report the difficulty of escaping the defences intact, but all managed to do so and provided positive feedback to the intelligence section at debriefing.

Orders were received on some 5 Group stations on the 10th to prepare for a joint 4 and 5 Group effort against Düsseldorf involving fifty-three aircraft, for which twenty-nine Hampdens were detailed. The other operation on this night was another assault on Brest and its guest enemy warships, for which fifty-three aircraft also were made ready, including five Manchesters of 97 Squadron to represent 5 Group. 49 Squadron sat out this night, while its 5 Group counterparts contended with thick industrial haze at Düsseldorf, which rendered their efforts largely ineffective. Meanwhile, at Brest, four bombs hit the under-repair Gneisenau on the starboard side of the forward superstructure, and, although only two detonated, seventy-two men were killed and ninety injured, sixteen of which would not survive.

It was the turn of Lindholme to stay at home on the 12th, while 5 Group split its forces to cover two bombing operations and mining. The main event would be played out once more at Brest, for which a force of sixty-six aircraft included a dozen Hampdens, six belonging to 49 Squadron, and six Manchesters, while six 49 Squadron Hampdens carried out the mining of the approaches in the Jellyfish garden. A second force of fifteen Hampdens and nine Wellingtons would bypass the Brest area on its way further south to attack Merignac aerodrome near Bordeaux. The 49 Squadron elements departed Scampton together between 00.30 and 00.57 with F/L Fisher the senior pilot on duty among the bombing brigade and crossed the Channel over ten-tenths cloud with a base at 3,000 feet. At the target the base had descended further, leaving the coastline completely obscured and the location of the port only identified by the volume of flak penetrating the cloud tops. A few crews found a fleeting gap in the clouds that revealed the docks area, among them the crews of Sgt Lamb and F/L Fisher, who dropped a stick each more in hope than expectation, while Sgt Pinney and crew bombed a flak concentration from 11,000 feet. The crews of Sgts Eshelby and Welch and P/O Mervyn-Jones eventually abandoned their search for a pinpoint and brought their bombs home. A post-raid analysis revealed that only thirty-seven crews had bombed in the area of the primary target, while many of the others had switched their attention to nearby Lorient.

The Manchester's Rolls Royce Vulture engines were proving to be problematic, with overheating and component failures seriously affecting the type's rate of serviceability. As a result, the first of a number of grounding orders was issued on the 13th, while investigations were carried out into the engine-bearing problem and modifications put in hand. This meant that no further operations would be undertaken by the type during what remained of the month. That night, seventeen Hampdens were dispatched for mining duties in the Cinnamon garden off the port of La Rochelle, the crews having been briefed to drop their wing-mounted bombs on a hotel south of Quiberon, which, presumably, was home to U-Boot personnel.

The pattern of operations was now set for the remainder of the month, in which Brest and Kiel would continue to be the principal objectives. The former was posted as the primary target for a force of ninety-four aircraft on the 14th, for which 5 Group contributed twenty-five Hampdens, ten of them representing 49 Squadron. They departed Scampton between 19.40 and 19.55 with no senior pilots on duty and lost the services of Sgt Eshelby and crew to the failure of their W/T equipment within the hour. A post-raid analysis would blame low cloud for an ineffective attack, but the experiences of the 49 Squadron crews cast doubt on that assessment, Sgt Beckett and crew reporting that the weather cleared as the target drew near. Even though they could not identify the cruisers, they saw enough detail to enable them to dive through the flak to release their bombs from 6,000 feet without observing them burst. Sgt Pinney and crew described the weather as very good and carried out a glide attack to 8,000 feet, while Sgt Lamb and crew reported that the visibility at the French coast was fair, and that they were untroubled by flak as they glided down from 12,000 to 7,500 feet to release their bombs with the cruisers clearly visible to the rear gunner as they sped away. P/O Kerridge and crew even claimed a cloudless sky and were prevented from identifying the vessels only because of searchlight glare. Sgt Merralls and crew probably were the closest physically to the cruisers after withholding their bombs until they were down to 4,000 feet over the docks, and they reported the flak from the vessels to be "not troublesome". There were others among the 49 Squadron element that did blame cloud for their inability to find the aiming point, P/O Bowden and crew claiming that the cloud increased as they arrived, and they ultimately bombed a flak concentration after a search lasting forty-five minutes.

Kiel was posted as the target for ninety-six aircraft on the 15th, 5 Group contributing nineteen Hampdens on a night when Scampton remained inactive. Cloud was again the decisive factor and returning crews were unable to offer an assessment of the outcome, while local reports suggested an ineffective raid that had caused little damage. The destination for 107 aircraft on the 16th was Bremen, where the shipyards were the aiming points. Scampton was back on the order of battle and 49 Squadron briefed ten crews for the main event and the freshman crew of Sgt Woolston for mining duties in one of the Nectarine gardens around the Frisians. The latter departed Scampton first at 20.00 and returned five-and-a-half hours later to report successfully delivering their mine from 800 feet. The bombing element took off at 22.49 and 23.45 with S/Ls Smith and Tench the senior pilots on duty and ran into thick cloud at the Dutch coast that persisted all the way to the target area. The only clue to their whereabouts for most crews was the flak coming up from Delmenhorst and Oldenburg and it was this that provided the reference for most crews to bomb on estimated positions after searching for up to ninety minutes. A number of crews were stalked by night-fighters but on a dark, moonless night, they were easily evaded.

Berlin would provide the target for 118 aircraft on the 17th, thirty-nine of them Hampdens, of which ten belonged to 49 Squadron. There were two aiming points, including the telephone exchange, but this was simply a euphemism for an attack on the city centre to cause as much destruction as possible. They departed Scampton between 20.08 and 20.34 with S/L Tench the senior pilot on duty and crossed the English coast over Skegness, running immediately into ten-tenths cloud at 12,000 feet until reaching Holland, where it began to disperse. Sgt Pinney had doubts about his fuel lasting and decided to bomb an aerodrome at Hoya, located between Bremen and Hannover before turning back and nursing a sick engine. Sgt Woolston and crew were uncertain of their position as they crossed the Dutch coast and eventually dropped a stick of bombs on a searchlight and flak position at Hamburg. There were clear skies over the border region between southern Denmark and Germany, but haze blotted out ground detail, and those reaching Berlin would find it difficult to locate the planned aiming points. The remaining 49 Squadron crews carried out their attacks on estimated positions and none was able to offer an assessment either because of cloud or the glare from searchlights.

While 49 Squadron spent a week away from the operational scene, eleven Hampdens joined fifty others to raid Cologne on the 20th and a further nine were detailed for mining duties in the Jellyfish garden off Brest. Hemswell maintained the pressure on the German warships at Brest on the 23rd, when sending ten Hampdens, the crews of which failed to identify the location of the vessels and bombed on approximate positions. In addition, fourteen Hampdens were assigned to gardening duties and were divided equally between Quiberon Bay, off the Biscay coast, and the Frisians. It was left to ten Hampdens from 49 Squadron to represent 5 Group in an overall force of sixty-nine aircraft with Kiel as their destination on the 24th. They departed Scampton between 20.30 and 20.52 with S/L Smith the senior pilot on duty and set course on a very dark, moonless night for the Danish coast, while the freshman crew of Sgt Huggett peeled off when they reached the northern Frisians and successfully planted their vegetable in the briefed location from clear skies. Despite the extreme darkness, the visibility was good, and the Kiel-bound force had little difficulty in locating it, although some blamed haze for their failure to establish a pinpoint. Sgt Lamb and crew were among these but glided down through a forest of searchlights from 15,000 to 12,000 feet to deliver their bombs on the general target area. S/L Smith and crew thought they were over Kiel but realised afterwards that they had bombed Flensburg to the north. Sgt Woolston and crew set a southerly course from Flensburg and dropped a stick of bombs and nickels across the target area. The others bombed from between 10,000 and 12,000 feet and were largely oblivious to the outcome as they dodged flak and searchlight beams. Local sources confirmed the scattered nature of the raid and the small amount of damage achieved.

A follow-up raid by sixty-two aircraft twenty-four hours later involved ten Hampdens from Coningsby and Hemswell and developed into a scattered affair that caused modest damage. Hamburg would be a frequent destination throughout the war and would receive its own mini campaign of six raids between the end of April and the middle of May. Twenty-eight Hampdens and twenty-two Wellingtons were prepared for an operation against it on the 26th, although, at this stage of the war, it is unlikely that they would have been over the target at the same time. Nine 49 Squadron crews were briefed to attack a specific area, probably the shipyards, and departed Scampton between 20.36 and 21.15 with S/L Tench the senior pilot on duty. The presence of ten-tenths ice-bearing cloud over Germany's north-western coast created challenges for navigation and crews experienced mixed fortunes as they sought out a pinpoint. S/L Tench identified Dollart as he passed south of Emden and only avoided the Bremen searchlights with difficulty as he pushed on eastwards to Hamburg, where his starboard engine cut as he carried out a dive approach from 14,000 feet. The bombs were released at 9,000 feet and two bursts observed near the river, and it was at this point that the dead engine coughed back to life. Two bursts were observed near the river but no detail, and severe static was responsible for inflicting two burns on the wireless operator. Sgt Lowe and crew also located the target with ease to bomb from 7,000 feet, while others struggled with the nine to ten-tenths cloud, intense darkness and searchlights and bombed on evidence of flak or on estimated positions. Local sources reported no more than sixteen bomb loads falling, no fires and only minor damage.

49 Squadron had now completed its operational activity for the month and watched from the sidelines as Mannheim was posted as the destination for seventy-one aircraft on the 29th, fourteen of them Hampdens. In the face of adverse weather conditions, only around fifteen crews reported bombing in the area of the city, and local sources reported fairly minor damage. Kiel was posted as the primary target for eighty-one aircraft including ten Hampdens on the 30th, and fewer than

fifty returning crews claimed to have attacked its estimated location. Local sources reported that no damage had resulted. During the course of the month, the squadron took part in fourteen operations and dispatched 103 sorties without loss.

# May 1941

The new month began with the posting of an operation to Hamburg on the 1st, but this was subsequently cancelled, only to be reinstated on the following day and a force of ninety-five aircraft assembled. The grounding order on the Manchester had been lifted, and three of the type representing 207 Squadron would join nineteen Hampdens as the 5 Group contribution. 49 Squadron briefed eleven crews for the main event and two freshman crews for mining duties in the Nectarine III garden and it was the latter, the crews of Sgts Bunn and Green, who took off first at 20.50 and 20.56 respectively. They were followed into the air by the main element between 21.03 and 21.31 with S/L Smith and F/L Howell the senior pilots on duty and flew out over the Lincolnshire coast before setting a course to follow the chain of the Frisian Islands. They would make landfall over the Elbe estuary, either to follow the river's course into the heart of the city or continue on to Neumünster, a town situated some thirty-five miles to the north of Hamburg to begin the bombing run from there. The weather for the outbound flight was fairly good with just a little low cloud, but this increased over Germany and combined with haze to create challenging conditions for some crews. Those from 49 Squadron mostly found the target without difficulty and all would comment on the intensity of the searchlights and flak that welcomed them to Germany's second city. F/L Howell and crew glided undetected from 12,000 down to 10,000 feet to release their single 2,000 and two 500 pounders, which were seen to detonate among buildings and hurl debris into the air, leaving a large fire that remained visible for sixty miles into the homeward flight. The others from the squadron attacked either their briefed aiming point or an alternative within the city and returned safely to report an effective raid. The local authorities confirmed twenty-six fires, half of them large, but no significant incidents. Meanwhile, the gardeners planted their vegetable each into the allotted locations from below 1,000 feet after pinpointing on Borkum and Juist and also returned safely having gained a tad more operational experience.

5 Group put up twenty-seven Hampdens and two Manchesters on the 3rd, in an overall force of 101 aircraft bound for Cologne, while a predominantly Wellington force of thirty-three aircraft continued the assault on Brest and its lodgers. On the following day, 5 Group detailed twenty-one Hampdens to take part in the next attack on the cruisers at Brest, the Group ORB offering the thought that the warships must be crippled by now following repeated attacks. Certainly, damage had been inflicted, but effective camouflage and smoke screens ensured that the British authorities actually had no clear picture of the vessels' state of serviceability, and the raids would continue. 49 Squadron made ready a dozen of its own as part of an overall force of ninety-seven aircraft and dispatched them between 21.25 and 21.40 with F/Ls Fisher and Howell the senior pilots on duty. Sgt Green and crew turned back after an hour because of an overheating engine, leaving the others to press on across the Channel towards the Finistere coast, P/O Henderson and crew reporting later that they could see Brest from seventy miles away, roughly from the Channel Islands, suggesting that the attack was already well under way. The visibility was so good in the target area under a bright moon that there were no navigational difficulties, and the vessels were positively identified

by some crews as they glided in to release their bombs from between 6,000 and 11,500 feet in the face of intense flak from the vessels and shore-based batteries. Bursts were observed by some crews across the docks and adjacent to the warships, and a number of returning crews from other squadrons claimed direct hits, which were not confirmed. Sgt Eshelby and crew were disappointed to watch their bombs splash into the water, but captured a bombing photograph, before becoming caught in a green flare at 4,000 feet, from where the flak chased them down to 1,500 feet to escape via Goulet-de-Brest on the southern side of the estuary.

The teleprinters on 1, 3, 4 and 5 Group stations began churning out the orders of the day on the 5th, to reveal that Mannheim was to be the destination for a force of 141 aircraft, of which 5 Group's contribution amounted to thirty-three Hampdens and four Manchesters. The outward flight was attended by ten-tenths cloud, which persisted in the target area, and despite the claim by 121 crews that they had attacked the city, local sources reported some twenty-five bomb loads falling and causing only minor damage. A force of 115 aircraft was assembled for an attack on the Blohm & Voss shipyards in Hamburg on the 6th, an operation supported by 5 Group with twenty-seven Hampdens and four Manchesters. 49 Squadron contributed eleven Hampdens to the main event and two freshman crews for mining duties in the Gorse garden in Quiberon Bay to the south of Lorient. The crews of Sgt Hannan and F/O Hirons departed Scampton first at 21.37 and 21.40 before pointing their snouts towards the south and were followed into the air between 21.50 and 22.15 by the main element, among which, P/Os Henderson and Kerridge were the only commissioned pilots. In the event, cloud up to 16,000 feet and poor visibility prevented any crews from identifying the aiming point and bombs were dropped on estimated positions or on alternative targets based largely on evidence of flak. When the map references were plotted later, it became clear that some crews had strayed up to fifty miles north of Hamburg and had entered the Kiel defence zone.

The eighteen Hampdens detailed for a raid on Brest on the 7th represented a reduced figure in the light of a forecast of adverse weather conditions. In the event, the weather turned out to be more favourable than expected, and those reaching the target area found moonlight that enabled some to identify the dry dock occupied by one of the vessels, while others were blinded by searchlight glare. Some bursts were observed in the docks area but claims of direct hits remained unconfirmed.

All 5 Group operational stations received orders on the following day to prepare aircraft for what would be a record-breaking night of activity involving 364 sorties. 188 aircraft were to attack Hamburg, 119 of them assigned to the Blohm & Voss shipyards and sixty-nine to target the city, while 133 Whitleys and Wellingtons attended to the A G Weser U-Boot construction yards in Bremen. 5 Group contributed a record seventy-eight Hampdens and nine Manchesters to the Hamburg forces, thirteen of the former representing 49 Squadron, their crews briefed for the shipyards. They departed Scampton between 22.08 and 22.35 with F/L Fisher the senior pilot on duty and flew out over the Lincolnshire coast on course initially for Jutland. As the drone of their engines faded, the freshman crews of Sgts Flint, Batchelor and Hind took off between 22.57 and 23.00 to deliver a mine each in the Nectarine I garden off the Frisian Island of Terschelling. Conditions over north-western Germany promised a reasonable chance of identifying the aiming points and this proved to be the case as the bombers made landfall at various points on the Danish and German coasts, some roaming far and wide over the Schleswig-Holstein peninsula as far as Kiel and Lübeck to the north and north-east of Hamburg. Sgt Woolston and crew crossed the

Danish coast at 18,000 feet before heading south to bomb the target from 20,000 feet. Others pinpointed on the town of Neumünster as the starting point for their bombing run and mostly found the target city laid out beneath them and throwing up an intense but inaccurate defence. Sgt Lowe and crew had lost their heating soon after take-off and were suffering from the extreme cold as they carried out their attack, observing that the searchlights were co-operating with night-fighters. Only Sgt Green and crew mentioned cloud compromising their view of the target and reported gliding down through it to release their bombs from 3,500 feet, before climbing out in a hail of flak, some of which found the mark. The others attacked from between 9,000 and 12,000 feet and registered bomb bursts in the general area of the briefed aiming point and in the docks, and fifty fires were counted by a 44 Squadron rear gunner.

Meanwhile the gardeners had crossed the North Sea at between 2,000 and 3,000 feet under bright moonlight and sought out pinpoints, Sgt Hind and crew finding one on Texel and coming under fire from a flak ship. After planting their vegetable as briefed, they descended to 100 feet to strafe a convoy, the position of which was reported back to 5 Group HQ. The crews of Sgts Batchelor and Flint delivered their mines unopposed off Terschelling and returned safely from uneventful sorties. Local sources in Hamburg confirmed that an accurate and effective raid had taken place that resulted in eighty-three fires, thirty-eight of them large, and the highest death toll yet in a German city of 185 people. Many of these may have resulted from the demolition of ten apartment blocks by a single 4,000 pounder.

While the Scampton squadrons were rested, a force of 146 aircraft was assembled on the 9th for that night's operation against the twin cities of Mannheim and Ludwigshafen, for which 5 Group made available twenty-four Hampdens and eleven Manchesters. The aiming point for the 5 Group element was the Badische Anilin & Soda-Fabrik (BASF) works in Ludwigshafen, which was part of the infamous I G Farben company, the largest manufacturer of chemicals and synthetic oil products in the world and major employer of slave workers. The operation took place under favourable conditions and local reports confirmed that some useful industrial damage had been inflicted on both cities, and more than 3,500 people had been left homeless.

Hamburg was posted to face its fourth major operation of the month on the 10th, for which a force of 119 aircraft was assembled and the crews briefed to aim for shipyards, the Altona power station (Tiefstack) and the general city area. 5 Group put up thirty-five Hampdens and a 97 Squadron Manchester for the main operation, and six Manchesters for Berlin as part of a force of twenty-three aircraft. 49 Squadron's fifteen crews were to target the Altona electrical power station, situated south-west of the city centre, north of the river, and departed Scampton between 22.02 and 22.55 with S/L Smith the senior pilot on duty. The recently commissioned P/O Hannan crossed the enemy coast north of Friedrichskoog before heading south-east to the target and reported an aircraft bursting into flames after being ensnared in searchlights. This may have been the same incident witnessed by Sgt Lowe and crew when they were some ninety miles out from Mablethorpe. They also were caught in searchlights near Büsum, the location of a lighthouse a few miles north of Friedrichskoog and descended to 500 feet to evade the attentions of a stalking fighter. An exchange of fire resulted in a fuel leak, which prompted Sgt Lowe to abandon the sortie and drop the bombs on a convoy. This was not the only crew to report the presence of night-fighters in bright moonlit conditions that were favourable to attackers and defenders alike. The remaining 49 Squadron crews delivered their bomb loads from between 9,000 and 13,000 feet, some after a shallow glide approach, and reported many bursts and fires, some in the area of the power station aiming point. Sgt Woolston and crew lost their port engine on the way home and he pulled off a forced-landing in a field near Martlesham Heath at 05.30. Returning crews were enthusiastic about the outcome, and local sources confirmed that 128 fires had broken out, forty-seven of them classed as large, with extensive damage resulting in the city centre.

There would be no respite for Germany's second city as plans were already in hand to send ninety-two aircraft back there twenty-four hours later, while eighty-one others, including thirty-one Hampdens and two Manchesters, sought out one of the Deutsche Schiff und Maschinenbau A G shipyards in Bremen. Abbreviated to Deschimag, this had been formed in the mid-twenties as a co-operation of eight shipyards to compete with the Blohm & Voss and Bremer Vulkan yards. The largest was the A G Weser company, which, after six of the others had fallen by the wayside before the outbreak of war, was partnered only by the Seebeckwerft, now as part of the Krupp empire, after that organisation was handed a controlling interest in 1941. 49 Squadron was not involved in this operation, which took place in favourable conditions, and was hailed as a success. Local reports confirmed that many bombs had fallen in the docks area, where a floating dock belonging to the A G Weser Company had been sunk. The main damage, however, was inflicted in the city, where housing was the principal victim. The Hamburg operation had also been effective, causing eighty-eight fires and damage mostly to residential property.

Mannheim and Ludwigshafen were posted again as the primary targets on the 12$^{th}$, for which a force of 105 aircraft was divided 65/40 between the two cities and would involve forty-one Hampdens and four Manchesters. 49 Squadron briefed fifteen crews to attack the BASF plant and dispatched them from Scampton between 21.50 and 22.30 with F/L Howell the senior pilot on duty. Ten minutes later, P/O Scorer and crew took off to deliver a mine to one of the nectarine gardens. They crossed the North Sea over ten-tenths cloud, which diminished as they traversed Belgium and some were able to pick up the Rhine and follow it to the target, where thick haze obscured ground features, and this combined with intense searchlight and flak activity to prevent some crews from identifying the aiming point. Any failing to establish their position in relation to the primary target turned to the north-west to head the 120 miles to the designated alternative target of Cologne. The arrival in the target area of F/L Howell and crew was delayed by inaccurately forecast winds, but once there they spent ninety minutes before gliding down from 12,000 to 9,000 feet to deliver the bombs. The return flight took place against a headwind, and they eventually touched down after nine hours aloft. A few of the other 49 Squadron crews spent a considerable time in the target area and attacks were delivered from between 6,500 and 12,000 feet. Bursts, explosions and fires were observed but no detail through the poor vertical visibility, and local sources estimated that only around ten bomb loads had fallen within the target area, causing minor damage. P/O Scorer and crew, meanwhile, had been accompanied by ten-tenths cloud until twenty miles from the Dutch coast and had delivered their mine into the allotted location from 750 feet.

The weather precluded operations on the following two nights, and it was the 15$^{th}$ when the northern city of Hannover was posted as the target for 101 aircraft, for which 5 Group detailed twenty-seven Hampdens, while a simultaneous raid on Berlin involved eight Manchesters and six 3 Group Stirlings. The briefed aiming points for the former were the main post office and telephone exchange, which, in reality identified this as an area attack. Scampton was not involved in the night's activities, which were compromised to an extent by ten-tenths cloud obscuring the ground and rendering accurate navigation something of a challenge. The cloud had reduced to five-tenths over Hannover, which was identified by the River Leine to the north-west and the Maschsee to the south-east, but, despite the improving conditions, only a handful of crews observed the burst of their bombs, and no local report was forthcoming to confirm the level of damage.

Cologne would be the object of Bomber Command's attentions on the following two nights as Scampton found itself back on the order of battle. A force of ninety-three aircraft was assembled on the 16th, of which twenty-four were Hampdens, a dozen of them provided by 49 Squadron, and they took off between 22.10 and 22.55 with S/L Tench the senior pilot on duty. They adopted a new route in an attempt to avoid searchlights when making landfall on the enemy coast, and this involved Aldeburgh in Suffolk as the starting point for the North Sea crossing and Nieuwpoort on the Belgian coast as the point of entry into Fortress Europe. They were then to head for Ghent before swinging south of Antwerp to approach Cologne from the south-west, which proved to be a successful ploy for the time being at least, and only those straying north over the Scheldt estuary found themselves in searchlights. F/L Howell and crew lost an engine at the enemy coast and turned east to attack Ostend docks as a last resort target. The others encountered ground haze and were guided to the target area by searchlights and flak, and although some picked up the Rhine as a reference, they were largely blinded by searchlight glare, and none was able to identify the planned aiming point even after flares had been deployed. Most remained in the target area for a considerable time searching for a recognisable ground feature, but ultimately bombed the general area or found an alternative on the way home. Returning crews were of the opinion that they had bombed within the city, while local sources suggested that, in fact, the majority of bomb loads had missed the city, and just eleven houses had been damaged.

There would be no further operational activity for 49 Squadron for nine days, during which period twenty-three Hampdens were involved in the second Cologne raid on the 17th and eighteen were sent to the Kiel shipyards on the 18th, neither of which produced more than light, scattered damage. On the 22nd, five 49 Squadron Hampdens were loaded with four 500 pounders each and put on stand-by along with others at Waddington for a possible operation against German surface raiders, which, although not named, were the battleship Bismarck and heavy cruiser Prinz Eugen. They had put to sea on operation "Rheinübung", which for Bismarck, would be its first offensive action, and were being shadowed by Coastal Command aircraft as they slipped out of Bergen, heading for the Denmark Straits between Greenland and Iceland. In the event, the 5 Group aircraft were not required, but the belief that Bismarck was racing for sanctuary at Brest with the Royal Navy snapping at its heels and determined to avenge the shocking sinking of HMS Hood on the 24th, prompted the detailing of forty-eight Hampdens for mining duties in the Jellyfish and Beech gardens off Brest and St-Nazaire respectively. Fourteen 49 Squadron aircraft departed Scampton between 22.00 and 22.35 with F/L Howell the senior pilot on duty and climbed into adverse weather conditions as they set course for Chesil Beach. The Channel crossing was undertaken in conditions of ten-tenths cloud, rainstorms and static and a 600-foot cloud base would prevent most from establishing a pinpoint once in the target area. In the event, only seven succeeded in planting their vegetable into the briefed location and the others brought theirs home. All landed away from Scampton, ten at Boscombe Down and Sgt Pinney and crew at Middle Wallop after surviving a loss of control and a spin.

In fact, the Bismarck's rudder would be crippled by a Fleet Air Arm torpedo during the 26th, rendering the vessel unable to manoeuvre and restricted to a top speed of ten knots. Later that night, 5 Group sent thirty-eight Hampdens to continue mining the approaches to Brest, and although 49 Squadron was not involved, six of its crews were put on stand-by from 03.00 on the 27th in the expectation of being called into action. At first light on the 27th, multiple units of the Royal Navy closed in on the helpless Bismarck, and from 08.47, engaged her with guns and torpedoes until she slipped beneath the waves at 10.39. This left her consort, Prinz Eugen, at large, and the mining at Brest would continue over the succeeding nights in case she put in an appearance. Nine 49 Squadron Hampdens were among thirty-six detailed for mining duties in the Jellyfish and Beech gardens on the evening of the 27th, and they departed Scampton between 22.30 and 22.50 with S/L Smith the senior pilot on duty. P/O Cooke and crew turned back after two hours because of an engine issue, and the crews of P/O Hirons and Sgt Flint failed to establish a pinpoint after spending an hour and fifty minutes and forty-five minutes respectively searching below the cloud base. The others found the conditions to be adequate and planted their vegetables off Brest, and some went on to deliver their wing-mounted 250 pounders on targets of opportunity. AD729 failed to return home and was lost without trace with the crew of S/L Smith.

During the course of the month, the squadron participated in twelve operations and dispatched 119 sorties for the loss of a single Hampden and crew.

## June 1941

June and July were to be significant months for the Command, as its performance began to be monitored in order to provide an assessment of its effectiveness for the War Cabinet. The project was initiated by Churchill's chief scientific advisor, Lord Cherwell, who handed the responsibility to David M Bensusan-Butt, a civil-servant assistant to Cherwell working in the War Cabinet Secretariat. The new month would be dominated by operations against Cologne, Düsseldorf and Bremen, with Kiel and Brest also receiving their share of attention. During the second half of the month Cologne and Düsseldorf would be attacked simultaneously on no fewer than eight nights by forces of varying sizes, and Bremen, including the shipbuilding yards at Vegesack, would host six raids. On, or soon after the 1st, the Hipper Class cruiser Prinz Eugen, which had been acting as consort to Bismarck, arrived at Brest having evaded detection by the Royal Navy following the sinking of the battleship. She would now join Scharnhorst and Gneisenau to form a powerful battle group that would continue to be a distraction for Bomber Command.

The month began for 5 Group with an operation against Düsseldorf on the night of the 2/3rd, for which forty-three Hampdens were detailed in an overall force of 150 aircraft. Bombing took place on estimated positions through cloud and in the face of considerable searchlight and flak activity, and returning crews were able to report fires in the centre of the target area, but no detail. Thereafter, the group, and, in fact, most of the Command, was kept on the ground by an unprecedented period of adverse weather conditions during the best part of the moon period. This was a source of monotony and massive frustration, until, finally, on the 10th, Brest was posted as the target for thirty-nine Hampdens in company with sixty-five Wellingtons and Whitleys, which would not have been over the target at the same time. Until the advent of the bomber-stream system introduced by Harris in 1942, groups, squadrons, and even, sometimes, crews, continued to determine for themselves the details of an operation with regard to timings, routes and attacking height, and, the likelihood is, that each group on this night attacked individually. 49 Squadron made ready thirteen Hampdens for the main event and three for freshman crews to employ in the Gorse garden in Quiberon Bay between Lorient and St-Nazaire. They departed Scampton together between 22.40 and 23.20 with F/L Fisher the senior pilot on duty and climbed through ten-tenths cloud until breaking into clear air at 5,000 feet as they headed for the Channel at Chesil Beach. The English coast was obscured, and it was only as they traversed the Brittany region that the cloud began to disperse to leave clear skies and bright moonlight, in which the target was easily located. The activation of the smoke screen did not prevent the crews from identifying the various docks and jetties in the early stages at least, but haze combined with intense searchlight and flak activity to create challenging conditions as the bombers bore down on the aiming point from a variety of headings. Some spent a considerable time in the target area before bombing from between 10,000 and 12,000 feet and most were too busy with evasive action to observe the results of their efforts. At debriefing it became clear that not one crew could claim to have positively identified any of the target vessels, which had been expertly camouflaged, and any claims by crews from other squadrons remained unconfirmed and doubtful. While this operation was in progress, the gardening element consisting of the crews of Sgts Latty and Tree and P/O Villiers had crossed the French coast at St-Brieuc and made their way to their target area some eighty miles south of the activity at Brest. They pinpointed on Belle Isle and made timed runs in bright moonlight to the release point, where they delivered their mine each from around 700 feet.

Düsseldorf and Duisburg were posted as the primary targets on the 11$^{th}$, for which forces of ninety-eight and eighty aircraft respectively were made ready, the latter provided by 4 and 5 Groups and involving thirty-five Hampdens, although none representing 49 Squadron. No reports came out of either city to shed light on the effectiveness of the raids, but a proportion of the predominantly Wellington force assigned to Düsseldorf strayed over Cologne and caused damage to the main railway station, the Rhine docks and housing.

The following night was devoted largely to attacks on railway yards at four locations in Germany to the east and north of the Ruhr, with 5 Group committing most of its available Hampden force, amounting to ninety-one aircraft, to attack the important hub at Soest, situated a few miles north of the Ruhr. 4 Group was to target the yards at Schwerte, south of Dortmund, while 1 and 3 Groups were handed those at Hamm and Osnabrück, and a small Halifax element was assigned to the "Buna" works, a chemicals and synthetic rubber plant at Marl-Hüls. Thirteen 49 Squadron Hampdens departed Scampton between 22.25 and 22.55 with S/L Tench the senior pilot on duty and flew out over Skegness on course for Den Helder. Having reached it, they turned to the south-east to bypass Zwolle, where Sgt Woolston and crew and, perhaps, others dropped a box of tea donated by the Dutch East Indies Company as a boost to morale for the beleaguered populace. Each teabag was imprinted with a message from Britain that the Netherlands would rise again. Pressing on into Germany, many crews employed the one-day-to-be-famous Möhne reservoir and its dam as a pinpoint for the six-mile run north to the target. S/L Tench and crew strayed too far south and ran into the flak at Gelsenkirchen, sustaining in the process shrapnel damage to the bomb doors. A layer of cloud at 2,000 to 3,000 feet obscured Soest and they bombed a large fire surrounded by flak batteries, probably at nearby Hamm. Sgt Green and crew also came under fire at 15,000 feet, and the wireless operator sustained a foot wound but continued with his duties. The other squadron participants experienced similar difficulties with vertical visibility and flak, many also reporting the presence of night-fighters, and only four crews would claim to have attacked the primary target, while others found alternatives at Hamm, Dortmund and Münster.

A major assault on the enemy warships at Brest was notified across 1, 3 and 5 Group stations on the 13th, and resulted in the assembling of a force of 110 aircraft, of which, thirty-seven were Hampdens, fourteen provided by 49 Squadron. They departed Scampton between 22.45 and 23.25 with F/L Fisher the senior pilot on duty and flew out over cloud that began to disperse as the French coast came into view. Largely clear skies and moonlight over the target allowed most crews to identify the docks and carry out their attacks on the general area from between 7,000 and 10,000 feet, some after spending a considerable time planning their approach, but haze and the need to take evasive action prevented most from observing the fall of their bombs. P/O Hannan and crew made three runs across the target at 14,000 feet and believed that the enemy vessels were in the bomb sight as they released their load. All returned safely to Scampton, where a number of crews reported bombing flak concentrations in the vicinity of the docks after failing to locate the warships.

Twenty-nine Hampdens were detailed on the 14th for a 5 Group operation that night, the first of four raids on consecutive nights against Cologne, a city that would continue to be a popular destination throughout the month. 49 Squadron was not involved in what turned out to be an indeterminate raid delivered through ten-tenths cloud, which caused only minor damage. The rest of the month would be devoted largely to eight simultaneous raids on Cologne and Düsseldorf, the first of which was posted on the 15th, and involved forces of ninety-one and fifty-nine aircraft respectively. 5 Group contributed forty-two Hampdens to the night's operations, but again none representing 49 Squadron, and it soon became clear that the prospects of locating the Derendorf marshalling yards at Düsseldorf through dense cloud at between 3,000 and 8,000 feet were nil, and most headed south down the Rhine for twenty miles to join their 5 Group colleagues at Cologne. They found conditions to be no better, and bombing took place on estimated positions over and in the vicinity of the city, guided to an extent by the flak coming up through the cloud.

Cologne and Düsseldorf were the principal targets again on the following night, for which 5 Group put up forty-seven Hampdens in an overall force of 105, all bound for the former. The fifteen-strong 49 Squadron element departed Scampton between 22.45 and 23.12 with S/L Tench the senior pilot on duty and set course for the Belgian coast, where some met intense searchlights and flak, while others remained unmolested until near the target. P/O Villiers turned back at Dunkerque because of an engine issue, and P/O Cooke and crew were also struggling to climb above 8,000 feet and decided to bomb Ostend as a last resort target. P/O Pratt and crew were delayed by an encounter with a night-fighter at the Belgian coast and also bombed Ostend, leaving the others to bypass Brussels on their way to picking up the Rhine, which provided a strong pinpoint through the thick haze and possibly even fog. Despite the poor vertical visibility, a few crews were able to establish their position and home in on the aiming point on the eastern side of the Rhine, which was probably the Kalk marshalling yards. S/L Tench described a bridge to the north-west of the aiming point, and this was almost certainly the Hohenzollern railway bridge that spanned the Rhine from the eastern bank to the main railway station on the western bank. At debriefing, he described his 2,000-pounder setting off a large fire, while others reported fires and many explosions after bombing from between 9,000 and 12,000 feet in the face of intense searchlight and flak activity.

P/O Kerridge and crew watched the glow in the sky recede until disappearing altogether after fifty miles, but the suggestion of a successful operation was not confirmed by local sources, which reported scattered damage but nothing of significance.

Forty-three Hampdens and thirty-three Whitleys took off to return to Cologne on the 17th in the absence of a contribution from 49 Squadron, while fifty-seven Wellingtons were dispatched to Düsseldorf. Poor visibility, caused by thick ground haze, prevented most crews from locating their respective targets, and neither operation produced meaningful results. An unspecified aiming point in Bremen was posted as the target for a hundred aircraft on the 18th, for which 5 Group contributed thirty-nine Hampdens, including fourteen representing 49 Squadron. They departed Scampton between 22.45 and 23.10 with F/L Fisher the senior pilot on duty and headed out over Skegness on course for Den Helder before crossing into Germany between Papenburg and Meppen. Sgt Lowe and crew wandered off track in poor visibility and made landfall near Bremerhaven well to the north, running into a wall of flak as they searched for a pinpoint to lead them to the primary target. Searchlights and flak proved to be the best guides to the general target area, but low cloud hindered attempts to locate the aiming point and flares were of little assistance. The 49 Squadron crews delivered their attacks from between 9,000 and 15,000 feet, and returning crews reported a ring of dummy fires up to twenty miles outside of Bremen, and the employment also of dummy flares to draw the bombing away from the city. P/O Villiers mentioned being targeted by flak from the aerodrome at the Focke-Wulf factory at Hemelingen to the south-east of the city centre, but whether or not this was the briefed aiming point is unclear, and he went on to bomb a flak concentration in the city from 9,000 feet.

The first casualty of the month resulted from a training flight involving P2068, which suffered engine failure and crash-landed near the airfield shortly after take-off on the 19th, injuring Sgt Alden and the other occupants. The country was now basking in a spell of very hot weather, which began on the 19th, and would continue through the 23rd. 115 aircraft set off for Kiel on the 20th in search of the battleship Tirpitz, and among them were twenty-four Hampdens, ten of which represented 44 Squadron. Ten-tenths cloud completely obscured the ground in the target area, preventing any hope of locating Tirpitz, and attention was turned instead upon the general area of the town. It was not until the 21st that the Manchester was once more declared fit for operations after almost five weeks on the side lines. During the course of the day, a record number of eighteen was made ready to target the docks at Boulogne, and this figure included a contribution from 61 Squadron, which would be blooding the type for the first time. The main operations on this night were against Cologne and Düsseldorf, the former the target for sixty-eight Wellingtons, while twenty-eight Hampdens and an equal number of Whitleys attended to the latter.

Bremen's dockyards were the destination for forty-five Wellingtons and twenty-five Hampdens on the 22nd, thirteen of the latter provided by 49 Squadron, which departed Scampton between 22.27 and 23.00 with F/O Hirons the senior pilot on duty. Some crews made landfall on the Dutch coast between Haarlem and Den Helder, while others opted to follow the Frisian Island chain to enter Germany from the sea between Wilhelmshaven and Bremerhaven. The conditions were generally favourable, but thick haze obscured the ground to create challenges and even the River Weser proved difficult to identify, leaving the crews reliant again upon searchlights and flak to point the way. Ten crews bombed on estimated positions from between 10,000 and 14,000 feet after searching for up to seventy-five minutes, some observing bursts but no detail, while Sgt Lowe and crew bombed a flarepath in the region of Farge on the eastern bank of the Weser to the north-west. F/O Hirons and crew were ensnared by searchlights as they passed over one of the Frisian Islands and spotted an enemy aircraft below. They unloaded the contents of the bomb bay on the island and fired two hundred rounds at the aircraft, which caught fire and broke up as it fell in flames. On the 24th, F/O Hirons was elevated to acting flight lieutenant rank to fill in as deputy flight commander on F/L Howell's temporary posting to 5 Group HQ.

Kiel, Cologne and Düsseldorf were posted as the targets for modest forces on the following night, the last-mentioned for a 5 Group effort against railway yards involving thirty Hampdens and eleven Manchesters. On the 24th, 5 Group assigned a force of twenty-five Hampdens to the docks at Kiel, while the Manchester brigade tried its hand at Düsseldorf, but none of these endeavours resulted in significant damage. While Bremen hosted a raid by sixty-four Wellingtons and Whitleys on the 25th, 5 Group prepared thirty Hampdens to target the Deutsche Werke shipyards at Kiel, for which 49 Squadron made ready thirteen aircraft along with another for the crew of P/O Falconer to take mining in one of the Nectarine gardens. P/O Falconer had been with the squadron for some time and had just been granted captain status after serving his apprenticeship as second pilot to F/L Fisher. The bombing element took off between 21.25 and 22.03 with no pilots above pilot officer rank on duty and exited the English coast near Skegness on course for Rømø island on the western coast of southern Jutland. They were well on their way when P/O Falconer and crew departed Scampton at 23.20 and headed towards Terschelling, where they ran into a weather front containing electrical storms and heavy rain. Unable to find a way round it and with little prospect of completing the sortie, they decided to bring their mine home but overshot the runway, crashed through a hedge and cartwheeled into a field at 04.30. X3060 was written off, but no injuries were reported among its occupants. The bombers, meanwhile, flew eastwards across southern Jutland to reach the Baltic and approach the target from the north in favourable conditions, which enabled most to identify ground features through the haze. After bombing, P/O Villiers and crew were forced down to 2,000 feet by searchlights and flak and only avoided a collision with an enemy aircraft by a whisker. Sgt Lowe and crew lost their oxygen and artificial horizon on the way out but pressed on to the target to bomb on estimated position. Flares assisted some crews to identify Kiel Harbour and the docks area, while dummy fires and flak guided others to the mark and bombing took place from between 9,000 and 15,000 feet. Sgt Green and crew watched an aircraft fall in flames before exploding in mid-air, and this may have been 49 Squadron's AD788, which was believed to have been shot down over the target. It was established later through correspondence from PoW camp, that Sgt Hind and his crew had fought valiantly to extinguish the fires, but when the tail boom broke away, the pilot was left with no option but to save himself. He survived with extensive burns to fall into enemy hands and was devastated by the loss of his crew. The Green crew also described an immense fire among dock buildings that remained visible for thirty minutes into the return flight and this may have been the one reported by Sgt Tree and crew that resulted from the detonation of their 2,000 pounder. Local sources reported a light raid and little damage.

Yet again, Kiel, Cologne and Düsseldorf were selected as the targets on the 26th, and, on this occasion, it was for the important naval stronghold on the eastern side of the Schleswig-Holstein peninsula that eighteen Manchester crews were briefed, while thirty Hampden crews learned of their part in the operation against marshalling yards at Düsseldorf. The Manchester crews were told that they would have fifteen Stirlings and eight Halifaxes for company, although, not necessarily over the target at the same time, and the Hampden crews would share their target with 1 Group Wellingtons. It was a night on which cloud, snow, electrical storms and icing conditions persuaded many crews to turn back from Düsseldorf or seek out alternative targets and the operation was another disappointing failure. Seventy-three Wellingtons and thirty-five Whitleys were made ready for operations on the night of the 27/28th, when Bremen was the target, while a force of Hampdens also visited the city to attack the shipbuilding yards at Vegesack further downstream of the Weser. They encountered very adverse weather, which included ten-tenths cloud with tops at 17,000 feet, storms and icing conditions, and if that were not enough, they would also face a concerted night-fighter response of unprecedented intensity. A new record for a single night of fourteen aircraft failed to return, and eleven of them were Whitleys, 31 % of those dispatched.

The night of the 28/29th was devoted to mining operations by thirty-four Hampdens in the Eglantine and Rosemary gardens, respectively in the Elbe estuary and the Heligoland Bight, for which 49 Squadron made ready thirteen of its own and dispatched them between 22.40 and 23.25 with S/L Tench the senior pilot on duty. They crossed the Lincolnshire coast at Mablethorpe and set course for their target area off the island of Heligoland, located some thirty-five miles north-west of Cuxhaven. They found it under ten-tenths cloud with a base sometimes as low as 500 feet and eleven crews were able to establish a pinpoint on the island from which to make a timed run and plant their vegetables as briefed from below 1,000 feet. On e.t.a., at Heligoland, F/L Hirons and crew found only sea and decided to continue on to the mainland in search of a recognisable pinpoint, which eluded them and persuaded them to abandon their sortie. On return, Sgt Latty and crew were dived upon by a BF109 three miles south of Mablethorpe, but their assailant was unable to bring his guns to bear and climbed away.

Bremen was chosen to be in the firing line again on the 29th, when thirty Hampdens were detailed to join seventy-six other aircraft, while six of the group's Manchesters took part in a small raid on Hamburg. Following a spate of engine failures, particularly some afflicting 61 Squadron aircraft, another Manchester grounding order was issued on the 30th. A conference was held at 5 Group HQ on this day, when it was decided that each Manchester squadron would select four aircraft for intensive flight testing. That night, 5 Group detailed fourteen Hampdens to attack a railway station in Düsseldorf, for which the 49 Squadron element of four departed Scampton between 23.10 and 23.18. They ran into intense searchlight and flak activity as they tried to skirt Cologne and before P/O Henderson and crew reached the target, they decided that the cloud would prevent them from locating the aiming point. They turned back towards Cologne and on dropping their bombs attracted searchlights and flak that drove them down to 8,000 feet as they made their escape. Sgt Huggett and crew were ensnared by searchlights soon after crossing the enemy coast and targeted by flak as they tried to follow the Rhine. Dazzled by the beams, they dropped their bombs on a concentration and photographed the area. Sgt Batchelor and crew reached the approximate position of the primary target and attacked it from 11,000 feet, before running into another nest as they crossed the coast homebound at Dunkerque. Sgt Woolston and crew failed to return in X3134, and nothing was heard from them until eight days later, when news came through that they had ditched and had spent eight days in their dinghy before being rescued, exhausted but safe, by an Air-Sea-Rescue launch.

During the course of the month, the squadron took part in eleven operations and dispatched 116 sorties for the loss of four Hampdens and one crew. 5 Group, meanwhile, added two new Dominion squadrons to its strength, 408 (Goose) Squadron RCAF at Lindholme on the 15th and 455 Squadron RAAF at Swinderby on the 30th.

# July 1941

On the 1st of July, a C Flight was added, which gave 49 Squadron a compliment of twenty-four aircraft. Having been prominent during the final few days of June, it fell to Bremen to open the Command's July account on the night of the 2/3rd, while smaller forces targeted Cologne and Duisburg. The last-mentioned was an all-Hampden affair involving thirty-nine aircraft and focused on the marshalling yards with Cologne and Düsseldorf as alternative targets. They found seven-tenths cloud hanging over the Ruhr at 6,000 feet, with thick industrial haze lurking beneath, and this left the crews with no prospect of identifying the briefed aiming point. Searches were carried out, some aided by flares, but it was a futile exercise, and only a small number of crews would claim to have bombed the estimated location of Duisburg.

Scampton and Hemswell combined on the following night to send twenty-three and seventeen Hampdens respectively to join Wellingtons in attacking shipyards at Bremen, while ninety Wellingtons and Whitleys attempted to hit the Krupp armament s works and railway installations at Essen. The fourteen-strong 49 Squadron element took off between 22.30 and 22.58 with S/L Tench and F/Ls Fisher and Hirons the senior pilots on duty and adopted a variety of courses. Some intended to pinpoint on Heligoland and others on the uninhabited Scharhörn Island located nine miles north of Cuxhaven or on the mainland coast itself, but all encountered the same conditions of ten-tenths cloud over the sea and the additional challenge of haze over land. P/O Henderson and crew reported the cloud to be at between 8,000 and 15,000 feet, which completely obscured all ground references and left the crews reliant on evidence of flak to guide them to the general area of the primary target and the briefed alternatives at Bremerhaven and Wilhelmshaven. They stooged around for up to sixty-five minutes, most eventually abandoning their sorties and bringing their bombs home in accordance with instructions. The exceptions were Sgt Tree and crew, who bombed a searchlight and flak concentration believed to be in Bremen, while F/L Fisher and crew caught a brief glimpse of the River Weser and followed it into the town area to deliver their bombs. P/O Pratt and crew flew to the enemy coast at 14,000 feet and pinpointed on Cuxhaven on the way to bombing a town believed to be Bremen, and Sgt Latty and crew made a positive identification of Bremen after also picking up the river. Curiously, all sixteen of the Hemswell crews to make it back reported carrying out an attack, mostly on Bremen city and the town area of nearby Bremerhaven, while fifteen crews from Scampton returned with their bombs, having been unable to see the ground and find something to aim at. It transpired that the Hemswell brigade had been searching at around 5,000 feet, while the Scampton crews had remained at 11,000 feet or above. Apparently, one did descend to a thousand feet and identified Bremerhaven, only to lose it again.

The Scampton squadrons were not involved on the 4th when twenty-five Hampdens were detailed to attack U-Boots at Lorient, where construction of the major new concrete structure was well under way on the Keroman peninsula. The operation took place in perfect weather conditions and, while no U-Boots were evident, the raid hit the general port area and was hailed as most successful. Marshalling yards in the cities of Münster and Osnabrück were the targets for two forces on the 5th, the former facing the larger one of sixty-five Wellingtons and twenty-nine Whitleys, while the latter would host an initial thirty-nine Hampdens, including eleven from each of the Scampton squadrons. Just thirty miles apart and located between the Ruhr and Bremen, Münster was more militarily significant as home to the HQ of the 6th Military District of the Wehrmacht and its extensive barracks accommodated infantry and armoured (Panzer) Divisions. Preceding the Scampton bombing element into the air, between 22.45 and 22.55, were the freshman crews of Sgts Gillies, Letford and Walker and two from 83 Squadron bound for the Beech garden off St-Nazaire. They would benefit from perfect moonlit conditions and easily establish their pinpoints on Pointe-Saint-Gildas before planting their vegetables according to brief from around 500 feet.

The bombing brigade departed Scampton between 23.20 and 23.41 with S/L Tench the senior pilot on duty and set course for the Dutch coast in ideal conditions, some employing the beacon on Texel as a guide to navigation before turning toward the south-east to run in on the target. Flares assisted crews to pick out the numerous waterways and railway tracks leading to the city, but searchlight glare played a part in preventing some from identifying the briefed aiming point and most bombed the built-up area generally. AD856 did not return with the others but news of the fate of Sgt Flint and his crew was soon communicated to Scampton. On crossing the Dutch coast outbound they had been attacked by enemy fighters and sustained damage, but not sufficient to prevent them from continuing on to the target to deliver their bomb load. They were homebound over the North Sea when spotted by intruder Me110s, one of them flown by Ofw Wilhelm Beier of I./NJG2, whose cannon shells knocked out the port engine and mortally wounded the wireless operator. They broke off the attack with the Hampden still airborne but struggling to maintain height, and it eventually ditched in shallow water some fifty yards off Cromer. All crew members were injured to some extent with only Sgt Flint able to render assistance, and through a superhuman effort he was able to manhandle the inert navigator to safety, assisted by a soldier who waded out. The second pilot/navigator, Sgt Benningfield, succumbed to his wounds within hours, while gunner, Sgt Atkinson, recovered from his wounds and returned to duty and the body of the wireless operator, Sgt Fitch, was recovered from the beach. For his airmanship, Sgt Flint was awarded a DFM, and for his courageous attempt to save the life of his crew member, the George Medal.

On the 6th, a 5 Group force of eighty-eight Hampdens was assembled for a raid on the German warships at Brest in company with twenty-one Wellingtons. Among the Hampdens were five 44 Squadron aircraft loaned to 207 Squadron crews to enable them to "keep their hand in" while their Manchesters were grounded. As the situation dragged on, they would continue to borrow from 44 Squadron, until receiving six Hampdens of their own as a stopgap measure. 49 Squadron supported the operation with ten aircraft, which departed Scampton between 22.20 and 22.56 with S/L Tench the senior pilot on duty and, according to the ORB Form 540, lost the services of one crew to engine trouble within an hour. However, the Form 541 records that all reached the target to carry out an attack and all landing times are consistent with completed sorties. They began the Channel crossing at Chesil Beach and crossed the French coast under clear skies and a full moon, which enabled them to map-read their way to the target area, where they encountered the usual intense searchlights and flak defence. Initially at least, the smoke generators were not active, allowing those arriving in the vanguard a clear run, but, for the 49 Squadron participants, the smoke screen proved to be highly effective and completely obscured Scharnhorst and Gneisenau. The Hampden force carried in its bomb bays a mix of 2,000, 500 and 250 pounders, and while the 49 Squadron ORB omitted details of its bomb loads, some crews were sitting on two 2,000 pounders. It must have been a chaotic scene above Brest as aircraft approached the aiming point from a variety of headings from east to west, north-east to south-west and south-west to north-east at altitudes of between 7,500 and 12,000 feet, dodging not only the searchlights and flak but also the bombs falling from as high as 17,000 feet. Searchlight glare and the need to take evasive action prevented any from observing more than bomb bursts and it was just another inconclusive raid during which, 5 Group delivered over three hundred high explosive, armour-piercing and semi-armour piercing bombs into the target area, sixty-seven of them 2,000 pounders, and returning crews reported fires in the town centre, in the northern outskirts and near the seaplane base. A number also reported an aircraft being hit at around 3,000 feet and crashing into the sea in flames, and this was probably one of two missing Hampdens, one from 144 Squadron and the other, AD739 of 49 Squadron containing the crew of P/O Henderson, whose fate has never been positively established and who are commemorated on the Runnymede Memorial. Despite the best efforts, the warships remained a threat as a "fleet in being", and the strategists at Bomber Command HQ continued to seek a solution.

Earlier in the day, F/L Drakes had been posted back to the squadron from 16 O.T.U. for a second tour and was immediately granted the acting rank of squadron leader to enable him to fill the vacancy for a C Flight commander. He would be allowed time to settle in as 49 Squadron was not required on the 7th, when four main targets were posted on stations across the Command, Cologne, Osnabrück and Münster for Wellingtons and or Whitleys, while forty Hampdens were to target marshalling yards in the town of Mönchengladbach on the south-western rim of the Ruhr. The outward flight took place under clear skies with a full moon to aid map-reading in coastal areas, until thick ground haze blotted out detail over land, and, ultimately, most crews turned their attention upon alternative targets at Düsseldorf, Neuss and Duisburg.

S/L Stubbs DFC was posted in from 97 Squadron on the 8th as commanding officer elect. He was a highly experienced officer, who had joined 207 Squadron from 144 Squadron as a flight commander and had been involved in the transfer of 207 Squadron's B Flight to form the nucleus of 97 Squadron a few weeks later. 5 Group was handed marshalling yards again that night, when forty-five Hampdens were detailed at Scampton, Waddington and Lindholme to target the northern half of those at Hamm, while twenty-eight Whitleys attended to the southern half. 49 Squadron made ready thirteen aircraft, which took off between 23.00 and 23.15 with S/L Bennett and F/L Hirons the senior pilots on duty and set course from Skegness to Enkhuizen on the eastern shore of the Den Helder peninsula. P/O Villiers and crew experienced severe engine vibration shortly after taking off, which was cured by throttling back, but after climbing through a heavy static storm, the pilot was unable to throttle up again to clear 10,000 feet and was forced to turn back. P/O Pratt and crew also abandoned their sortie after their compass proved to be unreliable and Sgt Batchelor and crew were defeated by the failure of their radio equipment. The others encountered cloud over the North Sea, which dispersed as they skirted the northern rim of the Ruhr, but thick ground haze rendered identification of ground features something of a challenge despite clear skies and bright moonlight. Sgt Huggett and crew were fifteen minutes from the target when intercepted by a Me110, which attacked six times in an engagement lasting twenty minutes. Sgt Huggett evaded the enemy's fire through a series of climbing turns, while the gunners fired 150 rounds each and believed that they may have shot their assailant down. The evasive action had thrown them off course and they unloaded the contents of their bomb bay on an unidentified town in the north-western Ruhr. Waterways to the north and the River Lippe provided strong references for navigation and the latter was followed by some crews into the heart of the town, where a few identified the yards in the face of intense searchlight glare and others attacked the built-up area generally from 8,000 to 14,000 feet.

A new Air Ministry directive was issued on the 9th, which alluded to the German transportation system and the morale of its civilian population as the enemy's weakest points. The C-in-C, Sir Richard Peirse, was consequently ordered to concentrate his main effort in these areas, which meant that from now on during the moon periods, he was to target the main railway centres ringing the Ruhr, to isolate it from the other regions of Germany, thus preventing the movement in of raw materials and the export of finished goods. On dark nights, the Rhine cities of Cologne, Duisburg and Düsseldorf would be easier to locate for area attacks, and, when unfavourable weather conditions prevailed, operations were to be mounted against more distant urban centres in northern, eastern and southern Germany. 49 Squadron remained at home on that night, buoyed by the news that Sgt Woolston and crew had been rescued from the North Sea after eight-and-a-half uncomfortable days adrift having survived on one-and-a-half pints of water, thirty-six Horlicks tablets and a little chocolate. A number of aircraft had passed close by, but they had only a mirror with which to signal and it was a Waddington Hampden crew who finally spotted them and reported their position to rescuers. Meanwhile, thirty-nine Hampdens joined forces with forty-three Whitleys and Wellingtons to target the Nazi Party HQ at Aachen, the first time that Germany's most westerly city had faced a major attack. This choice of aiming point meant, in reality, that it was intended as an area raid, which took place in favourable weather conditions and resulted in much destruction to housing, particularly in central districts.

On the 10th, nine airmen were attached to 49 Squadron from 207 Squadron to keep them busy until the Manchester grounding order was rescinded. That night, 5 Group detailed thirty-two Hampdens to join ninety-eight Wellingtons in attacking a number of aiming points in Cologne. One of the 5 Group targets was the Klöckner-Humboldt mechanical engineering works in the Deutz district, situated on the East Bank of the Rhine in the city centre, for which the fourteen 49 Squadron participants departed Scampton between 22.55 and 23.20 with F/Ls Fisher and Hirons the senior pilots on duty. They crossed the enemy coast between Ostend and Dunkerque and flew direct to the target, which they found largely hidden beneath eight-tenths cloud and thick haze extending up to 12,000 feet. This forced them to search for a pinpoint, some picking up the Rhine, while others were guided to the general area by searchlights and flak and spent up to forty minutes trying to establish their precise position. P/O Hannan and crew attacked from 12,000 feet on a south-to north heading, while Sgt Welch and crew ran across the city in the opposite direction at 10,000 feet. Sgt Huggett and crew flew north along the Rhine from Bonn and dropped their bombs to the east, roughly in the vicinity of the briefed aiming point. Sgt Tree and crew dropped their wing bombs on the estimated position of Cologne and the remaining bombs on a flak position, which responded by firing back. P/O Cooke and crew were another to follow the course of the Rhine northwards and delivered their attack without positively identifying what lay beneath, and it was a similar story that Sgt Bunn and crew told on their return. F/L Fisher and crew reported searching in vain for thirty minutes before being chased by a BF109 and heading for Calais, where they bombed the docks from 10,000 feet and then sustained flak damage after being held by an estimated fifty searchlights at 6,000 feet. Other crews reported bombing Koblenz and the Belgian town of Dinant, and an analysis revealed that barely half of the force had bombed in the general target area, a fact confirmed by local sources, who reported only a handful of bombs falling.

On the 11th, 5 Group called upon thirty-six Hampdens from Coningsby, Hemswell and Waddington to carry out an attack against the main railway station in the naval and shipbuilding port of Wilhelmshaven. The operation took place in generally favourable conditions and many bomb bursts were observed in the vicinity of the aiming point. Scampton was called into action on the 12th to provide twenty-two Hampdens to join forces with a dozen from Lindholme to target the main railway station in Bremen with Wilhelmshaven as the designated secondary target. The 49 Squadron ORB incorrectly recorded the latter as the primary target, for which the twelve-strong element took off between 22.27 and 22.50 with S/L Drakes the senior pilot on duty for the first time. They adopted the familiar outward route from Skegness to the Den Helder peninsula, where they ran into a towering bank of cumulonimbus cloud containing electrical storms, the circumnavigation of which would delay the arrival of many at the target. Sgt Huggett and crew were led astray by a compass, which had been affected by the static and abandoned their sortie after ending up too far north to reach the target and get home before daylight arrived. Those arriving early found Bremen under clear skies with visibility at twenty miles, which enabled them to pick up the River Weser and follow it right into the heart of the city to release their bombs. However, those delayed by the storms arrived to find conditions deteriorating and were confronted with thick ground haze that rendered target identification difficult. As a result, only the crews of S/L Drakes, P/O Villiers and Sgts Bunn, Gillies, Tree and Welch of 49 Squadron located Bremen, although not the briefed aiming point. Sgt Walker and crew were blown off track once over enemy territory, and an hour's search brought them to Wilhelmshaven, which they bombed through a gap in the cloud from 18,000 feet. Others also found Wilhelmshaven or Cuxhaven, among them P/O Hannan and crew, who bombed a railway line near the former before crossing paths with a Me110 while crossing Wangerooge on the way home. Steep diving turns prevented the night-fighter from scoring hits during five attacks, and the two rear gunners fired 150 rounds each, which they believed may have shot it down. Some crews were short of fuel as they arrived back over England, partly as a result of difficulty in navigating, and Sgt Batchelor wrote off AD910 in a forced-landing near Pocklington at 07.45 after nine hours aloft.

Scampton was not on the order of battle for the main event on the 14th, when briefings were held at Coningsby, Hemswell and Waddington to inform forty-four Hampden crews of their part in that night's operation to the northern city of Hannover as part of an overall force of eighty-five aircraft. The main railway station and post office building were designated as the aiming points, which disguised the actual intention to destroy the city centre. To what extent this was achieved is uncertain, as returning crews reported many fires, but few reports came out of Hannover to specify damage. While this operation was in progress, ten Scampton crews were sent mining in the Eglantine and Nectarine gardens, the four 49 Squadron freshman crews assigned to the former in the Elbe estuary and departing Scampton between 23.10 and 23.15. They benefitted from excellent conditions, and each established a pinpoint on Scharhörn and Trischen Islands or on the mainland to the north at Sankt Peter-Ording, before carrying out timed runs to deliver their stores completely unopposed into the briefed location.

Hamburg was posted as the target for 107 aircraft on the 16th, of which thirty-two Hampdens from Scampton and Lindholme represented 5 Group, eleven of them provided by 49 Squadron. The briefed aiming point was again the main railway station, for which the 49 Squadron element took off between 22.25 and 22.55 with no senior pilots on duty and headed for the Lincolnshire coast at Mablethorpe. Most set a course for the western coast of the Schleswig-Holstein peninsula to approach the target from the north, some climbing as high as 16,000 feet during the North Sea crossing and finding the enemy coastal region obscured by ten-tenths cloud. Sgt Batchelor and crew had turned back by this time after experiencing an engine issue. Sgt Broomfield and crew made landfall further south near Cuxhaven and followed the River Elbe into the heart of the city, which all found to be concealed beneath the layer of cloud that topped out at 13,000 feet. Sgt McMahon and crew searched for forty-five minutes before bringing their bombs home, while some glimpsed the Elbe and the distinctive Binnen and Aussen-Alster lakes but were unable to establish a firm pinpoint and had to direct their bombs at the estimated position of the city centre. Sgt Bunn and crew chanced upon a gap in the cloud and a flare offered them a full view of the town, which they attacked on a north-westerly heading and observed their bombs to burst among warehouses to the west of the city centre. Almost half of the force, including a number of 49 Squadron crews, attacked alternative targets in the form of flak concentrations and aerodromes and Wilhelmshaven also attracted attention. Local sources in Hamburg reported four fires and no significant damage.

On the 17th, W/C Jefferson concluded his command of the squadron on posting to 25 O.T.U., at Finningley having distinguished himself by not undertaking a single sortie during his tenure. S/L Stubbs was elevated to the paid rank of acting wing commander as his successor and would make his presence felt on the order of battle. However, he would have to wait a few days as Scampton was not required to contribute to the twenty-five Hampdens detailed to join fifty Wellingtons that night in a late take-off for the Gereon marshalling yards in Cologne. They encountered cloud and generally unfavourable conditions along with a hostile searchlight and flak defence and had little clue as to the outcome, which local sources would suggest had amounted to ten bomb loads falling within the city, causing little damage and no casualties. 5 Group issued orders to North Luffenham and Waddington on the 19th, to prepare for mining operations that night in the Eglantine and Yams gardens, respectively in the Elbe and Weser estuaries, which provided passage for shipping and U-Boots from the Hamburg and Bremen shipyards.

A force of 113 aircraft was assembled on the 20th for a return to Cologne for another swipe at marshalling yards, for which 5 Group contributed thirty-nine Hampdens, sixteen of them belonging to 49 Squadron. They departed Scampton between 22.58 and 23.28 with W/C Stubbs and S/L Drakes the senior pilots on duty and set course for the Belgian coast in the area of Blankenberg to swing past Brussels to the south and enter Germany near Aachen. Sgt Samuels and crew lost the use of their blind-flying instruments when south of Brussels and were unable to continue, leaving the others to approach the target in less than favourable weather conditions. Despite the challenges, all reached the target area to find seven to nine-tenths cloud with tops at 7,000 feet accompanied by haze, through which glimpses of the Rhine provided an approximate reference, but there was no possibility of identifying the marshalling yards. The 49 Squadron participants spent up to an hour searching for a pinpoint, before some decided to seek out alternatives and P/O Villiers and crew even descended to 5,000 feet in an attempt to locate Aachen but failed and brought their bombs home. Those able to pick up the Rhine followed its course and bombed the approximate area of Cologne, while the others mostly attacked Aachen. The operation was another failure that caused little damage, and the only positive was that no aircraft were lost.

Frankfurt and Mannheim were named as the targets for a mini-campaign on three consecutive nights from the 21/22nd, and it would be the former's first taste of a major Bomber Command assault. Thirty-seven Wellingtons and thirty-four Hampdens were made ready, the latter at Coningsby, North Luffenham and Waddington, while thirty-six Wellingtons and eight Halifaxes were prepared to attack Mannheim city centre some forty-five miles to the south. At 5 Group briefings, crews were instructed to aim for the post-office and main telephone exchange building, but the glare from an accurate searchlight and flak defence largely concealed the results. A number of bursts were observed along with fires, but the local reports spoke of minor damage, and the city of Darmstadt, situated some ten miles to the south, sustained a greater level of destruction. On the following night, while Scampton remained off the order of battle, thirty-four Hampdens were joined by twenty-nine Whitleys and Wellingtons in a return to Frankfurt, while a small force of Wellingtons attended to Mannheim. In the face of eight-tenths cloud, and, with no prospect of identifying the post office and telephone exchange, bombing was carried out on estimated positions and another inconclusive raid ensued.

The final raid of the series on Frankfurt on the 23rd involved thirty-one Hampdens from Scampton and Swinderby, 50 Squadron's new home, for the all-5 Group show, while fifty Wellingtons tried their hand at Mannheim. 49 Squadron detailed eighteen aircraft but listed only seventeen departing Scampton between 22.05 and 22.40 with S/Ls Drakes and Tench the senior pilots on duty. One unidentified Scampton aircraft, possibly the eighteenth from 49 Squadron, returned almost immediately after the rear gunner cut his finger on a tin containing the "decker" incendiary devices, which became scattered around the aircraft. The rest of the force crossed the enemy coast south of Dunkerque before entering Belgian airspace and pinpointing on Mons and Charleroi on their way to the German border west of Koblenz. They encountered a small amount of cloud, but it was the thick haze that blotted out most ground detail, leaving the Rivers Rhine and Maine the principal references for navigation. Flares provided some illumination, and most crews located the built-up area to bomb from between 8,000 and 14,000 feet and observe bomb bursts among buildings. Some descending to the lower altitude found themselves staring at barrage balloons tethered over the city. No local report emerged to shed light on the outcome, which suggests that the operation managed only a modest impact.

While the above was in progress, thirty Whitleys were sent to attack the dry dock at La Pallice, the deep-water port located west of La Rochelle on the Biscay coast between St-Nazaire to the north and Bordeaux to the south. It was home to the 3rd U-Boot Flotilla that was feeding wolfpacks into the Atlantic to savage Allied convoys bringing vital supplies to Britain. However, the objective for this operation was the cruiser Scharnhorst, which had slipped away from Brest unnoticed and was feared to be about to break out into the Atlantic for a campaign of surface raiding. Her disappearance from Brest had also caused a change of plans for a major raid on Brest due to take place on the following day.

Preparations and formation flying training had been ongoing for a number of weeks to carry out an audacious attack by daylight on the German warships at Brest under the codename Operation Sunrise. Scheduled for the 24th, as mentioned above, it had been discovered at the last minute that

Scharnhorst had slipped away to La Pallice, some two hundred miles further south, and this required an adjustment to the original complex plan of attack. The intention had been to send three 90 Squadron Fortress Is in to bomb from 30,000 feet to draw up enemy fighters, while 5 Group Hampdens performed a similar function at a less rarefied altitude under the umbrella of a Spitfire escort. While this distraction was in progress, it was hoped that Halifaxes and Wellington from 1, 3 and 4 Groups could sneak in unopposed to target the ships. Now that Scharnhorst had moved, it was decided to send the Halifax element to deal with her, while the rest of the original plan went ahead at Brest. 5 Group detailed six Hampdens each from Waddington, Coningsby and North Luffenham, and they had congregated at Coningsby on the previous day for the briefing, before taking off at 10.45 to proceed to Predannack in three boxes with Coningsby leading. They collected the Spitfire escort provided by 10 Group over Cornwall and were shepherded all the way to the target, which they reached at 14.15, seven minutes after the Fortresses had bombed. The enemy defence were fiercer than anticipated, and the Hampdens found themselves in a hornet's nest of single and twin-engine fighters. Ten of the seventy-nine Wellingtons were shot down by flak and fighters, along with two Hampdens, in return for six unconfirmed hits on the Gneisenau. The Halifaxes had also suffered the loss of five aircraft at La Pallice, and the ten survivors had all sustained damage to some extent, while scoring five confirmed hits on Scharnhorst to necessitate her return to Brest, where superior repair facilities existed.

The Deutsche Werke and Krupp Germania shipyards were the aiming points in Kiel for that night's main event, for which a force of thirty-four Wellingtons and thirty Hampdens was made ready, the latter on the stations at Coningsby, North Luffenham and Waddington. The weather conditions were favourable, and the visibility clear enough for ground features to be identified during the run in as they ran the gauntlet of an intense searchlight and flak barrage. Despite the enthusiastic claims of some crews, the bombing was scattered and inaccurate, and local authorities reported only a few bombs falling in the shipyards or the town.

Orders were received at Scampton and Swinderby on the 25th to provide thirty Hampdens to join forces with twenty-five Whitleys for an attack on Hannover. The crews were briefed to aim for the main railway station and post office, which meant that it was to be an area raid to target the city centre. Fourteen 49 Squadron Hampdens took off between 22.15 and 22.31 with F/L Fisher the senior pilot on duty and headed for the Frisian Island chain, where Ameland and Borkum provided a navigation pinpoint. Weather conditions over northern Germany were generally good but haze compromised the vertical visibility and a liberal employment of flares allowed crews to identify Steinhude Lake and then Hannover itself, although not with sufficient detail to pick out the briefed aiming points. Bombing took place from between 8,000 and 12,000 feet and a number of fires were observed, but, in truth, it was yet another inconclusive and probably ineffective raid, which failed to prompt a comment from local sources. X3151 ran out of fuel after reaching the Scampton circuit and P/O Cooke pulled off a forced landing in a field two miles south of the airfield at 05.14 from which the occupants emerged unscathed.

The 27th and 28th were devoted to mining operations off the Biscay ports and in the Baltic respectively. Scampton remained inactive on the former occasion and put up eighteen 49 Squadron Hampdens and a dozen from 83 Squadron on the latter, allotted to the Radish and Forget-me-not gardens in the Fehmarn Belt and Kiel Harbour, while twelve from 50 Squadron were assigned to the Quince garden in Kiel Bay. The 49 Squadron element took off between 22.13 and 22.40 with

S/L Tench the senior pilot on duty among the Forget-me-not element and S/L Bennett leading those bound for Radish, and all headed into adverse weather conditions of rain-bearing cloud and static, which would hamper the attempts of a few to identify pinpoints from which to time the runs. S/L Tench and crew spent seventy-five minutes searching in vain and retained their mine while dropping their wing bombs on a flak ship fifteen miles west of Sylt. Sgt Batchelor and crew reached Nakskov on Denmark's Lolland Island, at which point the port engine began to falter, forcing them to jettison all ordnance before beginning a tense homeward journey on one engine. P/O Hannan and crew failed to locate the Radish garden and set course westwards in search of Quince, but were again thwarted by the conditions and re-crossed the Schleswig-Holstein peninsula hoping to plant their well-travelled vegetable in the Rosemary garden in the Heligoland Bight. Despite their efforts the crew was destined to be disappointed and eventually dumped the mine and wing bombs "safe" to save fuel. In contrast, a dozen crews found favourable conditions once in their target areas and were able to fulfil their briefs, while seven found suitable targets for their 250 pounders. Overall, only twenty-five vegetables were planted in the allotted locations, while another was dropped in an alternative garden. Widespread mist and fog prevented all but four of the 49 Squadron participants from returning to Scampton, leaving the others scattered at airfields from Yorkshire to Cambridgeshire.

Scampton had now completed its operational activity for the month, and it was left to North-Luffenham and Waddington to provide forty-two Hampdens between them for a raid on marshalling yards in Cologne by an overall force of 116 aircraft. They encountered appalling weather conditions, and twenty-two crews bombed the estimated location of the city, while six others targeted Aachen or its approximate position. During the course of the month, the squadron took part in thirteen operations and dispatched 158 sorties for the loss of three Hampdens, one complete crew and two other crew members.

## August 1941

The policy of dispatching small numbers of aircraft to various targets simultaneously had rarely produced effective results, but it would be persisted with throughout the remainder of the year, and, in fact, until a new Commander-in-Chief arrived in 1942 to provide a different direction. 5 Group was informed that it would open its August account on the 2$^{nd}$ and sent instructions to Scampton and Coningsby to make ready twenty-nine and twenty-one Hampdens respectively to attack the town of Kiel and its shipyards, while larger forces attended to Hamburg and Berlin. During the course of the day, a new influx of crews arrived at Scampton from 16 O.T.U., at Upper Heyford to join 49 Squadron, and among the pilots was a Sgt Newmarch, who, four years, hence, would find himself in the rank of wing commander and commanding officer of 44 (Rhodesia) Squadron. 49 Squadron contributed sixteen Hampdens to Kiel and three for the crews of Sgts Bunn and Tree for mining sorties in the Quince and Wallflower gardens in Kiel harbour and Kiel Bay and F/L Hirons for Melon, located on the northern side of the headland off Eckernförde. They departed Scampton together over an extended period between 21.55 and 23.07 with S/L Tench the senior pilot on duty and climbed to between 10,000 and 14,000 feet over the North Sea, which was concealed by a blanket of low cloud that prevented most from pinpointing their positions at Rømø Island on the Danish coast. By the time they reached the Baltic coast north of Flensburg the skies had largely cleared to leave moonlight, and some crews were able to map-read their way south to the target area, where haze compromised the vertical visibility and flares were employed to improve illumination. The 49 Squadron crews mostly located the town, some after pinpointing on the Selenter Lake to the east, a few even identifying the dockyard area, and bombing was carried out from between 9,000 and 12,000 feet in the face of searchlights and accurate flak, the tracer element observed to reach 16,000 feet. Uncertain that they had located the primary target, F/L Fisher and crew delivered only their 250 pounders, before heading west towards Emden, where they let their 1,900 pounder go over a built-up area. At debriefing, bursts and fires were reported, but the need to take evasive action prevented most from making a detailed assessment. An incomplete report from Kiel sources suggested that the operation had failed, and mentioned a single house damaged, but did not refer to possible hits in the docks and shipyards.

Meanwhile, the gardeners had experienced mixed fortunes, Sgt Bunn and crew defeated by low cloud over the Quince garden, while Sgt Tree and crew found a wedge of eight-tenths cloud at between 800 and 1,500 feet over the Wallflower garden but came below the base to plant their vegetable in the briefed location. F/L Hirons and crew set course from Mablethorpe and made landfall over Rømø before traversing southern Jutland to reach the Baltic coast and map-read to the Melon garden to deliver their mine from 800 feet during what was an uneventful sortie.

The squadron now had twenty-four Hampdens IE and three IR, and nineteen were detailed on the 5th to support two of three operations planned for targets in south-central Germany at Mannheim, Karlsruhe and Frankfurt. A force of sixty-five Wellingtons and thirty-three Hampdens was made ready for the first mentioned and one of ninety-seven consisting of fifty Hampdens, twenty-eight Wellingtons and nineteen Halifaxes and Stirlings for railway targets at Karlsruhe, while eighty-eight Whitleys and Wellingtons attended to Frankfurt. 49 Squadron briefed fourteen crews for Mannheim, three for Karlsruhe and two for mining duties in the Baltic, one each for the Forget-me-not and Quince gardens off Kiel. They departed Scampton together between 21.30 and 22.10 with S/L Drakes the senior pilot on duty bound for the Forget-me-not garden. This crew attracted flak as they crossed the coast over Sylt and were fired upon again as they passed close to Kiel, at which point the mine was jettisoned and a course set for home. They ran into more flak at Neumünster and Cuxhaven on the way home and were struck by lightning, which cost them their trailing aerial. At debriefing, they reported that the altimeter had been unserviceable throughout, despite which, they were able to report being at 11,000 feet when outbound over Sylt. P/O Pratt and crew were the other gardeners and they flew over the Quince target area at 8,000 feet to avoid storms before establishing a pinpoint on the coast through a gap in the clouds. They descended to 1,000 feet to confirm their position and planted their vegetable into the briefed location from 600 feet.

When thirty miles from the enemy coast, Sgt McMahon's wireless operator picked up a recall signal, which he attempted unsuccessfully to challenge, leaving the crew with no alternative but to turn back. The others crossed the coast south of Dunkerque and passed to the south of Brussels under almost clear skies and bright moonlight, P/O Hannan and crew in a refrigerator after losing their heating system soon after taking off. Once in German airspace, the River Rhine guided them to Mannheim, where the bright moonlight revealed the built-up area and flares assisted in the search for the marshalling yards. Bombing was carried out from between 4,500 feet (P/O Falconer) and 9,000 feet (Sgt Letford) and many bomb bursts and explosions were observed, which developed into fires as the attackers turned away. Some thirty miles to the south, the crews of Sgts Batchelor and Samuel and P/O Cooke encountered five-tenths cloud at between 8,000 and 14,000 feet over Karlsruhe and identified the Rhine docks but not the railway workshops. They carried out their attacks from around 8,000 feet and observed bursts and fires as they headed for home, Sgt Gillies and crew claiming that the fires from Mannheim and Karlsruhe remained visible for a hundred miles into the return journey. Local sources reported serious damage in parts of Mannheim and eight days loss of production at a rubber and celluloid factory employing more than two thousand people. Reports coming out of Karlsruhe spoke of damage to the Rhine harbour and other locations on the western side of the city.

The same three targets were posted on the following night for smaller forces and thirty-eight Hampdens were detailed, predominantly from North Luffenham, to return to Karlsruhe for another shot at the railway workshops. A force of thirty-eight aircraft was assembled for freshman crews to employ against the docks and shipping at Calais, and five crews from each of the Scampton squadrons attended briefing. The 49 Squadron tyros took off between 22.05 and 22.10 and climbed through ten-tenths ice-bearing cloud as they headed south and broke into clear air at between 10,000 and 13,000 feet. The cloud persisted over the French coast in layers between 4,000 and 10,000 feet, which severely compromised target location. persuading Sgt Beck and crew to abandon the search for Calais and seek out Boulogne or Dunkerque as alternatives. These also were obscured, and they brought their bombs home as did Sgt Hiles and crew after cloud thwarted their efforts to locate the target. Sgt Rea and crew believed that they had bombed Calais docks and harbour, but after bombing an aerodrome and plotting their route home, they were unsure. The crews of P/Os Jenkins and Walker carried out a low-level and glide attack respectively at Calais but had no details to pass on at debriefing.

The troublesome operational career of the Manchesters got under way again on the night of the 7/8th, when three from 207 Squadron and fifty-four Hampdens were made ready to join forces with forty-nine other aircraft to attack the mighty Krupp munitions complex in Essen. 49 Squadron was called upon to provide a dozen Hampdens, which departed Scampton between 23.32 and 00.20 with S/L Bennett the senior pilot on duty and adopted a course to the Scheldt estuary, pinpointing on Tilburg as they crossed Holland to enter Germany near Wesel. The region was criss-crossed with waterways, including the Rivers Rhine, Ruhr and Lippe, that provided strong navigation references through the industrial haze once the cloud dispersed as the target area drew near. The density of Krupp buildings in the Borbeck districts should have guaranteed that some would be hit, if only the crews could pinpoint on that segment of the city. Bombing was carried out on a variety of headings and altitudes in the belief that Essen lay below, but local sources would report only thirty-nine high explosives bombs and two hundred incendiaries falling in the city, and other Ruhr locations would receive the rest.

Fifty Hampdens from North Luffenham, Swinderby and Coningsby were launched on the 8th to carry out a raid on the U-Boot construction yards at Kiel in company with four Whitleys, and in keeping with the level of performance established thus far during the year, little damage resulted. Poor weather kept 5 Group on the ground for the ensuing two nights, and it was the 11th when the next batch of orders was received, detailing an operation against marshalling yards in the Ruhr city of Krefeld for twenty Hampdens from North Luffenham, and docks in occupied ports for thirty freshman crews. The 5 Group ORB mentions only Rotterdam as the target, but six 49 Squadron crews were assigned to Calais and departed Scampton between 01.12 and 01.26. They were confronted over the enemy coast by ten-tenths cloud with tops at 7,000 feet, which prevented all but the crew of Sgt Robinson from identifying and attacking the target despite lengthy searches.

A plan to support the beleaguered Russians by persuading the Luftwaffe to withdraw fighters from the Russian front to protect economic targets in the west resulted in a number of daylight operations involving 5 Group Hampdens on the 12th. Waddington sent six to attack Longueness aerodrome at St-Omer in support of a 2 Group raid on Cologne's power stations at Knapsack and Quadrath and Coningsby dispatched a similar number to Gosnay power station, also in France, both elements protected by a fighter escort. The Waddington element encountered ten-tenths cloud with tops at 8,000 feet, which thwarted any hope of identifying the briefed target and the bombs were dropped on a stretch of railway track some two-and-a-half miles south of St-Omer.

The night of the 12/13th was to be a busy one for the Command, and, throughout the day, aircraft were made ready for attacks on Berlin, Hannover, Magdeburg and Essen. 5 Group detailed thirteen Hampdens to join sixty-five Wellingtons for Hannover, and thirty-six to operate on their own at Magdeburg, while a force of seventy aircraft assigned to the capital included nine Manchesters. Together with minor operations, the night's activities involved a total of 234 aircraft. Hannover lay on the route to both Magdeburg and Berlin, and the three forces would fly out together until reaching it, at which point the Berlin element would continue straight on for the 150 additional miles, while the Magdeburg element peeled off to the south-east with eighty miles still ahead of them. The 49 Squadron ORB did not provide a full picture of events, which, initially, had seen eleven of its aircraft detailed for Magdeburg, five for Hannover and three for gardening. However, six were cancelled and thirteen took off in extremely cloudy, wet and misty conditions, presumably bound for Magdeburg, only for five to be recalled shortly after crossing the coast. The Form 541 listed only the eight crews who continued on after taking off between 20.49 and 21.00, among which F/L Fisher was the senior pilot. The entire outward route was accompanied by ten-tenths cloud that topped out at between 12,000 and 15,000 feet, and crews decided for themselves whether to fly above or below. P/O Pratt and crew opted to climb to 16,000 feet and set course for Leiden on the Dutch coast to leave themselves a straight run on an almost due easterly heading to the target, while F/L Fisher and crew remained at 6,000 feet for the entire journey. The cloud dispersed to a large extent some twenty miles from the target, which enabled the River Elbe and other ground features to be identified. Sgt Samuel and crew were forced down from 11,000 to 800 feet by intense accurate flak and released their bombs in a dive rather than waste fuel in climbing back to the planned bombing altitude. Three crews failed to identify the primary target despite an extensive search and two of these attacked Bremen and one Wilhelmshaven on the way home. Bursts were observed in the built-up area but no detail, and no report emerged from Magdeburg to shed light on the outcome.

Orders were received across the Command on the 14th to prepare for operations that night against railway targets in three major cities in northern Germany to the north of the Harz mountains, Hannover the most westerly, Magdeburg the most easterly and Braunschweig (Brunswick) in-between. 5 Group detailed eighty-one Hampdens to operate alone against the main railway station in Braunschweig, while seven Manchester crews were briefed for Magdeburg as part of an overall force of fifty-two aircraft. 49 Squadron made ready a record twenty-four Hampdens and sent them on their way from Scampton between 20.30 and 21.03 with F/Ls Fisher and Hirons the senior pilot on duty. The crews of P/Os Jenkins and Walker returned immediately, leaving the others to cross the North Sea and make landfall on the Dutch coast between Amsterdam and Den Helder. Sgt Broomfield and crew lost their starboard engine at 14,000 feet as they entered German airspace and turned back to drop their bombs on an aerodrome at Arnhem. The others pressed on over a blanket of medium-level cloud, arriving in the target area at altitudes up to 17,000 feet with little prospect of identifying the aiming point. Thirteen crews delivered their bombs in the general area of Braunschweig, while four backtracked to Hannover and four others found alternative targets at Sarstedt, Minden, Lehrte and Bremen. On return at 03.20, Sgt Owen overshot his landing and wrote off AE262 without injury to the occupants. At debriefing, the crews of P/Os Pratt and Cooke reported an aircraft crashing in flames in the region of Osnabrück and P/O Harvey and crew described another exploding after a direct hit by flak. No report came out of Braunschweig to provide details of damage, and the likelihood is that very little occurred. The city would prove to be elusive, and it would be a further three years before it succumbed to a devastating Bomber Command attack.

On the 15th, the batch of 207 Squadron airmen returned to their parent unit and P/O Ralph Allsebrook was posted in from 44 (Rhodesia) Squadron, with two tours with 49 Squadron ahead of him, during which he would become a leading light before his untimely death two years hence while serving with a post-Operation Chastise 617 Squadron. Railway objectives featured again on the 16th, when orders went out to stations across the Command to prepare for attacks on installations in the Ruhr cities of Düsseldorf and Duisburg and nearby Cologne. Düsseldorf was to be a 5 Group show involving fifty-two Hampdens and six Manchesters. The bombing took place through cloud and industrial haze in the face of a spirited searchlight and flak defence, and although many fires were reported, no detail was gleaned and no report came out of the target city.

After two nights at home, 49 Squadron answered the call on the 17th to make ready ten Hampdens to contribute to the 5 Group force of thirty-nine assigned to the main goods railway station in Bremen, while twenty 4 Group Whitleys targeted the city's Focke-Wulf factory in the south-eastern Hemelingen district. The first departures from Scampton, however, were those of F/L Hodges and Sgt Robinson at 20.40, bound respectively for the Pumpkin and Kraut gardens in the Baltic's Great Belt (north) and Lim Fjord. They encountered little cloud and good visibility, despite the extreme darkness, and planted their vegetable each according to brief during uneventful and long sorties. The bombing element took off between 22.37 and 23.05 with no senior pilots on duty and benefitted from generally favourable conditions as they made their way via the Frisians to the target area, where cloud, haze and extreme darkness obscured ground detail. P/O Walker and crew followed the course of the River Weser into the city to bomb at 01.35, before being forced into extra-violent evasive action until gaining the sanctuary of the sea. It was a similar story for the others as they spent time seeking out a reference and most ultimately bombed the built-up area guided by evidence of searchlights and flak, while others found alternative objectives. Sgt Latty and crew were contending with an engine issue and a faulty artificial horizon, and despite reaching the target area, turned back without bombing. Sgt Tree and crew were unable to locate the briefed aiming point and bombed the approximate location of the Focke-Wulf factory. It was another inconclusive attack, and no results were observed by the 5 Group crews, while a number of those from 4 Group claimed hits on the aircraft factory.

On the 18th, the Butt Report on the Command's operational effectiveness was released, and it sent shock waves reverberating around the War Cabinet and the Air Ministry. Having taken into account around four thousand bombing photos produced during night operations in June and July, it concluded that only a fraction of bombs had fallen within miles of their intended targets, and the poorest performances had been over the Ruhr. It was a massive blow to morale, and demonstrated that thus far, the efforts of the crews had been almost totally ineffective in reducing Germany's capacity to wage war. The claims of the crews were shown to be wildly optimistic, as were those of the Command, and Sir Richard Peirse's tenure as Commander-in-Chief would forever be blighted by the report's revelations.

While the report was being digested that evening, 5 Group sent forty-two Hampdens from North Luffenham and Coningsby to attack the West Station at Cologne in company with twenty Whitleys and Wellingtons. Returning crews reported many fires on the western side of the Rhine, but local reports of nothing more than superficial damage suggested that a decoy fire site had attracted the main weight of bombs. The 49 Squadron ORB suggests that the squadron took part in the Cologne operation, when, in fact, Scampton remained inactive on that night. On the 19th, orders were received at Scampton and Waddington to prepare twenty-six and sixteen Hampdens respectively to join sixty-seven other aircraft for an operation against a railway junction at Kiel, for which 49 Squadron briefed fifteen crews plus two freshmen for mining duties in the Nectarine I garden off the southern Frisians. The bombing element took off between 20.20 and 20.55 with S/L Bennett the senior pilot on duty and were followed into the air at 21.00 by the crews of P/O Alfry and Sgt Donald. The frustrations that the C-in-C would experience over the ensuing three months were typified by this night's events, beginning with extremely poor weather conditions for the outward flight with severe icing and thunderstorms over the Danish coast extending as high as 18,000 feet. All ground features were obscured to leave crews struggling to establish their positions and a number turned back at this stage or when over the Schleswig-Holstein peninsula and attacked alternative targets at Sylt, Hamburg and Cuxhaven. Any reaching Kiel encountered nine to ten-tenths cloud with tops at around 8,000 feet and a base below 5,000 feet in places and bombed on the flashes from flak batteries. Meanwhile, Sgt Donald and crew successfully planted their vegetable off Terschelling and the rear gunner shot out a searchlight, but P/O Alfry and crew were unable to establish a pinpoint in the extreme darkness and returned their mine to store. At debriefings for the Kiel operation, twenty-one crews reported attacking the approximate location of the primary target, while six found last resort objectives and eleven jettisoned their bombs.

A series of three operations against Mannheim began on the night of the 22/23rd, for which 5 Group provided forty-one Hampdens from Coningsby, Syerston and Waddington, which were to join forces with fifty-six Wellingtons. Returning crews reported bomb bursts and fires, but local sources claimed that only one house had been destroyed and five others lightly damaged. S/L Tench was awarded a DFC on the 23rd at the conclusion of his tour and would be posted to 25 O.T.U. five days hence. It was left to Scampton to provide a dozen Hampdens to represent 5 Group at Düsseldorf on the 24th, when 4 Group Whitleys and Halifaxes completed the force of forty-four aircraft. Six additional Hampdens were assigned to searchlight suppression duties in the Wesel defensive belt, their task to attack with 40lb bombs and guns any battery holding a bomber in its beams. The intruder pair, the crews of F/L Hirons and Sgt Tree, took off at 20.20 to be followed into the air by the six-strong bombing section between 20.35 and 20.40 led by S/L Drakes. P/O Jenkins and crew returned after three hours because the starboard wing was low and becoming worse and its engine was overheating. The others checked what was beneath them on e.t.a. and had to peer through seven to eight-tenths cloud at 7,000 feet before bombing what they suspected was Düsseldorf. S/L Drakes remained unconvinced and headed to the north-west to bomb Duisburg from 13,000 feet. F/L Hirons and crew had made landfall on the Den Helder peninsula and pinpointed on Kampen on their way to their patrol area at Wesel, where they carried out eleven attacks with 40lb bombs, SBCs of incendiaries and six hundred rounds of ammunition from between 1,500 and 2,000 feet. Sgt Tree and crew spent seventy minutes in the patrol area, bombing two searchlights and two more in Holland on the way home. This activity turned out to be more effective than the raid on Düsseldorf and caused the beams either to become erratic or to be extinguished altogether. On return to the Scampton circuit, Sgt McMahon's AD967 collided with an 83 Squadron Hampden at 02.50 and both crashed without survivors at Whale Jaws Farm, Hackthorn, some seven miles north-north-east of Lincoln.

A 5 Group attack on Mannheim by thirty-eight Hampdens and seven Manchesters was briefed out on all stations on the 25th, when the main post office was specified as the aiming point for what was, in fact, an assault on the city centre. The outward flight was undertaken in conditions of cloud and icing, but gaps appeared over the target to enable crews to identify the city if not the briefed aiming point. Returning crews claimed a moderate success, but it was, in reality, another inconclusive affair.

Cologne was posted as the target on the 26th, and a force of ninety-nine aircraft made ready, which included twenty-nine Hampdens and a single Manchester drawn from Coningsby, Scampton and Syerston, while six other Hampdens were to carry out flak suppression sorties to the west of the city. 49 Squadron briefed seven crews for the main event, four as intruders and three for mining duties in the Nectarine I garden off the southern Frisians. The last-mentioned element departed Scampton first between 21.00 and 21.12 and was followed into the air by the intruders between 22.10 and 22.15, leaving the bombing brigade to bring up the rear between 22.24 and 22.44. P/O Jacobs and crew were greeted by searchlights and accurate light flak from Terschelling, which compromised their first two attempts to deliver their mine, throwing them of course and preventing them from re-establishing their pinpoint. They arrived back with their mine still on board, while P/Os Bromham and Jones pinpointed on Texel and flew north to plant their vegetables as briefed off Terschelling.

The intruders exited the English coast at Orfordness and made landfall on the Belgian coast south of Ostend, before passing to the south of Liege on their way to the German frontier near Aachen, where they were to take up station in the searchlight belt protecting Cologne and the southern Ruhr. When Sgt Broomfield and crew arrived, they descended to 3,000 feet and established their position in relation to the Rhine through gaps in the cloud. The searchlights were immediately extinguished and remained so for the forty-minute duration of their patrol, after which, they dropped their full load of incendiaries on the western side of Cologne, starting a fairly large fire, and the two 250 pounders on an existing fire on the eastern side. P/O Walker and crew carried out a number of dive attacks on searchlights, planting incendiaries among them and also causing a "nice" fire. On e.t.a. over the town of Düren, P/O Scorer and crew dived down to 3,000 feet and attacked searchlights with 250 pounders, incendiaries and machine guns and left a fire burning. The Germans were becoming accustomed to the Hampdens' new role and doused the lights on hearing the approach of low-flying aircraft. P/O Fournier and crew targeted a searchlight concentration on the very edge of Cologne, attacking it in a dive from 4,000 feet with bombs, incendiaries and guns and setting off a large red fire. When the lights were extinguished, they began chasing cars along the autobahns, forcing them to switch off their lights.

W/O Saunders and crew were contending with an overheating engine and low oil pressure and decided to abandon their quest to reach Cologne and dropped their bombs on a concentration of searchlights south-west of Ostend. The others assigned to bombing encountered cloud and haze over the Rhineland capital and found it difficult to establish a pinpoint other than the Rhine, which they followed either from the north or the south, guided to an extent by the searchlight and flak activity. Some bursts were observed, but there would be little useful information to pass on at debriefing.

Orders arriving on 5 Group stations on the 27th revealed a return to Mannheim for ninety-one aircraft, including thirty-five Hampdens from North Luffenham, Waddington and Swinderby. They were to attack the main railway station, while elements of 1, 3 and 4 Groups focused on other aiming points within the city and seventeen Hampdens from the same stations mined the waters of the Nectarine gardens around the Frisians. The benefits of clear skies over Mannheim were nullified by extreme darkness and haze, and many crews were prevented by searchlight glare from identifying the aiming point, forcing them to bomb the built-up area generally. There was some optimism among returning crews concerning the effectiveness of the raid, but local sources reported no significant damage.

Following its night's rest, 49 Squadron detailed five Hampdens on the 28th for a raid on marshalling yards in Duisburg, for which 5 Group put up thirty Hampdens and six Manchesters in an overall force of 118 aircraft. A further three 49 Squadron Hampdens containing the crews of Sgt Tree and P/Os Fournier and Pratt were to join three others from Coningsby for searchlight suppression duties in the Wesel area and took off first from 23.20, to be followed into the air between 23.50 and 00.05 by the bombing element. P/O Ratcliffe and crew found themselves behind schedule and decided not to press on to the city centre, stopping short and bombing a flak concentration at Hamborn, probably located on the aerodrome on the northern outskirts. The others found favourable conditions and five to eight-tenths cloud, but also thick industrial haze and an accurate and intense searchlight and flak defence. Flares were employed in an attempt to locate the briefed aiming point, and bombing was carried out from between 10,000 and 14,000 feet, Sgt Latty's under gunner sustaining a hand injury as an exploding flak shell took away his door. Meanwhile, Sgt Tree and crew spent around an hour in their patrol area and kept the searchlights quiet with two 250 pounders and incendiaries delivered from 6,000 feet. We will never know the details of the sorties of the other two intruders as they failed to return. AD971 coming down in the North Sea with no survivors from the crew of P/O Pratt, and their remains eventually came ashore for burial at Harlingen and on the Frisian Islands of Texel and Vlieland. They were probably victims of one of the night-fighters patrolling the Dutch coastal region, and this was certainly the fate of AE126 and the crew of P/O Fournier, who all lost their lives when shot down into the sea off Ameland at 03.40 by Oblt Helmut Lent of 4./NJG1. Returning crews claimed a successful raid, but, again, this was disputed by local reports, which suggested that only around a dozen bomb loads had hit the city.

The final raid of the Mannheim series was posted on Wellington stations on the 29th, while Frankfurt was notified as the destination for a 4 and 5 Group force of 143 aircraft. This would be the first time that this city had faced an attack by a hundred-plus aircraft, the crews of which had been briefed to use the inland docks as the aiming point. 5 Group would be contributing seventy-three Hampdens and three 207 Squadron Manchesters, 49 Squadron providing ten of the former, which departed Scampton between 20.55 and 21.15 with F/L Hodges the senior pilot on duty. Some crews adopted the briefed route from Orfordness to make landfall south of Ostend and bypass Namur, while others opted to fly directly to the target from the English coast, which meant landfall over the Scheldt estuary and skirting northern Belgium to pass south of Cologne. Cloud lay over most of the route, and icing became a problem, particularly for Sgt Donald and crew, whose aircraft was so weighed down that it was wallowing on the point of stall on e.t.a. and the bombs were jettisoned. Sgt Broomfield and crew picked up the River Rhine some fifteen miles short of the target, at which point the starboard engine began to falter and the bombs were dropped on a flare path that conveniently appeared 7,800 feet below. The remaining 49 Squadron crews reached the target area, where seven to nine-tenths cloud topped out at 10,000 feet and prevented many from identifying the planned aiming point. However, some were able to pick out the river and docks by running in from below 10,000 feet, and bombing was carried out on largely estimated positions. Some crews observed bursts in the built-up area but no detail, and local sources described scattered and insignificant damage, and certainly nothing commensurate with the size of the force and the effort expended.

The final operation of the month was notified to thirty-nine Hampden and six Manchester crews at briefings on the 31st, when railway targets in Cologne were revealed as the targets for an overall force of 103 aircraft. According to the Form 540, 49 Squadron put up nine Hampdens for the main event and five to perform a flak suppression role, but the Form 541 lists eleven for the bombing role and four for intruder duties. The latter departed Scampton first between 19.35 and 19.42 and headed for Schouwen in the Scheldt estuary and were followed into the air between 19.57 and 20.43 by the bombing element. They were routed out over southern Holland and would have to run the gauntlet of searchlights and flak in the Roermond area, where the ground was concealed by ten-tenths cloud, while bright moonlight above provided ideal conditions for night-fighters. Sgt Samuel and crew spent forty minutes in the patrol area and dropped eight 250 pounders singly, noting that some of the searchlights were operating against the intruders, perhaps luring them into the light flak guns. P/O Green and crew flew out at 10,000 feet, and on arrival in the patrol area found a searchlight cone to dive bomb, and then remained at between 1,000 and 3,000 feet to attack other lights with bombs and guns. They also noted that the lights were doused initially, but then remained illuminated to seek out the intruders. P/O Scorer and crew found themselves ensnared for considerable periods after stirring up a response by dropping a 250 pounder on a searchlight, and they became the target for a hail of flak shells. They attacked other locations and also reported that the lights remained on even as bombs detonated close by. Sgt Gillies and crew expended all of their bombs and ball ammunition in passes at 1,500 feet while dodging tracer and concluded that intruders were now expected, and that the Luftwaffe had developed new tactics to counter them. Those members of the bombing brigade arriving in the Cologne area did so by DR and evidence of searchlights and flak and were prevented by ten-tenths cloud from obtaining more than a fleeting glimpse of the ground. Most searched for a time before bombing the approximate location of the city and a few noted the glow of fires reflected in the cloud. Local sources reported a few bombs falling and no damage in what had been another ineffective and wasteful use of resources.

During the course of the month, the squadron carried out twenty operations and dispatched 182 sorties for the loss of four Hampdens and three crews. At some point, F/L Fisher was posted away at the conclusion of his tour. Born in western Australia in March 1917, Hurtle "Bill" Fisher had joined the RAF in 1939 and was still under training when war broke out. Initially with 185 Squadron, a 5 Group training unit, he had joined 49 Squadron in November 1940 and immediately demonstrated outstanding qualities as a Hampden pilot. He was awarded the DFC in November 1941 after completing twenty-seven sorties and the citation stressed his press-on spirit and determination to hit the target. He rose quickly through the ranks and as a squadron leader at 5 Group HQ, worked in Air Operations, during which period he authored an operational handbook for 5 Group. Following the loss of its commanding officer during the Peenemünde operation in August 1943, 57 Squadron appointed acting W/C Fisher as its new commander, a post he would occupy until his posting to HQ 21 Group eight months later.

## September 1941

5 Group was in action on the first night of the new month, when twenty Hampdens joined forces with Wellingtons to attack Cologne in what turned out to be favourable weather conditions. Despite this, few bombs found the mark, and the fires reported by returning crews were probably from decoy sites. Briefings took place across the Command on the 2$^{nd}$ for two operations to be carried out that night, both supported by 5 Group. The main operation would be conducted by 126 aircraft, including eleven Hampdens, against the inland docks at Frankfurt, while a force of forty-nine aircraft was to target the central railway station in Berlin, some 260 miles to the north-east. The bulk of the latter force, thirty-two Hampdens and four Manchesters, was provided by 5 Group, with a handful of 3 Group Stirlings and 4 Group Halifaxes in attendance. The 49 Squadron ORB Forms 540 and 541 contradict each other, but fifteen Hampdens were recorded with a take-off time between 19.30 and 20.25, a dozen of them bound for Berlin with F/L Hirons the senior pilot on duty, Sgt Hiles and crew for Frankfurt and the crews of Sgt Bow and P/O Andrews for mining duties in the Nectarine II garden.

The Berlin element set a course from the Lincolnshire coast to the east Frisians, and P/O Jenkins and crew were some one hundred miles out when intercepted by a Me110, which inflicted sufficient damage with cannons and machine-gun fire to persuade them to abandon all hopes of reaching Germany's capital and bomb an unidentified last-resort target. The rear gunners had returned fire and the enemy aircraft was last seen in a vertical dive. The outward flight was dogged by ten-tenths cloud at 6,000 to 8,000 feet, which prevented many from establishing their position at the Dutch and German coasts and not all would find a gap over Berlin to confirm their arrival. A few glimpsed the River Spree or other ground features to provide a reference, while Sgt Flint and crew saw nothing of Berlin on e.t.a., and decided to backtrack to Hamburg. In fact, they ended up over the Hansastadt city of Lübeck and dropped their bombs there. Sgt Broomfield and crew pinpointed on the Müritzsee, a large lake some sixty miles north of Berlin, but were concerned about the state of their fuel and bombed a railway junction at nearby Neubrandenburg. F/L Hirons and crew pinpointed on Bremerhaven on the way out, but then lost all sight of the ground until passing over a built-up area observed through a gap in the clouds on e.t.a. They swung back to bomb it and estimated later that they had probably been over Stettin, some sixty miles north-east of Berlin. By the time that returning crews reached England, many were flying on fumes and were in desperate need of somewhere to land. They lobbed down at the first airfields to present themselves or on any tract of level ground, Sgt Samuel and crew finding a piece of scrubland at Thornham Ling common in Norfolk on which to put down X3136 at 05.50 after ten hours aloft, while AE203 was crash-landed by Sgt Flint fifteen miles north-east of Stowmarket in Suffolk at 06.57 after eleven hours in the air. Both crews scrambled clear of the wreckage without injury and, unlike their Hampdens, would fly again. The crews of Sgt Gillies and P/O Jenkins also crash-landed, largely without injury, and their aircraft, AE194 and AD960, would be returned to flying condition. In contrast to the experiences of the Berlin force, Sgt Hiles and crew benefitted from more favourable conditions and crossed France over varying amounts of cloud between two and eight-tenths and experienced no difficulty in locating Frankfurt and pinpointing on the docks, which they bombed, setting off two fires. Meanwhile, Sgt Bow and crew had pinpointed on Ameland and delivered their mine from 800 feet, but P/O Andrews and crew had been defeated by a cloud base at 300 feet and brought their vegetable home.

The enemy warships at Brest returned to the spotlight on the 3rd after a respite in recent weeks, and a force of 140 aircraft was made ready to attack them. 5 Group contributed thirty Hampdens and two 207 Squadron Manchesters from North Luffenham, Coningsby and Waddington, which took off only for a recall signal to bring them home shortly afterwards, along with those from 1 and 4 Groups, because of deteriorating weather conditions. In the event, 3 Group and four other aircraft that had failed to pick up the signal carried on and fifty-three returning crews claimed to have bombed the estimated positions of the warships through an effective smoke screen, claiming no hits. On the 6th, 5 Group detailed eighteen Hampdens from Coningsby to join with sixty-eight other aircraft to target the I G Farben-controlled chemicals/synthetic rubber factory at Marl-Hüls on the northern edge of the Ruhr. Known locally as the "Buna" works because of the chemicals butadiene and natrium employed in the manufacturing process of synthetic rubber for tyres, the Chemische Werke-Hüls GmbH had been formed in 1938 after its acquisition by the I G Farben company in association with the Bergwerkgesellschaft Hibernia A G. Whether or not it was using slave workers at this time, the I G Farben company would become infamous for drawing its labour force from concentration camps and forcing tens of thousands to toil under the harshest conditions at its many manufacturing sites across Germany. *(In some of my previous books I have mistakenly located this factory in the Hüls district of Krefeld in the western Ruhr).*

Earlier in the day, thirty-four additional Hampdens had been sent to Kinloss and Lossiemouth as forward launching pads for mining operations that night in the Onion garden off Oslo, where the cruiser Admiral Scheer was believed to be at anchor. Six 49 Squadron Hampdens departed Kinloss between 20.30 and 22.00 with S/L Drakes the senior pilot on duty and set course for Kristiansand, before map-reading their way northwards along the coast to the target area in excellent conditions. Glide approaches were carried out from altitudes of between 2,000 and 9,000 feet and the vegetables planted from below 1,000 feet, after which, P/O Scorer bombed the flarepath on Tonsberg aerodrome, S/L Drakes another aerodrome at Ebjemoen (untraced) and P/O Falconer two flak ships. Sgt Robinson and crew ran out of fuel on the way home and all sustained injury when AD744 was force-landed eight miles south-west of Banff, one crew member suffering a fractured leg and arm.

Berlin was posted as the night's main target on the 7th, for which a force of 197 aircraft was made ready, while the Deutsche Werke U-Boot yards and the town of Kiel would occupy the attentions of a further fifty-one aircraft. 5 Group supported both operations, with eighteen Hampdens for the latter and forty-three Hampdens and four 207 Squadron Manchesters for Germany's capital. 49 Squadron made ready five Hampdens for Berlin and dispatched them from Scampton between 20.25 and 20.40 with W/C Stubbs the senior pilot on duty, leaving the crews of P/Os Bromham and Jacobs and Sgt Bow on the ground until taking off for Kiel at 22.00. The latter arrived in the target area to find favourable conditions with up to three-tenths cloud, and, according to most crews, good visibility, which they exploited to carry out their attacks. Curiously, after stooging around the Kiel area from 01.03 to 01.45, P/O Jacobs and crew failed to locate the target and cited poor visibility as the reason. They bombed the road to Flensburg after turning for home. AE236 crashed in the target area and there were no survivors from the crew of P/O Bromham. At debriefing, no claims were made of direct hits on the shipyard, but local sources reported damage in a number of locations to warehouses and housing and to two passenger vessels.

Meanwhile, the Berlin-bound force had also passed this way and had employed the Baltic coast as a strong navigation pinpoint that would aid them to reach the target area some 180 miles to the south-east. Sgt Gillies and crew had been delayed by a navigational error at the German coast at Sylt and, assessing that insufficient time remained in which to reach Berlin, they bombed Kiel as an alternative. Clear skies prevailed in the Berlin area and a hostile flak defence greeted the force, the searchlights to an extent nullified by the brightness of the moon. Despite that, Sgt Hiles and crew were among a few to positively establish a pinpoint, in their case Tempelhof aerodrome, upon which they left a red fire burning. The others bombed the built-up area generally and most ran into the defences at Hamburg and Bremen on the way home, before arriving in English airspace with empty tanks. Two-thirds of crews reported successfully bombing in the Berlin area, and the effectiveness of the attack was partly borne out by local descriptions of damage to several war-industry factories, housing, utilities and communications, mostly in the north and east of the city. Fifteen aircraft failed to return, and when added to three losses from other operations, this represented the highest number of bomber casualties in a single night.

The first large Bomber Command attack on the city of Kassel was briefed to crews of all groups on the afternoon of the 8th, and would involve ninety-five aircraft, including twenty-seven Hampdens. There were to be two aiming points, both of them belonging to the Henschel Company, the presence of whose numerous manufacturing sites dominated the city and employed eight thousand workers in addition to a large number of slaves. Aside from building the Dornier Do17Z bomber under license, Henschel was the main producer of the Panzer III tank and the Tiger I and II, as well as narrow-gauge locomotives. The force was to be divided, sixty-eight aircraft assigned to the tank works, and twenty-seven to the locomotive workshops, with the five 49 Squadron participants assigned to the former. The crews of P/Os Allsebrook and Scorer and a third unidentified crew were assigned to mining duties, respectively in the Nectarine III garden off the northern Frisians, the Verbena garden off Copenhagen and the Wallflower garden in Kiel Harbour, and the two elements departed Scampton together between 19.45 and 20.32. The gardeners headed east to their respective target areas, but the unidentified crew returned after ninety minutes with a violently ill wireless operator. P/O Allsebrook and crew had the night's shortest round-trip and reached the Borkum area to seek out a pinpoint for their timed run, only to be driven off by flak and having to make a second approach from north-east of Juist, this time successfully planting their vegetable. P/O Scorer and crew approached their target area in the Baltic in good visibility, gliding down from 6,000 feet to plant their vegetable in the briefed location, before attacking a ship, which responded with tracer.

The bombers, meanwhile, had adopted the briefed route from Orfordness to Dinant in Belgium, benefitting throughout from the fine weather conditions, which aided them in their search for the target. Kassel lay beneath clear skies, the excellent visibility enhanced by bright moonlight, which enabled crews to pinpoint on the River Fulda that runs from north to south through the city. The 49 Squadron crews experienced no difficulty in identifying and attacking the target and reported fires and smoke rising through 5,000 feet and light flak reaching 10,000 feet. Crews from other squadrons also observed bursts and fires, and a particularly large conflagration at the main railway station to the west of the aiming point. Local sources in Kassel reported serious damage to two industrial concerns and the destruction of eleven houses with more than seventy others requiring repair, which was a poor return for the size of the force operating in favourable conditions, but at least no aircraft were lost.

Orders were received on the 11th to prepare for an attack on the A G Neptun shipyards at Rostock, while the rest of the force targeted the nearby Heinkel factory and the town itself. A total force of fifty-six aircraft consisted of thirty-nine Hampdens and five 207 Squadron Manchesters from Coningsby, North Luffenham and Waddington, and a dozen Wellingtons. This was one of three Baltic coast targets for the night, the others at Kiel and Warnemünde, having been assigned to Wellingtons and Whitleys respectively. Other operations on this night involved eight freshman crews to attack the docks and shipping at Boulogne and twenty Hampdens mining off the Frisians, Heligoland and Warnemünde.

On the 12th, Scampton, Swinderby and Waddington were notified of an operation that night against marshalling yards in Frankfurt, for which 5 Group detailed thirty-one Hampdens in an overall force of 130 aircraft. 49 Squadron made ready eleven of its own for the main event and three for mining duties, one each in the Hollyhock and Radish gardens off Travemünde and in the Fehmarn Belt in the Baltic and one for one of the Nectarine gardens off the Frisians. One of the bombers was involved in a taxiing accident and had to be scrubbed, leaving the others to depart Scampton between 22.30 and 23.15 and head out over Orfordness for the North Sea crossing to the Scheldt estuary. They encountered cloud over the sea and for most of the outward flight via Namur in Belgium until it thinned to some extent, but as was usually the case, opinions varied as to the state of the conditions. The cloud density ranged at between six and ten-tenths in the target area at around 6,000 feet, and some crews also mentioned moonlight filtering through gaps to provide a glimpse of the ground. The visibility was described as both good and poor with searchlight dazzle cited as a major impediment to aiming point identification, but as far as the Scampton crews were concerned, they saw little of the ground through the cloud other than the Rivers Rhine and Main and observed only the flash of bomb bursts. Returning crews reported large fires, and local sources confirmed that thirty-eight blazes had to be dealt with and most of the damage had been in residential districts.

P/O Allsebrook and crew were again handed the shortest round-trip and, based on the seven-and-a-half-hour duration of their sortie, had been assigned to Nectarine III at the northern end of the island chain, where they found favourable conditions in which to fulfil their brief. P/O Jacobs and crew encountered cloud with a base at 1,500 feet over the coastal region to the north-east of Lübeck, which enabled them to fly over the mainland out of sight of the defences before descending to deliver their mine. Sgt Bow and crew found similar conditions, which thwarted their efforts to locate the drop zone and brought their mine home.

It was time for another attempt on the German warships at Brest on the 13th, for which a force of 147 aircraft of six different types was assembled across the Command. 5 Group contributed thirty-eight Hampdens and four Manchesters from North Luffenham, Coningsby and Waddington, all of which, like the rest of the participants, were thwarted by the smoke screen that engulfed the vessels and hid them from view. 49 Squadron remained at home on this night and on the 14th, welcomed F/L de Mestre DFC on posting from 44 (Rhodesia) Squadron to fulfil the role of deputy flight commander. Scampton was back in business on the 15th, when Hamburg was posted as the destination for a force of 169 aircraft of six different types, of which 5 Group contributed fifty Hampdens to target the city's Blohm & Voss shipyards in company with more than a hundred others, and four Manchesters to attack a railway junction. 49 Squadron made ready eleven Hampdens for the main event, another for the freshman crew of Sgt Davis to employ against the docks and shipping at Le Havre and four for mining duties off Germany's Baltic coast in the Jasmine and Radish gardens off Warnemünde and in the Fehmarn Belt. The ORB did not record a take-off time for Sgt Davis and crew, but it was almost certainly the same as for the 83 Squadron participants, at around 18.30, immediately preceding the departure of the main element between 18.35 and 18.45 with S/L Drakes the senior pilot on duty. The gardeners bound for the Jasmine garden followed between 19.45 and 19.55 and it would be 21.45 before Sgt Walker and crew set off for the Radish garden.

A layer of ten-tenths stratus cloud at 5,000 feet hid the North Sea and the German coastal region from view, but it dispersed sufficiently to allow some a sight of the Elbe Estuary, from which point, they would have to run the gauntlet of searchlights and flak all the way to the aiming points. Sgts Samuel and Gillies complained of inaccurate wind forecasts, and both ended up too far north over the island of Sylt, which the former bombed, while the latter retraced their steps to make landfall between Cuxhaven and Bremerhaven before carrying out a glide attack on Hamburg. According to most crews, the skies over the city were clear, but searchlight glare proved to be a serious impediment to aiming point identification and only six from 49 Squadron bombed in the general area of Hamburg, while others turned their attention upon Wilhelmshaven, Bremerhaven and Bremen. Light flak was reaching 10,000 feet, with searchlights co-operating with night-fighters to create the usual hostile environment for the attackers, and Sgt Donald and crew successfully evaded the attentions of an enemy aircraft. Returning crews reported the glow of fires visible for eighty miles, and a post-raid analysis and local reports confirmed that Hamburg had sustained quite severe damage in various residential districts. Seven large fires had erupted, and more than fourteen hundred people had been bombed out of their homes, while a 4,000lb blockbuster had destroyed a block of flats in Wandsbek, killing sixty-six residents.

The freshman crews had an easier time over Le Havre, where conditions were favourable, and Sgt Davis and crew reported five bursts in the vicinity of dock 1 and two large fires at a nearby location.

The gardeners had been given a route out from the Lincolnshire coast to make landfall on Sylt, before traversing the Schleswig-Holstein peninsula to reach the Baltic and establish a pinpoint at Nysted on Denmark's Lolland Island. Flying above ten-tenths cloud, Sgt Broomfield and crew failed to establish a pinpoint after Teschelling and abandoned their sortie, while the crews of Sgt Latty and P/O Andrews experienced no such difficulties and successfully planted their vegetables from low level under clear skies. Sgt Walker and crew enjoyed similar conditions over the Radish garden and delivered their mine into the briefed location from 700 feet.

The 16th was a momentous day in the history and fortunes of Bomber Command, with the arrival at Waddington of the first prototype Lancaster, BT308, for crew familiarization, in preparation for 44 (Rhodesia) Squadron to introduce the type into squadron service. This early Lancaster retained the three-fin configuration tailplane common to the Manchester, but, in time, would be replaced with the iconic two large fins, some of which would also be fitted to modified Manchesters. That was for the future, however, and, in the meantime, operations would continue with the magnificent and trusty, but, increasingly obsolete, Hampden.

Adverse weather conditions began to play a part in proceedings at this stage, and 5 Group squadrons were put on stand-by for a number of operations that were subsequently cancelled. Orders were received at North Luffenham, Swinderby and Waddington on the 20th to prepare for operations that night against Berlin and Frankfurt, and there would be more than an element of chaos surrounding the Berlin endeavour, when the force of seventy-four aircraft was recalled because of deteriorating weather conditions. 5 Group had sent thirty-six Hampdens to forward bases at Horsham-St-Faith and Swanton Morley, but ten of these were cancelled when they could not be refuelled in time.

49 Squadron would not be required to operate again for almost two weeks and during this period of inactivity the Scampton station sports day was held on the 18th, when 83 Squadron was beaten into second place by 724 Ground Defence Squadron and 49 Squadron's performance was not recorded. F/L Mundy DFC arrived on this day from 14 O.T.U., and P/O Falconer and Sgts Letford and Flint were posted to 14 O.T.U. at Cottesmore on the 19th at the conclusion of their tours. P/O Falconer would eventually join the Path Finder Force, and in late 1944, assume the command of 156 Squadron, with which he would lose his life over Cologne on the night of the 30/31st of December. Sgt Flint would rise through the ranks and be rewarded for his service and leadership qualities with the command of 50 Squadron in March 1945, seeing that famous 5 Group unit through to the end of hostilities. On the 26th, Marshal of the Royal Air Force Lord Trenchard paid Scampton a visit, when, in a speech to the assembled personnel, his main message was, to "keep the Jerries in their cellars". Also on this day, F/L Hirons was posted to 25 O.T.U. at Finningley at the conclusion of his tour and was accompanied by Sgt Tree.

Finally, on the 28th, after the unusually long lull in operations, 5 Group detailed forty-eight Hampdens from Coningsby, Scampton, Swinderby and Waddington for an attack that night on the main railway station at Frankfurt. However, continuing bad weather caused the withdrawal of the less experienced crews, and, together with accidents and incidents, this reduced the numbers to thirty Hampdens from Scampton, Coningsby and Waddington. The 49 Squadron effort was reduced from fourteen to eight, one of the cancellations caused by a tailwheel collapse during taxiing to take-off. They departed Scampton between 22.51 and 00.09 with S/L Hodges the senior pilot on duty and F/L Mundy undertaking his first operation with the squadron. Sgt Walker and crew were last away in AE376, and eleven minutes later, the Hampden impacted the ground and burst into flames at Burton Park near Lincoln following a shallow dive, and all on board lost their lives. The others made their way to the target area over ten-tenths cloud, that thinned to an extent over the target to be replaced by thick haze, which was equally efficient at concealing the aiming point. Flares were deployed in a vain attempt to improve visibility and a few bomb bursts and fires aside, there was nothing to report at debriefing and no information came out of Frankfurt. One Hampden and one Wellington failed to return, the former AD733 of 49 Squadron, from which the crew of F/L Mundy DFC survived in enemy hands.

On the 29th, six 49 Squadron crews were called to briefing to be told that a force of eighty-nine aircraft was being assembled to attack the Hamburger Flugzeugbau aircraft factory, a subsidiary of the Blohm & Voss company, situated in Hamburg's Finkenwerde district on the southern bank of the Elbe to the west of the city centre. 5 Group's contribution would be thirty-eight Hampdens and four Manchesters, while ten others, including P/O Jenkins and crew, attempted to hit the Admiral Scheer pocket battleship moored nearby. They departed Scampton between 17.54 and 18.06 with S/L Bennett the senior pilot on duty and soon lost the services of P/O Alfry to an engine issue. The others pressed on through ice-bearing cloud to make landfall on the German coast in the vicinity of Emden, Bremerhaven and Cuxhaven, where intense flak damaged S/L Bennett's starboard engine and forced him to jettison his bombs and turn for home, stalked by a night-fighter, which he succeeded in evading. Sgt Latty and crew had been forced to descend rapidly to 7,000 feet to escape the icing conditions and were unable to climb again so bombed the aerodrome on Borkum Island. Conditions over Hamburg were hazy, which made identification something of a challenge, and accurate searchlight and flak activity added to the difficulties. There was also some moonlight, but it was insufficient to allow a positive identification of the aircraft factory, and only Sgt Davis and crew from 49 Squadron positively identified the briefed aiming point and bombed it at 21.15, while the others attacked the built-up area generally. P/O Jenkins and crew located the Admiral Scheer, which did not return fire as they delivered what they reported was a successful attack but claimed no hits. Local reports confirmed nine fires within the city, but no damage worthy of particular mention.

Hamburg was posted as the destination again on the following night, this time for eighty-two aircraft again targeting the Blohm & Voss aircraft factory after the previous night's failure. 5 Group put up forty-eight Hampdens from Coningsby, Scampton, North Luffenham, Syerston and Swinderby, while sixteen freshman crews were briefed to bomb the docks and shipping at Cherbourg. According to the 49 Squadron ORB Form 540, seven crews were briefed for the main event and two freshmen to attack the docks and shipping at Cherbourg. However, the Form 541 recorded eight crews departing Scampton between 18.05 and 18.25, each of which would make reference to locations in north-western Germany. Sgt Rawstorne and crew took off at 19.30 and made no geographical reference to identify their destination, but the five-hour duration of the completed sortie confirms it to have been Cherbourg. They arrived to find favourable conditions and carried out an attack, and at some point, were engaged by a night-fighter, which they evaded by a steep diving turn to starboard. Meanwhile, some 560 miles to the north-east, the Hamburg force had contended with icing conditions to reach their objective and P/O Jones and crew had been forced to jettison their bombs and return home. The others were hampered over the target by varying amounts of cloud and intense searchlight and flak activity, through which some ground references were established. Five of the 49 Squadron crews bombed the general area of Hamburg, while two sought out alternatives, and it was another unsatisfactory endeavour which caused fourteen fires and some housing damage, but nothing commensurate with the effort expended.

During the course of the month, the squadron took part in eighteen operations and dispatched ninety sorties for the loss of five Hampdens and two crews.

## October 1941

The adverse weather conditions would continue to disrupt operations at the start of the new month, and the forty-four Hampdens dispatched to Karlsruhe on the night of the 1/2nd were recalled because of the risk of fog at the time of their return. Among these were six representing 49 Squadron, who had taken off between 18.25 and 19.00 and received the recall signal at various times between 21.00, when Sgt Davis and crew were over Luxembourg, and 21.45, by which time Sgt Hiles and crew were just ten minutes short of the target. P/O Andrews and crew had already reached the target area and had descended through the eight-tenths cloud to 5,000 feet but had not located Karlsruhe through the mist before the recall was picked up. They headed westwards for eighty miles and bombed an unidentified town, which might well have been Metz in France. All returned safely, mostly to diversion airfields between 23.40 and 02.40 after another wasted effort.

There were no operations for 5 Group and most other elements of the Command between the 2nd and 9th as the weather took a hand, and this would pave the way for a busy and record-breaking night of operations on the 12th. In the meantime, acting F/L Massey was posted in from 16 O.T.U. on the 6th, and on the 10th, an overall force of seventy-eight aircraft was assembled for an operation against the Krupp complex in the Borbeck districts of Essen. Sixty-nine others were assigned to attack Cologne, thirty-five miles away to the south, while eighty mostly freshman crews cut their teeth on occupied ports from Rotterdam to Bordeaux. 5 Group detailed forty-six Hampdens and ten Manchesters for Essen, six Hampdens for searchlight suppression duties in the Bocholt-Borken area on the northern approaches to the Ruhr and twenty-three freshmen for Dunkerque. Cloud and industrial haze created difficulties at both main targets and neither operation was effective.

The first major night of operations in the month was notified across the Command on the 12th, when a number of targets were posted in northern and southern Germany and the Ruhr in-between, which would require the highest number of sorties yet in a single night. The largest effort, for which 152 aircraft were detailed from 1, 3 and 4 Groups, was the first major assault of the war on the southern city of Nuremberg, the site of massive Nazi rallies during the thirties. The other targets were the Deutsche Schiff shipbuilding yards at Bremen, for which ninety-nine aircraft were detailed, including twenty-two Hampdens, and the Buna works at Marl-Hüls on the northern rim of the Ruhr, which was to be a 5 Group show involving seventy-nine Hampdens and eleven Manchesters. The total number of sorties for the night was 373, which included eight Hampdens to carry out an intruder role in the searchlight belt in the Bocholt area. 49 Squadron made ready a dozen Hampdens for the Buna works and four for the Bremen shipyards, and it was the latter, the crews of P/Os Wood and Rawstorne and Sgts Bow and Davis, that departed Scampton first between 18.45 and 18.50. They crossed the North Sea under clear skies until reaching the German coast, where they encountered ten-tenths cloud at around 5,000 feet with occasional gaps that afforded only the briefest glimpse of the River Weser and forced them to bombed on e.t.a., and searchlight and flak activity from as high as 18,000 feet.

They were homebound over the North Sea by the time that the Ruhr-bound element took off between 00.15 and 00.43 with S/L Hodges and the two new deputy flight commanders, F/Ls de Mestre and Massey, the senior pilots on duty. They benefitted from the same clear skies and a half moon as they crossed the North Sea, and P/O Jenkins and crew had reached the midpoint when R/T failure and a stalking night-fighter persuaded them to turn back. Sgt Hiles and crew were seventy miles out from Skegness when an engine cut and eventually caught fire to end their interest in proceedings. The others also ran into nine to ten-tenths cloud over the Dutch coast at 7,000 to 10,000 feet, which extended past their pinpoint at Enkhuizen on the eastern side of the Den Helder peninsula and all the way to the target, testing their ability to establish a position. Some dropped flares and all stooged around for up to fifty minutes searching for some kind of reference, which was provided generally by searchlights and flak. P/O Allsebrook and crew were ensnared in searchlights and fired upon by flak, escaping at 1,500 feet, before climbing again to bomb from 2,500 feet and observe three bursts. The others either attacked flak concentrations or brought their bombs home and many reported a strong enemy night-fighter presence. The Nuremberg raid was equally disappointing and the gloom and frustration at Bomber Command HQ deepened further.

Thirty Hampdens and nine Manchesters eventually made their way to take-off from 5 Group stations in the early hours of the 14th, after a number had been withdrawn for technical reasons. The target for this 5 Group operation was the main railway station in Cologne, situated in the shadow of the cathedral on the West Bank of the Rhine, while twenty miles to the north, elements of 1 and 3 Groups would be attending to Düsseldorf. The close proximity of the two operations would guarantee an intense searchlight and flak response. The eight-strong 49 Squadron element departed Scampton between 00.56 and 01.19 with S/L Drakes the senior pilot on duty and crossed the English coast at Orfordness, before heading for the Scheldt Estuary or Belgian coast in favourable weather. Severe icing conditions from the Belgian coast to twenty miles inland caused P/O Jenkins and crew to turn back and threw Sgt Hiles and crew into a righthand spin, during which they lost eight thousand feet, before pulling out at 6,000 feet and breaking the aileron control. They also turned back and Sgt Hiles pulled off a safe forced-landing at base, from which the Hampden was returned to service. Once in the target area, the others were greeted by haze and searchlight glare along with accurate flak that rendered identification of the aiming point almost impossible, and most bombed the built-up area generally or a last resort objective. Only Sgt Bow and crew made a positive identification of the briefed aiming point and carried out a glide attack without observing the results.

A force of eighty aircraft was assembled from 1, 3 and 4 Groups for a return to Nuremberg on the 14th for what turned out to be another disappointing effort, which was compromised largely by adverse weather conditions during the outward flight, and only a single 78 Squadron Whitley crew managed to identify and hit the Siemens factory and destroy a workshop. 3 Group sent thirty-four Wellingtons and Stirlings to Cologne on the 15/16th, and returning crews claimed large fires, while local sources reported only a few bombs and no damage.

On the 16th, 5 Group contributed twenty-six Hampdens from Scampton and Syerston to a force of eighty-one aircraft sent to attack railway yards at Duisburg, for which 49 Squadron contributed seven Hampdens and three others to operate as intruders in the searchlight belt in the Wesel-Borken-Bocholt area to the north. The crews of Sgts Newmarch and Donald and P/O Jones departed Scampton between 00.17 and 00.30 to take up station in the patrol area and they were followed into the air between 00.37 and 00.55 by the bombing element. The intruders were successful in disrupting searchlight activity, but not one of the Scampton crews was able to establish a position over Duisburg through the ten-tenths cloud and all bombed on estimated positions.

The weather intervened to keep the bomber force on the ground on the following three nights, until orders came through on the 20th to prepare for operations against the ports of Bremen, Wilhelmshaven and Emden in north-western Germany and Antwerp in Belgium for freshman crews. A force of 153 aircraft assembled for Bremen included a 5 Group contribution of eighty-two Hampdens and eight Manchesters, sixteen of the former representing 49 Squadron, which provided two more for the freshman crews of Sgts Watt and Williams to take mining in the Nectarine II garden off the central Frisians. They departed Scampton together over an extended period between 18.00 and 19.05 with S/L Bennett the senior pilot on duty and made their way across the North Sea under relatively clear skies and in the absence of a moon, extreme darkness. Sgt Latty's intercom broke down as they approached the target area and, unable to fix the problem, turned back, leaving the others struggling to establish themselves over the target in the face of six to seven-tenths cloud. They also had to contend with intense searchlight activity and light tracer reaching 10,000 feet, while the heavier calibre shells were climbing to 17,000 feet. Some picked up the River Weser to the north and south of city to aid navigation but the briefed railway junction aiming point remained elusive despite the deployment of flares and bombing was carried out by most on the general area of the city, although Wilhelmshaven, Oldenburg and Rotenburg were among alternative targets attacked. The gardeners experienced no difficulty in pinpointing on Texel and Schiermonnikoog and planted their vegetables as briefed.

Bremen was posted as the destination again on the 21st for a force of 136 aircraft, including eighteen Hampdens and two Manchesters, whose crews were briefed to attack shipyards. Conditions were similar to those of twenty-four hours earlier and local sources reported another scattered attack which hit largely housing but landed one bomb in the Vulkan shipyard. Mannheim was selected as the target for 123 aircraft on the 22nd, for which 5 Group put up forty-five Hampdens, thirty-three of them from Scampton, where the 49 Squadron element of sixteen took off between 17.50 and 18.20 with S/L Hodges the senior pilot on duty. Thick cloud, electrical storms and icing conditions up to 15,000 feet made life difficult during the outward flight, particularly as they crossed Belgium to pinpoint on Brussels on their way to the German frontier north of Luxembourg. F/L de Mestre and crew failed to obtain any ground reference through up to ten-tenths cloud, even on the River Rhine, and brought their bombs home. P/O Jacobs and crew were contending with an overheating engine and dropped their wing bombs on Ostend to lighten their load and enable them to climb to 18,000 feet, but the icing won out in the end and they abandoned their sortie. After all had landed at Horsham-St-Faith, only six crews asserted that they had bombed the target, while the others reported releasing their loads on estimated positions or on alternative targets. X3057 suffered an undercarriage collapse on landing, but Sgt Newmarch and crew were unhurt.

The squadron would not operate again until the last night of the month, and in the meantime the main operation on the night of the 23/24th was a two-wave attack on the shipyards in Kiel involving 114 aircraft, including thirty-eight Hampdens from Swinderby and Coningsby and six Manchesters from 97 Squadron. The two waves were widely separated, and it was the second one that gained some success by hitting the Deutsche Werke U-Boot yards. Orders were received across the Command on the 24th to prepare for that night's operation against railway workshops and marshalling yards in Frankfurt-am-Main, which would involve a force of seventy aircraft. They ran into ten-tenths cloud at around 8,000 feet shortly after crossing the enemy coast, and this persisted all the way to the target, which was located by just a fraction of the crews taking part. The dismal failure of the operation was typical for the period, and the situation continued to heap frustration on C-in-C, Sir Richard Peirse.

Hamburg was posted as the target for 115 aircraft on the 26th, for which 5 Group contributed an unknown number of Hampdens and six Manchesters, briefing the crews of the former to aim for the Blohm & Voss shipyards and the latter the main railway station. Those reaching the target area found good bombing conditions under moonlight and delivered a sharp and effective attack. Following two nights on the ground because of continuing adverse weather conditions, 5 Group detailed forty Hampdens and five Manchesters on the 29th to target the aerodrome at Schiphol, situated to the south-west of Amsterdam. It became another operation beset by the most difficult conditions of ten-tenths thick cloud and rain, and only six crews would report locating and bombing the primary target. Earlier in the day, a new influx of airmen from 16 O.T.U. at Upper Heyford had included wireless operator, Sgt John Minchin, whose life would end eighteen months hence a few miles beyond the Möhne Dam.

The month ended with a return to the Blohm & Voss shipyards at Hamburg on the 31st, for which a force of 123 aircraft was assembled. 5 Group called upon the services of Syerston, Coningsby and Swinderby to prepare forty-two Hampdens and five Manchesters, while a further eighteen Hampdens and a single Manchester were assigned to gardening duties in northern waters in the Forget-me-not garden in Kiel Harbour and Nectarine II off the central Frisians. Despite its long lay-off, 49 Squadron briefed only the freshman crews of Sgt Downes and P/O Cook for mining duties in the Nectarine garden, for which they departed Scampton at 17.50. They encountered four-tenths broken cloud above 2,000 feet and pinpointed on Juist, before heading south to the drop zone to release their vegetables from 800 feet. Two large ships opened up at the Downes crew, and the rear gunner responded with a hundred rounds.

During the course of the month, the squadron took part in nine operations and dispatched seventy-six sorties without loss.

# November 1941

On the 1st, preparations were put in hand to send a force of 132 aircraft to attack the Deutsche Werke shipyard and harbour installations at Kiel, for which 5 Group detailed thirty-two Hampdens from Scampton, North Luffenham and Waddington. It was a busy night for the 83 Squadron side of Scampton, which was to support the main event with a dozen aircraft, while dispatching three others on gardening sorties in the Forget-me-not garden in Kiel Bay and two on a shipping patrol off the Frisians. 49 Squadron, in contrast, briefed just four crews, those of P/O Wood and Sgt Newmarch for the former and F/L de Mestre and S/L Drakes for the latter and sent them on their way between 19.48 and 19.52. The gardeners ran in below the eight-tenths cloud at 2,000 feet, and benefitting from bright moonlight filtering through the gaps, established a coastal pinpoint before delivering their mines into the briefed location from 700 and 800 feet. They seemed to enjoy the best of the conditions as the bombers found the Kiel area to be completely obscured and bombs were delivered by most on e.t.a. Conditions around the Frisians were even less accommodating and forced F/L de Mestre and crew to fly through driving rain that reduced the visibility to no more than 1,500 yards. They spotted a convoy and attacked the third vessel in line from 1,000 feet, narrowly missing with one bomb and overshooting with the others. Return fire from the vessels hit the Hampden and wounded the rear gunner, P/O Holmes, who would require a spell in station sick quarters. AE224 failed to return with the crew of S/L Drakes after falling victim to flak, and no trace of them was found.

The weather kept most aircraft on the ground on the 2$^{nd}$, and only minor operations were mounted on the 3$^{rd}$, among them an anti-shipping patrol by six Hampdens off the Frisians, for which Sgt Robinson and crew alone represented 49 Squadron. They took off at 17.51 and encountered low cloud and poor visibility in the target area but sighted a flak ship during a two-and-a-half-hour patrol and attacked it with 250 pounders and machine guns from 800 feet. The conditions prevented them from finding other targets and they brought their four 500 pounders home with them.

While the rest of the bomber force remained on the ground, a busy night awaited 5 Group on the 5$^{th}$, the programme of operations involving six Hampden "sneakers", five on anti-shipping sorties, twenty-four gardeners and twenty-two freshmen to bomb the docks at Cherbourg. 49 Squadron detailed ten aircraft for mining duties in the Forget-me-not garden in Kiel Bay and five for Cherbourg. There was a late departure for all, the mining element taking off between 00.23 and 00.54 with F/L Massey the senior pilot on duty and the bombing brigade between 03.48 and 04.01, each with a sergeant pilot at the controls. They arrived at their respective targets at around the same time, the bombers to find up to nine-tenths cloud below 6,000 feet with bright moonlight filtering through to provide good visibility. Most crews were able most to identify the aiming point and deliver an attack from the land side between 10,000 and 14,000 feet in the face of a spirited flak defence. Bursts were observed across the docks and a number of fires were reported. Meanwhile, some six hundred miles to the north-east, the gardeners encountered similar conditions, which enabled them to identify the Baltic coastline and follow it to the chosen pinpoint from which to conduct the timed run. The vegetables were delivered from between 500 and 800 feet, but only Sgt Davis and crew found a target for their wing bombs in the form of a flak position, which they attacked from 1,000 feet.

No doubt still frustrated by his inability to deliver a telling blow on Germany during the extended period of unfavourable weather, and almost certainly eager to rescue the besmirched reputation of the Command after the damning Butt Report, Peirse planned a major night of operations for the night of the 7/8$^{th}$. The original intention had been to send over two hundred aircraft to Berlin, but continuing doubts about the weather prompted the 5 Group A-O-C, AVM Slessor, to question the wisdom of going ahead with that plan, and he was allowed to withdraw his force and send it instead to Cologne. A third operation, involving fifty-three Wellingtons and two Stirlings from 1 and 3 Groups was also to take place with Mannheim as the target. 169 aircraft eventually took off for Berlin, while sixty-one Hampdens and fourteen Manchesters set off for the Rhineland capital. In addition to the above, other small-scale operations would raise the number of sorties to 392. At Scampton, 49 Squadron made ready sixteen Hampdens for the Rhineland capital city, a further two to attack the Knapsack power station to the south-west and a singleton for a freshman crew to employ against the docks and shipping at Ostend. P/O Jenkins and F/L de Mestre took off first at 19.07 and 19.08 respectively, immediately ahead of the main element, which was safely airborne by 19.47 with F/L Massey the senior pilot on duty. The final departure was that of the freshman crew of Sgt Hamer at 19.52 bound for Ostend, where they would search in vain for seventy-five minutes in an effort to locate the target through ten-tenths low cloud before bringing their bombs home.

On a night of all-round disappointment, neither of the Knapsack crews identified the power station and sought out alternatives. P/O Jenkins and crew jettisoned their load "live" over Cologne as icing threatened to destroy their lift, while F/L de Mestre and crew spotted moonlight glinting off railway lines at Aachen railway station and released their bombs from 3,000 feet after a power-dive, probably overshooting. Sgt Freeman and crew had turned back early because of an unserviceable a.s.i., leaving the others to encounter up to nine-tenths cloud at 6,000 to 11,000 feet over Cologne together with haze, which prevented them from identifying the briefed city-centre aiming point, the main railway station. Bombing took place on estimated positions or on last resort targets between the city and Dunkerque from 1,600 to 15,000 feet and this reflected the performance of the 5 Group force generally. Returning 5 Group crews claimed to have observed the flashes as their bombs hit home and evidence of many fires, but local reports mentioned just eight high-explosive bombs and sixty incendiaries falling into the city, causing minor housing and no industrial damage. The only positive from this was the absence of casualties from among the 5 Group participants on a night when a new record loss would be established.

Once every aircraft from the night's endeavours had landed, it became clear that a record thirty-seven were missing, more than twice the previous highest loss in a single night. An analysis revealed that fewer than half of the Berlin force had managed to reach their objective, and twenty-one had failed to return. The Mannheim contingent missed its target altogether and suffered the loss of seven Wellingtons in the process and this proved to be the final straw for the Air Ministry. Sir Richard Peirse was summoned to an uncomfortable meeting with Churchill at Chequers on the 8th to make his explanations and on the 13th, he would be ordered to restrict future operations while the future of the Command was considered at the highest level.

In the meantime, on the 8th, 5 Group detailed twenty Hampdens for an attack on the Krupp complex at Essen in company with thirty-four other aircraft, ten Hampdens and five Manchesters for freshman sorties over Dunkerque and six for searchlight suppression duties in support of the Essen force. 49 Squadron briefed the crew of Sgt Freeman for Essen and those of P/O Jacobs and W/O Saunders to patrol the Bocholt area and they took off between 17.14 and 17.26. P/O Jacobs and crew returned almost six hours later to report spending an hour attacking searchlights from between 8,000 and 12,500 feet and causing many to be extinguished. P1206 failed to return with the crew of W/O Saunders DFM, and it was learned eventually that the Hampden had been shot down by a night-fighter while outbound over the Ijsselmeer and there had been no survivors. Sgt

Freeman and crew encountered eight-tenths cloud and ground haze, which prevented them from attacking the primary target and they bombed a searchlight concentration in the Duisburg area from 14,000 feet.

Hamburg was posted as the main target on the 9th, the aiming point for which was the Blohm & Voss shipyards in the Finkenwerder district. A force of 103 aircraft was assembled, thirty Hampdens and six Manchesters provided by 5 Group, of which seventeen of the former belonged to 49 Squadron. They departed Scampton between 17.10 and 17.30 with F/Ls Massey and Ratcliff the senior pilots on duty and found Germany's Second City basking under clear skies and bright starlight but no moon. The wide River Elbe provided a strong pinpoint for many crews, who followed its course to the aiming point, while others, unaccountably, struggled to identify any landmarks and sought out alternative objectives as they headed back towards the west, many selecting Cuxhaven. Eight 49 Squadron crews attacked the shipyards and four the city from between 7,500 and a lofty 22,000 feet and those not blinded by searchlight glare observed bursts and fires. According to local sources, the operation achieved only modest success, and just three large fires had to be dealt with.

Adverse weather conditions kept the bulk of 5 Group on the ground for the ensuing two weeks, during which period, on the afternoon of the 11th, Sgt Bryant took off to ferry X3135 to Dunholme Lodge with two members of ground crew on board. The Hampden was observed to stall out of a steep lefthand turn and crash at 16.16 at Hackthorne Hall, exploding on impact with fatal consequences for the occupants. The group's only operational activity involved small numbers against Emden on the night of the 15/16th, and it was the 23rd before orders were received on all 5 Group stations to make ready fifty-one Hampdens and two Manchesters for an all-5 Group attack on the docks and U-Boots at Lorient, while 3 Group focused on Dunkerque. 49 Squadron made ready eighteen aircraft for a late afternoon take-off and sent them on their way between 16.14 and 16.46 with S/L Bennett the senior pilot on duty. The freshman crew of Sgt Bond turned back after losing their bearings at the French coast and failing to establish a pinpoint, and P/O Allsebrook and crew experienced a similar problem and ultimately ran out of time. Sgt Stewart and crew brought their bombs home after losing their W/T, while Sgt Freeman and crew blamed cloud for their inability to locate the target on a night when their squadron colleagues reported largely clear skies and excellent visibility. Most ran in on the aiming point from the Ile-de-Groix and carried out their attacks from between 5,000 and 12,000 feet without observing bursts, although several fires were reported at debriefing and there were no losses.

Another non-operational accident took the lives of Sgts Hough and Smith when AD759 crashed at 14.55 on the 25th during a training flight. The Hampden was seen to approach the village of Scamblesby, the home of Sgt Smith's family, so low that a wing hit the ground and caused it to crash on farmland on the edge of the village. Scampton and Coningsby provided twenty Hampdens between them for an operation to attack shipping and dockyard installations at Emden on the 26th, the day on which 50 Squadron moved from Swinderby to a new station at Skellingthorpe situated on the western outskirts of Lincoln. 49 Squadron detailed fourteen of its own and dispatched them between 16.53 and 17.16 with S/L Hodges the senior pilot on duty and all reached the target area, where ten-tenths cloud at around 4,000 feet completely obscured the ground, while the crews themselves basked in bright moonlight. Not one was able to establish a position over the docks area and nine crews attacked the estimated position of the town, while five others brought their bombs home.

Most 5 Group stations were alerted on the 27th to prepare for a raid that night on marshalling yards in Düsseldorf in company with elements of 3 Group in an overall force of eighty-six aircraft. Thirty-four Hampdens and six Manchesters were made ready, 83 Squadron representing Scampton, while 49 Squadron remained on the ground. The southern Ruhr was found to be largely cloud-free, although some crews would report up to eight-tenths of the white stuff, but the usual blanket of industrial haze created poor vertical visibility. Despite claims of large fires in the railway yards, local reports detailed only light damage, while nearby Cologne attracted plenty of attention and recorded damage to 119 houses.

50 Squadron was ready to go to war again by the last night of the month, when a major raid was planned for Hamburg. A force of 181 aircraft was assembled that included forty-eight Hampdens and four Manchesters, whose crews had been briefed to aim for the Blohm & Voss shipyards. Eighteen 49 Squadron aircraft departed Scampton between 16.20 and 16.39 with the newly promoted S/L de Mestre the senior pilot on duty and lost the services of P/O Jenkins to an overheating starboard engine during the North Sea crossing. The others made landfall to the north of Hamburg, but S/L de Mestre and crew were unable to establish a pinpoint, and ended up near the Baltic coast, where they dropped two sticks of incendiaries south of Flensburg. They planned to drop the bombs on Cuxhaven on the way home but failed to locate it and brought them home. The rest of the squadron participants experienced no difficulty in locating the target under clear skies and in good visibility provided by bright moonlight, and most attacked either the shipyards or the city from between 9,500 and 15,000 feet, while Wilhelmshaven and Cuxhaven provided alternatives. Local sources confirmed twenty-two fires but only two classed as large, and there was sufficient housing damage to deprive 2,500 people of their homes.

During the course of the month the squadron took part in ten operations and dispatched 109 sorties for the loss of four Hampdens, two crews and four other airmen, including two pilots.

# December 1941

The dominant theme during December would be the continuing presence at Brest of Scharnhorst, Gneisenau and, sometimes, Prinz Eugen, and no less than fifteen operations of varying sizes would be mounted against the port and its guests during the month, some by daylight. The weather kept the entire Command on the ground for the first six nights of the new month, and it was not until the 7th that a posted operation would actually go ahead. The target for a force of 130 aircraft was Aachen, Germany's most westerly city, perched on the frontiers with both Holland and Belgium. A second target on this night involved 3 Group Wellingtons and Stirlings against Brest, during which the Stirling element would conduct the first operational trials of the Oboe blind bombing device, a game-changing system not destined to enter service for almost thirteen months. The briefed aiming point at Aachen was the Nazi Party HQ, which had no special significance other than the fact that it was situated in the city centre, at a time when it was still not admitted publicly that population centres were being bombed. 5 Group detailed fifty Hampdens and a dozen

Manchesters, six of the former provided by 49 Squadron and dispatched from Scampton between 01.58 and 02.10 with S/L Hodges the senior pilot on duty. They flew out initially in fair weather conditions with isolated clouds, which built up to nine to ten-tenths cloud in the target area with tops at 15,000 feet. S/L Hodges and crew interpreted it as dense ground haze, upon which the bright moonlight reflected to create an equally impenetrable visual barrier. They were one of three crews to bring their bombs home, while the others attacked last resort targets, and it became clear at debriefings that barely half of the force had attacked the city. Local sources estimated a raid by sixteen aircraft, which caused minimal damage and no casualties.

Daylight operations were a matter of course for 2 Group squadrons, and some, known as "Circus", had the purpose of tempting enemy fighters into the air to face RAF Spitfires in a war of attrition. These were, however, very different from the unescorted daylight operations known as "moling", conducted by the other groups, which relied on cloud and surprise to protect the crews. It was utter madness to put crews' lives at risk for a very small potential gain, but 5 Group ordered six crews into the air on the 10th to target ports and aerodromes in Germany and Holland. The crews of the newly promoted F/O Jenkins and P/O Walker took off at 11.47 and 11.50 respectively, the former setting course for Aurich, located in north-western Germany in the area sandwiched between Dollart and Jade Bays. The ten-tenths cloud that concealed them from the enemy defences also obscured the target, and they flew further east to Wittmund, where they bombed railway sidings and observed hits on sheds on the south side of the station. They followed up with two thousand rounds, which were seen to strike trains, buildings and the station. P/O Walker and crew must have been nearby, as they attacked a railway line, a factory and a station in an unidentified town after failing to locate Wilhelmshaven.

It was similar fare for six 5 Group crews on each of the following three days, with S/L Hodges and P/O Robinson and their crews representing 49 Squadron on the 12th with orders to attack naval barracks at Bremerhaven and Cuxhaven. They departed Scampton at 10.16 and 10.18, but S/L Hodges ran out of cloud cover and brought his bombs home, leaving the Robinson crew to fulfil its brief. Having failed to identify the primary target, they attacked Cuxhaven aerodrome at 100 feet in the face of intense ground fire, which killed the second pilot/navigator, Sgt Black RNZAF, and knocked out the Hampden's hydraulics system. In return, they set two, maybe three aircraft on fire, blew up a hangar and strafed the town, before crash-landing AD979 safely at Bircham Newton. The only night operation involving 5 Group during this period took place at Cologne on the 11/12th, when the main railway station was the target for fourteen Hampdens.

On the 14th, Scampton, Syerston and Waddington made ready twenty-two Hampdens to attack Scharnhorst and Gneisenau at Brest on a night of extremely unfavourable weather conditions including ten-tenths ice-bearing cloud at between 1,500 and 3,500 feet over the sea, which persuaded most to turn back after reaching a position west of the Channel Islands. A dozen Hampdens targeted the docks at Ostend on the 15th, and fourteen belonging to 49 Squadron were made ready to represent 5 Group at Wilhelmshaven on the 16th, while five others joined a contingent from Coningsby take care of mining duties in the Jellyfish garden off Brest. All but one of the bombing element departed Scampton between 17.44 and 18.03 with S/L de Mestre the senior pilot on duty and they were followed into the air between 18.13 and 18.17 by the gardening quintet, before F/Sgt Donald and crew took off last at 18.22. F/O Jenkins and crew were led astray by a navigational error and ran out of time to reach Brest, while the others located the target area under clear skies but extreme darkness and established pinpoints on Camaret-sur-Mer and at Pointe-Saint-Mathieu on the southern and northern headlands respectively of the estuary. The vegetables were planted unopposed and mostly according to brief from 600 to 800 feet, while 650 miles to the north-east, crews closing on Wilhelmshaven were experiencing wildly varying cloud conditions and visibility ranging from good to poor. P/O Allsebrook reported eight-tenths cloud with tops in places at 16,000 feet, while P/O Alfry described a clear starlit night with no cloud, but whichever was more accurate, most crews were able to map read their way by coastal references and carried out their attacks on the town or on nearby alternatives from between 10,000 and 17,000 feet. Some bomb bursts were observed and a number of fires, but local sources reported only slight damage and no casualties.

Another major assault on Brest was notified across the Command on the 17th, for which a force of 121 aircraft was assembled, among them twenty-five Hampdens from Waddington, Scampton (83 Squadron) and Syerston. Eleven Manchesters took part in the next attempt on Brest, by daylight on the 18th, when claims were made of at least one hit on Gneisenau. On the 19th, 5 Group added a new squadron to its strength with the formation of 420 (Snowy Owl) Squadron RCAF at Waddington under the command of W/C Bradshaw. A dozen daylight intruder ("moling") sorties by Hampdens over north-western Germany on the 21st came to nothing, after sufficient cloud failed to materialise to protect them. 49 Squadron had dispatched six crews between 12.23 and 12.32 with S/L de Mestre and F/L Massey the senior pilots on duty, all with an individual target to attack at Wittmund, Aurich, Dornum, Jever, Basbeck and Bedekesa. They turned back from positions over the North Sea, and all had returned home with their bombs by 15.38.

The crews of P/O Alfry and Sgt Stewart took off at 16.00 and 16.07 on the 23rd to deliver twenty-four bundles of nickels (leaflets) each to the residents of Rennes in north-western France. Clear skies, moonlight and moderate visibility enabled them to establish their positions upwind of the city and drop their reading matter from 10,000 feet. There was an early start for six crews on Christmas Eve, after they had been briefed for another attempt to complete the "moling" sorties abandoned on the 21st. They departed Scampton between 06.27 and 06.35 with F/L Massey the senior pilot on duty and were recalled within three hours in the absence of sufficient cloud cover.

The third wartime Christmas passed peacefully, and operations resumed on the 27th, when 50 Squadron supported the epic and successful Vaagso raid by Royal Marines off the Norwegian coast on the 27th, before Düsseldorf was posted as the target for 132 aircraft later that night. 5 Group contributed thirty Hampdens and seven Manchesters, whose crews were briefed to aim for the main marshalling yards, in what turned out to be another ineffective attack on a Ruhr target, which caused little damage at a cost of seven aircraft and crews. The two main operations on the 28th involved eighty-six Wellingtons at Wilhelmshaven, while eighty-one Hampdens returned to the synthetic rubber factory at Marl-Hüls on the northern edge of the Ruhr. 49 Squadron made ready twenty Hampdens and dispatched them from Scampton between 17.27 and 17.47 with S/Ls Hodges and de Mestre and F/Ls Massey and Ratcliff the senior pilots on duty. All reached the target area to find clear skies, bright moonlight glinting off the snow-covered landscape and perfect visibility, which enabled navigators to map-read their way to the aiming point. Seventeen crews carried out an attack on the primary target from between 6,500 and 17,000 feet, observing bursts and fires, and Sgt Newmarch and crew even picked out black debris flying into the air and described a fire as the largest they had witnessed. Many crews watched their bombs fall on or close to the factory and returning crews were confident of a successful outcome, although no local report emerged to confirm or deny. At debriefing, Sgt Freeman and crew reported that they had been unable to identify the primary target and had bombed Essen from 14,000 feet and Sgt Downs and crew attacked Dortmund from 10,000 feet. Sgt Watt and crew failed to return in AE419, and no trace of the aircraft and crew was ever found.

During the course of the month, the squadron took part in nine operations and dispatched sixty-three sorties for the loss of one Hampden and its crew and one other crew member. It had been a disappointing year for the Command, and despite the best efforts of the crews, one of under-achievement, with little to show in terms of an advance on the performance of 1940. The new aircraft types, the Stirling, Halifax and Manchester, introduced into operational service early in the year, had each failed to meet the requirements expected of them and had undergone long periods of grounding while essential modifications were carried out. 1942 would bring changes, however, chief among which were the arrival on the operational scene of the war-winning Lancaster, and a new Commander-in-Chief, who would know how to exploit it.

*W/C R A B Learoyd VC*
*Flew 30 operations with 49 Squadron including the Dortmund Ems raid for which he was awarded the Victoria Cross.*

*Members of 49 Squadron congratulate John Hannah (83 Squadron) who was the youngest recipient of the VC for aerial operations and the youngest for the Second World War. Those identified are Sgt Walter Ellis (left); F/Sgt F.R. Hibbert shaking hands with John Hannah VC, and Sgt W.R. Rich on the extreme right. October 1940*

*12/13th August 1940. The original shot of the destruction of the Dortmund-Ems Canal for which F/L R A B Learoyd was awarded the VC.*

*Modern views of the Dortmund Ems canal which was attacked by F/L Learoyd*

*Present day parts of the Dortmund Ems Canal which had been attacked in 1940.*

*(Andreas Wachtel)*

*Bombing up F-Freddie P1333 with EA-D in background*

*Hampden L4039 crash*
*Displaying the pre-war codes of XU, L4039 (the 8th production Hampden) is seen being dismantled after overshooting at Scampton on a night training exercise 1st August 1939. F/L Lerwill escaped uninjured.*

*Propaganda picture taken at Scampton late May or early June 1940. F/L Joe Collier (83 Squadron) is briefing 49 and 83 personnel. P/O Donald Parker, (wearing a cap), is standing at the rear. Leaning on the table in front of him is F/Sgt W.C. Ollason (83). On his left is Sgt W.T. Hills (49) with cigarette. P/O Ken Cook (83) is on the extreme right.*

*Ball brothers - both victims of war.*
*Sgt Leslie Ball (left) KIA 20th November 1940 while serving with 49 Squadron and his brother F/O Peter Ball KIA 5th August 1942 while with 44 Squadron.*

*Sgt M G P Stretton PoW 16th August 1940*

*Sgt Patrick Duffy KIA 8th September 1941*

*F/O John Bufton. KIA 28th October 1940 in Hampden X3027 on a Hamburg raid.*

*After being shot down, F/O Bufton managed courageously to force land his doomed Hampden in the sea, within a mile of the Skegness coast.*

*Despite the proximity of the ditching to the foreshore (it is said that the men's call for help could be heard from Skegness seafront) the rescue services were unable to reach the crew in time and tragically all perished; the body of P/O Ballas-Anderson was never recovered.*
*Crew:*
*F/O J.R. Bufton (Pilot)*
*P/O K. Ballas-Anderson (Pilot)*
*Sgt F.J.W. Bichard (Wop/AG)*
*Sgt R.F. Robertson (Wop/AG)*

*F/O John R. Bufton*

*Sgt Dennis Imber KIA 16th October 1940 When he was shot down on a Bordeaux raid.*

*F/O Kenneth Michie KIA 7th December 1940.*

*Remains of Hampden L4129 in which Sgt Imber and his crew died. Crew: Sgt Dennis Sydney Imber, Sgt Robert.Rose (observer), Sgt Frank Corbett (Wop/AG), Sgt Kenneth Friend (AG, aged 19).*

S/L David McClure. With 49 Squadron 1939/40 flying 40 operations on Hampdens. Killed 12$^{th}$ March 1943 while with 83 Sqn.

F/L Basil Mitchell. Taken prisoner on 26$^{th}$ June 1940 when shot down during mine-laying in the Kiel area.

F/L Nellis Timmerman RCAF receives the DFC from King George VI at Scampton on 26$^{th}$ May 1940. He flew 23 operations with 49 Squadron.

*4/5th September 1940, Stettin - Oil Target*
*Of the five 49 Squadron Hampdens dispatched, F/O Hodges P1347 failed to return. They had been flying for nine hours and needed to land. After holding his aircraft steady whilst his crew escaped, the pilot then elected to crash land (there being insufficient height for his own safe escape) on what he thought was Cornwall. A successful crash landing was made, but the aircraft had come to rest in a field in Brittany! The crew became prisoners or war, but while in a camp at Toulouse in southern France, F/O Hodges and Sgt Wyatt managed to escape and returned to England via Gibraltar.*

*S/L Lewis M Hodges*

*Bob Hodges (left) returned to continue his tour with 49 Squadron in August 1941. Now as S/L, he is seen here on a wintry Scampton day with his new crew. Bob completed a two-part tour in March 1942 and later resumed operations in command of 161 Special Duty Squadron flying Halifaxes and landing Hudsons in occupied Europe to pick up SOE agents. He flew a third tour with 357 Squadron out of Jessore near Calcutta operating Liberators. He retired as Sir Lewis Hodges KCB, CBE, DSO and bar DFC and bar. Also in the crew - third left is F/Sgt Walter Ellis DFC and bar (W.Op) who set out on 50 operations with 49 Squadron during two tours. The other two crew members are thought to be second left, Sgt Bill Rushton and extreme right Sgt Maurice Ash (AG) who was killed in action on the Cologne 1,000 bomber raid 30/31st May 1942.*

*F/O Hodge's Hampden P1347 in the field near Pordic.* (Oliver Clutton-Brock)

*49 Squadron Hampden AE224*

*Armourers prepare to load Hampden P1333 EA-F of 49 Squadron with 250lb general purpose (GP) bombs, Scampton, 6th June 1940*

*Hampden X2900 S-EA*

*49 Squadron WAAFs 1940*

*G/C Laurence Deane DSO, DFC and American Silver Star.*

*S/L J W Gillan. Flew nine operations with 49 Squadron. KIA 29th August 1941*

*W/C Peter Ward-Hunt DFC & Bar*
*Flew 32 Hampden operations with 49 Squadron and a further 23 with 106.*

*F/L Wilfred Burnett DSO, DFC, AFC, OBE*
*Flew 35 Hampden operations while with 49 Squadron.*

*AVM Walter Sheen*
*14th OC of 49 Squadron when Wing Commander 1939/40*

*Hampden AD896 EA-M after an attack on Cologne 16/17th May 1941. Sgt Frank Lowe (Pilot), Sgt Alan Littler (MUG), P/O Anthony Wilson (Nav and 2nd Pilot), Sgt Howlock (Wop/AG).*

*S/L David Drakes and his 49 Squadron Hampden crew went missing on 1st November 1941. L-R: P/O W.H. Cheetham (AG), P/O V.D. Beaney, (Nav/BA), S/L David Drakes (Pilot); F/Sgt W.A. Watson (AG). N.B. Golden Hind nose art in honour of S/L Drakes.*

*S/L Drakes and his crews in his 'Golden Hind' Hampden AE224*

*W/O Christopher Saunders DFM
KIA 8th November 1941.*

*P/O Bernard Fournier
KIA 29th August 1941.*

*Sgt Harry Irving KIA 12th January 1941*

*P/O Joseph Unsworth
Flew 13 operations with 49 Squadron. Killed 14th October 1941 while with 207 Squadron.*

*A fine photograph of three 49 Squadron Hampdens (AE240, AE354 and AD980)*

*Sgt James Flint GM, DFM*

*Sgt Flint was awarded the George Medal for actions that occurred in a Hampden, on the night of 5/6th July 1941. He was also awarded an immediate DFM for his 'cool courage and determination to strike at the enemy' during the flight. Citation:*

*One night in July 1941, this airman was captain and pilot of an aircraft which was attacked by two enemy aircraft whilst over the sea about 50 miles from the English Coast. As a result of the damage sustained, Sgt Flint was later compelled to descend on the water 800 yards from the shore. The wireless operator and air gunner were able to leave the aircraft but there was no sign of the navigator. Sgt Flint was unable to open the Astro hatch so he lowered the back of the pilot's seat, crawled through the aperture, and found the navigator, who had been badly wounded, helpless behind a spar where he had fallen. The aircraft was fast sinking, but Sgt Flint managed to drag the navigator out through the pilot's hatch. The dinghy had been punctured and, being only partially inflated, sunk at once with the aircraft. The air gunner, though wounded, swam towards the shore and Sgt Flint, at first assisted by the wireless operator until his wounds prevented him from continuing, supported the helpless navigator until they were within 50 yards of the shore where a soldier who had come out to render assistance relieved him. Sgt Flint then swam to the shore where, after seeing both the wireless operator and navigator safe and finding no sign of the air gunner, he asked for boats to be sent out to search for the missing man, at the same time giving clear instructions where to look for him. He would not leave the beach until he had seen that boats were searching for the air gunner who, it was subsequently found, must have succumbed to his wounds shortly after striking out for the shore. Sgt Flint then walked for over a mile to a waiting ambulance and was taken to hospital. This airman displayed great gallantry and disregard for personal safety in his efforts to save the helpless navigator who, unfortunately, has since died of his wounds.*

*Rear gunner in a Hampden*
Possibly John Kehoe, Wop/AG in 49 Squadron 8$^{th}$ November 1941 on an Essen operation. Killed with the other members of the crew. W/O C.A. Saunders DFM (Pilot), Sgt J.M. D'Arcy (Nav), Sgt J.E. Kehoe (Wop/AG), Sgt S.G. Mullenger (Wop/AG).

*Wireless Operator/Gunner Position in a Hampden.*
Possibly Stanley Mullenger killed with John Kehoe 8$^{th}$ November 1941.

*Navigator/bomb aimer's position in a Hampden*
*Possibly Sgt J.M. D'Arcy (Nav) killed 8$^{th}$ November 1941 in W/O Saunders' crew.*

*Hampden Navigator/Observer's position. Possibly Sgt D'Arcy.*

*Hampden Cockpit*

*Hampden Interior*

*The wing of Hampden AE126 being recovered from the Waddenzee. P/O Fournier's Hampden*

*De-briefing at Scampton 1941*

*Groundcrew of Hampden AE238 EA-P Scampton 1941 with nose art Popeye I*

S/L Kenneth Letford DSO, DFC, MiD flew seventeen Hampden operations as Second Pilot and thirteen operations as Pilot with 49 Squadron.

He went on to complete an amazing four tours of operations.

Awarded the DSO and DFC with 49 Squadron and DSO, DFC and Bar with 207 Squadron, and was also MID.

*S/L Kenneth Letford DSO, DFC, MiD*

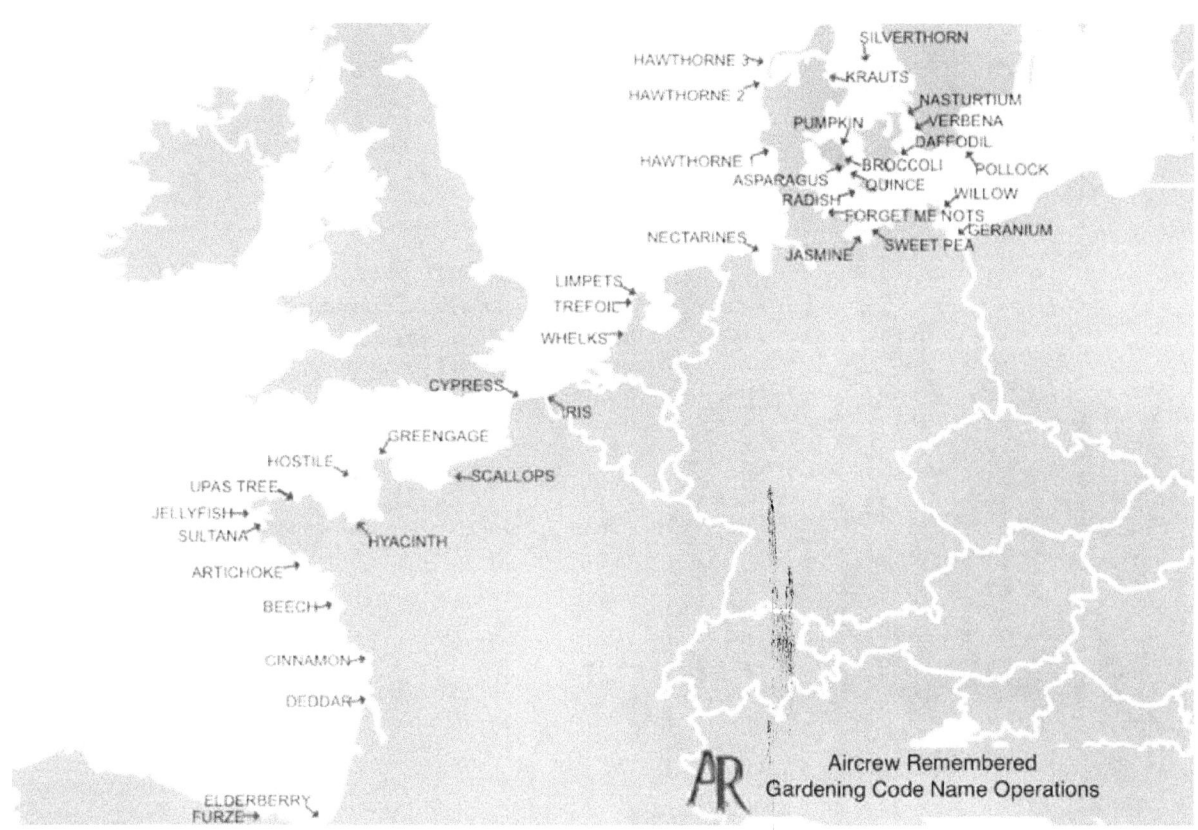

*'Gardening' Areas in Northern Europe (courtesy of Aircrew Remembered)*

*Sgt A C Watt from Rhodesia KIA on the 28th December 1941 on a Hüls raid.*

*Ken Bush, Terry Freeman and "Tubby" Gaunt with Hampden AE132.*

*G/C J N H Whitworth DSO, DFC, OC RAF Scampton OC RAF Scampton March 1942 – June 1943. Known as 'Charles', he spent his operational career in 4 Group and briefly commanded 78 and 35 Squadrons. In this photograph he is seen wearing the ribbon of the Czech MC..*

*G/C J N H Whitworth*

*F/L Keith Astbury DFC with G/C Leonard Cheshire VC, OM, DSO & Two Bars, DFC. 'Aspro' the well-known Australian bomb aimer joined 49 Squadron as a Sgt in April 1942.*

*W/C Leonard Slee DSO, DFC and Bar*
*With 49 Squadron from May 1942 to April 1943. He flew 26 operations with 49 Squadron and was the 18th CO. Below: W/C Slee (3rd from right) and crew*

*P/O Philip Floyd sacrificed his own chance of escaping from burning Manchester L7290 EA-K over Mulheim Oberhausen during Operation Millenium on Cologne on the 31st May 1942, to enable his crew to bale out. The crew, with the exception of one gunner Sgt J Smth who also remained in the aircraft, were captured.*

*P/O Philip Floyd*

F/L Dorian Bonnett KIA 24th October 1942.   P/O Stanley Way (Wop/AG) KIA 12th February 1942

*The Bonnett Crew*
Lancaster W4306 crashed 400 yards from Ford Airfield Sussex after a nine hour operation to Milan killing all but two of the crew on the 24th October 1942. One further died from his injuries. Back L-R: Sgt E Brookes (RG) (survived crash but died shortly after), Sgt W Myers DFM (BA); Sgt R Lawrence RAAF (W.Op), F/L D.Bonnett DFC (Pilot); Sgt R Wallis (FE); Sgt W Colquhoun (MUG) (survived), Sgt R Dangerfield DFM RAAF (Nav/Obs).

*Sgt R Gould*
*Flew 19 operations with 49 Squadron.*

*F/Sgt D C Pollitt*
*All crew of Hampden AE132 lost without trace 12th February 1942 on Fuller Operation.*

*The RAF pilots who stopped Hitler's broadcast on November 8th 1942. Hitler was stated to be speaking in the beer hall when our bombers attacked Munich.*

*His Majesty King George VI talks with G/C J.H.N. Whitworth, the Station Commander. L-R: W/C Slee, P/O C.K.Astbury, F/O A.S. Grant (hidden), F/L Bain, G/C Whitworth, AVM A. Coryton AOC 5 Group during a visit to Scampton 12th November 1942.*

*The Allsebrook Crew while serving with 49 Squadron
F/O Grant, F/Sgt Lulham, F/L Allsebrook, P/O Botting, F/Sgt Hitchen, Sgt Jones, F/ Sgt Moore*

*Completed two tours with 49 Squadron, surviving a ditching in Hampden AE397 on 14th February 1942 and managed a few trips while he was 'resting' on 25 OTU between tours. The son of a judge, he was killed in action in September 1943 leading 617 Squadron in an attack on the Dortmund-Ems canal.*

*F/L Ralph Allsebrook DSO DFC*

*F/L Edward Tickler and crew*
L-R: Sgt Jack Matthews RCAF (Nav), F/Sgt George Silvester (RG)(KIA 1943), F/Sgt Art Davies (MUG)(KIA 1943), Sgt Maurice Webb (W.Op), Sgt Dennis Downing (FE)(KIA 1943), F/L Ed Tickler (Pilot), F/Sgt Ted Lowans (BA). All with 49 Squadron 1943. Photo 26th December 1942.

*S/L Peter De Mestre KIA 7th June 1942 on an Emden operation in Manchester L7469. Lost with all crew. Four were buried in France but S/L De Mestre, P/O Thorndyke and Sgt Jones are commemorated on the Runnymede Memorial. Sgt Alfred Buttel was 2nd Pilot.*

*Crew: S/L P.M. De Mestre DSO DFC Pilot*
*Sgt A.F. Buttel RAAF 2nd Pilot*
*P/O R.H.J. Thorndyke A/OB*
*F/S M.E. Whitehill RAAF AG*
*Sgt G.C. Whitfield Wop/AG*
*Sgt L.J. Jones Wop/AG*
*Sgt D.S. Halliday Wop/AG*

*Funeral of Sgt Alfred Buttel RAAF of S/L De Mestre's crew. KIA 7th June 1942 during Emden raid. Manchester L7469 was intercepted by a night-fighter and shot down. The aircraft crashed into the North Sea with the loss of all seven crew, three of whom have no known grave. Sgt Buttel was 2nd pilot. His body was recovered from the sea on 22nd June 1942 by a German patrol boat and buried together with an unknown member of the RAF, in the Lutheran Cemetery with full military honours. The funeral was attended by a Guard of Honour from the Luftwaffe, headed by an officer, a German Naval Band, and the wreath bearers.*

*Triple fin Manchester L7389 EA-L of 49 Squadron above Scampton June 1942. The aircraft sequentially served 61, 207 and 83, 49 and 106 Squadrons.*

*Damage to the underside of the starboaard wing of Manchester L7287 after F/Sgt Freeman and crew were in collision over Grantham with another aircraft on the 19/20th May 1942. Both landed at Scampton after being airborne for about 40 minutes*

*Two 49 Squadron Manchesters and Lancasters of 83 Squadron prior to take off from Scampton's grass, bound for Bremen.*

*New-looking Manchester R5771 in final colour scheme. The EN5 front turret is fully skewed to the left.*

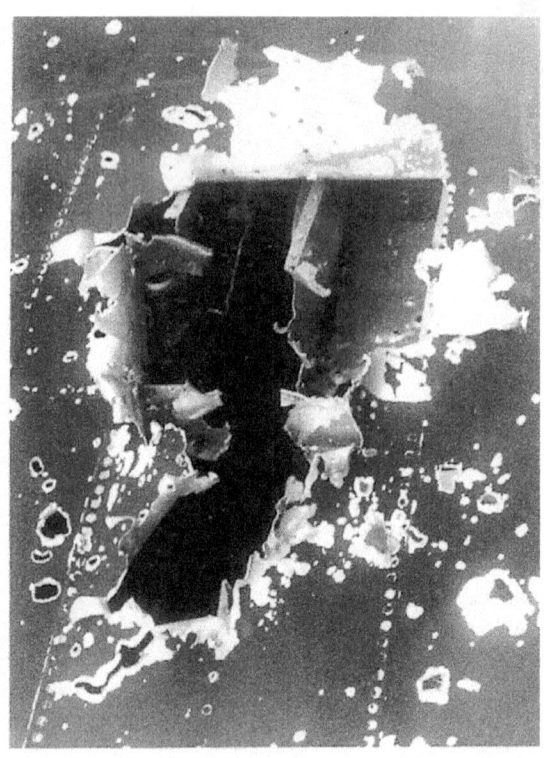

*Damage to Manchester L7453 prior to joining 49 Squadron.*

*The Webster Crew*
*Flew 32 operations with 49 Squadron 1942/43 and more in 1945 with 44 Squadron.*

*P/O Thomas Tomlin KIA 18$^{th}$ August 1943*

*Pilot Sgt James Thom lost without trace on a 6$^{th}$ March 1943 Essen operation together with all his crew.*

*Armourers loading a 0.303 ammunition belt into the rear turret of Mk1A Manchester L7526 of 49 Squadron at Scampton. It was the last Avro-built Manchester.*

*S/L Eric Couch DFC MBE*
*OC 'B' Flight and flew 26 operations with 49 Squadron. June 1942 - April 1943.*

```
        49                    Operation Robinson (Le Creusot)
     61    9           17th October 1942. A force of 88 Lancasters led by 49 Squadron on the way
      44    50         to attack the Schneider Factory in a low-level daylight operation. Photo
   97 106 57 207       taken from ZN-Y flown by W/C Guy Gibson of 106 Squadron.
The formation approach.
```

*Lancaster R5751 EA-E. 'A' Flight Lancasters at dispersal July 1942. The first all Lancaster operation by the Squadron was against Dusseldorf. The turrets are protected against an English summer.*

*The Stanton Crew*
*L to R: Sgt J Spiers, Sgt GA Bicknell, P/O Bale, F/Sgt David Stanton, Sgt E Howell*
*F/Sgt David Stanton, Sgts Joesph Spiers and Edward Howell were killed on the 23rd September 1943 while on a Mannheim raid. P/O Bale was not flying with F/Sgt Stanton on that operation.*

*The Robinson Crew*
*Sgt Robinson and crew were shot down after bombing Peenemünde on the 17/18th August 1943. Back L-R: Sgt D Parkin (KIA), Sgt Charles Robinson (PoW), F/Sgt J Wallner RCAF (KIA), F/O P. Duckham (PoW), F/O J Lowe (PoW), Sgt W Boyd (PoW).*

F/L Charles Dunnet
Lancaster ED497 shot down, killing him and all his crew on the 17th June 1943, during a Cologne raid. Crew: Sgt R.F. Middlebrook, Sgt R.G. Smith, Sgt M.Haley, P/O C.A. Edwards, Sgt W.A. Dutton Sgt R.M.W.Selby-Lowndes.

Sgt George Cole
Lancaster ED432 hit by flak and crashed in Holland while on an Oberhausen raid 15th June 1943. Crew: Sgt G Cole KIA, Sgts J P Harper KIA, C Barnett KIA, J Arnold (PoW) J Bryan (PoW), J Deacon, H Rhodes KIA, H Biggin KIA.

De-briefing at Fiskerton 14th February 1943 after a Lorient raid. F/O Eyre and crew tell their story. L-R: Sgt H.W. Mills, unknown, Sgt, Major John Mullock MC, Intelligence Officer; AVM Coryton, F/O J.N. Caty, F/O Eyre, G/C Charles Whitworth, unknown officer.

*Lancaster ED702 EA-D. W/C Slee's aircraft,. FTR Mannheim 23/24th September 1943 with Dams Raid survivors P/O C Anderson and crew.*

*Sgt C Kendrew KIA 4th September 1943*

*Sgt A Purrington KIA 18th August 1943*

*The Brunt crew at de-briefing with S/O Duncalfe.*
W/O R Brunt and crew of Lancaster JB362 EA-D of 49 Squadron on their return to Fiskerton, from a bombing raid on Berlin. On their next sortie to Berlin five days later, Brunt and his crew were shot down and killed.

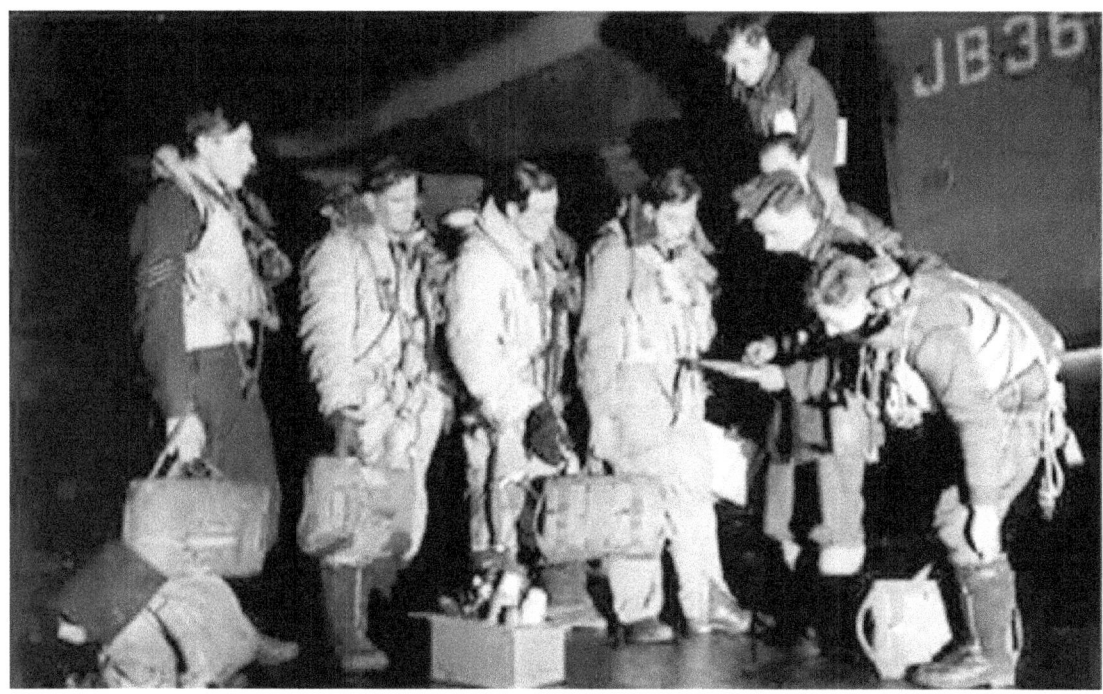

*W/O Ronald Brunt with crew*
Six of the crew were lost on the 26th November 1943 when their Lancaster JB362 crashed on a Berlin raid. The crew comprised W/O R Brunt, Sgt F Ashman, Sgt Harold Bronsky, Sgt R Norley, Sgt E Wilson and Sgt R O'Shea. Sgt Burrows became a PoW.

*F/O Gerald Fawke DSO, DFC and Crew*
L-R: F/Sgt Paul Fortin (WOP), Sgt R.G. Cole (FE), P/O Tom Bennett DFM (Nav), F/O G Fawke DFC, Sgt Erwin Osler DFM (BA), Sgt D. Bratt (MUG), Sgt L. Walters (RG). Flew 33 operations with 49 Squadron.

*An illustrious company*
Back L-R: W/C G.P. Gibson VC, DSO, DFC 617 Squadron, W/C P.C. Hopcroft DFC 57 Squadron, W/C P.W. Johnson AFC 49 Squadron, W/C J.D. Nettleton VC 44 Squadron.
Front L-R: G/C G.J. Grindell DFC, OC Fiskerton, G/C J.H.N. Whitworth DSO, DFC, OC Scampton and 52 Base and G/C L.C. Slee DSO, DFC OC Dunholme Lodge.

*P/O Cyril Thorpe Anderson*
Crew above are: Sgt Robert Paterson, Sgt Jimmy Green, Sgt Doug Bickle, Sgt Arthur Buck, P/O Cyril Anderson and Sgt John Nugent.

*P/O Anderson joined 49 Squadron on 23rd February 1943 and flew seven operations. He and his crew were then posted to the newly-formed 617 Squadron in readiness for the famous Operation Chastise. On the Dams raid, his Lancaster suffered many problems, forcing Sgt Anderson to return to Scampton, still carrying his Upkeep. W/C Gibson berated him and immediately dismissed him back to 49 Squadron. Here he carried out a further sixteen operations until the 23rd September 1943 when he and all his crew were lost on a Mannheim operation.*

*Left Top: P/O C Anderson*
*Below: Sgt Eric Ewan*

*March 1943, Fiskerton. Lancaster ED469. Crew and two passengers.*
*L-R: Sgt White- (BA), Sgt. W Beesley (FE), P/O F.C Ball (Wop/AG), Sgt. H Frost (RG), F/O Deloford (Nav), Sgt.A M MacDiarmid (MUG) S/L Douglas Cracknell -Pilot. The passengers were 8th & 9th from left - Intelligence.Officer and the Bombing Leader. This Lancaster was lost the same month but with a different crew. Note: Sgt Frost was KIA later on his tour with a different crew.*

*F/O Gordon Jeffreys and crew flew 27 operations with 49 Squadron in Hampdens and Manchesters.*

*Shot down by a night-fighter on the 17th January 1943 on a Berlin operation.*

*Crew of Lancaster ED444:*
*F/O G.S. Jeffreys Pilot (Killed)*
*Sgt R.S. Fermor FE (PoW)*
*F/O D.J. Robertson Nav (PoW),*
*F/S N.E. Mortimer W/Op (PoW)*
*Sgt H. Cowan AG (Killed)*
*F/O C.A. Watts BA (Killed)*
*Sgt J.E. Harrison AG (PoW)*

*F/O Gordon Jeffreys*

*F/O Alexander Bone, pilot of Lancaster ED427 lost with all crew on a Pizen raid 17th April 1943. F/O A.V. Bone (Pilot), Sgt R.N.P. Foster (FE), Sgt C.W. Yelland (Nav), Sgt R.C. White (Wop/AG) Sgt R. Cope (AG), Sgt R.J. Rooney (BA), P/O B. Watt RCAF (AG).*

*F/Sgt Bede King, RAAF, KIA 16th December 1943 on a Berlin raid. P/O G L Ratcliffe (Pilot), Sgt A E Marsland (FE), Sgt E Holloway (Nav), Sgt W T Rees (Wop/AG), F/Sgt R Losa RCAF (AG), Sgt W R Day (BA), F/Sgt B J V King RAAF (AG).*

*F/Sgt Gordon Cooper (Wop/AG), a veteran of 24 operations, poses for an official photograph with parachute packer LACW Radford. Fiskerton. December 1943.*

# January 1942

As far as most crews were concerned, the incoming year would look and feel exactly like the outgoing one, and still under the restrictions of the November directive, the Command's activities reflected the continuing obsession with the German raiders at Brest, against which a further eleven operations would take place during January. 5 Group would be without 44 (Rhodesia) Squadron until early March as it worked towards operational status on the Lancaster. 49 Squadron began 1942 with a strength of thirty-five officers and 630 airmen, with twenty-six Hampdens IE, and was detailed to contribute to 5 Group's first operational activity of the year. This involved four Hampdens each from 49, 106 and 144 Squadrons conducting daylight "moling" duties over Holland and north-western Germany. The 49 Squadron crews of Sgts Freeman and Hamer and P/Os Rawstorne and Allsebrook were assigned respectively to Luftwaffe aerodromes at Gilze-Rijen, Leeuwarden, Eindhoven and Soesterberg in Holland and departed Scampton between 11.36 and 12.14, only for three of them to turn back short of the enemy coast after finding insufficient cloud cover. Sgt Hamer and crew had the most northerly target, the infamous "Wespennest" or Wasps' Nest at Leeuwarden, which was home to some of the Luftwaffe's most skilled night-fighter pilots, and map-read their way before attacking from 50 feet and observing their bombs fall towards the runways.

5 Group detailed a dozen Manchesters for a raid that night on St-Nazaire, and thirty-six Hampdens for gardening duties off the Biscay ports and the Frisian Islands. 49 Squadron dispatched the freshman crew of P/O McGuffie at 16.46 bound for one of the Nectarine gardens, and they returned four-and-a-half-hours later with their mine still on board after searching in vain for thirty minutes in cloudy conditions that prevented them from establishing whether they were over sea or land. Another freshman crew, that of Sgt Burton, had taken off at 17.00 to deliver nickels to the Rennes area of north-western France, and they, too, were thwarted by cloud and brought their reading matter home to a landing at Exeter. Small-scale mining operations occupied elements of the group on the 3rd, and daylight "moling" operations on the 4th required a contribution of six Hampdens from 49 Squadron. The first departure from Scampton on that day, however, was by an unidentified crew, which took off at 07.00 on a meteorological flight that lasted five hours and was presumably to report on cloud conditions for the "moles". The targets were again in north-western Germany at Beverstedt, Dornum, Basbeck, Bederkesa, Bremervörde and Harsefeld, for which they took off between 10.14 and 10.22 with F/O Jenkins the senior pilot on duty. The cloud proved to be both a blessing and a curse as they emerged from it unsure of their bearings and searched for anything that resembled a worthwhile target. P/O Alfry and crew broke cloud on e.t.a. near the Elbe estuary and circled for fifteen minutes until a flak shell hit the mainplane and damaged an aileron, upon which the bombs were dumped "live". The others attacked unidentified built-up areas from between 50 and 500 feet, F/O Jenkins observing hits on two factories and a train between Bremerhaven and Cuxhaven, while the gunners expended all six thousand rounds of ammunition. P/Os Rawstorne and Jones returned with flak-damaged Hampdens, the latter also with a wounded gunner.

Twenty-seven Hampdens and twelve Manchesters took off on the evening of the 5th as part of a force of 154 aircraft targeting the Scharnhorst and Gneisenau at Brest and the naval docks area. It was well into the 6th before the first of two 49 Squadron elements took to the air between 02.23

and 02.38 with S/L Hodges the senior pilot on duty among five crews bound for the Gorse garden in Quiberon Bay off the Biscay coast. As AE372 lifted off last in the hands of Sgt Burton, the port engine cut, and the Hampden struggled into the air while the pilot fought to maintain control. According to the ORB, the Hampden was force-landed on the aerodrome at 02.55, suggesting that it had completed a circuit. The crew emerged unscathed, and the Hampden would fly again. The gardeners were followed into the air between 02.45 and 03.20 by the ten-strong bombing brigade, which lost the services of Sgt Bond and crew to an oxygen supply failure and an unreliable port engine. Many of the others were thwarted by an effective smoke screen and eight to ten-tenths cloud at around 10,000 feet, and three of the 49 Squadron crews returned with their bomb load intact. Flares dropped by other aircraft enabled P/O McGuffie and crew to identify the target, which they attacked from a lowly 2,500 feet, observing five or six bursts. The crews of Sgt Freeman and Stewart and P/O Andrews identified ground features and bombed the primary target from between 10,000 and 14,000 feet in the face of heavy flak, while the others attacked the vicinity of the docks area. Despite claims of large fires by some returning crews, no accurate assessment of results could be made.

The 6th began with the tragic crash of AD896 as it returned to Scampton following a night training sortie. Passing over the village of South Carlton, some four miles north-north-west of Lincoln, the port engine cut and caused a stall, which Sgt West was unable to recover, and the Hampden crashed at 07.00 in Middle Street, killing both occupants. That night, nineteen Hampdens were committed to roving commission sorties against targets of opportunity at specific locations in northern Germany, which were referred to in the 5 Group ORB as "Scuttle A" and appear to differ from "moling" only by relying on the cover of darkness rather than cloud. AM Sir Richard Peirse left his post as C-in-C Bomber Command on the 8th to be succeeded temporarily by AVM Baldwin, the A-O-C 3 Group. In February, Peirse would take up a new appointment as C-in-C Allied Air Forces in India and South-East Asia, but the sense that he had been "sacked" from Bomber Command would linger, and perhaps unjustly tarnish his legacy. Brest was posted as the target for a force of 151 aircraft that night, reconnaissance having revealed that Scharnhorst and Gneisenau had been joined by Prinz Eugen. 5 Group contributed thirty-seven Hampdens and ten Manchesters to the main event and six Hampdens and seven Manchesters for freshman crews briefed to target the docks and shipping at Cherbourg. 49 Squadron contributed a single unnamed crew to the latter, who departed Scampton at 04.12 in bright moonlight and reached the target area to find ten-tenths cloud that persuaded them to bring the bombs home.

A force of eighty-two aircraft was assembled for a return to Brest on the following night, for which 5 Group put up twenty-seven Hampdens and six Manchesters, 49 Squadron contributing nine of the former and five for mining duties in the Jellyfish garden on the approaches to the port. The bombing element departed Scampton between 23.51 and 00.20 with S/L de Mestre and F/L Massey the senior pilots on duty and was followed immediately into the air by the gardeners, among which F/L Ratcliffe was the senior pilot. The weather in the target area continued to be unhelpful with eight to ten-tenths cloud and poor visibility, and eight 49 Squadron crews brought their bombs home, while F/L Massey bombed a flak concentration in the target area from 8,000 feet. Meanwhile, over the sea a few miles to the west, bright moonlight filtered through four to six-tenths cloud, which enable the gardeners to establish a variety of pinpoints on Ushant Island, Pointe-Saint-Mathieu and St-Matlier to the north of the estuary and Pointe-de-Toulinguet and Camaret-sur-Mer to the south. Sgt Newmarch and crew attempted four timed runs before giving up and jettisoning their mine "safe", while the crews of F/L Ratcliffe, P/O Rawstorne and P/O Donald successfully delivered theirs into the briefed locations from between 500 and 700 feet. This left P/O Jacobs and crew unaccounted for in AD909, and it must be assumed that they found a final resting place on the bed of the Atlantic or English Channel.

Thirty-four Hampdens and nine Manchesters were detailed by 5 Group on the 10$^{th}$ to contribute to an overall force of 124 aircraft bound for Wilhelmshaven that night to attack the main railway station. 49 Squadron was not called into action, while the five Hampdens departing Scampton would be the last to operate with 83 Squadron, which was in the process of converting to the Manchester. Two crews close to the end of their tours would be posted across the tarmac to 49 Squadron on the 12$^{th}$. The Wilhelmshaven operation was another inconclusive affair, during which bombing took place through cloud and the outcome could not be determined.

Adverse weather conditions kept 5 Group on the ground for the next three nights, and when the faithful were called to prayer on the 14$^{th}$, it was to reveal Hamburg as the destination for an overall force of ninety-five aircraft. The targets were the Blohm & Voss shipyards situated on the Kuhwerder Island opposite the Sankt Pauli district to the west of the city centre and the nearby Hamburger Flugzeugbau airframe factory located on Finkenwerder Island. 5 Group was to have supported the operation with thirty-five Hampdens and fifteen Manchesters, but four of the former from 61 Squadron could not be made ready in time and three from 49 Squadron were cancelled after one crashed on take-off and prevented the other two from getting away. No mention of the aircraft and crew was recorded in the ORB, and we can assume that no casualties occurred and the Hampden was repaired. The incident left six aircraft to take off for the main event, along with five for mining duties, three in the Jasmine and two in the Forget-me-not gardens off Warnemünde and in Kiel Fjord respectively and two Freshman crews to attack the docks and shipping at Emden. They departed Scampton together between 16.44 and 17.35 with S/L Bennett and F/L Massey the senior pilots respectively among the bombing and gardening elements. The bombing element was reduced by two when Sgt Bond and crew were forced by severe icing conditions over the North Sea to dump their bombs in order to maintain height, while it was a misfiring engine at the German coast that persuaded Sgt Hamer and crew to jettison their bombs in the sea off Cuxhaven. Those reaching the target were challenged by extreme darkness and thick ground haze, which created challenging conditions for aiming point identification. That said, crews could always rely on the searchlight and flak batteries to guide them into the heart of the city, where large ground features like the Binnen and Aussen-Alster Lakes on the north-western edge of the centre were a good guide for non-precision bombing. P/O McGuffie and crew were unable to locate the aiming point through the haze, despite deploying flares, and their bomb load also ended up on the seabed. S/L Bennett and crew aimed at the primary target from 14,000 feet, but saw their bombs fall short and into the general built-up area and P/O Robinson and crew also hit the town, while P/O Rawstorne and crew attacked what they believed was Cuxhaven. It became clear at debriefings that only half of the force had attacked the Hamburg area and local sources confirmed seven large fires and hits on the Altona railway station but no significant damage.

Of the gardeners, only P/O Allsebrook and crew successfully planted their vegetable from 700 feet after finding good visibility below the 1,000-foot cloud base and identifying Rostock and the mouth of the Warnow river. F/L Massey and crew dropped their store from 500 feet into an alternative location off Kiel Fjord after being thwarted by cloud and extreme darkness and the others brought their mines home. Sgt Hill and crew attacked Emden docks from 13,000 feet after identifying numerous landmarks, and P/O Harvey and crew bombed the town through thick ground haze from 12,000 feet.

Hamburg was "on" again twenty-four hours later, for which a force of ninety-six aircraft was assembled with a 5 Group contribution of twenty-seven Hampdens and ten Manchesters. The crews had been briefed to attack the city centre, and again, only a little over a half returned to report bombing in conditions of poor visibility. The raid proved to be another in the long line of disappointments since the start of the autumn and, according to local sources, the emergency services dealt with thirty-six fires, only three of them classed as large, and there had been no major incidents. Having been selected as the third Lancaster unit, 207 Squadron set up a Conversion Flight on the 16th in preparation for the arrival of its first example of the type. The flight would be equipped, initially, with two Manchesters, the type it had introduced into squadron service and had struggled with for more than a year. Once the first Lancaster arrived on the 25th, the conversion programme would begin with selected second pilots and crews from the squadron.

Attention remained on north-western Germany on the 17th, when Bremen was posted as the target for eighty-three aircraft, including twenty Hampdens and six Manchesters. 49 Squadron made ready a dozen Hampdens for the main event, five for mining duties in the Rosemary garden in the Heligoland Bight and one for a freshman crew to take to Emden. They departed Scampton together between 16.46 and 17.42 with W/C Stubbs and S/L de Mestre the senior pilots on duty, the former making a rare appearance on the order of battle. On a night of poor serviceability for the squadron, the freshman crew of Sgt Williams lost their artificial horizon early on and turned back and the crews of Sgts Freeman, Hill and Hamer all experienced engine issues and abandoned their attempts to reach Bremen. Sgt Bond and crew were defeated by ice accretion that threatened to rob them of lift and S/L de Mestre and crew were attacked by a night-fighter off the Frisians and dumped their bombs as they took violent evasive action. This reduced the Bremen-bound element to seven aircraft, which found the city concealed beneath ten-tenths cloud at around 4,000 feet and the crews of P/Os McGuffie and Rawstorne dropped only their 250 pounders on flak concentrations. F/L Massey attacked a searchlight concentration from 11,000 feet, W/C Stubbs jettisoned his load after failing to locate the target and P/O Allsebrook bombed flak at Wilhelmshaven. Only P/O Donald and crew attacked the primary target after pinpointing on Borkum and following the River Weser into the city at 12,000 feet. They were among only eight returning crews claiming to have attacked the primary target, while Hamburg attracted others and reported eleven fires. The gardeners fared no better, three of them returning with their mines after ten-tenths low cloud and haze prevented them from establishing a pinpoint, leaving the crews of P/O Harvey and Sgt Rogers to find alternative locations off the Frisian Islands of Schiermonnikoog and Wangerooge.

Emden had been a regular destination for small forces since the 10th, sometimes with a contribution from 5 Group, and five 49 Squadron Hampdens were detailed to join twenty Wellingtons to attack it on the 20th, after snow and severe frost had kept aircraft on the ground for two nights. They departed Scampton between 17.05 and 17.15 with the newly promoted F/O Harvey the senior pilot on duty and lost Sgt Hamer and crew almost immediately after their heating system failed. The same issue curtailed the sortie of Sgt Rogers and crew sometime later as they climbed over the North Sea and recorded a temperature of minus 16 degrees. The others reached the target, where the crews of P/Os Donald and Jones attacked the docks from 11,500 and 12,000 feet respectively after identifying ground features, but neither crew was confident that their bombs had found the mark. F/O Harvey and crew failed to return after being intercepted homebound by the night-fighter of Ofw Paul Gildner of II./NJG2, which sent AT148 crashing to the ground some three miles northeast of Groningen in Holland at 20.58 without survivors.

Bremen and Emden shared the Command's attention on the night of the 21/22$^{nd}$, when eleven Hampdens joined in a raid by fifty aircraft on the former, while twelve Hampdens and three Manchesters plied their trade at the latter in an overall force of thirty-eight aircraft. The crew of Sgt Williams took off at 17.07 to represent 49 Squadron at Emden but returned after two hours because of an intercom issue. The garrison town of Münster was posted as the destination for forty-seven aircraft on the 22$^{nd}$, for what would be the first attack on a target in inland Germany since late December. 5 Group detailed twenty-two Hampdens and five Manchesters in an overall force of forty-seven aircraft, which found the many canals and rivers in this region of Germany, north of the Ruhr, standing out as dark lines in the snow-covered landscape, making navigation a simple task in cloud-free skies and under bright moonlight. There was no post-raid reconnaissance to assess the outcome, and a cursory local report mentioned five fatalities but no details of damage. In addition to the above, 5 Group sent five Hampdens each to the Yam and Nectarine III gardens, the latter the destination for Sgt Williams and crew, who were again the squadron's sole representatives. They departed Scampton at 16.52 and under clear skies, pinpointed on the eastern end of Juist in good visibility and planted their vegetable in the briefed location on a north-westerly heading at 19.09.

The seemingly interminable campaign against the enemy warships at Brest continued on the night of the 25/26$^{th}$, for which a force of sixty-one aircraft was made ready, 5 Group contributing thirty-five Hampdens and fifteen Manchesters, 49 Squadron responsible for seventeen of the former. They took off between 16.50 and 17.16 with S/L Bennett and F/Ls Massey and Ratcliff the senior pilots on duty and AT129 had covered some three miles towards the west before crashing south of the village of Sturton by Stow with fatal consequences for Sgt Stewart and his crew. The others made their way to the Cornish coast, where small amounts of cloud were encountered, but this increased during the Channel crossing to three to eight-tenths by the time that they arrived in the target area. The crews had a clear view of the coastline as they approached and were also guided to the aiming point by searchlights, flares and the heavy and accurate flak defence. It was at this stage that Sgt Newmarch and crew were attacked by a Me110, which they evaded without jettisoning the bombs, but turned back anyway and brought them home. A further six crews failed to carry out an attack in the face of ten-tenths cloud at around 8,000 feet, and S/L Bennett and crew were experiencing difficulties in establishing their position over the coast. They finally found what they were looking for at 20.20 only to be attacked by a BF109, which they shook off but left themselves with insufficient time to complete their attack. Sgt Burton and crew also failed to reach the target in time, and of the remaining crews, five attacked the general area of the port and only those of Sgts Downes and Freeman located and attacked the primary target from 11,000 and 14,000 feet respectively. It was another inconclusive and frustrating raid, of which returning crews were unable to offer any indication of the results.

50 Squadron represented 5 Group at Hannover on the 26$^{th}$ in a force of seventy-one aircraft, fewer than half of which attacked the primary target. The next assault on Brest was posted on the 27$^{th}$ and would involve thirty-two Hampdens and three Manchesters from Scampton, Syerston, North

Luffenham and Bottesford. *(The Bomber Command War Diaries does not record any operations taking place on this night).* It was reported that Prinz Eugen was also "still in town" as an added attraction for the force, which included seventeen Hampdens from 49 Squadron that took off between 00.04 and 00.40 with S/L Hodges the senior pilot on duty. Sgt Burton and crew turned back after persistent issues with the port engine, leaving the others to arrive in the target area under a bright half-moon and two to ten-tenths cloud with a base at 3,000 feet. Haze, or a smoke-screen, further obscured the docks area creating challenging conditions for target identification, and six of the 49 Squadron crews failed to deliver an attack despite some making repeated runs across the port. Three crews bombed the general area of the docks and six had the briefed aiming point in their bomb sight as they attacked it from between 10,000 and 13,000 feet. Not all observed the fall of their bombs as they concentrated on weaving their way out of the searchlight and flak defence and no claims were made of direct hits.

Orders were received on the 28th to prepare for a return to Münster, for which a force of fifty-five Wellingtons and twenty-nine Hampdens was prepared, while a second force consisting of four Hampdens, seven Manchesters and thirty-seven other aircraft was assembled for a freshman operation against the docks and shipping at Boulogne. It was for the latter that the 49 Squadron crews of P/Os Cook and Jeffreys and Sgt Holt departed Scampton between 19.06 and 19.11, and they were able to identify pinpoints on the coastline in conditions of five tenths cloud and good visibility. Sgt Holt overshot the target initially and was unable to find it again in increasing cloud, but his squadron colleagues delivered their bombs and nickels from 11,000 and 14,000 feet and observed bursts in the docks area.

On the last night of the month, a force of seventy-one aircraft took off for another tilt at Brest, and among them were forty-one Hampdens and eleven Manchesters representing 5 Group. The eighteen-strong 49 Squadron element departed Scampton between 17.05 and 17.20 with S/L de Mestre and F/L Ratcliff the senior pilots on duty and lost the services of Sgt Phillips and crew to engine trouble as they crossed the Channel. Sgt Slingo and crew abandoned their sortie when the oxygen supply failed, and Sgt Newmarch and crew were on their bombing run at 11,000 feet, when an engine failed, and they had to pull away. The target area was bathed in bright moonlight providing excellent visibility, but varying opinions as to the cloud conditions ranged from clear skies to eight-tenths. What was not in doubt was the smoke screen, which prevented five crews from establishing a pinpoint and carrying out an attack. Others had fixed their positions by coastal features and intense flak and searchlights pointed the way to the docks area for what would be an uncomfortable bombing run. Sgt Pollitt and crew attacked a ship in the reported location of Scharnhorst, but no bursts were observed, and the others bombed the docks area from 12,000 to 14,000 feet in the hope of hitting something. The inconclusive operation cost two Hampdens and three out of nine 61 Squadron Manchesters.

During the course of the month, the squadron took part in twenty-two operations and dispatched 135 sorties for the loss of four Hampdens and crews.

# February 1942

There were no operations for 5 Group during the first few days of the new month, and all available personnel were press-ganged into snow-clearing duties. Although the impending breakout from Brest by the three enemy warships would take the Royal Navy and the RAF by complete surprise in what would be a most humiliating episode for the government and the nation, there was clearly some advance warning, as three Manchesters were put on stand-by for daylight operations at Bottesford on the 4th in preparation for precisely that event, and six more on the 5th. 5 Group notified its stations on the 6th to prepare for daylight mining operations in the Nectarine I and II gardens off the southern and central Frisians, and between them they raised a force of thirty-three Hampdens and thirteen Manchesters. 49 Squadron dispatched ten Hampdens between 10.50 and 11.07 with S/L Hodges and F/L Massey the senior pilots on duty, and all reached the target area to find generally favourable conditions that enabled them to easily locate the drop zones off the island of Terschelling, mostly by an approach from the south via Vlieland. Nine found cloud to mask their approach and were able to make timed runs to their briefed release points at between 500 and 800 feet, while the newly promoted F/Sgt Pollitt and crew dropped theirs in a last resort location through the ice in the channel between Texel and Vlieland, sadly having forgotten to fuse it. That night, 3 Group sent fifty-seven Wellingtons and three Stirlings to continue the assault on Brest, but only a third of crews reported bombing through thick cloud.

The daylight gardening operation in the Frisians was repeated on the following day employing thirty-two Hampdens, when the target area on this occasion was further north in the Nectarine III garden off the island of Wangerooge in the Waddensee. 49 Squadron made ready five Hampdens and sent them on their way between 11.07 and 11.13 with S/L de Mestre the senior pilot on duty. On approaching the target area, he and F/Sgt Davis concluded that the 2,500-foot cloud base offered insufficient protection and they abandoned their sorties. P/O Allsebrook and crew carried out a timed run from the tip of Norderney and delivered their mine into the briefed location from 600 feet and F/Sgt Hill and crew were similarly successful from 900 feet off Wangerooge. P/O Alfry and crew dropped their mine in an alternative location off Schiermonnikoog from 600 feet under a 1,500-foot cloud base, and were then set upon by two BF109s, one of which they shot down in flames. The operation attracted some moderately accurate heavy flak from the western end of Wangerooge, but fighters were probably responsible for the loss of three Hampdens.

5 Group was not called into action again until the 10th, when a dozen 49 Squadron Hampdens were made ready to attack the main railway station in Bremen. The entire operation had descended into a shambles even before take-off, when the contributions from North Luffenham and Syerston were cancelled because of dangerous ice and water conditions on the aerodrome and a similar situation at Scampton delayed the preparation of six of the original eighteen Hampdens and led to them also being scrubbed. The others took off between 01.08 and 01.49 with F/L Massey the senior pilot on duty and over the next few hours five returned early, two with engine issues and the others with technical breakdowns caused largely by the freezing conditions. Six of those reaching the target area were unable to establish a position through cloud and haze, and any glimpses of the ground revealed a featureless blanket of snow. They bombed the general area of the city, guided by searchlight and flak activity, or sought out alternative targets at Wilhelmshaven or Borkum. Only

F/L Massey identified the primary target after spotting the River Weser and locks during the run-in, and attacked it from 7,500 feet, observing two bursts in the marshalling yards.

Orders were received at Bottesford, Coningsby and Swinderby on the 11th to prepare a dozen Hampdens and six Manchesters between them for an operation that night against a railway station at Mannheim. They were part of an overall force of forty-nine aircraft, which enjoyed favourable conditions, that enabled them to identify the target and release their bombs unopposed by flak in the vicinity of the briefed aiming point. Among other small-scale operations on this night was one against Brest by eighteen Wellingtons, the crews of which would have been unaware that they were the last to engage in this seemingly endless saga. As the sound of their engines receded into the eastern cloud-filled skies, Vice-Admiral Otto Cilliax, the Brest Group commander, whose flag was on Scharnhorst, put Operation Cerberus into action at 21.14, and Scharnhorst, Gneisenau and Prinz Eugen slipping anchor, before heading into the English Channel under an escort of destroyers and E-Boats. It was an audacious bid for freedom, covered by bad weather, widespread jamming and meticulously planned support by the Kriegsmarine and the Luftwaffe, all of which had been rehearsed extensively during January. The planning, and a little good fortune, allowed the fleet to make undetected progress until spotted off Le Touquet by two Spitfires piloted by G/C Victor Beamish, the commanding officer of Kenley, and W/C Finlay Boyd, both of whom maintained radio silence and did not report their find until landing at 10.42 on the morning of the 12th.

The British authorities had prepared a plan in advance for precisely this eventuality, under the Codename, Operation Fuller, but so secret was it, that few, it seemed, either knew of its full requirements or even of its existence. Once the enemy fleet was spotted in the late morning, frantic efforts were made to get Coastal and Bomber Command aircraft away, but only 5 Group was standing by at four hours readiness. It was after 13.00 hours before the first sorties were launched, and the 5 Group stations worked frantically to get sixty-four Hampdens and fifteen Manchesters into the air. 49 Squadron sent its twenty Hampdens away at intervals between 13.27 and 15.03 with S/Ls de Mestre and Hodges the senior pilots on duty and orders to make for a search position off The Hague and the Hoek of Holland. They were part of the largest commitment of aircraft by daylight in the war to date, amounting to 242 sorties, and arrived to find rainstorms and squally conditions that compounded the difficulties of locating a fleet at sea. Most crews would fail in that regard, among them eleven representing 49 Squadron, while the crews of P/O McGuffie and Sgt Burton attacked a 400-ton merchantman and two tramp steamers respectively but missed. F/Sgt Newmarch and crew spotted three large warships at the designated map reference and bombed them from 2,500 feet, before taking violent evasive action, which prevented them from observing bursts. S/L de Mestre and crew attacked from 3,500 feet in five-tenths cloud and heavy rain and watched the bombs detonate behind the trailing vessel. P/O Alfry and crew were scraping the cloud base at 2,000 feet when they came upon two large warships and three smaller vessels in line astern and attacked, only to observe their bombs undershoot. Sixteen Hampdens returned to Scampton between 16.50 and 19.18, leaving the crews of Sgts Downes, Holt and Phillips and F/Sgt Pollitt in P5324, AE240, AE396 and AE132 respectively unaccounted for. Three members of the Downes crew eventually washed ashore on the Dutch coast to confirm their fate, but no trace was ever found of the others. These were among fifteen failures to return, 5 Group alone posting missing nine Hampdens and crews, all lost in the North Sea, six of them without trace. They could be added to all of those others sacrificed to this endeavour over the past eleven months.

Despite the heroic effort and sacrifice of the Bomber Command, Coastal Command and Fleet Air Arm crews, the enemy fleet made good its escape into open sea, although, its own trials and tribulations were not yet over. Scharnhorst struck a mine in the late afternoon and began to fall back, and at 19.55, a magnetic mine detonated close enough to Gneisenau, when off Teschelling, to open a small hole in the starboard side, and temporarily slow her progress also. Later still, at 21.34, when passing through the same stretch of water, Scharnhorst hit another mine which stopped both engines and damaged steering and fire control. The vessel got under way again at 22.23 using its starboard engines and making twelve knots, while carrying an additional one thousand tons of seawater. The day's activities were not yet over for 5 Group, and the crews of fourteen Hampdens and nine Manchesters were briefed to lay mines in the Nectarines garden off the Frisians through which the enemy fleet would have to pass to reach safety.

Gneisenau and Prinz Eugen reached the Elbe Estuary at 07.00 on the 13th, and tied up at Brunsbüttel North Locks at 09.30, while Scharnhorst arrived at Wilhelmshaven at 10.00 with three months-worth of damage to repair. The mines had been laid almost certainly by 5 Group Hampdens over the preceding nights and demonstrated the remarkable effectiveness of this war-long campaign. The entire episode was a major embarrassment to the government and the nation, but on a positive note, this annoying and distracting itch had been scratched for the last time and the Command could now concentrate its forces against the strategic targets for which it was best suited.

A new Air Ministry directive, issued on the 14th, was to change the emphasis of bomber operations from that point until the end of the war. Lengthy consideration having been given to the Butt Report and the future of an independent bomber force, the new policy authorized the blatant area bombing of Germany's industrial towns and cities in a direct assault on the morale of the civilian population, particularly its workers. This had, of course, been going on since the summer of 1940, but no longer would there be the pretence of claiming to be attacking industrial and military targets. Waiting in the wings, in fact, at this very moment, four days into his voyage from the United States in the armed merchantman, Alcantara, was a new leader, a man well-known to 5 Group, who not only would pursue this policy with a will, but also possessed the self-belief, arrogance and stubbornness to fight his corner against all-comers on behalf of his beleaguered Bomber Command.

That night, a force of ninety-eight aircraft took off to employ the main post office and railway station as the aiming points for an area attack on Mannheim, to which 5 Group contributed twenty-five Hampdens and nine Manchesters. 49 Squadron dispatched a dozen Hampdens from Scampton between 18.00 and 18.08 and lost the services of P/O Alfry and crew to the failure of their heating system after about ninety minutes. The others reached the target area by homing in on the searchlight and flak activity and encountered four to ten-tenths cloud at between 2,000 and 12,000 feet, with fair visibility above and ground haze below. Such weather conditions proved to be unhelpful, and nine of the 49 Squadron participants abandoned their search for the station, while eight bombed the built-up area guided by flak and one attacked a flak concentration at Trier. P/O Andrews and crew dropped their bombs on the station through eight-tenths cloud and observed them to enter buildings and detonate. P/O Allsebrook and crew were drawn to a searchlight and flak concentration and saw their bombs hit the mark but had to undertake the final part of their return flight on one engine, which gave out and forced a ditching near the Isle of Wight. A passing Beaufighter relayed their position to the rescue services and a frost-bitten crew was picked up by a Coast Guard launch. Sgt Hamer and crew were contending with their own fuel emergency and an emergency landing took place at 03.20 on farmland near Upwood aerodrome in Cambridgeshire. AT112 would never fly again, but the crew emerged unscathed to fight another day. Despite the claims of sixty-seven crews to have bombed the city, local reports spoke of two buildings destroyed and fifteen damaged.

5 Group detailed thirty-seven Hampdens and twelve Manchesters on the 16th to carry out mining duties in the Nectarine I garden off Terschelling and Nectarine III garden, encompassing the east Frisian islands of Wangerooge, Juist and Borkum. Fourteen 49 Squadron Hampdens departed Scampton between 18.04 and 18.12 with S/L Bennett the senior pilot on duty and they were followed into the air at 19.20 by F/O Hooper and crew who were bound for the Paris area to deliver nickels. The gardeners reached the target areas to find eight to ten-tenths cloud at between 1,000 and 5,000 feet and generally poor visibility, which led to five of them planting their vegetables in alternative locations after failing to establish a pinpoint to drop as briefed. A further seven crews brought their mine home and only S/L Bennett and crew fulfilled their brief by delivering theirs from 600 feet after discerning Borkum dimly through the haze. In all, fourteen Hampden and seven Manchester crews returned to report a successful conclusion to their sorties. The experienced crew of F/O Jenkins failed to return in AT124, and no trace of the Hampden and its occupants was ever found. F/O Hooper and crew encountered eight-tenths cloud in the Paris area and successfully delivered their bundles of reading matter at five-mile intervals from 1,000 feet.

The night of the 18/19th was devoted to mining and nickelling operations, the former undertaken by twenty-five Hampdens off the Frisians in all three Nectarine gardens, the Rosemary garden in the Heligoland Bight and the Yam garden in the Schillig Roads approaches to Jade Bay and the Weser estuary. A dozen 49 Squadron Hampdens departed Scampton between 17.30 and 17.40 bound for the Nectarines with F/L Massey the senior pilot on duty and once in the target area, encountered ten-tenths cloud with a base in places as low as 600 feet. This led to three crews planting in alternative locations and one returning with their mine still on board, while eight were able to establish a firm pinpoint in their respective allotted garden and plant in the briefed locations from between 600 and 800 feet. According to the ORB Form 540, a single crew was sent nickelling in the Lille area on the 19th, but no mention was made on the Form 541 to offer a clue to its identity.

Air Chief Marshal Sir Arthur Harris took up his post as the new Commander-in-Chief of Bomber Command on the 22nd. He was a man well-known to 5 Group, having served as its A-O-C until November 1940, when he became second deputy to Sir Charles Portal, the Chief-of-the-Air-Staff. Harris arrived at the helm with firm ideas already in place on how to win the war by bombing alone, a pre-war theory, which no commander had yet had an opportunity to put into practice. It was obvious to him, that the small-scale raids on multiple targets favoured by his predecessor, served only to dilute the effort, and that such pin-prick attacks could not hurt Germany's war effort. He recognized the need to overwhelm the defences and emergency services, by pushing the maximum number of aircraft across the aiming point in the shortest possible time, and this would signal the birth of the bomber stream and an end to the former practice, whereby squadrons or even crews determined for themselves the details of their sorties. He knew also that urban areas are most efficiently destroyed by fire rather than blast, and it would not be long before the bomb loads carried in his aircraft reflected this thinking.

In the meantime, while he developed his ideas, he would continue with the fairly small-scale attacks on German ports favoured by his predecessor, and later on the evening of his appointment, he sent thirty-one Wellingtons and nineteen Hampdens to Wilhelmshaven to attack the floating dock likely to be employed during repairs to Scharnhorst and Gneisenau. 49 Squadron made ready a dozen of its own for the main event and another for the freshman crew of Sgt Carter to employ at Emden docks over to the west. They took off from Scampton together between 18.14 and 18.22 and were still climbing away over the station when an engine issue prompted P/O Alfry and crew to abandon their sortie. Sgt Carter and crew turned back within the hour because of an overheating port engine, and when they landed, found that a cold Sgt Bond and crew had beaten them home by ten minutes courtesy of the failure of their heating system. Sgt Davis and crew lost their heating system early on and were freezing by the time they reached the vicinity of the eastern Frisians, at which point the port engine began to falter and gave them an excuse to bomb the island of Norderney as a last resort before heading home to thaw out. The others ran into ten-tenths cloud that concealed the target area and, unable to establish any firm reference on which to base an attack, four gave up and returned their ordnance to store. Five bombed on estimated positions guided by searchlight and flak activity and their efforts were insufficient even to gain them a mention in the town diary.

On the night of the 23/24th, 5 Group detailed twenty-three Hampdens for mining duties in the Rosemary and Yams gardens in the Heligoland Bight and Schillig Roads respectively, and forty-two Hampdens and nine Manchesters on the 24/25th to return to the same gardens. 49 Squadron was called into action on the latter occasion to provide fourteen Hampdens for the Rosemary garden in Heligoland Bight, which departed Scampton between 18.00 and 18.10 with S/L de Mestre and F/L Massey the senior pilots on duty. Twenty-three minutes later, Sgt Carter and crew took off for the Nectarine I garden off Terschelling and like the others, would heed the 5 Group instructions to " not fight the weather", which in the North Sea and Waddenzee areas was unhelpful with six to ten-tenths cloud spewing out severe snow squalls from a base that in places was as low as 300 feet. The crews of F/L Massey, F/O Hooper, P/O Donald, F/Sgt Hill and Sgt Burton planted their vegetables according to brief from 400 to 1,000 feet, while seven others chose last resort locations mostly off the Frisians and three returned their mines to store after failing to establish a pinpoint.

On the 25th, 5 Group detailed a dozen Manchesters to target the Gneisenau, now believed to be at Kiel, while eighteen Hampdens and a Manchester took care of gardening duties in the Nectarines I and II, Yams and Rosemary gardens. The main event on the 26th was a raid on the floating dock at Kiel for which 49 and 144 Squadrons detailed four and six Hampdens respectively to join Wellingtons and Halifaxes in an overall force of forty-nine aircraft. A further twenty-seven Hampdens were made ready for mining duties in the Yam, Hawthorn and Rosemary gardens, respectively in the Jade/Weser estuary, in the Waddenzee off southern Jutland and in the Heligoland Bight, 49 Squadron supporting the Hawthorn and Rosemary endeavours with four aircraft each, although the ORB recorded the target area as the Heligoland approach. The Kiel-bound quartet consisting of the crews of S/L Hodges, Sgts Bond and Burton and P/O Andrews departed Scampton between 18.00 and 18.03 and were followed into the air between 18.03 and 18.09 by the gardeners led by F/L Massey. The bombing element encountered thin ice-bearing cloud topping out at around 19,000 feet as it approached the target area, and some crews were unable to climb through it to reach clear air. The crews of Sgts Bond and Burton were adversely affected by icing and turned back, leaving the remaining two to map-read their way to the Baltic coast and pinpoint on Flensburg Fjord before heading south. Kiel stood out against the snow-covered background as they delivered their bombs into the docks area without observing them burst. The gardeners experienced similar conditions and after P/O Williams and crew had returned early as a result of engine failure, six were able to plant their vegetables in the briefed locations from between 500 and 800 feet and one failed to establish a pinpoint and brought their mine home.

The Kiel operation threw up one of the war's great ironies, after a high explosive bomb struck the bows of Gneisenau, now supposedly in a safe haven after enduring eleven months of constant bombardment at Brest, and not only did it kill 116 of her crew, it also ended her sea-going career for good. Her main armament was removed for use in coastal defence, and she was towed to Gdynia, where she remained unrepaired for the remainder of the war. The British authorities were unaware of the success, however, and sent another raid of sixty-eight aircraft on the 27th, which included a 5 Group contribution of eighteen Hampdens and seventeen Manchesters. They encountered bright moonlight above the ten-tenths cloud in the target area, but poor visibility below, which offered no chance of identifying the floating dock, and most bombed the general area of the town, guided by the flashes of searchlights and flak.

During the course of the month, the squadron carried out fourteen operations and dispatched 127 sorties for the loss of seven Hampdens and five crews.

## **March 1942**

Adverse weather conditions welcomed in the new month and kept the bomber force on the ground on the 1st. It was the same on the 2nd, and it was the 3rd before orders were received across the Command to prepare for an operation, which, in its bold conception, was a clear indication of what was to come. Bomber Command's evolution to war-winning capability was to be long, arduous and gradual, but the first signs of a new hand on the tiller came early on in Harris's reign with this meticulously planned attack on the Renault lorry factory, which was located in a loop of the Seine in the district of Billancourt to the south-west of central Paris. The plant was capable of producing 18,000 lorries per year, which was a massive boon to the German war effort, and the attempt to destroy it came in response to an Air Ministry request. The operation would be conducted in three waves, led by experienced crews, and would involve extensive use of flares to provide illumination. In the face of what was expected to be scant defence, crews were also encouraged to attack from as low a level as practicable, both for the sake of accuracy and in an attempt to avoid civilian casualties. In time, such operations would be led by Gee-equipped aircraft, but the 3 Group squadrons already employing the device were forbidden from taking part on this occasion, lest one be lost over enemy territory and its secrets revealed.

A force of 235 aircraft was assembled, a new record for a single target, and among them were forty-eight Hampdens and twenty-six Manchesters representing 5 Group, nine of the former provided by 49 Squadron. They departed Scampton between 17.30 and 17.39 with S/Ls de Mestre and Hodges the senior pilots on duty and all reached the target area, where bright moonlight aided target location and most crews picked up the River Seine in good time to enable them to plan their bombing runs. The 49 Squadron crews delivered their bomb loads from between 1,000 and 4,000 feet and many bursts and explosions were observed. 223 crews reported successful sorties, many describing the factory buildings as well alight as they turned away, and post-raid reconnaissance confirmed the operation to have been an outstanding success for the loss of just one aircraft. 40% of the factory's buildings had been destroyed, and production was halted for four weeks, costing the Germans around 2,300 lorries, although, sadly, not all of the bombs had fallen precisely where intended. Inevitably, adjacent workers' housing had been hit by stray bombs, killing 367 French civilians, and severely injuring 341 others, some of whom would die. At the time, this was more than twice the heaviest death toll inflicted on a German target. It was somewhat paradoxical, that, as a champion of area bombing, Harris should gain his first major victory against a precision target.

While the above was in progress, some 330 miles to the north, four Lancasters taxied to the runway under the approving eyes of the 5 Group A-O-C, AVM Slessor, each carrying four mines for delivery to the Yams and Rosemary gardens in the Schillig Roads and Heligoland Bight in what would be the type's maiden operation.

It rained all day on the 4th and snowed all day on the 5th, and it was the 7th before orders came through from 5 Group to make ready seventeen Hampdens for gardening duties in the Artichoke garden, on the approaches to the port of Lorient, an operation not recorded in the 5 Group ORB. Despite the fact that Essen, as home to the Krupp organisation, was the beating heart of the Ruhr Valley's war production, it had not been paid particular attention thus far in the war. This was about to change as Harris fixed his attention upon it, and, like a dog with a bone, would not abandon his quest to destroy it until that aim had been achieved. It was a fight he would win, but the first twelve months would be frustrating, unrewarding and expensive, and began with the first of three raids on consecutive nights on the 8th. A force of 211 aircraft was assembled, of which thirty-seven Hampdens and twenty-two Manchesters were provided by 5 Group, while the leading aircraft, which belonged to 3 Group, would be those equipped with the new Gee navigation device. This carried the great hope that it could solve the problem of blind target locating. The twelve-strong 49 Squadron element departed Scampton between 23.43 and 00.22 with S/L Hodges and F/L Massey the senior pilots on duty and lost the services of P/O Jeffreys and crew to intercom failure. The others arrived over the Ruhr to find clear skies and good visibility provided by a half moon, but also the ever-present industrial haze, which obscured ground detail, including the assigned aiming point "B", the Krupp complex. Few crews were able to make a positive identification after pinpointing on the Rhine and most bombed the general city area, those from 49 Squadron from between 8,500 and 14,000 feet, some observing bursts and others not. Local sources reported a light raid with a little housing damage in southern districts.

The Krupp complex was back on twenty-four hours later as one of two aiming points at Essen, and a force of 187 aircraft made ready, which included a 5 Group contribution of fifteen Hampdens and ten Manchesters. This figure had originally been higher, but adverse weather conditions, technical difficulties and one unidentified Manchester becoming bogged down on the way to take-off at Bottesford, reduced the numbers significantly. 49 Squadron's original contribution of fourteen Hampdens was reduced to just three containing the crews of P/O Newmarch and F/Ls Massey and Ratcliff, who departed Scampton between 19.30 and 19.37. Some crews claimed to be able to see the flares over Essen even before reaching the Dutch coast, which confirmed that the horizontal visibility was reasonable, while vertical visibility at the target was again compromised by industrial haze. Major landmarks were identified through the five-tenths cloud with tops at around 8,000 feet, but not the Krupp districts in the western and north-western region of the city and the bombing was scattered over twenty-four other Ruhr towns and cities, with Hamborn and Duisburg the chief beneficiaries. The Essen authorities reported the destruction of two buildings, with seventy-two others damaged.

Essen was posted as the primary target again on the 10th, for which a force of 126 aircraft was made ready to attack two aiming points, the Krupp sector and the city centre. 5 Group provided almost half of the force in the form of forty-three Hampdens, thirteen Manchesters and, for the first time over Germany, two 44 (Rhodesia) Squadron Lancasters, which would be employing TR1335 (Gee) for the first time. 49 Squadron made ready eleven Hampdens and briefed the crews to attack aiming point B, the "old town", before sending them on their way between 19.10 and 19.17 with the newly promoted F/O Allsebrook the senior pilot on duty. P/O Cook and crew were soon on their way home with engine issues, while Sgt Slingo and crew had to contend with an undercarriage that refused to lock in the retracted position and protruded into the airflow to create drag. They pressed on but could not climb or maintain a satisfactory air speed and eventually turned back, as did P/O Jeffreys and crew after experiencing intermittent intercom failure. They must have been close to the target and would be last but one to land, but at least all three unsuccessful crews returned their bombs to store. The others reached the target area to find two to eight-tenths cloud at between 3,000 and 8,000 feet, extreme darkness and poor visibility, made worse by the glare from searchlights and flares and the attentions of intense and accurate flak. Unable to identify either the Krupp sector or the main square, most bombed the built-up area generally, before turning for home to report observing some bursts and fires but no detail. AT174 failed to return with the crew of P/O Andrews and was later found to have come down in the general target area without survivors. An analysis revealed that fewer than half of the crews had reached the primary target, while thirty-five others had bombed alternatives, and according to local sources, the nearest any bombs fell to the Krupp complex was on a railway line serving the area and one house was destroyed.

The Deutsche Werke and Germania Werft U-Boot construction yards at Kiel were the targets for a force of sixty-eight Wellingtons on the night of the 12/13th, while forty Wellingtons and Whitleys, probably crewed by freshmen, attended to Emden. 5 Group committed twenty-six Hampdens and a lone Manchester to mining duties in the Yams, Hawthorn and Rosemary gardens off Germany's North Sea coast and among them were eight representing 49 Squadron. They departed Scampton between 00.59 and 01.14 with F/L Massey the senior pilot on duty and were well on their way by the time that the recently-arrived crew of P/O Kay DFM took off at 02.30 to deliver what Harris described as "toilet paper" to the residents of the Lille region of north-eastern France. P/O Kay had earned his DFM while serving with 83 Squadron in 1941. Those arriving in the Hawthorn area found two to seven-tenths cloud with a base at between 1,000 and 1,500 feet and good visibility, while those in the Nectarine III garden encountered nine-tenths cloud at between 500 and 1,500 feet and poor visibility, which thwarted the efforts of P/O Rawstorne and crew to establish a pinpoint. The others carried out timed runs from Amrum, Norderney, Scharhörn and Spiekeroog Islands and delivered their mines into the briefed locations from between 500 and 1,000 feet. Meanwhile, P/O Kay and crew had successfully dispensed their leaflets over the Lille area from 10,000 feet and gained valuable experience in the process.

Cologne was posted on the 13th as the target for a force of 135 aircraft of six different types, which included a contribution from 5 Group of twenty-two Hampdens, sixteen Manchesters and a single Lancaster. Those reaching the target found the visibility to be good through the partial cover of three to five-tenths cloud at between 8,000 and 12,000 feet and had to run the gauntlet of intense searchlight and flak to arrive at the aiming point. Flares provided effective illumination, which contributed to an unusually effective raid that inflicted substantial damage on a number of war industry factories in the Nippes district located to the north of the city centre, west of the Rhine, where a major marshalling yard was also located. In addition to this, 1,500 houses were hit in what proved to be the first genuinely successful Gee-led raid.

49 Squadron was not involved at Cologne and would spend the next ten nights on the ground as the weather largely closed down all but small-scale bomber operations. Crews were put on stand-by daily for the possibility of an operation, only for them to be stood-down when they were cancelled. On the 17th, P/O Cook and crew were tasked to ferry P1226 from Exeter following repair, and Cook and second pilot, P/O Manders RCAF, took off in poor weather conditions to carry out an air-test, heading initially out to sea. At 11.25 the Hampden reappeared over the coast and immediately flew into a fog-shrouded hill near Branscombe, killing both occupants. A daylight mining operation by thirteen Manchesters and six Lancasters went ahead in the Nectarine region on the 20th, and on return, one of the Lancasters grazed a house roof with a wingtip and was crash-landed on a beach near Boston, where it was written off by the incoming tide to become the first Lancaster to be lost as a result of operations.

It was the 23rd before the next night operation was announced, which was to involve a dozen Hampdens, two Manchesters and three 3 Group Stirlings mining in the Artichoke garden off Lorient. 49 Squadron was not invited to take part, but training continued during the day and according to the ORB, F/O McGuffie was killed near Dunholme Lodge while engaged in blind approach practice. The squadron was called into action on the 24th to prepare six Hampdens for mining duties in the Artichoke garden that night. They departed Scampton between 18.27 and 18.33 with F/O Cumming the senior pilot on duty and soon lost the services of P/O Alfry and crew to port engine failure. The others arrived in the target area under bright moonlight and delivered their mines into the briefed locations after carrying out timed runs from the Ile-de-Groix, and all returned safely to land at Exeter.

Harris resumed his campaign against Essen on the night of the 25/26th, when sending the largest force yet to a single target of 254 aircraft. 5 Group played its part by contributing twenty Manchesters, nine Hampdens and seven Lancasters, and despite clear skies and good visibility, thick industrial haze thwarted the attempts of all crews to identify Essen. On return, crews commented that some of the Wellington-laid flares were burning at 18,000 feet, which was of no benefit in terms of illuminating ground features and the promise of Gee, demonstrated in the recent attack on Cologne, was not repeated, as much of the effort was wasted on a decoy site at Rheinberg, some eighteen miles away. It was a bad night for 5 Group, which posted missing six aircraft, two-thirds of the overall casualty figure, and among them were five of the twenty Manchesters dispatched, a loss rate of 25%. For 49 Squadron, there was a repeat of the previous night's fare, which involved six crews departing Scampton between 18.31 and 18.35 bound for the Artichoke garden, although the Form 540 states Bordeaux as the destination and also mentions a successful nickelling sortie by an unidentified crew in the Lille region of north-eastern France. All made it to the target area to be greeted by favourable conditions, which enabled them to pinpoint on the Ile-de-Groix before conducting timed runs and delivering their stores into the briefed locations from 600 to 1,000 feet between 21.25 and 22.23. Afterwards, all returned safely to a landing at Exeter.

On the 26th, instructions were received to withdraw Lancasters from operations and to restrict training flights to a fuel load not exceeding 580 gallons in inner tanks only. This resulted from an incident of wingtip rippling and loose rivets and brought an end to operations for 44 and 97 Squadrons for the remainder of the month. That night, a force of 115 Wellingtons and Stirlings returned to Essen, while 5 Group detailed thirty Hampdens and fifteen Manchesters to conduct mining operations in the Yams, Nectarines and Deodar gardens, respectively in Jade Bay/Weser estuary, off the Frisians and the Gironde estuary leading to the port of Bordeaux in south-western France. 49 Squadron supported the Deodar endeavour with five Hampdens, which took off between 18.44 and 18.48 with S/L de Mestre the senior pilot on duty. Sgt Carter and crew had reached the Vannes area before a defective starboard engine persuaded them to jettison their 250 pounders "safe" and bring their mine home. The others pinpointed on Pointe-de-la-Coubre and delivered their mines into the briefed locations from 600 to 800 feet between 22.43 and 23.30, before returning safely to Chivenor.

These operations preceded another foretaste of things to come, when Harris launched a major assault on the historic Hansastadt city of Lübeck on the north German coast, believing, that if he could provide his crews with the means to locate a target, they would hit it. Coastlines offered the most distinctive features for the purpose of identification, hence, Lübeck, which not only lay on the Baltic coast to the east of Kiel, but the narrow streets and half-timbered buildings in its old town also represented the perfect target for destruction by fire. The operation, to be carried out on the night of the 28/29th, was to be conducted along the same lines as the highly successful attack on the Renault factory at the start of the month, and a force of 234 aircraft was assembled, 5 Group represented by forty-one Hampdens and twenty-one Manchesters, ten of the former provided by 49 Squadron. They departed Scampton between 20.00 and 20.31 and Sgt Burton and crew were five miles east of Mablethorpe when engine issues ended their interest in proceedings. F/O Alcock and crew made it as far as Sylt before engine trouble and the failure of their heating system persuaded them to turn back also. The others pressed on in excellent visibility under bright moonlight that allowed them to map-read their way across the Schleswig-Holstein peninsula to gain the western Baltic. The target was identified easily by the coastline and the River Trave and the 49 Squadron crews attacked it from between 8,000 and 10,000 feet either side of midnight. Many fires were seen to develop, and returning crews reported the burning city to be visible from seventy miles into the homeward flight. Post-raid reconnaissance and local sources confirmed the operation to have been a major success, which destroyed almost fifteen hundred houses and seriously damaged almost two thousand more in a 190-acre area of devastation representing some 30% of the city's built-up area. It was the first major success for area bombing, and another sign of what was in store for the residents of Germany's towns and cities. There was an outcry following this unexpected attack on Lübeck, which was a city of culture and a vital port for the Red Cross. An agreement was struck that ensured its future protection from bombing, and, with a few exceptions, this was adhered to.

Eighteen Hampdens and eight Manchesters were made ready for further gardening operations on the 29th, all but two assigned to the Nectarine gardens, while two of the Manchesters ventured as far as the Bottle garden off Haugesund on Norway's western coast. A return to the madness of daylight "moling" cloud cover operations on the 31st involved eleven Hampdens and six Wellingtons, whose crews had been briefed to seek out railway targets in north-western Germany. 49 Squadron dispatched five crew between 12.08 and 12.15, which flew out over Skegness with the reassuring protection of ten-tenths cloud, but this began to disperse as they approached the Frisians and persuaded them to turn back. Some crews from other squadron pushed on across Holland to within ten miles of the German frontier, before they, too, decided to abandon their sorties.

At the end of the month, S/L Hodges was posted from 49 Squadron, initially as non-effective sick, but, in time he would resume his operational career and distinguished himself as a member of one of Bomber Command's SOE-supporting 138 and 161 Squadrons, known as the "Moon" Squadrons at Tempsford in Bedfordshire. He flew a number of types, including Lysanders to drop and pick up agents and resistance operatives, and in May 1943, began an eight-month tour as commanding officer of 161 Squadron. During the course of the month, 49 Squadron took part in a dozen operations and dispatched seventy-seven sorties for the loss of two Hampdens, one complete crew and three additional pilots.

# April 1942

The new month began for 5 Group with operations on the 1st in company with Wellingtons, although not operating together. Twenty-two Hampden crews were briefed to take part in a raid on the docks and shipping at Le Havre, while fourteen others were to be sent to carry out low-level attacks on railway targets in north-western Germany in the Meppen and Lingen region just over the frontier from Holland. In support of the latter, 49 Squadron dispatched the crews of F/O Alcock, P/O Williams and Sgt Burton between 20.00 and 20.10 and all reached the general target area in unhelpful weather conditions, which included electrical storms that interfered with the reliability of compasses. As a last resort target, F/O Alcock and crew attacked a coaster off the Frisians but failed to observe the outcome. P/O Williams and crew bombed lock gates, a small town and cross-roads and strafed barges on a stretch of canal. Sgt Burton and crew were following a south-to-north railway line on the Frisian Island of Langeoog when they were heavily engaged by flak. During violent evasive action, the bomb fell into the sea and the Hampden returned home with structural damage. At 00.17, F/Sgt Davis and crew took off on a nickelling sortie to the Paris region and made two runs at 10,000 feet to maintain stocks of toilet paper.

It turned into a disastrous night for 3 Group, whose railway targets were at Hanau and Lohr to the east of Frankfurt, from which five out of twelve 57 Squadron Wellingtons failed to return and seven of fourteen belonging to 214 Squadron. This caused a rethink by those responsible for planning operations, despite which, a similar disaster awaited 5 Group in December. On the following night, twenty-three Hampdens were detailed for mining duties in the Gorse garden in Quiberon Bay, situated on the western coast of Brittany, north-west of St-Nazaire. The operation took place in ideal, moonlit conditions, in which the crews established their positions without difficulty, pinpointing on Quiberon Point or the Ile-d'Houat, from where they carried out their timed runs to deliver the vegetables into the allotted locations. A daylight mining operation in one of the Nectarine gardens was planned for the late afternoon of the 4th, when crews would have to rely on cloud cover over the Frisians to provide protection. When this failed to materialize, the operation was abandoned, and all crews returned home with their stores.

The first major operation of the new month was directed at Cologne on the night of the 5/6th and involved a new record force of 263 aircraft, which included a 5 Group contribution of forty-four Hampdens and eleven Manchesters. The aiming point was the Klöckner-Humboldt engineering works in the Deutz district on the East Bank of the Rhine in the city centre, which manufactured aero-engines and a wide range of military vehicles. 49 Squadron supported the operation with eleven Hampdens, which departed Scampton between 00.15 and 00.38 with S/L Bennett the senior pilot on duty accompanied by the newly arrived F/L Cadman DFM. Another new arrival was F/L Marshall, who would be undertaking his first sortie with the squadron later on in the morning as the captain of one of four crews assigned to nickelling duties in the Lille area. The crews of Sgt Bond and F/Sgt Davis returned early because of engine issues, and AT156 was shot down by the Ju88 of Oblt Wilhelm Herget of II./NJG1, while flying at 14,500 feet over Belgium. The Hampden crashed at 02.10 four miles south-south-west of Philippeville, killing two members of the crew and delivering P/O Kay DFM into enemy hands. The fourth member of the crew managed to retain his freedom after receiving assistance from the local escape and evasion network. The others arrived in the target area to encounter bright moonlight, which penetrated the up-to-nine-tenths cloud and glinted off an S-bend in the Rhine to the south of the city centre, thereby assisting some crews to establish a position for the bombing run. Despite the advantages, however, many crews failed to identify Cologne and those that did scattered their loads right across the built-up area, destroying or seriously damaging ninety houses but nothing of industrial significance. Only P/O Williams and crew of the 49 Squadron contingent located the primary target and bombed it from 12,000 feet at 03.15, while the others sought out alternatives or brought their bombs home. The nickelling quartet departed Scampton between 03.35 and 03.45 and took advantage of the bright moonlight filtering through the nine-tenths cloud to pinpoint on the Lille region and deliver their bundles of leaflets from 10,000 feet between 05.15 and 06.00.

On the following night, Harris turned his attention back upon Essen, with the first of three raids against it in six nights, to which 5 Group contributed eighteen Hampdens and ten Manchesters. The five-strong 49 Squadron element departed Scampton between 23.45 and 23.56 with S/L de Mestre the senior pilot on duty and adopted the southerly route to the central Ruhr via Orfordness, Blankenberg on the Belgian coast and Nivelles to then swing south of Bonn before heading north to the target. They encountered electrical storms and severe icing conditions over the North Sea that threatened to destroy lift and forced S/L de Mestre and crew to abandon their sortie twenty miles short of the enemy coast. At about the same time, F/O Cumming lost control of his aircraft at 7,000 feet and pulled it out of a dive at 3,000 feet, and Sgt Bond and crew battled the weather for considerably longer before also turning back. On e.t.a., F/L Ratcliff and crew dropped their load from 13,000 feet, assuming that Essen lay beneath the ten-tenths cloud and were among only a third of crews to report bombing the primary target. Essen escaped with minor damage at a cost to the Command of five aircraft, three of them belonging to 5 Group, and one of them to 49 Squadron. No trace was ever found of AT126 and the crew of F/Sgt Davis, who may well have fallen victim to the weather on a night when the Luftwaffe was unlikely to have been operating.

Hamburg was posted as the target on the 8th, and yet another record force, this time of 272 aircraft, was made ready. 5 Group stepped up with thirty-two Hampdens and thirteen Manchesters assigned to the Blohm & Voss shipyards located to the west of the city centre, while the seven Lancasters and nine further Hampdens were to attack aiming point C, the industrial centre of the city. 49 Squadron detailed eleven Hampdens for the main event and five for nickelling duties in the Paris area, and it was the latter which departed Scampton first between 20.32 and 20.50 with F/L Marshall the senior pilot on duty. They were followed into the air between 21.15 and 22.02 by the bombing brigade with S/L de Mestre taking the lead, and lost the services of P/O Williams and crew to instrument failure during the climb-out. The others headed across the North Sea to encounter one of the towering electrical storms with icing conditions that frequently built up over it to bar the approaches to north-western Germany, and, on this night, not all who set out would reach their intended destination. F/O Alcock and crew turned back when ten miles west of Heligoland because of an ailing port engine and three others dumped their 250lb wing bombs in an attempt to reach clear air before seeking out alternative targets. In fact, only 188 crews would report bombing the general area of Hamburg on estimated positions through ten-tenths cloud, among them six of the 49 Squadron element from between 12,000 and 14,000 feet either side of midnight. The result was another poor performance, which deposited no more than the equivalent of fourteen bomb loads in the city and caused eight fires. Of the leafleteers, the crews of F/L Marshall and Sgt Gould returned early with intercom failure, leaving the others to fulfil their brief from 10,000 feet at around 23.30.

It was back to Essen for 254 aircraft on the 10th, an operation supported by 5 Group with forty-three Hampdens, ten Manchesters and eight Lancasters. 49 Squadron contributed thirteen Hampdens, but the first departure from Scampton was that of Sgt Gould and crew at 20.45, bound for the Paris region with a cargo of paper. The bombing element took off between 21.20 and 21.33 with F/L Marshall the senior pilot on duty and set course via Mablethorpe for Enkhuizen on the eastern shore of the Den Helder peninsula, before swinging round the eastern end of the Ruhr and running in on the target from east to west. On this night, they were expecting to find the clear skies forecast at briefing, but instead, were confronted by a layer of eight-tenths cloud across the central Ruhr at between 5,000 and 8,000 feet. The route in was described by F/L Sandford of 44 (Rhodesia) Squadron as "hot", with scores of searchlights from all sides working in conjunction with light and heavy flak. Sgt Hamer and crew turned back because of an issue with the starboard engine and eight others from 49 Squadron attacked alternative or last-resort targets from between 12,000 and 18,000 feet either side of midnight, and only Sgt James and crew claimed to have bombed the primary from 15,000 feet at 00.15. Returning crews reported bursts and the glow of fires beneath the cloud, but little of use to the intelligence sections at debriefing. It was a sad night for 49 Squadron, which waited in vain for the return of the crews of F/L Marshall and F/O Worthy in AT190 and AE421 respectively. The former was believed to have been shot down by flak when closing on the target, killing two members of the crew and delivering the pilot and one other into enemy hands, while the latter crashed into the Ijsselmeer some six miles east of Enkhuizen without survivors. Local reports confirmed the operation to have been another dismal failure, which destroyed only twelve houses and caused no industrial damage.

Orders were received across the Command on the 12th to prepare another large force to return to Essen that night, and 251 aircraft were made ready accordingly, 5 Group responding with thirty-one Hampdens and nine Manchesters, while the Lancaster element was busy training for an epic daylight raid five days hence. 49 Squadron made ready eleven of its own for the main event and one for mining, and it was the latter that started the ball rolling in the hands of Sgt Gould and crew at 20.36 bound for the Rosemary garden in the Heligoland Bight. The main element departed Scampton between 21.28 and 21.37 with S/L Bennett the senior pilot on duty on what would turn out to be a night of poor engine serviceability. The crews of F/O Alcock and P/O Williams turned back with the French coast in sight, while the crews of F/O Cumming, P/O Jeffreys and Sgt Bond were over France when the gremlins struck, and Sgt Slingo was approaching Koblenz. The Cumming crew was attacked by a night-fighter and sustained structural damage to the mainplane from cannon fire before evading further attention. Those reaching the target area found clear skies but were prevented by the industrial haze from identifying ground features, some picking up distinctive bends in the River Ruhr to the south of the city and employing already developing fires as a guide. The crews of P/O Floyd, Sgt James and P/O Rawstorne attacked the primary target from 15,000 and 14,000 feet at 01.40, 02.00 and 02.06 respectively, while S/L Bennett and Sgt Burton found alternatives to bomb from 15,000 and 9,000 feet. AT196 was flying on fumes as it crossed the Yorkshire coast north-east of Hull and Sgt James issued the order to abandon it before taking to his parachute. Sadly, when the Hampden crashed on farmland at Fitling, the remaining crew members were still on board and were killed. Meanwhile, Sgt Gould and crew had successfully delivered their mine into the briefed location from 700 feet at 00.40.

An analysis of the Essen raid revealed that 173 crews claimed to have bombed in the general area of the Krupp districts but bombing photos captured many Ruhr locations, while local sources confirmed a slight improvement in the bombing, reporting some damage and a large fire in the Krupp complex and the destruction of twenty-eight dwelling units. This brought to an end a series of eight heavy raids against the city since the night of the 8/9th of March, during which 1,555 sorties had resulted in fewer than two-thirds of the crews claiming to have bombed in the target area, and just twenty-two bombing photos being plotted to within five miles of Essen. In exchange for this, sixty-four aircraft had been lost, industrial damage had been slight, and housing damage modest in the extreme.

Dortmund was posted as the target for a force of 208 aircraft on the 14th, in what was by far the largest effort yet against this industrial giant situated at the eastern end of the Ruhr. 5 Group made a contribution to the operation of thirty-four Hampdens and four Manchesters, seven of the former provided by 49 Squadron, which departed Scampton between 21.28 and 21.34. Unfortunately, the engine serviceability issues had not been solved and F/O Floyd did not even leave the circuit before returning. Sgts Burton and Freeman progressed only a little further and were still over England when their sorties were abandoned. The rest of the force had to run the gauntlet of intense searchlight and flak activity as they traversed the most heavily defended region of Germany, and under clear skies, map-read their way by river and railway features to the aiming point. The 49 Squadron crews of F/O Cumming and Sgts Bond and Slingo were unable to identify the briefed aiming point and attacked the general city area from 12,000 and 16,000 feet at 02.18 and 02.20, while attempting to dodge some eighty searchlights in cones. P/O Williams and crew failed to return in AD931, and it was learned eventually that they had been shot down in the target area by a night-fighter and that P/O Williams and one other had survived to be taken into captivity. It would be established later that the bombing had been scattered over a forty-mile stretch of the region, with no significant damage to the intended target.

A reduced force of 152 aircraft was assembled for the same target twenty-four hours later, this time supported by 5 Group with nineteen Hampdens and seven Manchesters. 49 Squadron made ready six Hampdens for the main event and one for the crew of F/O Read to take to the Paris area to dispense morale-boosting propaganda. The latter took off at 21.00 and were already over France by the time that the five-strong bombing element departed Scampton between 22.31 and 22.55. The crews had to contend with severe icing conditions on the southern approaches to the Ruhr, only then to run into intense searchlight and flak activity over the target, where two-tenths low cloud combined with the industrial haze to muddy the vertical visibility. P/O Floyd and crew alone of the 49 Squadron participants attacked the primary target from 12,000 feet at 03.00, while Sgts Bond, Freeman and Burton found last-resort objectives to bomb from 16,000 to 18,000 feet between 01.45 and 02.45. Despite the effort and the courage of crews, this raid was another dismal failure that scattered bombs over a wide area and caused only the slightest damage in the target city.

Minor operations occupied the night of the 16/17th, for which 5 Group contributed ten Hampdens and two Manchesters for gardening duties and five Hampdens and two Manchesters for nickelling activities over Lille in north-eastern France. 49 Squadron dispatched the crews of F/O Read and Sgt James to the Artichoke garden off Lorient at 20.45, but neither was able to establish their precise position in poor weather conditions. The Read crew returned their mine to store, while the James crew pinpointed on Belle Isle and dropped their mine in an alternative location from 700 feet at 00.42.

At noon on the 17th, six crews each from 44 (Rhodesia) and 97 (Straits Settlement) Squadrons filed into the briefing rooms at Waddington and Woodhall Spa to be enlightened as to their immediate future. They were incredulous to learn that they were soon to embark on Operation Margin, an epic low-level deep-penetration flight to Augsburg in Bavaria, to attack the diesel engine assembly shop in the middle of a large factory complex belonging to the Maschinen Fabrik Augsburg Nürnburg Aktien Gesellschaft, otherwise known as the M.A.N. works, situated on the outskirts of the beautiful and historic city. Strategically, this particular shop was the most important part of the factory and was believed to be the bottleneck in the entire U-Boot industry at a time when the Battle of the Atlantic was the main preoccupation of both Britain and the United States. Four of the 44 (Rhodesia) squadron Lancasters were shot down over France on the way out and a fifth crashed beyond the target and two 97 (Straits Settlement) Lancasters were also lost, but some useful damage was inflicted upon the target and S/L Nettleton of 44 (Rhodesia) Squadron was awarded the VC. Harris disliked low-level operations in heavy bombers, particularly in daylight, and the Augsburg losses cemented that opinion.

Meanwhile, at Scampton, 49 Squadron received its first three examples of the Manchester, an aircraft with which it would have a brief and unhappy association. Fellow Scampton residents, 83 Squadron, had already gone through the ordeal of operating Manchesters, and were now in the process of converting to Lancasters. That night, according to Bomber Command War Diaries, Hamburg was selected to host a raid by a force of 173 aircraft including a contribution from 5 Group of five Manchesters but no Hampdens. However, 49 Squadron dispatched five of the type from Scampton between 22.24 and 22.47 and all reached enemy territory, where the crews of Sgts Slingo and Carter bombed last resort targets from 16,000 and 15,000 feet at 02.20 and 02.56 respectively. Germany's second city was found to be under clear skies but shrouded in haze and protected by the usual intense searchlight and flak barrage from both banks of the Elbe. The city-centre aiming point could not be identified, and the remaining three 49 Squadron participants attacked the built-up area generally from 12,000 to 17,000 feet at around 03.15, helping to set off seventy-five fires, thirty-three of which were classed locally as large. Even so, fewer than a third of the bomb loads had actually found the mark and local sources estimated a force of only fifty aircraft.

49 Squadron's fourth Manchester arrived on the 18th, and on the 19th, the crews of F/O Read and Sgts Burton and Slingo were detailed for mining duties in the Nectarine I garden off the southern Frisians as part of a 5 Group effort of twenty-five Hampdens, ten Manchesters and two Lancasters. They departed Scampton between 20.41 and 20.46 and headed out via Mablethorpe to pinpoint on the gap between Ameland and Terschelling, where the ten-tenths cloud base was at 2,000 feet and the visibility poor as a result of haze. The Read and Burton crews delivered their mine each off Terschelling from 800 and 700 feet at 22.36 and 22.32 respectively, but nothing was heard from the Slingo crew, who failed to return in AT217. The remains of the pilot and one other eventually washed ashore for burial, but their two crew mates were never found. On the 21st, four more Manchesters were taken on charge to bring the total to eight, and among the influx of airmen during the final third of the month were some from 144 Squadron, who were close to the end of their tour and were left behind when their former unit and 455 Squadron RAAF transferred to Coastal Command on the 20th and 21st respectively. Other airmen were posted in from 25 O.T.U to support the requirement for seven-man crews.

The first attempt to employ Gee as a blind bombing aid took place on the night of the 22/23rd, when Cologne was the target for a 3 Group force of sixty-four Wellingtons and five Stirlings. Fewer than 20% of the bomb loads fell into the city, and some landed up to ten miles away, proving that Gee was capable of guiding a force to a general area, but lacked the precision necessary to deliver a telling blow on an urban target. While this operation was in progress, 5 Group dispatched twenty-two Hampdens and a dozen Manchesters on gardening duties on both sides of the Schleswig-Holstein peninsula in Forget-me-not (Kiel Harbour), Quince (Kiel Bay), Radish (Fehmarn Belt) and Rosemary (Heligoland Bight). Those reaching the western Baltic encountered clear skies and good visibility and pinpointed on the southern tip of Denmark's Langeland Island and on the German mainland north-east of Kiel, before making their timed runs and dropping their mines into the briefed locations. The 49 Squadron crews of F/O Read and Sgts Bond and Hamer took off between 20.01 and 20.03 bound for the Quince garden in Kiel Fjord, but F/O Read turned back almost immediately because of an engine issue. The Bond and Hamer crews reached the western coast of Jutland and, for whatever reason, decided to plant their vegetables in the Hawthorn garden off Fanø Island as an alternative, dropping them from 600 and 800 feet at 22.56 and 23.00 respectively.

In an attempt to repeat the success gained at Lübeck, the nearby Baltic coastal town of Rostock was earmarked for a series of four raids on consecutive nights from the 23/24th, with the old town and the Heinkel aircraft factory on its southern outskirts the specific aiming points. A force of 161 aircraft was assembled, 143 of them assigned to the town and eighteen to the factory, and 5 Group managed to put up eleven Hampdens, six Manchesters and a single Lancaster. This would be the swansong for 49 Squadron Hampdens and the honour was handed to the same three crews who had operated on the previous night. They departed Scampton at 21.45 and all reached the target area to find favourable weather conditions and good visibility, despite which, the majority of crews failed to find the mark at either aiming point, and the bombing fell between two and six miles away. On return, the 49 Squadron trio reported bombing from 3,500, 6,000 and 8,000 feet at 02.05, 02.20 and 02.40 and observing bomb bursts and fires but no detail.

The 5 Group element for round two at Rostock amounted to thirty-four aircraft, including four Lancasters from the newly-converted 207 Squadron at Bottesford, and all were assigned to the Heinkel factory, while ninety-one aircraft from the other groups focused on the old town. Those reaching the target area were drawn on from many miles away by the fires already burning. Bright moonlight illuminated the Unterwarnow River running south from the coast to the heart of the town and provided excellent visibility for the low-level attacks. The town seemed to be ablaze as they crossed over it to reach the Heinkel factory, which most attacked on existing fires, while trying to evade the attentions of the many searchlights co-operating with light flak. According to the observations of returning crews, the Heinkel factory and adjacent aerodrome had been hit by many bombs and were left burning, and, while post-raid reconnaissance revealed extensive damage within the town, the factory buildings were revealed to be still intact, demonstrating that the impressions gained by crews in the heat of battle could be somewhat unreliable.

The third Rostock raid was launched on the night of the 25/26th and involved 110 aircraft assigned to the town, while eighteen from 5 Group targeted the Heinkel factory led by 106 Squadron's commanding officer, W/C Guy Gibson. Ideal weather conditions again prevailed, and post-raid reconnaissance revealed that the factory had, at last, been hit, and that the town had suffered severe damage without loss to the attackers. A force of 106 aircraft was detailed for the final raid of the series on the 26th, which included a contribution from 5 Group of nineteen Hampdens, nine Manchesters and a single Lancaster. Those reaching the target area found moonlight, excellent visibility and existing fires to aid target location, and another successful raid ensued. An analysis of the Rostock campaign revealed it to have been highly successful, destroying 1,765 buildings and seriously damaging five hundred more, which represented 60% of the town's built-up area. In his diaries, Propaganda Minister Goebbels used the phrase "Terrorangriff", terror raid, for the first time.

Earlier on the 26th, F/Ls Massey and Ratcliff had been posted to 24 O.T.U. at the conclusion of their tours and on the 27th, four further Manchesters arrived on squadron charge, at which point the ORB declared that 49 Squadron was now a Manchester unit. The Hampdens were transferred to 144 Squadron and would undergo conversion to enable them to carry torpedoes. Only 408 (Goose) and 420 (Snowy Owl) Squadrons RCAF now operated Hampdens and ten of them took part in a raid on the shipyards at Kiel on the 28th and contributed to damage to three of them. The month ended for 5 Group with a raid by nine 420 (Snowy Owl) Squadron Hampdens on the 29th against the Gnome & Rhône aero engine factory at Gennevilliers in Paris. During the course of the month, 49 Squadron took part in nineteen operations and dispatched ninety-six sorties for the loss of seven Hampdens, six complete crews and three other airmen.

# May 1942

On the 1st of May, 49 Squadron had eleven Manchesters on charge and awaited delivery of a further seven to complete its complement. The weather kept the Command on the ground on the night of the 1/2nd, but it had relented sufficiently on the following day for ninety-six aircraft from 3 and 5 Groups to be detailed for mining operations that night. 5 Group provided twenty-one Lancasters, eight Manchesters and twelve Hampdens for gardens in the Baltic and off the Biscay coast, and nine Manchesters for nickelling duties in the Rennes area of north-western France. Among the latter were five representing 49 Squadron, L7287, P/O Perry, L7386, P/O Jeffreys, L7469, P/O Farrington, L7484, F/S Carter and R5771, P/O Shackleton, which departed Scampton between 20.56 and 20.59 to launch the squadron's new and, thankfully, brief Manchester career. They crossed the French coast near St-Malo in extreme darkness under clear skies with haze below and four located the target area to dispense their leaflets from 8,000 to 11,000 feet between 23.24 and 23.42. P/O Jeffreys and crew had to contend with an unserviceable DR compass and dropped their bundles of reading matter on a last-resort area from 10,000 feet at 00.30.

Hamburg was posted as the primary target for a force of eighty-one aircraft on the 3rd, the numbers somewhat reduced in the face of a forecast of poor weather conditions. 5 Group contributed just five Hampdens from 420 Squadron RCAF, while other elements from the group were occupied by minor endeavours elsewhere. Orders were received on the 4th to make ready for the first of what would be a "Rostock-style" sustained assault on the important industrial city of Stuttgart over three consecutive nights. A force of 121 aircraft included a contribution from 5 Group of nineteen Hampdens and fourteen Lancasters, the crews of the former briefed to aim for the highly important Robert Bosch factory, which was engaged in the manufacture of dynamos, injection pumps and magnetos, while the Lancaster crews were briefed to attack military barracks. Meanwhile, 49 Squadron continued its gentle introduction to Manchester operations with two nickelling sorties to the Amiens region of north-eastern France involving the crews of P/O Floyd and Sgt Burton, who took off at 21.36. They were greeted by an absence of cloud and moon and had to contend only with ground haze as they delivered their cargos from 10,000 and 11,000 feet at 23.58 and 23.27 respectively.

At Stuttgart, very little was observed of the results, and all but one returning 5 Group crew reported bombing fires and red flares through the cloud, with just one Hampden crew claiming to have bombed the primary target. Local reports confirmed that the operation had scattered bombs over a wide area and onto a decoy site at Lauffen, fifteen miles to the north of the city, which was "defended" by thirty-five searchlights and fifty flak guns. It was a clever ruse that would lure away many bomb loads during the course of the war, that might otherwise have caused damage in Stuttgart. 5 Group contributed four 97 Squadron Lancasters to the same target on the following night, and they again bombed the town rather than the Bosch factory to which they had been assigned. Despite clear skies, ground detail was obscured by haze, and no bombs fell in the city. It was Stuttgart again on the 6th, for which 5 Group detailed ten Hampdens and ten Lancasters in an overall force of ninety-seven aircraft. They exited the English coast at Orfordness on course to traverse Belgium, and, after an outward flight lasting almost three hours, reached the target area to find largely clear skies, but haze again making target identification difficult. Most picked out a built-up area on e.t.a., backed up by evidence of searchlights, flak and burning incendiaries from other aircraft, and scattered their bombs over a wide area. The operation was another massively ineffective affair, which again failed to land a single bomb in Stuttgart, but did hit 150 buildings in Heilbronn, a large town situated five miles from the Lauffen decoy site and twenty miles from Stuttgart.

The night of the 7/8th was devoted to mining operations involving eighty aircraft of 3 and 5 Groups operating mostly in the Baltic, although 49 Squadron's four Manchesters were assigned to the Rosemary garden in Helgoland Bight, which would not require them to overfly enemy territory. They departed Scampton between 00.57 and 01.37 and lost the services of P/O Farrington to an engine issue when still some forty minutes from the target area. P/O Shackleton and crew had been last to take-off and decided that they had insufficient time to reach the target and return before the light of dawn. F/Sgt Carter and crew returned their mines to base after finding the conditions unfavourable, while P/O Jeffreys and crew described a successful sortie undertaken in ideal conditions.

The recent successes at Lübeck and Rostock may have encouraged the posting of another Baltic coast target on the 8th, this time, Warnemünde, situated on the West Bank of the estuary ten miles north of Rostock. The docks were the site of U-Boot crew training, and also supplied German forces on the Russian front, but, equally important was the Heinkel aircraft factory, the destruction of which was handed to 5 Group. An initial force of more than two hundred aircraft was detailed, among which 5 Group put up twenty-one Lancasters, nine Manchesters and nineteen Hampdens. The operation was only moderately successful and cost nineteen aircraft, eight of which belonged to 5 Group and included four Lancasters of 44 (Rhodesia) Squadron, one of which was captained by its newly appointed commanding officer.

The following night brought a small-scale mining effort by 5 Group in the Baltic, while the two 49 Squadron crews of P/O Floyd and F/Sgt Carter were assigned to the Rosemary II garden to the north of Heligoland. They departed Scampton at half-past midnight and this time both experienced ideal conditions, in which they planted their vegetables from 700 and 800 feet shortly before 03.00. This would prove to be the last operation to be undertaken by the squadron until almost the end of the month and in the meantime, all crews would be brought up to fully operational status.

Losses were a fact of life in Bomber Command and could not be allowed to interfere with the process of war. A team from the Committee of Adjustment would descend upon the billets of the missing men and remove all trace of them to prepare the way for the next occupants. Such was the size of a bomber squadron, and the constant turnover of arrivals and departures, that close friendships beyond one's own crew were discouraged. Perhaps it was different among officers, who were fewer, and were more frequently in each other's company in the officers' mess, but, generally, the faces of the missing soon faded from memory, and those returning within a matter of months after evading capture were often shocked to discover how few faces they recognised. On the 11th, changes were made to the make-up of a crew, which removed second pilots, second navigators and second wireless operators to create a crew consisting of a pilot (captain), flight engineer (pilot's mate), navigator, bomb-aimer, wireless operator/gunner and mid-upper and rear gunners. W/C Leonard Slee had arrived at Scampton from Coningsby on the 7th as commanding officer elect and would succeed W/C Stubbs DFC on his posting to HQ 92 Group on the 14th. W/C

Slee's previous role is uncertain, but he was probably a Senior Air Staff Officer (SASO) supporting operations by 97 and 106 Squadrons.

Small-scale mining operations aside on the 15th and 16th, 5 Group remained largely inactive until the 19th, when Mannheim was posted as the target for a force of 193 aircraft, which included a 5 Group contribution of fifteen Hampdens, thirteen Lancasters and four Manchesters. They flew to the French coast and continued south until crossing into Germany south of Luxembourg, where they had to run the gauntlet of masses of searchlights before finding the target area under clear skies, but, in the absence of a moon, in extreme darkness, which combined with haze to blot out all ground features. Most crews identified the city by means of a Gee-fix and the River Rhine but picking out the main post office aiming point was beyond them. Local reports claimed that only around ten bomb loads landed in the city, and this was after the force had been heard overhead for an extended period, as if searching for it. A 49 Squadron Conversion Flight had been formed on the 18th under S/L Peter Ward-Hunt, who had returned to the squadron after a spell at 207 Squadron. The flight initially boasted two Lancasters, R5850 and R5855, and two Manchesters, and an experienced Lancaster pilot, F/Sgt Rowlands, was brought in from 97 Squadron on the 24th to assist with the conversion programme.

There now followed another lull in major operations as Harris prepared for his master stroke. At the time of his appointment as C-in-C, the figure of four thousand bombers had been bandied around as the number required to wrap up the war. Whilst there was not the slightest chance of procuring them, Harris, with a dark cloud still hanging over the existence of an independent bomber force, needed to ensure that those earmarked for him were not spirited away to what he considered to be less-deserving causes. The Command had not yet achieved sufficient success to silence the detractors, and the Admiralty was still calling for bomber aircraft to be diverted to the U-Boot campaign, while others demanded support for the North Africa campaign. Harris was in need of a major victory, and, perhaps, a dose of symbolism to make his point, and, out of this was born the Thousand Plan, Operation Millennium, the launching of a thousand aircraft in one night against a major German city, for which Hamburg had been pencilled in. Harris did not have a thousand front-line aircraft and required the support of other Commands to make up the numbers. This was forthcoming from Coastal and Flying Training Commands, and, in the case of the former, a letter to Harris on the 22nd promised 250 aircraft. However, following an intervention from the Admiralty, the offer was withdrawn, and most of the Flying Training Command aircraft were found to be not up to the task, leaving the Millennium force well short of the magic figure. Undaunted, Harris, or more probably his able deputy, AM Sir Robert Saundby, scraped together every airframe capable of controlled flight, or something resembling it, and pulled in the screened crews from their instructional duties. He also pressed into service aircraft and crews from within the Command's own training establishment, 91 Group. Come the night, not only would the thousand mark be achieved, but it would also be comfortably surpassed.

During the final week of the month, the arrival on bomber stations from Yorkshire to East Anglia of a motley collection of aircraft from training units gave rise to much speculation among crews and ground staff alike, but, as usual, only the NAAFI staff and the local civilians knew what was really afoot. The most pressing remaining question was the weather, and, as the days ticked by inexorably towards the end of May, this was showing no signs of complying. Harris was aware of the genuine danger, that the giant force might draw attention to itself, and thereby compromise security, and the point was fast approaching when the operation would have to take place or be abandoned for the time being. Harris released some of the pressure by sanctioning operations on the night of the 29/30th, for which the Gnome & Rhone aero-engine and Goodrich tyre factories at Gennevilliers in Paris were the main targets. A force of seventy-seven aircraft included a contribution from 5 Group of fourteen Lancasters and three Hampdens, the crews of which found it difficult to gain an accurate picture of the outcome. Despite the claims of a successful operation, the only damage caused was to eighty-seven houses, in which thirty-four people were killed and 167 injured.

It was in an atmosphere of frustration and hopeful expectation, that "morning prayers" began at Harris's High Wycombe HQ on the 30th, with all eyes turned upon the civilian chief meteorological adviser, Magnus Spence. After careful deliberation, he was able to give a qualified assurance of clear skies over the Rhineland, while north-western Germany and Hamburg would be concealed under buckets of cloud. Thus, did the fickle fates decree that Cologne would bear the dubious honour of hosting the first one thousand bomber raid in history. At briefings, crews were told that the enormous force was to be pushed across the aiming point in just ninety minutes. This was unprecedented and gave rise to the question of collisions as hundreds of aircraft funnelled towards the aiming point. The answer, according to the experts, was to observe timings and flight levels, and they calculated also that just two aircraft would collide over the target. It is said that a wag in every briefing room asked, "do they know which two?"

5 Group had seventy-three Lancasters, forty-six Manchesters and thirty-four Hampdens bombed up and ready to go, and at Scampton, thirteen 49 Squadron Manchesters and an equal number of 83 Squadron Lancasters awaited the arrival of their crews, who had been briefed to attack one of three areas spanning the city centre from north to south, in their case, aiming point Y, bordering the western and southern extremities on the West Bank. After one aircraft became unserviceable just before take-off, the 49 Squadron order of battle for this momentous occasion comprised the following aircraft and crews; L7526 S/L Bennett, L7287 F/L Paramore, L7479 P/O Farrington, L7290 P/O Floyd, R5775 P/O Jeffreys, L7524 P/O Perry, R5794 P/O Shackleton, L7421 F/Sgt Lewis, L7429 F/Sgt Carter, L7389 Sgt Burton, and from the Conversion Flight, L7493 S/L Ward-Hunt with W/C Slee as second pilot and L7398 F/Sgt Rowlands. Late that evening, the first of an eventual 1,047 aircraft took off to deliver the now familiar three-wave-format attack on the Rhineland capital, the older training hacks struggling somewhat reluctantly into the air, lifted more by the enthusiasm of their crews than by the power of their engines, and some of these, unable to climb to a respectable height, would fall easy prey to the defences or would simply drop from the sky through mechanical breakdown.

The 49 Squadron element departed Scampton between 22.50 and 23.31 and soon lost the services of P/O Perry and crew, when their aircraft began to vibrate and lose height, forcing them to land at Docking after just forty-five minutes flying time. The remainder pressed on across Belgium, drawn on for the last seventy miles by the glow of the already burning city, and were greeted at the target by precisely the weather conditions of clear skies and bright moonlight predicted by Magnus Spence. Returning crews described a city on fire from end to end and never-before-witnessed scenes, but the only detail recorded by the recently appointed new 49 Squadron adjutant was S/L Ward-Hunt's bombing height of 10,000 feet at 01.16 and S/L Bennett's claim that the glow could be seen from a hundred miles into the return journey. Not among those at debriefing to express their views were the crews of P/O Floyd and F/Sgt Carter, the former having been hit by flak as they headed home over the Ruhr and lost their starboard engine. A Manchester with only one good engine possessed the flying characteristics of a brick, and the captain ordered his crew to bale out while he attempted to maintain control. Five managed to get out in time, before the Manchester rolled over and crashed in the Mülheim/Oberhausen area in the central Ruhr with fatal consequences for the pilot and bomb-aimer. News would eventually arrive via the Red Cross to the effect that the five survivors were now in enemy hands. The fate of F/Sgt Carter and crew remains unknown after they disappeared without trace in a Manchester borrowed from the Conversion Flight.

Post-raid reconnaissance confirmed that the operation had, by any standards, been an outstanding success, and had destroyed more than 3,300 buildings, while inflicting serious damage to two thousand others. Although the loss of forty-one aircraft represented a new record high, the conditions had favoured both attackers and defenders alike, and in the context of the scale of success and the numbers dispatched, it could not be considered an inordinately high figure. 5 Group registered a loss of four Manchesters, one Lancaster and one Hampden, but it was the training units that sustained the greatest losses amounting to twenty-one aircraft.

During the course of the month, the squadron took part in five operations and dispatched twenty-five sorties for the loss of two Manchesters and crews.

# June 1942

While the Millennium force remained assembled, Harris wanted to exploit its potential again immediately, and was no doubt excited about the prospect of visiting upon the old enemy of Essen a similar ordeal to that just experienced by Cologne. A force of 956 aircraft was the best that could be achieved during the 1$^{st}$, 5 Group managing seventy-three Lancasters, thirty-three Manchesters, nine of them belonging to 49 Squadron, and twenty-six Hampdens. Seven of the 49 Squadron element departed Scampton between 23.30 and 00.11 with F/L Paramore the senior pilot among them, while the crews of P/O Farrington and S/L de Mestre were delayed until 00.50 and 00.56 respectively, the latter by engine trouble, and neither would have sufficient time to complete their sortie. Crews had been briefed to employ the sprawl of the Borbeck district Krupp sector as the aiming point and flew out under favourable weather conditions that promised the possibility of actually being able to identify ground detail. They ran into five to ten-tenths cloud at 4,000 to 6,000 feet over the target, which combined with industrial haze and smoke drifting over from Cologne to muddy the vertical visibility, and bombing took place largely on TR (Gee) supported by occasional visual references on waterways. The 49 Squadron participants delivered their attacks from 9,000 to 16,000 feet between 01.06 and 02.15 on a variety of headings ranging from north-east, through east to due west and most observed bursts and fires. An SOS message was received from P/O Shackleton and crew at 02.19 stating that the starboard engine had failed, but nothing further was heard and it was sometime later that news arrived to shed light on their fate. R5794 had been shot down by a night-fighter and crashed seven miles east-north-east of Turnhout in Belgium killing all but the bomb-aimer and wireless operator, who were taken into captivity. An accurate assessment of results was not possible, and crews returned with reports of many fires, some identified as dummies, but no detail and the authorities would have to wait for post-raid reconnaissance before they could assess what had happened on the ground. In the meantime, a counting of the cost revealed the loss of thirty-one aircraft, and sadly, there would be no major success to mitigate the scale of the loss, local reports confirming that only eleven houses had been destroyed in Essen, and fewer than two hundred others damaged, mostly in southern districts. A greater number of bomb loads had actually fallen on the nearby locations of Oberhausen, Duisburg and Mülheim-an-der-Ruhr.

A follow-up raid was planned for twenty-four hours later, and a much-reduced force of 197 aircraft made ready, with 5 Group providing twenty-seven Lancasters and a dozen Hampdens. They found clear skies over the Ruhr with the usual industrial haze, but a low moon provided some illumination and most crews would describe the visibility as good. The deployment of flares proved beneficial as they highlighted the Rhine over to the west, and those equipped with Gee confirmed their positions over what they believed to be the Krupp works aiming point. Despite the apparent confidence of the crews that they had attacked Essen, local authorities reported just three high explosive bombs and three hundred incendiaries falling in the city to cause only minor damage. Such was the density of the Ruhr, with overlapping town and city boundaries, it was difficult not to hit something urban, but concentration was the key to success, and the scattering of bombs over a wide area was never going to achieve a knock-out blow. Harris was stubborn and would keep trying, but it would be a further nine months before the means were to hand to make a genuine impact.

For the next operation, on the 3rd, Harris turned his attention upon Bremen, which, along with Essen and Emden, would share the Command's attention for the remainder of the month. A force of 170 aircraft was made ready for the first major attack on the port-city since the previous October, for which fifteen Lancasters, nine Hampdens and six Manchesters were provided by 5 Group. 49 Squadron was not invited to take part and instead dispatched the crews of Sgt Webster and P/O Elliott at 01.21 and 01.58 respectively to deliver propaganda to the residents of Lille. The residents of north-eastern France were probably by now relying on Bomber Command to supplement their stocks of toilet paper, which fluttered down from 10,000 feet out of cloudless skies between 03.00 and 03.30. Crews returning from Bremen lacked confidence in the effectiveness of the raid, but local reports told a story of heavy damage to housing in six streets and to harbour installations, and there were also hits on U-Boot construction yards and the Focke-Wulf aircraft factory, although, any loss of production was slight.

A force of 180 aircraft was prepared for the next intended assault on Essen on the 5th, for which 5 Group put up thirteen Lancasters and eleven Hampdens. 49 Squadron was once more excluded, but W/C Slee decided to undertake his first sortie with the squadron as crew captain with a nickelling sortie to Rennes, for which he took off at 23.34 and returned at 02.55 having fulfilled his brief from 15,000 feet in excellent conditions under clear skies. Those bound for the main event flew out over Belgium, and some identified a bend in the River Ruhr to the south-east of the target, while others relied on a TR-fix, flares or evidence of searchlight and flak concentrations to establish their positions in conditions of poor vertical visibility. Local sources again confirmed an ineffective and wasteful raid, which caused only minor damage in Essen at a cost of twelve aircraft and crews.

The first of four attacks during the month on the naval port of Emden was posted on the 6th, and a force of 233 aircraft made ready, 5 Group contributing twenty Lancasters, fifteen Hampdens and seven Manchesters. 49 Squadron made ready five Manchesters and sent them on their way from Scampton between 23.13 and 23.37 with S/L de Mestre the senior pilot on duty. P/O Farrington was unable to coax sufficient height out of L7479 and invited the bomb aimer to jettison a bomb or two to lighten the load, only for the entire contents of the bomb bay to fall out. The others found the skies over the coast of north-western Germany to be clear of cloud and the visibility to be good, which enabled those dropping flares to illuminate the docks area for the bomb-aimers. F/Sgt Lewis and crew attacked from 10,000 feet at 01.30 and Sgt Webster from 14,000 feet fifteen minutes later and smoke was rising through 8,000 feet as they retreated to leave a glow in their wake that remained visible for up to eighty miles into the return journey. L7287 and L7469 failed to return with the crews of F/L Paramore DFC and S/L de Mestre DSO DFC, both having crashed into the sea, the former without trace, while the remains of four from the latter came ashore in the target area for burial. Oblt Ludwig Becker of 6/.NJG2 claimed to have shot down L7469 from 11,500 feet some twelve miles north-west of the Frisian Island of Borkum. Photographic reconnaissance and local reports confirmed that the raid had been responsible for the destruction of some three hundred houses, with a further two hundred severely damaged in return for the loss of nine aircraft.

The Command entered a period of gardening and minor operations, thereafter, punctuated by two further attacks on Essen and it was at this point, on the 8th, that S/L Barnard was posted in to fulfil the role of flight commander. The first of the Emden raids, by an initial force of 170 aircraft, took place that night, and was supported by 5 Group with thirteen Lancasters and nine Hampdens. It was another disappointing and widely scattered raid, which caused only minor housing damage. After spending four nights on the ground because of adverse weather conditions, the Command stirred itself on the 16th at Harris's behest to have another crack at Essen, for which 106 aircraft were made ready, 5 Group contributing fifteen Lancasters. All crews had been briefed to employ TR to locate the target and bomb blindly based on that, which, under the conditions of up to eight-tenths cloud on a moonless night with visibility down to three miles, was the best that could be expected. It emerged at debriefing that only sixteen crews claimed to have bombed the primary target, while fifty-six others had found alternatives, mostly the city of Bonn. This concluded a series of five raids on Essen in sixteen nights, during which 1,607 sorties had been dispatched and eighty-four aircraft lost. The city had sustained no industrial damage, and a few wrecked houses was all that Bomber Command had to show for the massive effort expended.

Having hosted an effective attack earlier in the month, Emden became the focus for three raids in the space of four nights, beginning on the 19th, for which a force of 194 aircraft was assembled. 49 Squadron remained at home while nine Lancasters and eleven Hampdens from other units represented 5 Group, their crews having been briefed to switch to Osnabrück, eighty miles to the south, if the weather conditions over the coastal region became troublesome. Part of the flare force did, indeed, initiate an attack on Osnabrück by twenty-nine aircraft, leaving 131 others to claim that they had bombed the primary target. Despite the numbers, the Emden authorities reported only a handful of high-explosive bombs falling and a few hundred incendiaries. 185 aircraft were made ready to return to the port on the following night, among them twenty-four Lancaster and a dozen Hampdens provided by 5 Group. The docks were the briefed aiming point and the town the alternative, and positions were established by TR-fix and glimpses of the coastline. Local reports confirmed that only a proportion of the force had located the target, and around a hundred houses had been damaged. On the following morning, the squadron dispatched four Manchesters on a sea search for any crews that might have ditched. The identity of three of those involved was not recorded, but we are told that L7387 took off from Scampton at 11.30 with the crew of Sgt O'Brien RAAF on board and failed to return. It is believed that the Manchester crashed into the North Sea off the Frisians and the remains of two of the occupants, both members of the RAAF, eventually came ashore for burial, one in Sweden and the other on Schiermonnikoog.

A force of 227 aircraft took off on the 22$^{nd}$ to deliver the third raid of the series on Emden, for which 5 Group contributed eleven Lancasters and eight Hampdens. Most crews established their approach to the target by identifying the coastline and confirming it via a TR-fix backed up by flak and fires, before running in on the aiming point in good visibility under moonlight. Some returning crews had been able to distinguish between genuine and decoy fires, but the latter succeeded in drawing off many loads, and those finding the target destroyed fifty houses and damaged a hundred more.

On the 25$^{th}$, S/L Bennett DFC was posted out at the conclusion of his tour and S/L Couch arrived to succeed him as a flight commander. In keeping with the practice of the incumbent adjutant, no details were provided of S/L Bennett's new post or from whence his successor had come. The time had now arrived for the final deployment of the Thousand Force, and, indeed, of the Manchester in operational service. A force of 960 aircraft was assembled on the 25$^{th}$, 142 provided by 5 Group in the form of ninety-six Lancasters, twenty-six Hampdens and twenty Manchesters. It was an indication of the failure of the Manchester, that the aircraft it had been intended to replace, the Hampden, would continue to serve 5 Group in small numbers until mid-September. To the above numbers were added five aircraft from Army Co-operation Command and 102 aircraft from Coastal Command, which had been ordered by Churchill himself to take part, although, its contribution was to be deemed a separate operation. However, the 1,067 aircraft from all sources would represent a larger combined force than that sent to Cologne at the end of May. 49 Squadron dispatched the crews of Sgts Heard and Webster and P/O Elliott between 23.22 and 23.24 and W/C Slee at 00.02, but the last-mentioned lost their hydraulics system as they climbed out and were soon back on the ground. According to the 5 Group ORB, 49 Squadron also detailed its first Lancaster sortie on this night, and although it was not mentioned in the squadron ORB, 44 (Rhodesia) Squadron recorded that a 49 Squadron aircraft was among those departing Waddington but did not identify the pilot.

The briefed aiming point was the Focke-Wulf aircraft factory in the south-eastern district of Hemelingen on the East Bank of the Weser, for which the 5 Group crews set course after crossing the English coast between Mablethorpe and Skegness. They flew out above the ten-tenths cloud that persisted all the way from the English coast to the target area and occupied a sky that was extremely bright, courtesy of a full moon and the Northern Lights. A band of nine to ten-tenths cloud lay over Bremen at between 3,000 and 5,000 feet, completely obscuring ground detail, which precluded any chance of picking up the Focke-Wulf aircraft factory and positions were established by TR-fix, the glow of fires on the ground and the volume of flak coming up through the cloud. The crews of Sgts Heard and Webster attacked the city area of Bremen from 8,000 and 12,000 feet respectively at 01.40, while P/O Elliott and crew went for Emden as an alternative. Returning crews could only estimate that they had hit the city and reported several areas of fire, but none of the 696 crews claiming to have attacked the primary target had any real clue as to the outcome.

Local sources confirmed a number of hits on the Focke-Wulf aircraft factory and some shipyards, along with the destruction of 572 houses and damage to more than six thousand others, mostly in southern and eastern districts, but estimated the size of the bomber force to be around eighty. The level of success fell well short of that achieved at Cologne, but surpassed by far the failure at Essen, albeit at a new record loss of forty-eight aircraft, which represented 5% of those dispatched. The O.T.Us of 91 Group suffered the highest casualty rate of 11.6%, largely because they were employing tired, old Whitleys, Wellingtons and Hampdens, which were not up to the task, while 5 Group lost one Lancaster and one Manchester.

There would be no further operations for 49 Squadron as its conversion to the Lancaster gathered pace, and in the meantime, the first of a number of follow-up operations against Bremen was mounted on the night of the 27/28th involving 144 aircraft, including twenty-four Lancasters from 5 Group. Weather conditions were very much as those of two nights earlier, with ten-tenths cloud up to around 4,000 feet and decreasing amounts thereafter as high as 15,000 feet. The sky above was as bright as day under a large moon, even though the Northern Lights, on this occasion, were masked by high cloud. Most located the target area by TR-fix, and crews could only estimate that they were over the target. Local reports confirmed hits on the previously damaged Atlas Werke shipyard and the Korff refinery, but further details were scant and of little value.

It was Bremen again on the 29th, for which a force of 253 aircraft was assembled, including sixty-four Lancasters as the 5 Group contribution. They flew out over six to ten-tenths cloud at between 3,000 and 5,000 feet with excellent visibility above and found around seven to ten-tenths cloud in layers up to 16,000 feet in the target area, with large gaps that afforded some a glimpse of the ground. They delivered their loads from 15,000 and 16,000 feet at 01.24 and 01.27 respectively, and, in keeping with other returning crews, could provide only impressions of the raid. Local reports, however, spoke of extensive damage to the Focke-Wulf factory, the A G Weser U-Boot construction yard and three other important war-industry premises, along with the local gas works and some limited destruction of housing.

During the course of the month, the squadron took part in five operations and dispatched twenty-one Manchester sorties and one by a Lancaster for the loss of four Manchesters and crews.

# July 1942

A gentle start to the new month had 5 Group operating alone on the night of the 1/2nd, when sending two Lancasters each from 97 and 106 Squadrons to mine the waters of the Great Belt in the western Baltic. The campaign against Bremen continued on the 2nd, with the preparation of a force of 325 aircraft, more than half of which were Wellingtons. 5 Group squadrons contributed fifty-three Lancasters and twenty-eight Hampdens, and those reaching the target found favourable weather conditions with excellent visibility, no low cloud, high cirrus at around 22,000 feet and only a little haze to spoil the view below. Positions were established by TR-fix confirmed by a visual check, but searchlight glare created great difficulty for the bomb-aimers trying to identify the Focke-Wulf aircraft factory aiming point, and most would settle for estimating the fall of their bombs. Local reports spoke of a thousand houses damaged, along with four small industrial premises, while three cranes and seven ships were hit in the port, one of the vessels sinking and becoming a danger to navigation. The likelihood is, however, that much of the effort was wasted beyond the city's southern boundary.

The remainder of the first half of the month would be low-key, with mining operations occupying much of the night-time activity. 5 Group detailed fifty-two Lancasters and twenty-four Hampdens on the 8th to attack Wilhelmshaven as part of an overall force of 285 aircraft. Those reaching the target encountered around three-tenths thin cloud at 10,000 feet and haze below, which made it almost impossible for most to identify ground detail, including the docks and shipyards aiming points, and positions were established on e.t.a. and by TR-fix, some backed up through a visual check assisted by the use of flares. Local reports confirmed some damage in Wilhelmshaven, but post-raid reconnaissance revealed that much of the bombing had missed the town to the west.

The first daylight foray deep into enemy territory by Lancasters, the previously mentioned raid on the M.A.N diesel engine factory at Augsburg in April, had cost seven of the twelve aircraft dispatched, and Harris, despite his antipathy to such operations, sanctioned a similar plan by 5 Group for an attack on the U-Boot construction yards in the distant port of Danzig on the 11th. The forty-four Lancasters of 61, 83, 97, 106 and 207 Squadrons were to fly out in formation at low level, before splitting up to cross Denmark and the Baltic independently, and then climb to bombing altitude and make their own individual approaches to the target. The attack was to be carried out in the fading light, to allow a withdrawal to take place under the cover of darkness, and the 1,500-mile round-trip would be the longest yet attempted by the Command. An unanticipated band of ten-tenths ice-bearing cloud was encountered over the North Sea extending from 1,000 to 14,000 feet, and this ruined the plan as aircraft lost contact with each other, forcing the individual crews to break formation and make their way independently to the target. This would have a detrimental effect on the raid and cause some crews to abandon their sorties or arrive late, when darkness had already settled over the area to make identification a challenge. Twenty-six aircraft bombed either the ship-building wharfs or the town, and two of them were shot down by flak.

The first of a series of five operations over a four-week period against Duisburg was mounted on the night of the 13/14th and involved 194 aircraft, including thirteen Lancasters from the 5 Group stations of Bottesford and Coningsby. The operation failed to find the mark in adverse weather conditions consisting of electrical storms and heavy cloud, and the bombing became widely scattered and ineffective. A force of ninety-nine four-engine types was assembled on the 19th to send that night against the Vulkan U-Boot construction yards at Vegesack, situated on the River Weser a few miles to the north-west of Bremen city centre. 5 Group contributed twenty-eight Lancasters to the attack, and those arriving in the target area were met by up to ten-tenths cloud with tops at 10,000 to 12,000 feet and delivered their attacks on the basis of a Gee-fix (TR). They gained an impression that a lot was going on beneath the cloud, but, in reality, the raid had completely missed the target, confirming the fact that Gee was useful as a guide to navigation, but was not precise enough to employ as a blind-bombing device.

A force of 291 aircraft was assembled on the 21st for the second raid of the series on Duisburg, and this number included twenty-nine Lancasters and seventeen Hampdens representing 5 Group. It was a moonless night, and, despite the presence of clear skies over the target, extreme darkness and the usual industrial haze took their toll on vertical visibility, the effects of which, it was hoped, would be negated by flares dropped from the leading aircraft by TR. However, these proved to be not entirely accurate, and some illuminated an area of open country on the West Bank of the Rhine. Returning crews could offer no useful information to the intelligence section at debriefing, but local reports confirmed extensive damage in residential districts, with ninety-four apartment buildings destroyed and 256 seriously damaged, and there was also mention of damage to the Thyssen steel works and to two other important war-industry factories.

A reduced force of 215 aircraft was made ready to continue the assault on Duisburg on the 23rd, and forty-five of these were Lancasters, those reaching the target encountering seven to ten-tenths cloud with tops as high as 12,000 feet in places but a large gap that afforded some crews a sight of the ground. Despite that, for many, there was little chance of locating the briefed aiming point, which was probably the Thyssen steel works, and the Gee-based (TR) flares were again scattered and largely ineffective, leaving most crews to carry out their attacks on their own TR-fix. Returning crews were confident that they had hit the city's built-up area, many claiming to have identified specific ground features, and the outcome of the raid was similar to the previous one, with residential property sustaining the bulk of the damage.

The fourth raid on Duisburg was posted on the 25th, for which the largest force yet of the series was assembled amounting to 313 aircraft, among which were 177 Wellingtons and fourteen Hampdens, with the four-engine types, including thirty-three Lancasters, making up the numbers. They ran into around seven-tenths cloud over the target, with fair visibility, which enabled a visual confirmation of the TR-based approach, but not the briefed aiming point D, and the extensive and distinctive Ruhrort inland docks complex provided a solid reference point to bomb the built-up area generally for those unable to identify the briefed aiming point. It was left to local reports to confirm further damage to residential property, but less extensive than in the two previous attacks.

A maximum effort was planned on the 26th for the annual last-week-of-July attack on Germany's second city, Hamburg, and 404 aircraft answered the call, among them seventy-seven Lancasters and thirty-three Hampdens. The 5 Group elements flew out over the Lincolnshire coast, and once over the North Sea, had to negotiate the frequently met conditions on this route of towering cloud, electrical storms and severe icing. The skies over the target were clear, however, and the visibility excellent, which allowed the crews to confirm their positions by visual reference, with the docks area standing out particularly clearly in the bright moonlight. They had been handed aiming point D, which was probably the shipbuilding yards to the west of the city centre but found smoke already drifting across the built-up area to obscure some ground detail. The glow from the resultant fires remained visible for around seventy miles into the homeward journey, and returning crews reported bomb bursts and thirty to forty fires seeming to merge into one single conflagration. The effectiveness of the raid was borne out by local reports, which spoke of eight hundred fires, more than five hundred of which were classed as large, and it seems that the residential and semi-commercial districts bore the brunt of the raid. When the flames had died down and the smoke cleared, 823 houses were found to have been reduced to ruins, with five thousand others damaged to some extent. It was a highly successful raid for the period, which the Command hoped to build upon forty-eight hours later until the weather took a hand to reduce the number of aircraft available.

Another maximum effort was called for on the 28th, and a force well in excess of four hundred aircraft was assembled for the return to Hamburg that night, 256 of them provided by 3 Group and the operational training units. It was to have been the debut in numbers of 49 Squadron Lancasters, but the weather conditions over the 1, 4 and 5 Group stations prompted the withdrawal of their contributions to the operation, and as conditions worsened over the North Sea, the O.T.U aircraft were recalled. Many of the 3 Group crews turned back also, and only sixty-eight would claim to have attacked the primary target, where fifteen large fires and forty smaller ones were reported. This modicum of success was gained at the high cost of twenty-five aircraft, 15% of those dispatched, and four O.T.U Wellingtons also failed to return, while a fifth, a Whitley, ditched, and its crew was picked up safely.

Saarbrücken was posted as the target on the 29th, and a force of 291 aircraft assembled, which would be the largest raid by far on this major industrial and coal-producing Saarland capital city, situated right on the frontier with France in south-western Germany. 5 Group contributed sixty-nine Lancasters and seventeen Hampdens, the crews of which had been briefed to attack aiming point C, and in the expected absence of a strong searchlight and flak defence, the intention was to attack from a lower level than customary for the period. They made landfall on the French coast, before following the frontier with Belgium and entering Germany south of Luxembourg. At the target, they encountered a layer of four to eight-tenths low cloud at between 2,000 and 9,000 feet, below which the visibility was good, and this enabled crews to confirm their TR positions by visual references on ground features like the River Saar. Returning crews were confident that their bombs had found the mark, and this was confirmed by local reports of severe damage in central and north-western districts, where almost four hundred buildings had been destroyed in return for the loss of nine aircraft.

Eleven Lancasters were detailed by 49 Squadron for an operation on the 30th, but the weather intervened again, and the crews were stood-down. The month ended with a major assault on the Ruhr city of Düsseldorf, for which a force of 630 aircraft was assembled, the numbers bolstered by a large contribution from the training units. 5 Group offered 113 Lancasters, the first time that the one hundred figure had been reached, and they would be accompanied by twenty-four Hampdens belonging to the two Canadian squadrons, 408 and 420. 49 Squadron was finally able to make its presence felt after more than a month on the side lines and made ready eleven Lancasters, dispatching them from Scampton between 00.33 and 00.01 with the new leadership well represented in the form of W/C Slee and S/Ls Barnard and Couch. P/O Farrington and crew returned after a little more than three hours because of the failure of the fuel transfer system, leaving the others to benefit from bright moonlight, clear skies and good visibility over the southern Ruhr, which enabled the crews to confirm their TR-fixed positions visually by an S-bend in the River Rhine. Seven of the 49 Squadron participants carried out their attacks on the primary target from 8,500 to 17,000 feet between 02.35 and 02.56 in the face of an intense and accurate searchlight and flak defence and observed a large number of explosions and fires. Most crews were confident in the quality of their work, some commenting on a column of black smoke rising through 10,000 feet as they turned away. More than nine hundred tons of bombs were dropped, some wasted in open country, but the remainder had been scattered across all parts of the city and the neighbouring city of Neuss on the opposite bank of the Rhine. The crews of P/O Green and F/Sgt Webster attacked the general built-up area, while F/Sgt Lewis and crew found a last resort objective in the form of Texel aerodrome and bombed it from 4,000 feet at 03.27. Local sources confirmed the destruction of 453 buildings, with varying degrees of damage to fifteen thousand more, and sixty-seven large fires had to be dealt with. The success came at the cost of twenty-nine aircraft, including five Hampdens and two Lancasters, and the O.T.U.s were again hit disproportionately hard, losing fifteen of their number.

During the course of the month, the squadron carried out a single operation in which it dispatched eleven sorties without loss.

# August 1942

A gentle start to the new month saw the heavy brigade remain at home because of unfavourable weather on the first two nights, before 5 Group sent out orders to Swinderby and Woodhall Spa on the 3rd to prepare small numbers of Lancasters for mining duties in the Forget-me-not and Radish gardens, respectively Kiel Harbour and the Fehmarn Belt in the western Baltic. On the following night, 5 Group contributed a handful of Lancasters and Hampdens for mining duties around the Frisians and off the Biscay coast. Meanwhile, ten Lancasters from 44 (Rhodesia) and 97 (Straits Settlements) Squadrons had been briefed to join twenty-eight other aircraft in a blind attack on Essen employing Gee. Once over enemy territory, they found in their path a towering, ice-bearing front with electrical storms, which topped out at 22,000 feet and extended over the Ruhr. Some crews opted not to press on to the primary target and dropped their bombs on alternatives, and just eighteen claimed to have attacked Essen based on TR readings. The authorities deeming it necessary to repeat the exercise twenty-four hours later, when eight Lancasters were among seventeen aircraft assigned to Essen along with eight for Bochum, the crews of which were to employ Gee to locate the target before bombing visually through gaps in the cloud. Only one Lancaster bombed the target and three Halifaxes, a Lancaster and a Wellington failed to return, 20% of those dispatched.

5 Group's contribution to the fifth and final operation of the three-week campaign against the Ruhr industrial giant of Duisburg amounted to forty-seven Lancasters and ten Hampdens, which were part of an overall force of 216 aircraft assembled on the 6th. Those reaching the target area reported cloud conditions at zero to ten-tenths with tops at 10,000 feet and barrage balloons tethered as high as 12,000 feet. Positions had to be established by TR-fix confirmed by visual reference aided by fires, flak and flares, and the bombs were delivered from 14,000 to 21,000 feet, mostly without their fall being plotted. According to local reports, eighteen buildings were destroyed and sixty-six seriously damaged, giving a sum total over the five raids of 212 houses destroyed, 741 seriously damaged, and significant industrial damage resulting from just one raid. In return for this modest gain, Bomber Command had lost forty-three aircraft.

Earlier on the 6th, 420 (Snowy Owl) Squadron RCAF had vacated Waddington on transfer to 4 Group, where it would convert to Wellingtons, and on the 7th, 9 Squadron arrived from 3 Group to begin conversion to the Lancaster as the replacement for 83 Squadron, which was about to leave 5 Group for pastures new. The garrison town of Osnabrück was posted as the target on the 9th, and a force of 192 aircraft assembled accordingly, 5 Group contributing forty-two Lancasters, to attack a specific "special" aiming point, which the 5 Group and squadron ORBs failed to identify. There were clear skies over the Münsterland region of Germany to the north of the Ruhr, but haze contributed to the poor visibility that awaited the approaching bombers. They all found that they were unable to establish their positions by TR after it was jammed by the enemy on crossing the Dutch coast. Flares were dropped to illuminate the area, and some crews picked out railway lines and the River Hase, but it was mainly the fires, searchlights and flak that pointed the way to the aiming point. The fires resulting from the ensuing attack remained visible for eighty to a hundred miles into the return flight, and TR functioned again once the Dutch coast had been crossed homebound. Local sources confirmed an effective raid, which destroyed 206 houses and a military building, and damaged a number of industrial premises along with four thousand other buildings, mostly lightly.

Having spent the first ten days of the month operationally inactive, 49 Squadron finally received orders to prepare three Lancasters for action on the 11th, but not for the main event, which was the first of two raids on consecutive nights against the city of Mainz, situated to the south-west of Frankfurt-am-Main in southern Germany. A force of 154 aircraft was assembled, the number including a contribution from 5 Group of thirty-three Lancasters, for what would be the first large-scale operation against this target. The raid was highly successful, and caused major destruction in the central districts, where many historic and cultural buildings were damaged or destroyed. In the excellent tome, Bomber Command War Diaries by Martin Middlebrook and Chris Everitt, the losses from this operation are put at six aircraft, but the actual number failing to return was fourteen, while four others were lost in crashes at home. Meanwhile, the freshman crews of P/Os Fawke, McDonald and McIntyre had departed Scampton between 21.22 and 22.05 to deliver nickels to the residents of Vichy in central France and returned within seven hours from uneventful sorties to report fulfilling their brief unopposed from 11,000 to 15,000 feet between 00.57 and 01.07.

The ordeal was not yet over for Mainz, which was posted as the primary target again on the following day and a force of 138 aircraft made ready, to which 5 Group contributed thirty-three Lancasters and ten 408 (Goose) Squadron Hampdens. 49 Squadron was still not required for bombing and loaded a single Lancaster with leaflets for the freshman crew of P/O Lowrie to take to the Amiens region of north-eastern France. They set off at 20.57, dropped their nickels from 10,000 feet at 22.43 and returned safely at 00.48. Post-raid reconnaissance and local reports from Mainz confirmed further heavy damage in central and industrial areas, and the main railway station was also a casualty.

A new era for Bomber Command began on the 15th, with the formation of the Path Finder Force, and the arrival of the four founder heavy squadrons on their stations in Huntingdonshire and Cambridgeshire. 83 Squadron moved into Wyton, the Path Finder HQ, as the 5 Group representative operating Lancasters, and it would be the responsibility of 5 Group's front-line units to provide a steady supply of their most promising crews. The other founder members were 35 (Madras Presidency) Squadron, which took up residence at Graveley with Halifaxes to represent 4 Group, while 156 Squadron retained its Wellingtons for the time-being at Warboys, drawing fresh crews from 1 Group, and 3 Group would be represented by the Stirling-equipped 7 Squadron at Oakington. In addition to the above, 109 Squadron was posted to Wyton, where it would spend the next six months developing the Oboe blind-bombing device and marrying it to the Mosquito under the command of W/C Hal Bufton. The new force would occupy 3 Group stations, falling nominally under 3 Group administrative control and receiving its orders through that group, which was commanded by AVM Baldwin, whose tenure, which had lasted since just before the outbreak of war, was shortly to come to an end.

A "Path Finder Force" was the brainchild of the former 10 Squadron commanding officer, G/C Sid Bufton, Hal's brother, and now Director of Bomber Operations at the Air Ministry. He had used his best crews at 10 Squadron to find targets by the light of flares and attract other crews by firing off a coloured Verey light, and it could be said, that the concept of target-finding and marking had been born at 10 Squadron. Once at the Air Ministry, Bufton promoted his ideas with vigour and gained support among the other staff officers, culminating with the idea being put to Harris soon after his enthronement as Bomber Command C-in-C. Harris rejected the principle of establishing an elite target-finding and marking force, a view shared by the other group commanders with the exception of 4 Group's AVM Roddy Carr. However, once overruled by higher authority, Harris gave it his unstinting support, and his choice of the former 10 Squadron commanding officer, and still somewhat junior, G/C Don Bennett, as its commander was both controversial and inspired, and ruffled more than a few feathers among more senior officers. Australian, Bennett, was among the most experienced aviators in the RAF, a pilot and a Master Navigator of unparalleled experience, with many thousands of hours to his credit. He also had the recent and relevant experience as a bomber pilot through his commands of 77 and 10 Squadrons and had demonstrated his strong character when evading capture and returning from Norway after being shot down while attacking the Tirpitz in April. Despite his reserve, total lack of humour and his impatience with those whose brains operated on a lower plane than his, he would inspire in his men great affection and loyalty, along with enormous pride in being "Path Finders". He would forge the new force into a highly effective weapon, although this would not immediately be apparent.

There is some confusion surrounding 5 Group operations on the night of the 15/16th, the group ORB recording no operations because of the weather conditions, while at least five squadron ORBs revealed that their aircraft had contributed to an overall force of 131 aircraft bound for Düsseldorf. 49 Squadron made ready eleven Lancasters for the main event and two for mining duties in one of the Nectarine gardens. The bombing element took off first between 00.33 and 01.13 with W/C Slee and S/L Couch the senior pilots on duty and was followed into the air at 01.22 by the freshman crews of P/Os Lowrie and McDonald. Their take-off having been delayed for more than thirty minutes by technical malfunctions, F/L Cooke and crew turned their attention upon the docks at Rotterdam, which they bombed from 16,000 feet at 02.23. Those reaching the southern Ruhr encountered six to nine-tenths cloud at 10,000 feet with poor to modest visibility and not all were able to establish their position in relation to the briefed aiming point. Most employed a TR-fix confirmed by a visual confirmation on the River Rhine, while others simply relied on e.t.a. Eight of the 49 Squadron crews bombed at Düsseldorf from 9,000 to 17,000 feet between 02.16 and 02.34, while W/C Slee and crew attacked an unidentified built-up area within the Ruhr and F/Sgt Lewis and crew a flak concentration in the Düsseldorf area. At debriefing, a number of bursts and flashes were reported, and the abiding impression was of a scattered attack, which was confirmed by local reports from Düsseldorf and its neighbour across the Rhine, Neuss, which described a light raid and no damage of note. P/O McDonald and crew, meanwhile, had planted their vegetables from 2,500 feet at 03.05 but P/O Lowrie and crew had been hampered by the failure of their Gee and abandoned the search for a pinpoint after spending fifty minutes in low cloud and rain.

Orders were received at five 5 Group stations on the 17th to prepare for a return to Osnabrück that night as part of a 5 Group effort of thirty-two Lancasters and ten Hampdens in an overall force of 139 aircraft. It had been intended that the Path Finder Force would make its debut on this night, but the commanding officers decided that the squadrons were not yet ready, and the operation would have to go ahead without them. A dozen 49 Squadron crews attended briefing to learn of their part in the grand plan, while out on the dispersals, their Lancasters were having a 4,000lb "cookie" and SBCs of incendiaries winched into the cavernous 33-foot bomb bay. They departed Scampton between 21.47 and 22.26 with W/C Slee and S/Ls Barnard and Couch the senior pilots on duty and all reached the target area, most after making a timed run from the Dümmer Sea, a large lake situated some twenty miles to the north-east. They were greeted by three to five-tenths cloud at between 11,000 and 14,000 feet with haze at 4,000 feet to compromise the vertical visibility, but some crews were able to identify the river and railway lines and bombing by the 49 Squadron crews was carried out either on the briefed aiming point or on the built-up area generally between 23.56 and 00.44. Local reports confirmed a moderately destructive raid, which fell mainly into northern and north-western districts, and thereby, built on the damage inflicted eight nights earlier.

The Path Finders took to the air in anger for the first time on the 18th, when contributing thirty-one aircraft to an overall force of 118, of which twenty Lancasters and sixteen Hampdens were provided by 5 Group. They were bound for the naval and shipbuilding port of Flensburg, situated on the eastern coast of the Schleswig-Holstein peninsula close to the border with Denmark, where the U-Boot pens were the briefed aiming point. Eleven 49 Squadron Lancasters departed Scampton between 20.58 and 21.17 with S/L Barnard and F/L Cooke the senior pilots on duty and lost the services of P/O Perry and crew to the failure of the air-pressure system when over the North Sea. The others pressed on to the west coast of Jutland before traversing the peninsula to what had been selected as a worthwhile and easy-to-locate target. Sadly, the planners had not factored in an incorrect wind forecast, which pushed the bomber stream north of the intended track and over southern Denmark, a situation that the Path Finders failed to notice. As a result, in conditions of haze and two-tenths cloud at 6,000 feet, they illuminated an area of similar coastal terrain north of where they believed themselves to be, which led to a scattering of bombs across Danish territory up to twenty-five miles north of the frontier and into the towns of Abenra and Sønderborg. The 49 Squadron crews were unable to positively identify Flensburg and trusted that they were over its approximate location as they delivered their cookie and incendiaries from either side of 10,000 feet between 23.25 and 23.52. It was an inauspicious operational debut for a force, which in time, would become a highly efficient, successful and vital component in Bomber Command's armoury.

On the 20th, 5 Group detailed fifteen Lancasters for mining duties in a number of gardens in the Baltic, for which 49 Squadron put up the largest contribution of nine, four assigned to the Pollock garden off Bornholm Island situated to the south of Sweden, three to Geranium off the port of Swinemünde and two to Willow, located off Arkona on the Island of Rügen. They departed Scampton between 20.13 and 20.47 with S/Ls Couch and Barnard the senior pilots on duty, bound for Pollock and Geranium respectively. The squadron scribe recorded little detail, but all but one reached their respective garden, those off Bornholm noting lights on the Swedish mainland despite the poor visibility and P/O Perry and crew were engaged with some intensity by a flak ship. P/O Elliott and crew ran into ten-tenths cloud with a base at sea-level, which led to them dropping three mines in the Radish garden in the Fehmarn Belt, some way short of the Geranium garden. P/O McIntyre and crew had been hounded by flak all the way from the Danish coast and jettisoned their load after the constant evasive action wrecked their gyro and DR compass.

Frankfurt was selected on the 24th to host the second Path Finder-led operation, for which a force of 226 aircraft was assembled. 5 Group contributed forty-seven Lancasters, six of them made ready at Scampton, which took off between 21.26 and 21.33 with W/C Slee and S/Ls Barnard and Couch the senior pilots on duty. They headed out across The Wash on course for the Belgian coast and reached the target area to find five to nine-tenths cloud at between 7,000 and 9,000 feet, with ground haze adding to the difficulties experienced by the Path Finders in locating the aiming point. Not all of the 49 Squadron crews positively identified the primary target, but most picked up glimpses of the Rivers Rhine and Main, which led them on e.t.a. to a built-up area, where they bombed, and in some cases, observed bursts and fires. Opinions at debriefing would be mixed, some satisfied with the results and others not and no mention was made of the Path Finder contribution, which, at this early stage of its development was restricted to identifying and then illuminating the target. Sixteen aircraft failed to return, 7.1% of those dispatched, and among them were five Path Finders.

The third Path Finder-led operation was to be directed at the city of Kassel, the home to three Henschel aircraft and tank factories and other important war-industry concerns, as well as being the HQ for the military's Wehrkreis IX and the site of a subcamp of the Dachau concentration camp, which supplied slave labour to the factories. A force of 306 aircraft was assembled on the 27th, 5 Group detailing seventy-five Lancasters and a dozen Hampdens, thirteen of the former made ready at Scampton, which took off between 21.00 and 21.27 with W/C Slee the senior pilot on duty. He was demonstrating excellent leadership and endearing himself to the crews by frequently leading from the front in a way that his recent predecessors had failed to do. They all arrived at the target to be greeted by minimal cloud, bright moonlight and good visibility, with only ground haze between them and the aiming point. The Path Finder flares assisted greatly in enabling the crews to pick out ground detail, like a bend in the River Fulda and lakes to the south-west, and all of the Scampton crews took advantage to deliver their cookies and incendiaries from medium level either side of midnight. Local reports confirmed the effectiveness of the raid, which was spread across the city and destroyed 144 buildings, while causing serious damage to more than three hundred others. Among those afflicted to some extent were all three Henschel factories and a number of military establishments, and the fire services had to deal with seventy-three large blazes. However, the success was gained at the high cost of thirty-one aircraft, twenty-one of them Wellingtons, of which fifteen belonged to 1 Group.

A force of 159 aircraft was assembled on the 28th to send to the city of Nuremberg, deep in southern Germany, which had been the scene of massive Nazi Party rallies during and after Hitler's rise to power during the thirties. The Path Finders were to employ target indicators (TIs) for the first time in adapted 250lb bomb casings. 5 Group detailed sixty-three Lancasters, while also contributing seventeen Hampdens to a simultaneous raid on Saarbrücken by a force of 113 "oddments", which included 4 Group Halifaxes and new crews from other groups, but no Path Finders. 49 Squadron made ready ten Lancasters, listing only nine on the Form 541, and sent them on their way from Scampton between 21.04 and 21.23 with W/C Slee and S/Ls Barnard and Couch the senior pilots on duty. The squadron's recent excellent rate of serviceability continued on this night, and all completed the six-hundred-mile outward leg across France and into the target area, which was found to be under clear skies. A four-fifths moon aided a visual identification of the city and enabled the Path Finder element to exploit the conditions to deliver their TIs with great accuracy. The Scampton crews pinpointed on waterways and autobahns leading into the city, and the only detail recorded by the squadron scribe was that P/O Perry and crew attacked from a lowly 2,500 feet at 23.46 and P/O Green and crew counted twenty-four fires, half of them large. There was no question in their minds as they withdrew, that they had hit the target, a belief confirmed by fires remaining visible for some seventy miles into the return flight. Twenty-three aircraft failed to return, 14.5% of the force, and the Wellingtons were hit particularly hard again, losing a third of their number. It was a sad night for 49 Squadron, which had two empty dispersal pans to contemplate in the cold light of dawn. L7567 crashed in Holland killing F/O Lowrie RNZAF and four others and delivering the two survivors into enemy hands. R5897 came down in southern Germany and took with it to their deaths the crew of Sgt Burton. Both crews were a mix of RAF, RAAF and RCAF airmen. Local reports suggested that about a third of the force had landed bombs within the city, causing damage to the Altstadt, but that others had wasted their effort on communities up to ten miles to the north.

During the course of another busy month, the squadron took part in ten operations and dispatched seventy-eight sorties for the loss of two Lancasters and crews.

## September 1942

The first half of the new month would distinguish itself through an unprecedented series of effective operations, although, it would begin ignominiously for the Path Finder Force, when posting a "black" on the night of the 1/2nd by marking the wrong town. The city of Saarbrücken had been briefed out to 231 crews, of which sixty-nine represented 5 Group, sixty-two to fly Lancasters and seven in Hampdens, a type with just two more weeks of front-line service ahead of it. 49 Squadron made ready eight Lancasters and dispatched them from Scampton between 23.46 and 00.06 with F/L Cooke the senior pilot on duty and a S/L Meston on board, presumably as second pilot. All reached south-western Germany to find the target under clear skies with good visibility, and established their positions by TR, confirmed by visual identification of the River Saar and other ground features and Path Finder flares. They bombed from medium level from around 02.00 onwards and most observed the burst of their cookie, while some crews from other squadrons reported the entire area of the North Bank of the Saar to be on fire and commented on a very large explosion occurring in the midst of the conflagration. There was no question in the minds of the crews as they retreated to the west, that this had been an outstandingly accurate attack, and some claimed to be able to see the glow of fires from up to 140 miles into the return flight. It was only later that the truth emerged, that the Path Finders had marked not Saarbrücken, but the non-industrial town of Saarlouis, situated thirteen miles to the north-west, which lay in a loop of the river similar to that at the intended target. Much to the chagrin of its inhabitants and those in surrounding communities, the main force bombing had been particularly accurate and concentrated, and heavy damage had been inflicted.

This could have been an ill-omen for the month's efforts but, in fact, the Command now embarked on the unprecedented run of effective operations mentioned above. It began at Karlsruhe on the night of the 2/3rd, a city that was home to a factory belonging to the Deutsche Waffen und Munitionsfabriken A G, better known as DWM, which manufactured all types of firearms from pistols to automatic weapons for infantry and aircraft. A force of two hundred aircraft was made ready, the 4 Group Halifax brigade having now returned to operations following intensive training to restore confidence in the type after a period of above average losses and a series of design-flaw accidents. 5 Group put up sixty Lancasters and five Hampdens, of which nine of the former were provided by 49 Squadron and departed Scampton between 23.11 and 23.30 with no senior pilots on duty. The target lay some fifty miles beyond Saarbrücken, which enabled the force to adopt the same route as on the previous night, passing south of Liege in Belgium and entering Germany north of Luxembourg. It was a three-hour outward flight, and at 02.15, three hours after departing Scampton, R5763 was shot down by the night-fighter of Oblt Martinek of III./NJG4 and crashed at Abée in Belgium, some thirty-five miles from the German frontier, which suggests that F/Sgt Lewis and crew had turned back with some kind of technical difficulty. The pilot and both gunners lost their lives, while three others were captured, and the bomb-aimer evaded a similar fate to arrive in Spain three weeks later. The rest of the force reached the target area under clear skies, where they found Karlsruhe basking in moonlight and naked to the eyes of the bomb-aimers high above. The autobahn and the Rhine and its docks stood out clearly as a guide to the aiming point, and bombing was carried out generally from medium level. The only details recorded by the 49 Squadron scribe inform us that P/O Gerry Fawke and crew attacked from 5,000 feet at 01.55 on a north to south heading, while P/O Perry and crew were pointing due east when they delivered their cookie and incendiaries from 9,000 feet fifty-two minutes later. The city appearing to be swallowed by a sea of flames, before becoming obscured by smoke and returning crews reported as many as two hundred fires, the glow from which remained visible for a hundred miles into the homeward journey. Post-raid reconnaissance confirmed much residential and some industrial damage, and local reports mentioned seventy-three fatalities.

Scampton welcomed a new resident unit on the 4th when 57 Squadron arrived on transfer from 3 Group to begin conversion to the Lancaster. When Bremen was posted as the target for that night, 5 Group responded with a contribution of forty-six Lancasters in an overall force of 251 aircraft. Crews were told at briefing that the Path Finders would be rolling out a new three-phase technique based on illumination, visual marking and backing-up, which, if successful, would form the basis of Path Finder operations for the remainder of the war. Nine 49 Squadron crews attended briefing, five to learn that their aiming point was the city, while four were assigned to the Focke-Wulf aircraft factory at Hemelingen. In the event, only eight Lancasters departed Scampton between 00.15 and 00.35 after one became unserviceable at the last minute. F/L Cooke was the senior pilot on duty and his navigator on this night was the legendary F/O Tommy Blair, one of the Command's characters. Enemy night-fighters were operating over Holland and R5894 was intercepted by a Ju88 as it closed on the German frontier. The Lancaster was raked with cannon fire, which persuaded P/O Perry to order the bombs to be jettisoned "live" and prompted mid-upper gunner, Sgt Steer, to bale out and drift down into the arms of his captors. Meanwhile, his colleagues completed a safe return to base. The others reached the target area to find cloudless skies and good visibility, although ground haze and smoke created challenging conditions for target identification. The first Path Finder flares and incendiaries went down at around 01.50, after which the bombing of the Focke-Wulf factory was carried out from 7,000 to 17,500 feet, and the only records of the

49 Squadron effort revealed that the crews of F/Sgts Webster and Heard attacked the city from 13,000 and 17,000 feet at 02.04 and 02.15 respectively. Generally, crews noticed a less-intense flak defence over the city than usual, but much increased hostility as they withdrew towards the Frisian island of Norderney. Twelve aircraft failed to return from this successful operation, and debriefing reports of fires in the central districts were confirmed by a local assessment, which listed 460 dwelling houses, six large/medium industrial premises and fifteen small ones destroyed, and a further fourteen hundred buildings seriously damaged.

The next operation was to be directed at the Ruhr city of Duisburg on the night of the 6/7th for which a force of 207 aircraft was assembled, fifty-four Lancasters and four Hampdens representing 5 Group, nine of the former provided by 49 Squadron. The first departure from Scampton was that of the freshman crew of Sgt Thom at 01.00, bound for a successful and uneventful toilet paper drop over the Reims area of north-eastern France. They were followed into the air between 01.10 and 01.32 by the main element with S/L Barnard the senior pilot on duty, and all reached the target area to find it partially concealed by cloud, below which, the usual industrial haze rendered ground detail indistinct. Positions were established by TR and confirmed as far as possible by visual reference in the light of flares, and the 49 Squadron crews attacked from around 8,000 to 10,000 feet either side of 03.00 in the face of a searchlight and flak defence operating to its usual high standard. W4183 was hit three times and lost two engines and the second pilot, Sgt Gregory-Coleman RAAF, was mortally wounded. P/O Jeffreys nursed the Lancaster home and ordered his crew to bale out shortly after they crossed the Suffolk coast, while he prepared to land at Martlesham Heath. On approach, the Lancaster ploughed through treetops before crashing at 04.34 a short distance from the airfield, injuring the pilot, who would spend some time in station sick quarters. The Duisburg authorities reported the heaviest raid to date, which destroyed 114 buildings and seriously damaged more than three hundred others, and, while this was only fairly modest, it still represented something of a victory at this notoriously elusive target.

There was no pattern to the choice of targets thus far in the month, southern and north-western Germany and the Ruhr all featuring during the busy first week, and Frankfurt in south-central Germany was posted as the latest target on the 8th, for which a force of 249 aircraft was assembled. 5 Group contributed sixty-two Lancasters and nine Hampdens, the eight participants from 49 Squadron departing Scampton between 20.27 and 20.46 with S/L Couch the senior pilot on duty. An engine issue during the climb-out ended the sortie of F/Sgt Heard and crew and they headed directly to the jettison area some twenty miles off Mablethorpe to dump their four 2,000 pounders. The others reached the target area, where, according to some, the skies were clear of cloud and the visibility good, while others reported up to eight-tenths cloud at 2,000 feet and poor to moderate visibility. Another factor was the intensity of the searchlight and flak activity, which should, perhaps, have helped to guide the Path Finders to the aiming point but, surprisingly, they failed to locate the city. Path Finder flares were in evidence but scattered over a wide area, and it was clear that they were by no means certain of their position in relation to Frankfurt. Crews established their own positions by what they could glimpse on the ground and the dozens of searchlights fingering the darkness and those from 49 Squadron bombed the primary target from 9,500 to 14,000 feet between 23.28 and 23.58, observing fires in what appeared to be the built-up area. According to local reports, only a handful of bomb loads hit the intended target, and this halted the run of successes thus far in the month. The majority of bombs appeared to have fallen to the south-west of Frankfurt as far as Rüsselsheim, fifteen miles away, where the authorities confirmed damage to the Opel tank works and a Michelin tyre factory, which compensated in small measure for the failure to hit the primary target.

5 Group devoted the 9th to mining operations in the Baltic, for which 49 Squadron briefed the crews of P/O Eyre and Sgt Mant and sent them on their way to one of the Silverthorn gardens in the Kattegat region at 23.35. They encountered favourable conditions and established firm pinpoints from which to begin their timed runs. P/O Eyre and crew were frustrated by the failure of their bomb doors to open and eventually jettisoned their mines off northern Jutland at 03.01, by which time the Mant crew had planted theirs in the briefed location from 700 feet at 02.36.

The Path Finder Force was constantly evolving in tactics and equipment and had a new weapon in its armoury for the next operation, which was to be against the Ruhr city of Düsseldorf on the 10th. "The Pink Pansy", which weighed in at 2,800lbs, was the latest attempt to produce a genuine target indicator and used converted 4,000lb cookie casings. A force of 479 aircraft included a contribution from the training units of 91, 92 and 93 Groups, and eighty-one Lancasters and eight Hampdens from 5 Group. 49 Squadron put up a dozen Lancasters, which set off from Scampton between 20.33 and 20.58 with S/Ls Barnard and Couch the senior pilots on duty and each carrying a cookie and all-but one, twelve SBCs of incendiaries. They all reached the target area to encounter clear skies with the usual industrial haze muddying the vertical visibility, but fires were already burning to help them identify the target visually and pick out major features like a bend in the Rhine and the docks complex. The red flares were reported by some to be a little north of the main city area with the greens over to the west, while the white illuminators highlighted the more central districts. The 49 Squadron crews bombed from 9,000 to 16,000 feet between 22.24 and 22.46, observing fires to develop, and they turned away believing the attack to have been successful. Returning crews made complimentary comments about the performance of the Path Finders and reported the glow of the fires to be visible from the Scheldt on the way home. Post-raid reconnaissance and local reports confirmed this operation to have been probably the most successful since Operation Millennium at the end of May. Other than the northern districts, all parts of the city and its neighbour, Neuss, had been hit, and 911 houses had been destroyed with a further fifteen hundred seriously damaged. In addition to the destruction also of eight public buildings, fifty-two industrial firms in the two cities sustained damage sufficient to cause a total shut down of production for varying periods. It had been an expensive victory for the Command, however, with thirty-three failures to return, of which sixteen were from the training units.

Thirteen 49 Squadron crews attended briefing on the 13th to learn that Bremen was to be their target for that night and for the second time during the month. A force of 446 aircraft was assembled, again bolstered by aircraft and crews from the training groups, and there was a contribution from 5 Group of ninety-eight Lancasters and seven Hampdens. The Scampton element took off between 23.12 and 23.37 with W/C Slee and S/L Couch the senior pilots on duty and all reached the target area to find clear skies but considerable ground haze, which made pinpointing something of a challenge. Some major ground features, like the docks, could be identified visually, otherwise it was down to flares and fires to point the way, and the 49 Squadron participants mostly believed that they were over the built-up area as they carried out their attacks from 11,000 to 16,000 feet between 01.10 and 01.30. A number of crews were convinced that some early arrivals had bombed at Delmenhorst, a few miles to the south-west of Bremen, and the 5 Group ORB described the Path Finder performance as unhelpful. However, the success of the operation suggested otherwise and by far exceeded the destruction resulting from June's Thousand Bomber raid. A total of 848 houses was destroyed and much damage was inflicted on the city's industry, including to the Lloyd Dynamo works, where two weeks production was lost and parts of the Focke-Wulf factory were put out of action for between two and eight days. Of the twenty-one aircraft lost, fifteen belonged to the training units.

The end of the Hampden era arrived on the following night, when the naval and shipbuilding port of Wilhelmshaven was posted as the target for 202 aircraft. Sixty-two Lancasters and four Hampdens were made ready as the 5 Group contribution, the latter from Syerston's 408 (Goose) Squadron RCAF. The twelve 49 Squadron aircraft were loaded with a cookie and either 900 x 4lb or 90 x 30lb incendiaries and departed Scampton between 20.27 and 20.40 with S/L Couch the senior pilot on duty. P/O McIntyre and crew were skirting the Frisians when the starboard-outer engine failed and compelled them to turn back. The others arrived to find clear skies over the coastal region of Jade Bay, with extreme darkness and ground haze to impede vertical visibility, but the shoreline and the docks provided an adequate pinpoint for the Path Finders to establish their position and mark accurately. The Scampton crews carried out their attacks from 9,000 to 15,000 feet between 22.14 and 22.33 with light flak bursting around them at between 15,000 and 17,000 feet. It was difficult to distinguish individual bomb bursts, but the consensus was of a successful outcome and crews from other squadrons reported an enormous explosion, believed to be from an ammunition dump. It lit up the ground for five seconds and emitted flames a hundred feet into the air along with a cloud of smoke that rose to several thousand feet. Local sources confirmed that this had been the port's most destructive raid to date.

After such a run of successes, Harris had to have another go at Essen, and a force of 369 aircraft was assembled on the 16th, which again called upon the training units to supply aircraft and crews. Ninety-three Lancasters represented 5 Group, eleven of them provided by 49 Squadron, and two 9 Squadron crews would be undertaking the unit's first Lancaster sorties in aircraft borrowed from 44 (Rhodesia) Squadron. The Scampton contingent took off between 20.17 and 20.43 with W/C Slee and S/Ls Barnard and Couch the senior pilots on duty and lost the services of P/O Fawke and crew to problems with a starboard engine and fuel pump. The others reached the target area to encounter between three and ten-tenths cloud, but generally good visibility despite the industrial haze, which could be penetrated sufficiently for some ground detail to be identified visually by the light of Path Finder flares. Even so, the overlapping boundaries of the Ruhr towns and cities made it difficult to establish positions with absolute certainty, and some of the crews dropping their bombs on e.t.a. would find, from the evidence of their bombing photos, that they had been over Bochum, Oberhausen or some other built-up expanse. Some of the Path Finder flares were estimated to be falling some twenty miles to the east of Essen, which would have put them over Dortmund and Hagen. W/C Slee and crew searched for twenty minutes before taking their bombs home, and we are told that the crew of Sgt Gould bombed from 13,000 feet at 22.10 and Sgt Mant from 12,000 feet at 22.16, so must assume that the others followed suit in the face of an intense searchlight and flak response. Returning crews reported the glow of fires visible for a hundred miles into the return journey, and local sources would confirm this to be Essen's worst night of the war to date. In addition to much housing damage and more than a hundred medium and large fires, fifteen high-explosive bombs had found their way onto the Krupp complex, as did a crashing bomber loaded with incendiaries. A post-raid analysis revealed that bombs had been scattered across a large part of the Ruhr, with Bochum, Wuppertal and Herne among the hardest hit, and, until the advent of Oboe in the coming spring, such inaccuracies remained a fact of life. It was far from a one-sided affair, and cost the Command a massive thirty-nine aircraft, 10.6% of those dispatched, nineteen of them from the training units. R5890 crashed in the target area and there were no survivors from the crew of S/L Barnard MiD, whose presence would be missed by the squadron and Scampton communities.

If any period in the Command's gradual evolution to war-winning capability could be seen as a turning point, then perhaps, the first half of September 1942 qualified. It can be no coincidence, that the Path Finder Force was emerging from its hesitant start as the crews got to grips with the complexities of their demanding role, and new tactics and aids were being brought to bear against the enemy. It would be no overnight transformation, and failures would still outnumber victories for some time to come, but the encouraging signs were there that all of the elements of technical and tactical advance were coming together, and, with other technological wizardry in the pipeline, it boded ill for Germany's industrial towns and cities.

Extensive mining operations occupied 115 aircraft on the night of the 18/19th, 5 Group supporting the effort with forty-nine Lancasters, ten of them representing 49 Squadron and assigned to three separate gardens in the Baltic. They departed Scampton between 19.30 and 20.04, five bound for the Geranium garden off Swinemünde, four for one of the Silverthorn gardens in the Kattegat and one for Tangerine, the most distant of all gardens off Pillau, now known as Baltiysk in Russia, located on the eastern seaboard of Danzig Bay. W/C Slee had been briefed for Pillau, but his Lancaster became unserviceable shortly before take-off and his participation had to be scrubbed. All five crews arrived off Swinemünde to find three-tenths cloud at 6,000 feet and good visibility and F/O Bonnett and crew delivered their mines into the briefed location, before bombing and strafing the aerodrome at Bad Berg and the town of Binz on Rügen from 200 feet. P/O Elliott and crew bombed Wittow, near the island's northern tip, while the crews of Sgts Miller and Gould and P/O Fawke restricted themselves to mining from 700 to 900 feet between 23.07 and 23.35. R5898 was hit by flak in the tailplane and the rudder jammed, but Gerry Fawke brought it home to a safe landing. Five to ten-tenths low cloud in the Silverthorn area was of no great consequence and the mines went down mostly according to brief. P/O McDonald and crew pinpointed on Pillau and ran north-north-west for ten miles to deliver their stores and landed back at Scampton after nine-and-three-quarter-hours aloft.

Munich was posted as one of two targets on the 19th, and would involve sixty-one 5 Group Lancasters, seven Lancasters from 83 Squadron of the Path Finders and twenty-one Stirlings from 3 Group and 7 Squadron of the Path Finders. A simultaneous operation by 118 aircraft of 1, 3 and 4 Groups would target Saarbrücken, also with Path Finder support. The two forces followed a common route as far as Saarbrücken, leaving the 5 Group element a further 220 miles to travel to reach the Bavarian capital, the birthplace of Nazism and a city of cultural and industrial significance. 49 Squadron was called upon to contribute ten Lancasters, which departed Scampton between 19.25 and 19.42 with W/C Slee and S/L Couch the senior pilots on duty and the newly promoted F/L Bonnett and F/L Cooke in support. They flew out across France, entering southern Germany near Strasbourg to be greeted by clear skies and good visibility, which enabled them to identify the lakes to the south-west of the target city. Most crews adopted a time-and-distance run from Lake Constance to bring them to the aiming point, which had been well-illuminated by Path Finder flares, and the cookies and incendiaries were released from 7,000 to 12,000 feet between

23.23 and 00.04. Bomb bursts were observed in the city centre, along with a large explosion to the north and numerous fires, including an extensive one to the south-west, and 40% of returning crews would claim to have bombed within three miles of the city centre. Saarbrücken was reported to be well-alight by crews passing by on the way home, and the Path Finders were complimented on their performance at debriefings. Bombing photos revealed that the main weight of the attack had fallen into western, southern and eastern suburbs of Munich, but there was no confirmation from local sources, and Saarbrücken had largely escaped damage after the bombing became widely scattered.

The squadron was notified on the 23rd, that it would be operating that night against the Baltic coastal town of Wismar and the nearby Dornier aircraft factory as part of an all-5 Group affair involving eighty-three Lancasters. Two-thirds of the force was assigned to the town, situated some thirty miles east of Lübeck, and a third to the factory, and 49 Squadron made ready ten Lancasters, six loaded with incendiaries to employ against the town and four with six 1,000 pounders with an eleven-second delay fuse for the factory. They departed Scampton between 23.02 and 23.21 and ran into a violent electrical storm when around a hundred miles short of Denmark's western coast. This caused many to turn back and added to a total of twenty-one early returns from all causes, while it was flak damage that caused Sgt Gould and crew to jettison their load near Rendsburg on the Schleswig-Holstein peninsula at 01.30, having been forced down to 5,000 feet. Those reaching the target found ten-tenths cloud with tops in extreme cases at 20,000 feet but more generally at around 12,000 feet and a base just above the rooftops, with intense and accurate searchlight and flak activity awaiting any crews brave enough to venture so low. P/O Fawke's was such a crew and watched their bombs straddle the factory from 300 feet at 02.05 but had to bring home sixteen 30lb incendiaries after they hung up. P/O Green and crew were the only others from the squadron to carry out an attack, in their case from 12,000 feet at 02.15, while the others either bombed unidentified alternatives or brought their bombs home. Returning crews reported fires in the town and at the Dornier factory at a cost of four Lancasters, while local reports listed thirty-two houses and eight industrial buildings seriously damaged.

On the following night, five 49 Squadron crews were briefed to join others from the group to conduct mining sorties in the Baltic. F/L Cooke and crew were assigned to the Jasmine garden off Warnemünde, P/O Elliott and crew to Spinach off Gdynia, P/O McDonald to Tangerine off Pillau and P/O Armstrong and Sgt Townsend to Pollock off Bornholm Island. They departed Scampton together between 19.50 and 20.01 and all but one reached their respective target areas to find excellent conditions and deliver four mines each from 600 to 1,000 feet between 23.18 and 00.15. The McDonald crew selected the alternative garden of Silverthorn V in the Kattegat and delivered their stores six miles west of Kullen point on the Swedish coast. On return, F/L Cooke and crew reported dropping two 250 pounders on Præstø aerodrome on Denmark's Sjælland Island and strafing a mile-and-a-half-long German army convoy from 400 feet.

During the course of the month, the squadron carried out fifteen operations and dispatched 129 sorties for the loss of three Lancasters, two crews and two other airmen.

# October 1942

The new month opened with a number of operations including a further attempt by 4 Group to hit the U-Boot construction yards at Flensburg, while elements of 3 and 5 Groups turned their attention upon other Baltic coast objectives at Lübeck and Wismar respectively. 5 Group detailed a force of seventy-eight Lancasters, a dozen of them made ready by 49 Squadron at Scampton, where the crews learned that the plan called for three-quarters of the force to attack the town, with the main square as the aiming point, while the remainder targeted the Dornier aircraft factory. The 49 Squadron crews of W/C Slee, F/L Bonnett, P/O McDonald and Sgt Mant were briefed to attack the factory and the remainder the town and took off between 18.28 and 18.38 on what would be a round trip of some eleven hundred miles. They crossed Jutland seemingly without incident, arriving at the target area to encounter three to ten-tenths cloud with a base at between 1,500 and 7,000 feet. Poor visibility over the town was caused by heavy ground haze and an effective smoke screen, which combined with intense searchlight glare to blot out identifying features. Brief glimpses of the coastline provided a scant reference by which to establish position, despite which, W/C Slee and crew attacked the factory in a number of passes at 5,000 feet between 21.15 and 21.40, while Sgt Mant and crew bombed its proximity from 10,000 feet at 21.34. F/L Bonnett and crew were unable to locate the factory after searching for forty-five minutes and bombed the town instead from 6,000 feet at 21.46, and experiencing similar difficulties, P/O McDonald and crew found an aerodrome to the north of the town and attacked it through a smoke screen from 6,000 feet at 21.39. Most of the others bombed the town area from 6,000 to 11,000 feet between 21.10 and 21.50 after a DR run from the coastline, while P/O Green and crew bombed Travemünde after mistaking it for Wismar. Sgt Miller and crew used up too much fuel searching and had to jettison their bomb load in order to get home. The unfavourable conditions led to the bombing of a number of locations along a 150-mile stretch of coastline from Wismar eastwards, and the entire undertaking proved to be a wasted effort that cost just two Lancasters.

The Ruhr city of Krefeld was posted as the target for a force of 188 aircraft on the 2nd, for which 5 Group contributed twenty-four Lancasters from Waddington, Coningsby and Syerston, while the rest of the group stood down. Located at the western edge of the Ruhr, a few miles to the south-west of Duisburg, Krefeld's industry had been based on silk and velvet textiles, but the presence of a Thyssen-Krupp steelworks was sufficient to attract the attention of Bomber Command. The force encountered dense industrial haze, which thwarted the Path Finders' best efforts to provide a reference for those following behind and most crews were reduced to bombing on estimated positions on DR and isolated Path Finder flares from 8,500 to 16,000 feet either side of 21.00. Returning crews reported some scattered fires, and local sources confirmed that three streets in the northern part of the city had sustained damage, but nothing commensurate with the size of the force and the effort expended.

All heavy groups were alerted on the 5th to an operation that night against the city of Aachen, for which a force of 257 aircraft was put together, 5 Group detailing sixty-nine Lancasters, ten of them from 49 Squadron. They departed Scampton between 19.16 and 19.28 with F/L Bonnett the senior pilot on duty and headed south on course for landfall on the French coast, passing through electrical storms and icing on the way. The stormy weather extended inland, which encouraged some of the force to descend for the rest of the journey to the target, Germany's most westerly city, nestling just inside the German borders with southern Holland and Belgium. On arrival in the target area, flares were visible, but up to nine-tenths cloud at between 8,000 and 14,000 feet with haze below created poor visibility and challenging conditions. The Scampton element arrived intact, mostly to search in vain for a reference on the ground but, of course, opinions of cloud conditions were rarely unanimous. According to F/L Bonnett there was no cloud and his bomb-aimer was able to pinpoint on the river to begin a DR run, and had the town in his bombsight as he released the bomb load on e.t.a. from 11,000 feet at 21.40. The others attacked the primary or alternative objectives from 9,000 to 14,000 feet between 21.32 and 21.55, few of them catching a glimpse of the ground but some observed bursts and at least one large fire. Local sources reported that Aachen's southern district of Burtscheid had suffered quite extensive damage to housing and industry, and five large fires had required attention. Even so, they estimated the attack to have involved only around ten aircraft. Some bombs fell seventeen miles away onto the small Dutch town of Lutterade, and this would have minor consequences for the trials of the Oboe blind-bombing device in late December.

Osnabrück was posted as the target on the 6th, for which 237 aircraft were made ready, including fifty-nine Lancasters of 5 Group. 49 Squadron loaded eight of its aircraft with a cookie each and twelve SBCs of either 30lb or 4lb incendiaries and dispatched them from Scampton between 19.14 and 19.23 with F/L Bonnett the senior pilot on duty. Sgt Gould and crew lost the port engine that provided power to the rear turret, and they were back in the circuit within two-and-a-half hours. The Path Finders dropped flares over Makkum in Holland and the Dümmer See to the north-east of the target as route markers, and these proved to be very effective in guiding the main force in, although, inevitably, some bomb loads were released early during the twenty-mile leg between the Dümmer See and the town. Four to eight-tenths cloud lay over the town at 8,000 feet and provided challenging conditions for accurate bombing, although opinions varied as to the quality of the visibility. The 49 Squadron crews carried out their attacks from 9,000 to 12,000 feet between 21.31 and 21.50 and much of the effort fell into the central and southern districts. Returning crew described many fires and a glow visible by some from the Dutch coast homebound, and most had confidence in the effectiveness of the raid. According to local reports, 149 houses and six industrial buildings were destroyed, 530 houses seriously damaged and more than 2,700 others slightly damaged.

On the 7th, the first of daily "Dixon" exercises was carried out in preparation for an as yet undisclosed operation to be conducted ten days hence. The weather conveniently precluded operational activity for 5 Group until the 12th, allowing squadrons to focus on the daylight formation flying that was going to be necessary. On the 10th, the high standards set by F/L Cooke and crew were recognised with a posting to 83 Squadron at Wyton to take up duties as Path Finders.

5 Group notified its stations on the 12th that another shot at Wismar and the Dornier aircraft factory was to be launched that night, for which a force of fifty-nine Lancasters was assembled, ten of them provided by 49 Squadron and a dozen by 57 Squadron for its maiden Lancaster operation. At the Scampton briefing, the crews of Sgts Miller and Thom, F/Sgt Heard and F/O Elliott were assigned to the factory and the remainder to the town, and they took off between 17.47 and 17.56 before setting course for the coast of Jutland. Difficult weather conditions over the North Sea prevented many from establishing a pinpoint on their arrival at the enemy coast and forced them to navigate by DR. The town lay under six to ten-tenths cloud in a band between 1,000 and 7,000 feet with extreme darkness adding to the challenges, and the lack of pinpoints forced some crews

to search for up to thirty minutes before bombing on estimated positions, those representing 49 Squadron carrying out their attacks from 9,000 to 14,000 feet between 20.44 and 21.03. This inevitably led to a scattered and probably ineffective attack, despite which, some returning crews reported that the factory had been left burning furiously and the flames had remained visible for seventy miles into the homeward journey. W4116 failed to return home with the crew of twenty-one-year-old F/O Richard Elliott after disappearing without trace in the sea.

S/L Cracknell and his crew were posted in from 1654 Conversion Unit on the 13th and he would assume the duties of a flight commander. The naval and shipbuilding port of Kiel was posted as the target for a force of 288 aircraft that night, for which 5 Group weighed in with sixty-nine Lancasters, eight of them provided by 49 Squadron and loaded with a cookie and 4lb or 30lb incendiaries. They departed Scampton between 18.40 and 18.52 with no senior pilots on duty and reached the target area to find almost clear skies and good visibility and red and white flares marking out the Selenter Lake, some ten miles to the east. Illuminator flares were also deployed over the town to reveal a built-up area, which the 49 Squadron crews attacked from 10,000 to 17,000 feet between 21.20 and 21.30, some observing the fall of their bombs close to the aiming point and others not. Probably 50% of crews were deceived by a decoy fire site, but the rest hit the town and caused an appropriate amount of damage. Returning crews reported a much-reduced searchlight and flak defence, and conscious that defensive measures attracted attention, this was a tactic employed occasionally and effectively by the Luftwaffe.

A force of 289 aircraft was assembled on the 15th to send against Cologne, which had been left in peace for a considerable time, and the operation was supported by sixty-two Lancasters of 5 Group from Coningsby, Scampton, Syerston and Waddington. 49 Squadron made ready nine Lancasters and sent them on their way between 18.47 and 19.15 with no senior pilots on duty and set course for the Scheldt estuary, flying for a time through icing conditions. Some crews were eased off track by inaccurately forecast winds as they crossed northern Belgium, but the force arrived at the Rhineland capital to find it concealed beneath a layer of ten-tenths cloud. The Path Finder flares were scattered, and a large, effective decoy fire site combined with that to attract the main force crews away from the target. The 49 Squadron participants mostly caught a glimpse of the Rhine in the light of flares and carried out their attacks from 10,000 to 15,000 feet between 20.50 and 21.06, some after stooging around for twenty minutes. Few observed anything of the results, and it was left to local sources to mention that 224 houses had sustained slight damage from the single 4,000 pounder and three other high-explosive bombs and 210 incendiaries that had landed within the city, and this was out of a total of seventy-one 4,000 pounders, 231 other high explosive bombs and more than 68,000 incendiaries expended. It was a disappointment compounded by the loss to the Command of eighteen aircraft.

On the 17th, the purpose behind the "Dixon" formation-flying training that had been causing speculation for more than a week was revealed to crews in 5 Group briefing rooms. They learned that Operation Robinson was a daylight attack on the Schneider armaments works at Le Creusot, deep in eastern France, and the nearby Henri Paul transformer station at Montchanin, which provided its power. Often referred to as the French "Krupp", the company belonged to the Schneider family, which had donated the famous aviation trophy bearing its name. The Schneider Trophy was initially a prize to encourage technical advances in civil aviation, but eventually, became a speed contest for float and seaplanes competed for biannually by Britain, France, Italy and the USA. It was a massively prestigious and popular spectator event that drew crowds of up to 200,000 people. Britain claimed it outright after three consecutive wins culminating in 1931, when the revolutionary Supermarine S6B triumphed in the hands of the future first wartime commanding officer of 44 Squadron, W/C Boothman. Ninety-four Lancasters were to take part in the operation, which required an outward flight at low level by daylight, the attack at dusk, and a return under the cover of darkness. It was a bold plan to commit such a large force, which would be difficult to conceal, and it was only six months since the excessive losses from Augsburg.

The plan called for eighty-eight aircraft to bomb the factory complex from as low as practicable, led by W/C Len Slee of 49 Squadron, while six others, two each from 106, 61 and 97 Squadrons went for the power station in a line-astern attack led by W/C Gibson. The 49 Squadron contribution of eleven Lancasters departed Scampton between 12.09 and 12.20 with S/L Couch and F/L Bonnett the other senior pilots on duty and F/L Tommy Blair navigating for the former. They headed south to join up with the rest of the force over Upper Heyford and take the lead, before setting course for Land's End at below 1,000 feet. Once over the sea, they were to aim for a point just south of the Ile d'Yeu to cross the French coast midway between St Nazaire and La Rochelle at around 100 feet. Shortly before the sea crossing began, Coastal Command Whitleys had carried out a sweep to force enemy U-Boots beneath the surface and prevent them from spotting the force and transmitting a warning.

For most, the three-hundred-mile low-level dash across France would be relatively uneventful, but bird strikes became a constant threat, causing injury to a number of crewmen as they smashed Perspex, while others became ingested in engines. P/O Green and crew had both their front and mid-upper turret Perspex broken in this manner. A pilot from 44 (Rhodesia) Squadron complained that the lead section was too low, which placed upon him an exhausting physical strain as he wrestled with slipstream turbulence, and others commented on bunching-up and occasional congestion, but there was also praise for 49 Squadron's leadership during the outward flight. Despite the challenges, this middle leg terminated successfully at the predetermined point some forty-five miles from the target, and it was at this juncture that the main force broke up to form into a fan and climb to a bombing height of between 4,500 and 7,000 feet. The target was reached at dusk under clear skies and in good visibility, and crews were able to follow a railway line directly to the heart of the factory complex, where the 49 Squadron crews bombed as briefed from 4,000 to 7,000 feet between 18.08 and 18.13. Not all were able to plot the fall of their bombs, but W/C Slee watched his five RDX 1,000 pounders fall towards what he believed to be locomotive machine shops, while those from S/L Couch's bomb bay appeared to strike the roof of the factory's turbine shed. Some crews commented on blue flashes as bombs hit the central power station on the south-eastern corner of the site and others described explosions and smoke rising through 3,000 feet that eventually obscured the entire target area. S/L Burnett of 44 (Rhodesia) Squadron claimed that it was the most successful of the many operations that he had participated in. All but a 61 Squadron Lancaster from the Montchanin element returned safely home after a round-trip of ten hours, and at debriefing on all stations it was unanimously believed that the target had been utterly devastated. The apparent success prompted a message from the A-O-C 5 Group, AVM Coryton, who added to his own congratulations with similar sentiments from the Secretary of State for Air, Sir Archibald Sinclair. W/C Slee's leadership was rewarded with a DSO. Unfortunately, it would be discovered later, that the damage had been less severe than first thought, and production had soon returned to normal. Another raid would be mounted against the plant eight months hence.

A new campaign, against Italian cities in support of land operations in North Africa under Operation Torch began on the night of the 22/23rd against the city-port of Genoa and the naval dockyard, where part of the Italian fleet was sheltering. It was the eve of the opening of the Battle of El Alamein, which, after twelve days' fighting, would see Montgomery push Rommel's forces all the way back to Tunisia and out of the war. Ten 5 Group squadrons mustered between them 101 Lancasters, while 83 Squadron of the Path Finders contributed eleven more to take care of target marking. 49 Squadron made ready eleven Lancasters and sent them on their way from Scampton between 17.12 and 17.21 with W/C Slee and S/L Cracknell the senior pilots on duty and set course for the French coast. There were no early returns from the 49 Squadron element, and all passed south-west of Paris on the way to the wall of rock that was the Alps, which glistened under clear skies and an almost full moon. Crews found the clear air and perfect visibility over Italy a joy to behold after contending with the industrial haze at German targets and the Path Finder flares could be seen by approaching main force crews from sixty miles away. On arrival over the city, they found the flak defence to be wildly inaccurate, while a smoke screen proved ineffective as the wind blew it straight out to sea and they were able to establish their positions visually on the layout of the docks and the city. All of the 49 Squadron crews carried out their attacks from 8,000 to 11,500 feet between 21.19 and 21.45, and observed many bursts, explosions and fires, some returning crews on other stations describing the raid as a "miniature-Cologne". Local sources confirmed heavy damage in central and eastern districts, which, because of the need for fuel over bombs, had been achieved with just 180 tons of high-explosives and incendiaries, and remarkably, without loss.

Twenty-four hours later, a force made up of elements from 3 and 4 Groups and the Path Finders attempted to follow up at Genoa, but, in cloudy conditions, attacked in error the town of Savona, thirty miles to the west.

Milan would host two raids on the 24th, the first in daylight by 5 Group, and while that was in progress, back home, seventy-one aircraft were being made ready by 1, 3 and 4 Groups and the Path Finders for a night attack. The city was home to many war factories, including the Isotta Fraschini luxury car works, which had been converted to military vehicle and aero engine manufacture, the Pirelli rubber works, Alfa Romeo, the Caproni aircraft plant, the Breda locomotive, armaments and aircraft works and the Innocenti machinery and vehicle factory. Eighty-eight 5 Group crews attended briefings on the morning of the 24th to learn that they would be undertaking the first daylight crossing of the Alps on their way to the target. This would require an even longer flight over fighter-defended territory than the Le Creusot operation a week earlier, however, it had been forecast that cloud would protect them for most of the way. The nine 49 Squadron Lancasters departed Scampton between 12.16 and 12.24 with W/C Slee and S/L Cracknell the senior pilots on duty, and headed for Selsey Bill, from where they would cross the Channel at very low level with the rest of the loose formation under a Spitfire escort. S/L Cracknell lost his port-outer engine before reaching the French coast and was compelled to abort his sortie. Crews had been briefed to expect the cloud of a warm front awaiting them at the Normandy coast, however, to their discomfort, they saw that it had formed further inland, and they had to run the gauntlet of anti-aircraft fire as they raced over the clifftops with three hours to go to the Alps. A bank of cloud could be seen in the distance, to which the force climbed as rapidly as possible, and once reached, the crews had to plot their own individual course until rendezvousing over Lake

Annecy, sixty miles short of the target. From there they formed a loose formation and lost height, until reaching the target to find eight to nine-tenths cloud with a base at 3,000 feet but sufficient gaps through which to establish their positions visually. The marshalling yards, a seaplane base and an aerodrome were among ground features identified as the 49 Squadron crews delivered their high-explosive and incendiary payloads from 2,000 to 6,000 feet between 17.03 and 17.07. Some squadrons had loaded their Lancasters with a cookie, which required a minimum clearance of 4,000 feet, demonstrating the disregard for their safety of those attacking from such a low height, and even down to a few hundred feet to strafe factories and other targets of opportunity. The sun was setting ahead of them as they crossed the Alps homebound, and France passed beneath them unseen in darkness, with enemy night-fighters waiting over the coastal region as the returning bombers passed through. W4306 was hit by flak, which set an engine on fire and knocked out the hydraulics system, preventing the bomb doors from closing and leaving them without undercarriage for a landing. Doubting that they would make it home, they began the return flight at rooftop height, before F/L Bonnett eventually coaxed the Lancaster up to around 7,000 feet, which meant that they would have to find a path through rather than over the Alps. Miraculously, they reached England's south coast and prepared for a crash-landing at Ford, which, sadly, did not play out as intended and the Lancaster came to grief four hundred yards north of the airfield at 21.38, killing F/L Bonnett DFC and four members of his crew. The two gunners sustained serious injury, to which the rear gunner, Sgt Brookes, succumbed six days later. At debriefing, crews were enthusiastic about the effectiveness of the raid, from which three Lancasters had failed to return, each of them shot down into the Channel. Post-raid reconnaissance revealed that the 135 tons of bombs had caused extensive damage to housing, public buildings and a number of war-industry factories, including the Caproni aircraft works, and had also seriously affected railway communications between Italy and Germany. Local reports confirmed a figure of 441 houses destroyed or seriously damaged along with nine public buildings.

There were no further operations for 5 Group before the end of the month, and 49 Squadron welcomed Sgt "Barney" Gumbley RNZAF and his crew on the 27th from 1654 Conversion Unit. Gumbley was one of a number of members of the squadron at this time who would eventually end up at 617 Squadron, pilot, Sgt Bill Townsend and four of his crew, Gerry Fawke and navigator, Keith Astbury and F/L Ralph Allsebrook and crew among them. During the course of the month, the squadron took part in nine operations and dispatched eighty-eight sorties for the loss of one Lancaster and all but one of its crew.

## November 1942

There would be no operations for the majority of the Command during the first week of the new month, largely as a result of the weather, and 5 Group crews were put on stand-by three times, only to be stood-down as the operations were cancelled. The first major operation to be posted was against Genoa on the 6th, but first, the 49 Squadron crews of W/C Slee, S/L Cracknell and Sgt Mant and two from 57 Squadron were briefed at Scampton for a "moling" operation to Osnabrück with the intention of employing Gee (TR) as a blind-bombing aid. Their Lancasters were loaded with ten 1,000 pounders each and the 49 Squadron trio took off between 11.15 and 11.35, to be followed minutes later by the 57 Squadron pair. Sgt Mant and crew were unable to pick up a Gee signal and the density of the cloud prevented them from establishing a visual pinpoint, forcing them to change their plans. They headed north to within four miles of Emden, but still were unable to pick up a signal and brought their bombs home. The others also lost Gee as the signal faded at 04.30 degrees east at the Dutch coast, but pinpoints were established by dropping to beneath the very low cloud base, where W/C Slee and crew were trailed by two BF109s. When they opened fire, W/C Slee took appropriate evasive action and climbed into the cloud base, which shook off their pursuers but also messed up their navigation and it became necessary to descend to 100 feet to re-establish their whereabouts. They found that they were north of the target and circled 180 degrees before running up the railway line from the east, and with the railway station in view, pulled up to 700 feet to release the bombs at 13.08. Faced with solid cloud from 1,000 to 10,000 feet, S/L Cracknell and crew bombed completely blind on e.t.a. from 4,000 feet at 13.34.

Meanwhile, on 5 Group stations in Lincolnshire, the preparation of a main force of fifty-seven Lancasters was well under way and similar activity at Wyton in Cambridgeshire ensured that fifteen Path Finder Lancasters belonging to 83 Squadron would be available for target-marking duties. The five-strong 49 Squadron element departed Scampton between 21.23 and 21.35 and all reached the target after an uneventful outward flight of four hours in favourable weather conditions. The excellent visibility, along with accurate Path Finder flares, enabled them to locate the aiming point visually after identifying ground features like the breakwater, harbour and town, and they carried out their attacks from 9,500 to 12,500 feet between 01.38 and 01.55. Fires of increasing intensity were concentrated in the docks area and a number of ships appeared to be burning in the harbour, and a pilot from another squadron counted a total of 116 fires across the city. Those arriving in the rear-guard found the effectiveness of the attack laid out before them and described a colossal fire on a hill near the city centre. The glow from the burning city remained visible from the Alps and Nice, some eighty miles away, but no local report emerged to reveal the full extent of the damage.

A follow-up raid on Genoa was posted on 3, 4 and 5 Group stations on the 7th and a force of 175 aircraft assembled, which included Halifaxes, Stirlings and a handful of Wellingtons to join eighty-one Lancasters of 5 Group. The eleven 49 Squadron participants departed Scampton between 17.21 and 17.35 with S/Ls Couch and Cracknell the senior pilots on duty and Sgt Gumbley flying as second pilot with Sgt Mant. The crews of F/O Perry and P/O McIntyre dropped out early on because of engine failures, leaving their colleagues to cross France without incident until reaching the Dijon region with the foothills of the Alps beyond, when it became necessary to climb and pass through a patch of extreme icing conditions. Having made it through, they experienced the same ideal conditions as on the previous night, particularly on the far side of the Alps, and they were able to make a visual identification of the coastline, harbour and aiming point in the light of the punctual and accurately delivered Path Finder flares. A smoke screen failed to shield the city, and the flak defence seemed to give up once the bombing began, although light flak from rooftops continued to fire, even if inaccurately. The 49 Squadron crews bombed from 7,000 to 11,000 feet between 21.35 and 21.59, and would report bombs exploding in the built-up area causing numerous fires. Many crews brought home an aiming point photograph to add to those from reconnaissance flights, which confirmed the operation to have been highly successful. On return from Genoa, Australian, Sgt Mant, and his crew were posted across the tarmac to join 467 Squadron RAAF, which had been formed at Scampton on that very day and would shortly be moving to Bottesford on the Leicestershire/Nottinghamshire border.

The campaigns against Italy and Germany would have to run side-by-side for the time being, and in a break from Italy, Hamburg was posted as the target on the 9th. No mention was made by the "met boys" during briefing of strong winds and ice-bearing cloud of the type that often lay in wait across the bombers' path to Germany's second city. The four heavy groups put together a force of 213 aircraft, of which, sixty-seven Lancasters were provided by 5 Group, eight of them by 49 Squadron. They had been loaded with a cookie and incendiaries each before departing Scampton between 17.46 and 17.54 with S/Ls Couch and Cracknell the senior pilots on duty. The crossed the Lincolnshire coast on course for a point on the German coast to the north of the target and soon encountered the troublesome weather front of towering cumulonimbus cloud. Most negotiated it successfully to reach the target area, which they found to be completely hidden by ten-tenths cloud with tops at 16,000 feet. P/O Eyre and crew failed to locate the target and ran into icing conditions when the attempted to descend to the cloud base, which persuaded them to jettison their bomb load forty miles south of the target. The others were forced to bomb on e.t.a. from 9,000 to 15,000 feet between 20.41 and 21.10 in the absence of Path Finder flares but in the presence of heavy flak, particularly from naval guns, the shells from which were detonating above the bombing height. They found it impossible to assess what was happening beneath the cloud and a strong wind from the north almost certainly pushed the bombing south of the intended aiming point, a fact seemingly confirmed by local reports, that many bombs had fallen into the River Elbe or into open country, and only three large fires had required attention. Five of the fifteen failures to return were from 5 Group.

Mine-laying would occupy the ensuing two nights, and 5 Group detailed a dozen Lancasters on the 10th to send that night to the Biscay coast to the Deodar, Elderberry and Furze gardens, located respectively in the Gironde estuary, off Bayonne further south and a dozen miles further south still at St-Jean-de-Luz, right down on the border between France and Spain. 49 Squadron asked for a volunteer crew for Deodar and W/O Mapp offered his, which departed Scampton at 17.29 and arrived in the target area to find a band of cloud at between 1,000 and 4,000 feet. They pinpointed on Pointe-de-Grave as the start of the timed run and delivered their mines into the briefed location from 700 feet at 20.48.

Orders were received at Scampton on the 13th to prepare three aircraft for a 5 Group operation against Genoa that night involving sixty-one Lancasters, supported by a Path Finder element comprising six Lancasters of 83 Squadron and nine Stirlings of 7 Squadron at Oakington. Nineteen of the 5 Group element were to attack the Ansaldo engineering works, which could be viewed as the Italian "Krupp", while the remainder had their own aiming point in the town. The 49 Squadron trio consisting of the crews of Sgts McDonald, Gumbley and Johnstone departed Scampton between 18.17 and 18.28 and set course for Selsey Bill for the Channel crossing. They negotiated France without incident and traversed the Alps in good weather conditions that allowed the target to be identified visually from cloudless skies. The bombing by the 49 Squadron crews was carried out from 8,000 and 9,000 feet between 22.28 and 22.47 in the face of a "beefed-up" searchlight and flak defence, and high explosive and incendiary bursts were observed right across the target area. Those plotted were found to be at least a thousand yards from the aiming point, but there was no attempt to assess the outcome through reconnaissance. Some returning crews reported the glow of fires to be visible for 130 miles into the return flight, and confidence was high that the loss-free raid had been successful.

Two days later, a force of seventy-eight aircraft was made ready to continue the assault on Genoa, and twenty-one of twenty-seven Lancasters were provided by 5 Group. 49 Squadron contributed eight Lancasters, which departed Scampton between 17.49 and 17.56 with S/L Cracknell the senior pilot on duty and enjoyed an uneventful outward flight across France. The ten-tenths cloud to the south of the Alps stopped just short of the target to provide clear skies and moonlight, which the Path Finders exploited to illuminate the aiming point, allowing it to be identified visually for a force largely untroubled by the defences. The 49 Squadron crews attacked from 9,000 to 11,500 feet between 22.04 and 22.12 and observed their bombs mostly to fall close to the aiming point. Six large fires were counted in the built-up area, and the glow was still visible from up to a hundred miles into the return journey.

Attention turned upon the northern powerhouse of Turin on the 18th, which was home to Fiat's Lingotto and Mirafiori car plants, the Lancia motor works, the Arsenale army munitions factory, the Nebioli foundry and plants belonging to the American Westinghouse company. The force of seventy-seven aircraft made ready to attack the Fiat motor works had originally been significantly larger, but forty-two 5 Group Lancasters, including all six from 49 Squadron, had been withdrawn because of doubts about the weather over their stations. Those arriving at the target some three-and-at-half hours after taking off found clear skies that left the city naked to the eyes of the bomb-aimers, who benefitted from another excellent performance by the Path Finders. The aiming point was squarely in their bomb-sights as the main force element ran in and many fires broke out in the city centre, the Fiat works sustaining an unspecified degree of damage, which was confirmed by bombing photographs.

Tommy Blair was posted to 1660 Conversion Unit on the 19th, from where he would find his way to the Path Finder Force to continue his operational career. Following the recent run of relatively small-scale operations to Italy, the 20th brought a return to the Fiat works at Turin with greater numbers, amounting this time to 232 aircraft, of which seventy-eight Lancasters were provided by 5 Group. 49 Squadron made ready eleven of its own and dispatched them from Scampton between 18.08 and 18.24 with W/C Slee and S/L Cracknell the senior pilots on duty. It would take almost four hours to reach the target, but all from the squadron negotiated the seven-hundred-mile outward leg without incident, and those arriving at the front end of the attack were able to establish their position by following the autostrada and identifying ground features in the light of flares. By the time that the majority of the Scampton crews reached the city, smoke was already drifting across it, and ground features appeared fleetingly, which created challenging conditions for target identification. Ground haze added to the difficulties, but even so, by running in at low to medium level, some crews were able to identify the factory visually and deliver the bombs with some degree of accuracy. The 49 Squadron participants attacked from 6,000 to 7,000 feet between 22.08 and 23.05 and left behind them massive fires raging in the city centre, from which smoke was already rising through 6,000 feet. Returning crews were confident in the effectiveness of their work and a death toll of 117 would provide evidence of a damaging attack.

Sixty-four 5 Group crews attended briefings on the 22nd to learn that their destination that night was to be Stuttgart as part of an overall force of 222 aircraft. 49 Squadron made ready eight Lancasters, which departed Scampton between 18.16 and 18.33 with W/C Slee and S/L Cracknell the senior pilots on duty. They flew out over Dungeness on the Kent coast and made landfall at

Cayeux, before pinpointing on Châtillon-sur-Seine and turning east to cross the German frontier. Located in a series of valleys, Stuttgart was always a difficult city to identify, but three hours and fifteen minutes after take-off, the first of the main force crews had Path Finder flares in their sights, illuminating the target area to apparently enable a visual identification of the aiming point. The bombs were dropped by the 49 Squadron crews from 5,000 (W/C Slee) to 12,000 feet between 21.51 and 22.28, and their bursts observed, before a safe return was made from what they described as a quiet trip with a satisfactory result. It was soon discovered that a thin layer of cloud and ground haze had prevented the Path Finders from identifying the centre of the city, and much of the bombing had fallen onto south-western and southern districts and outlying communities up to five miles from the city centre. Local reports confirmed that a modest eighty-eight houses had been destroyed and described two bombers attacking the city centre at low level and causing extensive damage to the main railway station. 49 Squadron was represented among the ten failures to return by W4107, which initially disappeared without trace with the crew of F/Sgt Singleton. It would be some time before the Red Cross reported the entire crew to be safe but in enemy hands and not until after the war that the circumstances of their capture came to light. They had been hit by flak after bombing and a fire threatened to blow the Lancaster apart. Four members of the crew baled out before the fire was extinguished and F/Sgt Singleton decided to see how much distance he could coax out of his aircraft. After crossing the French coast, they came upon land, which they took to be England, and crash-landed in a field, only to discover that they were on the occupied Channel Island of Sark, where a reception by German soldiers awaited them.

Aircraft actually became airborne for operations on the 26th and 27th, only to be recalled immediately on receipt of a cancellation order. On the latter occasion, five 49 Squadron Lancasters were outbound for Stettin when the raid was cancelled. Instructions came through to all heavy groups on the 28th to prepare its aircraft and crews for operations that night against Turin, and during the course of the day a force of 228 aircraft was made ready, ninety-one of the Lancasters on 5 Group stations. *(1 Group was in the process of converting from Wellingtons to Lancasters, and 101, 103 and 460 Squadrons had begun to operate the type in the past week).* 49 Squadron made ready ten aircraft, their bomb bays containing either a cookie and three SBCs of 30lb incendiaries or all-incendiary loads and launched them from Scampton between 18.37 and 18.53 with S/L Couch the senior pilot on duty. P/O Eyre and crew were three miles south of Reading when engine trouble ended their interest in proceedings, leaving the others to continue on to cross France without incident to reach the target area under clear skies and just a little haze to mar the vertical visibility. Despite this, they were able to establish their positions by visual reference of the River Po assisted by Path Finder flares and the 49 Squadron crews bombed their briefed aiming point of the city centre from 6,000 to 10,000 feet between 22.25 and 22.35, observing bursts in the town and on the Fiat works being targeted by other elements. One returning crew counted forty-seven fires when they were fifteen minutes into the homeward journey and others confirmed that the city was a mass of flames, commenting on a particularly large blaze in the centre and some others around the Royal Arsenal. W/C Gibson and F/L Whamond of 106 Squadron dropped the first two 8,000 pounders to fall on Italy, and all indications were that the operation had been entirely successful.

During the course of the month, the squadron undertook eleven operations, including the recall from Stettin, and dispatched seventy-three sorties for the loss of a single Lancaster and crew.

# December 1942

The weather at the start of the new month restricted operations, and an unsuccessful raid on Frankfurt involving 112 aircraft on the 2nd did not include a contribution from 5 Group. Squadrons were warned of operations daily between the 2nd and 5th, but each was cancelled and it was the 6th before a bombing operation involving 5 Group would actually go ahead. Mannheim was revealed as the target for seventy-four 5 Group Lancasters in an overall force of 272 aircraft, and 49 Squadron would contribute six of its own. They departed Scampton between 17.37 and 17.45 with P/O Eyre the only commissioned pilot on duty, and all reached the target to encounter eight to ten-tenths cloud at between 4,000 and 12,000 feet. This rendered ineffective the Path Finders' efforts to mark the city with flares and a decoy site was also operating some twenty miles to the south, which, inevitably, attracted a proportion of the bombing. Crews could bomb only on DR and e.t.a., in the case of the 49 Squadron element from 7,000 to 13,000 feet between 20.17 and 20.42. They had no clue as to the fall of their bombs, but a few crews from other squadrons descended to the cloud base, from where the Rhine and a built-up area were visible and scattered fires were observed along with blazing square factory buildings. Most returning crews had little of interest to report to the intelligence section at debriefing.

On the following night, 5 Group called for nine crews to carry out gardening duties in the Elderberry and Furze gardens off the south-western coast of France. Group enquired of 49 Squadron whether they had an experienced gardening crew for Elderberry, and that of P/O perry departed Scampton at 16.31 with a long round trip ahead of them. They found up to three-tenths cloud and good visibility in the target area off Bayonne, and lights from the notoriously poor blackout at Biarritz to provide a solid reference. They established a pinpoint north of the River Adour, guided by the glow from a factory blast furnace and delivered their mines at five-second intervals into the briefed location from 1,000 feet at 21.57. Further south, lights were blazing in Spain and a steel works at Bilboa appeared to be in full production.

Notification was received on 5 Group stations on the 8th that Turin was to be the target for that night, in an operation to be conducted by a 5 Group main force of ninety-eight Lancasters, supported by thirty-five Path Finder aircraft of all types. The 49 Squadron element of nine departed Scampton between 17.28 and 17.55 with W/C Slee and S/L Cracknell the senior pilots on duty and lost the services of Sgt Gumbley and crew to engine failure when thirty miles east of Troyes. The remainder all reached the eastern side of the Alps to find clear skies and good visibility, and the city visible to the south as they approached the final turning point. Swinging towards the start of their bombing run, over to port to the east of the city a large bend in the River Po provided a strong reference, which enabled the Path Finders to identify the aiming point and deliver their flares right on the mark. The 49 Squadron crews followed in their wake and registered that the aiming point was well-defined by two arcs of Path Finder flares and one massive explosion a mile-and-a-half to the south-west. The bombing was carried out from 7,500 to 10,000 feet between 21.04 and 21.29, and the city could be seen to be well-alight. Those arriving when the attack was already well underway reported smoke drifting across the aiming point and counted thirty to forty sizeable fires burning across the city. A huge pall of smoke was rising through 8,000 feet as the force retreated towards the Alps, and the fires would still be burning when the next bomber force arrived twenty-four hours later.

Orders came through on the 9th to prepare for another assault on Turin that night, and eight 49 Squadron crews attended the briefing at Scampton to learn that they would be part of a 5 Group effort of eighty-two Lancasters in an overall force of 227 aircraft. S/Ls Couch and Cracknell were the senior pilots on duty as they took off between 17.26 and 17.41, and it was not long before F/O McDonald and crew turned back with the floor of their Lancaster awash with leaking hydraulic fluid. The others enjoyed an uneventful outward flight and were guided the final few miles to the target by the fires still burning from the previous night. This, however, proved to be a double-edged sword as the smoke hanging over the city created challenging conditions for the Path Finders, who failed to deliver as strong a performance this time. The identity of the aiming point was not recorded but it was almost certainly the Fiat works, and the raid was spread out over more than thirty minutes, during which the 49 Squadron crews attacked the general city area from 6,000 to 13,000 feet between 21.35 and 21.47. They contributed to the creation of many more fires that produced even larger volumes of smoke to obscure much of the ground from those arriving at the tail end of proceedings. Returning crews reported explosions and fires, but the consensus was of a less effective raid than that of the previous night.

For the third night in succession the torment of Turin continued, although at the hands of a reduced force of eighty-two aircraft drawn from 1 and 4 Groups and the Path Finders. They had to fight their way through severe icing conditions over France, and more than half of the force turned back before reaching the Alps. Those completing their sorties failed to inflict more than the slightest damage on the city, in what proved to be the final raid of this first Italian campaign. Sixty-eight aircraft were sent mining on the night of the 14/15th, but the twenty-three 5 Group Lancasters were recalled after an hour because of concerns about the weather for their return.

The weather curtailed 5 Group operations from the 10th to the 16th inclusive and on the 17th, twenty-seven Lancasters were detailed to target eight small German towns for what was referred to in the 5 Group ORB as "Batter", against Soltau, some forty miles east of Bremen, and Neustadt-am-Rübenberge and Nienburg, located between Bremen to the north-west and Hannover to the south-east. A further ten Lancasters were assigned to "moling" sorties over five other towns in north-western Germany including, Cloppenburg, Diepholz and Quakenbrück, and one wonders if, in the cold light of dawn, anyone in raid planning recalled the disaster that had afflicted 57 and 214 Squadrons of 3 Group as a result of similar operations on the first night of April. Nine Lancasters failed to return, three belonging to 44 (Rhodesia) Squadron and two each to 9, 50 and 97 Squadrons.

Apart from isolated "moling" daylight operations, the Ruhr had been left in peace since Krefeld at the start of October, while attention had been focussed on Italian targets. Now, on the 20th, Duisburg was posted as the target, and this would mask another operation of great significance for the Command that was taking place at the same time over Holland. Although, in the event, not all would proceed according to plan, it would be a mere blip in the development of the Oboe blind-bombing device. Having sat out the carnage of the 17th, 49 Squadron prepared eleven of its Lancasters to contribute to the seventy-five-strong 5 Group contingent in an overall force of 232 aircraft assembled for the main event. They departed Scampton between 17.54 and 18.17 with S/L Cracknell the senior pilot on duty and may have witnessed a tragic collision between two Waddington Lancasters over Lincoln, which resulted in the deaths of all fourteen occupants. There were no early returns among the 49 Squadron element, which crossed the North Sea to make landfall on the Den Helder peninsula, pinpointing on Enkhuizen before turning to the south-east for the run on the target. Favourable weather conditions prevailed in the target area, where bright moonlight provided the good visibility that enabled crews to identify the River Rhine and the Ruhrort docks through the industrial haze. Having established a firm visual reference, bombing was carried out by the 49 Squadron crews from 8,000 to 14,000 feet between 19.50 and 20.11, and at least fifteen fires were observed, many of them large. Sgt Johnston RCAF and crew were homebound over Holland in R5762, when it was hit by flak from the Ijmuiden defence zone and crashed without survivors on dunes to the south of the town at 20.42.

Meanwhile, six 109 Squadron Oboe-equipped Mosquitos had targeted a power station at Lutterade in Holland, believing the target to be free of bomb craters so as not to impair the data gleaned from a calibration test to gauge the device's margin of error,. Unfortunately, three of the Mosquitos suffered Oboe failure and went on to bomb Duisburg instead, leaving W/C Hal Bufton and two other crews to deliver the bombs. What they hadn't bargained for was a whole carpet of bomb craters left over from the attack on Aachen, seventeen miles away, in October, and it proved impossible to identify those aimed by Oboe. The calibration tests would continue, however, and come the spring, Oboe would be ready to unleash with devastating results against the Ruhr.

The 21st brought instructions to 1 and 5 Groups and the Path Finders to prepare a force of 137 aircraft for an operation that night against Munich, deep in southern Germany. As already mentioned, a few 1 Group squadrons had begun to receive Lancasters during the autumn, and would contribute in small numbers, but eighty-two of the 119 of the type made available for this operation were provided by 5 Group and some others by the 83 Squadron of the Path Finders. 49 Squadron briefed eleven crews, who were in their aircraft and lined up for take-off behind W/C Slee by 17.19. The commanding officer had a highly experienced crew around him, which on this night included F/L Ralph Allsebrook as second pilot and Keith Astbury as navigator. Sgt Thom and crew took off at 17.29 and had reached 1,000 feet when the starboard-inner engine failed, and they proceeded directly to the jettison area. The others were safely airborne by 17.33 and made their way across France to enter Germany north of Strasbourg with Munich 180 miles away a little to the south of due east. P/O Eyre and crew had covered around sixty of those miles when they were attacked by a night-fighter, which they evaded at a cost of their starboard-inner engine. Unable to regain the altitude lost during the engagement, the bombs were jettisoned "live" over the town of Reutlingen before they set off for home. The others arrived in the target area after a three-and-a-half-hour outward journey, only to find it concealed beneath ten-tenths cloud with tops at a lowly 2,000 feet. The Path Finders illuminated the Ammersee to the south-west of the city, and crews carried out a time-and-distance run from there to the aiming point, the 49 Squadron crews bombing from 7,000 and 12,000 feet between 21.07 and 21.25. There were plenty of flashes below the cloud, together with the glow of fires to convince the crews that they had found the mark, but it is likely that these came from a decoy site, as most bombing photos would reveal open country. Twelve aircraft failed to return, six of them belonging to 5 Group, but all from 49 Squadron made it back from what turned out to be their final operational activity of the year.

The fourth wartime Christmas was celebrated in traditional style across the Command, and operational activity ceased until the 29th, when fourteen 5 Group Lancasters were sent mining off France's Biscay coast. On New Year's Eve, eight Lancasters and two Mosquitos of the Path Finder

Force carried out the first live trial of Oboe at Düsseldorf. During the course of the month, the squadron took part in six operations and dispatched forty-six sorties for the loss of one Lancaster and crew.

As the New Year beckoned, a great responsibility lay on the nine operational Lancaster squadrons of 5 Group to carry the war to the enemy. There was no question that the Stirling and Mk II and V Halifaxes were inferior aircraft, and their limited availability and restricted bomb-carrying capacity meant that the Command still had to rely very much on the trusty but aging Wellington to make up the numbers if the defences were to be overwhelmed. That said, the advent of Oboe and the yet-to-be-introduced ground-mapping radar, H2S, would greatly enhance the Command's ability to deliver a telling blow, and 1943 would see the balance of power shift massively in the Command's favour.

## January 1943

The year began with the official formation on New Year's Day of the Canadian 6 Group, and the handing over to it of the former 4 Group stations in North Yorkshire on which its squadrons had been lodging. Eventually, all Canadian squadrons would find a home in the group, which was financed by Canada and controlled by Harris, but initially, there were eight founder members, including 408 and 420 Squadron, which had left 5 Group during the autumn. Further south, a continuation of the Oboe trials would occupy the first two weeks, during which 109 Squadron marked for small forces of 1 and 5 Group Lancasters at Essen on seven occasions and Duisburg once. For the first time, the cloud cover and ever-present blanket of industrial haze would have no bearing on the outcome of the raid as reliance on e.t.a., DR and Gee was cast aside in favour of Oboe, at least, that is, at targets within the device's range. Until the advent of mobile transmitter stations late in the war, Oboe would be restricted by the curvature of the earth and the altitude at which Mosquitos could fly, but this meant that the entire Ruhr lay within range of Harris's bombers. That said, the success of a raid would still rely on the ability of the Path Finders to back up the initial Oboe markers and maintain a supply of target indicators (TIs) on the aiming point.

49 Squadron began 1943 with a complement of thirty-seven officers and 602 other ranks and a dozen Mk I Lancasters and eight of the Mk III variant powered by American-built Packard Merlin engines. There would be no operations for the squadron for more than two weeks while it moved out of Scampton and took up residence at Fiskerton, situated five miles east of Lincoln. Quite why it took so long to settle in is uncertain, when most moves were not allowed to interfere with operations for more than a day. This meant that the squadron would not be involved in the above-mentioned round of Oboe trials, the first of which was mounted against Essen on the 3rd by a 5 Group force of nineteen Lancasters and three Mosquitos. On the 8th, the Path Finder Force was granted group status as 8 Group, and the stations it occupied were transferred from 3 Group. For the purpose of this book, the titles Path Finder and 8 Group are interchangeable.

A new Air Ministry directive was issued on the 14th, which authorised the area bombing of the French ports with concrete bunkers and support facilities providing a home for U-Boots. A list was drawn up accordingly, headed by Lorient and included St-Nazaire, Brest and La Pallice. As mentioned earlier, between February 1941 and January 1942, the Germans had built three giant concrete structures K1, K2 and K3 on the southernmost point of Lorient's Keroman Peninsula. They were capable of housing and servicing thirty U-Boots and providing accommodation for their crews and were impregnable to the bombs available to Bomber Command at the time. The purpose of this new campaign, therefore, was to render the town and port uninhabitable and block or sever all road and rail communications to them. The first of the series of nine attacks on the port over the ensuing four weeks took place that very night at the hands of a force of 122 aircraft in the absence of 5 Group, and, despite accurate marking by the Path Finder element, the main force bombing was scattered and destroyed a modest 120 buildings.

5 Group's involvement with Lorient would come in February, and in the meantime, Harris planned two operations against the "Big City", Berlin, beginning on the 16th, for which a force of 201 aircraft was made ready. This would be the first raid on Germany's capital for fourteen months and would bring with it the first use of custom-designed target indicators (TIs). The main force would be made up predominantly of 5 Group Lancasters, with others from 1 Group, while eleven Halifaxes of 35 (Madras Presidency) Squadron would be included in the Path Finder element. Those reaching the target would share the airspace over it with the broadcaster, Richard Dimbleby, who was in a 106 Squadron Lancaster captained by W/C Guy Gibson. *(In some of my previous books, I have fallen into the trap of repeating the errors of others by recording Dimbleby's participation during the second Berlin raid that took place on the following night. This could not be the case, as Gibson was not involved in the second Berlin raid.)* 49 Squadron detailed sixteen Lancasters, which departed Fiskerton between 16.36 and 16.59 with W/C Slee and S/Ls Couch and Cracknell the senior pilots on duty and F/L Allsebrook undertaking the first sortie of his second tour. They headed for Mandø Island off the west coast of Jutland, from where the route would take the bomber stream across southern Jutland to the western Baltic, to follow the coastline eastwards until reaching Swinemünde, from where they would swing to the south for the run on the target. It was not to be an outstanding night of serviceability for 49 Squadron as first Sgt Thom and crew returned after two hours because of port-outer engine failure. An hour later, it was Sgt Gumbley and crew who touched down after an early return for which no reason was recorded. S/L Cracknell and crew fell victim to engine gremlins two hours into the outward flight and brought their incendiaries home after jettisoning their cookie. F/O Jeffreys and crew had been outbound for around three hours when excessive petrol consumption persuaded them not to go on.

The remaining twelve crews pressed on to reach the target under moonlight, with good visibility above six-tenths cloud at 10,000 feet, through which the built-up area could be seen clearly. The 49 Squadron crews mostly failed to observe the red warning flares and picked up the lakes and autobahns to reach the city, and it was then that red and green TIs could be seen bursting on what was assumed to be the aiming point. They dropped their cookie and incendiary bomb loads from 15,000 to 21,000 feet between 20.04 and 20.45, not all with a clear view of the ground, although some recognised that they were over the southern outskirts of the city, where the Tempelhof district could be identified. At debriefing, some crews reported black smoke rising through 5,000 feet as they turned away, but many were unconvinced of the effectiveness of the raid, and this was borne out by local sources. One notable scalp was the ten-thousand-seater Deutschlandhalle, the largest covered venue in Europe, which was hosting the annual circus as the bombers approached and was efficiently emptied of people and animals with only a few minor injuries. Shortly afterwards, incendiaries set fire to the building and reduced it to ruins. Remarkably, only a single Lancaster failed to return from this operation, but the balance would be redressed somewhat twenty-four hours later.

170 Lancasters and seventeen Halifaxes were made ready on 1, 4, 5 and 8 Group stations for the return to Berlin that night, when they would follow the same route as for twenty-four hours earlier with a three-and-a-half-hour outward flight ahead of them, stalked constantly by night-fighters once they reached western Denmark. 49 Squadron's nine Lancasters departed Fiskerton between 16.50 and 17.17 with S/L Cracknell and F/L Allsebrook the senior pilots on duty. The latter turned back because of oxygen system failure shortly after crossing the coast, leaving the others to press on across southern Jutland, to bypass the searchlights and flak in the Kiel defence zone and reach the Baltic. F/O McDonald and crew must have had Berlin in sight when they too suffered oxygen failure and turned back towards the German coast, where the bombs were dropped from 6,000 feet at 20.40 and seen to burst on the seafront of an unidentified location. Those reaching the target area were greeted by eight to ten-tenths cloud with tops at between 10,000 and 14,000 feet, through which it was possible for most to pick out the Müggelsee to the south-east of the capital, from where a timed run was carried out to the aiming point. Some crews failed to see any flares, which was understandable as the Path Finders arrived thirty-seven minutes late, and so bombed on e.t.a. or DR. Some did benefit from target marking, which sadly, was once more concentrated over the southern fringes of the city rather than over the centre. The 49 Squadron crews carried out their attacks from 15,000 to 21,000 feet between 20.35 and 21.04, and by the latter time, some Path Finder flares were evident. Little was seen of the results of the bombing, and local reports confirmed that the operation had not been successful, and no significant damage had occurred. The disappointment was compounded by the loss of twenty-two bombers, 11.8% of those dispatched, and many of these disappeared without trace in the Baltic or North Sea. 49 Squadron's ED444 was shot down by a night-fighter near Flensburg with fatal consequences for F/O Jeffreys DFC and two members of his crew, while the four survivors were taken into captivity.

A force of seventy-nine Lancasters and three Mosquitos was detailed to resume the Oboe trials programme at Essen on the 21st, for which 49 Squadron briefed seven crews and dispatched them from Fiskerton between 17.27 and 17.50 with W/C Slee and S/L Cracknell the senior pilots on duty and F/L Allsebrook in support. W/O Mapp and crew returned early as oxygen failure struck again, but the others reached the target area, noting that condensation trails were forming at 18,000 feet to advertise their presence to the German defences. There was a question as to the cloud conditions, some reporting clear skies and others ten-tenths cloud, neither of which would have mattered if the Oboe marking had worked and been visible to all. In the event, the entire Ruhr was concealed beneath thick industrial haze, which proved to be impenetrable, and the 49 Squadron crews could only estimate that they were over Essen when they let their bombs go from 15,000 to 22,000 feet between 19.45 and 20.00 in the face of an intense flak barrage. As far as many returning crews were concerned, there had been no Path Finder markers to point the way and the outcome of the raid remained undetermined at a cost of four Lancasters.

The Oboe trials programme moved to Düsseldorf on the 23rd, the huge industrial city situated some fifteen miles south-south-east of Essen, for which 1, 5 and 8 Groups assembled a force of eighty Lancasters and three Mosquitos. At Fiskerton, 49 Squadron loaded eight of its Lancasters with a cookie each and a dozen SBCs of 4lb incendiaries and sent them on their way between 17.30 and 17.56 with S/Ls Couch and Cracknell and F/L Allsebrook the senior pilots on duty. They lost the services of Sgts McDonald and Gumbley after their guns failed to function when tested over the North Sea. Those reaching the target area found ten-tenths cloud at 12,000 feet, heavy, accurate flak and Path Finder release point flares drifting towards the cloud tops. The 49 Squadron element bombed on these from 15,600 to 22,000 feet between 19.35 and 19.58 but saw nothing of the outcome through the cloud. Lorient had faced another assault on this night with a token Lancaster presence in a force of 121 aircraft, which inflicted further heavy damage. The fourth raid took place on the night of the 26/27th at the hands of an initial force of 157 aircraft, which attacked in poor weather conditions.

Düsseldorf was selected again as the primary target on the 27th, when the Path Finders were to use ground marking for the first time rather than skymarking. Ground markers, which were TIs fused to burst and cascade just above the ground, could be seen through thin or partial cloud and industrial haze and were much more reliable than the previously-employed parachute flares, that drifted in the wind. However, skymarkers would remain an indispensable part of target marking techniques on nights of heavy cloud or to use in combination with ground markers. From this night onwards, Path Finder heavy aircraft would back-up the Mosquito-laid Oboe markers to ensure that the aiming point remained marked throughout the operation. A heavy force of 124 Lancasters and thirty-three Halifaxes was made ready on 1, 4, 5 and 8 Group stations, 49 Squadron providing ten of the Lancasters, which departed Fiskerton between 17.37 and 18.11 with S/L Couch and F/L Allsebrook the senior pilots on duty. Sgt Gilmore and crew were forced to turn back when the rear gunner's oxygen tube was severed by the rotating turret, leaving the others to press on and reach the target to be greeted by a thin layer of five to ten-tenths cloud at 10,000 feet, through which the red and green TIs could be seen burning on the aiming point. They carried out their part in the proceedings from 16,500 to 22,000 feet between 20.04 and 20.11, S/L Couch requiring three passes before his cookie deigned to leave the bomb bay. All returned safely, impressed by the potential of ground marking and confident that they had hit the aiming point, a fact confirmed by local reports, which spoke of widespread destruction in southern districts amounting to 456 houses, ten industrial premises and nine public buildings destroyed or seriously damaged, and many others afflicted to a lesser extent.

Seventy-five aircraft of 1, 4 and 6 Groups carried out the fifth attack of the series on Lorient on the night of the 29/30th. Another new blind-bombing device, the ground-mapping H2S radar, was to be employed operationally for the first time at Hamburg on the 30th, for which a force of 135 Lancasters of 1, 5 and 8 Groups would be joined by thirteen H2S-equipped Path Finder Stirlings and Halifaxes of 7 and 35 Squadrons respectively. The H2S equipment was housed in a cupola aft of the bomb bay and projected an image of the terrain onto a cathode-ray tube in the navigator's compartment. It was the job of the operator to interpret what he was seeing and guide the pilot to the aiming point, but this was no easy task, particularly with the Mk I set, and it proved difficult to distinguish particular ground features in the jumble of images presented to him. It would take much practice and experience to master the device, but, in time, and once the Mk III set became available, H2S would become an indispensable tool. Initially employed only by Path Finder aircraft, it would eventually become standard equipment in main force squadrons also.

49 Squadron made ready eleven Lancasters for Hamburg, loading each with a cookie and incendiaries before sending them on their way from Fiskerton between 23.46 and 00.31 with S/Ls Couch and Cracknell the senior pilots on duty. As mentioned frequently before, north-western

Germany had a "gatekeeper" in the form of weather fronts, which on this night, contained severe icing conditions and electrical storms for the bombers to negotiate as they made their way across the North Sea. A few aircraft dropped out of the bomber stream at this stage, but all from 49 Squadron made it through the conditions to reach the target, where they encountered cloud ranging between zero and ten-tenths with tops at between 6,000 and 15,000 feet. They bombed on flares or TIs from 18,000 to 23,000 feet between 03.03 and 03.15 and observed the reflections of explosions in the cloud. On return, a flak-damaged ED428 hit trees as Sgt Cole was making an approach to land and crashed at 07.15 at Reepham Crossing, two miles east-north-east of Lincoln, killing all but the mid-upper gunner. A consensus that the operation had been effective was partially confirmed by local reports that mentioned seventy-one large fires, but much of the bombing had fallen either into the Elbe or into marshland outside of the city. This would have been disappointing to the raid planners, as Hamburg, with the nearby coastline and wide River Elbe, was an ideal target for H2S and should have been easy to identify on the cathode-ray tubes.

During the course of the month, the squadron took part in six operations and dispatched sixty-one sorties for the loss of two Lancasters and their crews.

## February 1943

It was a time of honing and refining for Bomber Command in preparation for the launching of a major campaign a month hence and February would bring an increase in operations. It opened with the posting of Cologne as the target for an experimental operation on the $2^{nd}$, in which two marking methods were to be employed. Situated just to the south of the Ruhr, the Rhineland capital city was within range of Oboe Mosquitos, and these were to be supplemented by Path Finder aircraft relying on H2S. A force of 159 heavies included seventy-four 5 Group Lancasters, seven of them provided by 49 Squadron, while two Path Finder Mosquitos of 109 Squadron carried the Oboe markers. The Fiskerton contingent took off between 18.24 and 18.59 with S/L Cracknell the senior pilot on duty, and all made it through a cold front, which caused many guns to freeze solid. They reached the target to find a layer of two to five tenths thin cloud up to 8,000 feet and patches above, which afforded good vertical visibility and a clear sight of the red and green skymarkers even from some distance on approach to the bombing run. There was some debate as to the accuracy and concentration of the markers, which a few crews from other squadrons would report as five to ten miles to the north-west of the city, while others described them as scattered. Most of the 49 Squadron crews picked up the red flares with green stars and cascading TIs above the ground and had them in the bomb sight as they delivered their cookie and incendiaries from 20,000 to 22,000 feet between 21.04 and 21.09. Although few were able to observe their own bombs burst, many scattered fires were evident, the glow from which could be seen from a hundred miles into the return journey. Local reports confirmed bombs falling all over the city, but nowhere with concentration, and damage was, consequently, not commensurate with the size of the force and the effort expended. Five aircraft failed to return, and among the three missing Lancasters was ED440, which had been shot down by a night-fighter while homebound and crashed four miles south-west of the Dutch town of Venlo at 21.13, killing F/O Jackson and all but the flight engineer, who was taken into captivity. They had been on their first operation together.

Hamburg was posted as the target on the 3rd, for which a force of 263 aircraft was made ready, unusually, with Halifaxes representing the most populous type followed by Stirlings. 5 Group contributed forty of the sixty-two Lancasters, five of them belonging to 49 Squadron, and they departed Fiskerton between 18.21 and 18.51 with F/L Allsebrook the senior pilot on duty. Fifteen of the 5 Group crews turned back on encountering the towering cloud and severe icing conditions common to this route over the North Sea, and most of them cited frozen guns. F/O Fawke was contending with a faltering starboard-inner engine and turned back when unable to coax ED427 above 16,000 feet. At about the same time, F/O Armstrong abandoned his attempt to climb over the front and jettisoned his load into the North Sea, while F/Sgt Miller and crew had entered the cloud and were thrown about violently to the point where control was almost lost. Once the bombs had been jettisoned, the Lancaster became more stable and they were able to make it home. The crews of Sgt McDonald and F/L Allsebrook arrived in the target area to find nine to ten-tenths cloud, which they estimated topped out at 12,000 feet, while 207 Squadron crews reported the cloud to be at 17,000 to 20,000 feet. Scattered red and green Path Finder H2S-laid skymarker flares were in the bomb sights as the 49 Squadron pair bombed from 21,000 and 22,000 feet respectively at 21.01 and 21.13. No results were observed, and the impression was of an ineffective attack, which was confirmed by local reports of forty-five large fires but no concentration or significant damage, and this disappointing outcome cost the Command sixteen aircraft. The losses by type made interesting reading and would reflect the trend for the remainder of the year, with the Stirlings suffering the highest numerical and percentage casualties, followed by the Halifaxes and Wellingtons, with the Lancasters clearly at the top of the food chain.

A return to Italy was posted on the 4th with Turin the target for a force of 188 aircraft, while 128 others, mostly Wellingtons, were prepared to continue the assault on Lorient. 5 Group contributed forty-eight Lancasters to the former and eight with freshman crews to the latter, 49 Squadron putting up three Lancasters for Italy. They departed Fiskerton between 18.05 and 18.16 containing the crews of S/L Cracknell, F/Sgt Miller and Sgt Gilmore, and followed the usual route across France. After crossing the Alps in cloud at 21,000 feet, they found conditions on the Italian side much improved with clear skies and excellent visibility, which facilitated a visual confirmation of the accuracy of the Path Finder TIs. An estimated one hundred searchlights were active, and the flak defence had also been "beefed-up" but was still inaccurate and in keeping with expectations at an Italian target. *(Following a raid on a German target, a bomb symbol was painted on the forward fuselage below the glasshouse, but after a raid on an Italian target, the symbol would be an ice-cream cone.)* Red TIs were much in evidence in the city centre as the Fiskerton trio carried out their attacks from 12,000 to 16,500 feet between 21.47 and 21.50, and returning crews were enthusiastic about the effectiveness of their work. Local sources confirmed later that serious and widespread damage had resulted.

According to Form 541 of the 49 Squadron ORB for this night, three freshman crews went to Lorient. However, the Form 540 makes no mention of them, but does for the night of the 7/8th, the squadron scribe having failed to add the date on the Form 541 and simply dittoing the 4/5th date. This was the seventh raid in the series on Lorient and was by far the largest to date, employing 323 aircraft, of which forty-three of eighty Lancasters were provided by 5 Group. It was to be conducted in two waves, an hour apart, and it was for the second wave that 49 Squadron made ready three Lancasters for the crews of F/O Armstrong and Sgts Duncan and Hogg, before sending them on their way from Fiskerton between 19.06 and 19.23. The first wave had arrived in the target area to find clear skies and ideal bombing conditions, which they exploited after making a visual identification of the aiming point confirmed by Path Finder TIs. As they were returning home to report an outstandingly destructive raid, they left behind them a glow in the sky visible from the English coast, which acted as a beacon for the second-phase element to home in on. They encountered heavy smoke and haze over the target, through which the 49 Squadron trio bombed from 11,000 and 12,000 feet between 21.30 and 21.37, before heading home to confirm a devastating raid.

Before the penultimate raid on Lorient took place, attention was switched to the important naval and shipbuilding port of Wilhelmshaven, situated on the north-western coast of Jade Bay, some sixty miles to the west of Hamburg. A force of 177 aircraft was put together on the 11th, of which 129 were Lancasters, sixty-eight of them representing 5 Group. Six Lancasters were made ready by 49 Squadron at Fiskerton, and they took off between 17.23 and 17.47 only to lose the services of Sgt Townsend and crew to a rear turret malfunction. The others reached the target area to find ten-tenths cloud with tops at around 10,000 feet, and the least reliable marking method, H2S skymarking, in progress. On the credit side, at a smaller, more compact urban target, like Wilhelmshaven, it was easier to interpret the images on the cathode-ray screens, and on this night, great accuracy was achieved. The red and green flares were right over the aiming point as the Fiskerton crews delivered their cookies and incendiaries from 12,000 to 16,000 between 20.05 and 20.10, but it was impossible to assess what was happening beneath the cloud until an enormous explosion took place, the glow from which lingered for ten minutes. Many crews commented on this at debriefings across the Command, and there must have been much speculation about the source, which turned out to be the naval ammunition depot at Mariensiel, situated to the south of the town. It blew itself into oblivion, devastating 120 acres and causing widespread damage in the dockyard and town.

It was back to Lorient for ten 49 Squadron crews on the 13th, who learned at briefing that they were to be part of the largest force yet sent to the port of 466 aircraft, 103 of them 5 Group Lancasters. The Fiskerton brigade took off between 18.49 and 19.10 as part of the second wave with S/L Couch and F/L Allsebrook the senior pilots on duty and there were no early returns to deplete the squadron's impact. As they began the Channel crossing in the Exmouth area, some crews reported observing flares going down over the target as the first wave attacked. It had been planned to station a number of Path Finder aircraft over the Ile-de-Groix, an island situated some five miles off the mouth of the estuary leading to the port and illuminate it continuously as a navigation point. The other Path Finder crews followed up over Lorient itself with flares, green TIs and 1,000 pounders in a number of passes from 11,000 to 14,000 feet between 20.35 and 20.56, paving the way for the main force element to carry out their attacks. The target was located with ease in excellent visibility under clear skies, which allowed them to make a visual identification of both aiming points, the U-Boot pens on the Keroman peninsula and the town, before smoke began to drift across the area. The 49 Squadron crews bombed from 11,000 to 14,500 feet between 21.05 and 21.19 and all but one returned safely to report massive fires right across the town and the port area. Tragically, ED450 had collided with barrage balloons on the Devon coast on return and crashed into the Channel off Plymouth with no survivors from the crew of F/Sgt Miller.

Orders came through from 5 Group on the 14th to make ready for a return to Italy that night for a crack this time at Milan. A force of 142 Lancasters of 1, 5 and 8 Groups was assembled to carry out the attack, while 243 Halifaxes, Stirlings and Wellingtons were made ready to try their hand at Cologne. Among the eighty-nine 5 Group Lancasters were eight representing 49 Squadron, which took off from Fiskerton between 18.27 and 18.45 with S/L Couch and F/L Allsebrook the senior pilots on duty. F/O Eyre and crew abandoned their sortie after the rear turret became unserviceable, leaving the others to continue on across France and reach the target area after a trouble-free outward flight. They were guided to the aiming point by green and red Path Finder route-marker flares and were able to identify the aiming point visually before carrying out their bombing-runs from 8,500 to 15,000 feet between 22.37 and 22.52. Most loads were observed to hit the city, and many fires were reported, the glow from which remained visible for at least a hundred miles into the return journey. The operation was hailed as a success, although no local report was forthcoming to confirm or deny.

The final raid of the series on Lorient was posted on the 16th, for which another large force was made ready, this time of 377 aircraft. Of seventy-five Lancasters offered by 5 Group, seven were made ready by 49 Squadron at Fiskerton and took off between 18.44 and 19.04 with F/L Allsebrook the senior pilot on duty. They were among the earlier arrivals at the target and found clear conditions aided by an almost full moon, which enabled them to deliver their cookies and SBCs of incendiaries on red TIs onto the Keroman peninsula from 11,000 to 15,000 feet between 20.51 and 20.56. The majority of the force dropped incendiaries into the town, which, after nine attacks, 1,926 sorties and four thousand tons of bombs, was now a desolate and deserted ruin.

Preparations were put in hand on the 18th to make ready 195 aircraft for the second of four raids on Wilhelmshaven during the month. 5 Group contributed seventy-nine Lancasters, including eight belonging to 49 Squadron, which departed Fiskerton between 18.08 and 18.30 with S/L Cracknell the senior pilot on duty. All reached the target area, which was identified visually in excellent conditions, and red TIs were in the bomb sights as the 49 Squadron bomb bays were emptied from 15,000 to 22,000 feet between 20.31 and 20.37. Bombs were observed to burst and fires to spring up and returning crews were confident that an accurate and concentrated attack had taken place. However, bombing photos revealed that the operation had been a failure, after the main weight of bombs had fallen into open country to the west of the town, and this demonstrated how easy it was to be misled by what the eye saw. Local reports admitted to a number of bombs hitting the town, causing no serious damage or casualties.

Twenty-four hours later a force of 338 aircraft set off to return to Wilhelmshaven, with Wellingtons and Halifaxes accounting for 230 of the number and Stirlings and Lancasters the rest. 5 Group dispatched thirty-three Lancasters, with only those of S/L Couch, F/O Fawke and Sgt Duncan representing 49 Squadron. They departed Fiskerton between 17.57 and 18.01 and once again found the conditions to be excellent with visibility that enabled crews to identify the coastline and line themselves up on the target, which was marked by green TIs. Bombing took place from 11,000 and 13,600 feet at 20.06 and 20.07, and the bursts and fires observed in the docks area and the town left the crews with the impression that another successful raid had taken place. However, bombing photos told a different story, and revealed that the Path Finder marking had fallen to the north of the built-up area, partly through reliance upon outdated maps, which would now be replaced. Of the twelve missing aircraft, five were Stirlings and represented 8.9% of those dispatched, thus confirming the type's vulnerability compared with the Lancaster and Halifax. The four missing Lancasters represented a 7.7% loss rate, while no Halifaxes failed to return, but this would prove to be a blip. During the course of the year, the food chain would become established with Lancasters firmly at the top, Halifaxes in the middle and Stirlings at the bottom, when all types operated together.

On the 21st, an all-Lancaster main force from 1 and 5 Groups was made ready to attack the U-Boot construction yards at Vegesack, situated on the East Bank of the Weser to the north-west of Bremen. Path Finder Lancasters, Halifaxes and Stirlings were to provide the marking in an overall force of 143 aircraft of which, seventy-four of the Lancasters were put up by 5 Group. Seven of these departed Fiskerton between 18.20 and 18.46 to represent 49 Squadron with S/Ls Couch and Cracknell the senior pilots on duty. Sgt Townsend and crew were defeated by W/T failure early on and turned back, but their colleagues all reached the target area after attempting to follow scattered route-marker flares. They were greeted by ten-tenths cloud at 3,000 feet, above which, red and green skymarker flares drifted down, also in a somewhat scattered manner and up to nine minutes late to join the dimly visible TIs burning on the ground. The 49 Squadron crews carried out their attacks from 15,000 to 18,000 feet between 20.50 and 20.56, and a considerable glow from beneath the clouds suggested a successful outcome. Bombing photos depicted only cloud, and no local report was available to provide details of damage.

115 aircraft of 6 and 8 Groups concluded the current series of raids on Wilhelmshaven on the night of the 24/25th with indeterminate results, and the port would now be left in peace until October 1944. A major operation against Nuremberg was posted on stations across the Command on the 25th, and 5 Group responded with a maximum effort of 101 Lancasters, eight of them made ready by 49 Squadron at Fiskerton. They took off between 19.22 and 19.47 with S/L Cracknell the senior pilot on duty and the other crews captained by a sergeant pilot. Each Lancaster was carrying a cookie and SBCs of 4lb and 30lb incendiaries, and after Sgt Stables and crew had turned back with engine trouble, the rest of it made it to the target area, where cloudless skies and good visibility prevailed. They had to wait for the Path Finder element to turn up some sixteen to twenty minutes after the raid was due to begin and drop marker flares on the approach, from which the 5 Group crews carried out a time-and-distance run to the aiming point marked by red and green TIs. The 49 Squadron element bombed from 8,400 to 15,000 feet between 23.20 and 23.30, and all of the indications, including what looked like an oil-depot exploding, suggested a concentrated attack, which fell predominantly in northern and western districts. This was confirmed by local reports, which mentioned damage to three hundred buildings but also revealed that bombs had fallen onto other communities and open country up to seven miles to the north.

When Cologne was posted as the target on the 26th, 5 Group responded with ninety Lancasters, nine of which were made ready by 49 Squadron at Fiskerton as part of an overall force of 427 aircraft. They took off between 18.59 and 19.29 with S/L Couch and F/L Allsebrook the senior pilots on duty and all reached the Cologne area on a night of almost perfect serviceability for the group and good vertical visibility for the bomb-aimers, some of whom were able to identify the bridges over the Rhine. It seems from some comments from other squadrons that a proportion of the force bombed before the Path Finders had a chance to mark, but once the red and green TIs appeared on the ground, the 49 Squadron crews aimed their cookies and incendiaries at them from 16,000 to 18,000 feet between 21.15 and 21.27. Fires were reported in the city centre, as were decoys to the west of the city, and bombing photos showed fire tracks and smoke that suggested an effective raid. In fact, a large proportion of the effort had fallen to the south-west of the city, and perhaps only a quarter had landed in the built-up area, causing much damage to housing, minor industry and public buildings.

On the following night, 5 Group detailed thirteen Lancasters for mining duties in one of the Nectarine gardens off the Frisians and it provided the opportunity for Sgt Tickler to operate as crew captain for the first time. They departed Fiskerton at 18.59 and arrived in the target area in poor visibility, and after alerting a flak ship to their presence, an exchange of fire took place that resulted in a little damage to the rear turret. Undaunted, they continued on and ran into searchlights and light flak, which hit the cockpit, port wing and rear turret. The pilot sustained wounds to his shoulder and side and momentarily lost control but recovered the situation with assistance from the navigator. The flight engineer was found to have received a severe head wound, which would prove fatal, and he was tended by the wireless operator as the sortie continued and the mines were delivered into the briefed location. The bomb-aimer helped to fly the Lancaster while Sgt Tickler received first aid and having reached the northern coast of Lincolnshire near North Coates, they landed at Donna Nook, only to swing off the grass track and collide with a military vehicle that had come to their aid. ED434 was repaired and returned to duty, while Sgt Tickler was awarded a CGM, three crew members a DFM and two were Mentioned in Despatches. Sgt Tickler would return to operations with a new crew and serve with 57 Squadron until failing to return from the infamous Nuremberg raid at the end of March 1944, although, happily, he would survive with two members of his crew and end the war as a PoW.

Having dealt with Lorient under the January Directive, attention now turned upon St-Nazaire, situated further south along the Biscay coast. The force of 437 aircraft assembled on the 28th included a contribution from 5 Group of eighty-nine Lancasters, of which eight represented 49 Squadron. They departed Fiskerton between 18.24 and 18.41 with W/C Slee and F/L Allsebrook the senior pilots on duty, and all reached the target area to find clear skies and good visibility with only a little ground haze to contend with. They bombed on red TIs from 13,000 to 16,000 feet between 21.11 and 21.25, and it was clear from the many explosions and at least forty fires burning in the docks that the port was undergoing an ordeal of destruction. ED467 failed to return with the crew of Sgt Duncan RCAF, after crashing into the sea in the target area with no survivors. The remains were eventually recovered for local burial. Post-raid reconnaissance revealed that the marking had been concentrated and the bombing accurate, and local reports confirmed that 60% of the town had been destroyed. This concluded the month's activity, during which, the squadron had taken part in fifteen operations and had dispatched ninety-four sorties for the loss of three Lancasters and crews.

# March 1943

March would bring with it the opening rounds of the Ruhr campaign, the first for which the Command was adequately equipped and genuinely prepared, with a predominantly four-engine bomber force at its disposal to carry an increasing weight of bombs and Oboe to provide accuracy. First, however, the crews would have to negotiate operations to Germany's capital and second cities, and it was the "Big City" itself, Berlin, that opened the month's account on the 1st. The crews learned at briefing that six Path Finder Halifaxes and ten Stirlings equipped with H2S were to drop a "landmark" yellow TI each at Butzow, situated some eighty miles north of Berlin, which were to be backed up by seven Halifaxes and sixteen Lancasters. The "special" (H2S-equipped) aircraft were then to release red warning flares twelve miles short of the target followed by red TIs on the aiming-point at the time-on-target of 22.00, which the seven Halifaxes and sixteen Lancasters would back-up with green TIs. As always, the plan was based on a forecast of favourable conditions, in the absence of which, skymarkers would substitute for TIs. A force of 302 aircraft was assembled, made up of 156 Lancasters, eighty-six Halifaxes and sixty Stirlings, 5 Group putting up a maximum effort of ninety-eight Lancasters, of which nine represented 49 Squadron. They departed Fiskerton between 18.47 and 19.03 with W/C Slee and S/L Cracknell the senior pilots on duty and lost the services of F/O Eyre and crew after they were coned by searchlights and bombarded with flak at Kiel and had to jettison their bombs in order to escape. They were one of eleven early returns by 5 Group aircraft, while those reaching the target found it to be under clear skies with only haze to impair the vertical visibility. However, reliant upon H2S, the Path Finder navigators experienced great difficulty in establishing their positions based on the images on their cathode-ray tubes over such a massive urban sprawl, and this led to scattered marking. As a result, the main weight of the attack fell into south-western districts, where the 49 Squadron crews bombed on red and green TIs from 17,000 to 21,000 feet between 22.07 and 22.18. Seventeen aircraft failed to return, and some crews among those that made it back reported the glow of fires to be visible from two hundred miles into the return flight. A post-raid analysis based on bombing photos revealed the attack to have been spread over an area of a hundred square miles, but because of the increasing bomb tonnage now being carried, more damage was inflicted on the city than on any previous raid. 875 buildings, mostly houses, were destroyed and twenty factories seriously damaged, along with railway workshops in the Tempelhof district. It is interesting to analyse the percentage loss rate of each type on this night, as it would be an accurate indicator of their future fortunes. The statistics revealed the loss rate of Lancasters to be 4.5%, and those of the Halifaxes and Stirlings to be 7%.

A force of 417 aircraft was assembled to send against Hamburg on the 3rd, and eighty-nine of 149 Lancasters were provided by 5 Group, eight of them by 49 Squadron at Fiskerton, where each had a cookie and twelve SBCs of incendiaries winched into its cavernous thirty-three-foot-long bomb bay. They took off between 19.05 and 19.23 with S/L Cracknell and F/L Allsebrook the senior pilots on duty and all negotiated the North Sea crossing to find the target basking under clear skies and in good visibility. Sgt Price and crew were attacked by night-fighters as they bore down on the target at 20,000 feet at 21.50 and sustained damage including the loss of their starboard-inner engine. They were forced to jettison their bombs fused in order to maintain height, but still lost three thousand feet and had to contend with severe vibration during the return flight. Meanwhile, some Path Finder and main force crews had identified the primary target's Hamburg-America landing stage, the Blohm & Voss shipyards, the Binnen-Alster Lake and the main railway station and had carried out their attacks from 18,000 to 21,000 feet between 21.33 and 21.45, aided by the H2S-laid Path Finder TIs. On return, crews reported numerous fires in the docks area along with black smoke rising to meet them as they turned away. What was not appreciated, was the fact that a proportion of the markers had fallen onto the town of Wedel, situated some thirteen miles downstream of the Elbe, and had attracted perhaps the bulk of the bombs, while those hitting the primary target had caused a hundred fires that needed to be dealt with before the fire services could go to the aid of their neighbour. Ten aircraft failed to return, but there were no empty dispersal pans at Fiskerton.

On the following night, 5 Group sent six Lancasters to mine the waters of Danzig Bay and two others for similar duties in the Kattegat. The night off for most of the Command provided the opportunity for maximum serviceability as the decks were now cleared for the opening of the Ruhr offensive, which over the ensuing months, would change the face of bombing and provide for the enemy an indication of the burgeoning power of the Command. This was a culmination of all that had gone before during three and a half years of Bomber Command operations, the backs-to-the-wall desperation of 1940, the tentative almost token offensives of 1941, the treading water and gradual metamorphosis under Harris in 1942, when failures still far outnumbered successes. It had all been leading to this night, from which point would begin the calculated and systematic dismantling of Germany's industrial and population centres. The only shining light during these dark years had been the quality and spirit of the aircrew, and this had never faltered. It would begin on the 5th at Essen, Harris's nemesis thus far and the home of the giant armaments-producing Krupp complex occupying the Borbeck districts, and for the first time since the war began, the Command would have at its disposal a device which would negate the industrial haze protecting this city and its neighbours. The magnificent pioneering work on Oboe by W/C Hal Bufton and his crews at 109 Squadron was about to bear fruit in spectacular fashion, and the towns and cities of Germany's arsenal would suffer destruction on an unprecedented scale.

A force of 442 aircraft included ninety-seven Lancasters representing 5 Group, 49 Squadron contributing eight Lancasters on this momentous occasion containing the crews of F/L Allsebrook in ED597, F/O Eyre in ED445, F/Sgt Gilmore in ED584, Sgt Gumbley in ED416, Sgt McDonald in ED438, Sgt Penry in ED487, Sgt Thom in ED431 and Sgt Townsend in ED432. The main force element was to bomb in three waves, Halifaxes first, followed by Wellingtons and Stirlings with Lancasters bringing up the rear. Six Path Finder Halifax and fifteen Lancaster crews had been briefed to drop a warning yellow TI each when fifteen miles from the target, before backing up the Mosquitos' red TIs on the aiming-point with greens, and the force was to adopt the southern route to the central Ruhr, making landfall over the Scheldt estuary. The Fiskerton contingent took off between 19.13 and 19.31 and was not involved in the unusually high number of early returns, including a modest seven from 5 Group, which, together with those bombing alternative targets, would reduce the size of the force reaching Essen and bombing as briefed to 362 aircraft. 5 Group favoured a time-and-distance approach to the aiming point, and the 49 Squadron crews employed the Path Finders' yellow route markers as the initial reference point, before exploiting the good visibility to bomb through the industrial haze onto red and green TIs from 18,000 to 21,000 feet between 21.20 and 21.27. The overwhelming impression was of a concentrated attack, which left many fires burning and a glow in the sky reported by some to be visible from the North Sea homebound. At debriefing, crews across the Command reported terrific explosions among fires, which lit up the sky and a pall of smoke hanging above the dull, red centre of the conflagration. The operation cost the Command an acceptable fourteen aircraft, among which was the squadron's ED431, which disappeared without trace with the crew of Sgt Thom. Post-raid reconnaissance revealed 160 acres of devastation and damage to fifty-three buildings within the Krupp district, and the success of the operation was confirmed by local reports of 3,018 houses destroyed and more than two thousand others seriously damaged. It was a most encouraging start to what would become a five-month-long offensive.

It would be a further week before round two of the Ruhr offensive was mounted, and in the meantime, Harris turned his attention upon southern Germany, beginning with Nuremberg on the 8th. A force of 338 aircraft included 105 Lancasters of 5 Group, the crews of which learned at briefing that zero hour was to be 23.15 and that three Path Finder Stirlings and two Halifaxes were to drop illumination flares across the target in two sticks by H2S, to be followed by six Stirlings and three Halifaxes dropping green TIs on the aiming-point, also by H2S, and employing additional flares if necessary. The remaining Path Finder markers were to back up with green TIs, unless cloud negated the illuminator flares, in which case, red TIs were to be dropped by the H2S-equipped aircraft and backed up by the others with greens. All Path Finder aircraft were to deliver yellow route markers on the way in and out. The eight-strong 49 Squadron element departed Fiskerton between 19.47 and 20.01 with F/Ls Allsebrook and Green the senior pilots on duty, each carrying a cookie and assorted incendiaries. Sgt Penry and crew were unable to fix their position over the North Sea and lost so much time in trying that they ran out of time and abandoned their sortie. The others reached the target area by following yellow route markers and encountered clear skies with ground haze and extreme darkness. This seemed to impede the Path Finders' ability to locate the city centre blind by H2S, and the main force crews experienced the same difficulty in identifying ground detail, allowing themselves to be guided to the aiming point by a few red and green TIs, which appeared to lack concentration and soon burned out. The 49 Squadron crews had predominantly red TIs in the bombsights but also a few scattered greens and carried out their attacks from 16,000 to 19,000 feet between 23.27 and 23.44. The initial impression was of a scattered raid, but a greater concentration of fires developed and the glow from these was reported by some to be visible for two hundred miles into the return journey. At debriefing, 83 Squadron's S/L Cooke, formerly of 49 Squadron, reported that a cookie and yellow TIs had been jettisoned east of Heilbronn, some forty miles short of the target and accurately backed-up by other Path Finders. Inevitably, this would have drawn off other bomb loads and local sources confirmed the marking and bombing of Nuremberg to have been spread along a ten-mile stretch, half of it falling short of the city boundaries, while the rest destroyed six hundred buildings and damaged fourteen hundred others, including a number of important war-industry factories.

On the following day, preparations were put in hand to return to southern Germany to attack the city of Munich, situated deep in the Bavarian mountains of south-eastern Germany, a round-trip of more than 1,200 miles. A force of 264 aircraft included a 5 Group contribution of eighty-one Lancasters, eight of them made ready at Fiskerton and loaded with a cookie each and SBCs of incendiaries, while their crews learned at briefing the details of the plan of attack. White TIs were to be dropped by the Path Finders as route markers to aid the main force crews, and white and green flares over the northern tip of the Ammersee, a large lake situated some twenty miles to the west-south-west of the city centre, which the 5 Group crews, in particular, would use as the starting point for their time-and-distance runs. Nine Stirlings and four Halifaxes were to ground mark by H2S with red TIs at the same time as releasing white flares, and four Lancasters were to drop flares also, if required, and then join with eleven Lancasters and four Halifaxes to back up with green TIs. The 49 Squadron element took off between 20.42 and 21.14 with F/Ls Allsebrook and Green the senior pilots on duty and lost the services of F/O Eyre and F/L Green to engine and intercom failures respectively. The others reached the target area, where clear skies and good visibility prevailed, and the Path Finder green and white TIs could be seen to have fallen within the built-up area. An enormous orange explosion occurred in a south-western district as crews were carrying out their timed runs to the aiming point from the Ammersee, and those from 49 Squadron had the

TIs in the bomb sights as they released their loads from 14,000 to 16,000 feet between 00.19 and 00.41. Another huge explosion at 00.25 lit up the sky for twenty seconds and illuminated an area of ground with a ten-mile radius, described by some as the largest they had experienced, and another particularly large one occurred at 00.43. Fires were taking hold and sending a large pall of smoke rising above the city as the bomber force withdrew to the west, and one 5 Group crew counted eighteen blazes in or close to the city centre. A relatively modest eight aircraft failed to return, and only two of these were from 5 Group. A post-raid analysis concluded that a strong wind had pushed the attack into the western half of the city, where 291 buildings had been destroyed and 660 severely damaged. The aero-engine assembly shop at the B.M.W factory was put out of action for six weeks, and many other industrial concerns also lost vital production.

The trio of operations to destinations in southern Germany concluded with the highly industrial city of Stuttgart, for which a force of 314 aircraft was assembled on the 11th, 5 Group contributing ninety-six of 152 Lancasters, ten of them belonging to 49 Squadron. Briefings revealed that the Path Finders were to deliver flares and red TIs by H2S across the aiming point, and that these were to be backed up visually with green TIs. At Fiskerton, take-off was accomplished safely between 19.59 and 20.10 with F/Ls Allsebrook and Green the senior pilots on duty and it was to be a night of good serviceability for the squadron. They crossed the English coast over Eastbourne, heading for the French coast near Dieppe, before pushing on across France to enter Germany in the Strasbourg area with Stuttgart fifty miles straight ahead. The main force element arrived late because of inaccurately forecast winds and found excellent visibility but the Path Finder TIs already burning out on the ground. This left the way clear for dummy TIs to lure the bombing away from the city centre, and in this endeavour, they were largely successful, although to the bomb-aimers high above, the green TIs appeared to be legitimate and were bombed by the 49 Squadron crews from 13,200 to 16,000 feet between 23.11 and 23.50. Most of the effort was wasted in open country but the south-western suburbs of Vaihingen and Kaltental were hit and 118 buildings, mostly houses, were destroyed. It was a disappointing outcome, which cost eleven aircraft, only one of which was from 5 Group.

Round two of the Ruhr campaign was posted on the 12th, when 457 crews learned at briefing that Essen was once more to be their destination with a time-on-target for the Path Finders of 21.15. They were to adopt the northern route to the Ruhr, and sixteen Path Finders were to ground mark the town of Dorsten with white TIs as a track guide before backing up the Mosquito-borne Oboe red TIs with greens to provide the main force crews with a solid aiming point. 5 Group detailed ninety-five Lancasters, of which ten were made ready by 49 Squadron and took off from Fiskerton between 19.42 and 19.53 with S/L Green the senior pilot on duty. Undertaking his first sortie as crew captain was Sgt Cyril Anderson, a Yorkshireman who had flown his first two sorties as second pilot to Barney Gumbley at the end of February. They all reached the target, where fierce fires were already burning beneath clear skies, the smoke from which combined with industrial haze to blot out ground detail. Oboe rendered this of little consequence as the red and green Path Finder TIs identified the aiming point for the 49 Squadron crews to attack from 14,000 to 19,000 feet between 21.33 and 21.47. It was clear that the bombing was accurate and mostly concentrated around the Oboe-laid TIs, and this time, the Krupp complex found itself in the centre of the area of destruction. The defences fought back to claim twenty-three bombers, in return for which, according to post-raid reconnaissance, another highly successful assault on this centre of war production had been achieved. In fact, substantially fewer buildings had been destroyed, but a greater concentration of bombs had inflicted 30% more damage on Krupp than the raid of a week earlier.

Following the commitment of seventeen Lancasters to mine the waters in the Baltic on the 13th, 5 Group stood down for a week during a spell of adverse weather and it was the 22nd before orders came through to prepare for the next assault on St-Nazaire. A force of 357 aircraft was assembled, including a contribution from 5 Group of 120 Lancasters, of which fourteen were provided by 49 Squadron. They departed Fiskerton between 19.18 and 19.33 with W/C Slee and S/L Cracknell the senior pilots on duty and Bill Townsend flying his final sortie with the squadron, while Cyril Anderson was undertaking his last until returning to the squadron in June. They flew out over Portland Bill, and all reached the target area, where F/L Green and crew were two miles shy of the aiming point at 10,000 feet when struck by a rocket-propelled projectile, which severed the rudder controls and knocked out the pilot's and bomb-aimer's intercom. The SBCs of 30lb incendiaries were jettisoned and a tense return flight begun. The others attacked from 5,000 to 11,500 feet between 21.55 and 22.33 from under clear skies and moonlight that had enabled the target to be identified visually and by the abundance of red and green TIs. Despite the recall of the 3 Group Stirlings, to which fifty-five crews responded, the main force bombed with accuracy and concentration, leaving the town and port areas in flames and massively damaged.

Squadron X, soon to be given the number 617 Squadron, was formed at Scampton under W/C Guy Gibson on the 21st, and the first crews arrived on posting on the 24th. Among them was that of Sgt Cyril Anderson, a remarkable fact since he had only four sorties under his belt, two as "second dickey" and two as crew captain, and this shatters the myth that only experienced crews were invited to join what would become a special squadron. One is left with a feeling that W/C Slee, for whatever reason, saw an opportunity to get rid of a crew that he didn't want, when there were plenty of others vastly more experienced and better qualified than the Anderson crew. They were joined on the 25th by Sgt Bill Townsend and crew, who were, at least, deep into their first tour and had demonstrated their effectiveness.

Duisburg was selected as the host for the third operation of the Ruhr offensive, for which a force of 455 aircraft was assembled, ninety-four of them Lancasters provided by 5 Group. Crews learned at briefing that the Oboe Mosquitos were to drop warning flares five and two-and-a-half minutes before the aiming-point, and then employ the "Musical Wanganui" marking method, the code for Oboe skymarking, releasing red flares with green stars at regular intervals thereafter. 49 Squadron contributed ten Lancasters, which departed Fiskerton between 19.08 and 19.17 with F/Ls Allsebrook and Green the senior pilots on duty but lost the services of Sgts Price and Stables and their crews to port-outer engine failure and Sgt Miller and crew to an unserviceable artificial horizon. The others pressed on to the target area, where they found ten-tenths cloud with tops at 10,000 feet and good visibility above. They were greeted by the Oboe release-point parachute flares, which were in the bomb sights as they dropped their cookies and incendiaries from 18,000 to 21,000 feet between 21.37 and 22.11, and a large explosion was witnessed at 21.53. What the crews couldn't know, was that five of the Oboe Mosquitos had returned early with equipment failure and a sixth had been shot down, leaving just three to deliver what could only be sparse marking. This was insufficient and led to a scattered and ineffective attack, which, according to local reports, caused only minor damage. Fortunately, the failure cost a modest six aircraft, none of them belonging to 5 Group.

Orders were received on stations across the Command on the 27th to prepare for a trip to the "Big City" that night, and a force of 396 aircraft was duly assembled. At briefings, the Path Finder crews were told of their part in the plan, which required eleven Stirlings and eight Halifaxes to drop green route marker flares and yellow warning flares by H2S, before marking the aiming-point with red TIs for two Stirlings, five Halifaxes and twenty-one Lancasters to back up with green TIs. In the event of cloud blotting out the ground, skymarking would be employed. 5 Group contributed 111 Lancasters, nine of them made ready by 49 Squadron, which departed Fiskerton between 20.25 and 20.49 with W/C Slee and F/Ls Allsebrook and Green the senior pilots on duty, the commanding officer demonstrating good leadership at what was among the most demanding targets. The route took them into enemy territory between the Frisian Islands of Texel and Vlieland and then on a course a little north of Hannover to a point to the south-west of the capital for the run-in to the intended city-centre aiming-point. The Path Finders were reliant upon H2S and established two areas of marking, both well short, and the main force crews had little choice but to aim for them. There was the usual discrepancy in the reported cloud state of zero to nine-tenths as the Fiskerton crews tracked in across yellow TIs and carried out their attacks from 18,000 to 22,500 feet between 23.12 and 23.22. From bombing altitude, the attack appeared to be effective but local reports confirmed that the main weight of bombs had fallen between seven and seventeen miles short of the target, and 25% of those hitting the city had failed to detonate.

There would be a chance to rectify the failure two nights hence, but in the meantime, St-Nazaire would face its third heavy assault under the January Directive, for which a force of 323 aircraft was made ready on the 28th. 5 Group detailed twenty-one freshman crews, while 49 Squadron remained on the ground, and those reaching the target area encountered good visibility and red and green Oboe-laid TIs marking out the aiming point. Returning crews reported concentrated fires, and post-raid reconnaissance confirmed the accuracy and effectiveness of the raid.

The month's final operation was posted on the 29th, when the red tape on the briefing-room wall maps ended again at Berlin. A force of 329 aircraft was made ready, of which 106 Lancasters were provided by 5 Group, a dozen of them representing 49 Squadron, while 149 Wellingtons were prepared for an attack on Bochum in the central Ruhr. The plan for the main event required all Path Finder aircraft to drop yellow route markers at predetermined points, and the marker crews to illuminate the Müggelsee to the south-east of Berlin with sticks of white flares and bundles of green flares with red stars by H2S, before they and the backers-up carried out a DR run to the aiming-point to deliver red TIs. The 49 Squadron contingent departed Fiskerton between 21.28 and 22.12 with F/Ls Allsebrook and Green the senior pilots on duty and crossed the English coast over Mablethorpe on course for Mandø Island off Jutland's western coast. They met bad weather in the form of heavy ice-bearing cloud and static electricity extending from the North Sea to the Baltic, which forced many crews to turn for home, among them eighteen belonging to 5 Group and a massive twenty-four from 4 Group. Sgt Gumbley and crew were back home within ninety minutes as a result of a.s.i. failure, and Sgt Miller and crew landed an hour later after temporarily losing flying controls and engine power due to icing. The latter dumped their cookie but retained the twelve SBCs of 30lb incendiaries for future use. This was not the final "boomerang" on what was a bad night for the squadron, and twenty-five minutes later, Sgt Price and crew touched down with an indisposed navigator on board.

The others continued on across Jutland and traversed Kiel Bight and Mecklenburg Bay, before crossing the German coast between Wismar and Rostock on track for the "Big City", where good visibility enabled them to identify the Müggelsee to the south-east of the city as a reference point from which to run in on the aiming-point. The Path Finders were again short with their marking, and the main force arrived late after some of the markers had already burned themselves out. The Fiskerton crews bombed from 19,000 to 21,000 feet between 01.04 and 01.14 in the face of a heavy searchlight and flak defence and set off home in the belief that the fires they had left behind, the glow from which was still visible from 150 miles away, indicated that an effective attack had been delivered. ED469 was homebound north of Hannover when shot down by a night-fighter to crash four miles north-north-west of Neustadt am Rübenberge at 03.26. Only the rear gunner survived in enemy hands from the crew of F/O Mabee RCAF, who was operating as crew captain for the first time. It is believed that Sgt Jones was severely injured and possibly repatriated in 1944. ED435 was hit by flak over the target and control temporarily lost, and during those tension-filled few minutes, three members of the crew were ordered to take to their parachutes to fall into enemy hands. Sgt Fyffe, another flying as crew captain for the first time, regained control and the Lancaster was flying westwards across north-central Holland when intercepted by the night-fighter of Hptm Herbert Lütje of III./NJG1 and shot down to crash at 04.27 six miles south-east of Raalte without survivors. An analysis of the operation revealed that most of the bombing had been wasted in open country to the south-east of the city, and an accurate figure for damage was not forthcoming.

During the course of the month, the squadron took part in eleven operations and dispatched 106 sorties for the loss of three Lancasters and their crews.

## April 1943

April would be the least rewarding month during the Ruhr offensive, principally, because of the number of operations directed at targets in regions of Germany beyond the range of Oboe. On the 2nd, orders were received to prepare for the final raids on St-Nazaire and Lorient that night, which would bring down the curtain on the January directive. Forces of fifty-five and forty-seven aircraft were made ready with eight 5 Group Lancasters included in the former and the operations took place in favourable conditions in the face of heavy and accurate flak. No reports came out of the towns, which had long since been abandoned by the civilian populations.

The next round of the Ruhr campaign was announced across the Command on the 3rd, when Essen was posted as the target for the third time and a force of 348 aircraft made ready. The heavy brigade consisted of 225 Lancasters and 113 Halifaxes, 123 of the former representing 5 Group, and this would be the first occasion on which more than two hundred Lancasters had operated against a single target. The Path Finder contribution amounted to ten Oboe Mosquitos and twenty Lancasters from 83 and 156 Squadrons, the crews of which were to identify the Krupp complex as the aiming-point, and in the event of cloud, sky mark it with coloured flares, or if clear skies prevailed, ground mark with red TIs. The ten-strong 49 Squadron element departed Fiskerton between 19.37 and 20.04 and joined the bomber stream over the North Sea on their way to make landfall on the Dutch coast near Haarlem and uncomfortably close to the Amsterdam defences. Almost clear skies prevailed over the Ruhr region as Sgt Penry and crew approached from the north, contending with a loss of power from the starboard-inner engine, which prevented them from maintaining height. They dropped their bombs on the town of Haltern on the Ruhr's northern rim from 12,500 feet at 22.25 and reported the glow from Essen to be visible from a hundred miles into the return flight. The others arrived in the target area, where the anticipated industrial haze was negated by the accuracy of the Oboe markers falling around the aiming-point. The attack began slowly, some crews apparently confused by the employment of both sky and ground markers on a clear night, but it built to a crescendo, during which a massive explosion was observed by many crews in the centre of the bombing. The 49 Squadron crews attacked from 18,000 to 20,500 feet between 22.00 and 22.17, aiming mostly at the TIs burning on the ground and many explosions were witnessed, with fires emitting large volumes of smoke. Returning crews echoed the remarks of the Penry crew that the glow from the burning city was still visible from the Dutch coast homebound and the consensus was of a successful raid. This was confirmed by bombing photographs and local reports, which spoke of widespread destruction in central and western districts, where 635 buildings had been reduced to rubble and many more seriously damaged. The searchlight and flak defence had been intense, and it became an expensive night for the Command, which registered the loss of a dozen Halifaxes and nine Lancasters. This represented 6% of those dispatched, but it was the respective loss rates of the types that was most telling, with the Halifaxes suffering 10.62% compared with 4% for the Lancasters.

The largest non-1,000 force to date of 577 aircraft was made ready on the 4th for an attack that night on the naval and shipbuilding port of Kiel, for which 5 Group detailed 112 Lancasters. Nine of these belonged to 49 Squadron, whose crews learned at briefing that the plan of attack called for a time-on-target of 23.00 and for yellow TIs to be dropped by the Path Finders as route markers, before the H2S marker crews in ten Stirlings and six Halifaxes illuminated the aiming-point with flares and marked it with red TIs. Two Stirlings, five Halifaxes and fifteen Lancasters were then to back up with green TIs, leaving two of each type to bomb with the main force. The Fiskerton contingent took off between 20.58 and 21.08 and all reached the target area, where they were guided towards the aiming point by yellow route marker flares, released by the Path Finder heavy brigade either side of 23.00. Kiel was found to be concealed beneath ten-tenths cloud with good visibility above, and the cookies and incendiaries were released by the 49 Squadron participants from estimated positions onto the glow of fires below the cloud from 11,000 to 19,000 feet between 23.24 and 23.38. It was not possible to assess the outcome, and as bombing photos revealed only cloud, it was left to a post-raid analysis to conclude that decoy fires had been operating and had probably lured away a proportion of the effort, while the strong wind caused the markers to drift, leading the remainder astray and resulting in most of the bombs missing the target altogether. According to local reports, only eleven houses were destroyed, and this was a major disappointment in view of the size of the force involved.

On the 5th, W/C Johnson was posted in from 1660 Conversion Unit to succeed W/C Slee DSO DFC, whose tenure as commanding officer had come to an end. After undertaking twenty-six operations with the squadron, Slee was posted to 5 Group HQ while his future was considered and was installed as station commander at Dunholme Lodge on the 17th of May in the rank of group captain. While in that post, he would lead Operation Bellicose in June, (described at the appropriate juncture in this narrative) before another posting in August took him to the Path Finder station at Bourn in Cambridgeshire, home at the time of 97 (Straits Settlement) Squadron. Later in the month, he would lead an element of 139 Squadron Mosquitos in a spoof raid on Berlin in support of Operation Hydra, the raid on the secret weapons and rocket research facility at Peenemünde.

W/C Slee was a hard act to follow, and W/C Johnson put himself on a fighter affiliation exercise on the 8th to hone his skills, before presiding over his first briefing that afternoon. The Ruhr offensive was to continue at Duisburg that night, for which a mixed force of 379 Lancasters, Wellingtons, Halifaxes and Stirlings was assembled as the heavy element, while ten Oboe Mosquitos would provide the initial marking, backed up by the Path Finder heavy brigade consisting of four Stirlings, twenty Lancasters and eight Halifaxes. 5 Group contributed eighty-four of the Lancasters, seven of them belonging to 49 Squadron, which departed Fiskerton between 21.10 and 21.20 with W/C Johnson flying as second pilot to Sgt Hogg and the standard Ruhr payload of a cookie and assorted 4lb and 30lb incendiaries in the bomb bays. They headed out over Sheringham on the Norfolk coast and had to climb through ten-tenths ice-bearing cloud over the North Sea before breaking into clear air at 12,000 feet. They made landfall at Egmond with a time-on-target set for 23.15, before which, the ten Oboe Mosquitos were to drop red warning flares and then greens with red stars and green TIs over the aiming-point. If the weather conditions permitted, one Stirling, seven Halifaxes and fourteen Lancasters would back up with red TIs, while the remaining 8 Group aircraft supported the main force. The bomber stream reached the western Ruhr to encounter ten-tenths cloud with tops in places as high as 20,500 feet, such conditions completely nullifying the Path Finders' attempts to mark either the route or the target, and the bombing had to be carried out on e.t.a., some crews embarking on a time-and-distance run from as far away as the Dutch coast as the last visual reference. The 49 Squadron crews attacked from 20,000 to 21,000 feet between 23.36 and 23.51 and had nothing of value to pass on to the intelligence section at debriefing. Absent from that process was the crew of F/O Southern DFM, who had all lost their lives when ED590 crashed in the target area at 23.45. They were one of three missing 5 Group crews in an overall loss of nineteen aircraft, in return for which, local sources confirmed a widely scattered raid that hit at least fifteen other Ruhr locations and destroyed just forty buildings in Duisburg.

Not content with the outcome, Harris ordered another raid twenty-four hours later, only this time, employing a much-reduced force of 104 Lancasters and five Mosquitos. 5 Group detailed seventy Lancasters, of which five represented 49 Squadron and departed Fiskerton between 20.40 and 20.47 with no senior pilots on duty and each Lancaster carrying a cookie and twelve SBCs of incendiaries. Sgt Penry and crew experienced starboard-out engine issues and had to turn back, while the others were guided to the target by red route-marker flares and then red and green skymarkers over the aiming point, which was hidden by ten-tenths cloud with tops at 5,000 to 15,000 feet. They delivered their bomb loads from 20,500 and 21,000 feet between 23.08 and 23.11, some observing a large red glow reflected in the clouds. Local reports confirmed that this was another highly scattered raid, which spread bombs over a wide area of the Ruhr and destroyed only fifty houses in Duisburg.

Frankfurt was posted as the destination on the 10th for 502 aircraft, of which the 144 Wellingtons would represent the most populous type, demonstrating that this trusty old warhorse still had an important part to play in Bomber Command operations. 5 Group provided sixty-six of 136 Lancasters, just four of them belonging to 49 Squadron, which departed Fiskerton between 00.17 and 00.24 with W/C Johnson leading the squadron into battle for the first time. The plan was standard for a target beyond the range of Oboe and required eleven Stirlings and six Halifaxes to drop yellow TIs as route markers by H2S, followed by preliminary warning flares, all of which were to be backed up by two Stirlings, ten Halifaxes and seventeen Lancasters. Cloud conditions permitting, the aiming-point was then to be marked by red TIs on H2S, and if not, by green flares with red stars and a white flare, with appropriate backing up with green TIs or coloured flares. They adopted the usual course to this region of Germany, following the line of the Franco/Belgian frontier to cross into Germany on an east-north-easterly heading north of Saarbrücken. The H2S marker crews arrived in the target area to be confronted by ten-tenths cloud with tops at between 8,000 and 12,000 feet but found that their red TIs were visible and opted not to sky mark. This was fine in the early stages, until it became impossible to distinguish the genuine TIs from decoys, incendiaries and searchlights, and the backer-up crews experienced great difficulty in establishing an aiming-point. The 49 Squadron crews went in at 14,000 to 16,000 feet between 02.58 and 03.05, having been guided by preliminary warning flares, and some bombed at whatever was glowing beneath the cloud or on e.t.a., without being able to assess the outcome. Bombing photos revealed nothing but cloud, and local sources confirmed that only a few bombs had fallen into the southern suburbs.

On the 11th, S/L Gilpin was posted in from 61 Squadron and S/L Couch left Fiskerton for 1654 Conversion Unit at the end of his tour. On the 13th, 208 Lancaster crews were notified of a change of scenery for their next operation, which was to be against the docks at La Spezia on Italy's northern coast some forty miles south-east of Genoa. 5 Group detailed 124 of the Lancasters, with the remainder provided by 1 and 8 Groups, the latter also sending three Halifaxes as part of the marker force. 49 Squadron loaded nine of its aircraft with 1,000 pounders and SBCs of incendiaries and two others with mines to plant in the Mullet garden on the approaches to the port. The latter departed Fiskerton first at 20.32 with the crews of Sgts Price and Gumbley on board, and they were followed into the air between 20.35 and 20.48 by the main element with W/C Johnson the senior pilot on duty. F/O Bone and crew were over northern France when the starboard-inner engine burst into flames, and they were forced to jettison their load and return home. Sgt Morrison and crew were on course as they traversed France but lost their way as they tried to pinpoint on the Italian coast. The navigator became confused, until it was discovered that the DR compass was unreliable, by which time they were lost. The bombs were jettisoned, and the navigator performed outstandingly to work out a course and bring the crew home on dead reckoning. Meanwhile, the others arrived on the Italian side of the Alps to find almost cloudless skies and only haze and smoke to mar the vertical visibility. They established their positions by visual reference of ground detail, such as rivers and the docks, confirmed by Path Finder flares and bombing by the 49 Squadron element took place from 8,000 to 9,000 feet between 01.49 and 02.15. Three large vessels observed tied together east of the outer harbour were seen to be on fire, and the naval oil stores were targeted by some crews. By the later stages of the raid, many fires had added to the smoke obscuring the town, and a number of large explosions encouraged the crews' belief that a successful operation had taken place, which, ultimately, would be confirmed. The crews of Sgts Gumbley and Price planted their vegetables into the briefed locations from 4,000 and 3,500 feet at 01.54 and 01.56 respectively after pinpointing on Palmaria and Tino Islands and returned safely with all but one of the other squadron crews. Sgt Nixon and crew knew that they could not reach home and landed at Maison Blanche, one of the captured former enemy airfields in Algeria, along with two others in what was the first unofficial "shuttle" raid.

The busy round of non-Ruhr operations continued with the posting of Stuttgart as the target on the 14th, for which a force of 462 aircraft was made ready, 5 Group providing fifty-seven Lancasters, six of them made ready by 49 Squadron and loaded with a cookie and twelve SBCs of incendiaries. At briefing, they took in the details of the plan, which involved Path Finder aircraft dropping yellow TIs as route markers at two locations, while, at the target, nine Stirlings and eight Halifaxes were to ground mark the aiming-point with red TIs on H2S, at the same time as releasing a short stick of flares. One Stirling and four Lancasters were then to identify the aiming-point visually, and mark it with green TIs, for three Stirlings, six Halifaxes and eleven Lancasters to back up also with greens. This would leave three Stirlings, three Halifaxes and five Lancasters to bolster the efforts of the main force. The Fiskerton sextet took off between 22.14 and 22.35 with S/L Gilpin the senior pilot on duty for the first time and lost the services of Sgt Millar and crew to surging engines before crossing the coast. Sgt Tolchard and crew were last away eleven minutes late and were twenty minutes behind schedule at the final turning point, leaving them with no prospect of making up the time and no option other than to turn back. The others followed the Franco/Belgian frontier and passed beyond Luxembourg to enter Germany in the Strasbourg area before approaching the city from the north-east to find an absence of cloud. The Path Finder ground marker crews established their positions by H2S confirmed by visual reference, but as evidence of the shortcomings of H2S in its early form, they were actually short of the city centre when they delivered bundles of white flares, red TIs and 1,000 pounders between 00.47 and 00.56. The backers-up were carrying four green TIs, one of them of the long-burning variety, four 1,000 pounders and a single 500 pounder each, which they dropped between 00.50 and 01.14, also to the north-east of the planned aiming-point. The main force crews were greeted by plentiful red and green TIs concentrated in a built-up area, and some would claim later to have picked out ground details such as marshalling yards, the railway station, the river and the Bosch factory through the copious volumes of smoke rising through 8,000 feet. This reinforced their belief that they were over the briefed aiming-point, where the TIs had mostly burned out by the time that the Fiskerton crews delivered their attacks on concentrations of fire from 10,000 to 15,500 feet between 01.25 and 01.35, and there was little information to glean and pass on at debriefing. Bombing photos and post-raid reconnaissance confirmed that the Path Finders had not marked the centre of the city, and that a "creep-back" had developed, which had spread along the line of approach. Creep-back was a feature of many large raids and was caused by crews bombing the first fires they came upon, rather than pushing through to the planned aiming-point. It could work for or against the effectiveness of an attack, and on this night, worked in the Command's favour by falling across the industrial district of Bad-Canstatt, situated to the north-east of the city centre on the East Bank of the River Neckar. The bombing continued to spread further back along the line of approach onto the residential suburbs of Münster and Mühlhausen, and it was here that the majority of the 393 buildings were destroyed and more than nine hundred others severely damaged.

On the 15th, F/O Gerry Fawke was posted to 1660 Conversion Unit, where he would remain until joining 617 Squadron in the rank of flight lieutenant on the 6th of April 1944. It was at this time that 617 Squadron was experimenting with Mosquitos for use in a low-level marking role, and F/L Fawke would be selected as one of the pilots.

Two major operations were planned for the 16th, the main one employing 327 Lancasters and Halifaxes to target the Skoda armaments factory at distant Pilsen in Czechoslovakia, while a force of 271 aircraft, consisting predominantly of Wellingtons and Stirlings, created a large-scale diversion at Mannheim some 240 miles to the west. A force of 197 Lancasters and 130 Halifaxes was detailed for Pilsen, of which 102 of the former were provided by 5 Group, seven of them made ready by 49 Squadron at Fiskerton. In an unnecessarily complicated plan, the Path Finders were to drop yellow route markers at the final turning point, seven miles from the target, which the main force crews were to then locate visually in the anticipated bright moonlight and bomb from as low a level as practicable. The plan briefed out to the Path Finder crews was more detailed and seems to contain elements that were not part of the main force briefings. It called for six 35 (Madras Presidency) Squadron crews to employ H2S to drop long sticks of flares from south-west to north-east across the city and green TIs on the south-western edge of the Skoda works as a rough guide. These were to be backed up by green TIs delivered by two Halifaxes and twenty Lancasters, unless cloud conditions rendered this impossible, in which case, red TIs were to be employed by both the markers and backers-up. Two further Halifaxes and five Lancasters were to attack with the main force. It was a plan of attack that invited confusion and failure, and the outcome would question the quality of some of the briefings.

The 49 Squadron element took off between 21.11 and 21.17 with W/C Johnson and S/L Gilpin the senior pilots on duty supported by F/L Allsebrook with a roundtrip of some 1,500 miles to negotiate. They headed for Dungeness on the Kent coast to make landfall on the French coast in the area of Cayeux-sur-Mer, before swinging round Amiens and tracking eastwards towards the German frontier near Saarbrücken. It is believed that all from Fiskerton reached the target area to find the forecast favourable weather conditions, with a layer of eight-tenths cloud at around 9,000 feet, below which, visibility was good and ground features could be made out clearly in bright moonlight. They delivered their bomb loads from 6,000 to 8,000 feet between 01.44 and 01.59 and in their debriefing reports would make reference to green TIs and flares and the fact that they had positively identified the factory buildings despite copious amounts of smoke and dust.

The briefings should have made clear that the bombing was to be carried out visually from below the cloud base after making a timed run from the turning-point, which had been marked by yellow TIs. Many 5 Group crews reported bombing on TIs, proving that they had failed to understand and comply with the instructions at briefing and had bombed the turning point and not the target. Some, like those from 49 Squadron, made reference to yellow and green TIs and white illuminator flares, but all described difficulty in locating and identifying the factory buildings, some after spending time searching while having to dodge searchlights and flak. The details of the crew reports across the groups demonstrated that they could not have related to the Skoda works. Post-raid reconnaissance revealed the truth, that, despite the claims of returning crews, no bombs had fallen within miles of the factory and had been concentrated instead around an asylum at Dobrany, some seven miles to the south-west. This failure was compounded by the loss of thirty-six aircraft, split equally between the two types, and this represented a massive 11% of the force. ED441 crashed on the eastern outskirts of Amiens, almost certainly while homebound, and only the rear gunner survived in enemy hands from the crew of Sgt Penry, while ED427 disappeared without trace with the crew of F/O Bone. The losses from Pilsen had to be added to the eighteen aircraft also missing from the Mannheim contingent, which had, at least, achieved the destruction of 130 buildings and damage to some degree to three thousand others. The combined casualty figure of fifty-four aircraft represented a new record for a single night.

Later, on the 17th, F/L Scorer arrived from 1661 Conversion Unit as a deputy flight commander and F/L Green went in the opposite direction at the conclusion of his tour. A return to the docks at La Spezia was notified to the Lancaster squadrons of 1, 5 and 8 Groups on the 18th, and 8 Group would also contribute five Halifaxes to the overall force of 178 aircraft. The eighty-nine 5 Group Lancasters included four representing 49 Squadron, which departed Fiskerton between 20.49 and 21.00 with S/L Storey and F/L Allsebrook the senior pilots on duty, the former having just arrived from Scampton to fulfil the role of flight commander. Also taking off at this time were the crews of Sgts Price and Tolchard, who were bound for the Mullet garden in the approaches to the port. They all negotiated the outward flight across France and the Alps and found the weather to be ideal and visibility good in the target area, although an effective smoke screen partially obscured the town and docks until it drifted to the south to hang over the gulf. The aiming point was identified visually after a timed run from Palmaria Island to the south, and confirmed by red Path Finder TIs, on which they bombed from 8,000 to 9,500 feet between 01.44 and 02.02. The fires were becoming concentrated as they turned away and set course for home, completely satisfied with their night's work. The gardeners had also fulfilled their brief by planting their vegetables in the allotted locations from 4,000 and 5,000 feet at 01.51. Photographic reconnaissance revealed that the marking and bombing had fallen to the north-west of the dockyards but had caused extensive damage to the railway station and public buildings in the town centre.

On the 20th, F/O Eyre was posted to the Bombing and Gunnery Unit at the conclusion of his tour, while his former colleagues attended briefing to learn of their part in that night's operation to Stettin. This port city is situated 640 miles from the Lincolnshire bomber stations as the crow flies and at the midpoint of Germany's wartime Baltic coast. A force of 339 aircraft included ninety-one Lancasters representing 5 Group, and as they were being prepared for battle, their crews were devouring the details of the route that would take the bomber stream across the North Sea to a point north of Esbjerg on the Danish coast, before traversing Jutland to then head south-east towards the target. The distance, which was similar to that for Pilsen, would keep some crews in the air for more than nine hours, and would require a small reduction in bombs among the main force element in favour of fuel. Navigation by coastline was expected to be simple in the prevailing conditions, which negated the need for route markers, and once illuminating flares had laid bare the aiming point, the marking would be by H2S-based TIs backed up by greens. The nine-strong 49 Squadron element took off between 21.41 and 21.51 with W/C Johnson and F/Ls Allsebrook and Scorer the senior pilots on duty, the latter undertaking the first sortie of his second tour. They headed out over Mablethorpe to rendezvous with the rest of the bomber stream and completed the outward flight under clear skies which persisted all the way to the target, where they benefitted from bright moonlight and horizontal visibility estimated to be fifty miles. They were able to identify ground features as they bore down on the aiming point and the Fiskerton crews bombed on green TIs from 10,000 to 12,000 feet between 01.10 and 01.33. There were targets, like Duisburg and, later, Braunschweig, that, for a period at least, seemed to enjoy something of a charmed life and managed to dodge the worst ravages of a Bomber Command attack, but Stettin was not among them, perhaps because of its location near an easily identifiable coastline. On this night, the perfect conditions paved the way for the Path Finders to deliver a flawless marking performance, which was exploited by the main force crews to devastating effect. Returning crews reported fires raging across the built-up area and the glow from the burning port-city visible for ninety miles into the return journey. The success cost the Command twenty-one aircraft, four of which belonged to 5 Group, and among these was 49 Squadron's ED620, which was hit by flak at the Danish coast outbound and crash-landed eight miles north-north-west of Ringkøbing at 23.35. Pilot, Sgt Anderson, who had only just qualified as crew captain, was mortally wounded and died in hospital within hours and was the fourth member of the crew to perish. The three survivors were treated in hospital before being moved to PoW camps, from where one was repatriated in 1944. It was thirty-six hours before a reconnaissance aircraft captured photographs of the still-burning city, and these revealed an area of one hundred acres of devastation across the centre. Local reports confirmed that thirteen industrial premises and 380 houses had been destroyed.

On the 25$^{th}$, Sgt Gumbley RNZAF was posted to Scampton at the conclusion of his tour and would return to the operational scene in the rank of flight lieutenant and with a DFM to his name late in September 1944, when joining 617 Squadron at Woodhall Spa. Tragically, he would lose his life on the 21$^{st}$ of March 1945, while flying a grand Slam-carrying Lancaster B I "Special" during an operation to Bremen, just five weeks from the end of the bombing war.

Orders on the 26$^{th}$ signalled a return to the Ruhr and Duisburg, for which a large force of 561 aircraft was assembled, the numbers bolstered by the inclusion of 135 Wellingtons, while 215 Lancasters represented the largest contribution by type. 8 Group was boosted by the operational debut of 97 (Straits Settlement) Squadron and 405 (Vancouver) Squadron RCAF in a plan that called for eight Oboe Mosquitos to drop yellow route markers and red TIs on the aiming-point. The yellows were to be backed up by others of the same colour delivered by a dozen Lancasters, while three Stirlings, five 35 (Madras Presidency) Squadron Halifaxes and seven Lancasters backed up at the aiming-point with green TIs. 5 Group was responsible for 105 of the Lancasters and 49 Squadron seven, which departed Fiskerton between 00.04 and 00.16 with F/L Scorer the senior pilot on duty. After climbing out, they set course for the Dutch coast near The Hague for the northern approach to the Ruhr and reached the target area after approaching from the north-east. They found largely clear skies and good visibility and were guided to the aiming point by red and green TIs, upon which the bombing by the Fiskerton element was carried out from 17,500 to 19,000 feet between 02.34 and 02.55. A large orange explosion was witnessed to the east of the aiming point at 02.34, but fires had not fully gained a hold by the time that the force withdrew, although black smoke was rising through 7,000 feet. Opinions were divided as to the degree of concentration achieved, but what was not in doubt was the failure to return of seventeen aircraft, just one of which belonged to 5 Group. Post-raid reconnaissance revealed that the attack had fallen short of the city centre and had been focused on the north-eastern districts under the line of approach, thus sparing Duisburg yet again from the full weight of a Bomber Command heavy raid. Even so, local reports confirmed the destruction of more than three hundred buildings, which represented something of a telling blow at this target.

The 27$^{th}$ was devoted to the largest mining operation of the war to date, which involved 160 aircraft targeting the waters off the Brittany and Biscay coasts and the Frisians. Twenty-eight 5 Group Lancasters were detailed, four of them representing 49 Squadron, which departed Fiskerton between 01.30 and 01.44 bearing aloft the freshman crews of Sgts Cole, Morrison, Nixon and Robinson, each pilot operating as crew captain for the first time. They were bound for the Nectarine II garden off the central Frisians, where low cloud and poor visibility hampered attempts to locate a pinpoint for a timed run. Sgts Cole and Morrison returned their six mines each to store, while Sgt Nixon and crew delivered theirs into the briefed location from 2,000 feet at 03.23 after pinpointing on Juist and Borkum. Sgt Robinson and crew established their position from Schiermonnikoog and planted their vegetables in an estimated position from 2,000 feet at 03.35.

The following night brought an even larger gardening effort involving 207 aircraft, of which forty-one Lancasters were provided by 5 Group on a night when Fiskerton remained dormant. The 5 Group crews operating over the Baltic experienced favourable conditions, while elsewhere, low cloud was encountered and flak proved to be troublesome, contributing to the loss of twenty-two aircraft, just one of them from 5 Group. This would be the largest-ever loss to result in a single night from mining, but, on the credit side, the number of mines delivered, 593, was also a record for one night and would not be surpassed.

F/L Munro and crew arrived on posting from 1661 Conversion Unit on the 30th, the day on which Essen was posted as the target as attention swung once more towards the Ruhr and would remain upon it almost exclusively now until well into July. A force of 305 aircraft included 101 Lancasters of 5 Group, of which six were loaded with a cookie and twelve SBCs each at Fiskerton and dispatched between 23.53 and 00.08 with F/L Scorer the senior pilot on duty. A layer of ice-bearing cloud lay across the bomber stream's path over the North Sea, which most crews negotiated to reach the target to be greeted by ten-tenths cloud with tops in places as high as 21,000 feet and red and green Oboe-laid Wanganui flares (skymarkers) identifying the aiming point. Some crews carried out a time-and-distance run from green tracking markers, and all had some kind of flare in the bomb sight, or at least the glow of one, as the 49 Squadron crews released their loads from 19,000 to 22,000 feet between 03.00 and 03.10. Returning crews reported the glow of fires beneath the cloud and a number of large explosions, but it was impossible to determine whether or not concentration had been achieved, particularly as bombing photos showed only cloud. Post-raid reconnaissance and local reports confirmed a lack of concentration and the liberal distribution of bombs onto ten other Ruhr locations, particularly Bottrop to the north, but 189 buildings were destroyed and 237 severely damaged in Essen, and importantly, Krupp sites sustained further damage.

During the course of the month, the squadron took part in fifteen operations and dispatched ninety-one sorties for the loss of three Lancasters and crews.

# May 1943

May would bring a return to winning ways, with a number of outstanding successes and new records as the Ruhr offensive expanded its horizons to include targets other than Essen and Duisburg. It was, in fact, Duisburg that was posted as the target for each of the first three nights of the new month, before the operations were cancelled. The first of the "new" targets was Dortmund, which had been attacked many times before, but not on the scale that it was about to face on the 4th, when the force of 596 aircraft represented the largest non-1,000 effort to date. 5 Group made available 125 Lancasters, of which a dozen were prepared at Fiskerton and loaded with a cookie and twelve SBCs each, while their crews were being informed of the plan at briefing. Oboe Mosquitos were to drop yellow track markers, before eight of them ground-marked the aiming-point with green TIs, leaving two in reserve to bomb with the main force if not required for marking duties. Twenty-two Lancasters and two Halifaxes were to back up with red TIs, and all remaining Path Finder aircraft were to bomb with the main force. The 49 Squadron participants took off between 21.14 and 21.49 with S/Ls Gilpin and Storey the senior pilots on duty and flew out over the Lincolnshire coast to rendezvous with the bomber stream over the North Sea. There were no early returns from the Fiskerton brigade, and they pushed on across Holland to enter Germany to the north of the Ruhr and make their way to the eastern end, where they found clear skies, good visibility and only industrial and smoke haze to spoil the vertical view. Yellow Path Finder tracking skymarkers were used as the starting point for a timed run to the target, while the defences responded with many searchlight cones and intense heavy flak, and much evasive action would be required after bombing to vacate the target area intact. The initial Path Finder marking was accurately placed around the city centre, but some of the backing-up fell short and a decoy site was also successful in luring away a proportion of the bombing. The 49 Squadron crews aimed at red or green TIs from 18,000 to 21,000 feet between 01.05 and 01.36, many leaving a gap of up to ten seconds between the release of the high explosives and incendiaries. On return, they reported many sizeable explosions, including a particularly large on at 01.12, which may have been the one reported by a 50 Squadron crew that threw flame to a height of 2,000 feet and burned for ten seconds. They also described developing fires, the glow from which could be seen, according to some, from 150 miles into the return flight. ED597 landed with a burst tyre, which was a surprise to Sgt Moss, who lost control as the Lancaster dug in and careered off the runway, shedding the port-outer propeller in the process. The crew emerged unscathed, if shaken, and were pleased to have their first sortie together under their belt, while the Lancaster would be repaired and find its way eventually to 619 Squadron. Post-raid reconnaissance revealed that approximately half of the force had bombed within three miles of the aiming point and had destroyed 1,218 buildings and seriously damaged more than two thousand others. Local reports confirmed a death toll of 693 people, which was a record from a Bomber Command attack. It was not a one-sided affair, however, and the loss of thirty-one aircraft was a foretaste of what was in store for the bomber crews operating over "Happy Valley".

There would be no major operations during the ensuing week, and when the Command as a whole was next called into action, on the 12$^{th}$, it was for a major assault on Duisburg, for which a heavy force of 562 aircraft was assembled. Nine Oboe Mosquitos were to drop yellow TIs on track as a preliminary warning and red TIs on the aiming-point, which would be backed up with green TIs by five Stirlings, five Halifaxes and twenty Lancasters. 5 Group detailed 119 of the 238 Lancasters, and they would be accompanied by 142 Halifaxes, 112 Wellingtons and seventy Stirlings. The seven 49 Squadron Lancasters departed Fiskerton between 23.58 and 00.30 with S/L Storey and F/L Munro the senior pilots on duty, and after climbing out over the station, they headed for the North Sea to rendezvous with the bomber stream and make landfall on the Dutch coast in the area of Castricum-aan-Zee. They reached the target area guided by the yellow tracking flares and found ideal bombing conditions with no cloud and good visibility, which helped the Oboe and H2S crews to mark with great accuracy and focus. The main force crews were able to identify ground features and exploit the opportunity to produce a display of unusually concentrated bombing, those from Fiskerton delivering their attacks onto red and green TIs from 18,000 to 20,000 feet between 02.03 and 02.35. Perhaps, for the first time at this target, the attack proceeded according to plan, and Duisburg finally succumbed to a devastating assault. Returning crews described a large explosion at 02.30, streets outlined by fire and a highly successful outcome, the best yet witnessed by some, and their impressions were confirmed by photo-reconnaissance, which revealed extensive damage in the city centre and the Ruhrort Rhine docks, the largest inland port in Germany. 1,596 buildings were totally destroyed and the Thyssen steelworks was hit, while dozens of barges and ships were sunk or damaged. However, many crews were absent from debriefing at stations across the Command, and it soon became clear that the success had been gained at the high cost of thirty-four aircraft. The loss rates by type again made interesting reading and confirmed the established food chain, the Lancasters sustaining a 4.2% loss, compared with 8.9% for Wellingtons, 7.1% for Stirlings and 6.3% for Halifaxes. Such was the level of destruction that Duisburg would now be left in peace for a year.

On the following night, the squadron contributed fourteen aircraft to a 5 Group force of 124 Lancasters, which, with thirty-two other Lancasters and twelve Halifaxes of 8 Group, would attempt to rectify the recent failure at the Skoda armaments works at Pilsen. A simultaneous raid was planned against the Ruhr city of Bochum, another new target for the campaign, and would involve 442 aircraft from the other groups. The Fiskerton element took off between 21.37 and 21.52 with W/C Johnson and S/Ls Gilpin and Storey the senior pilots on duty and lost the services of Sgt Morrison and crew to the failure of their port-inner engine within ninety minutes. The others completed the 650-mile outward leg across France and southern Germany and reached the target to find clear skies and good visibility, but with ground haze and a smokescreen to impair the vertical visibility. The Path Finders dropped yellow and white track markers and red TIs with a fairly good concentration that would have been perfectly adequate over a built-up area, while at a precision target like the Skoda works, they were too scattered to be effective. Bombing by the 49 Squadron crews was carried out from 7,000 to 11,000 feet between 01.19 and 01.43, although Sgt Tolchard's bombing height was recorded at an unlikely 21,000 feet. The impression was that most of the hardware fell among the TIs and the opinion was voiced that if the TIs had been on the target, the operation had been successful. Sadly, they were found to have missed the factory complex, and most of the bombs had fallen into open country to the north. Some compensation was gained at Bochum, where almost four hundred buildings were destroyed and seven hundred seriously damaged at a cost of twenty-four aircraft, and these were added to the nine Lancasters missing from Pilsen.

The above operations proved to be the last major outings for the Path Finders and main force squadrons for nine days, and it was during this lull, that 617 Squadron entered bomber folklore with its epic attack on the Ruhr Dams under Operation Chastise on the night of the 16/17$^{th}$. Among those taking part were the former sons of 49 Squadron, the crews of F/Sgts Bill Townsend and Cyril Anderson and wireless operator Sgt John Minchin. The Townsend and Anderson crews had been assigned to the third wave, taking off after midnight to be told which target to attack only once they were over Germany, by which time a clearer picture of the conduct of the operation would be apparent. There is uncertainty as to which dam the Townsend crew attacked after being directed to the Ennepe, one of the reserve targets. The likelihood is that they attacked the nearby Bever Dam in error, but the truth will never be positively established. The Anderson crew, the least experienced of those taking part, fell behind schedule and unsure of their position with mist filling the valleys, dawn creeping ever closer and an unserviceable rear turret, took the brave decision to abandon the search for the Sorpe Dam and return the Upkeep to Scampton, making them the only crew to reach Germany and not complete their sortie. This compared them unfavourably with the other two surviving crews from the third wave, who had carried out an attack. In any other squadron and on any other operation, Anderson's actions would have been considered reasonable and would not have been questioned, but this was 617 Squadron and Operation Chastise and W/C Guy Gibson was a man with an intense dislike of NCOs, treating most of them with disdain. He admitted to an inability to relate to such lowly beings and firmly believed that an officer, by virtue of a commission, was a better human being than those without one. From the moment Anderson landed, his future at 617 Squadron was over, but he would have to endure an uncomfortable two weeks under a cloud before being shipped back to 49 Squadron.

Perhaps the saddest death on this night was that of the 27-year-old Sgt John Minchin, who hailed from the Cotswold town of Bourton-in-the-Water and as a wireless operator was the least likely to be recognised for his skills, courage and dedication. He had begun his operational career with 49 Squadron in October 1941 and completed a tour on Hampdens and Manchesters achieving the distinction of being on board the very last Hampden sortie and taking part in the first Manchester operation. He got married on the 28th of May, but the first of the "thousand bomber raids" two days later dashed any hopes of a proper honeymoon. At the end of his tour, he was posted to 26 O.T.U., and it was from there that he joined the newly forming 617 Squadron in April 1943 to become a member of the crew of F/L John Hopgood, one of Gibson's closest friends. As they skirted the northern rim of the Ruhr on their way to the Möhne Dam, AJ-M was hit by flak and Hopgood sustained a face wound, while Tony Burcher in the rear turret picked up flak splinters in the lower torso and Minchin suffered massive trauma to a leg from which he would almost certainly not have survived, even had he made it home. Minchin remained silent about his predicament and continued at his post as Hopgood bore down on the dam as the second to attack, the defenders now aware of where to aim their guns. Flying into a stream of light flak from the dam's towers, the Lancaster was soon on fire from two engines and the bomb bounced over the parapet of the dam to detonate on the power station on the dry side. During the ensuing twenty-five seconds, Hopgood strove to drag sufficient height out of the crippled Lancaster to enable his crew to bale out, while Minchin somehow dragged himself and his parachute pack over the main spar and crawled towards the rear exit, where Burcher had opened the door. Burcher was shocked by Minchin's plight and was unsure what to do, but noticing that his crew mate was now motionless, clipped on his parachute and rolled him out of the door, firmly grasping the D-ring. Burcher had already separated his parachute from its pack, when a blast of air blew him out into space to strike the starboard fin and possibly thrust him upwards a few extra feet. He felt the jerk of the chute filling with air and at the same instant landed in a freshly ploughed field, which cushioned his fall. Moments later still, the Lancaster exploded and fell in pieces within about five hundred yards of the village of Ostönnen, bomb-aimer, John Fraser, having dropped clear from 300 feet perhaps a second or two earlier. Burcher and Minchin landed in the same field, which contained a large oak tree known as Frielings Eichen, located a few hundred yards south-east of the village of Sieveringen. Burcher had fallen into a hollow to the east of the tree and benefitted from perhaps an additional fifteen feet of height, but Minchin's body was found on the crown of the field, and whether he died on impact or succumbed to his injuries is uncertain. It seems clear that he was already beyond help before leaving the Lancaster and his life ended just eleven days short of his first wedding anniversary.

By the time that the next major operation was posted on the 23rd, the day on which F/L Dunnett arrived on posting from 1654 Conversion Unit, main force squadrons had undergone an expansion with the addition to many units of a third or C Flight, which, in most cases, would eventually be hived off to form the nucleus of a brand-new squadron. The giant force of 826 aircraft was the largest non-1,000 force to date and surpassed the previous record set three weeks earlier by a clear 230 aircraft. The number of available Lancasters had leapt by eighty-eight, Halifaxes by forty-eight, Stirlings by forty and Wellingtons by forty-one, and their destination for the second time in the month was to be Dortmund. The Command had been restored to full health and vigour and activity on all participating stations was hectic as preparations were put in hand to resume the Ruhr offensive. The ground crews and armourers worked tirelessly, while the crews attended briefings to learn of their part in that night's grand plan, which called for eleven Mosquitos to drop yellow preliminary warning TIs on track, before marking the aiming-point with Oboe-laid red TIs, which eight Stirlings, eleven Halifaxes and fourteen Lancasters were to back up with green TIs. 5 Group detailed a record 154 Lancasters, thirteen of which were made ready at Fiskerton, where they were loaded with the standard Ruhr load of a cookie and twelve SBCs of incendiaries. They took off between 22.30 and 22.51 with W/C Johnson and F/L Munro the senior pilots on duty and headed out over Skegness to join up with the bomber stream. Having made landfall near Castricum-aan-Zee, they adopted a south-easterly course to the eastern Ruhr, which all from the squadron reached to find clear skies but considerable industrial haze. Before the advent of Oboe, this would have rendered the attack a lottery, now, however, the thirteen Path Finder Mosquitos marked the centre of the city accurately and the Path Finder heavy brigade backed-up to maintain the aiming point with red and green TIs. These could be seen from twenty miles away on approach, as could the yellow track markers assisting the early 5 Group arrivals for their time-and-distance runs. The Fiskerton crews bombed largely on the clusters of red and green TIs from 14,000 to 20,000 feet between 01.35 and 01.43, observing many explosions and fires, which were merging into a large area of conflagration with thick columns of black smoke rising up through 18,000 feet as the bombers turned away. Returning crews reported fierce night-fighter activity over the target and on the way home, and this was reflected in the high casualty rate of thirty-eight aircraft, the largest loss of the campaign to date. Almost half of these were Halifaxes and eight were Lancasters, four belonging to 5 Group, among them 49 Squadron's ED813, which crashed at Essen, killing four members of the crew and delivering Sgt Thomas and his flight engineer and navigator into enemy hands. The rear gunner, Sgt Ancell, hailed from Argentina, and at 39 years of age was among the oldest to serve as aircrew in Bomber Command.

The Ruhr offensive continued with the posting of Düsseldorf as the target on the 25th, for which a force of 759 aircraft was assembled, 5 Group contributing 139 Lancasters, eleven of them representing 49 Squadron. Briefings revealed the standard procedure of Mosquito-laid yellow preliminary warning TIs on track and red TIs delivered by Oboe onto the aiming-point, after which eight Stirlings, twelve Halifaxes and twenty-three Lancasters were to back these up with green TIs, leaving five Stirlings, fourteen Halifaxes and twenty-five Lancasters to bomb with the main force. The Fiskerton element took off between 23.10 and 23.40 with W/C Johnson and S/L Gilpin the senior pilots on duty and each Lancaster loaded with a cookie and ninety-six 30lb incendiaries. Sgt Tomlin and crew dropped out early when the rear turret failed, leaving the others to continue on to the Dutch coast, where some crews claimed that they were able to observe feverish activity at the target some one hundred miles and thirty minutes flying time away. Düsseldorf lay beneath two layers of thin cloud, and the generally poor visibility impacted the Path Finders' ability to back up the Mosquito-laid TIs to the extent that two red TIs were seen to be thirty miles apart. There were also decoy markers and dummy fire sites operating, which succeeded in causing confusion and prevented a concentration of bombing. The 5 Group crews carried out time-and-distant runs from yellow track markers, before identifying the target visually and by red and green TIs and the

49 Squadron participants bombed from 18,500 to 22,000 feet between 01.47 and 02.24. Post-raid reconnaissance and local reports confirmed that the raid had failed to achieve concentration and had developed into an "old-style" scattering of bombs across a wide area, leading to the destruction in Düsseldorf of fewer than a hundred buildings. Twenty-seven aircraft failed to return, five of them belonging to 5 Group and among them was the one containing 207 Squadron's commanding officer.

Harris was not yet done with Essen and the fifth visitation by the bomber force during the campaign was notified to stations on the 27th, for which a force of 518 aircraft was assembled, 5 Group putting up 133 Lancasters, a dozen of them from Fiskerton. 8 Group prepared two plans of attack, one for ground marking and an alternative for skymarking in the event of cloud cover, and in the event, the latter would be employed, involving a dozen Oboe Mosquitos to drop red flares nineteen miles short of the target and green ones ten-and-a-half miles short as a preliminary warning. Continuing on to the target, they were to sky mark the aiming-point with red flares with green stars and two white flares for the rest of 8 Group to bomb with the main force. The 49 Squadron element became safely airborne between 21.40 and 22.56 with F/L Munro the senior pilot on duty and all reached the target to be greeted by six to eight-tenths cloud with tops at 12,000 feet. Tracking flares guided them in with, ahead of them, Wanganui skymarkers gently descending into the cloud tops over the aiming point. The 5 Group crews carried out time-and-distance runs and bombed on white flares and red parachute markers with green stars, those from 49 Squadron from 18,000 to 23,000 feet between 00.41 and 00.53. Post-raid reconnaissance revealed that much of the bombing had fallen short, but 488 buildings had been destroyed, mostly in central and northern districts, and ten nearby towns reported themselves to be victims of collateral damage. Twenty-three aircraft failed to return, and the Halifaxes again represented almost half of the casualties.

A force of 719 aircraft was assembled on the 29th to pitch against another new Ruhr target, the conurbation known as Wuppertal, perched on the southern rim of the Ruhr Valley east of Düsseldorf. It consisted of the towns of Barmen and Elberfeld, which had grown wealthy on the proceeds of rich coal deposits. The aiming-point for this night's attack was to be the Barmen half at the eastern end, for which 5 Group detailed 129 Lancasters, a dozen of them representing 49 Squadron and departing Fiskerton between 21.47 and 22.01 with F/L Munro the senior pilot on duty and F/L Dunnett flying as second pilot to F/O Taylor. On a night of poor serviceability for the squadron, the crews of Sgts Tolchard, Moss and Robinson arrived back at base between 00.09 and 01.58, two with engine failure and one with a compass issue. On this occasion, the route markers were to be dropped by two 8 Group Stirlings and two Halifaxes, while ahead, the Oboe Mosquitos took care of ground marking with red TIs. These would be backed up by four Stirlings, eleven Halifaxes and twenty-three Lancasters with greens, at the same time as thirteen Stirlings, twenty Halifaxes and twenty-one Lancasters acted as fire raisers by dropping incendiaries, leaving two Stirlings, five Halifaxes and seven Lancasters to bomb with the main force. Having negotiated the southern approach to the Ruhr, running the gauntlet of searchlights and flak in the Cologne and Düsseldorf corridor, crews were greeted by clear skies in the target area, with the usual industrial haze extending up to 10,000 feet. The yellow tracking flares clearly identified the final turning-point, and the backers-up went in at 16,000 to 18,000 feet between 01.03 and 01.51 to reinforce the red TIs with greens. Meanwhile, the thirteen fire-raisers had attacked with a 2,000 pounder and 1,164 x 4lb incendiaries each, leaving the way clear for the main force to exploit the opportunity to deliver a massive blow. The depleted Fiskerton element delivered their cookies and incendiaries from 18,000 to 21,000 feet between 00.57 and 01.27 and it was clear to all that something extraordinary was taking place as the built-up area beneath them became a sea of explosions and flames with smoke rising very rapidly through 15,000 feet. Post-raid reconnaissance revealed this to be the most awesomely destructive raid of the campaign thus far, which devastated by fire a thousand acres, or around 80% of the built-up area, and destroyed almost four thousand houses, five of the six largest factories and more than two hundred other industrial buildings. It would be some time before the human cost could be established, but it is now accepted that 3,400 people lost their lives during this savage Saturday night. The defenders had their say also, and fought back to claim thirty-three bombers, including seven Lancasters, of which three were from 5 Group.

During the course of the month, the squadron carried out seven operations and dispatched eighty-one sorties without loss.

## June 1943

Sgt Cyril Anderson and crew arrived back at 49 Squadron on the 2nd to resume their first tour of operations, and despite their, perhaps, less than fulfilling experiences with 617 Squadron, they would forever be members of the most exclusive club in the RAF. They were Dambusters, which, at the time, meant a lot less than it does now. There were no major operations at the start of June because of the moon period, and, although 5 Group stations were alerted on most of the first ten days, no operations actually took place. This kept the Path Finder and main force crews kicking their heels on the ground until the 11th, when Düsseldorf was briefed out to 783 crews. The plan would follow the standard pattern, in which Mosquito yellow preliminary warning flares would be backed up by the other 8 Group aircraft and the Oboe-laid red TIs on the aiming-point backed up with greens. However, uncertainty concerning the weather conditions resulted in the Mosquitos also carrying target-marking red flares with green stars. 5 Group was responsible for 162 of the 326 Lancasters, and seventeen of them were loaded with a cookie, four 500 pounders and ten SBCs of incendiaries each at Fiskerton and dispatched in two waves between 22.19 and 23.09 with W/C Johnson and S/Ls Storey and Gilpin the senior pilots on duty. F/Sgt Curton and crew turned back within ninety minutes after their a.s.i. failed and they were followed home by Sgt Morrison and crew, whose wireless operator had tried in vain to fix the intercom. The bomber stream adopted the southern approach to the Ruhr via the Scheldt estuary and had to contend with static and lightning conditions in towering ten-tenths cloud as they made their way across the North Sea, some reporting the tops to be at 23,500 feet. This had largely dissipated to leave just small amounts at 2,000, 5,000 and 10,000 feet over the southern Ruhr, dependent upon the time of arrival on final approach. Those in the vanguard of the main force were drawn on by yellow tracking flares from 01.05, and red skymarkers with green stars at 01.16, while those a little further back in the bomber stream were guided to the mark by red and green skymarkers. The Paramatta marking (ground-marking TIs) did not seem to appear until these crews were turning away, but they were clearly visible to those in the rear-guard, by which time a sea of flames had spread over a massive area with columns of smoke rising through 21,000 feet. The 49 Squadron crews delivered their attacks on red TIs from 18,000 to 22,500 feet between 01.22 and 02.16, before returning safely to report a successful night's work. When all aircraft had been accounted for, thirty-eight were found to be missing, a figure that equalled the heaviest loss of the offensive to date. Post-raid reconnaissance revealed an area of fire across central districts measuring eight by five kilometres, and local reports confirmed 8,882 individual fire incidents. More than seventy war-industry factories suffered a complete or partial loss of production, 140,000 people were bombed out of their homes and 1,292 lost their lives. Had it not been for an errant Oboe marker attracting a proportion of the bombing onto open country some fourteen miles to the north-east, the destruction would have been greater.

Bochum would face its second heavy visitation of the campaign on the 12$^{th}$, and a force of 503 aircraft was made ready for the purpose, 5 Group contributing 165 Lancasters, fourteen of them provided by 49 Squadron. Briefings revealed that two Mosquitos were to drop yellow preliminary warning TIs, before joining seven others to mark the aiming-point with red TIs, which twenty-five Lancasters would back up with greens. The Fiskerton crews took off between 22.13 and 22.46 with S/L Storey and F/Ls Dunnett and Munro the senior pilots on duty and set course via Texel to pass over central Holland and enter Germany to the west of Münster, before turning south for a direct run on Bochum, situated between Essen to the west and Dortmund to the east. Sgt Powell became indisposed and brought his crew home early and F/L Dunnett and crew touched down ninety minutes later blaming a defective rear turret. It is believed that night-fighters were waiting in Dutch airspace and over the frontier region, and a number of bombers fell victim at this stage of the operation, including, it is believed, 49 Squadron's ED584, which crashed near Raalte in north-central Holland with no survivors from the freshman crew of Sgt Hutchinson. The leading Path Finder crews encountered clear skies but eight to ten-tenths stratocumulus drifted across the city during the course of the raid with tops at 14,000 feet and obscured ground detail. The Fiskerton crews attacked from 16,500 and 22,000 feet with red and green TIs in their bomb sights, and on return reported concentrated fires, the glow from which was visible for up to a hundred miles into the homeward journey. Twenty-four aircraft failed to return, at least nine of them having fallen victim to night-fighters, and there were six empty dispersal pans on 5 Group stations. Photo-reconnaissance revealed 130 acres of devastation, backed up by local reports that 449 buildings had been destroyed and more than nine hundred severely damaged.

Following a night's rest, the Ruhr offensive continued at Oberhausen, situated between Duisburg to the west and Essen to the east and home of the Ruhr Chemie synthetic oil plant at Sterkrade-Holten on the northern outskirts. Although the town itself had not been targeted in numbers before, it had been hit by many bombs intended for its near-neighbours, and on this night would face an all-Lancaster heavy force numbering 197 aircraft, 108 of them provided by 5 Group. A dozen belonging to 49 Squadron departed Fiskerton between 22.11 and 22.32 with S/L Storey and F/L Dunnett the senior pilots on duty and each carrying a cookie, four 500 pounders and a mix of 4lb and 30lb incendiaries. They set course for the Scheldt estuary to bypass Antwerp on their way to the Belgian/German frontier and soon lost the services of F/O Millar and crew to a defective compass. They were among fifteen 5 Group crews to turn back on what would be a bad night for the squadron and the group. The main force element reached the target area to find three to ten-tenths cloud with tops in places at 18,000 feet, which were bathed in very bright moonlight. Tracking flares were drifting down to provide a reference for the start of the time-and-distance runs, and over the aiming point, the 49 Squadron crews aimed at reds with green stars and white skymarkers dropped by the six Oboe Mosquitos and backed-up by 8 Group heavies. They delivered their loads from 20,000 to 22,000 feet between 01.24 and 01.38 in the face of intense heavy flak, which continued to chase them out of the target area into the guns of night-fighters. Between them, the defences accounted for seventeen Lancasters, 8.4% of the force, ten of which belonged to 5

Group and there were three empty dispersal pans at Fiskerton. ED432 was carrying the eight-man crew of Sgt Cole and was shot down by flak to crash three miles west of Arnhem, killing all but the wireless operator and mid-upper gunner, the former, Sgt Arnold, surviving with shrapnel wounds after being thrown clear on impact. They were taken into captivity, where they were joined by Sgt Frost and his flight engineer, who were the only survivors after ED434 had been shot down by the night-fighter of Hptm Hans-Dieter Frank of I./NJG1 and crashed at 01.13 nine miles north-west of Nijmegen. There were no survivors from the eight-man crew of W/O Nixon in ED453, which came down near Lembeck on the northern fringe of the Ruhr while homebound. Local reports confirmed that the Wanganui flares had been right over the city centre, where 267 buildings had been destroyed and 584 seriously damaged.

On the 16th, 1, 5 and 8 Group stations were notified that Cologne was to be the target for that night, for which a force of 202 Lancasters and ten Halifaxes was made ready. They learned at briefings that there would be no Oboe Mosquitos on hand to mark the target, as that role was to be undertaken by the Path Finder Halifax element and six Lancasters employing H2S. 5 Group detailed eighty Lancasters, of which nine at Fiskerton were loaded with the usual mix of high explosives and incendiaries and dispatched between 22.10 and 22.28 with W/C Johnson and S/L Storey the senior pilots on duty supported by F/L Dunnett. They arrived in the target area to find six to ten-tenths cloud and green tracking flares from which to make a time-and-distance run to the aiming point. The Path Finders were late on target, and problems with some of the H2S sets led to sparse and scattered marking with solid white flares and reds with green stars. The 49 Squadron crews bombed from 20,000 to 24,000 feet between 01.11 and 01.20, and a number witnessed a large orange explosion at 01.08, although generally, they were unable to assess the outcome. Of five missing 5 Group Lancasters, two belonged to 49 Squadron and were among its most experienced crews. S/L Storey's ED785 was homebound over the Scheldt estuary when shot down by a night-fighter to crash into the water a mile south-west of Vlissingen (Flushing), killing seven of the eight occupants and delivering the wireless operator into enemy hands. ED497 was shot down by the night-fighter of Hptm Manfred Meurer of I./NJG1 and crashed at 01.41 six miles north-west of Helmond, also in Holland, with no survivors from the crew of F/L Dunnett. The impression was that a proportion of the bombing had been concentrated where intended, but that some crews had been lured away by dummy markers, and local reports suggesting that only around a hundred aircraft had been involved, tended to support this view. Residential districts bore the brunt of the raid, and 401 houses were destroyed, with 13,000 others sustaining damage to some extent, mostly lightly, while sixteen industrial premises and nine railway stations were hit, along with public and utility buildings.

A large influx of personnel on the 18th brought five new crews to Fiskerton from 1654 Conversion Unit, and they would undergo further training before being unleashed upon the enemy. The recent successes in the Ruhr had been aided by the sheer size of the urban areas below, which all but guaranteed that the bombs would hit something useful, even after smoke had obscured the aiming point TIs. It was a different matter at a small or precision target, however, which would rapidly be enveloped in smoke from the first bombs before the rest of the attacking force had a chance to draw a bead on the aiming point. When, on the 20th, therefore, an attack was mounted under the codename Operation Bellicose against the production site of the Würzburg radar sets, which the enemy was employing very successfully to warn of and intercept Bomber Command raids, a plan was already in place to combat the problem by adopting the oft-used and still-under-development

5 Group time-and-distance method. Briefings actually took place on the day before, when crews learned that the factory was housed in the old Zeppelin sheds at Friedrichshafen, situated on the shore of Lake Constance (Bodensee) on the frontier with Switzerland, and represented a very small target. The plan was to use a designated "Master of Ceremonies" to direct the bombing, much in the manner of Gibson at the Dams, and the officer chosen was the highly experienced G/C Len Slee, the former 49 Squadron commanding officer, with the popular W/C Gomm, commanding officer of 467 Squadron RAAF, as his deputy. 5 Group was to provide the main force element of fifty-six Lancasters, six of them from 49 Squadron, with four others from 8 Group's 97 (Straits Settlement) Squadron to provide the marking for the selected crews at the head of the stream. The plan called for the Channel to be crossed at a standard altitude, before descending gradually to 10,000 feet by the time that Orleans was reached, and thereafter, to fly at between 2,500 and 3,000 feet all the way to the Rhine. After crossing the Rhine, they were to climb to their briefed bombing height of between 5,000 and 10,000 feet for the rendezvous over the north-western shore of Lake Constance, and then circle until receiving the start signal.

The Fiskerton sextet took off between 21.33 and 21.47 with G/C Slee in his favourite ED702 but with F/O Gerry Fawke in the pilot's seat and Keith Astbury at the navigator's table, and they were accompanied by the crews of S/L Gilpin, F/Ls Munro and Taylor, P/O Price and Sgt Millar. All would make it to the target on a rare night when not a single aircraft from the entire force turned back, despite encountering electrical storms and having to adjust the briefed course. That said, ED702 lost an engine to flak over France, and Slee was forced to drop back into the formation and hand over the lead to W/C Gomm, who, on arrival at the target under clear skies and in bright moonlight, became concerned about the hostility of the searchlight and light flak defences. In order to reduce the very real risk of heavy casualties, he decided to add five thousand feet to the bombing height, where, unknown to him, the wind was stronger and would push the bombing towards the north-east. The Path Finder element also had little time to climb to the new height, and this caused a slight delay in the opening of the attack. The first TI fell wide of the aiming point, but the second one was assessed by W/C Gomm to be accurate, upon which he called in the first crews, whose high explosives and incendiaries created the expected smoke and obscured the target. He decided that another TI on the aiming point might still provide a reference for some crews, but the Path Finders were driven off by the searchlights and light flak and abandoned the attempt. They were then ordered to drop flares along the shore of Lake Constance, to enable the remaining crews to begin their runs from a pre-determined landmark, fly across the lake to the opposite shore, pick up another landmark 2,000 yards from the target and continue at a constant speed for the requisite number of seconds to cover the distance to bomb release. The 49 Squadron crews carried out their attacks on cascading green TIs from 11,000 to 13,000 feet between 02.45 and 02.58 and observed explosions and fires, some of which remained visible for eighty miles into the onward flight to landing grounds in North Africa, in what was the first official shuttle operation of the war. Post-raid reconnaissance revealed that a proportion of the bombs had hit the target, causing extensive damage, and there had been no losses among the attacking force.

While these crews were absent from England, a hectic round of four major operations to the Ruhr in the space of five nights began at Krefeld on the 21st, for which a force of 705 aircraft was assembled. 5 Group contributed ninety-two Lancasters, of which seven represented 49 Squadron, and they departed Fiskerton between 22.45 and 23.24 with the now P/O Cyril Anderson and crew operating for the first time since their return from 617 Squadron. There were no early returns, and all reached the target, situated a short distance to the south-west of Duisburg and on the opposite side of the Rhine. Conditions in the target area were ideal, with small amounts of thin cloud at between 6,000 and 10,000 feet and bright moonlight, which would benefit attacker and defender alike. The Path Finders delivered a near-perfect marking performance, red TIs falling in concentrated fashion to clearly identify the city centre aiming point for the main force crews, among which the 49 Squadron crews carried out their attacks from 15,000 to 22,000 feet between 01.36 and 02.25 and described a sea of red fire giving off masses of smoke, with one particular jet-black column rising through 18,000 feet as they turned away. All were convinced of the success of the operation, and one crew likened it to the Wuppertal-Barmen raid. There was no hint of troublesome flak or night-fighters, and yet forty-four aircraft failed to return, the heaviest casualties of the campaign to date. Many of these were lost to the Nachtjagd but 5 Group escaped relatively lightly with the loss of three Lancasters.

The medium-sized town of Mülheim-an-der-Ruhr, a close neighbour of Duisburg, Oberhausen and Essen, lies around a dozen miles to the north-east of Krefeld, and it was here that the red ribbon terminated on the target maps at briefings across the Command on the 22nd. A force of 557 aircraft was prepared, of which ninety of the Lancasters were provided by 5 Group, six of them representing 49 Squadron. The plan of attack called for eight Oboe Mosquitos plus two in reserve to drop yellow preliminary warning TIs on track, before marking the aiming-point with red TIs for twenty-nine Path Finder Lancasters to back up with greens. The 49 Squadron element departed Fiskerton between 22.30 and 23.00 but lost the services of Sgt Robinson and crew to port-outer engine failure. The others made their way via the Scheldt through the Cologne corridor and arrived at the target to find small amounts of cumulostratus cloud at between 5,000 and 10,000 feet, with red and green TIs clearly visible and defining the aiming point. The Fiskerton crews bombed from 18,000 to 20,000 feet between 01.21 and 01.48 and witnessed the development of a concentrated area of fire, which was visible from the Dutch coast homebound. Returning crews commented on the intense searchlight and flak response and the number of night-fighters, and reported that Krefeld was still burning from the night before. Local reports confirmed that the town had suffered severe damage, particularly in the northern districts, where 1,135 houses had been destroyed and more than 12,000 others damaged to some extent. The road and telephone communications to Oberhausen had been cut, preventing any passage out of the town other than on foot. In fact, some of the bombing had spilled into the eastern districts of Oberhausen, which was linked to Mülheim for air-raid purposes. It was another expensive night for the Command, however, which registered the loss of thirty-five aircraft, with the Halifaxes and Stirlings representing two-thirds of them and suffering a respective loss rate of 7.7% and 11.8%.

Later, on the 23rd, S/L Day arrived on posting from 1661 Conversion Unit to replace the missing S/L Storey. While the Path Finder and main force units were enjoying a night off and girding their loins for the next round of the Ruhr offensive, fifty of the 5 Group Lancasters that had landed in North Africa following the Friedrichshafen raid took off with two 97 (Straits Settlement) Squadron Path Finder aircraft to bomb the docks at La Spezia on the way home to England. The 49 Squadron crews of F/Ls Munro and Taylor and Sgt Millar took off from Blida in Algeria between 19.35 and 19.44, leaving behind S/L Gilpin and Sgt Price, whose aircraft were unserviceable, and arrived in the target area to find clear skies but hazy conditions made worse by a smoke-screen. There appeared to be a degree of confusion in getting the raid started, but a lucky hit on an oil storage facility resulted in a large explosion at 23.41 just as the main force was running-in, and most crews were able to identify the target visually, thereafter, and by red, green and white Path Finder flares. Bombing was carried out by the 49 Squadron trio in accordance with instructions from a Master Bomber from 9,000 to 10,250 feet between 23.45 and 00.05, and all returned safely home to moan about the length of time it had taken for the raid to develop and the poor communications with the raid controller. The authorities seemed happy to claim the destruction of the oil depot and an armaments store and declared the operation to be a success.

Having destroyed the Barmen half of Wuppertal at the end of May in one of the most devastating attacks to date, it was time to visit the same catastrophe on the western half, Elberfeld, for which a force of 630 aircraft was made ready on the 24th. 5 Group supported the operation with 103 Lancasters, seven of which were provided by 49 Squadron, and they departed Fiskerton between 22.12 and 22.51 with W/O "Chuffy" Bull and Sgt Jupp operating as crew captains for the first time. On this occasion, six Lancasters, three Stirlings and three Halifaxes of 8 Group were to deliver the yellow route markers on H2S, while seven Oboe Mosquitos marked the aiming-point with red TIs and eighteen Lancasters, seven Halifaxes and three Stirlings backed them up with greens. They made landfall over the Scheldt estuary and ran the usual gauntlet of searchlights and flak from the Cologne and Düsseldorf defence zones, the crews of which were aided by the formation of condensation trails at between 18,000 and 21,000 feet to advertise the presence of the bomber stream. There seemed to be fewer guns firing at them over the target, where small amounts of cloud with tops at 17,000 feet were insufficient to obscure the ground and the 5 Group crews carried out time-and-distant runs from yellow tracking flares until observing cascading red and green TIs. The 49 Squadron element bombed from 17,000 and 20,000 feet between 01.07 and 01.41 and those arriving at the tail end of the attack, when the built-up area was well-alight, described thick columns of smoke already passing through 19,000 feet and the glow of fires visible from the Dutch coast. Post-raid reconnaissance revealed another massively concentrated and accurate attack, which had reduced to rubble an estimated 90% of Elberfeld's built-up area, including three thousand houses and 171 industrial premises. It had also severely damaged 2,500 houses and dozens of important factory buildings, and the fact that more buildings were destroyed than damaged, provided a telling commentary on the conditions on the ground. The number of fatalities stood at around eighteen hundred, and some of the survivors might have been cheered to know that thirty-four bombers, containing 240 of their tormentors, would not be returning to England that night. Remarkably, only two of these belonged to 5 Group.

Instructions were received across the Command on the 25th to prepare for the first major attack on the Ruhr city of Gelsenkirchen since 1941, when it had been a regular destination under the Oil Directive. A force of 473 aircraft was assembled, and the crews briefed to focus on the Nordstern synthetic oil plant (Gelsenberg A.G.), which was a Bergius-process manufacturer of high-grade petroleum products, particularly aviation fuel. 8 Group was to provide seven Oboe Mosquitos plus two in reserve to drop route markers and sky mark the aiming-point, and two others to bomb after the main force had finished, but none of its heavy aircraft was to be involved. 5 Group stations bombed up 114 Lancasters, seven at Fiskerton with a cookie, four 500 pounders and thirteen SBCs of 4lb and 30lb incendiaries each and they were dispatched between 22.25 and 22.55. F/O Randall and crew were closing on the Dutch/German frontier when attacked by a Ju88, at which the gunners opened fire at four hundred yards range and seemed to have shaken it off. As they completed an orbit to resume course, the enemy reappeared from the starboard beam, flew over the Lancaster's cockpit and collided with the port wing, tearing off the aileron and damaging the flaps and a fuel tank. They were left with no choice but to jettison the load and turn for home. The others reached the target area to find ten-tenths stratus lying over the region with tops at 10,000 to 15,000 feet, which would not have been a problem for Oboe, had five of the twelve participating Mosquitos not suffered equipment failures. This caused tracking flares to be late and to drop in the wrong sequence in a somewhat scattered manner at a time when the crews were contending with an intense flak barrage. Searchlights illuminated the cloud as those from 49 Squadron bombed on red flares with green stars from 18,500 to 20,000 feet between 01.29 and 01.54. A large explosion was witnessed at 01.43, and the glow from the target was visible from the Dutch coast, to which the returning bombers were chased by a large deployment of enemy night-fighters. Post-raid reconnaissance and local reports confirmed that the operation had failed to achieve accuracy and concentration, and in an echo of the past, bombs had been sprayed all over the Ruhr, leaving Gelsenkirchen largely untouched. Thirty aircraft were missing, and this time eight of them were from 5 Group, four alone from 106 Squadron.

A series of three operations against Cologne would span the turn of the month and began on the night of the 28/29th, when 608 aircraft took off in the late evening to deliver what would be the Rhineland capital's greatest ordeal of the war to date. At briefings, crews took in the details, which, for those of 8 Group, involved nine Mosquitos dropping green flares as route markers sixteen miles short of the target, and then red TIs and red flares with green stars on the aiming-point, which four Stirlings, ten Halifaxes and eighteen Lancasters were to back up with green TIs. 5 Group contributed 131 Lancasters, the 49 Squadron element of nine departing Fiskerton between 22.26 and 23.21 with W/C Johnson the senior pilot on duty and S/L Day flying as second pilot to F/L Taylor. P/O Moss and crew dropped out within ninety minutes after their rear turret became unserviceable, leaving the remainder to press on to the target area, where they encountered ten-tenths cloud below them at 8,000 to 10,000 feet and good visibility above. The main force crews were unaware that five of the Oboe Mosquitos had turned back and a sixth was unable to drop its skymarkers, leaving just six to do so, and these were behind schedule by seven minutes and could manage only intermittent flares. The omens for a successful attack were not good, particularly as skymarking was the least reliable method because of drift, but by the time the Fiskerton crews arrived, they were greeted by red and white flares. They carried out their attacks from 17,000 to 22,000 feet between 01.50 and 02.21 and deduced from the glow beneath the clouds and the presence of smoke rising through them that they had contributed to a successful operation. This was confirmed by post-raid reconnaissance and local reports, which provided details of forty-three industrial buildings and 6,374 others completely destroyed, and a further fifteen thousand sustaining damage to some extent. The death toll was put at 4,377, the greatest by far from a Bomber Command attack, and 230,000 others had lost their homes for varying periods. By recent standards, the figure of twenty-five missing aircraft could be considered moderate, but that was no consolation to the individual stations with an empty dispersal pan.

During the course of the month the squadron participated in eleven operations and dispatched ninety-seven sorties for the loss of six Lancasters and their crews.

# July 1943

The first two days of the new month were beset by poor weather conditions, which kept all but a few gardeners and Mosquitos on the ground. The second attack of the current campaign against Cologne was scheduled for the night of the 3/4th, and crews were called to briefings on all operational stations during the late afternoon as a force of 653 aircraft was assembled. The Path Finder crews listened with interest as they were told that ten Mosquitos would drop green flares four-and-a-half miles from the target as a preliminary warning, and red, green and white flares and red TIs on the aiming-point. On this night, the aiming-point was on the East Bank of the Rhine in the industrial Deutz district, where the Klöckner-Humboldt-Deutz works manufactured aero-engines and heavy and tracked vehicles for the Wehrmacht, served by the nearby Kalk and Gremberg marshalling yards. Nine Halifaxes and twenty-four Lancasters were to back up the red TIs with greens, but in the event that cloud concealed the TIs, they were to bomb on H2S with the main force, along with the remaining nine Halifaxes and seventeen Lancasters. 5 Group contributed 141 Lancasters, the thirteen made ready at Fiskerton taking off in two phases between 22.17 and 23.11 with W/C Johnson and F/L Munro the senior pilots on duty. The meteorological experts had forecast nine-tenths cloud from the English coast all the way to the target, but what the leading Path Finder heavy crews actually encountered was a clear sky and red Oboe-laid TIs in the bomb sights, which they backed up with greens. There was a certain amount of haze or perhaps, two to three-tenths cloud at 8,000 feet, but this did not interfere with the accuracy of the attack, which developed in concentrated form in the face, initially, of an intense flak defence. The crews of W/C Johnson, F/L Munro and P/O Tolchard were drawn on by green tracking flares and bombed in the first phase from 19,000 to 21,000 feet between 01.20 and 01.29. By the time the raid reached its crescendo, Cologne was visible to approaching crews from a hundred miles away and it was nine-tenths smoke rather than cloud that greeted them and through which the later-arriving 49 Squadron participants delivered their bombs on red and green TIs from 18,000 to 21,000 feet between 01.51 and 02.04. Returning crews described a highly successful raid, which left the city a mass of flames visible from 170 miles into the homeward flight, with smoke rising to 10,000 feet and blotting out ground detail. F/L Munro and crew reported that they had witnessed a large explosion to the west of the Rhine and a mile from the planned aiming point at 01.18 and noted that the early bombing had been falling short. Some other crews also noticed a creep-back, while the overall impression was of another operation more successful than the Thousand raid against this city at the end of May 1942. Post-raid reconnaissance and local reports confirmed another stunningly accurate and concentrated attack, in which twenty industrial premises and 2,200 houses had been destroyed and 72,000 people bombed out of their homes at a cost to the Command of thirty aircraft.

Some crews commented on the presence of day fighters over the target, and this was clear evidence of a new tactic being employed by the Luftwaffe. The newly formed JG300 was operating for the first time, employing the Wilde Sau (Wild Boar) tactics, which was the brainchild of former bomber pilot, Major Hans-Joachim (Hajo) Herrmann. The unit had been formed in June with borrowed standard BF109 and FW190 single-engine day fighters to operate directly over a target, seeking out bombers silhouetted against the fires and TIs. On this night, the unit would claim twelve victories but would have to share them with the flak batteries, which claimed them also. Unaccustomed to being pursued by fighters over a target, it would take time for the bomber crews to work out what was happening, and until they did, friendly fire would often be blamed for damage incurred by unseen causes.

The series against Cologne would be completed on the 8th by an all-Lancaster heavy force of 282 aircraft drawn from 1, 5 and 8 Groups, with six Oboe Mosquitos to carry out the initial marking. 5 Group provided 151 Lancasters, of which fourteen were made ready at Fiskerton and dispatched between 22.10 and 22.25 with S/L Day and F/L Taylor the senior pilots on duty. They had to fly through the tops of towering cumulonimbus as they made their way to the target, where ten-tenths cloud at around 10,000 to 15,000 feet concealed the ground from view. Tracking flares guided the main force crews to the aiming point, but the release-point flares were late and some crews bombed on e.t.a. before they were deployed. The 49 Squadron crews mostly carried out their attacks on red flares with green stars from 20,000 to 21,000 feet between 01.17 and 01.30 in the face of an intense flak barrage. The Anderson crew witnessed a large explosion at 01.17, which lit up the clouds for eight seconds and another very large orange explosion was observed by other crews at 01.23. Post-raid reconnaissance and local reports revealed a highly successful operation, which had caused extensive damage in north-western and south-western districts, where nineteen industrial premises and 2,381 houses had been destroyed. The success cost a modest seven Lancasters, five of them from 5 Group, among which was 49 Squadron's ED663 containing the crew of Sgt Eyles. The Lancaster was shot down by the night-fighter of Oblt Heinz-Wolfgang Schnaufer of II./NJG1 and crashed without survivors some ten miles east of Antwerp at 02.53. When the dust had settled over Cologne, the local authorities catalogued the destruction over the three raids of more than eleven thousand buildings and a death toll of almost 5,500 people, with a further 350,000 rendered homeless.

The Ruhr campaign was winding down by the time that Gelsenkirchen was posted across Lancaster and Halifax stations on the 9th as the target for that night, for which a heavy force of 408 aircraft was made ready. At briefings, the crews learned of the plan, which required seven Oboe Mosquitos to drop red flares twenty miles short of the target and green flares nine miles further on, before marking the aiming-point with white flares and reds with green stars. Eleven 49 Squadron Lancasters were among 112 representing 5 Group, and they departed Fiskerton between 22.07 and 22.43 with F/L Munro the senior pilot on duty. Sgt Coxhill and crew turned back after around one hour because of an unserviceable rear turret as the others made their way to the target above ten-tenths cloud, which stretched over the Ruhr at around 16,000 feet and topped out in places at 20,000 feet. The Oboe skymarkers were several minutes late, partly as a result of a 50% failure rate of the Oboe equipment, while a sixth Mosquito dropped its markers ten miles to the north. The 49 Squadron crews carried out their attacks mostly on red and green skymarkers or on e.t.a. from 20,000 to 22,300 feet between 01.12 and 01.46 and reported large explosions at 01.22, 01.38 and 01.41, the last one lighting up the sky like day for ten seconds. A red glow beneath the cloud suggested that an extensive fire was developing, but returning crews could offer only impressions at debriefing and none was certain as to the outcome. According to local reports, it had appeared that the attack had been meant for Bochum and Wattenscheid, which received more bombs than Gelsenkirchen, where limited damage occurred in southern districts.

Although two more operations to the region would be launched late in the month, Harris was already planning his next attempt to shorten the war by bombing and was buoyed by the success of the spring offensive. He could look back on the past four and a half months with genuine satisfaction at the performance of his squadrons, and as a champion of technological innovation, take particular pride in the performance of Oboe, which had been the decisive factor. Although losses had been grievously high and the Ruhr's reputation as "Happy Valley" well earned, its most important towns and cities had suffered catastrophic destruction. In Britain, the aircraft factories had more than kept pace with the rate of attrition, while the training units both at home and overseas were pouring eager new crews into the fray to fill the gaps. With confidence high in the ability of his Command to destroy almost any target at will, Harris prepared for his next major campaign, the erasure from the map of a prominent German city in a short, sharp series of maximum effort raids to be launched during the final week of the month.

In the meantime, 1, 5 and 8 Groups were alerted to prepare for a trip to Italy to attack the city of Turin, for which 295 Lancasters were made ready on the 12th, 130 of them provided by 5 Group. The twelve-strong 49 Squadron element departed Fiskerton between 22.10 and 22.29 with S/L Gilpin and F/Ls Munro and Taylor the senior pilots on duty and set course for Dungeness on the Kent coast with the intention of making landfall on the French coast at Cayeux-sur-Mer. S/L Gilpin and crew turned back when their rear turret became unserviceable, leaving the others to negotiate poor weather conditions, including icing over France. They pinpointed on Lake Annecy in the foothills of the Alps before arriving in the target area to be greeted by clear skies, good visibility and defences up to their usual poor standard, characterised by ineffective searchlights and inaccurate light flak rising to 15,000 feet. The marking was punctual, accurate and concentrated, inviting the bombing by the 49 Squadron crews to be carried out from 16,300 to 18,000 feet between 01.50 and 02.17, and a column of black smoke was observed rising through 12,000 feet as they withdrew. The return route involved a low-level circumnavigation of the Brest peninsula, and many of the thirteen missing Lancasters disappeared without trace into the sea after running into enemy night-fighters in this area. This may have been the fate of the crew of F/O Millar AFM in ED726, which disappeared without trace, and was certainly where W/C Nettleton VC, the veteran of the Augsburg raid and commanding officer of 44 (Rhodesia) Squadron went down. Reconnaissance showed the main weight of the attack to have fallen just north of the city centre, and a local report stated that 792 people had lost their lives, the largest number of fatalities from a Bomber Command attack on Italy.

Aachen, Germany's most westerly city and an important railway hub between Germany and the occupied countries, was posted as the target on the 13th and a force of 374 aircraft made ready. This consisted largely of Halifaxes, Wellingtons and Stirlings and in the absence of a 5 Group presence, just eighteen Lancasters among the 8 Group contribution. It was left to local sources to confirm the severity of the damage inflicted upon the city, which amounted to 2,927 buildings completely destroyed, with many industrial, public and cultural buildings seriously damaged.

On the 15th, a dozen 617 Squadron crews carried out the squadron's first operation since the Dams in company with twelve others from 5 Group, when targeting two electrical transformer stations near Bologna and Genoa to disrupt railway movements of enemy reinforcements to Sicily. The operations were only modestly effective, and it was decided to attack two similar targets on the following night, one at Cislago and the identity of the other was unrecorded. Eighteen crews from 44 (Rhodesia), 49 and 57 Squadrons flew over to Scampton for briefing and learned that 57 Squadron's W/C Hopcroft had been appointed to command with S/L Gilpin as his deputy. The 49 Squadron trio, which included the crews of F/L Munro and P/O Tomlin, took off between 22.00

and 22.30 and all reached the target area to find a full moon, clear skies and excellent visibility. S/L Gilpin attacked the Cislago site, situated on the north-western outskirts of Milan, from 1,000 feet, before bombing the secondary target at Reggio Nel Amelia from 1,500 feet. The crews of F/L Munro and P/O Tomlin also attacked the secondary target in accordance with the instructions of W/C Hopcroft, before all flew on to Blida in Algeria, where they landed between 08.45 and 08.50 after more than ten hours aloft.

Hamburg had been a regular target for the Command throughout the war to date, and had been attacked, amongst other occasions, during the final week of July in 1940, 1941 and 1942. It had been spared by the weather from hosting the first "One Thousand" bomber raid at the end of May 1942, but Harris now identified it as the ideal candidate for destruction under Operation Gomorrah, the intention of which was to cause the maximum impact to the enemy's morale in a short, sharp campaign employing ten thousand tons of bombs. Hamburg's political status was second only to Berlin's, and its value to the war effort in terms of ship and U-Boot construction and other war production was undeniable, but it suited Harris's criteria also in other respects. Its location close to a coastline aided navigation and made it accessible from the North Sea without the need to spend time over hostile territory, and its relatively short distance from the bomber stations enabled a force to approach and retreat during the few hours of darkness afforded by mid-summer. Finally, lying beyond the range of Oboe, which had proved so decisive at the Ruhr, Hamburg had the wide River Elbe to provide a solid H2S signature for the navigators high above.

There had been no operations for most squadrons for nine days, despite a number being posted, and by the time that 791 crews trooped into their respective briefing rooms on the 24th, they probably expected the day to end with yet another scrub. Instead, they were read a special message from the commander-in-chief, to announce the beginning of the Battle of Hamburg. They listened intently to the revelation that they would be aided by the first operational use of "Window", aluminium-backed strips of paper of precise length, which, when released in bundles into the airstream at a predetermined point, would drift down slowly in vast clouds to swamp the enemy night-fighter, searchlight and gun-laying radar with false returns and render it blind. The device had actually been available for a year, but its use had been vetoed in case the enemy copied it for use against Britain. It was not realized that Germany had, in fact, already developed its own version called Düppel, which it had withheld for the same reason.

The plan of attack called for eleven Lancasters and nine Halifaxes to drop yellow TIs as route markers, before continuing on to mark the aiming-point with yellow TIs, and if conditions permitted, illuminator flares. The route markers were to be backed up by six Stirlings, thirteen Lancasters and nine Halifaxes, and six Lancasters and two Halifaxes were to use the yellow TIs as a guide, and with the aid of flares, mark the aiming-point with red TIs, which would be backed up with green TIs by the remaining marker crews. 5 Group supported the operation with 143 Lancasters, a dozen of them belonging to 49 Squadron, which departed Fiskerton between 22.20 and 23.04 with W/C Johnson and S/L Day the senior pilots on duty. Meanwhile, almost twelve hundred miles to the south, the crews of S/L Gilpin, F/L Munro and P/O Tomlin were taking off from Blida to bomb the docks at Leghorn on their way back to Fiskerton. They would arrive home safely in a fifteen-minute window from 05.35 and report that they had attacked the target in generally poor visibility from 15,000 to 18,000 feet between 00.51 and 00.57. F/L Munro's bomb-aimer had a large factory in the bomb sight and his counterpart in P/O Tomlin's aircraft an iron foundry, while S/L Gilpin reported two large fires and smoke rising through 8,000 feet, probably from an oil refinery that was seen to explode to the north of the town.

There were no early returns to deplete the squadron's contribution to the main event, and at a predetermined point over the North Sea, wireless operators began to dispense Window through the flare chute, beginning shortly after 00.30, and the effects appeared to be immediate as few fighters rose to meet the approaching bombers. A number of aircraft were shot down over the sea during the outward flight, two of them 103 Squadron Lancasters, but these were off course and outside of the protection of the bomber stream and may well have been among those returning early with technical difficulties. The efficacy of Window was made more apparent in the target area, where the crews noticed an absence of the usually efficient co-ordination between the searchlights and flak batteries and defence appeared random and sporadic. This offered the Path Finders the opportunity to mark the target by visual reference and H2S virtually unmolested, and although the red and green TIs were a little misplaced and scattered, they landed in sufficient numbers close to the city centre to provide the main force crews with ample opportunity to deliver a massive blow. It rarely happened that aircraft arrived in strict bands according to their task, and some main force crews were already over the target from the opening of the raid at 01.00. The 49 Squadron crews carried out their attacks from 17,000 and 21,000 feet between 01.04 and 01.45 and returning crews reported a successful operation that had left part of the city ablaze with a column of smoke rising through 20,000 feet. Post-raid reconnaissance revealed that a six-mile-long creep-back had developed, which cut a swathe of destruction from the city centre along the line of approach, out across the north-western districts and into open country, where a proportion of the bombing had been wasted. In fact, less than half of the force had bombed within three miles of the city centre during the fifty-minute-long raid, in which 2,284 tons of bombs had been delivered, despite which, the city had suffered a telling blow, and fifteen hundred of its inhabitants lay dead. For the Command it was an encouraging start to the campaign, particularly in the light of just twelve missing aircraft, for which Window was largely responsible.

P/O Tolchard and crew were rewarded for their efforts thus far with a posting on the 25th to 97 (Straits Settlement) Squadron of the Path Finder Force. That night, and in the expectation that Hamburg would be covered by smoke, Harris switched his force to Essen, where he could take advantage of the body blow dealt to the enemy defensive system by Window. A force of 705 aircraft was made ready and a plan prepared, which called for Halifaxes and Lancasters of 35 (Madras Presidency) and 156 Squadrons to drop preliminary yellow warning TIs on track by H2S, which would be backed up by elements of 7 and 156 Squadrons. Ahead, fourteen Oboe Mosquitos would mark the aiming-point with red TIs, which nineteen Lancasters, nine Halifaxes and five Stirlings were to back up with greens. 5 Group detailed 136 Lancasters, the fourteen at Fiskerton taking off between 21.32 and 22.19 with no senior pilots on duty and over the ensuing two hours lost the services of the crews of P/O Anderson and Sgt Hales to a faulty bomb sight, double engine failure and an engine fire respectively. They were among seventeen early returns from the 5 Group contingent, the remainder arriving in the target area to find four to five-tenths cloud to the west but clear skies over the aiming-point, with just the usual ground haze to spoil the vertical visibility. The Fiskerton crews carried out their bombing runs at 17,000 to 21,500 feet between 00.32 and 01.12 and watched a highly concentrated attack develop, which left the ground enveloped in smoke from the many fires and explosions. Returning crews reported concentrated fires around the aiming-point in a one-and-a-half-square-mile area of the city, two large, red explosions at 00.36

and 00.39 and a column of smoke rising through 20,000 feet as they withdrew to the west, the glow remaining visible from as far away as the Dutch coast. Post-raid reconnaissance confirmed the raid to be another outstanding success against this important war materials producing city, with more than 2,800 houses destroyed, while the complex of Krupp manufacturing sites suffered its heaviest damage of the war to date. Twenty-six aircraft failed to return, only two of which belonged to 5 Group.

During the course of the 27th, a force of 787 aircraft was assembled for round two of Operation Gomorrah, for which 5 Group detailed 155 Lancasters, sixteen of them made ready by 49 Squadron. They attended briefing to learn that yellow route markers would be dropped by H2S on the enemy coast and backed up, and that "Y" aircraft (H2S blind markers) were to deliver red TIs and a stick of flares over the aiming-point for visual markers to confirm and back up with green TIs. They departed Fiskerton between 22.15 and 23.05 with S/L Day the senior pilot on duty and all reached the Schleswig-Holstein coast to the north of Hansastadt Hamburg, none of them having any concept of the events that were to follow their arrival. A previously unknown and terrible phenomenon was about to present itself to the world and introduce a new word "firestorm" into the English language. A number of factors would conspire on this night to seal the fate of this great city and its hapless inhabitants in an orgy of destruction that was quite unprecedented in air warfare. An uncharacteristically hot and dry spell of weather had left the city a tinderbox, and the spark to ignite it came with the Path Finders' H2S-laid yellow and green TIs, which fell with almost total concentration some two miles to the east of the intended city-centre aiming-point and into the densely populated working-class residential districts of Hamm, Hammerbrook and Borgfeld. To compound this, the main force, which had been drawn on to the target by yellow release-point flares, bombed with rare precision and almost no creep-back and deposited much of its 2,300 tons of bombs into this relatively compact area. The 49 Squadron crews delivered their bomb loads from 16,000 to 21,500 feet and observed many explosions and a sea of flames developing below. Those bombing towards the later stages of the raid observed a pall of smoke rising through 20,000 feet, and the glow of fires was reported to remain visible for up to two hundred miles into the return journey.

On the ground, individual fires began to join together to form one giant conflagration, which sucked in oxygen from surrounding areas at hurricane speeds to feed its voracious appetite. Trees were uprooted and flung bodily into the inferno, along with debris and people and temperatures at the seat of the flames exceeded one thousand degrees Celcius. The defences were overwhelmed and the fire service unable to pass through the rubble-strewn streets to gain access to the worst-affected areas. Even had they done so, they could not have entered the firestorm area, and only after all of the combustible material had been consumed did the flames subside. By this time, there was no-one alive to rescue and an estimated forty thousand people died on this one night alone. A mass exodus from the city, which would ultimately exceed one million people, began on the following morning and this undoubtedly saved many from the ravages of the next raid, which would come two nights hence. Seventeen aircraft failed to return, reflecting the enemy's developing response to the advantage gained by the Command through Window. No gain was ever permanent, however, and the balance of power would continue to shift from one side to the other for the next year. For a change, it was the Lancaster brigade that sustained the highest numerical casualties on this night, accounting for eleven of the failures to return.

Bomber Command's heavy brigade stayed at home on the following night, while four Mosquitos carried out a nuisance raid on Hamburg to ensure that the residents' sleep was disturbed. A force of 777 aircraft was put together to continue Hamburg's torment on the 29th, while the crews attended briefings to learn of their part in the proceedings. They were told that red TIs and flares were to be employed as route markers, before seventeen Lancasters and eight Halifaxes marked the aiming-point with yellow TIs by H2S to be backed up by thirty-four Lancasters, six Stirlings and nine Halifaxes. 5 Group contributed 148 Lancasters, of which sixteen were made ready by 49 Squadron and departed Fiskerton between 22.14 and 22.55 with no senior pilots on duty. After thirty-five minutes, Sgt Greig's rear gunner reported that his turret was not fully functional and the decision was taken to turn back, leaving the others to press on across the North Sea and reach the target area to find clear skies and the city protected only by slight ground haze. The plan involved approaching from due north to hit the northern and north-eastern districts, which, thus far, had escaped serious damage, but the Path Finders strayed two miles to the east of the intended track and dropped their markers just to the south of the already devastated firestorm area. A four-mile creep-back rescued the situation for the Command, by spreading along the line of approach into the residential districts of Wandsbek and Barmbek and parts of Uhlenhorst and Winterhude. The 49 Squadron crews carried out their attacks from 17,000 to 22,500 feet between 00.44 and 01.20 and released their loads on yellow and green TIs, before returning home to report smoke rising through 17,000 feet and fires visible for two hundred miles into the homeward journey. It was another massive blow against this proud city, but as the defenders began to recover from the effects of Window, so the bomber losses began to creep up, and twenty-eight aircraft failed to return home on this night, five of them from 5 Group.

Before the final round of Operation Gomorrah took place, the curtain on the Ruhr offensive was brought down finally with a raid on the town of Remscheid, situated on the southern edge of the region some six miles south of Wuppertal, where the main industries were mechanical engineering and tool-making. Up until this point, only twenty-six people had lost their lives in this town as a result of stray bombs, but it was now to face a modest force of 273 aircraft consisting of roughly equal numbers of Lancasters, Halifaxes and Stirlings with six Oboe Mosquitos to mark out the aiming-point with red TIs. 5 Group put up thirty-nine Lancasters, four of which were loaded with a cookie and up to seventeen SBCs of various incendiaries at Fiskerton and sent on their way between 21.00 and 22.03 bearing aloft the crews of S/L Day, F/L Taylor, P/O Tomlin and F/Sgt Kirton. They all reached the target area to find clear skies and good visibility and bombed on red TIs from 17,500 to 19,500 feet between 01.04 and 01.10, observing the burst of many cookies and a pall of smoke rising through 5,000 feet. They returned home with a red glow in the sky behind them that remained visible as they crossed the enemy coast homebound and gave promise of another Ruhr town in ruins. It would be left to a post-war bombing survey to establish that a mere 871 tons of bombs had laid waste to around 83% of Remscheid's built-up area, destroying 107 industrial buildings and 3,117 houses. Three months war production was lost, and the town's industry never recovered fully. Fifteen aircraft failed to return, and the Stirling brigade suffered 10% casualties.

During the course of the month, the squadron carried out ten operations and dispatched 118 sorties for the loss of two Lancasters and crews.

*The Sgt K R Millar Crew*
L-R: Unknown, Sgt M H King, Sgt R H Pennells, Sgt K R Millar, Sgt F R Birks, F/Sgt W Foster, unknown, Sgt J H Harsley. (One of the unknowns will be Sgt F Earnshaw).
P/O Millar, Sgt Birks, F/Sgts Pennells DFM, King and Harsley all killed 26th November 1943 while with 83 Squadron on a Berlin operation.

*F/Sgt Webb and Crew. Fiskerton August/September 1943.*
Successfully carried out their tour between August 1943 and January 1944. Back L-R Harold Hayes (FE), Fred Woodhouse, (MUG), Harold Ollerenshaw, (BA), Percy Horton (RG). Front Eric Lovick, (W/O), Ernie Webb (Pilot), Johnny Chaloner.(Nav).

*49 Squadron Lancasters at Fiskerton 1944. The FIDO pipeline can be seen in the foreground.*

*Rear Gunner in Lancaster EA-D*

*Sgt George Boulton*
*Navigator/Bomb Aimer with Sgt Armstrong's Crew. PoW then repatriated May 1944.*

*Crash site of Lancaster ED620*
Sgt Adam Anderson's Lancaster ED620 was hit by flak and crashed in Denmark on what was the crew's $2^{nd}$ operation on the 20/21$^{st}$ April 1943. Three crew members were killed and Sgt Anderson died later in hospital; the remaining three crew members survived to become PoW's. Their comrades rest in Lemvig Cemetery. Sgt A. Anderson (Pilot) KIA, Sgt A. Telfer (FE) KIA, Sgt G. Boulton (N/AB) PoW, Sgt G.J. Evans Wop/AG, (KIA) Sgt G. Barclay (AG) PoW, Sgt W.A. Cook (BA) KIA, Sgt W.P. Hayworth (AG) PoW.

*F/Sgt Gordon Edy DFM*
*Completed tour with 49 Squadron December 1943.*

*P/O A H Blackmore DFC*
*KIA 20th December 1943.*

*F/Sgt John Turner and Sgt Edward Pope*
Lancaster ED719 was shot down on the 9th August 1943 on a Mannheim raid. All crew survived and air gunner John Turner is pictured above 2nd from left. 4th is Eddie Pope, a 49 Squadron PoW since November 1942. Taken at Stalag Luft 1 at Barth near the Baltic coast in October 1943.

*The Taverner Crew*
*P/O Philip Taverner and F/Sgt E Parker were both killed on the 22$^{nd}$ October 1943 during a Kassel raid. The remaining members of the crew became PoW's.*

*P/O Philip Taverner far right.*

*The Tolchard Crew*
*Possibly L-R: Sgt G H Porter, Sgt D Doe. F/Sgt GW Coburn, P/O L H Tolchard, F/O L R Hastings, Sgt W George Sgt A E Best in front of Lancaster ED448.*

*Examining a rear turret 1943/44*
*U.S Capt. Stevenson, S/L Denis Miller CO 'B' Flight, W/C A.A.Adams, CO 49 Squadron*

*Sgt James Milburn*
*Flew 32 operations with 49 Sqn*

*Cpl Mary Pratt and F/L Evans in Scampton's Intelligence Section.*

*F/O Hinderley*

Debrief with F/O Hinderley. Back from Berlin 23rd November 1943. L-R Intel Officer, navigator, F/O Hidderley - pilot of Lancaster JB339, G/C Grindell, AOC RNZAF Navigator may be P/O Wittmer.

*The F/O John Millar Crew*

Lancaster ED726 was lost without trace on the 13$^{th}$ July 1943 during a Turin raid. All are commemorated on the Runnymede memorial. It was their 13$^{th}$ operation.

Above: In hatch, Sgt John Crabb (not on raid) with Sgt Paul Goodyear (KIA) on right. Front L-R: Sgt Reginald Burnett (KIA), F/O John Millar AFM (KIA), Sgt Leslie Phillips (not on raid), Sgt Donald Bettinson. (KIA). Also lost was F/Sgt J.W. Gillin RCAF, F/O G. Lockie and Sgt H Read. Crew on their 13$^{th}$ operation.

*Debriefing the Tancred crew following a raid to Berlin on 22/23$^{rd}$ November 1943. L-R: Intelligence Officer, F/L Andrew Lawson-Tancred (Pilot), Sgt T Smith (face obscured), F/Sgt W. Branigan (drinking), Sgt R Phipps, Sgt D Shaw (standing at the rear), Sgt E Sullivan (wearing the red scarf) and Sgt H Jerrard (smoking with back to the camera). All lost on a Brunswick operation 14/15$^{th}$ January 1944.*

*The crews of Lancaster ED721 taken at Fiskerton, Summer 1943.*
*Rear row: 4th from left is Sgt Jock Stopani, 5th is Sgt Bob Seddon, 6th is Sgt John Costello.*
*Front row 2nd from left Sgt George Boag, 3rd Sgt Steve Sherman, 4th Sgt Eric Winstanley, 5th P/O Tommy Taylor (Pilot).*

*RAF reconnaissance photograph of V-2 rockets at Peenemünde Test Stands I and VII*

*S/L George Gilpin DFC & Bar
Flew nine operations with 49 Squadron.*

*F/L William Townsend DFM
Flew 27 operations with 49 Squadron. He was
posted to 617 Squadron and took part in and
survived the famous Dambusters raid. Pilot of
Lancaster AJ-O, he attacked the Ennepe Dam.*

*Unknown crew on the transport at Dunholm Lodge*

*Sgt John Minchin*
*Flew 28 operations with 49 Squadron.*
*Killed on Dams Raid 16/17th May 1943.*

*S/L James Warwick DFC.*
*Flew 27 operations with 49 Squadron from May 1943 to January 1944. He was was killed on 19th September 1944 flying as Navigator with W/C Guy Gibson in a Mosquito of 627 Squadron on a Rheydt operation.*

*The Munro Crew*
*L-R: F/S B. Dreaver, Sgt Jim Rushton, F/O B.L. Schauenberg, F/L R.C. Munro, Wood (MUG), F/O J.D. Harris.*

*Sgt Gilbert Green and Sgt William Powell*
*Both killed in action. F/Sgt Green, bomb aimer with P/O C Anderson's crew on Mannheim raid September 1943 and F/L William Powell on the 29$^{th}$ July 1944 during a Stuttgart raid.*

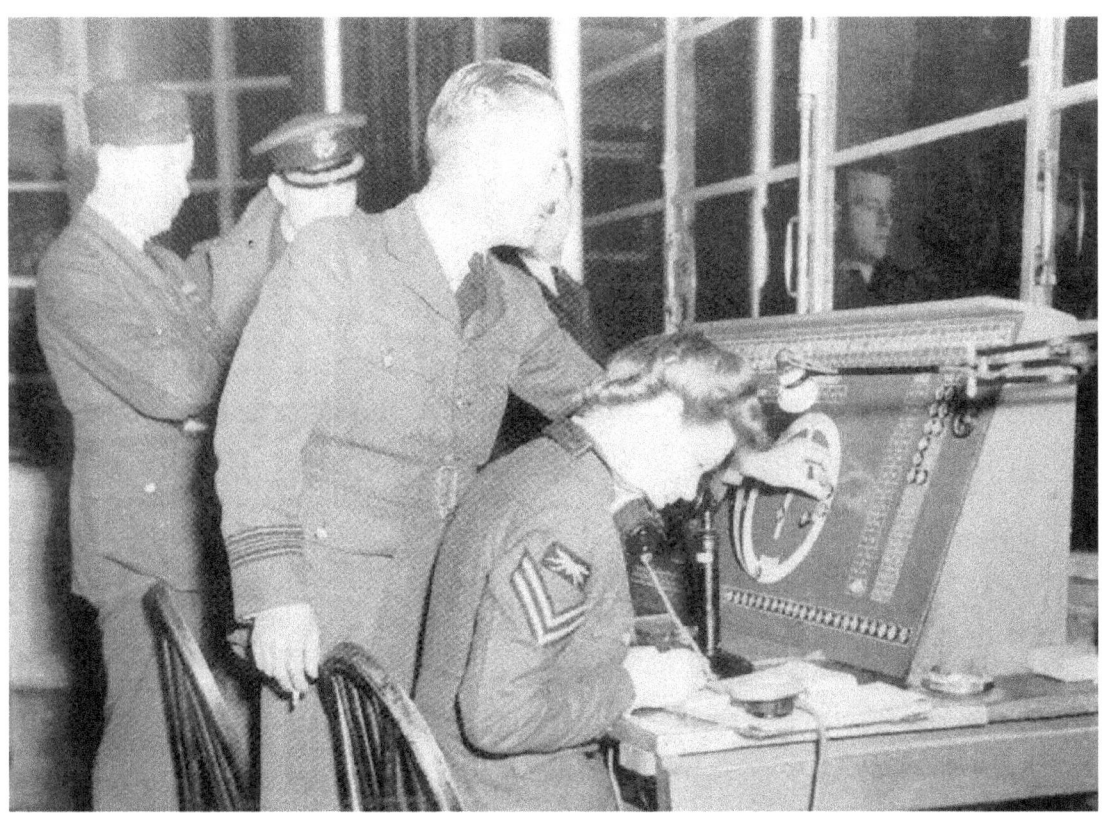

*Fiskerton Control*

Pilot: Sgt "Jock" Morrison | Flight Engineer: Sgt Tom J Page | Navigator: Sgt Jimmy Dorian | Bomb Aimer: Sgt Hughie C Annett

Wireless Operator: Sgt Ralph I Green | Mid Upper Gunner: Sgt Ernie Green | Rear Gunner: Sgt "Taffy" Maggs

*The Morrison Crew –*
*On the 20th October 1944 after a raid on Leipzig, W/O Morrison completed his tour of 30 operations.*

*F/L Norman Carfoot KIA 3rd November 1943.*

*F/L J R Hill. KIA 22nd June 1944.*

*Fiskerton Motor Transport Section*

*49 Squadron in formation*

*Riddled with bullets from a night-fighter, Lancaster ED438 of 49 Squadron came to grief on 3/4th November 1943, the target being Düsseldorf. The aircraft was shot down on its 57th operation. Five of the crew including pilot F/L Cecil Thomas were killed.(Below).*

Lancaster ED438 (EA-R)
F/L C.G. Thomas Pilot (KIA), P/O J.E. Teager 2nd Pilot (PoW), Sgt N.D. Panter FE (PoW), F/Sgt W.G. Clutterbuck Nav (KIA), Sgt W.A. Payne Wop/AG (PoW), Sgt H. Minns AG (KIA), F/O C.P. Ross BA (KIA), Sgt G.E. Boxer AG (KIA)

*Avro Lancaster D for Donald returns to RAF Fiskerton after bombing Berlin, 22nd November 1943. A month later the aircraft and crew were lost as a result of another Berlin operation.*

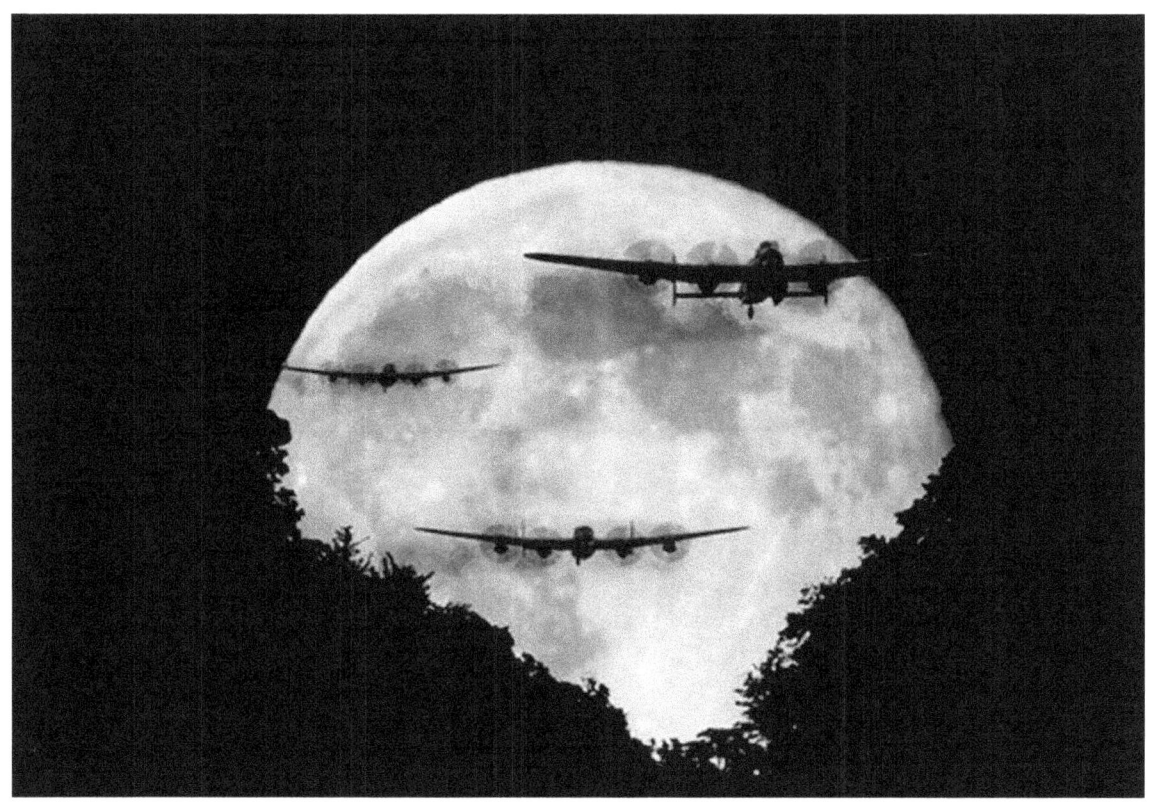

*Bomber Moon*

*Some of the ground staff at Fiskerton in the summer of 1943.*
Back L-R: Arnold Hazelwood, Joe Steel, Bill Wooton, Rex Yates, Chas Allen, Derek Richmond, Fred Cheadle, Les Jarvis, Bill Hyland, 'Pash' Palmer. Front L-R:.Unknown, Harry Williams, Brandon, Charley Grossey, Ted Ousten, Jack Barnes, Bill Fox, Ted Paling.

*49 Squadron Line-up with W/C Slee*

*P/O John Lett*  *Sgt Frank Campbell*

Flying in Lancaster JB421, P/O Jack Lett and crew made a successful attack when the main entrance door blew open. Sgt Campbell had passed out from lack of oxygen, but Sgt Alan Morgan managed to connect him up to the supply at the rest bed and he soon regained consciousness. Then Alan too passed out, close to the open rear door with an outside temperature of -42°. After an emergency landing at Ford, Alan was taken to Chichester Hospital suffering from severe frostbite to his hands.

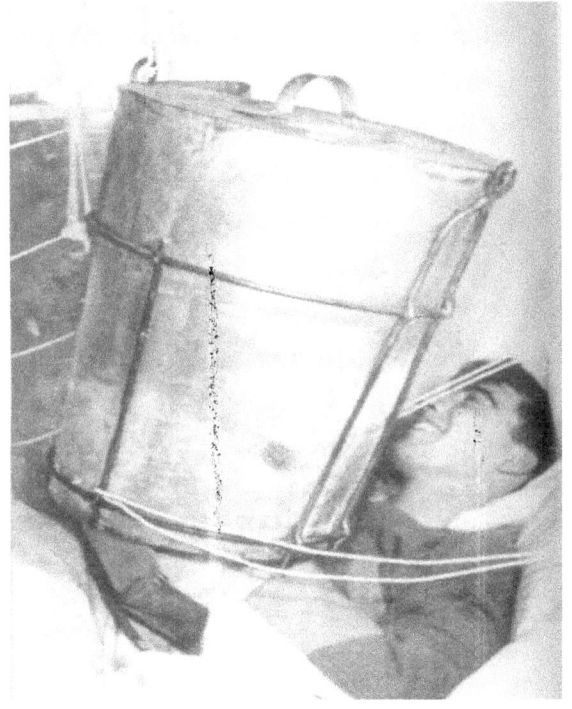

*Sgt Alan Morgan*

Alan Morgan's frost bitten hands were kept in buckets of ice. Unfortunately, all his fingers had to be amputated and Alan became a patient of Sir Archibald McIndoe and a member of the famous Guinea Pig Club.

*Fiskerton. 16th March 1944. P/O Russ Ewens and crew disembarking from Lancaster JB714 after a Stuttgart operation. L-R: Sgt Doug Tritton, Sgt Maurice Laws, P/O Ewens, Sgt Phil Griffiths in doorway, F/O Bob Granger. The crew successfully completed their tour.*

*F/O Healey & crew*

*Lancaster JB679 EA-D at Fiskerton 20th February 1944. This aircraft had collided with a JU88 over Leipzig the previous night. D-Dog spun rapidly for several thousand feet before the pilot regained control. F/O W.A. Healey points out the damage to his crew, F/O J. Bailes (Nav)); Sgt P. Boardman (FE); F/Sgt T. Thompson (W.Op), Sgt J.A. Kirwan (MUG); F/Sgt S. Noble (BA), Sgt G. J. Parkinson (RG),. F/L Woodroffe had flown as second pilot but is not in the photograph. F/O Healey was awarded the DFC for this action but was killed while on detachment along with Sgt J Jones, Sgt F Boardman and F/O R Bailes, on 30th April 1944.*

*Remains of Lancaster LM541 7/8th July, 1944 - St-Lue-D'esserent (Criel).*
*A very experienced crew, F/L George Ball DFC was flying his 30th operation, and most of his crew their 29th. Tragically they were all killed and are buried in Le Chesne Cemetery, Eure, France.*
*Crew: F/L G.E. Ball DFC Pilot, Sgt E. Wardman, P/O G. Millar, P/O J. Kernahan, Sgt J.A. Kirwan DFM, P/O G.A. Rae RCAF, F/Sgt G.J.W.Parkinson DFM .*

He flew from bases in North Africa, Italy, and England and took part in raids over Germany as captain of a Lancaster.

W/C Crocker and all crew in Lancaster LL900 were shot down on the 11/12th June 1944 during a Wesseling operation. A BBC correspondent also died.
Crew:
W/C M. Crocker DFC & Bar
F/L A.E.A. Matthews DFC FE
P/O L.B. Benson DFM Nav
F/O J.R. Worthington DFC W/Op
P/O A.D. Creighton RCAF AG
F/O K. Dutton BA
P/O D.H. Carr DFM AG
Mr Kent Stevenson BBC

W/C Malcolm Crocker DFC and Bar

P/O Leslie Kellow KIA 31st March 1944

F/L Cecil Palmer KIA 3rd January 1944

*The Roantree crew*
*With Lancaster ND792 at Fiskerton March/April 1944. L-R  Sgt Jack Grimshaw; Sgt John Peaker BA;  P/O Clive Roantree pilot;  Sgt Hugh Laurie W/Op;  Sgt Ern Paddick Nav; Sgt Ken Nelson (sitting).*

*The Roantree crew at de-brief following a Stuttgart operation 21$^{st}$ February 1944.*

*The Nowrie Crew*
*Served in 49 Squadron 1944-45. In no order: F/O Bob Barlow (Nav); P/O Bert Weatherley (Wop/AG), F/O F Ford (Pilot/AG), Sgt Colin Burridge (AG), P/O Stan Goldsworthy (BA), F/O Jack Nowrie Pilot), Sgt Cliff Palmer (FE)*

*The Russell crew, nicknamed, 'The Gen Crew'*
*At Winthorpe HCU just before the crew were posted to 49 Squadron at Fiskerton in July 1944. Back L-R: Sgt D G Hird (WO), Sgt B A Frost (MUG), Sgt G (Dusty) Miller (Nav), F/O T Russell (Pilot). Front L-R: Sgt A R Boyce (FE), Sgt R W Reid RCAF (BA), Sgt J O'Callaghan (RG). The aircraft is a Short Stirling code letters GP-L.*

*The Bacon Crew*
*All crew killed on an Aachen operation when shot down over Belgium on 11th April 1944. Back L-R: Sgt John Hennessey (FE), Sgt Stan Weedon (MUG), Sgt Peter Monck W /AG), F,Sgt Clarence Richard (RG). Front L-R: P/O Cliff Coward (Nav), F/L Don Bacon (Pilot), F/O William Fitch (BA). F/O Fitch was not on the operation. His replacement, F/O Nicholas Melnick also died.*

*P/O Bill Fitch was posted to 49 Squadron Fiskerton from 1660 HCU, RAF Swinderby on 29th October 1943. He joined F/O Don Bacon's crew as their BA although he wore Pilot's Wings. His first two operations were as 2nd pilot with the Hidderley crew but he then reverted to being a bomb aimer in the Bacon crew. Bill also flew an operation in August 1943 before joining 49 Squadron where he flew another seventeen operations. He was killed on the 21st February 1945 while with 83 Squadron.*

*F/L William Fitch DFC, GM*

*F/Sgt Ronald Greig*
*Killed with all his crew on the 22$^{nd}$ March 44 most of whom were on their 7$^{th}$ operation. Sgt W.F. Edwards (FE), F/Sgt K. Anderson (Nav). F/Sgt C. Peacock Wop/AG, P/O O.R. Rogers RAAF (AG), F/S L.J. Phillips (BA), F/Sgt H. Whiteley (AG).*

*Sgt Colin Gesch*
*Pilot/gunner. Carried out 30 operations. Involved with the development of AGLT*

*An onboard camera captures the bombing of an enemy ship. Aircraft probably flown by Sgt Colin Gesch.*

*S/L Graham Day*
*Flew 11 operations with 49 Squadron.*

*S/L James Evans DFC & Bar*
*He took over as 49 Squadron's 'A' Flight Commander from S/L Day and between February to May 1944, he flew eighteen operations.*

*49 Squadron Lancaster EA-E.*
*W/C Alex Adams (third from left in peaked cap) chats with P/O John 'Jock' Simpson before being introduced to his crew, and the ground crew who service his Lancaster ND383 E-Easy. On the far left of the picture is OC 'A' Flt, S/L Jim Evans, who most unusually was a navigator. He succeeded S/L Graham Day. The Simpson crew consisted of: F/Sgt Denis Hiscock, Nav (fourth from left); Sgt Frank Wheeler, (BA); Sgt Bob Mower, (FE); Sgt Arthur Highman, (W/Op); Sgt Colin Winterborn, (RG); Sgt Dennis 'Johnny' Walker, (MUG).*

*The Powell Crew*
*Lancaster JB701 EA-G crashed at Yonne, France on a Stuttgart operation, 29th July 1944. F/L W.L. Powell (Pilot), Sgt J.F. West (FE), F/O G.E. Franklin (Nav), F/S D.C. Stephens (W/Op.), Sgt G.E. Kirkpatrick (AG), F/O A.S. Cole (BA), Sgt T. Moore (AG) were all lost.*

*Memorial to the crew of Lancaster JB 701, St Martin sur Creuse, Yonne, France*

*The Simpkin Crew*
Lancaster NE128 was brought down on the 22$^{nd}$ June 1944 while on a Wesseling operation. Five of the crew survived to be taken into captivity but the pilot and the rear gunner were killed. F/O L.N. Simpkin (Pilot) KIA, Sgt A. Ladkin (FE) PoW, F/S T.A. Wilson (Nav) PoW, W/O R.S. Phillips RAAF (Wop/AG) PoW, Sgt W. Watson (AG) PoW, W/O E. O'Reilly RCAF (BA) PoW, Sgt J.A.T. Maton (AG) KIA. Photographed under a Stirling.

*P/O Robert Montgomery KIA 27$^{th}$ April 1944.*

*Sgt Robert Thompson KIA 25$^{th}$ June 1944.*

*The Maul Crew*
*All crew killed on the 21st November 1944 during a Gravenhorst Raid. Back L-R: Sgt E Battye (AG), Sgt S D Bolton (Nav), Sgt J Houghton (AG), Sgt W Cooper (FE). Front L to R: P/O I G Williams (W/Op), F/O E C Maul, F/Sgt A L Jackson.(BA). Both gunners were 19 years old.*

*The Brady Crew*
*Not in order -  Sgt KF Errey (FE), F/O R Bullock , (Wop/AG), Sgt JA Castles (BA), P/O David Brady (Pilot) F/O HM Peddie RAAF (Nav), Sgt JL Wright RCAF (MUG), Sgt R J Spicer (RG)*

*F/Sgt Edward White and Crew*
*Outward-bound on the 19th February 1944 for a Leipzig raid, the aircraft was attacked by two night fighters. The subsequent crash killed all the exceptionally young crew. F/Sgt White (centre back) was 20, the crew's average age.*

*Edward White is second from right in front of a Harvard.*

*F/Sgt Edward White*

*P/O Alan Edgar and crews*
*Back L-R: Sgt Don Harwood with unknown aircrew/groundcrew, Front L-R: Sgt Alf Ridpath, Sgt Alan Millard, P/O Edgar, F/Sgt Bob Brooks, Sgt George Bedford.*

*F/O David Hytch and crew*
*Back L-R: Unknown, Ken Read, David Hytch, Geoff Brunton, Tom Scott, "Blondie" Broadbent" and unknown rear gunner.*

*The Sullings Crew*
Back: Sgt D Simmons, F/Sgt J Skidmore, Sgt J Richards, Sgt C Wright. Front: F/Sgt J Christian, F/L Alan Sullings, F/Sgt E Haines.

*S/L Dudley Pike and Crew*
The crew carried out seven operations with 49 Squadron before a posting to 207 Squadron. They were all killed on a Clermont-Ferrand raid on the 10$^{th}$ March 1944. Crew: S/L D G H Pike (Pilot), Sgt N C New (FE), F/O A A Boad (Nav), P/O E H Moulden (BA), F/S R A Wheeler (W/O, Sgt J Hesketh (AG), Sgt A J Little (AG). Also F/L J G Moore (Air Gunner - ex 50 Squadron)

*Crew of Lancaster JB727 S for Sugar*
*(Not in order) F/L C.J.E. Palmer, (Pilot), Sgt P.O. Camm, (FE), F/O G.T. Young, (Nav), Sgt H. Conrad, (W/Op), Sgt D.D.R. Dallaway (AG), F/O R. Stobo, (BA), Sgt D.F. Prusher, (AG). All lost without trace on a Berlin operation 3$^{rd}$ January 1944.*

*The Lee Crew*
*Back L-R: F/l George Lee (Pilot), Sgt Bert Ashcroft (FE), Sgt Frank Smith (MUG), P/O John Amato (BA). Front L-R: Sgt Bert Gordon (W.Op), Sgt Hugh Trimnell (Nav), F/Sgt Jack Townsend RCAF (RG)*

*P/O H Carrington Crew*
*Lancaster LM539 crashed on 22<sup>nd</sup> May 1944 while on a Duisburg operation. Only F/Sgt Silver survived. Back: Sgt Bob Berry (MUG) KIA, Sgt Harry Hales (Nav) KIA, Sgt Ron Coleman (FE) KIA, Harry James (BA) (Replaced by F/Sgt S A Silver who survived and became PoW), Front: Sgt Lawrence Foulkes (RG) KIA, P/O Harry Carrington (Pilot) KIA, Sgt Ron Hill (W.Op), KIA.*

*The Buchanan Crew*
*F/O Walter Buchanan and crew failed to return from a Stuttgart operation 26<sup>th</sup> July 1944 in Lancaster PE250 EA-J. Back L-R: F/S Kitto (Nav), Sgt G W Picker (W/Op), Sgt C J Crane (AG), Sgt Greenwood (RG), Front L-R: Sgt Ashby (FE), F/O Buchanan, (Pilot), F/Sgt E Shackleton (BA).*

*The F/L G W Green Crew*

*Lancaster PB799 EA-G was lost on a training flight over the North Sea. All crew commemorated on the Runnymede Memorial. Crew : F/L G.W. Green (Pilot), Sgt A. Blanchard, Sgt E.C. Charles, F/O H.H.S. Gwyer, Sgt R.W. Henson, Sgt J.A. Rudd, Sgt H. Stobart.*

*The Carlyle Crew*

*Probably, E J Thompson, W/O A M Kalinski, F/O J R Furness, F/L K Carlyle, Sgt J G Kenrick, F/O L Lewtas, F/L M W Maxwell.*

*The Ross Crew*
*All crew lost without trace in Lancaster ND695 EA-B on the 21ˢᵗ June 1944 on a Wesseling raid. Crew: P/O A.R. Ross (Pilot), Sgt D.W. Palmer (FE), F/S C.G. Morton (Nav), Sgt C.C. Holden (Wop/AG), Sgt A.D. Griffin (AG), P/O G.F. MacGregor RCAF (BA), Sgt D.W.E. Hardy (AG)*

*F/L John Woodroffe (left) flew nine operations with 49 Squadron. With him are W/C Guy Gibson and G/C Anthony Evans-Evans DFC who was the base commander at Coningsby and would often fly on operations.*

*Driver LACW Lillian Yule*

*F/O Edward Essenhigh and his Crew*
F/O Edward Essenhigh and crew in Lancaster PB355 had turned back after take-off, and crashed on Worthing beach en route to Munich on the 17th December 1944. Crew which were all killed: Sgt H. Varey (FE), Sgt L.B. Bourne (Nav), F/Sgt F.B. Rees (W.Op), Sgt J.W. Moore (AG), F/O J.A. Thomson (BA), F/Sgt G.F. Callon (Sgt Callon was one of the volunteer pilot/rear gunners operating the 'Village Inn' turret and therefore wore pilot's wings).

*Lancaster LM190 of 49 Squadron over Sequeville 7/8th August 1944. Bombs falling from above and hitting aircraft flying at a lower level were always a hazard during concentrated bombing raids.*

*49 Squadron Lancaster photographed over a V-site, northern France.*

*F/O William Green DFC RAAF and Crew*

All killed 19th July 1944 on a Revigny operation when they were shot down by a night fighter. Back L-R: Sgt Alan Ansell (MUG), Sgt Geoff Brunton (Sgt Brunton was not on raid - Sgt Francis Seymour took his place), Sgt Reg Neal (Nav), F/Sgt Mervyn Holland (BA). Front L-R: F/Sgt Colin Davison (W.Op/AG), F/O William Green (Pilot), Sgt Gordon Hands (RG).

*The Alty Crew*

L – R: Sgt D H 'Dave' Millett (RG), Sgt AP 'Alf' Lewis (MUG), Sgt K N 'Ken' Manning (W/Op), Sgt LF 'Les' Hauser (FE), P/O AE 'Ted' Parker DFC (Nav), Pilot F/O NH 'Norman, Nobby' Alty DFC, F/O R W 'Bob' Waggett (BA).

*J H Evans*

*Shot is almost certainly F/O Jack Adams (including S/L Jimmy Evans) and crew returning from Schweinfurt 24/25th February 1944 in JB466 EA-A - their first trip with 49 Squadron.*

*The Weir Crew*

*G/C C T Weir became a PoW while the remainder of the crew perished on 21st November 1944. Crew who died: F/O F.A. Wooding (FE), S/L P. Kelly (Nav), P/O A.W. Bishop (W/Op), Sgt P. Telford (AG), F/O H.W. Hayward (BA), F/O A.R. Verrier (AG).*

*The Rowley Crew. Flew 31 operations with 49 Squadron.*

*The F/O D Talbot crew.*
*All killed 5th November 1944 on a Dortmund Ems Canal Raid, their 5th operation.*

*The Automatic Gun-Laying Turret (AGLT), also known as the Frazer-Nash FN121, was a radar-directed, rear gun turret fitted to some British bombers from 1944*

*Lancaster ME 308 equipped with AGLT (Village Inn), a radar aided rear turret. The radome can be seen near the tail fin. This was manned by a pilot/rear gunner. Oddly on 49 Squadron - at the bottom of the crew ladder can be seen heads of sweeping brushes which have been added by the ground crew so that boots could be cleaned before climbing aboard. ME 308 joined 49 Squadron in November 1944 and flew on 30 operations before her demise.*

*Fiskerton Snows*

*British Bomb Loads*

*The Galloway crew failed to return from Politz 8th February 1945. There was just one survivor. Back row L-R: F/O George Kydd, F/S Tom Bolton, F/L Sam Galloway, F/Sgt Les Randall, Sgt John Hardy. Front: L-R F/O Billy Dron. F/Sgt Ernie Ellis became a PoW*

*Somerville Galloway*
*Dressed up against the harsh winter weather while training at Moose Jaw, Canada.*

*The Stark Crew*

F/O Roussel Stark in Lancaster PB537 is believed to have come down on a Harburg operation on the 7/8th March 1945. L-R: F/O Roussel Stark RAAF KIA, Sgt Joe Dixon PoW, Sgt Fred Brennan PoW, W/O Ralph Bairnsfather KIA, F/Sgt Gus Lovett KIA, Sgt Paddy Gilbert KIA W/O Johnny Yeoman PoW.

*W/C David Balme DSO DC*
*C/O 18th June -16th November 1945*

*The Whent Crew*
*Four members of F/O Doug Whent's Lancaster ME454 crew survived being brought down on the 16th March 1945. Back L-R: Sgt F.P. Anderson (Nav) (Injured), Sgt G.C. Leeke (AG) KIA, Sgt H. Darbyshire (AG) KIA, F/S R.H. Usher (W/Op) (Injured), Front L-R: Sgt F.R. Haylock (FE) KIA, F/O D.I. Whent (Pilot) Injured, Sgt E.J. Sullivan (BA) Injured.*

*The Hammond Crew of Lancaster EA-B*
*L-R  F/Sgt  G. Woodland  (BA), F/Sgt R. Menhinick (RG), F/Sgt 1945(Pilot),   F/Sgt N. Smith (Nav),  F/Sgt F. Woolsey  (MUG). F/Sgt G. Moses W/Op was on leave.*

*F/O C. Corley and crew.*
*L-R Sgt W. Richie (FE), Harry Cowan (Nav), F/O C. Corley (Pilot), F/Sgt McHale (BA), Sgt Howells (RG) Sgt D.W. Tester (W/Op). The Mid-Upper Gunner was absent.*

*The Babb Crew*
*Back L-R: Sgt W B M McDonald, F/O E H Boyle, Sgt A R Swann. Front L-R: F/O N Hewitt, F/L R V Babb, F/O H N Savinson*

*The Mallinson Crew*
*Believed to have been on their 35th operation on the 12th February 1945 when they were reported as missing. The crew: Back L-R: Sgt Ernie Stansill (FE), PoW, John McHeffey (BA) (Not on raid had been replaced by F/Sgt J F McQuand (PoW), F/O Ray Mallinson (Pilot), PoW,, F/Sgt John Gascoyne (RG) KIA. Front: P/O Hank Eberley (Nav) Evaded, F/Sgt Max Makofski (W.Op), Evaded , P/O Fred Grimsdale (MUG) PoW.*

*F/L Leslie Hay DFC 1945*

*F/O Alec Bolter KIA 8th January 1945*

*The Browning Crew*
*After the raid to Nordhausen on the 4th April 1945. Back L – R: Sgt Walters, P/O Wells, F/O Bromfield, F/O Browning, Sgt McLeod. Front L – R: (kneeling): Sgt Palmer, F/S Johnson*

*The Botting Crew*
*P/O A W Bishop KIA 21st November 1944, F/L J A Edwards, P/O J H Willmot, P/O W J Bennett RCAF, W/C L E Botting, P/O R P Timms*

*Memorials to 49 Squadron*
*Above at the Alrewas National Arboretum and below Fiskerton Airfield*

# August 1943

Briefings for the final act of Operation Gomorrah took place on the 2nd, and a force of 740 aircraft was assembled, 128 of them Lancasters belonging to 5 Group. 49 Squadron briefed fifteen crews, setting out the intention for the Path Finders to mark the aiming-point with red TIs by H2S and for the visual markers to follow up with yellow TIs for the backers-up to reinforce with greens. They lifted off from Fiskerton between 23.28 and 00.15 with W/C Johnson the senior pilot on duty and headed for the Lincolnshire coast to begin the North Sea crossing and rendezvous with the bomber stream. The weather conditions, initially, were favourable, until coming into contact with a towering bank of ice-bearing cumulonimbus cloud at 7 degrees east, a not unusual feature of this regular route into north-western Germany, but on this occasion, a particularly imposing one, which could not be circumnavigated and stretched upwards to 20,000 feet and beyond. Upon entering it, aircraft were thrown around by violent electrical storms and it was a hugely terrifying experience beyond anything that most crews had ever experienced, with enormous flashes of lightning, thunder, electrical discharges and instruments going haywire. W/C Johnson's experience told him that to continue on would be futile and he turned back, as did F/Sgt Watson and crew after severe icing shut down both inboard engines. P/O Tomlin became afflicted with a severe migraine that took away his vision and the flight engineer assisted him in flying the Lancaster home. Those battling through the conditions to reach the target area found seven to ten-tenths cloud, and while some caught a glimpse of the Elbe and isolated yellow and green Path Finder flares, which might have been jettisoned rather than placed, the majority bombed on e.t.a., those from Fiskerton attacking from 16,000 to 19,000 feet between 02.25 and 02.44. Bombs were spread over a hundred miles of the Schleswig-Holstein peninsula, the town of Elmshorn, some fifteen miles to the north-west of Hamburg, seeming to attract the most attention and 254 houses were destroyed. Few crews had any idea of their precise location and bombed on the glow of fires beneath the cloud and the smoke rising through it. On return, they expressed themselves to be shaken by their experience and were unanimous in their conviction that the operation had been a total failure. The outcome was of little consequence in view of what had gone before, but the Command suffered the relatively heavy loss of thirty aircraft, some of them having fallen victim to the weather conditions. During the course of the four raids of Operation Gomorrah, the squadron despatched fifty-nine sorties, fifty-three of which bombed as briefed and suffered no losses. (The Battle of Hamburg. Martin Middlebrook).

On the 6th, S/L Gilpin was posted to 5 Group HQ, and his replacement as a flight commander, S/L Todd-White, would arrive with his crew from 1660 Conversion Unit three days hence. Italy was now teetering on the brink of capitulation and Bomber Command was invited to help nudge it over the edge with a short offensive against its major cities, beginning with the preparation of an all-Lancaster force drawn from 1, 5 and 8 Groups for an attack on Genoa, Milan and Turin on the 7th. With preparations already in hand for, perhaps, the most important operation of the war to date to be launched in ten days' time, the Turin raid was to be used to test the merits of employing a raid controller, or Master of Ceremonies, in the manner of W/C Gibson during Operation Chastise. The man selected for the job was Group Captain John Searby, currently serving as commanding officer of 83 Squadron, and before that, Gibson's successor as commanding officer of 106 Squadron. It is believed that all 197 aircraft reached their respective targets after flying out in excellent weather conditions, and although the Master Bomber experiment at Turin was not entirely successful, experience was gained which would prove useful for the forthcoming Operation Hydra.

Following a week's operational inactivity after Hamburg, seventeen 49 Squadron crews were called to briefing on the 9th to learn of their part in a raid on Mannheim that night as part of a 5 Group contribution of 143 Lancasters in an overall force of 457 aircraft. They departed Fiskerton between 23.00 and 23.26 with F/L Munro the senior pilot on duty and S/L Todd-White flying as second pilot. After climbing out, they headed for the rendezvous point over Reading, before exiting England via Beachy Head on course for the French coast at Boulogne. F/Sgt Stanton and crew lost their port-outer engine after an hour and turned back, while the others pushed on across the Channel and France, and it was at this stage that ED719's port-outer engine had to be shut down because of overheating. Sgt Watson and crew debated whether or not to press on, and with a strong tailwind to speed them on, decided in the affirmative and jettisoned the incendiaries to lighten the load. When the port-inner engine also failed, they felt that they were too close to the target to turn back and doggedly flew on. The others were greeted at the target by a five-tenths layer of broken cloud at 4,000 feet and eight-tenths at 10,000 feet, despite which, the visibility was fair and the conditions were irrelevant as far as the H2S-equipped Path Finder marker crews were concerned anyway. The Fiskerton crews attacked from 15,000 and 21,000 feet between 01.43 and 02.17 aiming at yellow and green TIs and set off home to report a number of very large fires but what appeared to be a generally scattered raid. The Watson crew, meanwhile, found themselves in an underpowered Lancaster alone over Mannheim and dropped their cookie unopposed until being picked up by the flak batteries as they retreated to the west. As the wallowing aircraft became more difficult to control, the decision was taken to abandon it to its fate and all seven occupants drifted down into the hands of their captors. According to local sources and against expectations, 1,316 buildings had been destroyed in Mannheim, forty-two industrial concerns had lost production and more than fifteen hundred fires of varying sizes had required attention. Six Halifaxes and three Lancasters failed to return, two of the latter belonging to 5 Group.

The following night brought a return to southern Germany, this time to Nuremberg, for which a force of 653 aircraft was made ready. The presence of Stirlings, the type usually at the bottom of the food chain, might provide respite for the Halifax crews, which, in a Lancaster/Halifax force, invariably came off second best. 5 Group contributed 128 of the Lancasters and 49 Squadron briefed a dozen crews while their Lancasters were being loaded with a cookie and up to twelve SBCs of incendiaries and sufficient fuel and reserves for the 1,300-mile round-trip. The Fiskerton contingent took off between 21.40 and 22.13 with W/C Johnson and S/L Day the senior pilots on duty, and after climbing-out set course for Beachy Head to follow a route similar to that of the previous night. The conditions in the target area also reflected those of twenty-four hours earlier with eight to ten-tenths cloud at 12,000 feet, despite which, the Path Finders elected to ground-mark. There were no release-point flares to draw the main force on but the green TIs were visible to most, and the 49 Squadron crews delivered their bombs from 18,000 to 21,000 feet between 01.04 and 01.40. At debriefing, crews reported a good concentration of fires, the glow from which remained visible for 150 miles into the return journey. Sgt Moss and crew were absent from the post-raid ritual and ED625's dispersal pan stood empty on the following morning. It would be some time before news came through from the Red Cross that they had crashed in Germany and that only the pilot and bomb-aimer had survived to fall into enemy hands. It would be longer still before the full story emerged that they had been shot down by two Ju88s and that the Lancaster had blown itself apart just as the crew was leaving it. The operation was moderately successful and caused substantial housing damage in central and southern districts, while a death toll of 577 people was evidence of the intensity of the bombing. It was achieved for the relatively modest loss of sixteen aircraft, seven Halifaxes, six Lancasters and three Stirlings, which, in percentage terms, was respectively 3.2, 1.9 and 2.5.

The Italian campaign continued on the 12th, when Milan and Turin were the targets, the former for a force of 504 aircraft including 130 Lancasters provided by 5 Group, while 152 aircraft from 3 and 8 Groups attended to the latter. 49 Squadron made ready thirteen Lancasters, which departed Fiskerton between 21.20 and 21.47 and set course for the south coast at Selsey Bill to begin the Channel crossing that would terminate on the Normandy coast at Cabourg. Thereafter, they headed south-east in a straight leg across central France to the northern tip of Lake Bourget, before traversing the Alps and skirting southern Switzerland. The final run-in on the target was conducted under clear skies with just ground mist to spoil the vertical view, and on arrival, the Fiskerton crews bombed visually or on yellow flares and green TIs from 15,600 to 19,000 feet between 01.17 and 01.50 in accordance with the instructions of the "Master of Ceremonies". They observed large fires in the city centre, which could be seen for a hundred miles and more into the return flight, and local reports, though short on detail, confirmed that four important war-industry factories had sustained serious damage during August and most of it probably occurred on this night.

Milan would face two further attacks before the Command's interest in Italy ceased for good, and the first of these was posted on the 14th, for which 1, 5 and 8 Groups put together a force of 140 Lancasters, fifty-nine of them representing 5 Group. 49 Squadron made ready six of its own and sent them on their way from Fiskerton between 21.21 and 21.32 with S/L Todd-White the senior pilot on duty for the first time. F/Sgt Coxhill and crew arrived back with a defective rear turret three hours after taking off, leaving the others to reach the target under clear skies and in good visibility aided by a brilliant moon and Path Finder route markers. The Path Finder target marking with green TIs was accurate and concentrated and was exploited by the 49 Squadron crews from 15,000 to 18,000 feet between 01.29 and 01.40. Many fires were seen to take hold as the force turned away, and the glow remained visible for a considerable distance into the return flight.

There was to be no respite for Milan as a force of 199 Lancasters was made ready later on the 15th for a return that night for what would be the last time over Italy for main force Lancasters. 49 Squadron provided eight of the eighty-five 5 Group Lancasters, and they took off from Fiskerton between 20.19 and 20.31 with F/L Taylor the senior pilot on duty. They passed over Reading on their way south to Selsey Bill to make landfall at Cabourg on the French side of the Channel and make for the northern tip of Lake Bourget. All reached the target area to find clear skies and the Path Finder green flares guiding them over lake Bourget to encounter haze and smoke hanging over the city from the previous night to spoil to an extent the vertical visibility. The Path Finders marked the city-centre aiming point with green TIs, and these were bombed to good effect by the 49 Squadron crews from 13,700 to 18,000 feet between 00.05 and 00.25. Enemy night-fighters were waiting over France to catch the bombers as they returned home, and among the seven missing aircraft was that of 467 Squadron's popular commanding officer, W/C Cosme Gomm DSO, DFC, who died with all but one of his crew. It is believed that flak accounted for 49 Squadron's LM337, which crashed at 02.45 near Rugles some thirty miles short of the Normandy coast, killing P/O Gospel and all but two of his crew, who evaded capture. The consensus of returning crews was of a concentrated attack, but no local report was forthcoming to confirm or deny.

The final raid of the war on an Italian city was carried out by 154 aircraft of 3 and 8 Groups against Turin on the following night. A successful raid was claimed at the modest cost of four aircraft, but many of the participating Stirlings were diverted on return and did not reach their home stations in time to be made ready for the night's highly important operation, for which a maximum effort had been planned. This would deplete the available number of Stirlings by sixty and heap an even greater responsibility upon the rest of the force to destroy the Peenemünde site, ideally, at the first attempt, otherwise, crews were told at briefing, they would have to go back. A force of 596 aircraft was assembled made up of 324 Lancasters, 218 Halifaxes and fifty-four Stirlings, 117 of the Lancasters provided by 5 Group.

Since the very beginning of the war, intelligence had suggested that Germany was researching into and developing rocket technology, and although scant regard was given to the reports by some of the leading scientific experts, photographic reconnaissance had confirmed the existence of an establishment at Peenemünde at the northern tip of the island of Usedom on the Baltic coast. The activities there were monitored through Ultra intercepts and surreptitious reconnaissance flights, and the V-1, known to the photographic interpreters at Medmenham because of its wingspan as the "Peenemünde 20", was captured on a photograph. The brilliant scientist, Dr R V Jones, had been able to gain vital information concerning the V-1's range, which would ultimately be used to feed disinformation to the enemy, largely through the double agent "Zigzag", otherwise known as Eddie Chapman. Unfortunately, Churchill's chief scientific adviser, Professor Lindemann, or Lord Cherwell as he became, steadfastly refused to give credence to the existence and feasibility of rocket weapons and held stubbornly to his viewpoint even when presented with a photograph of a V-2 on a trailer, taken by a PRU Mosquito in June 1943. It required the combined urgings of Duncan Sandys and Dr Jones to persuade Churchill of the urgency to act, and Operation Hydra was planned for the first available opportunity, which occurred on the night of the 17/18th. Earlier in the day, the USAAF 8th Air Force had carried out its first deep-penetration raids into Germany to attack ball-bearing production at Schweinfurt and the Messerschmidt aircraft plant at Regensburg, and to the shock of its leaders, had learned the harsh lesson that unescorted daylight raids in 1943 were not viable. The folks at home would not be told that sixty B17s had failed to return. A force of 596 aircraft and crews answered the call to arms for Peenemünde, 5 Group contributing 117 of the 324 Lancasters, with Fiskerton making ready twelve, and the rest of the force was comprised of 218 Halifaxes and fifty-four Stirlings.

The operation had been meticulously planned to account for the three vital components of Peenemünde, the housing estate, where the scientific and technical staff lived, the factory buildings in which the weapons were assembled and the experimental site, where testing took place. Each was assigned to a specific wave of aircraft, which would attack from medium level, with the Path Finders bearing the huge responsibility of re-directing the point of aim accordingly, for which each squadron was to provide one crew as a "shifter". That apart, once route markers had been dropped on Rügen island, the Path Finder markers and backers-up were to follow the standard routine of red, yellow and green TIs. After last minute alterations, 3 and 4 Groups were given the first mentioned, 1 Group the second, and 5 and 6 Groups the third. The whole operation was to be overseen by a Master of Ceremonies (referred to hereafter as Master Bomber), and the officer selected for this hazardous and demanding role was G/C Searby of 83 Squadron, who, as already mentioned, had stepped into Gibson's shoes at 106 Squadron after Gibson was posted out to form 617 Squadron. Searby's role was to direct the marking and bombing by VHF and to encourage the crews to press on to the aiming-point, a task requiring him to remain in the target area and within range of the defences throughout the attack. In an attempt to protect the bombers from the attentions of enemy night-fighters for as long as possible, eight Mosquitos of 139 Squadron were to carry out a spoof raid on Berlin beginning at 23.00, seventy-five minutes before the opening of the main event, and would be led by the highly experienced and former 49 Squadron commander, G/C Len Slee. In the expectation of encountering drifting smoke as the last wave on target, the 5 Group crews were instructed to employ their oft-used time-and-distance approach to the aiming-point and had practiced this over a stretch of coast near the Wainfleet bombing range at the mouth of the Wash in Lincolnshire, progressively cutting the margin of error from one thousand to three hundred yards.

The 49 Squadron element took off between 21.35 and 22.57 with W/C Johnson and S/Ls Day and Todd-White the senior pilots on duty on a night when many squadron commanders elected to fly, in some cases, with fatal consequences. There were no early returns to Fiskerton, and the overall early-return rate was lower than normal, three from 5 Group, suggesting that crews had taken to heart the importance of the operation. The various groups made their way individually to a rendezvous point some ninety minutes flying time or three hundred miles from the English coast and sixty miles from Denmark's western coast, where they formed into a stream. Darkness had fallen as they crossed the North Sea, and twenty miles short of landfall over the southern tip of Fanø island, south of Esbjerg, windowing began in order to simulate a standard raid on a northern or north-eastern city. Southern Denmark was traversed by the Lancaster brigade at 18,000 feet, twice the altitude required for the attack, but worryingly, in a band of cloudless sky under a bright moon. They adopted an east-south-easterly course and began to shed altitude gradually during the 240-mile run to the target a little over an hour away, and at the rear of the stream, the 5 Group crews focused on the island of Rügen, the ideal starting point for their timed run to Peenemünde, which lay some fifteen miles beyond to the south-east.

The initial marking of the housing estate went awry, and some target indicators fell onto the forced workers camp at Trassenheide, more than a mile south of the intended aiming point. Many of the 3 and 4 Group bombs fell here, inflicting grievous casualties on friendly foreign nationals, who were trapped inside their wooden barracks. Once rectified, however, the attack proceeded according to plan and a number of important members of the technical staff were killed. The 1 Group second-wave crews encountered strong crosswinds over the narrow section of the island where the construction sheds were located, but this phase of the operation largely achieved its aims and they were on their way home before the night-fighters arrived from Berlin, having been attracted by the glow of fires well to the north. On arrival at Rügen, the 5 Group crews began their timed run, reaching the experimental site to encounter the expected smoke and bombed on green TIs, in the case of the 49 Squadron element, from 6,500 to 8,000 feet between 00.43 and 01.04. They and the 6 Group Halifaxes and Lancasters then ran into the night-fighters, which proceeded to take a heavy toll of bombers both in the skies over the target and on the route home towards Denmark.

Twenty-nine of the forty missing aircraft came from this third wave, seventeen of them belonging to 5 Group and twelve to 6 Group, which represented a loss rate for the Canadians of 19.7%. The first of the 49 Squadron Lancasters to go down was JA892 containing the crew of P/O Robinson, who were twenty miles into the homeward flight when falling to the guns of a night-fighter near Greifswald. Both gunners lost their lives, possibly during the engagement, while those in the front of the aircraft survived to fall into enemy hands. In the sequence of the operation's losses, they were fourteenth, and sixteenth was ED805, which crashed into the Baltic and took with it the crew of S/L Todd-White, who were on the second operation of their second tour. The body of the pilot eventually came ashore for burial in Sweden and that of the mid-upper gunner in Poland. JA851 had reached southern Denmark when crossing paths with the night-fighter of Oblt Hans Meissner of II./NJG3, which sent it crashing into the coastal region near Nordborg at 02.56 with no survivors from the crew of P/O Tomlin DFC, the thirty-sixth loss of the operation. Five minutes later, Meissner also accounted for the thirty-seventh, JA691, which came down four miles north-east of Abenra and fifteen miles west of Nordborg, killing F/O Randall and his crew, whose flight engineer, Sgt Henley, was forty-three years old. Many crews brought home aiming point photographs, despite the fact that the time-and-distance method was found to have been not entirely effective. Returning crews praised the work of the Path Finders and the Master Bomber, and post-raid reconnaissance revealed the raid to have been sufficiently effective to delay the V-2 development programme by a number of weeks and ultimately to force the manufacture of secret weapons underground. The flight testing of the V-2 was eventually withdrawn eastwards into Poland, beyond the range of Harris's bombers, and thus Peenemünde had been nullified as a threat.

Before the next campaign began, Leverkusen was posted on the 22$^{nd}$ as the target for a heavy force of 449 Lancasters and Halifaxes with 8 Group Oboe-Mosquito to provide the initial marking. Situated on the Rhine just a stone's throw north of Cologne, the city was home to a factory belonging to the infamous I G Farben chemicals company, which was engaged in the development and production of synthetic oil and employed slave labour at all of its factories across Germany, including 30,000 from the Auschwitz concentration camp, where it had built a plant. One of the company's subsidiaries manufactured the Zyklon B gas used during the Holocaust to murder millions of Jewish victims. 49 Squadron made ready nine Lancasters in a 5 Group contribution of 108, which departed Fiskerton between 20.59 and 21.32 and after climbing out, headed for the Belgian coast at Knokke, to follow a well-worn route to the southern Ruhr, which would require them to pass through the searchlight and flak belt near Cologne that was guaranteed to provide a hot welcome. They all made it safely through the narrow searchlight and flak corridor to reach the target, where ten-tenths cloud with tops at 18,000 feet blanketed the area. Oboe-equipment failures forced most crews to bomb on e.t.a. in the absence of markers, until the glow of fires came to their aid as the raid developed, although a small number of crews spotted green TIs on the ground and aimed for them. Bombing was carried out by the 49 Squadron crews in the face of intense flak from 18,000 to 20,000 feet between 00.06 and 00.39, and the glow of fires and the flash of explosions were initially the only confirmation of something happening under the cloud until a column of smoke was observed to be rising through 12,000 feet. Local reports revealed that up to a dozen neighbouring towns had been hit, Düsseldorf suffering the destruction of 132 buildings.

Harris had long believed that the key to ultimate victory lay in the destruction of Berlin, the seat of the Nazi government and the symbol of its power. On the 23$^{rd}$, orders were received on stations across the Command to prepare for a maximum effort that night against Germany's capital city, which had not been visited by the heavy brigade since the end of March. The crews, of course, could not know that this was to be the first of an eventual nineteen raids on the "Big City", in an offensive which, with an autumn break, would drag on until the following spring. It was a campaign that would test the resolve of the crews to the absolute limit, whilst also sealing the fate of the Stirlings and the Mk II and V Halifaxes as front-line bombers. There are varying opinions concerning the true start date of what became known as the Berlin offensive or the Battle of Berlin, some commentators believing these first three operations in August and September to be the start, while others point to the sixteen raids from mid-November. However, there was little doubt in Bomber Command circles that this was it, a fact demonstrated by the comments in numerous squadron ORBs, which spoke of the "long-awaited Berlin campaign" and similar sentiments. There would be a Master Bomber on hand for this operation and the officer chosen was Canadian W/C "Johnny" Fauquier, the tough, grizzled and one-time bush pilot and frequent brawler, who was enjoying his second spell as the commanding officer of 405 (Vancouver) Squadron, once of 4 Group, but since April, proud to be the only Canadian Path Finder unit. The route had been planned to take the bomber stream to a rendezvous point over the North Sea, before crossing the Dutch coast near Haarlem and entering Germany between Meppen to the north and Osnabrück to the south. It would then pass between Bremen and Hannover to bypass the southern rim of Berlin, before turning back sharply on a north-westerly course across the city centre. After bombing, aircraft were to pass out over the Baltic coast in the direction of the Schleswig-Holstein peninsula. Finally, seventeen Mosquitos were to precede the Path Finder and main force elements to drop route markers at key points in an attempt to keep the bomber stream on track.

A force of 727 aircraft was assembled, of which 124 Lancasters represented 5 Group, nine of them belonging to 49 Squadron, and they departed Fiskerton between 19.36 and 20.35 with F/Ls Munro and Taylor the senior pilots on duty. Those reaching the target area found clear skies and moonlight, but the Path Finders were unable to identify the aiming point in the centre of the city, a result of the inherent difficulties of interpreting the H2S images over such a massive urban sprawl and marked the southern outskirts instead. Many main force crews then cut the corner to approach the city from the south-west rather than south-east, and this would result in the wastage of many bomb loads in open country and on outlying communities. The Fiskerton crews each delivered their cookie and incendiaries visually and on red and green TIs from 19,000 to 22,000 feet between 23.49 and 00.23 in the face of intense searchlight activity with moderate flak. Returning crews reported large explosions and many fires, the glow from which was visible for at least 140 miles, and a pall of smoke had already risen to meet them as they turned towards the north-west. Curiously, only a few crews commented on hearing the Master Bomber and finding his instructions helpful. A new record of fifty-six aircraft failed to return, twenty-three Halifaxes, seventeen Lancasters and sixteen Stirlings, representing a percentage loss rate respectively of 9.1, 5.1 and 12.9, which perfectly reflected the food chain when all three types operated together. Berlin experienced a scattered raid, but because of the numbers attacking, extensive damage was caused, a little in or near the centre but mostly in south-western residential districts and industrialized areas a little further east. 2,611 buildings were reported to have been destroyed or seriously damaged, and the death toll of 854 people was surprisingly high, caused largely, perhaps, by a failure to heed the alarms and go to the assigned shelters.

Orders were received on the 27th to prepare for an operation that night against Nuremberg, the plan for which included an additional ten 139 Squadron Mosquitos to provide a "Window" screen in advance of the bomber stream. The Oboe Mosquitos were to mark the route with red and green TIs, backed up by H2S Lancasters, but as Berlin was beyond the range of Oboe, the aiming-point was to be marked with red TIs by H2S, backed up by greens. A force of 674 aircraft lined up for take-off in mid-evening, 5 Group contributing 140 Lancasters, the dozen provided by 49 Squadron taking to the air between 20.42 and 21.23 with F/L Munro the senior pilot on duty accompanied by F/L Pike, who had been posted in with his crew from 1661 Conversion Unit on the 23rd. After climbing out, they headed for the French coast and once there, followed the line of the frontier with Belgium until crossing into Germany south of Luxembourg on course for the target, where clear skies and intense darkness prevailed. The Path Finders had been briefed to check their H2S equipment by dropping a 1,000 pounder on Heilbronn, and some crews complied, while others, it seems, experienced technical difficulties. The initial marking was accurate, but a creep-back developed, which the backers-up and the Master Bomber could not correct and this resulted in many bomb loads falling into open country, while others hit Nuremberg's south-eastern and eastern districts. The Fiskerton crews aimed at green TIs from 20,000 to 22,000 feet between 00.32 and 01.02, and generally gained an impression of a fairly concentrated and accurate attack, which produced many fires. They reported searchlights and night-fighters to be numerous and evidence of this came with the failure to return of thirty-three aircraft, eleven of each type, which again confirmed the vulnerability of the Stirlings and Halifaxes when operating alongside Lancasters. The loss rate on this night was 3.1% for the Lancaster, 5% for the Halifax and 10.6% for the Stirlings.

The main event on the night of the 30/31st was a two-phase attack on the twin towns of Mönchengladbach and Rheydt, the first time that either would experience a major Bomber Command assault. Situated some ten miles west of the centre of Düsseldorf in the south-western Ruhr, they would face an initial force of 660 aircraft of four types, in what for the crews, was a short-penetration trip across the Dutch frontier and a welcome change from the recent long slogs to eastern and southern Germany. The plan called for the first wave to hit Mönchengladbach, before a two-minute pause in the bombing allowed the Path Finders to head south to mark Rheydt. 49 Squadron made ready fifteen Lancasters as part of a 5 Group contribution of 138 and took off in two phases between 23.21 and 23.29 and 23.49 and 00.09 with F/L Pike the senior pilot on duty. There were no early returns to Fiskerton, and they reached the target area to find good visibility above the seven to ten-tenths cloud at 8,000 feet, and a near-perfect display of target-marking by Oboe delivered red and green flares to draw on the main force to bomb with scarcely any creep-back. The 49 Squadron element carried out their bombing runs from 18,000 to 21,000 feet between 02.02 and 02.42, four crews joining in at Rheydt, and on return reported many fires, the glow from which could be seen from the Dutch coast homebound. Photo-reconnaissance confirmed a highly accurate and concentrated attack, which destroyed more than 2,300 buildings in the two towns, 171 of them of an industrial nature, along with 869 residential properties. Twenty-five aircraft failed to return, and Halifaxes narrowly sustained the highest numerical casualties.

The month ended with preparations for the second of the Berlin operations on the night of the 31st, for which 622 aircraft were made ready, more than half of them Lancasters, of which 129 were provided by 5 Group. 49 Squadron loaded sixteen of its own with a cookie and nine SBCs of incendiaries each and dispatched them between 19.30 and 20.17 with W/C Johnson and F/Ls Munro and Taylor the senior pilots on duty. The route on this night took the bomber stream on an east-south-easterly heading across Texel to a position between Hannover and Leipzig, before turning to pass to the south-east of Berlin and approach the city-centre aiming point on a north-westerly track. The return leg would involve a south-westerly course to a position south of Cologne for an exit over the French coast, but despite the attempts to outwit the enemy night-fighter controller, he would be able to predict to some extent where to concentrate his fighters. P/O Blackmore and crew abandoned their sortie early on when their intercom failed, leaving the remainder to press on, and for the first time to report the use by the Germans of "fighter flares" to mark out the path of the bombers to and from the target. The Path Finders encountered five to six-tenths cloud in the target area and this combined with H2S equipment failure and a spirited night-fighter response to cause the markers to be dropped well to the south of the planned aiming point. The main force crews became involved in an extensive creep-back, which would stretch some thirty miles into open country and outlying communities. The 49 Squadron crews reported up to eight-tenths thin cloud and bombed on red and green TIs from 19,000 to 21,500 feet between 23.29 and 00.14, observing many fires over a wide area. It was noted by some that two groups of green TIs were ten miles apart and both attracted attention from the main force. The outcome of the raid was a major disappointment, brought about by woefully short marking and a pronounced creep-back and resulted in the destruction of just eighty-five houses, a figure in no way commensurate with the effort expended and the loss of forty-seven heavy bombers. The percentage loss rates made alarming reading at Bomber Command HQ, the Lancasters with an acceptable and sustainable 3%, the Halifaxes with 11.3% and the Stirlings with 16%.

During the course of the month the squadron participated in twelve operations and dispatched 144 sorties for the loss of seven Lancasters and their crews.

## September 1943

The new month began operationally for fifteen 5 Group freshman crews on the 2$^{nd}$ with a mining operation in the Nectarine I garden, situated a fraction north of due east on the other side of the North Sea. The 49 Squadron crews of Sgts Kerr and Taverner departed Fiskerton at 20.22 and 22.24 and found four to eight-tenths cloud in the target area with tops at around 3,000 feet and good visibility despite the absence of a moon. They homed-in on the drop zone by Gee-fix to plant their vegetables into the briefed locations from 5,300 and 5,700 at 21.48 and 21.45 respectively.

Probably as a result of the heavy losses recently incurred by the Halifaxes and Stirlings, an all-Lancaster force of 316 aircraft was assembled on the 3$^{rd}$ to conclude the current series of operations against the "Big City". 5 Group contributed 121 aircraft, including thirteen representing 49 Squadron, which departed Fiskerton between 19.33 and 19.55 with S/L Day and F/L Pike the senior pilots on duty. F/Sgt Barnes and crew were over the North Sea when the rear turret let them down and ended their interest in proceedings. After the rest of the force had rendezvoused over the North Sea, the bomber stream crossed the Dutch coast over the Den Helder peninsula and adopted a direct course of 350 miles, which took them north of Hannover to Brandenburg, some thirty-five miles short of the target. Long, straight legs were rarely employed because of the risk of interception by the Luftwaffe, but the forecast heavy cloud with tops at 18,000 feet accompanied the stream all the way from the Dutch coast to the target area and helped to keep the enemy at bay. The Path Finders had been briefed to use H2S to navigate their way via the region's lakes to the city centre aiming point, but the cloud miraculously dispersed in time to leave clear skies and allow them to drop ground-marking TIs rather than the less reliable skymarkers. The first TIs fell right over the aiming point, before others crept back for between two and five miles along the line of approach from the west. Fortunately, the backers up maintained the marking as the main force Lancasters came in in a single wave, and, although much of the bombing fell short of the city centre, most of it landed within the city boundaries, falling principally into the largely residential districts of Tiergarten, Wedding, Moabit and Charlottenburg and the industrial Siemensstadt, where much useful damage occurred that resulted in a loss of war production. The 49 Squadron crews carried out a time-and-distance run from yellow track markers and bombed on red and green TIs from 18,000 to 20,000 feet between 23.24 and 23.39. Many fires were observed, which appeared to be merging as the bombers turned towards the north for a return route that would intentionally violate Swedish airspace. Four Mosquitos laid spoof route marker flares well away from the actual track to mislead the night-fighters, but in the absence of the poorer performing Halifaxes and Stirlings, twenty-two Lancasters failed to return, almost 7% of those dispatched. JB126 had been hit by flak and was still fifteen miles short of the Tyneside coast at Blythe when F/O Coates was forced to ditch in unfavourable sea conditions at 03.57. The Lancaster broke up and the pilot went down with the nose section, while the flight engineer was swept away and three others succumbed before the rescue launch arrived on the scene. The two survivors were only slightly injured and were taken to hospital to recover.

Whether by design, or as a result of the losses sustained, Berlin was now shelved for the next ten weeks, while Harris sought other suitable targets, of which there were many. He would shortly begin a four-raid series against Hannover stretching over a four-week period but first he focused on southern Germany, beginning on the 5$^{th}$ with the twin cities of Mannheim and Ludwigshafen, which face each other from the East and West Banks respectively of the Rhine. The plan was to exploit the creep-back phenomenon that attended most large operations, by approaching the target from the west and marking the eastern half of Mannheim, with the expectation that the bombing would spread back along the line of approach across western Mannheim and into Ludwigshafen. A force of 605 aircraft was assembled, which included 108 Lancasters of 5 Group, a dozen of them at Fiskerton loaded with a cookie each and a variety of incendiaries packed in up to eighteen SBCs. They took off between 19.32 and 20.08 with F/L Pike the senior pilot on duty, and after climbing out, set course for Beachy Head and the Channel crossing. There were no early returns and all tracked across France to a point five miles south of Luxembourg, where route markers established the final turning point for a direct run on the target. The Path Finders were routed in over Kaiserslautern some thirty miles due west of Mannheim, from where they were to carry out a timed run to the aiming-point. The main force crews arrived to find clear skies and the Path Finders performing at their absolute best, and after first observing red and yellow markers, the 49 Squadron crews had green TIs in their bomb sights as they let their loads go from 20,000 to 22,000 feet between 23.06 and 23.37. Those arriving towards the later stages of the raid were drawn on by the burgeoning fires fifty miles ahead, and a number of large, red explosions were observed at 23.12, 23.23 and 23.27, the last of which was followed by a purplish-red mushroom of fire. Searchlights were numerous but the flak negligible, and it was the abundance of night-fighters that posed the greatest risk to life and limb, although most of the Fiskerton crews appeared to avoid any contact. Black smoke was rising through 15,000 feet as the bombers withdrew to the west, and the glow from the burning cities was visible for 150 miles and more into the return journey, which thirty-four aircraft would fail to complete. Thirteen Lancasters, an equal number of Halifaxes and eight

Stirlings were missing, and the percentage loss rates continued to tell the same story. 49 Squadron posted missing the crew of F/Sgt Kirton in ED416, which was attacked by a night-fighter when leaving the target and set on fire in the bomb bay and a wing. The crew was in the process of abandoning ship when the Lancaster was rent by an explosion and only the pilot and navigator survived to fall into enemy hands. Local reports confirmed that both Mannheim and Ludwigshafen had suffered catastrophic destruction, with almost two thousand fires in the latter alone, 986 of them classed as large. Mannheim's reporting system broke down completely and little detail emerged of this raid, although it would recover in time for the next assault in fewer than three weeks' time. What is known, is that the main railway station in Mannheim and three suburban stations were destroyed and the tank and military tractor factories belonging to Heinrich Lanz and Josef Vogele respectively sustained serious damage, as did the Rashig & Sulzer chemicals plant.

Munich was posted as the target on the 6th, for which the squadron made ready ten Lancasters as part of the ninety-two-strong 5 Group element in an overall force of 257 Lancasters and 147 Halifaxes, the Stirling brigade made conspicuous by its absence. The Fiskerton crews were airborne between 19.28 and 19.41 with S/L Day the only commissioned pilot on duty, each carrying a similar bomb load and adopting the same route as for the previous night. Again, there were no early returns, and all arrived at the Bavarian capital city under conditions that were not ideal. The cloud varied between five and nine-tenths, although some ground features, like the River Isar, could be identified and the red, yellow and green TIs observed. The 49 Squadron crews were among those carrying out a timed run from the Ammersee, located twenty-one miles away to the south-west, and bombed from 19,000 to 22,000 feet between 23.34 and 23.55. A large number of fires was observed to be grouped around the markers, but an accurate assessment was not possible, and local reports would suggest that the attack had been scattered across southern and western districts. The searchlights were ineffective because of the cloud but large numbers of night-fighters were again evident and sixteen aircraft failed to return, thirteen of them Halifaxes, a percentage loss rate of 8.8, compared with 1.2 for the Lancasters.

While 5 Group left the war to the other groups for the ensuing two weeks, a series of operations against French targets began on the night of the 8/9th with the bombing of heavy gun emplacements near the small coastal resort town of Le Portel. This was the final phase of Operation Starkey, a rehearsal for invasion, which had begun on the 16th of August and which was intended to deceive the enemy into believing that the invasion was imminent. Harris was less than enthusiastic about allowing his squadrons to participate in what he considered to be "play-acting" and managed to restrict Bomber Command's involvement to token gestures as on this night. The batteries, codenamed Religion and Andante, were to be attacked forty minutes apart, but much confusion surrounded the marking and the subsequent inaccurate bombing caused massive destruction to the town of Le Portel and many casualties. (For a detailed analysis of this operation, see the excellent book, The Starkey Sacrifice, by Michael Cumming, published by Sutton).

Despite having been laid down only nine months earlier, the Fiskerton main runway was showing signs of wear and tear that rendered it unfit for operational purposes. On the 10th, it was decided to launch operations from the nearby 52 Base station, Dunholme Lodge, the home of 44 (Rhodesia) Squadron, which, however, was not able to accommodate an influx of personnel. The solution was to conduct the briefings, pre-operational meal and kitting out at Fiskerton and bus the aircrew to their aircraft through the outskirts of Lincoln, and reverse the process on return for debriefing, post-operational meal and bed. On the 15th, ED448 crash-landed at Dunholme Lodge at the end of a ferry flight, and while the Lancaster would never fly again, F/Sgt Oglesby and crew were unhurt. It appears that the crew was broken up and F/Sgt Oglesby officially left the squadron in November, perhaps after undertaking additional training. It was on this day that W/C Johnson concluded his outstanding tour as commanding officer and was rewarded with promotion to group captain rank and command of Woodhall Spa, home at the time of 619 Squadron. His operational days were not over, however, and he would be appointed commanding officer of 97 (Straits Settlement) Squadron at the start of October 1944 and remain in post until the end of hostilities. His successor at 49 Squadron was W/C Alex Adams, whose arrival was not recorded in the ORB. On the night of W/C Johnson's departure, 617 Squadron carried out an operation against the earthen banks of the Dortmund-Ems Canal near Ladbergen and lost five of the eight crews taking part. Among them was the crew of S/L Ralph Allsebrook, whose Lancaster was hit by flak at ultra-low-level, bounced off the roof of a house, knocked a quayside crane into Das Nasse Dreieck (The Wet Triangle) a basin at the confluence of the Dortmund-Ems and Mittelland Canals and followed it into the water inverted. There were no survivors, and a memorial to the eight-man crew was unveiled at the crash site at Bergeshövede in June 2022.

It was not until the commencement of the series of raids on Hannover that 5 Group, as a whole, was roused from its slumber. The irony of such long layoffs was that airmen, despite occupying the most dangerous jobs in the fighting services, grew listless and bored when left to kick their heels, attend lectures and take part in PT, and no doubt cheered when the tannoys called them to briefing on the 22nd. They learned that they were to be part of a force of 711 aircraft to attack the ancient city of Hannover, situated in northern Germany midway between the Dutch frontier and Berlin. They were told that it was home to much war industry, and it was also the location of seven Nazi concentration camps, although, this was not known at the time among the Allies. According to Martin Middlebrook and Chris Everitt in Bomber Command War Diaries, the first two operations produced concentrated bombing but mostly outside of the target, while only the third one succeeded in causing extensive damage, which, if the figures are to be believed, seem to be massively out of proportion. The author contends that the reports of the crews after the first two operations suggest strongly that the damage to Hannover was accumulative over the first three raids and did not result from just one, as will be explained in the following narrative. The telling feature is, perhaps, that no reports came out of Hannover to corroborate the testimony of the crews on the first two raids, although post-raid reconnaissance by the RAF after the second one did show that some of the bombing had fallen into open country, and the Path Finders did admit to at least one poor performance.

Eleven 49 Squadron Lancasters were prepared at Dunholme Lodge and took off between 18.50 and 19.24 with F/Ls Munro and Thomas the senior pilots on duty, before climbing out and joining up with the other 135 participants from 5 Group for the 430-mile outward leg. The excellent serviceability continued and all from Dunholme Lodge reached the target area, where good visibility prevailed but stronger-than-forecast winds would play their part in pushing the marking and bombing towards the south-east. The attack was scheduled to begin at 21.30 and the first red TIs were observed three minutes later, before another was seen to cascade after overshooting the aiming point by an estimated four miles. This was followed by other red TIs overshooting by one to four miles with many greens falling among them, while the yellows seemed to be undershooting the reds by two miles and were closer to the city centre aiming-point. The 49 Squadron crews carried out their bombing runs from 18,000 to 21,500 feet between 21.31 and 21.47, aiming at red and green TIs and dodging the intense searchlights and heavy flak, which was bursting at around 18,000 feet. Some returning crews observed a line of fires developing from west to east, with smoke rising through 14,000 feet, while others claimed that fires ran from the aiming point in a north-north-westerly direction across the city. All were unanimous, however, that the raid had been highly successful and that the glow of fires was still visible from the Dutch coast, a distance of two hundred miles. Twenty-six aircraft failed to return, twelve of them Halifaxes, which again sustained the highest numerical losses, and this time, at 5.3%, even exceeded the Stirling's loss rate.

Let us now examine the claim that the main weight of bombs fell two to five miles south-south-east from the city centre and that the operation largely failed. Firstly, two to five miles in any city means that the bombing fell within the boundaries and, therefore, within the built-up area. Secondly, the majority of crews, if not all, reported a highly successful raid with fires right across the city, smoke rising to 14,000 feet as they left the scene and the glow visible from the Dutch coast. It is true that crews were very frequently mistaken in their belief that an attack had been successful, but the evidence on this occasion would seem to confirm their testimony. Decoy fire-sites do not produce a glow visible from a distance of two hundred miles or sufficient volumes of smoke to reach bombing height during the short duration of a raid and be dense enough to be visible at night.

On the 23$^{rd}$, and for the second time in the month, Mannheim was posted as the target and would face a force, which, at take-off, numbered 628 aircraft, 139 of them 5 Group Lancasters. Thirteen of these were made ready by 49 Squadron at Dunholme Lodge, while the crews attended briefing to learn that Mosquitos were to drop red and green route markers, before the Path Finder blind marker crews delivered flares and red TIs over the target by H2S to guide the visual markers to the precise aiming-point. This had been placed in the less-severely afflicted northern districts, which they would mark with yellow TIs, followed by the backers-up with greens. The 49 Squadron element took off between 18.33 and 18.59 with no senior pilot on duty and there were no early returns from either squadron as the bomber stream pushed on across France and into southern Germany to encounter largely clear skies and good visibility. At the head of the stream, the Path Finders had marked out the northern districts, which had not been hit so severely during the previous operation. The marking was accurate and concentrated, allowing the 49 Squadron crews to attack on red, green and yellow TIs from 16,000 to 21,000 feet between 21.55 and 22.15. Later bombing spilled over into the northern fringe of Ludwigshafen and out into the nearby towns of Oppau and Frankenthal, where much damage resulted. Returning crews reported that smoke had reached around 6,000 feet as they turned away and that the glow of fires remained visible for 150 miles into the return journey. Thirty-two crews were absent from debriefing, and this time eighteen of them were in Lancasters, compared with seven each for the Halifaxes and Stirlings. This provided a somewhat topsy-turvy and unusual loss-rate of 5.7%, 3.6% and 6% respectively. Among the missing Lancasters were two from 49 Squadron, including ED702, the aircraft favoured by the two previous commanding officers. On this night it contained the crew of P/O Cyril Anderson, the Yorkshireman whose legacy and that of his crew as Dambusters has been unfairly darkened by the class attitude of W/C Guy Gibson. There were no survivors and the fact that they are buried in the Rheinberg Cemetery, close to John Minchin, Hopgood and three other members of that crew, suggests that they were homebound near the Ruhr when the end came.

JB301 came down in southern Germany some twenty miles south-west of Mannheim and there were no survivors from the crew of F/Sgt Stanton. Post-raid reconnaissance and local reports revealed that 927 houses and twenty industrial premises had been destroyed in Mannheim and that the I G Farben factory in Ludwigshafen had sustained serious damage.

The Dortmund-Ems Canal disaster had left 617 Squadron with a need to recruit new crews and it was decided to do so on a volunteer basis as the squadron had now acquired a reputation as a "chop" unit. Among those eager to put themselves forward was the crew of W/O "Chuffy" Bull and they were posted on the 27th after a successful interview with "Mick" Martin at Coningsby. That night, Hannover was posted again as the target and a force of 678 aircraft made ready, which included a 5 Group contribution of 141 Lancasters, a dozen belonging to 49 Squadron. The crews learned at briefing that the Steinhude Lake to the north-west of the city was to be employed again by the Path Finder blind marker crews as the starting point for a timed run to the aiming point, which would be marked with yellow TIs on H2S and identified visually by the backers-up and marked with reds and greens. They departed Dunholme Lodge between 19.21 and 19.46 with W/C Adams the senior pilot on duty for the first time and followed in the wake of the Path Finders, who were unaware that the weather forecasts on which their performance would be based were incorrect. The result of that would be to push the marking some five miles from the city centre towards the north, but at least the weather improved markedly over Germany to present the crews with clear skies at the target. As JB229 closed on the target at 21,000 feet shortly before 22.20, it was fired upon by another Lancaster, wounding the rear-gunner and knocking out the pilot's intercom. The bomb-aimer believed that the pilot, F/Sgt Jupp, had been hit and jettisoned the bomb load, while the flight engineer shut down a damaged engine. As they turned for home, the other crews were delivering their cookie and 4lb and 30lb incendiaries mostly on green TIs from 19,000 to 21,000 feet between 22.04 and 22.24 and observed many fires with smoke rising to 15,000 feet. Returning crews again reported the glow of fires visible from the Dutch coast, and confidence in the success of the operation was unanimous across the Command, giving lie to the claim that little damage resulted. Post-raid photos did reveal many bomb craters in open country, but the fire and smoke evidence did not support decoy fire-sites, and no local report was forthcoming to shed further light. The loss of thirty-eight aircraft was probably something of a shock, but at least common sense returned to the statistics to re-establish the status-quo after the topsy-turvy outcome of the Mannheim raid. Seventeen Halifaxes, ten Lancasters, ten Stirlings and one Wellington failed to return, giving loss-rates for the four-engine types of 9% for the Stirling, 7.3% for the Halifax and 3.2% for the Lancaster.

The month ended with an operation to Bochum in the central Ruhr on the 29th, for which 49 Squadron made ready seven Lancasters in a 5 Group effort of 111, and they were part of an overall heavy force of 343 aircraft. The plan of attack required the Mosquito element to drop green warning flares, before Oboe-marking the aiming-point with red TIs, and in case they could not be seen through cloud, with red flares with green stars. The 49 Squadron element departed Dunholme Lodge between 17.57 and 18.24 with F/L Thomas the senior pilot on duty and proceeded to the target, kept on track by two route-marker flares at 20,000 feet, and after a two-and-a-half-hour outward flight, established their positions visually in good visibility. The Path Finders marked the aiming point with green TIs and the bombing was carried out from 17,500 to 20,500 feet between 20.51 and 21.08 in the face of a strong searchlight and moderate flak defence. Some returning crews described the target as a mass of flames with smoke rising rapidly to meet them, while local reports confirmed the destruction of 527 houses, with 742 others seriously damaged.

While this operation was in progress, fourteen 5 Group Lancasters were sent to the Baltic to mine the waters of the Privet I garden off distant Danzig (Gdansk). P/O Coxhill and crew had taken off at 17.59 and arrived at their destination under clear skies and in extreme darkness to deliver their mines into the briefed location in the Gulf of Pucka from 3,000 feet at 22.14. During the course of the month, the squadron carried out nine operations and dispatched eighty-one sorties for the loss of four Lancaster, three complete crews and five members of another.

## October 1943

The start of October was a busy time for the Lancaster squadrons, which would be called upon to participate in six major operations in the first eight nights. The month's account was opened at Hagen at the eastern end of the Ruhr on the 1st, for which a moderately sized heavy force of 243 Lancasters was drawn from 1, 5 and 8 Groups. 5 Group contributed 125 aircraft, eleven of them representing 49 Squadron, and they were loaded with a cookie and up to sixteen SBCs of incendiaries each, before departing Dunholme Lodge between 08.19 and 18.24 with W/C Adams and F/L Thomas the senior pilots on duty. They flew out over Skegness aiming for Egmond on the Dutch coast, to then skirt the northern edge of the Ruhr as far as Werl, a town to the north of the now famous Möhne reservoir, from where they would turn sharply to the south-west to run in on the target. F/Sgt Webb and crew lost the use of their rear turret and the mid-upper operated only sluggishly, forcing them to abandon their sortie. Meanwhile, W/C Adams and crew had been straying off course without noticing that their compass may have been defective, and they ended up bombing the estimated position of Cologne, some thirty-six miles from their intended target from 18,000 feet at 21.02. The others arrived in the target area to find ten-tenths cloud with tops at 8,000 feet and red and green Oboe-laid skymarkers to aim at and carried out their attacks from 18,000 to 21,000 feet between 20.59 and 21.10. Returning crews reported a column of black smoke rising through the clouds and some described a large bluish-green explosion at 21.03, the glow of fires beneath the cloud and an effective Path Finder performance. In addition to the usual housing damage, local reports confirmed the destruction of forty-six industrial firms, among them a manufacturer of accumulator batteries for U-Boots, and this would have an impact on U-Boot production. W/C Adams and his navigator had the sortie disallowed, the former for not having a drill in place for checking the accuracy of the compass and the navigator for complacency, while the rest of the crew were able to count it towards the completion of their tour.

294 crews from 1, 5 and 8 Groups were called to briefings on the 2nd to learn that Munich was to be their target for that night. 5 Group detailed 113 Lancasters, among them eleven representing 49 Squadron, whose crews, like the others of 5 Group, were to adopt the time-and-distance method of bombing. Their Lancasters were loaded at Dunholme Lodge with a cookie and ten SBCs each before taking off between 18.28 and 18.49 with F/L Thomas the senior pilot on duty. He was forced to turn back early because of an unserviceable rear turret and intercom issues, while the others set a course to the south coast to begin the Channel crossing to the Dunkerque region, before traversing France to enter Germany south of Strasbourg. They reached the target area after an

outward flight of some three-and-a-half hours and encountered cloud over the Wörthsee, situated some fifteen miles west-south-west of the centre of Munich, which had been selected as the starting point for the time-and-distance run. The skies over the city were clear of cloud, but the marking was scattered and led to most of the early bombing falling into southern and south-eastern districts. The 5 Group crews were unable to establish a firm fix on the Wörthsee, and this would lead to a creep-back of up to fifteen miles along the line of approach. The 49 Squadron crews bombed on red and green TIs from 19,000 to 21,000 feet between 22.34 and 22.48, but it was not all plain-sailing and eight Lancasters were lost. Returning crews suggested that the raid appeared to be concentrated on the eastern side of the city, and local authorities reported that 339 buildings had been destroyed.

Kassel, the industrial city located some eighty miles to the east of the Ruhr, would receive two visits from the Command during the month, the first on the 3rd, for which a force of 547 aircraft was assembled consisting of 223 Halifaxes, 204 Lancasters and 113 Stirlings. 5 Group supported the operation with ninety-two Lancasters, of which seven were made ready by 49 Squadron at Dunholme Lodge. At briefing at Fiskerton, the crews learned of the plan of attack, which called for the Mosquitos to provide route markers and for the Path Finder H2S crews to mark the target blind with yellow TIs and flares. The visual markers were then to identify the aiming-point and mark it with red TIs for the backers-up to maintain with greens. The 49 Squadron element took off between 18.19 and 18.36 with F/Ls Munro and Taylor the senior pilots on duty and there would be no early returns. Arriving in the target area, they found largely clear skies but thick ground haze, which may have been responsible for the Path Finder H2S "blind" markers overshooting the planned aiming point, and because of the haze and, possibly, decoy markers, the backers-up, whose job was to confirm their accuracy by visual means, were unable to correct the error. The 49 Squadron crews identified the target visually and by green TIs and bombed from 19,000 to 21,000 feet between 21.17 and 21.35, reporting on their return what appeared to be a good concentration of fires and a pall of smoke rising to meet them. In fact, the main weight of the attack had fallen onto the western suburbs, where the Henschel aircraft and tank factories and the Fieseler aircraft plant were hit, but a stray bomb load had also detonated an ammunition dump at Ihringshausen, situated close to the north-eastern suburb of Wolfsanger, which was left devastated by the blast. Twenty-four aircraft failed to return, fourteen Halifaxes, six Stirlings and four Lancasters, which gave a loss-rate of 6.3%, 3.2% and 2.9% respectively.

The busy schedule of operations was to continue at Frankfurt on the 4th, for which a force of 406 aircraft was made ready. The American confidence in the ability of its forces to deliver daylight attacks on military and war production targets in Germany had been shaken by the high loss rates, which were not sustainable. Since the first Hannover raid, a small number of 8th Air Force B17s had been flirting with night raids alongside their RAF colleagues and this night would bring their final involvement. 5 Group detailed ninety-five Lancasters, of which eight would represent 49 Squadron, and they departed Dunholme Lodge between 18.08 and 18.25 with F/L Pike the senior pilot on duty. They had to follow a somewhat circuitous route, which departed England over the Sussex coast and tracked across Belgium as if heading for southern Germany, before swinging to the north-east and passing to the west of Frankfurt for the final run-in of around eighty miles. This added significantly to the mileage but avoided the flak hotspots from the Dutch coast and north of the Ruhr. There were no early returns among the 49 Squadron element, and the target was reached after a four-hour outward flight, although an hour of that was generally accounted for in climbing-out and gaining height before setting course. Frankfurt was found to be clear of cloud, and the Path Finders produced a masterful marking performance to leave the city at the mercy of the main force, among which, the 49 Squadron crews bombed on red and green TIs from 17,500 to 22,400 feet between 21.35 and 22.00. They witnessed a highly-concentrated attack that left the eastern half of the city and the docks area a sea of flames and noted a large red explosion at 21.37, which threw flames up to 3,000 feet, while a column of smoke was rising through 8,000 feet. Some crews reported the glow from the burning city to be visible for 120 miles into the homeward leg and the successful outcome was gained for the modest cost of ten aircraft.

The squadron welcomed the crew of F/L Carfoot on posting from 1654 Conversion Unit on the 6th, his previous and extensive operational experience having been gained with Coastal Command. The busy first week of the month concluded with an operation against Stuttgart, for which a force of 343 Lancasters was drawn from 1, 3, 5, 6 and 8 Groups on the 7th. A new weapon in the Command's armoury was introduced for the first time in numbers on this night with the participation of a night-fighter-communications-jamming device called "Jostle" fitted in Lancasters of 1 Group's 101 Squadron. It required a specialist operator in addition to the standard crew of seven, who, though not necessarily a German speaker, could recognise the language and on hearing it, jam the signals on up to three frequencies by broadcasting engine noise over them. At 101 Squadron the device was referred to as ABC or Airborne Cigar, and once proved to be effective, ABC Lancasters would be spread through the bomber stream for all major operations, whether or not 1 Group was otherwise involved. The Lancaster would also carry a full bomb load reduced by 1,000lbs to compensate for the weight of the equipment and its operator.

5 Group put up 128 Lancasters for this operation, of which eleven were made ready by 49 Squadron at Dunholme Lodge and took off between 20.26 and 20.51 with S/L Day the senior pilot on duty. F/Sgt Jupp and crew were well into the outward leg when engine problems forced them to turn back, leaving the others to reach the target area, where ten-tenths cloud at 10,000 feet concealed the ground from view. The Path Finders employed H2S and established two areas of marking, which led to bombs falling in many parts of the city from the centre to the south-west. The 49 Squadron crews bombed from 18,000 to 22,500 feet between 00.11 and 00.25, before returning safely to report their impressions of a scattered attack, which cost a remarkably modest four aircraft. Among these, however, was ED426, which was damaged homebound by a combination of flak and a night-fighter and was flying a few feet off the ground on two engines over Commercy Forest, before scraping the treetops and crashing into a hill at Bezimont at 02.00. P/O Wares, the wireless operator and both gunners survived the impact, the first two-mentioned evading capture, while the gunners were taken into captivity. Whether or not the presence of the radio-countermeasures Lancasters was responsible for the low casualty rate could not be certain, but it was a promising start and would lead, ultimately, to the formation of a dedicated RCM force, 100 Group, in November.

Later, on the 8th, S/L Miller and crew were posted in from 44 (Rhodesia) Squadron to fulfil the role of flight commander. The third raid of the series on Hannover was posted to take place that night, and a force of 504 aircraft duly assembled, 5 Group contributing eighty-four Lancasters, ten of them made ready by 49 Squadron at Dunholme Lodge. A large diversionary raid was planned for Bremen to begin at 01.15, five minutes ahead of zero-hour at the main event and would involve seventeen 8 Group Halifaxes and seven Lancasters marking for a main force of ninety-five

Stirlings. The 49 Squadron element took off between 22.30 and 23.03 with F/L Munro the senior pilot on duty and after climbing out, set course for the northern tip of Texel to traverse northern Holland and enter Germany north of Meppen. All reached the target area to find largely clear skies and red and green TIs marking out the city-centre aiming point, inviting the bombs of the main force crews, those from 49 Squadron delivering theirs from 18,000 to 22,500 feet between 01.32 and 01.58. Having arrived in the early stages of the attack, they saw fires just beginning to take hold and it became clear as they retreated westwards, that the fires were developing into a serious conflagration. Curiously, despite the claim by some commentators that this was the one successful raid of the series, there was no mention of the glow being visible from a considerable distance, as had been the case with the first two operations. This time a local report did emerge, which described heavy damage in all districts except for those in the west, with a large area of fire engulfing the central districts. A total of 3,932 buildings was destroyed, while thirty thousand others were damaged to some extent and the death toll amounted to 1,200 people. These statistics seem somewhat excessive for a single operation by fewer than five hundred aircraft, particularly in the absence of the kind of crew reports common to the first two raids, and this adds weight to the author's contention, that the damage was accumulative over the three operations. Twenty-seven aircraft failed to return, but there were no empty dispersals at Dunholme Lodge.

F/L Tancred and crew were posted in from 1654 Conversion Unit on the 12th, during what was effectively a stand-down for the Path Finder and main force squadrons that would last for a period of ten days. In the meantime, it was left to the Mosquitos of 8 Group to take the war to Germany. JB411 was a brand-new Lancaster that had been delivered to Fiskerton on the 5th and had been "operationalised" by the ground crew before being handed over to F/Sgt Brunt and crew to ferry over to Dunholme Lodge. Halfway into its take-off run, the Lancaster swung off course and completed a 180-degree change of direction, before, it is alleged, continuing backwards along the runway at ninety miles per hour. Had the tailwheel not caught in a drainage ditch alongside the runway and been ripped off, it might have escaped serious damage, but the main undercarriage collapsed and ended the Lancaster's career before it had begun. The occupants were unhurt, but their reprieve would prove to be only temporary. If that excitement were not enough, the squadron was called to briefing along with the rest of 5 Group, no doubt to the relief of the crews who had become bored with filling their days with routine non-operational tasks. The wall map revealed Hannover as the target for the fourth and last time in this series, and the crews learned that this was to be an all-Lancaster affair involving 360 aircraft. 5 Group provided 143 of them, fourteen made ready by 49 Squadron, which departed Dunholme Lodge between 17.24 and 17.47 with S/L Miller and F/L Pike the senior pilots on duty. They made landfall over Texel and continued on an easterly track across Holland aiming for Cloppenburg and thence Nienburg and Celle, before turning to the south-west to run in on the target close to the Misburg oil refinery. They remained unmolested by the defences until encountering a nest of night-fighters on crossing the frontier into Germany, and at least thirteen aircraft were brought down during the ensuing forty-five minutes encompassing the approach and withdrawal phases. A layer of eight to ten-tenths cloud hung over Hannover with tops at 12,000 to 15,000 feet, and these conditions made it difficult for the Path Finders to establish the aiming point. It resulted in them dropping both sky and ground markers that lacked concentration, which would lead to a scattering of the effort. The 49 Squadron crews bombed mostly on red and green TIs or on release-point flares from 19,500 to 21,600 feet between 20.17 and 20.31, and a colossal explosion was observed at around 20.19. The strong night-fighter presence dissuaded crews from hanging around to assess the outcome further, and the impression of those returning was of a scattered attack. It was established later that most of the bombs had fallen into open country, a disappointment compounded by the loss of eighteen Lancasters. The four raids on Hannover had cost the Command 110 aircraft from 2,253 sorties, a loss rate of 4.9%, but much of the city now lay in ruins and would receive no further attention for a year, when the oil offensive and the close proximity of the Misburg synthetic oil plant to the east would return the region to prominence.

The first major attack of the war on the eastern city of Leipzig was planned for the 20th, for which an all-Lancaster force of 358 aircraft was assembled from 1, 5, 6 and 8 Groups. 5 Group was responsible for 140 Lancasters and 49 Squadron fifteen, which took off from Dunholme Lodge between 17.04 and 17.32 with F/Ls Carfoot and Thomas the senior pilots on duty. The crews of P/O Blackmore and F/Sgt Jones were back in the circuit within an hour because of compass and fuel pump failure and avoided the atrocious weather conditions encountered by the others outbound, with a towering front of ice-bearing cumulonimbus east of Hannover extending beyond 20,000 feet. Many crews were persuaded to turn back as engines began to falter and ice-accretion destroyed lift and four 49 Squadron crews took that decision in an eighteen-minute window between 20.22 and 20.40. P/O Kerr and crew were some forty miles north-west of Magdeburg when dumping their bomb load from a lowly 9,500 feet, while W/O Hales and crew attempted to climb into clear air and had reached 26,500 feet before accepting defeat and dropping their bombs in the region of Stendal, still some one hundred miles north of Leipzig. W/O Petty and crew were twenty miles north of Magdeburg when they let their bombs go over Colbitz from 18,000 feet and F/O Palmer and crew were only twenty miles behind them when they became the last 49 Squadron "boomerang". The others pushed on through the front to reach the target after a three-and-a-half-hour outward flight, to then encounter seven to ten-tenths cloud with tops as high as 14,000 feet. The Path Finders had been unable in the conditions to establish and mark the aiming point, leaving crews to bomb on e.t.a., on fires glimpsed through the cloud or on scattered skymarkers, the 49 Squadron element from 18,000 to 23,000 feet between 21.05 and 21.44. Sixteen Lancasters failed to return, and those crews that did make it home were unable to offer any useful details at debriefing.

The final major operation of the month was the second one against Kassel, for which preparations were put in hand on the 22nd. A force of 569 aircraft ultimately stood ready to take off in the early evening, 133 of them 5 Group Lancasters, eleven provided by 49 Squadron, which departed Dunholme Lodge between 17.56 and 18.30 with S/L Miller and F/Ls Pike and Tancred the senior pilots on duty. Some ran into an electrical storm over the North Sea but emerged on the other side to traverse Belgium, still in continuing unfavourable weather conditions, which miraculously improved in the target area to leave clear skies between the bombers and the target but ten-tenths cloud above them at 24,000 feet. At the opening of the raid, the H2S "blind" markers overshot the city-centre aiming point, leaving the success of the operation reliant upon the visual marker crews' backing up, and they did not disappoint. The red and green TIs were concentrated right on the aiming point and the main force crews followed up with accurate and concentrated bombing with scarcely any creep-back. The 49 Squadron crews carried out their attacks from 19,000 to 22,400 feet between 21.04 and 21.20 and observed the fires just beginning to take hold as they turned away. It was after the sound of their engines had receded that the fires joined together to engulf the city in what, in some areas, developed into a firestorm, though not one as fierce as that experienced in Hamburg. The massively successful operation was achieved at a high cost of forty-three bombers, twenty-five of them Halifaxes. Among nine missing 5 Group Lancasters were two belonging to 49 Squadron, JB416 and JB413, the former exploding over the target and crashing in the north-western suburb of Harleshausen with no survivors from the crew of F/Sgt Hodgkinson. The latter was set upon twice by a night-fighter shortly after leaving the target area and the rear gunner was killed during the first attack, while the second set a fuel tank on fire, which could not be extinguished. They were heading north and had reached the Wunstorf area by the time the order was given to abandon ship and five crew members landed safely to be taken into captivity. It seems that P/O Philip Taverner remained at the controls too long to ensure the safety of his crew, and his remains were found in the wreckage of the Lancaster. In Kassel, the shell-shocked inhabitants emerged from their shelters to find their city devastated and unrecognizable. After 3,600 fires had been dealt with, it would be established eventually that more than 4,300 apartment blocks containing 53,000 dwelling units had been destroyed or damaged, leaving up to 120,000 people without homes and in excess of six thousand others killed. 155 industrial buildings had also been destroyed or severely damaged, along with numerous schools, hospitals, churches and public buildings.

During the above operation, a 207 Squadron flight commander was lost, and F/L Pike was rewarded for his outstanding service and leadership qualities with promotion to acting squadron leader rank and a posting to Spilsby on the 28th. Sadly, he would fail to return from an operation in early March 1944, by which time he had been Mentioned in Despatches. During the course of the month, the squadron participated in nine operations and dispatched ninety-eight sorties for the loss of four Lancasters and three crews.

## November 1943

November brought with it the long, dark, cloudy nights which enabled Harris to return to his main theme, the destruction of Germany's capital city. The next four months would bring the bloodiest, hardest-fought air battles between Bomber Command and the Luftwaffe Nachtjagd and test the hard-pressed crews to the limit of their endurance. In a minute to Churchill on the 3rd, Harris stated, that with the participation of the American 8th Air Force, he could "wreck Berlin from end to end". He estimated that the campaign would cost the two forces between four and five hundred aircraft, but that it would cost Germany the war. This would remove the need for the kind of bloody, expensive and protracted land campaign, which he had personally witnessed during the Great War and had prompted him to "get into the air" at the earliest opportunity. It should be remembered that this was the first time in the history of air warfare, that the means had existed to prove the theory, that an enemy could be defeated by bombing alone. It is only in the light of more recent experiences that we have learned of the need, in a conventional conflict at least, to occupy the enemy's territory to secure submission. The Americans, however, were committed to victory on land, where film cameras could capture the glory and would not accompany Harris to Berlin.

While 49 Squadron had been absent from Fiskerton, not only had the main runway been repaired, but the FIDO fog-dispersal system was in the process of being installed, making the station one of only fifteen to be so equipped. 49 Squadron operations had returned to Fiskerton by the time that Düsseldorf was selected to open the month's operational account that very night, and no doubt, while the Prime Minister was digesting Harris's epistle, a force of 589 Lancasters and Halifaxes was being prepared for action. 5 Group's contribution amounted to 147 Lancasters, of which eighteen represented 49 Squadron, and they were each loaded with a cookie and SBCs of various incendiaries before taking off between 16.45 and 17.14 with F/Ls Carfoot, Tancred and Thomas the senior pilots on duty. F/Sgt White and crew were twenty miles off the Norfolk coast when engine issues ended their interest in proceedings, while the rest of the squadron joined the bomber stream over the North Sea and approached the south-western Ruhr after flying out over Belgium and through the concentration of fifty to sixty searchlights in the Mönchengladbach-Cologne corridor, some fifteen miles from the target. Small patches of cloud below them at 12,000 feet were drifting across the target along with smoke from the early fires, despite which, the visibility remained generally good and the Path Finders employed both sky and ground markers to good effect to identify the aiming point in the city centre. Bombing took place by the 49 Squadron crews on red and green TIs and skymarkers from 20,000 to 22,500 feet between 19.43 and 20.00, although F/O Cottingham's bombing height was recorded as an unlikely 29,200 feet. Fires were observed to be developing on both sides of the Rhine with black smoke rising through 6,000 feet as the bombers turned away. Eighteen aircraft failed to return, and, unusually, eleven were Lancasters and only seven Halifaxes. There were two empty dispersal pans at Fiskerton that should have been occupied by ED438 and JB305 and the station community would have to wait for the Red Cross to shed light on their fate. It turned out that the former had failed to survive the attentions of a night-fighter near Cologne and had exploded, killing F/L Thomas and four others, while three, including the second pilot, survived to fall into enemy hands. The latter crashed in the target area after being set on fire by flak and attacked by a Ju88, and it took the lives of F/L Carfoot and three of his crew, while the three survivors joined their squadron colleagues in enemy hands. It was on this night, that 61 Squadron's F/L Bill Reid earned the award of a Victoria Cross for pressing on to bomb the target after his Lancaster, LM360, had been severely damaged and a number of his crew either killed or wounded. Post-raid reconnaissance revealed that central and southern districts had sustained widespread damage to industry and housing, but no report came out of Düsseldorf to provide detail.

F/L Munro was posted to 1661 Conversion Unit on the 7th at the end of his first tour of operations. The only serious activity for 5 Group squadrons, thereafter, until the resumption of the Berlin campaign, was an operation on the night of the 10/11th in company with 8 Group against railway yards at Modane, situated in the foothills of the Alps in south-eastern France. A force of 313 Lancasters included a contribution from 5 Group of 136, of which it was intended, sixteen would represent 49 Squadron. The first five departed Fiskerton between 20.20 and 20.34 before W/O Webb and crew began their take-off run in JB533, during which it seems, the port tyre deflated and caused the Lancaster to career off the runway and ground-loop before catching fire. The crew had all scrambled clear and were safe by the time that the station fire department gave up on trying to extinguish the flames, which consumed the Lancaster before the bomb load went up and spread it around the airfield. The remaining ten take-offs had long since been cancelled and the Lancasters removed to a safe distance from the pyre. Ahead of the others lay an outward flight of more than 650 miles, which all from Fiskerton completed in around four-and-a-quarter hours to be rewarded by the presence of a full moon shining brightly from a cloudless sky. They pinpointed on Lake Bissorte, from where they carried out a time-and-distance run to the target, which they identified visually and by red and green TIs, before bombing from an almost uniform 15,000 feet between 01.01 and 01.13. The attack seemed to be concentrated around the markers and fires appeared to be taking hold, while a large explosion was observed at 01.13. Returning crews were fairly confident in the quality of their night's efforts and brought back two hundred bombing photos that revealed extensive damage to track and installations within one mile of the aiming point, a success gained at no cost in aircraft and crews.

On the 12th, the highly experienced navigator, F/L Pat Kelly, was posted to 617 Squadron, with which he would continue his illustrious career. On the 15th, a new 5 Group squadron, 630, was formed at East Kirkby around a nucleus from 57 Squadron, and F/Sgt White and crew were donated by 49 Squadron. Undaunted by the American response to his invitation to join the Berlin party, Harris would return alone, and the rocky road to the Germany's capital was re-joined by an all-Lancaster heavy force on the night of the 18/19th, while a predominantly Halifax and Stirling contingent of 395 aircraft acted as a diversion by raiding Mannheim and Ludwigshafen three hundred miles to the south-west. The Berlin-bound crews would benefit from four Mosquitos dropping dummy fighter flares, while other Mosquitos carried out a spoof raid on Frankfurt to protect the Mannheim force. The two formations would cross the enemy coast simultaneously some 250 miles apart to confuse the enemy night-fighter controllers, the route chosen for the Berlin brigade taking it via the Frisian island of Texel to a point north of Hannover, and thence to the target to pass over the centre on an east-north-easterly heading. The return route would pass south of Berlin and Cologne, before crossing central Belgium to gain the English Channel via the French coast. An innovation for this operation was a shortening of the bomber stream to reduce the time over the target to sixteen minutes. When the first Thousand Bomber raid had taken place in May 1942, with an unprecedented twelve aircraft per minute crossing the aiming point, there was considered to be a high risk of collisions. The number had since been increased to sixteen per minute, with large raids lasting up to forty-five minutes, but on this night, twenty-seven aircraft per minute were to pass over the aiming point.

49 Squadron made ready nineteen Lancasters as part of a 5 Group force of 182, and take-off from Fiskerton was accomplished without incident between 16.57 and 17.20 with W/C Adams and S/L Day the senior pilots on duty. A blanket of cloud covered the whole of northern Germany and crews were grateful for the red spotfire route marker dropped by the Path Finders north-east of Hannover, which confirmed that they were on track. They benefitted from good horizontal visibility despite the absence of a moon, while they were denied sight of the ground by the presence of cloud all the way to the target with tops at 6,000 feet. Searchlights illuminated the cloud as the 49 Squadron crews carried out their attacks on H2S-laid red and green skymarkers from 20,000 to 26,000 feet between 21.01 and 21.26. All returned home with nothing useful to pass on to the intelligence section at debriefing, and most considered the bombing to have been scattered and probably ineffective. The only casualty was P/O Hales' rear-gunner, Canadian, W/O Fraser, who had been airsick, and a particle of vomit had lodged in his oxygen tube, restricting the flow until he passed away quietly between checks from the front. Local sources confirmed that there had been no concentration of bombing and confirmed the destruction of 169 houses and a number of industrial units, with many more damaged to some extent. The diversion at Mannheim was deemed to have been successful in its purpose and caused some useful industrial damage, most seriously to the Daimler-Benz motor factory, which suffered a 90% loss of production for an unknown period. In addition to this, more than three hundred buildings were destroyed at a cost of twenty-three aircraft, while the losses from Berlin were encouragingly low at just nine.

The Lancasters stayed at home on the 19th, while 3, 4, 6 and 8 Groups combined to put 170 Halifaxes, eighty-six Stirlings and 10 Mosquitos into the air for a raid on the Ruhr city of Leverkusen. They were greeted in the target area by ten-tenths cloud and an absence of marking, which was caused by equipment failure among the Oboe Mosquitos. A few green TIs were spotted some five to ten miles to the north-west of the target during the approach, but the crews were left to establish their positions on the basis of their own H2S, which, over a region as densely built-up as the Ruhr, was a challenge. As a result, the operation was a complete failure, which sprayed bombs over twenty-seven towns in the region, mostly to the north of Leverkusen. Fiskerton's FIDO system was fired up in earnest for the first time on the 21st for night flying training and proved to be effective, and the station could now expect to be a welcome haven for crews across the Command seeking somewhere to land on a foggy night.

Harris called for a maximum effort on Berlin on the 22nd, and 764 aircraft were made available, of which sixteen of 5 Group's 166 Lancasters were provided by 49 Squadron. They departed Fiskerton between 16.35 and 17.04 with F/L Tancred the senior pilot on duty and after climbing out, adopted an outward route similar to that employed by the all-Lancaster force four nights earlier. This took them from Texel to a point north-west of Hannover, where a slight dogleg to port put them on a due-easterly heading directly to the target. Unlike the previous raid, however, rather than the circuitous return south of Cologne and out over the French coast, they would come home via a reciprocal route. This was based on a forecast of low cloud and fog over Germany, which would inhibit the night-fighter effort, while broken, medium-level cloud over Berlin would facilitate ground marking. An additional bonus was the availability to the Path Finders of five new H2S Mk III sets, while a new record of thirty-four aircraft per minute passing over the aiming point would be achieved by abandoning the long-standing practice of allocating aircraft types to specific waves. On this night, aircraft of all types would be spread through the bomber stream, and this was bad news for the Stirlings, which, by the very nature of their design, would be below the Lancaster and Halifax elements and in danger of being hit by friendly bombs.

W/O Webb and crew were back home within two-and-a-quarter hours after their rear turret became unserviceable, leaving the others to discover that the meteorological forecast had been inaccurate, and that the city was hidden under a blanket of ten-tenths cloud with tops at around 12,000 feet. This meant that ground marking would be largely ineffective, and that the least reliable Wanganui (skymarking) method would have to be employed. Crews ran into intense predicted flak and a mass of searchlights as they began their bombing runs, and those from 49 Squadron, which were allotted to waves 1, 4 and 5, aimed at red and green TIs and release-point flares from 18,500 to 22,100 feet between 20.04 and 20.29. The glow of fires was observed beneath the clouds and a very large explosion lit up the sky at 20.10. The impression was of a successful operation, but an assessment through the clouds was impossible and it was only once post-raid reconnaissance had taken place and local reports had filtered out that the scale of success would be realised. In the meantime, the families of twenty-six crews had to be informed that their son, husband or brother was missing as a result of air operations and teams from the Committee of Adjustment had to eradicate all trace of them from the billets. Eleven Lancasters, ten Halifaxes and five Stirlings had failed to return, which amounted to a loss-rate among the types respectively of 2.3%, 4.2% and 10.0%. 49 Squadron's JB368 disappeared without trace with the eight-man crew of F/O Cottingham, one of four members of the RCAF on board. The Stirling losses proved to be the final straw for Harris because of its short wing design, which restricted it to a low service ceiling, and the configuration of its bomb bay to small calibre bombs. Unlike the Lancaster and Halifax, it lacked development potential and was immediately withdrawn from future operations over Germany. It would still have an important role to play on secondary duties, however, bombing over occupied territory, mining, and in 1944, it would replace the Halifax to become the aircraft of choice for the two SOE squadrons, 138 and 161, at Tempsford. Many of those released from Bomber Command service would find their way to 38 Group, where they would give valuable service as transports and glider-tugs for airborne landings.

Reconnaissance photos revealed this last raid on Berlin to have been the most effective against it of the war to date and had caused a swathe of destruction from the city centre through the western residential districts of Tiergarten and Charlottenburg as far as the suburb town of Spandau. A number of firestorm areas were reported, and the catalogue of destruction included three thousand houses and twenty-three industrial premises. Many thousands more sustained varying degrees of damage, costing 175,000 people their homes and an estimated two thousand their lives, and by daylight on the 23rd, the smoke had risen to almost 19,000 feet.

A heavy force of 365 Lancasters and ten Halifaxes was made ready with some difficulty on the 23rd for a return to Berlin. Back-to-back long-range operations put a strain on those charged with the responsibility of getting the aircraft off the ground and the Ludford Magna armourers were unable to load all nineteen 101 Squadron Lancasters with the intended weight of bombs, sending them off 2,000lb short. 5 Group detailed 141 Lancasters, of which the fourteen belonging to 49 Squadron were each loaded with a cookie, and some had a 1,000 pounder along with their SBCs of incendiaries. They took off between 17.00 and 17.22 with no senior pilots on duty, and lost P/O Hales and crew after an hour to severe icing that coated the mid-upper and rear turrets and prevented them from functioning. There were eighteen 5 Group early returns among forty-six from the force as a whole, which was a further indication of the strain of back-to-back long-range operations. Another was the dumping of bombs over the North Sea by crews intending to push on to the target but wanting to gain more height. It involved largely those from 1 Group, who were shedding their cookies in protest at their A-O-C's policy of loading each Lancaster to its maximum all-up weight at the expense of altitude. The slogan "H-E-I-G-H-T spells safety" could be found on the walls of most bomber station briefing rooms at the time. The target was reached by way of the same route adopted on the previous night and was found to be covered by ten-tenths cloud with tops at between 10,000 and 15,000 feet. Guided by the glow of fires still burning beneath the clouds from the night before, and the presence of red and green TIs, the 49 Squadron crews bombed from 19,100 to 24,000 feet between 20.02 and 20.31 to contribute to another stunning blow. Returning crews described a column of smoke reaching 20,000 feet and the glow of fires visible again from the Hannover area some 150 miles from the target. It was on this night that fake broadcasts from England caused annoyance to the night-fighter force by ordering them to land because of fog over their bases, despite which, they still had a major hand in the bringing-down of twenty Lancasters. On return, JB229 was flying a thousand feet lower than indicated on the altimeter and hit the sea before coming to rest on the shoreline of the beach at Chapel St Leonards on the Lincolnshire coast. The crew scrambled out shaken and bruised to find themselves waist-deep in freezing cold seawater and spent a couple of days recovering in Scampton sick bay. Post-raid reconnaissance and local reports confirmed that this operation had destroyed a further two thousand buildings and killed around fifteen hundred people.

While 1, 3 and 5 Groups enjoyed a night off on the 25th, 216 Halifaxes of 4 and 6 Groups and forty-six 8 Group Halifaxes and Lancasters carried out an operation against Frankfurt, where the blind markers established a firm H2S fix and delivered yellow TIs and red flares with green stars to coincide with the e.t.a. of the main force crews. Local reports described a modest amount of housing damage and 3,500 people bombed out of their homes, in return for which, eleven Halifaxes and a single Lancaster failed to return.

After a three-night rest for most of the Lancaster crews, 443 of them were briefed on the 26th for a return to the "Big City" for the fourth attack since the resumption of the campaign. 5 Group detailed 161 Lancasters, fourteen of them made ready by 49 Squadron, which departed Fiskerton between 17.15 and 17.32 with no senior pilot on duty. A diversionary raid on Stuttgart by a predominantly Halifax force followed the same route as those bound for Berlin, which involved an outward leg across the French coast and Belgium to a point north of Frankfurt, where they diverged. An indication of the beneficial effects of the three-day lay-off was a 44% reduction in early returns by 5 Group crews compared with the previous Berlin raid. P/O Ratcliffe and crew were late setting course after obtaining a doubtful Gee-fix, and unable to make up time, jettisoned their load and returned home. The remaining 49 Squadron crews, who were spread among the first three waves in the bomber stream, found Berlin under clear skies, but despite the favourable conditions, the Path Finders overshot the city centre aiming point by six or seven miles and marked an area well to the north-west, which happened to contain many war-industry factories. The Fiskerton crews bombed on red and green TIs from 19,500 and 24,500 feet between 21.19 and 21.30 and on return spoke of a mass of fires and thick smoke rising to 15,000 feet. JB235 contained the eight-man crew of Sgt Richardson RAAF, who were on their first operation together and had a "spare bod" in the rear turret. They had survived a brush with a Me110 shortly after leaving the target, and despite the rear turret jamming, the mid-upper gunner believed that they may have shot their assailant down. They were on final approach to Fiskerton, "in the funnel", at 01.03, when the Lancaster's main undercarriage suddenly made contact with the ground more than two miles short of the threshold. A crash was inevitable, and the aircraft broke apart behind the trailing edge as it slid across the farmland, catching fire as it went. Despite the heroic efforts of the surviving crew members and the station fire brigade, the pilot and four others perished in the wreckage. Other pilots commented on the glare from the FIDO installation and the thought was that this may have contributed to the tragedy. Night-fighters took a heavy toll of bombers during the return flight and among twenty-eight missing Lancasters was 49 Squadron's JB362, which crashed south of Lake Gransee, some thirty-five miles north of Berlin and only the bomb-aimer survived from the crew of W/O Brunt. It was learned later that thirty-eight war-industry factories had been destroyed and many others damaged.

These last three operations against Berlin undoubtedly represented the best phase of the entire campaign, and according to local reports, the total death toll on the ground resulting from them amounted to 4,330 people, while the destruction of 8,700 apartment buildings containing more than 104,500 flats and damage to several times that number, robbed 450,000 residents of their homes for varying lengths of time. However, Berlin was not Hamburg, where narrow streets had aided the spread of fire. Berlin was a modern city of concrete and steel with wide thoroughfares and open spaces to create natural firebreaks, and each building destroyed added to these, so that the campaign would become a bitter struggle of ever decreasing returns. During the course of the month the squadron took part in six operations and dispatched eighty-six sorties for the loss of seven Lancasters, four complete crews and six other airmen.

# December 1943

Berlin would continue to be the dominant theme during December, and, as November had ended, so December would begin. A heavy force of 443 aircraft stood ready to take off in the late afternoon of the 2nd, all but fifteen of them Lancasters, after the main Halifax element had been withdrawn because of fog over their Yorkshire stations. 5 Group contributed 145 Lancasters, of which fourteen represented 49 Squadron, and they departed Fiskerton between 16.21 and 16.45 with F/L Tancred the senior pilot on duty. After climbing out, they headed for the Lincolnshire coast to rendezvous over the North Sea with the rest of the force for a straight-in-straight-out route across Holland and northern Germany with no feints or diversions. First, however, the crews had to negotiate a towering front of ice-bearing cloud over the North Sea, which would contribute to a 10% rate of early returns, although none from 49 Squadron. They pushed through the challenging conditions and made it to the target area, although mostly south of track after variable winds had thrown them off course and dispersed the bomber stream. They also had to contend with large numbers of enemy night-fighters that would harass the bombers all the way to the target, after the controller had been able correctly to predict it. The Path Finders employed H2S to establish their position at Stendal, but had strayed some fifteen miles south of track and mistakenly used the town of Genthin as their reference for the run-in. The 49 Squadron crews were spread among the three waves and found good visibility as they were guided by release-point flares to the aiming point, where they encountered a thin layer of two to three-tenths cloud at around 5,000 feet but up to nine-tenths between 10,000 and 12,000 feet, which the searchlights were able to pierce. They bombed on skymarkers and red and green TIs and where possible ground detail like burning streets, from 20,000 to 23,500 feet between 20.14 and 20.33. They reported observing scattered fires and a number of large explosions and some claimed the glow to be visible from 120 miles into the homeward leg. F/L Tancred and crew returned on three engines after the starboard-outer was lost to flak. It was a bad night for the bomber force, which lost forty aircraft, mostly in the target area and on the way home. W/O Petty and crew had lost the use of the rear turret on the way out but elected to continue and were attacked twice by night-fighters over the target, when they had only intermittently jamming guns in the mid-upper turret with which to defend themselves. While in the throes of evasive action, they were hit by flak, which set the starboard-inner engine on fire and persuaded the captain to issue a bale-out order. Six drifted down into the arms of their captors, leaving the bomb-aimer and rear gunner unaccounted for, the latter having been observed to leave the Lancaster. Bombing photographs suggested that the raid was only partially successful, causing useful damage in industrial districts in the west and east, but scattering the main weight of bombs over the southern districts and outlying communities to the south.

Having been spared by the weather from experiencing an effective visitation from the Command in October and exploiting the enemy's expectation that Berlin would be the target again, Leipzig found itself at the end of the red tape on briefing-room wall-maps from County Durham to Cambridgeshire on the 3rd. A force of 527 aircraft was made ready, which included 103 Lancasters of 5 Group, eleven of them belonging to 49 Squadron, which departed Fiskerton between 00.10

and 00.33 with S/L Miller the senior pilot on duty. The bomber stream headed for Berlin as a feint, passing north of Hannover and Braunschweig with ten-tenths cloud beneath them and an hour's journey to Leipzig still ahead of them. Then, as they turned towards the south-east, the Mosquito element continued on to carry out a diversion at the capital. Night-fighters had already infiltrated the stream at the Dutch coast, but the feint had the desired effect, and few night-fighters were encountered in the target area, where two layers of ten-tenths cloud prevailed with tops at around 7,000 and 15,000 feet. The Path Finders marked by H2S with green skymarkers and the 49 Squadron crews bombed on these from 20,000 to 23,100 feet between 04.05 and 04.13, observing explosions and a strong glow beneath the clouds. The emergence through the cloud tops of black smoke suggested that an accurate and concentrated attack had taken place and the smoke and glow remained visible for 150 miles into the return journey south-east towards the French frontier. Had many aircraft not then strayed into the Frankfurt defence zone, the losses may have been fewer, but twenty-four aircraft failed to return, fifteen of them Halifaxes. Local reports confirmed this as a highly successful operation, which had hit residential and industrial areas and was the most destructive raid visited upon this eastern city during the war. Sadly, for the Command, it would take its revenge in time.

Thereafter, minor operations carried the Command through to mid-month, and during this period, 617 Squadron lent a number of crews to Tempsford, home to the highly secret "Moon" squadrons, 138 and 161, which operated on behalf of Special Operations Executive (SOE) and Secret Intelligence Service (SIS) to deliver and collect agents from the Continent and maintain a supply of arms and equipment to the resistance organisations. Such was the high demand for operations, that the resident squadrons frequently supplemented their numbers by importing aircraft and crews from less busy units, which at the moment meant 617 Squadron and soon the Stirlings of 3 Group. On the night of the 10/11th, W/O "Chuffy" Bull and crew were sent on a supply drop to France in Bill Townsend's Dams Lancaster, ED886, and failed to return after falling victim to flak. Two members of the crew were killed, one evaded capture and Bull and three others were taken into captivity.

On the 16th, the Lancaster stations were roused and instructed to prepare 483 of the type for that night's operation to Berlin for the sixth time since the resumption of the campaign. 5 Group put up 165 aircraft, sixteen of them representing 49 Squadron, which took off between 16.01 and 16.35 with S/L Miller and F/L Tancred the senior pilots on duty. They were to cross the Dutch coast in the region of Castricum-aan-Zee, and then head due east all the way to the target with no deviations. A three-quarter moon would rise during the long return leg over the Baltic and Denmark, but it was hoped that the very early take-off and the expectation of fog over enemy night-fighter stations would reduce the risk of interception. Night-fighters were sent to meet the bomber stream at the Dutch coast, and P/O Ratcliffe and crew had the misfortune to cross paths with the one captained by Oblt Heinz-Wolfgang Schnaufer of IV./NJG1, who shot down JB545 to crash without survivors at 18.32 near Sonnega, in the Friesland region of northern Holland. The others pressed on to find Berlin obscured by ten-tenths cloud with tops at around 5,000 feet, but still identifiable by red and green skymarkers, which were bombed from 18,500 to 22,000 feet between 20.01 and 20.11. The return over Denmark passed largely without major incident, but the greatest difficulties awaited the 1, 6 and 8 Group crews as they arrived home to find their airfields covered by a blanket of dense fog. With little reserves of fuel, the tired crews began a frantic search to find somewhere to land, stumbling blindly through the murk to catch a glimpse of the ground.

For many, this proved fatal, while others gave up any hope of landing and abandoned their aircraft. Twenty-nine Lancasters and a mine-laying Stirling were thus lost and more than 150 airmen killed in these most tragic of circumstances. To this number was added the twenty-five Lancasters failing to return from the raid, many of which were accounted for by night-fighters while outbound. Returning crews reported the glow of fires, while others saw nothing through the cloud and it was a local report that confirmed a moderately effective raid, which had fallen principally onto central and eastern districts, where housing suffered most.

A three-day stand-down allowed the crews to recover from the Berlin operation and it was the 20th when all stations were notified of an operation that night to Frankfurt, for which a force of 390 Lancasters and 257 Halifaxes was assembled. 5 Group made ready 168 Lancasters and at Fiskerton, fifteen 49 Squadron Lancasters were loaded with the requisite amount of fuel and a cookie and sixteen SBCs of incendiaries each and dispatched between 16.57 and 17.12 with F/L Tancred and the recently promoted F/L Bacon the senior pilots on duty. While the main operation was in progress, forty-four Lancasters and ten Mosquitos of 1 and 8 Groups were to carry out a diversion at Mannheim, some forty miles to the south. After climbing out, the crews set course for Southwold and the North Sea-crossing to the Scheldt estuary, before passing north of Antwerp and flying the length of Belgium to the German frontier north of Luxembourg. The German night-fighter controller had picked up transmissions from the bomber stream as soon as it left the English coast and was able to track it all the way to the target and vector his fighters into position. Many combats took place during the outward flight and the diversion failed to draw fighters away from the main action. The problems continued at the primary target, where the forecast clear skies failed to materialize and the crews were greeted by four to nine-tenths cloud at between 5,000 and 10,000 feet. This allowed some of them to pick out ground features, while others fixed their positions by H2S, if so equipped, and the main force Lancaster crews simply waited for TIs on e.t.a. The Path Finders had prepared a ground-marking plan in expectation of good vertical visibility, and dropped red, green and yellow TIs, while the Germans lit a decoy fire-site five miles to the south-east of the city. Some crews described the marking as late and erratic, and those from 49 Squadron bombed on red and green TIs from 19,000 to 23,000 feet between 19.41 and 19.55. Most thought the attack to be scattered in the early stages, becoming more concentrated as it progressed, and many commented on the new cookies detonating with a brighter flash than the old ones. All but one of the 49 Squadron Lancasters returned safely to Fiskerton, JB467 having crashed a few miles to the north-east of Hanau with no survivors from the crew of P/O Blackmore DFC. They had contributed to a moderately successful raid, and at least one crew reported the glow of fires remaining visible for 150 miles into the return journey. Any success was achieved largely as the result of the creep-back from the decoy site, which fell across the suburbs of Offenbach and Sachsenhausen, situated on the southern bank of the River Main. 466 houses were destroyed and more than nineteen hundred seriously damaged, despite which, the operation fell well short of its aims and the loss of forty-one aircraft was a high price to pay. The Halifaxes suffered heavily, losing twenty-seven of their number, a loss-rate of 10.5% compared with the Lancasters' 3.6%.

Just two more operations remained before the year ended and both were to be directed against Germany's capital city. The first was posted on the 23rd and would involve an all-Lancaster heavy force with seven Halifaxes among the Path Finder element and eight Mosquitos to provide a diversion. The 130 Lancasters of 5 Group included thirteen representing 49 Squadron, which were loaded with a cookie and eleven SBCs each and launched into the cold night air between 23.57

and 00.16 with S/L Miller and F/L Tancred the senior pilots on duty. The route to the target was somewhat circuitous and took the bomber stream in a south-easterly direction to the Scheldt estuary, before hugging the Belgian/Dutch frontier to cross into Germany south of Aachen, as if threatening Frankfurt. When a point was reached south of Leipzig, the route turned sharply towards the north and Berlin, while the Mosquito feint threatened Leipzig. P/O Ewens and crew were thwarted by the failure of navigation equipment and turned back, while the vanguard of the bomber stream reached the target to find it enveloped in up to eight-tenths cloud at between 5,000 and 10,000 feet. This might not have been critical had the Path Finders not suffered an unusually high failure rate of their H2S equipment, which resulted in scattered and sparse sky-marking. The 49 Squadron crews found red and green skymarker flares at which to aim their bombs from 19,500 to 23,500 feet between 04.00 and 04.15 and observed well-concentrated fires and at least four large explosions, one described as orange and red and lasting for thirty seconds. A relatively modest sixteen Lancasters failed to return, but all from Fiskerton landed safely in time to observe the fifth wartime Christmas. A local report named the south-eastern suburbs of Köpenick and Treptow as the ones to sustain the most damage, with 287 houses and other buildings suffering complete destruction.

The "Big City" was posted as the target again on the 29th, for what, for the Lancaster operators, would be the first of three raids on it in five nights spanning the turn of the year. A force of 712 aircraft included 163 Lancasters of 5 Group, of which fifteen represented 49 Squadron and departed Fiskerton between 16.40 and 17.00 with the newly promoted F/L Palmer the senior pilot on duty. It was from this juncture that the intolerable strain on the crews of successive long-range flights in difficult weather conditions would begin to become manifest in some squadrons through the rate of early returns, which on this night reached forty-five or 6.3%. The bomber stream was routed out over the Dutch Frisian islands pointing directly for Leipzig and having reached a point just to the north of that city, was to turn to the north towards Berlin, while Mosquitos carried out spoof raids on Leipzig and Magdeburg. 49 Squadron was exempt from early returns, and its crews reached the target area to find ten-tenths cloud with tops at anywhere between 7,000 and 18,000 feet. Red and green Path Finder release-point flares could be seen hanging over the city, upon which they aimed their bombs from 20,000 to 22,000 feet between 20.06 and 20.24. At debriefing, crews reported a considerable red glow beneath the clouds, which remained visible for a hundred miles and gave the impression of a concentrated and successful assault. This was not entirely borne out by local reports, which revealed that the main weight of the raid had fallen onto southern and south-eastern districts and also into outlying communities to the east. 388 buildings were destroyed, although none of significance, and ten thousand people were bombed out of their homes. Eleven Lancasters and nine Halifaxes failed to return, a loss-rate of 2.4% for the former and 3.5% for the latter.

During the course of the month the squadron participated in six operations and dispatched eighty-four sorties for the loss of three Lancasters and their crews. It had been a testing end to a year which had brought major successes and advances in tactics, but it had also been a year of high losses, particularly among the Stirling and Halifax squadrons. While Window had been an instant success, it had also caused the Luftwaffe to rethink and reorganise and the night-fighter force which emerged from the ruins of the old system was a leaner, more efficient and altogether more lethal beast than that of before. As far as the crews of Bomber Command were concerned, the New

Year offered the same fare as the old one, which few would view with relish and the next three months would see morale at its lowest ebb as the winter campaign ground on.

# January 1944

The change of year was not destined to effect a change in the emphasis of operations, and this was, no doubt, a disappointment not only to the hard-pressed crews of Bomber Command but also to the beleaguered residents of Germany's capital city. Proud of their status as Berliners first and Germans second, they were a hardy breed and just like their counterparts in London during the Blitz of 1940, would bear their trials with fortitude and humour and would not buckle under the constant assault from above. "You may break our walls", proclaimed banners in the streets, "but not out hearts", and the most popular song of the day, "Nach jedem Dezember kommt immer ein Mai", "After every December there's always a May", was played endlessly over the airwaves, its sentiments hinting at a change in fortunes with the onset of spring. Harris allowed the Berliners little time to enjoy New Year, and as New Year's Day dawned, plans were already in hand to continue the onslaught. Before it ended, the first of 421 Lancasters, 161 representing 5 Group, would be taking off and heading eastwards to arrive over the city as the clock showed 03.00 hours on the 2nd.

Take-off had actually been delayed because of doubts over the weather, and this meant that insufficient hours of daylight remained to allow the planned outward route over Denmark and the Baltic. Instead, the bomber stream would adopt the previously used almost direct route across Holland and northern Germany, but return as originally planned more circuitously, passing east of Leipzig, before racing across Germany between the Ruhr and Frankfurt and traversing Belgium to reach the Channel near the French port of Boulogne. 49 Squadron's fifteen participants departed Fiskerton between 00.06 and 00.31 with S/L Miller and F/L Palmer the senior pilots on duty and each carrying a mix of high explosives and 4lb and 30lb incendiaries. The force was gradually depleted by twenty-nine early returns, one of them, that of P/O Simpson and crew, who made it as far as Stendal, some fifty miles short of Berlin, before a fuel leak in the port-inner engine feed persuaded them to return home on three. The bomber stream had covered the four-hundred-mile leg from the Dutch coast to Berlin in under two hours without once catching a glimpse of the ground through the dense cloud, and it was no different at the target, which was completely obscured by a layer of ten-tenths cloud with tops in places as high as 19,000 feet. The Path Finders had to employ skymarking (Wanganui), which was somewhat scattered, and the 49 Squadron crews aimed for these parachute flares from 19,000 to 22,100 feet between 02.55 and 03.30. They observed the glow of fires and smoke rising through the cloud tops and a huge explosion was witnessed at 03.07, which lit up the clouds for three seconds, but it was impossible to assess what was happening on the ground. It was established, ultimately, that the operation had been a failure, which had scattered bombs across the southern fringes of the city causing only minor damage, while the main weight of the attack had fallen beyond the city boundaries into wooded and open country. The disappointment was compounded by the loss of twenty-eight Lancasters, a dozen of them belonging to 5 Group.

During the course of the 2nd, a heavy force of 362 Lancasters and nine of the new Mk III Hercules-powered Halifaxes was made ready for a return to Berlin that night. There was snow on the ground, and many of the crews called to briefing were still tired from being late to bed following the almost-eight-hour round trip the night before. Some of these were in a mutinous frame of mind at being on the order of battle again so soon. 5 Group cancelled twenty-five of its intended contribution, leaving 119 to take part, the twelve-strong 49 Squadron element departing Fiskerton between 23.42 and 23.56 with S/L Day and F/Ls Bacon and Palmer the senior pilots on duty. The outward route crossed the Dutch coast near Castricum and took the bomber stream to a point south-east of Bremen, followed by a dogleg to the north-west and, finally, a ninety degree change of course to the south-east in the Parchim area to leave a ninety-mile run to the target. The crew of P/O Ewens was the only 49 Squadron representative among a massive sixty early returns, 15.7% of those dispatched, and that was caused by the indisposition of the navigator. Many were defeated by severe icing conditions, while others abandoned their sorties because of minor problems that might have seen them carry on had they been fully rested. The route changes worked well to throw off the night-fighters, but they would congregate in the target area after the controller correctly identified Berlin as the target forty minutes before zero-hour. Ten-tenths cloud with tops at 16,000 feet forced the bombing to take place on the red skymarkers with green stars or on the glow of fires, the 49 Squadron crews carrying out their attacks from 20,000 to 21,500 feet between 02.46 and 02.59. They reported smoke rising to 20,000 feet as they turned away, but it was not possible to make an accurate assessment of the outcome and the impression was of an effective attack, when, in fact, it had been another failure. Bombs had been scattered across the city and destroyed just eighty-two houses for the loss of twenty-seven Lancasters, most of which had fallen victim to night-fighters in the target area. Two Lancasters failed to return to Fiskerton, JB231 and JB727, and the fate of their crews demonstrated the diverse fortunes of war. The former was the victim of a head-on collision with another Lancaster on approach to the target and F/O Young RCAF and his crew all survived to be taken into captivity, while the latter was lost without trace and took with it the crew of F/L Palmer.

After three trips to the "Big City" in five nights, it would now be left to the Mosquitos of 8 Group's Mosquito squadrons to disrupt the resident's sleep with cookies until the final third of the month, allowing Harris to turn his attention on the 5th upon the Baltic port-city of Stettin, which had not been attacked in numbers since the previous April. It was to be another predominantly Lancaster affair involving 348 of the type accompanied by ten Halifaxes, 5 Group putting up 120 aircraft and 49 Squadron five. An additional six Lancasters were prepared for a mining operation in the Geranium I and II gardens to the north of the port in the region of the Baltic that was known at the time as the Gulf of Pomerania. The two elements took off from Fiskerton together between 23.54 and 00.12 with W/C Adams leading the bombing brigade and F/L Bacon the gardeners, and in contrast to the seventeen early returns by 5 Group crews during the last Berlin operation, only one came home early on this night. Those continuing on found themselves in thick cloud at cruising altitude, some struggling to find a clear lane even when as high as 23,000 feet, but on the plus side, they all benefitted from a Mosquito diversion at Berlin, which kept the night-fighters off the scent. Stettin was found to be partially visible through five-tenths thin cloud with tops at around 10,000 feet, and crews were able to identify some ground features before focusing on H2S-laid flares and green TIs, which the 49 Squadron crews bombed from 20,000 to 22,300 feet between 03.53 and 03.57. The gardeners, meanwhile, established their positions by H2S before five of them planted their vegetables into the briefed locations from 12,000 feet. W/O Jupp and crew lost their H2S in the target area, and unable to plant with guaranteed accuracy, jettisoned their mines "safe" away from the area. The bombing element returned home to provide the intelligence section with accounts of a highly accurate and concentrated attack, which seemed to leave the entire city on fire. Fourteen Lancasters and two Halifaxes failed to return, in exchange for which, post-raid reconnaissance and local reports confirmed heavy damage in central and western districts, where 504 houses and twenty industrial buildings had been destroyed, a further 1,148 houses and twenty-nine industrial buildings seriously damaged and eight ships sunk in the harbour.

Following this operation, the crews of the heavy squadrons were rested until mid-month, while the Halifax units would spend three weeks in virtual hibernation apart from isolated mining forays. When briefings finally took place on the 14th, there was doubtless some relief to see the red tape on the wall maps terminate some way short of Berlin. It led, in fact, to Braunschweig (Brunswick), the historic and culturally significant city situated some thirty-five miles to the east of Hannover. It had not been attacked by the Command in numbers before, and on this night, would face a force, which, at take-off, numbered 496 Lancasters and two Halifaxes. 5 Group supported the operation with 153 Lancasters, of which nine represented 49 Squadron and departed Fiskerton between 16.22 and 16.34 with F/Ls Bacon and Tancred the senior pilots on duty and Lt Stevens of the USAAF operating for the first time as crew captain. After climbing out they headed towards Germany's north-western coast, where they were met by part of the enemy night-fighter response, which would harass the bomber stream all the way to the target and back. Complete cloud cover at the target, in places up to around 15,000 feet, dictated the use of red skymarkers with green stars, at which the 49 Squadron crews aimed their cookies and incendiaries from 20,000 and 22,000 feet between 19.16 and 19.26. The enemy fighters scored consistently and accounted for the majority of the thirty-eight missing Lancasters, many of which came down around Hannover. 49 Squadron's JB295 crashed at 19.15 at Reppner to the south-west of Braunschweig, close to the Herman Göring steelworks at Salzgitter. F/L Tancred and four of his crew lost their lives, while the flight engineer and navigator survived to fall into enemy hands. The attack almost entirely missed the city, falling mostly onto outlying communities to the south and was reported locally as a light raid. This would be a continuing theme in future attacks up to the autumn, as Braunschweig enjoyed something of a charmed life, leading to a belief among the populace of the surrounding villages that they were being targeted intentionally in an attempt to drive them into the city, before a major operation destroyed it with them in it!

The Path Finders, in particular, had been taking a beating since the turn of the year, with 156 Squadron alone losing fourteen Lancasters and crews in just three operations, four and five on Berlin, and five again on Braunschweig. This was creating something of a crisis in Path Finder manpower, particularly with regard to experienced crews, and a number of sideways postings took place between the squadrons to ensure a leavening of experience in each one. One of the solutions was to take the cream from among the crews emerging from the training units, rather than wait for them to gain experience at a main force squadron.

Another lull in operations kept the bomber force on the ground until the 20th, when orders were received to prepare for a maximum effort for the next round of the Berlin offensive. The Halifax squadrons, which had largely remained dormant since late December, were roused from their slumber and 264 of them joined 495 Lancasters to constitute the Path Finder and main force elements, while two small Mosquito sections carried out spoof raids on Kiel and Hannover. 5

Group weighed in with 155 Lancasters, a dozen of them made ready by 49 Squadron and assigned to the first, fourth and fifth waves, and they took off between 16.04 and 16.36 with no senior pilots on duty. It was a rare pleasure for them to be taking off in daylight, and they circled as they climbed out above Fiskerton before setting course, while observing the dozens of Lancasters rising up into the dusk to join them from the neighbouring stations. They turned their snouts towards the west coast of the Schleswig-Holstein peninsula at a point opposite Kiel, rendezvousing with the other groups over the North Sea and all the time shedding individual aircraft as a hefty seventy-five crews abandoned their sorties and turned back. They others made landfall over the Nordfriesland coast, before turning to the south-east on a more-or-less direct course for Berlin and soon found themselves being hounded by night-fighters. The enemy controller had fed a proportion of his resources into the bomber stream east of Hamburg, and they would remain in contact until a point between Leipzig and Hannover on the way home, although, curiously, the 5 Group brigade saw nothing of this and would lose just a single 57 Squadron Lancaster. The two Mosquito diversions had been completely ignored by the Luftwaffe controller, who knew well in advance that Berlin was to be the target. The Path Finders arrived over the Müritzsee to the north of Berlin with a sixty-mile run-in to the aiming point, and they found this to be concealed beneath the same ten-tenths cloud that had accompanied them for the entire outward leg. The tops of the cloud lay beneath the bombers at up to 15,000 feet as the main force crews carried out their attacks on red skymarkers with green stars, those from 49 Squadron from 20,000 to 22,000 feet between 19.35 and 19.51. On return, the crews commented on the lack of flak activity over Berlin and reported the glow of large fires under the cloud and smoke rising through the tops. Thirty-five aircraft failed to return, twenty-two of them Halifaxes, which represented an 8.3% casualty rate compared with 2.6% for the Lancasters. It took a little time for an assessment of the operation to be made because of continuing cloud over north-eastern Germany, by which time four further raids had been carried out. It seems from local reports that the eastern districts had received the heaviest weight of bombs in an eight-mile stretch from Weissesee in the north to Neukölln in the south, although no details of destruction emerged.

On the following day, the city of Magdeburg was posted to host its first major attack of the war. The city had, in fact, been a regular destination for small forces as far back as the summer of 1940, when the Command targeted a ship lift at the eastern end of the Mittelland Canal at its junction with the River Elbe and the important Bergius-process Braunkohle A G synthetic oil refinery (hydrogenation plant), both located in the same Rothensee district to the north of Magdeburg city centre. Situated some fifty miles from Braunschweig and slightly to the south of east, it was on an increasingly familiar route as far as the enemy night-fighter controllers were concerned, and within easy striking distance of the night-fighter assembly beacons. In an attempt to deceive the enemy, a small-scale diversion was planned at Berlin involving twenty-two Lancaster of 5 Group and twelve Mosquitos of 8 Group. 5 Group contributed 122 Lancasters to the main event, ten of them made ready by 49 Squadron, which were loaded with a cookie and SBCs of incendiaries each. The Lancasters of the crews of P/O Meggeson and Sgt Keeling were loaded with a cookie and a few 1,000 and 500 pounders to drop on Berlin as part of the diversionary force. The two elements took off together between 19.56 and 20.13 with F/Ls Bacon and Hidderley the senior pilots on duty and flew out over the North Sea to a point some one hundred miles off the west coast of the Schleswig-Holstein peninsula, before turning to the south-east to pass between Hamburg and Hannover. P/O Harford and crew lost their starboard-outer engine during the sea crossing and were forced to turn back. Enemy radar was able to detect H2S transmissions during night-flying tests and equipment checks, and the night-fighter controller was, thereby, always aware of an imminent heavy raid. On this night, the night-fighters were able to infiltrate the bomber stream even before the German coast was crossed and the recently introduced "Tame Boar" night-fighter system provided a running commentary on the bomber stream's progress, enabling the fighters to latch onto it and remain in contact. The final turning-point was twenty-five miles north-east of the target, and this was identified both by Path Finder markers and the bombing of twenty-seven main force aircraft. These had been driven by stronger-than-forecast winds to arrive ahead of schedule and contained crews anxious to get the job done and get out of the target area as soon as possible. They bombed using their own H2S without waiting for the TIs to go down, and together with dummy fires, would be blamed by the Path Finders as the reason for their failure to produce concentrated marking.

The conditions over Magdeburg varied according to the time of arrival, the early birds encountering seven to nine-tenths thin cloud at around 6,000 feet, while those turning up towards the end of the raid found the northern half of the city completely clear with cloud over the southern half only. The 49 Squadron crews experienced a mixture of eight-tenths cloud and relatively clear skies, and in the face of fairly modest opposition, bombed on green TIs from 20,000 to 21,500 feet between 23.01 and 23.15, all gaining the impression that the attack was concentrated around the markers. Returning crews from other groups reported explosions and fires or their glow, and smoke beginning to rise as they turned away. A number reported a flash some twelve minutes after bombing that lit up the clouds for seven seconds, and two large explosions were witnessed at 23.15. Fires that initially seemed to be scattered, appeared to become more concentrated as the crews headed for home and the impression was of a successful operation. While all of this was in progress, the diversionary force arrived at Berlin, some seventy miles away to the north-east, where the 49 Squadron duo found a layer of eight to ten-tenths cloud at 10,000 feet, through which they bombed from 20,500 and 22,300 feet at 22.56. The 5 Group ORB expressed the opinion that the diversion had succeeded in the early stages in reducing the impact of the Nachtjagd, although this was not borne out by the figures. In the absence of post-raid reconnaissance and a local report, the outcome at Magdeburg was not confirmed and it is generally believed now that most of the bombing fell outside of the city boundaries. A record fifty-seven aircraft failed to return, thirty-five of them Halifaxes, and this provided another alarming statistic of a 15.6% loss-rate compared with 5.2% for the Lancasters.

The end of the month would bring the final concerted effort to destroy Berlin and involve three trips in the space of an unprecedented four nights. This hectic round of operations began on the 27th, after five nights of rest since the bruising experience of Magdeburg and involved an all-Lancaster heavy force of 515 aircraft. 5 Group put up a record 172, thirteen of them belonging to 49 Squadron, which departed Fiskerton between 16.56 and 17.37 with F/Ls Bacon and Hidderley the senior pilots on duty. After climbing out and rendezvousing with the rest of the group, they set course on a complex route that would take the bomber stream towards the north German coast, before swinging to the south-east to enter enemy territory over the Frisians and northern Holland. Having then feinted towards central Germany, suggesting Leipzig as the target, the force was to turn north-east to a point west of Berlin, from where the final run-in would commence. The long return route passed to the west of Leipzig before turning due east to miss Frankfurt on its northern side and traverse Belgium to gain the Channel south of Boulogne. P/Os Jones and Harford turned back early on, both with starboard-outer engine issues that suggested icing had affected the fuel feed. The others pressed on towards the target, while a mining diversion off Heligoland and the dispensing of dummy fighter flares and route-markers partially succeeded in reducing the numbers of enemy night-fighters making contact. It was, therefore, a relatively intact bomber force that approached the target over ten-tenths cloud with tops at 15,000 feet. This required the Path Finders to use sky-marking, and it was the red Wanganui flares with green stars that led the 49 Squadron crews to the aiming point, where all bombed from 18,500 to 22,000 feet between 20.34 and 20.44. At debriefings, crews reported the glow of fires and the appearance of a successful raid, but no detailed assessment was forthcoming. Of course, not all would make it back to tell their stories at debriefing, and thirty-three Lancaster dispersal pans stood empty in dawn's early light. JB360 crashed somewhere in the target area, killing P/O Barnes DFC RAAF and two of his crew and delivering the others into enemy hands. Reports from Berlin described bombs falling over a wide area, more so in the south than the north, and damage to fifty industrial premises, a number of them engaged in important war work, while twenty thousand people were bombed out of their homes. A feature of the campaign was the number of outlying communities suffering collateral damage, and on this night sixty-one such hamlets recorded bombs falling.

The early time-on-target had allowed crews to get a full night in bed and they were, hopefully, fully rested, when news came through on the 28th that many of them would be returning to the "Big City" that night. A heavy force of 673 aircraft was assembled, of which 432 were Lancasters and 241 Halifaxes, 155 of the former provided by 5 Group. 49 Squadron made ready eleven Lancasters, which departed Fiskerton between 00.15 and 00.34 with no senior pilots on duty. They were routed out over southern Denmark before turning south-east on a direct course for the target, with an almost reciprocal return and various diversionary measures to distract the night-fighter controller. Sixty-six crews turned back early, suggesting some adverse reaction to the back-to-back operations. Those reaching the target area encountered ten-tenths cloud and a mixture of sky and ground-marking to aim at, the 49 Squadron crews delivering their bombs on red and green release-point flares from 19,000 to 22,000 feet between 03.12 and 03.35. Some crews reported huge explosions at 03.15, 03.18 and 03.25, the second-mentioned one described by a 10 Squadron crew as lighting up the sky over a radius of fifty miles. Forty-six aircraft failed to return, twenty-six of them Halifaxes as the defenders fought back to exact another heavy toll of bombers, but all of Fiskerton's dispersal pans were occupied come the morning. The impression gained from returning crews at debriefing was of a concentrated and effective attack, and this was partly borne-out by local reports of heavy damage in western and southern districts, where 180,000 people were bombed out of their homes. However, as had been the pattern throughout the campaign against Berlin, seventy-seven outlying communities had also been afflicted.

On the 29th, S/L Day was posted to 54 Base at the completion of his tour. After a night's rest a force of 534 aircraft was made ready on the 30th for the final operation of this concerted effort against Berlin. 5 Group offered 156 Lancasters, of which thirteen were made ready at Fiskerton and took off between 16.54 and 17.23 with S/L Miller and F/L Bacon the senior pilots on duty. After climbing out, they joined with the rest of the group to follow a route similar to that adopted two nights earlier. The bomber stream remained relatively free of harassment and on reaching the target was greeted by ten-tenths cloud at around 8,000 feet and the sight of Path Finder skymarking in progress. The 49 Squadron crews bombed on these from 19,500 and 22,000 feet between 20.20 and 20.51, and all commented on the smoke rising through 12,000 feet and the glow of fires beneath the cloud, which, according to some, was still visible from a hundred miles into the return flight. Thirty-two Lancasters and a single Halifax failed to make it home, among them eleven belonging to 5 Group. In return for these significant losses and according to local reports, central and south-western districts suffered heavy damage and serious areas of fire. Other parts of the city were also hit, while many bomb loads were again scattered liberally onto outlying communities, and at least a thousand people lost their lives. 112 heavy bombers and their crews had been lost to the Command as a result of these three operations, and with the introduction of the enemy's highly efficient Tame Boar night-fighter system based on running commentaries, the advantage had swung back in the defenders' favour.

Two further heavy raids would be directed at Berlin before the end of the winter offensive, one in February and the other in March, but they would be almost in isolation. There is no question that Germany's Capital had been sorely afflicted by the three latest operations, but it remained a functioning city and showed no signs of imminent collapse. During the course of the month the squadron participated in ten operations and dispatched 103 sorties for the loss of four Lancasters and their crews.

## February 1944

Bad weather during the first two weeks of February allowed the crews to draw breath and the squadrons to replenish. Harris had intended to maintain the pressure on Berlin and would have launched a further attack had he not been thwarted by the conditions, and as a result, the time was filled with training and mining operations. When the Path Finder and main force squadrons next took to the air, it would be for a record-breaking effort to Berlin on the 15$^{th}$ and would also be the penultimate operation of the campaign, and indeed of the war by Bomber Command's heavy brigade against Germany's capital city. The force of 891 aircraft represented the largest non-1,000 force to date, and, therefore, the greatest-ever to be sent against the Capital, and it would be the first time that more than five hundred Lancasters and three hundred Halifaxes had operated together. 5 Group would surpass its previous best effort by fifty Lancasters when putting 226 of them into the air and eighteen of them would be representing 49 Squadron. The bomb bays of this huge armada would convey to Berlin the greatest-ever tonnage of bombs to any target to date, and 49 Squadron's contribution would be eighteen cookies and 1,050 x 30lb and 16,350 x 4lb incendiaries. They departed Fiskerton between 17.11 and 17.44 with W/C Adams and S/L Miller the senior pilots on duty and a G/C Hawtry flying as an observer with the former. After joining up with the rest of the 5 Group squadrons, they set course for the western coast of Denmark, before crossing southern Jutland and entering Germany via the Baltic coast between Rostock and Stralsund on a direct heading for the target. The return route would require the bombers to pass south of Hannover and Bremen and cross Holland to the North Sea via Castricum. Extensive diversionary measures included a mining operation in Kiel Bay ahead of the arrival of the bombers, a raid on Frankfurt-an-Oder to the east of Berlin by a small force of 8 Group Lancasters and Oboe Mosquitos attacking five night-fighter airfields in Holland. The force had been depleted by seventy-five early returns by the time the remainder homed in on the target, where ten-tenths cloud at around 10,000 feet concealed it from their view, but those with H2S were able to confirm their positions, while the others relied on the Path Finders' red release-point flares with green stars and red and green TIs on the ground. The 49 Squadron crews bombed on these from 20,000 to 24,000 feet between 21.14 and 21.33, and on return reported the markers to be highly effective and well-concentrated. The burgeoning glow beneath the clouds convinced them that they had taken part in a successful operation, and this was borne out by local reports, which confirmed that the 2,642 tons of bombs had caused extensive damage in central and south-western districts but had also spilled out into surrounding communities. A thousand houses and more than five hundred temporary wooden barracks were destroyed and important war-industry factories in the Siemensstadt district were damaged in return for the loss to the Command of forty-three aircraft, twenty-six Lancasters, (4.6%) and seventeen Halifaxes, (5.4%). Perhaps slightly disturbing was the fact that eight of the missing Halifaxes were Mk IIIs, only one fewer than the nine now obsolete Mk II/Vs.

Despite the recent heavy losses, when orders were received on the 19$^{th}$ to prepare for another major assault that night, this time on Leipzig, where four Messerschmitt aircraft factories were the principal targets, the heavy squadrons were able offer 816 aircraft, 561 Lancasters and 255 Halifaxes. 5 Group managed 209 Lancasters and 49 Squadron fifteen, which departed Fiskerton between 23.41 and 00.05 with W/C Adams and S/L Miller the senior pilots on duty. After climbing out over the station, they joined up with the others heading for the Dutch coast near Groningen, where a proportion of the Luftwaffe Nachtjagd was waiting for them, while others had been drawn away by a mining diversion off Kiel. S/L Miller's generators failed after crossing the English coast, forcing him to turn back, and after landing he described a chaotic scene over the North Sea, with aircraft flying in every direction, the wiser crews with their navigation lights on but most without and he witnessed three aircraft exploding, possibly as a result of collision. F/O Healey had F/L Woodroffe on board as second pilot, the latter destined to become a member of 5 Group's Master Bomber fraternity later in the year, and this was a prospect which almost ended when they collided with what they believed was a Ju88 at 21,000 feet at 02.01, still some two hours from the target. The badly damaged Lancaster lost a large amount of altitude after entering a spiral dive, but F/O Healey recovered the situation and turned for home, while the enemy aircraft was seen to impact the ground. The bomber stream continued on to pass south of Bremen and north of Hannover on a south-easterly course, parts of it to become embroiled in a running battle with night-fighters all the way into eastern Germany, and it was during this phase that 49 Squadron's JB469 and ND516 ran into trouble. The former crashed three miles east of Bröckel, ten miles south-east of Celle, with no survivors from the crew of F/Sgt White, while the latter was at 20,000 feet when shot down by a night-fighter to crash near Burg, north-east of Magdeburg, killing four members of P/O Mackenzie's crew and delivering him and two others into enemy hands.

Inaccurately forecast winds caused some aircraft to reach the target early, forcing them to orbit while they waited for the Path Finders to arrive, and the local flak batteries accounted for around twenty of these, while four others were lost through collisions. The 49 Squadron crews arrived to find ten-tenths cloud with tops at around 10,000 feet and bombed on green Wanganui flares and red and green TIs from 20,500 to 24,000 feet between 03.59 and 04.16. It seems that there was a brief period during the attack when skymarking stopped and led to some scattering of bombs, but the marker-flares were soon replenished with the arrival of more backers-up and a considerable glow beneath the cloud remained visible for some fifty minutes into the return journey, giving the impression of a successful assault. When all of those aircraft returning home had been accounted for, there was a massive shortfall of seventy-eight, a record loss by a clear twenty-one aircraft. Forty-four Lancasters and thirty-four Halifaxes had failed to return, with a loss-rate of 7.8% and 13.3% respectively, prompting Harris to immediately withdraw the Mk II and V Halifaxes from further operations over Germany, which at a stroke, removed a proportion of 4 Group's fire-power from the front line until they could be re-equipped with the Mk III. In the meantime, the Mk II and V operators would focus their energies for the remainder of the month on gardening duties.

Despite this depletion of available numbers, a force of 598 aircraft was made ready on the 20th for an operation that night against Stuttgart, which would be the first of three against the city over a three-week period. 49 Squadron detailed fifteen Lancasters, the first twelve of which departed Fiskerton without incident between 23.37 and 00.05 with S/L Miller the senior pilot on duty, F/L Woodroffe again accompanying F/O Healey and each carrying a cookie and eleven SBCs of incendiaries. As P/O Clark and crew began their take-off run at 00.07, ND498 began to swing, which caused the undercarriage to collapse and the Lancaster to catch fire. The crew scrambled clear and the station fire brigade attempted to douse the flames before the cookie exploded, but were forced to abandon the attempt and clear the area as it became clear that they were fighting a losing battle. The remaining two sorties were scrubbed, and the airborne crews were well on their way as part of the 5 Group contribution of 176 Lancasters by the time that the cookie exploded and distributed the once proud Lancaster over a wide area. The bomber stream crossed the Channel to make landfall over the French coast, from where the cloud remained at ten-tenths with tops at 8,000 feet all the way into southern Germany. A North Sea sweep and a diversionary raid on Munich two hours ahead of the main activity had caused the Luftwaffe to deploy its forces early, and this allowed the bomber stream to push on unmolested to the target. By the time it hove into view, the cloud had thinned to five to eight-tenths at around 6,000 feet and the excellent visibility enabled the crews to draw a bead on the Path Finder red and green sky-markers and similar-coloured TIs on the ground. The 49 Squadron crews bombed from 18,000 to 24,500 feet between 04.00 and 04.10, observing many large fires, and on return there were reports that the glow from the burning city was still visible from 250 miles into the return flight. Despite some scattering of bombs, local reports described central districts and those in a quadrant from north-west to north-east suffering extensive damage, and a Bosch factory was one of the important war industry concerns to be hard-hit. In contrast to twenty-four hours earlier, a modest nine aircraft failed to return.

In an attempt to reduce the prohibitive losses of recent weeks, a new tactic was introduced for the next two operations. A force of 734 aircraft was assembled on the 24th for an operation to the centre of Germany's ball-bearing production, Schweinfurt, situated some sixty miles to the east of Frankfurt in south-central Germany. The plan called for 392 aircraft to depart their stations between 18.00 and 19.00 and to be followed into the air two hours later by 342 others in the hope of catching the night-fighters on the ground refuelling and re-arming as the second wave passed through. While this operation was in progress, extensive diversionary measures would be put in hand that involved more than three hundred other aircraft, including 179 from the training units conducting a North Sea sweep and 110 Halifaxes and Stirlings mining in northern waters. 5 Group contributed 204 Lancasters, of which sixteen were made ready by 49 Squadron, five assigned to the first phase and eleven to the second. They were sent over to Dunholme Lodge for bombing-up and the first wave participants took off between 18.24 and 18.33 with F/Ls Bacon and Woodroffe the senior pilots on duty to be followed by the second wave element between 20.16 and 20.39 led by F/O Healey. F/O Healey and P/O Jones and their crews were to perform the role of Path Finder supporters, which required them to accompany the target-marking force across the target to beef up the numbers and prevent searchlights and flak from latching onto individual aircraft. They would retain their bombs and release them during a second pass. W/O Jupp and crew were in the second phase and were heading south some fifteen miles north of Brighton when misidentified by a friendly night-fighter and attacked. Firing the colours of the day had the desired effect, but not before ND533 had been damaged and had lost its hydraulics system. They turned back and headed for the North Sea jettison area, before selecting the long runway at Wittering as a suitable destination to land without brakes and flaps and with the bomb bay doors open. The first phase bombers reached the target to find three-tenths cloud at 3,000 to 4,000 feet, with haze spoiling the vertical visibility. The aiming point was identified by red and green TIs and already established fires towards the south-western edge of the town as the 49 Squadron crews bombed from 21,000 to 23,000 feet between 23.09 and 23.31. Other crews over the target at this time saw no cloud and described the visibility as excellent, enabling them to pick out the River Main as they ran in to bomb. Two columns of black smoke were observed to be rising through 5,000 feet as they turned away, and the consensus was of an effective, if, somewhat scattered attack.

Meanwhile, the second phase crews were well on their way and picked up the glow of fires from the earlier raid at a distance of two hundred miles. The visibility in the target area remained good, despite the rising smoke, and bombing by the 49 Squadron crews took place out of almost cloudless skies onto red and green TIs from 20,000 to 24,000 feet between 01.03 and 01.18. All indications suggested an effective raid, but unfortunately, both phases of the operation had suffered from undershooting after some Path Finder backers-up failed to press on to the aiming point. In that regard, it was a disappointing night, but an interesting feature was the loss of 50% fewer aircraft from the second wave in comparison with the first in an overall casualty figure of thirty-three, and this suggested some merit in the tactic. Since the turn of the year, a wind-finder system had been in use, which employed selected crews to monitor wind speed and direction and pass their findings back to HQ, where the figures were collated and any changes from the briefed conditions re-broadcast to the bomber stream. This had been found to be extremely useful, but as would be discovered in the ensuing weeks, the system had its limitations.

The main operation on the following night was directed at the beautiful and culturally significant southern city of Augsburg, situated around thirty miles north-west of Munich. It was home to a major Maschinenfabrik Augsburg Nuremberg (M.A.N) diesel engine factory, which had been the target for the previously mentioned epic low-level daylight raid by 44 and 97 Squadron in April 1942. On this night, 594 aircraft were divided into two waves, and among them were 164 Lancasters of 5 Group, including fourteen representing 49 Squadron. Ten of these were assigned to the first phase, taking-off between 18.19 and 18.34 with F/Ls Bacon and Woodroffe the senior pilots on duty, while the four second-phase crews got away between 21.08 and 21.19. The ORB mentioned that two additional unidentified 49 Squadron crews operated with 44 (Rhodesia) Squadron. The first wave bomber stream flew out over Belgium with ten-tenths cloud beneath them, but that had dissipated by the time the target drew near, and on arrival, it was possible for crews to gain a visual reference. The Path Finders' red and green TIs were in the bomb sights as the 49 Squadron crews carried out their attacks from 20,000 to 23,500 feet between 22.40 and 22.51, and fires were beginning to take hold as they turned away. The second wave crews were drawn on by the glow in the sky from a hundred miles away and arrived to find visibility still good despite copious amounts of smoke rising through 10,000 feet. Those from 49 squadron bombed on existing fires and red and green Wanganui flares and TIs from 21,000 to 22,000 feet between 01.15 and 01.18. The loss of twenty-one aircraft seemed to confirm the benefits of splitting the forces, and this tactic would remain an important part of Bomber Command planning for the remainder of the war. It had been a devastatingly destructive operation, in which all facets of the plan had come together in near perfect harmony, spelling disaster for this lightly defended historical treasure trove. Its heart was torn out by blast and fire that destroyed almost three thousand houses along with buildings of outstanding historical significance, and centuries of irreplaceable culture was lost forever. There was also some industrial damage, and around ninety-thousand people were bombed out of their homes.

During the course of the month the squadron carried out five operations and dispatched seventy-five sorties for the loss of two Lancasters and their crews.

# March 1944

March would bring an end to the winter campaign, but a long and bitter month would have to be endured first before any respite came from long-range forays into Germany. The crews had enjoyed a few nights off when the second raid of the series on Stuttgart was posted on the 1st, for which a force of 557 aircraft was made ready. This number included 178 Lancasters representing 5 Group, thirteen of which were provided by 49 Squadron and dispatched from Fiskerton without incident between 23.20 and 23.37 with W/C Adams the senior pilot on duty and supported by F/Ls Adams, Bacon, Healey and Woodroffe. They flew out over ten-tenths cloud with tops at between 12,000 and 17,000 feet and encountered similar conditions in the target area, where the Path Finders employed a combination of sky and ground-marking. This, unfortunately, became scattered, and the bombing was directed between two main concentrations, the 49 Squadron crews carrying out their attacks on Wanganui red markers with green stars from 20,500 to 24,000 feet between 02.59 and 03.18. It was not possible to assess the accuracy of the attack, although a column of smoke had reached 25,000 feet by the end of the raid and large fires were evident from the glow in the sky visible from up to 150 miles away. The presence of thick cloud all the way there and back made conditions difficult for enemy night-fighters and a remarkably modest four aircraft failed to return. It was eventually established that the raid had been an outstanding success, which had caused extensive damage in central, western and northern districts, where a number of important war-industry factories, including those belonging to Bosch and Daimler-Benz, had sustained damage.

At the end of the first week, the Halifax brigade, particularly those withdrawn from operations over Germany, fired the opening salvoes of the pre-invasion campaign, the purpose of which was to dismantle by bombing thirty-seven railway centres in France, Belgium and western Germany. It began on the night of the 6/7th at Trappes marshalling yards, situated some ten miles west-south-west of Paris and continued at Le Mans in north-western France on the following night. For most of the heavy crews, however, there was no employment following Stuttgart, until a return there in mid-month, but in the meantime, matters were afoot at 5 Group, and had been ever since a frustrating series of operations against flying bomb launching sites conducted by 617 Squadron since December had failed to achieve the desired results. The problem had been an inability to put markers right on the aiming point, which was vital to destroy small, precision targets, and Oboe was just not precise enough. Effective though Oboe undoubtedly was at an urban target, where a margin of error of 400 to 600 yards represented pinpoint accuracy, precision targets required more. 617 Squadron had obliterated the Oboe markers, only for bombing photos to show that the targets, situated only a matter of yards away, had remained intact. W/C Cheshire and S/L Martin experimented with a dive-bombing technique, which had proved to be successful but impracticable in a Lancaster and Cheshire had borrowed a Mosquito for further trials. These were so promising, that the 5 Group A-O-C, AVM Cochrane, authorized a number of operations by the squadron against factory targets in France, before taking the idea to Harris. Harris approved, paving the way for 5 Group to become effectively independent of the main bomber force and begin larger-scale trials.

Orders were received at Bardney, Skellingthorpe and Waddington on the 9th to prepare eleven Lancasters each for a 5 Group attack that night against the Lioré et Olivier aircraft factory at Marignane, situated a few miles to the north of Marseilles in southern France. The area had been the main pre-war hub for commercial flying boat operations, particularly for the Pan American Clipper Class flights, and the factory had been engaged in the manufacture of the LeO 45 twin-engine medium bomber for the French Air Force. They took off in mid-evening with a round-trip ahead of them of some 1,350 miles if they flew direct and arrived in the target area under clear skies and bright moonlight, which facilitated an easy identification of the factory buildings marked by red spotfires. The bombing was carried out from medium level either side of 01.30, and the high-explosives were seen to fall among the buildings, while the incendiaries appeared to be a little scattered. A large explosion was witnessed at 01.24 and a huge pall of smoke was rising through 6,000 feet as the force turned away. All arrived home safely, most having spent more than nine hours aloft.

5 Group received orders on the 10th to prepare 102 Lancasters to form four small forces, each to attack a specific factory in France that night. The targets were the Michelin tyre factory at Clermont-Ferrand, the Bloch aircraft factory at Châteauroux, which was the first to be set up by the famed designer, Marcel Dassault, in 1935, the Morane Saulnier aircraft plant at Ossun, just north of the Pyrenese and the Ricamerie needle-bearing works at St-Etienne, the last-mentioned, the objective for sixteen Lancasters from 617 Squadron. 52 Base was assigned to the Ossun target, for which a dozen 49 Squadron crews were briefed at Fiskerton and eleven by 44 (Rhodesia) Squadron at Dunholme Lodge. S/L Miller was appointed Master Bomber with F/L Adams as his deputy and F/L Bacon as supporter, and all got away safely between 19.58 and 20.21 for the three-and-a-half-hour outward flight. They arrived in the target area to find bright moonlight and circled, while flares were released over the town of Tarbes, a few miles to the north-east, to provide a rally point for the run on the aiming point. There was, apparently, some disagreement between 44 (Rhodesia) Squadron's W/C Thompson and F/L Adams but all was resolved and the Fiskerton crews carried out their attacks on red spotfires from 6,000 to 8,100 feet between 23.50 and 00.01, observing some buildings to disintegrate and others to catch fire. There was no opposition and all four operations were concluded successfully for the loss of a single Lancaster occupied by the crew of a 207 Squadron flight commander.

Now that the Mk III Halifax was becoming available in larger numbers, the Command was quickly returning to full strength, and it was a force of 863 aircraft that set out for Stuttgart in the early-evening of the 15th. This number included 206 Lancasters provided by 5 Group, eighteen of them departing Fiskerton between 19.01 and 19.24 with S/L Miller the senior pilot on duty. They rendezvoused with the rest of the force as they passed over Reading on their way to the south coast, and an elongated bomber stream crossed the French coast at 20,000 feet over broken cloud with clear conditions above. It maintained a course parallel with the frontiers of Belgium, Luxembourg and Germany as if heading for Switzerland, before crossing the German border between Strasbourg and Freiburg and turning towards the north-east for the run-in to the target. It was during this final leg that the night-fighters managed to infiltrate a section of the stream and score heavily, and among the victims was 49 Squadron's ND474, which crashed three miles south-west of Saulgau with fatal consequences for Sgt Waugh and his crew, who were operating together for the first time. Adverse winds were responsible for the Path Finders arriving up to six minutes late to open the attack, when they employed both sky and ground-markers in the face of seven to ten-tenths cloud at between 8,000 and 15,000 feet. The Wanganui flares drifted in the wind, marking an area to the north-east of the River Neckar, while the TIs landed far apart in the north and south of the city. The 49 Squadron crews bombed on whatever markers presented themselves, mostly red TIs, from 19,500 to 23,000 feet between 23.10 and 23.29 and observed a spread of fires, including two large ones ten miles apart and smoke rising to bombing altitude. It would be established later that some of the early bombing had been accurate, but that most of the loads had undershot and fallen into open country, a disappointment compounded by the loss, mostly to night-fighters, of thirty-seven aircraft.

On the 17th, 52 Base welcomed 619 Squadron to Dunholme Lodge to share the facilities with 44 (Rhodesia) Squadron. Many operations had been mounted against Frankfurt during the preceding two years, only a small number of which had been really effective. This state of affairs was about to be rectified, however, and the first of two raids against this south-central powerhouse of industry was posted on the 18th, for which a force of 846 aircraft was made ready. 5 Group supported the operation with 212 Lancasters, sixteen of which belonged to 49 Squadron and they were loaded at Fiskerton with a cookie each and a variety of incendiaries, before taking off between 18.52 and 19.18 with F/Ls Bacon, Healey and Woodroffe the senior pilots on duty. They benefitted from favourable weather conditions as they pressed on across France and entered Germany, where they encountered a layer of haze 20,000 feet thick over the target, and according to most, no more than three-tenths cloud. This allowed the Path Finders to employ the Newhaven ground marking technique (blind marking by H2S, followed by visual backing-up), which the 49 Squadron crews exploited when carrying out their attacks on red and green TIs from 20,000 to 23,000 feet between 21.58 and 22.07. A large explosion was witnessed at 22.05, and the participants in the raid flew home confident that their efforts had been worthwhile. They had, indeed, contributed to an outstandingly successful raid, during which, 5 Group alone dropped more than one thousand tons of bombs for the first time at a single target. Local reports calculated that six thousand buildings had been destroyed or seriously damaged in predominantly eastern, central and western districts, and this was in return for the loss of twenty-two aircraft, five of which were from 5 Group.

Frankfurt was named again on the 22nd as the target for that night, and 217 crews of 5 Group learned that they were to be part of another huge force of 816 aircraft. The nineteen participants from 49 Squadron took off between 18.40 to 19.12 with W/C Adams the senior pilot on duty and after climbing out above their stations and forming up, adopted an unusual route for a target south of the Ruhr, crossing the enemy coast over Vlieland and Teschelling, before passing to the east of Osnabrück on a direct course due south for the target. P/O Jones and crew soon lost their port-outer engine and turned back, leaving the others to arrive at the target and find five to six-tenths thin, low cloud at around 4,000 feet and Paramatta marking (blind marking by H2S) in progress. They focussed their attention on the release-point flares and red and green TIs marking out the aiming point, before bombing from 20,000 to 22,700 feet between 21.47 and 22.04. A massive rectangular area of unbroken fire was observed across the centre of the city, the glow from which could be seen for at least a hundred miles into the return flight. Returning crews reported numerous searchlights lighting up the cloud, and moderate to intense flak that reached up to the bombers' flight level. Local reports confirmed the enormity of the devastation, which was particularly severe in western districts and left this half of the city without electricity, gas and water for an extended period. More than nine hundred people lost their lives and a further 120,000 were bombed out of their homes at a cost to the Command of twenty-six Lancasters and seven Halifaxes, a loss-rate of 4.2% and 3.8% respectively. 49 Squadron was represented among the missing by ND536 and ND672, the latter crashing outbound near Beckum on the northern rim of the Ruhr and only the mid-upper gunner survived in enemy hands from the crew of F/O Turner. The former was homebound when it came down three miles east of Baumholder, some thirty miles short of the Luxembourg frontier, and there were no survivors from the crew of F/Sgt Greig. It was a bad night for senior officers, 207 and 7 Squadrons losing their commanding officers, while Bardney's station commander, G/C Norman Pleasance, failed to return in a 9 Squadron Lancaster. What was about to happen over the next week and a half, however, would overshadow anything that had gone before and would certainly not fall within what might be considered acceptable.

It was more than five weeks since the main force had last visited the "Big City", and 811 aircraft were made ready on the 24$^{th}$ for what would be the final raid of the war upon it by RAF heavy bombers. 5 Group put up 193 Lancasters, of which seventeen were made ready by 49 Squadron and departed Fiskerton between 18.47 and 19.09 with F/Ls Adams, Bacon, Healey and Woodroffe the senior pilots on duty. They had a long flight ahead of them, which would take them across the North Sea to the Danish coast near Ringkøbing and then to a point on the German Baltic coast near Rostock. When north-east of Berlin they were to adopt a south-westerly course for the bombing run, and once clear of the defence zone homebound, dogleg to the west and then north-west to pass around Hannover on its southern and western sides, before heading for Holland and an exit via the Castricum coast. The extended outward leg provided a time-on-target of around 22.30, but an unexpected difficulty would be encountered, which would render void all of the meticulous planning. The existence of what we now know as "Jetstream" winds was unknown at the time, and the one blowing from the north with unprecedented strength on this night pushed the bomber stream south of its intended track. Navigators, who were expecting to see the northern tip of Sylt on their H2S screens, were horrified to find the southern end, which meant that they were thirty miles south of track and about to fly over Germany rather than Denmark. The previously mentioned "wind-finder" system had been set up for precisely this eventuality, but the problem on this night was that the wind-finders refused to believe what their instruments were telling them. Winds in excess of one hundred m.p.h had never been encountered before, and fearing that they would be disbelieved, many modified the figures downward. The same thing happened at raid control, where the figures were modified again, so that the information rebroadcast to the bomber stream bore no resemblance to the reality of the situation.

P/O Simpson and crew turned back within two hours as a result of starboard-inner engine failure, and by the time that the others had reached Westerhever on the west coast of the Schleswig-Holstein peninsula, most realized that they were some distance south of track and set course for the north to try to regain the planned route and avoid the defences that would be met if they turned east over Germany. Many commented on the inaccurate wind information received during the outward journey, and having arrived in the target area, some were convinced that the Path Finders were up to ten minutes late in opening the raid. This was confirmed to some by the voice of the Master Bomber exhorting them to hurry up. Crews reported a variety of cloud conditions from three to ten-tenths at between 6,000 and 15,000 feet, but most were able to pick out the red and green TIs on the ground, and if not, found red Wanganui flares with green stars to guide them to the aiming point. The 49 Squadron crews confirmed their positions by H2S before bombing from 20,000 to 22,000 feet between 22.27 and 22.45 and observed what appeared to be a scattered attack in the early stages, until fires began to become more concentrated in three distinct areas and large explosions were witnessed at 22.42 and 22.54. The defences were very active with moderate flak bursting at up to 24,000 feet and light flak attempting to shoot out the skymarkers, but night-fighter activity was described by the 5 Group ORB as unusually quiet. There was a shock awaiting the Command as the returning aircraft landed to leave a shortfall of seventy-two, and it would be established later that two-thirds of them had fallen victim to the Ruhr flak batteries after being driven into that region's defence zone by the wind on the way home. 49 Squadron came through unscathed, while 5 Group posted missing eleven crews. Post-raid analysis revealed that the wind had also played havoc with the marking and bombing and had pushed the attack towards the south-western districts of the capital, where most of the damage occurred, while 126 outlying communities also received bombs. 49 Squadron had been present on each of the nineteen main raids to Berlin from August onwards, and the diversion there on the night of the Magdeburg debacle in January and had despatched 273 sorties for the loss of seven of its Lancasters. It ended the campaign with the lowest percentage loss rate in Bomber Command. (The Berlin Raids. Martin Middlebrook).

Twenty 5 Group Lancasters were invited to take part in an attack on the extensive railway yards at Aulnoye in north-eastern France to be carried out on the evening of the 25th, while twenty-two 617 Squadron Lancasters returned to the Sigma aero-engine factory at Lyons. The 49 Squadron crews of P/Os Hodgson and Cornish departed Fiskerton at 19.05 and 19.25 respectively and arrived in the target area to encounter clear skies and favourable conditions. The Hodgson crew was in the first wave and bombed the centre of three green TIs from 8,500 feet at 21.51, while the Cornish crew were part of the second wave and aimed at the centre of three red TIs from the same altitude at 22.06. The bombing appeared to be well concentrated on the south-western aiming point and started a fire that remained visible from a hundred miles away. Returning crews reported large explosions at 22.04 and 22.50 and fifteen crews brought back an aiming point photo.

Although Berlin had now been consigned to the past, the winter campaign still had a week to run, and two more major operations for the crews to negotiate. The first of these was posted on the 26th and would bring a return to the old enemy of Essen that night, for which a force of 705 aircraft was made ready. 5 Group contributed 172 of the 476 Lancasters, seventeen of them provided by 49 Squadron, which departed Fiskerton between 19.35 and 20.06 with the usual suspects, F/Ls Adams, Bacon, Healey and Woodroffe, the senior pilots on duty. They climbed out over the station and set course for the Dutch coast to pass north of Haarlem and Amsterdam, before swinging to the south-east on a direct run to the target. There were no early returns, and all reached the target to find it covered by eight to ten-tenths cloud with tops in places as high as 14,000 feet, but Oboe performed well and enabled the Path Finders to mark the city with red and green TIs and Wanganui flares. P/O Shinn and crew had just settled on their bombing run when attacked by an unidentified enemy night-fighter, which knocked out the starboard-inner engine, left the starboard-outer on reduced power and set the rear turret on fire. The Lancaster plummeted five thousand feet and by the time that the dive was arrested, the bomb load had been jettisoned. The Lancaster was then hit by flak or a fighter and lost intercom, hydraulics, H2S and Gee and the wireless operator sustained a severe head wound to which he would succumb. The controls became very heavy, and P/O Shinn struggled to complete the sea crossing, eventually making landfall on the Norfolk coast and ordering his crew to bale out over Swanton Morley. P/O Shinn pulled off a crash-landing at Coltishall at 01.00 with the mortally wounded wireless operator on board and his efforts would be recognised. Meanwhile, the other 49 Squadron crews had bombed from 18,500 and 22,000 feet between 22.00 and 22.14, before returning safely, having been unable to assess the results of their efforts. The impression was of a successful raid, and this was based on a considerable glow beneath the clouds as they withdrew. Post-raid reconnaissance soon confirmed another outstandingly destructive operation against this once elusive target, thus continuing the remarkable run of successes here since the introduction of Oboe to main force operations a year earlier. Over seventeen hundred houses were destroyed in the attack, with dozens of war industry factories sustaining serious damage, and on a night when the night-fighter controllers were caught off guard by the switch to the Ruhr, the success was gained for the modest loss of nine aircraft. Among these was P/O Hodgson's JB680, which was shot down by a night-fighter and exploded on impact at Ahrbrück, some twenty miles south-west of Bonn, killing all on board.

The period known as the Battle of Berlin, but which was better referred to as the winter campaign, was to be brought to an end on the night of the 30/31$^{st}$ with a standard maximum-effort raid on Nuremberg. The plan of operation departed from normal practice in only one important respect, and this was to prove critical. It had become standard practice for 8 Group to plan operations and to employ diversions and feints to confuse the enemy night-fighter controllers. Sometimes they were successful and sometimes not, but with the night-fighter force having clearly gained the upper hand with its "Tame Boar" running commentary system, all possible means had to be adopted to protect the bomber stream. During a conference held early on the 30$^{th}$, the Lancaster Group A-O-Cs expressed a preference for a 5 Group-inspired route, which would require the bomber stream to fly a long straight leg across Belgium and Germany to a point about fifty miles north of Nuremberg, from where the final run-in would commence. The Halifax A-O-Cs were less convinced of the benefits, and AVM Bennett, the Path Finder chief, was positively overcome by the potential dangers and predicted a disaster, only to be overruled. A force of 795 aircraft was made ready, of which 201 Lancasters were to be provided by 5 Group, sixteen of them representing 49 Squadron, and the crews attended briefings to be told of the route, wind conditions and the belief that a layer of cloud would conceal them from enemy night-fighters. Before take-off, a Meteorological Flight Mosquito crew radioed in to cast doubts upon the weather conditions, which they could see differed markedly from those that had been forecast. This also went unheeded, and from around 21.45 for the next hour or so, the crews took off for the rendezvous area, and headed into a conspiracy of circumstances, which would inflict upon Bomber Command its heaviest defeat of the war.

At Fiskerton, eight crews, including those of F/Ls Adams, Bacon and Healey, were assigned to Path Finder support duties, while F/L Woodroffe and crew were allotted to wave 1, and all others to waves 3, 4 and 5. They took off between 21.55 and 22.21, and it was not long into the flight before they and the rest of the force began to notice some unusual features in the conditions, which included uncommonly bright moonlight and a crystal clarity of visibility that allowed them the rare sight of other aircraft in the stream. On most nights, crews would feel themselves to be completely alone in the sky all the way to the target, until bang on schedule, TIs would be seen to fall, and other aircraft would make their presence known by the turbulence of their slipstreams as they funnelled towards the aiming point. Once at cruising altitude on this night, however, they were alarmed to note that the forecast cloud was conspicuous by its absence, and instead lay beneath them as a white tablecloth, against which they were silhouetted like flies. Condensation trails began to form in the cold, clear air to further advertise their presence to the enemy and the Jetstream winds, which had so adversely affected the Berlin raid a week earlier, were also present, only this time blowing from the south. As then, the wind-finder system failed to cope, and this would have a serious impact on the outcome of the operation. The final insult on this sad night was the route's close proximity to two night-fighter beacons, which the enemy aircraft were orbiting while they awaited their instructions, unaware initially that they were about to have the cream of Bomber Command handed to them on a plate.

The carnage began over Charleroi in Belgium, and from there to the target, the route was sign-posted by the burning wreckage on the ground of eighty Bomber Command aircraft. P/O Dickenson and crew were attacked by a Ju88 as they flew south of Bonn at 21,000 feet at 00.12 and damage to the hydraulics system robbed them of both turrets, but not before return fire had damaged their assailant. The pilot corkscrewed continuously for eight minutes assisted by a running commentary from his gunners, whose input was crucial to their escape from its clutches. They dropped their bombs over a built-up area believed to be Bonn as they made their way home with a holed fuel tank. JB314 contained the crew of P/O Kellow, who were on their first operation and were the thirty-seventh to go down, shot out of the sky by a night-fighter to crash at Quotshausen, between Siegen and Marburg. The navigator and mid-upper gunner were the only survivors, and both were severely injured to the extent that the former succumbed on the following day and the latter would be repatriated in early 1945. JB466 became the sixty-fifth victim when it crashed at Schleusingen close to the final turning point some seventy miles north of Nuremberg, killing F/O Colhoun and all but the flight engineer and navigator, who fell into enemy hands. The wind-finder system broke down again, and those crews who either failed to detect the strength of the wind, or simply refused to believe the evidence, were driven up to fifty miles north of their intended track, and as a result turned towards Nuremberg from a false position. This led to more than a hundred aircraft bombing at Schweinfurt in error, which combined with the massive losses sustained before the target was reached to reduce considerably the numbers arriving at the primary target. The remaining 49 Squadron crews arrived over Nuremberg to encounter eight to nine-tenths cloud with tops as high as 16,000 feet and bombed from 19,000 to 22,500 feet between 01.01 and 01.20, aiming at red and green TIs and sky-markers after confirming their positions by H2S. Many fires were observed, the glow from which, according to some reports, remained visible for 120 miles into the return journey. Ninety-five aircraft failed to return home, twenty-one of them from 5 Group, and many others were written off in landing crashes or with battle damage too severe to repair. The shock and disappointment were compounded by the fact that the strong wind had driven the marking beyond the city to the east, and Nuremberg had, consequently, escaped serious damage.

During the course of the month, the squadron participated in nine operations and dispatched 130 sorties for the loss of six Lancasters and their crews and one other airman.

# April 1944

The winter campaign had brought the Command to its low point of the war and was the only time when the morale of the crews was in question. What now lay before the hard-pressed men of Bomber Command was in marked contrast to that which had been endured over the seemingly interminable winter months. In place of the long slog to Germany on dark, often dirty nights, shorter range hops to France and Belgium in improving weather conditions would become the order of the day. However, these operations would be equally demanding in their way, and require of the crews a greater commitment to accuracy to avoid casualties among friendly civilians. Despite this, a decree from on high insisted that such operations were worthy of counting as just one third of a sortie towards the completion of a tour, and until this flawed policy was grudgingly rescinded late in the war, a sense of injustice pervaded the crew rooms. In fact, the number of sorties to complete a tour would fluctuate up and down between this point and the end of hostilities. Despite the horrendous losses of the winter campaign, the Command was in remarkably fine fettle to face its new challenge, with 3 Group gradually changing to Lancasters and the much-improved Hercules powered Halifaxes equipping 4 Group and most of 6 Group. Harris was now in the enviable position of being able to achieve what had eluded his predecessor, namely, to attack multiple targets simultaneously with enough strength to be effective. Such was the hitting-power now at his disposal, that he could assign targets to individual groups, to groups in tandem or to the Command as a whole, as dictated by operational requirements. Although invasion considerations would come first, while Harris was at the helm, his favoured policy of city-busting would never be entirely shelved.

5 Group returned to operations on the 5th, with an undertaking involving 144 Lancasters and a Mosquito flown by W/C Cheshire of 617 Squadron. The target was the former Dewoitine aircraft factory at Toulouse in south-western France, which, under a nationalization plan in 1936 involving six aircraft companies, including Lioré et Olivier and Potez, was now operating under the name SNCASE, or Sud Est for short. Cheshire was to mark it with spotfires from low level, using the system that he was instrumental in developing, and one which would become an integral part of 5 Group operations, with refinements, from this point on. This would be Cheshire's first operational flight in a Mosquito and the first time that he marked a target for 5 Group rather than just 617 Squadron. Much depended upon its success if Harris were to become sold on the idea of the low-level visual marking technique and give it his backing. At Fiskerton, 49 Squadron bombed up ten Lancasters and sent them on their way between 20.20 and 20.42 with W/C Adams and S/L Miller the senior pilots on duty. The squadron participants had been assigned to specific roles, W/C Adams, S/L Miller and F/L Adams respectively as Master Bomber and Deputies, Lt Stevens and P/O Ewens as supporters and the remainder as part of the main force. Ahead of them lay an outward flight of more than four hours, which all of the 49 Squadron crews negotiated and arrived in time to watch Cheshire lob two red spotfires onto the roof of the factory at 00.17 during his third pass. So accurate were they, that the two 617 Squadron Lancaster backers-up were not required, and bombing took place in bright moonlight, the 49 Squadron crews delivering their loads from 8,900

to 12,000 feet between 00.11 and 00.26 and observing large fires with smoke rising through 7,000 feet. One 207 Squadron Lancaster was hit by flak over the target at 00.30 and exploded, killing all on board, and this was the only loss from an outstandingly successful operation. Within hours, Harris gave the go ahead for 5 Group to take on its own target marking force, and become, in effect, an independent entity.

It would be almost two weeks before the necessary moves took place, and in the meantime, the pre-invasion campaign got into full swing with the posting of two operations on the 9th. The Lille-Delivrance goods station in north-eastern France was assigned to 239 aircraft from 3, 4, 6 and 8 Groups, while the marshalling yards at Villeneuve-St-Georges, on the southern outskirts of Paris, were to be targeted by 225 aircraft drawn from all groups. The weather conditions were excellent, and clear skies greeted the latter force as it crossed the French coast at around 14,000 feet. The target could be identified visually, but crews aimed for the red and green TIs that had been accurately placed by the Path Finders, delivering their hardware from between 13,000 and 14,500 feet in the face of little opposition. Many bomb bursts were observed along with orange explosions, and to those high above, the raid appeared to be highly successful. In fact, many bomb loads had fallen into adjacent residential districts, where four hundred houses had been destroyed or seriously damaged, and ninety-three people killed. This was far fewer than had died in the simultaneous operation at Lille, many miles to the north-east, where over two thousand items of rolling stock had been destroyed and buildings and installations seriously damaged, but at a collateral cost of 456 French civilian lives. Civilian casualties would prove to be an unavoidable by-product of the campaign.

While the above operations were in progress, 103 Lancasters of 1 and 5 Groups were engaged in mining activities in the Baltic off Danzig (Gdansk), Gdynia and Pillau (Baltiysk). Nine 49 Squadron Lancasters departed Fiskerton between 21.14 and 21.26, six of them carrying eight-man crews after the addition of a second pilot and assigned to the Privet garden in the Gulf of Danzig, while the three seven-man crews had the Königsberg (now Kaliningrad) Canal further east as their destination in what was an extension of the Tangerine garden. S/L Miller was the senior pilot on duty and accompanying F/L Adams was his namesake and commanding officer. They noted night-fighter activity over Denmark, while the accurate Swedish flak discouraged them from straying too close to neutral airspace, and all arrived in their respective target areas to find bright moonlight and only high cirrus cloud. The main 49 Squadron element delivered their mines as briefed and unopposed from 15,000 feet between 01.43 and 01.46, while the canal-bound trio map-read their way to the target area, where P/O Roantree and crew dropped their mines into the briefed location from 200 feet at 01.52. As P/O Simpson and crew began their run, they were immediately engaged by around six flak guns, the fire from which forced them down to zero feet under cover of an island and then into a searchlight cone and more flak. The mines were jettisoned "live" and they made their escape unscathed to claim a completed sortie. Lt Stevens and crew carried out runs at 150 and 500 feet but were unable to locate the release point in time and eventually jettisoned their load at 02.15 after climbing to 10,000 feet. Nine Lancasters failed to return, having been intercepted by night-fighters on the route home over the western coast of Denmark, and it was a reminder that this most productive of enterprises could, on occasions, be as dangerous as the bombing of a city.

On the following day, Monday the 10th, a further five railway yards, four in France and one in Belgium, were posted as the targets for that night and assigned to individual groups. 5 Group was handed those at Tours in the Loire region of western France, for which 180 Lancasters were made ready, eleven of them on the 49 Squadron dispersal pans at Fiskerton. They took off between 22.44 and 23.25 with no senior pilot on duty and set course for England's south coast and the Channel crossing. There were no early returns and all arrived at the target to find bright moonlight and red spotfires marking the aiming point. Master Bombers were on hand to direct the two phases of the attack, the first against the western side of the yards and the second its eastern counterpart, but comments from returning crews revealed a somewhat chaotic raid, in which a good plan was hampered by poor communication. Having received no instructions from the Master Bomber, P/O Roantree and crew made a run at 02.00 without releasing any of their mixed high-explosive and incendiary load and eventually let it all go from 7,000 feet at 02.14 after pinpointing on the town. P/O Simpson and crew complained first about congestion at the datum point reaching suicidal proportions, and then the delay in receiving W/T instructions, which had crews orbiting for an extended period. The 49 Squadron crews attacked aiming point "B" mostly from 7,000 feet between 01.52 and 02.46 and found smoke from aiming point "A" completely obscuring it for a considerable time. This may have been the reason that some crews made two passes, up to twenty-five minutes apart, and smoke rising through 7,000 feet eventually persuaded the Master Bomber to call a halt to proceedings at 02.48. Any crews with bombs still on board were sent home and P/O Simpson and crew were among them. There were mixed opinions as to the effectiveness of the operation, some gaining the impression that the eastern half of the yards had not been touched, but others claimed the attack to have been accurate and concentrated within the yards, and two large fires were observed. Post-raid reconnaissance confirmed the success of the attack, but the Germans would round up local civilians and force them into repairing the damage to get the yards working again before long.

Aachen was a major railway centre with marshalling yards at both the western and eastern ends, but the attack planned for the night of the 11/12$^{th}$ was clearly designed as a city-busting exercise for which a force of 341 heavy aircraft was drawn from 1, 3, 5 and 8 Groups. 49 Squadron detailed four Lancasters, which took off between 20.19 and 20.35 bearing aloft the experienced crews of S/L Miller, F/Ls Adams and Bacon and P/O Shinn. The bomber stream climbed to between 18,000 and 20,000 feet by the time it reached the Belgian coast at 3 degrees east and maintained that altitude all the way to the target, where six to ten-tenths thin cloud was encountered at 7,000 to 8,000 feet. Red and green TIs identified the aiming point and the 49 Squadron crews attacked it from 17,000 feet between 22.37 and 22.45, observing many bomb bursts and fires, which suggested that the attack was accurate. The crews maintained height on the way home until fifty miles from the coast, at which position they began a gentle descent to exit enemy territory at 15,000 feet or above. Nine Lancasters failed to return, and among them was 49 Squadron's LL899, which was shot down by Oblt Heinz-Wolfgang Schnaufer of Stab IV./NJG1 while homebound at 17,500 feet. It crashed at 23.26 some fifteen miles north of Antwerp and there were no survivors from the crew of F/L Bacon DFC. Reports coming out of Aachen revealed this to be the city's worst experience of the war to date, with extensive damage in central and southern districts, disruption of its transport infrastructure and a death toll of 1,525 people. However, post-raid reconnaissance revealed that the railway yards had not been destroyed and would require further attention.

On the 14$^{th}$, the Command became officially subject to the orders coming from the Supreme Headquarters of the Allied Expeditionary Force (SHAEF), under General Dwight D Eisenhower, and would remain thus shackled until the Allied armies were sweeping towards the German frontier at the end of the summer. On the 18th, 83 and 97 Squadrons were loaned to 5 Group from the Path Finders, on what amounted to a permanent detachment, along with the Mosquito unit, 627 Squadron. The Lancaster units were to become the 5 Group heavy markers, while the Mosquitos would eventually take over the low-level marking role currently performed by 617 Squadron. This was a major coup for AVM Cochrane and 5 Group and a bitter blow to AVM Bennett, the Path Finder Force chief. Relations between Cochrane and Bennett had never been cordial, but this plunged them to new depths. Both were brilliant men, Bennett, an Australian, in particular, a man of the greatest intellect, who, despite his total lack of humour, commanded the deepest respect and loyalty from his men. He and Cochrane possessed vastly different opinions on the subject of target marking, Bennett believing that a low-level method exposed the crews to unnecessary danger, while Cochrane insisted that the risks in a fast-flying Mosquito were negligible and would produce greater accuracy. Though 83 and 97 Squadrons were formerly of 5 Group, and, at that time, had undoubtedly considered themselves part of the elite, most of the current crop of crews, despite beginning their operational careers in 5 Group, had come to see 8 Group as the pinnacle and were upset at being removed from what they considered to be an elevated status. They were fiercely proud, once qualified, to wear the Path Finder badge and enjoyed the enhanced benefits of their status, although, happily for them, as the squadrons were only officially on loan to 5 Group, they would retain these privileges.

Any resentment might have been smoothed over had their reception at Coningsby been handled better, but as the newly arrived crews tumbled out of their transports, they were summoned immediately to the briefing room to be lectured by the 54 Base commander, Air Commodore "Bobby" Sharp. Rather than welcoming them as brothers-in-arms, he harangued them over their bad 8 Group habits and ordered them to buckle down to learning 5 Group ways. This was an insult to experienced airmen, for whom the task of illuminating targets for 5 Group would be a piece of cake compared with the complexities of their 8 Group duties. The fact that the insult was being delivered by a pompous, self-important man with no relevant operational experience made it doubly unpalatable. From this point on, 5 Group would be known in 8 Group circles somewhat disparagingly as the "Independent Air Force", or "The Lincolnshire Poachers".

The 5 Group target on the 18th was the marshalling yards at Juvisy, situated on the West Bank of the Seine south of Paris, which was one of four similar targets for the night. The intention had been for the new arrivals to participate, but the disgruntled commanding officers, G/C Lawrence Deane of 83 Squadron and W/C Jimmy Carter of 97 Squadron, announced that they were not yet ready, and the operation would have to go ahead without them. 202 Lancasters and four Mosquitos were made ready, the latter belonging to 617 Squadron, and 8 Group would provide three Oboe Mosquitos to deliver the initial marking. 49 Squadron made ready nine Lancasters for the main event and ten for mining duties in the Geranium garden in Pomeranian Bay off Swinemünde. The two elements departed Fiskerton together between 20.48 and 21.20 with W/C Adams and S/L Miller the senior pilots on duty among the gardeners and F/L Armstrong among the bombing brigade. The latter reached their target to find clear skies and ideal bombing conditions, in which they observed W/C Cheshire's red spotfires in the process of being backed up by green TIs. Despite black smoke drifting across the aiming point and upwards from the destruction of a fuel dump at 23.32, the 49 Squadron crews were able to hit the markers from 7,000 to 11,000 between 23.34 and 23.53, and returning crews were enthusiastic about the success of the operation. This was confirmed by post-raid reconnaissance and prompted the crews to make the valid comment that, to count this operation as just one-third of a sortie was undervaluing it, a sentiment shared by all whose job involved putting their lives on the line.

Meanwhile, the gardeners had also encountered conditions ideal for the purpose of laying mines from altitude and were greeted by flak from shore-based batteries in the Peenemünde area and from ships moored in the bay. They established firm pinpoints from which to carry out their timed runs and delivered their payloads as briefed from 15,000 feet between 00.33 and 00.43, before returning safely, satisfied with their night's work.

Briefings on 5 Group stations on the 20th informed crews of their part in the first operation to include the three newly transferred squadrons, which was a two-phase attack on railway yards at La Chapelle, situated just to the north of Paris, while the night's main event was to be conducted by a force of 357 Lancasters and twenty-two Mosquitos drawn from 1, 3, 6 and 8 Groups against Cologne. A meticulous plan had been prepared for 5 Group, in which the phases were to be separated by an hour, each with its own specific aiming point, and 83 Squadron's W/C Deane was to be the Master Bomber with S/L Sparks his deputy. The plan called for 8 Group Mosquitos to drop cascading flares by Oboe to provide an initial reference and for a Mosquito element from 627 Squadron to lay a Window screen ahead of the main force Lancasters. Once the target had been identified, the first members of the 83 Squadron flare force were to provide illumination for the low-level marker Mosquitos of 617 Squadron, which would mark the first aiming point with red spot fires for the main force element to aim at. The whole procedure would then be repeated at the second aiming point. At Coningsby, W/C Deane conducted the briefing, and at its conclusion, wished the assembled throng good luck, before dismissing them, whereupon a voice from the back declared that the briefing wasn't over and that the base and station commanders wanted their say. This had not been standard practice in 8 Group, and it left Deane mystified and a little humiliated. The senior officers had only waffle to offer, but it made them feel important, while confirming the first impressions of the crews, that A/C Sharp was a self-important and irrelevant link in the chain of command.

49 Squadron made ready seventeen Lancasters as part of the overall force of 247 representing 5 Group and twenty-two Mosquitos of 5 and 8 Groups, and they departed Fiskerton between 22.05 and 22.34 with F/Ls Adams and Armstrong the senior pilots on duty. They were assigned to various waves attacking the first aiming point with a mix of 1,000 and 500 pounders and arrived at the target to find largely clear skies, good visibility and only some ground haze to mar the view. Zero hour for the opening phase was set for 00.05, but the Oboe Mosquitos were two minutes late and some communications problems had to be ironed out before matters began to run smoothly. The 49 Squadron crews bombed from 7,000 to 11,600 feet between 00.24 and 00.42, and a large, orange explosion at 00.28 sent a column of black smoke skyward, impairing visibility to some extent. Even so, those attacking afterwards were able to identify a red spotfire and bomb it, observing large explosions and fires that were visible to the second phase crews as they approached. Following the second phase attack, the fires remained visible for a hundred miles into the return flight and at debriefing, crews expressed confidence that they had contributed to a successful operation. Post-raid reconnaissance confirmed the success of both phases of the raid, which had left the yards severely damaged for the loss of six Lancasters. A congratulatory message from A-O-C Cochrane was received on all participating stations.

The real test for the 5 Group low-level marking system would come at a heavily defended German target, for which Braunschweig was selected on the 22nd, while the rest of the Command targeted the Ruhr city of Düsseldorf. 5 Group put together a force of 238 Lancasters and seventeen Mosquitos, with ten ABC Lancasters of 1 Group's 101 Squadron to provide radio countermeasures (RCM) cover. 49 Squadron contributed eighteen Lancasters, which took off between 23.01 and 23.20 with F/L Adams the senior pilot on duty. P/O Rowley and crew were fifteen miles east-south-east of Osnabrück when intercepted by a night-fighter at 01.23, which left a fire burning amidships and filled the fuselage with smoke. The assailant was evaded through violent corkscrewing but not before both turrets had been put out of action and the rear gunner mortally wounded. The flight engineer succeeded in extinguishing the flames and they were able to return safely to base. The others reached the target area after being guided by route-markers and found six to eight-tenths thin cloud at between 8,000 and 10,000 feet and accurate marking by the 617 Squadron Mosquito element. Despite this, the main force crews were unable to properly identify the target, a situation again compounded by communications problems between various controllers, caused by the failure of VHF and the consequent need to pass on instructions instead by W/T. This led to confusion, and many crews were forced to orbit for up to fifteen minutes before bombing. The 49 Squadron crews carried out their attacks on green TIs and red spotfires from 15,000 to 22,000 feet between 01.57 and 02.06 and most returned safely to report what appeared to be a successful operation, while also complaining about the dangers of orbiting a target with aircraft heading in a variety of directions. A minute after bombing, P/O Lett's ND695 was peppered by shards of hot metal from an exploding flak shell when at 19,500 feet at 02.05, damaging the fuselage and mortally wounding the bomb-aimer. A post-raid analysis revealed that some bombs had fallen in the city centre, but most were directed at reserve H2S-laid TIs to the south of the city, and damage was less severe than might otherwise have been.

On the 23rd, 114 Halifaxes, Stirlings and Lancasters were sent mining in the Baltic, 5 Group making a small contribution, which included 49 Squadron's F/O Ewens and crew, who departed Fiskerton at 21.00 bound for the Geranium garden off Swinemünde. They established a pinpoint on Liepe Point and delivered their mines into the briefed location from 15,000 feet at 01.32.

When Munich was posted across 5 Group as the target on the 24th for another live test of the low-level visual marking method, it might have been seen as somewhat ambitious to select such a major city, that was protected by two hundred flak guns. The main operation on this night was to be conducted by a force of 637 aircraft against Karlsruhe, 150 miles to the north-west, which would help to distract the night-fighters. 234 Lancasters were made ready by 5 Group and supplemented by ten of the ABC variety from 101 Squadron, while four Mosquitos of 617 Squadron were loaded with spotfires to carry out the marking and twelve of 627 Squadron with Window to dispense during the final approach to the target. 49 Squadron's sixteen Lancasters took to the air between 20.46 and 21.15 with F/Ls Adams and Armstrong the senior pilots on duty and headed for the south coast before setting course across France towards the south-east and feinting towards Italy. The 617 and 627 Squadron Mosquitos took off three hours after the heavy brigade and adopted a direct route, the latter laying a Window screen from high level six minutes from the target to mask the arrival of the flare force that was to provide seven minutes of illumination for the 617 marker Mosquitos. P/O Green and crew had reached central France when the port-outer engine failed and forced them to turn back, while the others reached the target area to encounter clear skies and good visibility. W/C Cheshire dived onto the aiming point in the face of murderous light flak, before racing away across the rooftops to safety ahead of the arrival of the main force element, those of 49 Squadron bombing on the red spotfires and green TIs from 15,200 to 21,500 feet between 01.46 and 01.56 in the face of intense searchlight and flak activity. Many fires were seen to take hold, and as the bombers pointed their snouts back towards France to eventually pass to the north of Paris, Karlsruhe could be seen burning over to starboard. Among ten missing Lancasters was 49 Squadron's ND537, which was rent by an explosion following a night-fighter attack as it left the target and crashed at 01.53 near Pastetten, some twelve miles east-north-east of Munich, without survivors from the crew of P/O Clark. Post-raid reconnaissance and local reports confirmed the success of the raid, which left 1,104 buildings in ruins and a further thirteen hundred severely damaged. It was probably this operation that sealed the award to Cheshire of the Victoria Cross at the conclusion of his operational career of one hundred sorties.

At briefing on the 26$^{th}$, fifteen 49 Squadron crews were told that Schweinfurt was to be their target that night, after the failure of the RAF to destroy it in February and the American 8$^{th}$ Air Force just two weeks ago. The tone was very much, "leave it to RAF Bomber Command", and with the satisfaction of Munich still fresh in the mind and the natural rivalry between the two Allied bomber organisations keen, such attitudes were to be expected. They learned that, for this operation, 627 Squadron would act as the low-level marker force for the first time and for a main force of 215 Lancasters, including nine from 101 Squadron to provide RCM protection. This was just one of three major operations taking place, the main event at Essen involving 493 aircraft from all but 5 Group, while the railway yards at Villeneuve-St-Georges was the objective for a predominantly Halifax main force. The 49 Squadron element departed Fiskerton between 21.23 and 21.40 with F/Ls Adams and Armstrong the senior pilots on duty and joined up with the bomber stream as they headed south. Stronger-than-forecast head winds delayed the arrival in the target area of the heavy brigade, but once there they found generally clear skies and good visibility, which the 627 Squadron crews failed to exploit as their debut marking effort proved to be inaccurate. The 83 Squadron crews remarked on the lack of illumination and those carrying hooded flares were called in a number of times to back-up. The 49 Squadron crews bombed from 14,500 to 21,000 feet between 02.22 and 02.44 aiming at red spotfires and green TIs, some following the instructions of the Master Bomber to overshoot by a thousand yards. A large white explosion was witnessed at 02.29, and many fires were reported, but once again at this target, most of the hardware fell outside of the target area, leaving ball-bearing production more or less unscathed. Night-fighters got amongst the heavy force on both sides of the Franco-German frontier and twenty-one Lancasters were shot down, a hefty 9.3%, among them three representing 49 Squadron, each containing a highly experienced crew. LL908 came down at Ugny-sur-Meuse in north-eastern France some twenty miles west of Nancy and there were no survivors from the crew of P/O Dickinson, who were on their twenty-fifth sortie. JB679 crashed some fifteen miles to the south-west at Bure killing P/O Montgomery and all but the two gunners, one of whom evaded capture. They had been on their nineteenth sortie. ND687 contained the crew of F/L Armstrong DFC, who were on the fifth sortie of their second tour, and all lost their lives when shot down by a night-fighter to crash at Igelsloch, twenty miles west of Stuttgart.

5 Group made preparations on the 28$^{th}$ to send a force of eighty-eight Lancasters and four Mosquitos to attack the Alfred Nobel Dynamit A G explosives works at St-Médard-en-Jalles, situated in a wood on the north-western outskirts of Bordeaux in south-western France. A further fifty-one Lancasters and four Mosquitos would head in the opposite direction to target an aircraft

maintenance facility at the Kjeller Flyfabrikk, some ten miles north-east of Oslo, which had been occupied by the Germans since April 1940 and was used by Junkers, Daimler-Benz and BMW. This was the destination for eleven 49 Squadron Lancasters, which departed Fiskerton between 21.12 and 21.27 with F/L Adams the senior pilot on duty. They all arrived in the target area to find clear skies and excellent visibility and identified the target by H2S, confirmed by yellow TIs at the start of the bombing run and flares and red spotfires. A two-thousand-yard correction was broadcast to compensate for a poor marking performance, and the 49 Squadron crews carried out their attacks from 5,000 to 7,000 feet between 01.27 and 01.46, many making more than one pass to take in a number of aiming points. Explosions were observed on the airfield and runway and among barrack buildings and some of the sheds, and an ammunition dump went up at 01.40. On return, the 44 (Rhodesia) Squadron commanding officer, W/C Thompson, was scathing about the quality of marking and control and the amount of smoke given off by too many hooded flares. Meanwhile, the attack near Bordeaux had also been spoiled by smoke and haze from a wood burning nearby, and only twenty-six aircraft had bombed before the Master Bomber called a halt.

The operation was rescheduled for the following night, when the Michelin tyre factory at Clermont-Ferrand was added to the target list and the 52 Base squadrons stayed at home. Sixty-eight Lancasters were assigned to the explosives works and fifty-four to the tyre factory, with five 627 Squadron Mosquitos at each to provide the low-level marking. The aiming point was identified both visually and by red spotfires and red and green TIs, which could be seen burning between factory buildings, and returning crews were filled with enthusiasm at the explosions that had ripped the site apart, some commenting that it was the most destructive attack they had taken part in. Post-raid reconnaissance confirmed that both targets had been severely damaged with a massive loss of production.

News came through on the 30th of a particularly sad incident involving a scratch crew in a 460 Squadron RAAF Lancaster engaged in trials of the Automatic Gun-Laying Turret (AGLT), coded Village Inn, on behalf of the Bombing Development Unit at Newmarket. F/L Healey DFC, formerly of 49 Squadron, took off from Binbrook in the afternoon for a fighter affiliation exercise in Lancaster ND553, and on board were four other former members of 49 Squadron, including F/O Brian Jagger DFM, who had been Shannon's front gunner on Operation Chastise and was currently attached to the BDU. At some point during vigorous evasive manoeuvres, the dinghy broke loose from its wing stowage and fouled the tailplane, causing the Lancaster to flip onto its back. There was insufficient altitude to provide F/L Healey with the time to rescue the situation and the Lancaster crashed near Witchford at 16.55, killing all six occupants.

Sometime towards the end of the month, W/C Adams was posted away and was succeeded by American, W/C Malcolm Crocker DFC, who had been rejected by his own Army Air Force and had been picked up by the RAF and sent to Canada for training in 1942. He rose quickly through the ranks after joining 57 Squadron as a flying officer in April 1943 and was promoted to acting flight lieutenant rank in June. He was appointed flight commander in the rank of acting squadron leader in July and acting wing commander in November on his posting across the tarmac at East Kirkby to assume command of the newly formed 630 Squadron. He occupied that post only for a month before his posting to a staff job for a rest from operations. During the course of the month the squadron carried out twelve operations and dispatched 131 sorties for the loss of five Lancasters and crews and two additional airmen.

## May 1944

With the invasion now just five weeks away, the new month would be devoted to attacks on railway targets and coastal defences. In the case of the latter, the focus would be on the Pas-de-Calais region of France, to try to reinforce the enemy's belief that the landings would take place there. Twelve 49 Squadron crews were called to briefing at Fiskerton on the 1st to learn that they would be going to Toulouse in southern France that night as part of a 5 Group force of 131 Lancasters and eight Mosquitos to attack two targets, the Proudrerie explosives works and a SNCASE aircraft assembly factory in the western suburb of Saint-Martin-du-Touch. At the same time, a third 5 Group force of forty-six Lancasters and four Mosquitos would be sent against an aircraft repair workshop at Tours in western France. The 49 Squadron crews took off between 21.27 and 21.52 with F/L Botting the senior pilot on duty and employed Gee for the first part of the outward flight until it was jammed, relying, thereafter, on good navigation, green track markers provided by the Path Finders, and H2S. They all reached the target to find moonlight, clear skies and excellent visibility, with flares and red spotfires marking out the aiming point, and carried out their attacks from 6,150 to 8,000 feet between 01.37 and 01.47 in accordance with the instructions of the Master Bomber. The attack was clearly focused on the aiming point, where many bomb bursts and large explosions were observed and the glow of the burning site remained visible for a hundred miles into the return journey. All crews returned to their respective stations confident of a successful outcome, and post-raid reconnaissance revealed all three factories to have been heavily damaged.

Briefings took place on 1 and 5 Group stations on the 3rd, for what would become a highly contentious operation that night against a Panzer training camp and transport depot at Mailly-le-Camp, situated some seventy-five miles east of Paris in north-eastern France. The units based there posed a potential threat to Allied forces as the invasion unfolded and needed to be eliminated. The events of the operation proved to be so controversial that recriminations abound to this day concerning the 5 Group leadership provided by W/Cs Cheshire and Deane. Although the grudges by 1 Group aircrew against them can be understood in the light of what happened, they are unjust, and based on emotion and incorrect information and it is worthwhile to examine the conduct of the operation in some detail. W/C Cheshire was appointed as marker leader, and was piloting one of four 617 Squadron Mosquitos, while 83 Squadron's commanding officer, W/C Deane, was overall raid controller with S/L Sparks his Deputy. Deane and Cheshire attended separate briefings, and neither seemed aware of the complete plan, particularly the role of the 1 Group Special Duties Flight from Binbrook, which was assigned to its own specific aiming point to mark for an element of the 1 Group force.

The fourteen 49 Squadron participants became airborne between 21.49 and 22.09 with W/C Crocker demonstrating good leadership qualities by putting himself on the order of battle for the first time, supported by F/Ls Adams and Botting. All reached the target area to find clear skies, moonlight and excellent bombing conditions, but confusion already beginning to influence events. 617 Squadron's W/C Cheshire and S/L Shannon were in position before midnight, and as the first flares from the 83 and 97 Squadron Lancasters illuminated the target below, Cheshire released his two red spot fires onto the first aiming point at 00.00½ from 1,500 feet. Shannon backed them up from 400 feet five and a half minutes later, and as far as Cheshire was concerned, the operation was bang on schedule at this stage. A 97 Squadron Lancaster also laid markers accurately to ensure a constant focal point, and Cheshire passed instructions to Deane to call the bombers in. It was at this stage of the operation that matters began to go awry, when a commercial radio station, believed to be an American forces network, jammed the VHF frequencies in use. Deane called in the 5 Group element, elated that everything was proceeding according to plan, but nothing happened. He checked with his wireless operator that the instructions had been transmitted and called up S/L Sparks, who was also mystified by the lack of bombing.

Post raid reports are contradictory, and it is impossible to establish an accurate course of events, particularly when Deane and Cheshire's understanding of the exact time of zero hour differed by five minutes. Remarkably, it also seems, that Deane was unaware that there were two marking points, or three, if one includes 1 Group's Special Duties Flight. Cheshire, initially at least, appeared happy with the early stages of the attack and described the bombing as concentrated and accurate. It seems certain, however, that many minutes had passed between the dropping of Cheshire's markers and the first main force bombs falling, during which period, Deane was coming to terms with the fact that his instructions were not getting through. A plausible scenario is, that in the absence of instructions, and with red spot fires clearly visible in the target, some crews from 9, 207 and 467 Squadrons opted to bomb and others followed suit. The crews of W/C Crocker and five others from 49 Squadron attacked from 6,400 to 8,000 feet between 00.11 and 00.17, Crocker describing the target as well-marked and the air above it as ridiculously congested. It was at this point that W/C Deane attempted to control the operation by W/T, which also failed.

Now a new problem was arising as smoke from these first salvoes threatened to obliterate the entire camp, and Cheshire had to decide whether or not to send in Fawke and former 49 Squadron pilot, Gerry Kearns, to mark the second aiming point. His feeling and that of Deane, as it later transpired, was that it was unnecessary as the volume of bombs still to fall into the relatively compact area of the target would ensure destruction of the entire site. By 00.16, the first phase of bombing should have been completed, leaving a clear run for Fawke and Kearns across the target, however, the majority of 5 Group crews were still on their bombing run, a fact unknown to Cheshire, who asked Deane for a pause in the bombing while the two Mosquitos went in. As far as Cheshire was concerned, there was no response from Deane, who would anyway have been confused by mention of a second aiming point. In the event, Deane's deputy, S/L Sparks, eventually found a channel free of interference, and did, in fact, transmit an instruction to halt the bombing both by W/T and R/T, and some crews reported hearing something. While utter chaos reigned, Kearns and Fawke dived in among the falling cookies at 00.23 and 00.25 respectively to mark the second aiming point on the western edge of the camp. At 2,000 feet, they were lucky to survive the turbulence created by the exploding 4,000 pounders, when 4,000 feet was considered to be a minimum safe height. They were not entirely happy with their work, but F/O Edwards of 97 Squadron dropped a stick of markers precisely on the mark, and S/L Sparks was then able to call the 1 Group main force in along with any from 5 Group with bombs still on board. Among the latter were the remaining 49 Squadron crews who attacked from 6,800 to 7,900 feet between 00.27 and 00.34. P/O Ball and crew were among those sent to orbit a yellow marker fifteen miles away and they spent an uncomfortable thirty minutes watching Lancasters fall from the sky in flames. Finally called in, they were about to drop their bombs when ND647 was hit by flak and filled with smoke. The bombs were jettisoned, and the order given to don parachutes, at which point the intercom failed completely and the two gunners left the aircraft. P/O Ball brought the Lancaster home on two-and-a-half engines, and he would be awarded an immediate DFC. Meanwhile, the night-fighters continued to create havoc among the Lancasters as they milled around in the target area, and as burning aircraft were seen to fall all around, some of 1 Group's Australian crews succumbed to their anxiety and frustration and in a rare breakdown of R/T discipline, let fly with comments of an uncomplimentary nature, many of which were intended for, and, indeed, heard by Deane.

Despite the problems, the operation was a major success, which destroyed 80% of the camp's buildings and 102 vehicles, of which thirty-seven were tanks, while over two hundred men were killed. Forty-two Lancasters failed to return, however, two thirds of them from 1 Group, and 50 Squadron was 5 Group's most afflicted unit with four Lancasters and crews unaccounted for. At debriefing, S/L Blome-Jones of 207 Squadron described the situation as a complete shambles and chaos, the controller as inefficient and the discipline of some crews as bad. Others voiced the opinion that this was a trip worthy of more than one-third of a sortie. On the following day, an inquest into the conduct of the raid revealed that the wireless transmitter in Deane's Lancaster had been sufficiently off frequency to allow the interference from the American network to mask the transmission of instructions and prevent the call to bomb from reaching the main force crews. The 1 Group A-O-C, AVM Rice, decided he would not participate in further operations organized by 5 Group, which was probably not a blow to Cochrane, who was confident that his group did not need back-up.

On the 6th, 1 and 5 Groups were invited to send a modest force each to attack ammunition dumps in France, 5 Group detailing sixty-four Lancasters and four Mosquitos for a site at Louailles, situated some four miles south-east of the town of Sable-sur-Sarthe, south-west of Le-Mans. Clear skies and excellent visibility provided ideal conditions, and a Master Bomber was on hand to direct the attack, which resulted in numerous bomb flashes that lit up the long storage sheds. Two enormous explosions were each followed by a large mushroom of smoke rising through 3,000 feet as the force withdrew. 52 Base (Fiskerton and Dunholme Lodge) sat this one out but was alerted on the 7th to prepare for its part in five small-scale operations to be mounted against airfields, ammunition dumps and a coastal battery in support of the coming invasion. 5 Group was involved in two raids, the airfield at Tours and an ammunition dump at Salbris, some sixty miles to the east, and it was for the latter that 49 Squadron made ready fourteen Lancasters. They took off between 21.54 and 22.08 with F/L Botting the senior pilot on duty on what turned out to be another night of perfect conditions and headed south to pass by Reading on their way to Selsey Bill for the Channel crossing and landfall on the French coast at Cabourg. They set course for the target with Gee working perfectly all the way out, and with twenty miles horizontal visibility under bright moonlight, the red spotfires were observed well in advance of arrival at the aiming point. The Fiskerton crews carried out their attacks from 6,000 to 8,000 feet between 00.24 and 00.32 and observed large, vivid explosions and a column of smoke rising through 11,000 feet as they withdrew. JB421 was one of seven missing Lancasters and was almost certainly the victim of a night-fighter patrolling over the Loire region. P/O Anderson and crew were on their maiden operation, and all lost their lives in the crash a mile-and-a-half west-north-west of the town of Bourges. Post-raid reconnaissance confirmed that both targets had been bombed accurately and effectively to leave them severely damaged.

Another small-scale operation was mounted by the group on the 8th against the airfield and seaplane base at Lanveoc-Poulmic, located on the northern side of the peninsula forming the southern boundary of the L'Elorn estuary opposite Brest. A force of fifty-eight Lancasters and six

Mosquitos identified the target easily by the coastline and layout of the hangars, which they left on fire along with other buildings and the entire site was enveloped in smoke as they withdrew.

The night of the 9/10th brought attacks on seven coastal batteries in the Pas-de-Calais by four hundred aircraft, the purpose of the operations to confirm in the mind of the enemy the belief that the Allied invasion forces would land at Calais. Right up to D-Day itself, the coastal region between Gravelines to the east of the port and Berck-sur-Mer to the south-west would be subjected to constant bombardment. 5 Group, meanwhile, prepared fifty-six Lancasters and eight Mosquitos to attack two factories, the Gnome & Rhône aero-engine works and the Goodrich tyre factory at Gennevilliers in northern Paris, while a second force of thirty-nine Lancasters and four Mosquitos targeted a small ball-bearing factory at Annecy, situated in south-eastern France close to the frontiers with Switzerland and Italy. 49 Squadron made ready thirteen Lancasters for Paris, and they departed Fiskerton between 22.06 and 22.20 with W/C Crocker and F/L Botting the senior pilots on duty. They rendezvoused with the other squadrons over Reading, before beginning the Channel crossing at Shoreham-on-Sea and making landfall on the French coast near Dieppe. Moonlight and clear skies enabled them to map read after Gee was jammed at the French coast, and H2S proved useful as they closed on Paris. Yellow TIs and red spotfires identified the aiming point, and the bombing by the 49 Squadron crews proceeded from 7,000 to 8,650 feet between 00.34 and 00.41. Local sources confirmed damage to the target, but also collateral damage that killed twenty-seven French civilians and injured more than a hundred. Post-raid reconnaissance confirmed the Annecy site also to have been severely damaged.

Five railway targets were selected for attention on the night of the 10/11th, among them the marshalling yards at Lille for 5 Group on a night when 52 Base squadrons stayed at home. Bomb bursts were seen across the tracks, and two large explosions were observed to confirm a successful assault on this important hub linking north-eastern France with Belgium. Night-fighters were out in force, and most of the night's casualties resulted from this operation, from which a dozen Lancasters failed to return.

5 Group put together a force of 190 Lancasters and eight Mosquitos on the 11th to target a military camp at Bourg-Leopold in north-eastern Belgium, for which 49 Squadron made ready fourteen Lancasters. They departed Fiskerton between 22.28 and 22.45 with F/L Botting the senior pilot on duty and all reached the target to find hazy conditions and a little thin cloud at around 10,000 feet, despite which, they would be able to identify ground detail in the form of buildings and huts in the light of illuminating flares. Three Oboe Mosquitos were on hand to deliver the initial marking, but inaccurately forecast winds caused the 83 Squadron element to arrive late, by which time the main force crews had begun to orbit to await instructions. A communications problem prevented some crews from hearing the Master Bomber's broadcasts, but the aiming point could be seen to be marked by red spotfires and green TIs. From the Master Bomber's perspective, the initial Oboe marker had been visible only to a few crews and quickly burned out, and so he called for another Mosquito to drop a red spot fire onto the aiming point. Before this was accomplished, however, the main force began to bomb, and among ninety-four crews to do so were eight from Fiskerton, who attacked from 14,250 to 17,000 feet between 00.20 and 00.27. As smoke began to obscure the ground, the Master Bomber, S/L Mitchell, quickly became uncomfortable about the close proximity of civilian residential property and called a halt to the bombing at 00.35, before sending the rest of the force home, some of them after circling for more than twenty minutes.

Minor operations occupied elements of the Command, thereafter, until the 19th, when the station teleprinters worked overtime dispensing the details of five operations for that night against marshalling yards, two on coastal batteries and one against a radar station. 5 Group detailed 225 Lancasters, 112 to be sent to Amiens with eight Mosquitos and 113 for Tours with four Mosquitos, the 49 Squadron element of sixteen assigned to the former. They departed Fiskerton between 22.57 and 23.17 with F/Ls Adams, Botting and Powell the senior pilots on duty and set course for north-eastern France via Hastings and Dieppe to find the target shrouded in a layer of eight to ten-tenths cloud between 6,000 and 11,000 feet. The aiming point was identified by red spotfires, but when checked on H2S, these appeared to be up to five miles from the planned aiming point. Thirty-seven aircraft had bombed when instructions came through by W/T at 01.25 to terminate the attack and return home, by which time, seven 49 Squadron crews had already carried out their attacks from 5,800 to 8,500 feet between 01.21 and 01.24. The others either jettisoned their loads on the way home across the Channel or brought them back. The Tours raid had been directed at the marshalling yards in the centre of the city, which required great precision on the part of the marker and main forces, both of which performed magnificently to leave the target severely damaged without causing collateral damage.

For the first time in a year, Duisburg was posted as the target for a heavy raid on the 21st, for which a force of 510 Lancasters was drawn from 1, 3, 5 and 8 Groups. They would be supported by twenty-two Mosquitos, and while this operation was in progress, seventy Lancasters, including some from 5 Group, and thirty-seven Halifaxes would undertake gardening duties off the Frisians and Heligoland and in the Baltic. 49 Squadron would support both operations, assigning seven Lancasters to the main event and a dozen to the gardening effort in the Forget-me-not garden in Kiel Bay, and it was the latter which departed Fiskerton first between 21.38 and 21.54 with F/L Powell the senior pilot on duty.

Those bound for the Ruhr took off between 22.14 and 22.23 led by W/C Crocker and the newly promoted S/L Botting, having been told at briefing to adhere to the plan for the outward route, which involved a few aircraft from 3 Group gaining height as they adopted a north-westerly course as far as Sleaford, so as not to cross into enemy radar cover earlier than necessary. The groups would rendezvous at 18,000 feet over the North Sea at 3 degrees east to cross the enemy coast via the western Frisians at 20,000 feet and climb to 22,000 or 23,000 feet, before increasing speed for the run across the target. All of the 49 Squadron participants reached the Ruhr, which they found to be concealed beneath ten-tenths cloud with tops at between 11,000 and 20,000 feet, into which the red Wanganui markers with-yellow-stars fell almost before they could be seen. A number of crews commented on the data provided by the wind-finder system to be inaccurate, and this made it a challenge to establish positions. The Fiskerton crews used the explosion of cookies, the glow of fires and the evidence of intense flak as references and bombed from 18,500 to 22,000 feet between 01.10 and 01.34, before returning home with little useful information to impart. W/C Crocker complained bitterly about the lack of coherent marking and described it as the poorest show ever seen after eventually bombing a built-up area on H2S, which may have been Duisburg. The loss of twenty-nine Lancasters was a reminder to the Command that the Ruhr remained a dangerous destination, although most of the missing had come down onto Dutch and Belgian soil or into the sea homebound after falling victim to night-fighters. Martin Drewes of III./NJG1 alone accounted for at least three Lancasters. 49 Squadron's LM539 crashed near Roosendaal in south-western Holland within sight of the Scheldt estuary, killing P/O Carrington RAAF and all but his bomb-aimer, who fell into enemy hands. Returning crews were not enthusiastic about the outcome, and post-raid reconnaissance confirmed that a modest 350 buildings had been destroyed in the southern half of Duisburg and 665 others had been seriously damaged. While this operation was in progress, the gardeners had encountered up to six-tenths cloud in the western Baltic, through which they established a pinpoint on Dovns Klint, the most southerly point of Denmark's Langeland island and planted their six vegetables each into the allotted positions from 14,000 to 15,000 feet between 00.52 and 01.08.

Just like Duisburg, Dortmund was posted on the 22nd to host its first large-scale visit from the Command for a year and would face an all-Lancaster heavy force of 361 aircraft drawn from 1, 3, 6 and 8 Groups. While this operation was in progress, 220 Lancasters of 5 Group and five from 101 Squadron were to target Braunschweig, which, thus far, had evaded severe damage at the hands of the Command. 49 Squadron made ready seventeen Lancasters, which departed Fiskerton between 21.59 and 22.26 with F/Ls Matheson and Powell the senior pilots on duty. F/Sgt Baker and crew lost their DR compass on take-off and soon afterwards their intercom and turned back, while the others pressed on across the North Sea and through the clearly evident night-fighter activity from the Dutch coast all the way to the target. They negotiated the patches of ten-tenths cloud over northern Germany and intense searchlight activity as they passed between Bremen and Osnabrück. The forecast at briefings had suggested clear skies over Braunschweig, but in fact, the marker force encountered four to seven-tenths drifting cloud with tops up to 7,000 feet. Although highly effective in the right weather conditions, the 5 Group low-level visual marking method could easily be rendered ineffective by cloud cover. The blind heavy markers dropped skymarkers by H2S, while the 627 Squadron Mosquito element went in at low level to release red spotfires. Some crews described "hopeless confusion" with flares and incendiaries spread over a distance and many had to rely on their own H2S to establish their position. Some found a complete absence of marking and orbited for up to fifteen minutes until a few green TIs appeared, after which, the bombing by the 49 Squadron element took place on these or on incendiary fires from 19,000 to 22,000 feet between 01.16 and 01.40. Considerable interference over R/T communications added to the problems, and although the Master Bomber could be heard in discussions with his Deputies, no instructions were received from him and the attack lacked cohesion. Post-raid reconnaissance confirmed that most of the bombing had fallen onto outlying communities, confirming in the minds of the residents that this was an intentional ploy by the Command. It was a relatively expensive failure that cost thirteen Lancasters, including 49 Squadron's NE125, which crashed somewhere in north-western Germany with no survivors from the crew of P/O Graves-Hook, who were operating for the seventh time.

The main operation on the 24th involved 442 aircraft in an attack on two marshalling yards at Aachen, Aachen-West and Rothe-Erde in the east. As the most westerly city in Germany, sitting on the frontiers of both Holland and Belgium, it was a major link in the railway network that would be a route for reinforcements to the Normandy battle front. Other operations on this night were directed at coastal batteries in the Pas-de-Calais and war-industry factories in Holland and Belgium. 5 Group detailed forty-four Lancasters to attack the Ford Motor works in Antwerp and fifty-nine for the Philips electronics factory at Eindhoven in southern Holland, while 52 Base remained off the order of battle. Those bound for Eindhoven were more than an hour into the outward journey when the Master Bomber sent them home by W/T, presumably after a Met Flight

Mosquito crew had found poor visibility in the target area. There were no such difficulties at Antwerp, where the target was identified by illuminating flares, a yellow TI and red spotfires, despite which, post-raid reconnaissance revealed the factory to be intact.

The night of the 27/28th was to be one of feverish activity, which would generate more than eleven hundred sorties, reflecting the close proximity of the invasion, now just ten days away. The largest operation would bring a return to the military camp at Bourg Leopold in Belgium, the previous attack on which, two weeks earlier, had been abandoned part-way through. There was also a repeat of the Aachen attack of the 24th, which had failed to destroy the Rothe-Erde marshalling yards at the eastern end of the city and needed further attention. 5 Group was not involved in either of the above, and instead prepared forces of one hundred Lancasters and four Mosquitos and seventy-eight Lancasters and five Mosquitos respectively to target marshalling yards and workshops at Nantes and the aerodrome at Rennes, situated some fifty miles apart in north-western France. The group would also support operations against coastal batteries, of which there were five on this night, including one at Morsalines, situated on the eastern seaboard of the Cherbourg peninsula, some ten miles north of what, during the forthcoming Operation Overlord, would be the Americans' Utah landing ground. This was the target for the 52 Base squadrons and eighteen 49 Squadron Lancasters departed Fiskerton between 22.49 and 23.07 with the recently posted-in S/L Bazin the senior pilot on duty. S/L Bazin was thirty-one years of age and had served with Fighter Command during the Battle of Britain, flying Hurricanes with 607 Squadron, and had occupied staff jobs thereafter until a posting to Bomber Command late in 1943. He volunteered for flying duties, undergoing Lancaster training before arriving at 49 Squadron as a flight commander. All reached the target area on Gee-fix to find seven tenths cloud at 3,000 to 4,000 feet, but fair visibility and the aiming point identified by flares, red spotfires and green TIs. The Fiskerton participants carried out their attacks from 5,000 to 7,000 feet between 00.55 and 01.12 in accordance with the instructions of a Master Bomber and observed the bombing to be concentrated around the markers. Cloud and smoke obscured much of the detail, but the consensus was, that if the markers had been accurate, the target had been hit.

On the 28th, 181 Lancasters and twenty Mosquitos continued the attacks on coastal batteries overlooking the Normandy beaches, which, a week hence, would be the scene of Operation Overlord. The 52 Base squadrons were not called into action on this night or on the following two nights, and it was on the 31st when the next operational orders were received to prepare for further operations that night against coastal batteries covering the Normandy beaches. 5 Group was to send a force of eighty-two Lancasters and four Mosquitos to attack a railway junction at Saumur in the Loire Valley, and another of sixty-eight Lancasters to a coastal battery at Maisy, overlooking what would be the Americans' Omaha Beach. It was for the latter that 49 Squadron prepared fourteen Lancasters, which departed Fiskerton between 22.59 and 23.13 with W/C Crocker and S/L Bazin the senior pilots on duty. They had to pass through a belt of storm-bearing clouds as they flew from base to Reading, and the foul weather continued as they passed over Selsey Bill to start the Channel crossing. The leading crews were within seven miles of the French coast when the Master Bomber cancelled the operation by W/T at 01.51 and sent everyone home.

There was no further operational activity for 49 Squadron, which watched from the side-lines as eighty-two Lancasters and four Mosquitos dealt with a railway junction at Saumur in western

France. During the course of the month, the squadron took part in eleven operations and dispatched 151 sorties for the loss of three Lancasters and their crews and two gunners.

# June 1944

June was to be a hectic month, which would make great demands on the crews for whom the bombing of coastal batteries was to be the priority during the first few days leading up to D-Day. However, 5 Group opened its account by returning to Saumur to attack a second railway junction on the 1st, a day which dawned cloudy and cold, and such conditions would persist throughout the first week of the month, causing concern among the invasion planners. The 52 Base squadrons remained at home, while fifty-eight Lancasters took off in the late evening to find ten-tenths cloud covering the route out to within twenty miles of the town, where it dispersed completely to leave clear skies and good visibility under a three-quarter moon. Returning crews reported little opposition, fires in the yards and a large explosion at 01.35, and the success of the raid was confirmed by photographic reconnaissance, which showed severe damage to the track.

Seventeen 49 Squadron crews were among sixty-one from 5 Group to be called to briefings on the 2nd, when they were told that they would be attacking a heavy battery mounted on a rail platform at Wimereux, situated south-west of Calais. They departed Fiskerton between 23.52 and 00.12 with W/C Crocker and S/L Bazin the senior pilots on duty, and all reached the French coast to encounter the most unfavourable weather conditions including ten-tenths cloud at 10,000 feet. The glow of red TIs greeted their arrival, but the Master Bomber was uncomfortable with the conditions and called a halt to proceedings at 01.45, by which time seven 49 Squadron crews had bombed from 17,700 to 19,500 feet between 01.39 and 01.42. The crews had not been told the date of the invasion or where the landings would take place, and were not, therefore, aware that the operation was a smoke screen as part of the deception plan. The Squadron remained off the order of battle thereafter until D-Day Eve, while ninety-six Lancasters of the group carried out an operation on the 3rd against a listening station at Ferme-d'Urville, situated on the Cherbourg peninsula to the west of the port. It had escaped damage when attacked by Halifaxes two nights earlier, but this time the bombing was focused within a five-hundred-yard radius of the aiming point and was confirmed by post-raid reconnaissance to have obliterated the site.

Orders came through on the 4th to prepare for attacks that night on coastal batteries, three in the Pas-de-Calais to maintain the deception, and the one at Maisy, overlooking the Utah and Omaha beaches. 259 aircraft of 1, 4, 5, 6 and 8 Groups were made ready, the majority for the deception targets, while fifty-two of the Lancasters, all representing 5 Group, were assigned to Maisy. 52 Base was not involved in these pre-dawn attacks, which took place through ten-tenths cloud with a base at around 4,000 feet. This necessitated the use of Oboe skymarkers and positions were confirmed by Gee-fix and a faint red glow, before the bombing was carried out from just above the cloud tops. It was impossible to assess the outcome, and similar cloudy conditions had thwarted two of the three attempts in the Pas-de-Calais area.

The 5th was D-Day Eve, and during the course of that night, a record number of 1,211 sorties would be flown against coastal defences and in support and diversionary operations. Twenty 49 Squadron crews attended briefing at Fiskerton, where in keeping with all briefings, no direct reference was made to the invasion, but unusually, they were given strict altitudes at which to fly and were told not to jettison bombs over the sea. They learned also that they would be among more than a thousand aircraft targeting ten heavy gun batteries along the Normandy coast, and that their specific objective was at La Pernelle, some three miles north of the recently attacked Morsalines battery, which, although not disclosed to them, was close to Utah Beach. The plan called for 5 Group to provide 122 Lancasters and four Mosquitos for this site, and 115 Lancasters and four Mosquitos for a second target at Saint-Pierre-du-Mont, which was the closest to Omaha Beach. 83 Squadron would provide the illumination and the marking for the former, while 97 Squadron took care of business at the latter, led by W/C Jimmy Carter. 49 Squadron loaded its Lancasters with a mixture of 1,000 and 500 pounders and launched them from Fiskerton between 01.15 and 01.37 with S/L Bazin the senior pilot on duty. They all arrived in the target area to find a layer of ten-tenths cloud with a base at around 7,000 feet and tops at 12,000 feet with broken cloud below, through which the glow of the red and green TIs and red spotfires could be seen. The bombing was carried out by all but one of the 49 Squadron crews from 8,000 to 12,000 feet between 03.37 and 04.01, the exception that of P/O Sullings, whose bomb-aimer was trying to fix his bomb sight when the Master Bomber called a halt to bombing and sent them home. Any homeward-bound crews looking down through the occasional gaps in the clouds were rewarded by the incredible sight of the greatest armada in history ploughing its way sedately southwards towards the French coast. A total of five thousand tons of bombs was dropped during the night, and this was a new record. Only seven aircraft failed to return from these operations, three of them from Sainte-Pierre, including the one containing 97 Squadron's W/C Carter and seven highly experienced crewmen, all but one of whom held either a DFC or DFM.

As the beachheads were being established during the course of the 6th, preparations were put in hand to support the ground forces by attacking nine road and railway communications centres through which the enemy could bring reinforcements. 5 Group was assigned to two targets, Argentan supply depot and railway centre located some thirty miles south-east of Caen, and a road bridge in Caen itself, for which forces of 112 Lancasters and six Mosquitos and 120 Lancasters and four Mosquitos respectively were assembled. 49 Squadron made ready nineteen Lancasters for the latter, and they departed Fiskerton between 00.23 and 00.46 with S/Ls Bazin and Botting the senior pilots on duty. The Channel crossing began at Bridport, from where the route bypassed the Channel Islands before turning sharply to the east to cross the Cherbourg peninsula. All reached the target area to find ten-tenths cloud with a base at 5,000 to 6,000 feet, whereupon the 627 Squadron Mosquitos ran in at low-level to drop red spotfires, which were then supplemented by red TIs from the heavy marker element. The 49 Squadron crews attacked the aiming point from below the cloud base from 2,500 to 5,000 feet between 02.40 and 02.50 in accordance with the Master Bomber's instructions, and were able to clearly pick out the river, marshalling yards and town detail. Six Lancasters failed to return from the Caen raid, largely as the result of the need for the force to orbit while the markers were assessed.

Four railway targets were earmarked for attention by a force of 337 aircraft on the 7th, while elements of 5 Group were being prepared to join forces with 1 and 8 Groups to attack a six-way road junction at Balleroy, situated fifteen miles west of Caen on the approach to the Foret-de-Cerisy, where it was believed the enemy was concealing a fuel dump and tank units. The 52 Base squadrons were not involved in the operation, which took place in conditions of ten-tenths cloud with a base at 8,000 to 10,000 feet and haze below. The initial Oboe markers appeared to be accurate and on time, but another marker fell simultaneously some five miles to the south-west and attracted some bomb loads. The Master Bomber quickly gained control of the situation and directed the bombing to the correct marker, which was pounded by concentrated bombing. Dense clouds of black smoke and one particularly large explosion were evidence of a successful outcome, during which the gunners in the crew of the 207 Squadron commanding officer shot down three enemy fighters in a twenty-minute period.

The night of the 8/9th was devoted to the disruption of railway communications, for which 483 aircraft were detailed and assigned to five centres. Orders were received at Fiskerton for 49 Squadron to prepare twenty-one Lancasters as part of a 5 Group force of fifty-four and four Mosquitos assigned to railway installations at Pontaubault, while a second force of ninety-seven Lancasters and four Mosquitos attended to a similar objective at Rennes in Brittany, thirty miles to the south-west. 617 Squadron would also operate on this night to deliver the very first Barnes Wallis-designed 12,000lb Tallboy earthquake bombs against the railway tunnel at Saumur. The 49 Squadron element took off between 22.08 and 22.36 with W/C Crocker and S/Ls Bazin and Botting the senior pilots on duty, and lost P/O Smiley and crew to faulty navigation equipment, which put them too far behind schedule to continue. The others reached the target area to encounter up to six-tenths stratocumulus cloud at 6,000 feet and a layer at 2,000 feet, and the first attempt to mark was cancelled with yellow TIs. The second attempt with red spotfires and TIs was successful, and the bombing took place in accordance with the instructions of the Master Bomber from 3,200 to 7,700 feet between 00.45 and 00.58. Returning crews reported concentrated bombing on or near the markers, and the operation was deemed to have been successful.

While 5 Group concentrated on a railway junction at Etampes, south of Paris on the 9th, a force of 401 aircraft from 1, 4, 6 and 8 Groups was to target airfields in the battle area. 108 Lancasters and four Mosquitos were to take part in the former, twenty-one of them representing 49 Squadron, which departed Fiskerton between 21.13 and 21.42 with W/C Crocker and S/Ls Bazin and Botting the senior pilots on duty. Those reaching the target found eight to ten-tenths cloud with a base at 8,000 feet and patches of two to three-tenths lower down at 4,000 feet, but this had no effect on the marking with red spotfires, backed up with green and yellow TIs and illumination flares. Some crews thought that they had picked up a recall signal and others a message at around midnight to orbit until being called in to bomb. W/C Crocker and crew orbited eight times before bombing in the first wave from 5,000 feet at 00.10 and were then set upon by a night-fighter, which they would claim as a "probable" after their Lancaster sustained some damage. The remaining 49 Squadron participants carried out their attacks from 4,800 to 7,000 feet between 23.59 and 00.18, P/O Sullings and crew after the Master Bomber had called an end to bombing at 00.17. It appeared to be a successful operation, which cost six Lancasters, including two belonging to 49 Squadron. JB714 was shot down by a night-fighter to crash at Morigny-Champigny on the north-eastern edge of the target, and there were no survivors from the crew of P/O Smiley. A 44 (Rhodesia) Squadron aircraft crashed nearby and both crews were buried in the local cemetery. ND533 came down a mile-and-a-half from Rosay-sur-Lieure, thirty miles short of the Normandy coast at Dieppe and only the bomb-aimer survived from the crew of F/O Bell. Somehow, F/O Hemmens ended up in Buchenwald concentration camp, where he died in October. Photo-reconnaissance confirmed that all tracks had been cut for a distance of four hundred yards to the north-east of the junction, but it revealed also that the town had sustained collateral damage, which caused many civilian casualties.

5 Group detailed 108 Lancasters and four Mosquitos on the 10th and briefed the crews for an attack on a railway junction at Orleans, situated some thirty miles south-west of Paris. The 52 Base squadrons were not involved in this operation, which took place under clear skies and in good visibility and appeared to be successful. The campaign against communications targets continued on the 12th at six locations, including Caen and Poitiers, for which 5 Group detailed forces of 109 Lancasters and four Mosquitos and 112 Lancasters and four Mosquitos respectively. 49 Squadron made ready eighteen Lancasters to take part at the former, where road bridges were the specific targets, and they departed Fiskerton between 23.32 and 23.52 with F/Ls Edwards, Matheson and Powell the senior pilots on duty and the newly posted-in S/L Cox flying as second pilot with the Edwards crew. All reached the Caen area, where they encountered six to ten-tenths cloud with tops at between 4,000 and 6,000 feet, which provided difficult conditions in which to spot the TIs on the ground. A strict timing was imposed for the duration of the attack and fourteen 49 Squadron crews delivered their loads from 5,000 to 10,000 feet between 02.18 and 02.28 before the Master Bomber called a halt and sent more than thirty Lancasters home without bombing. Three of the four Fiskerton crews failing to bomb were unable to find markers in the conditions and had insufficient time to plan a visual attack. In contrast, clear conditions attended the raid on Poitiers, and photo-reconnaissance revealed the Paris to Bordeaux line to have been cut in seven places.

A new oil campaign began on this night, prosecuted by 286 Lancasters and seventeen Mosquitos of 1, 3 and 8 Groups, the target for which was the Nordstern (Gelsenberg A.G.) plant at Gelsenkirchen. Such was the accuracy of the attack, that all production of vital aviation fuel was halted for a number of weeks at a cost to the Germans of a thousand tons per day.

The 14th brought the Command's first daylight operation since the departure of 2 Group twelve months earlier. The target was the port of Le Havre, from where the enemy's fast, light marine craft were posing a threat to Allied shipping supplying the Normandy beachheads. The two-phase operation was conducted by predominantly 1 and 3 Groups with 617 Squadron representing 5 Group and took place in the evening under the umbrella of a fighter escort. The attack was highly successful, and few craft survived the onslaught. Other operations on this night were directed against railway installations at three locations in France, while elements of 4, 5 and 8 Groups attended to enemy troop and vehicle concentrations at Aunay-sur-Odon and Évrecy near Caen. 5 Group assembled a force of 214 Lancasters and five Mosquitos for the former, of which eighteen of 49 Squadron departed Fiskerton between 22.00 and 22.40 with F/Ls Ball, Matheson and Powell the senior pilots on duty. The weather was generally clear with some low cloud, but this did not hamper the marking process, which proceeded punctually and accurately. W/C Jeudwine was the Master Bomber, with 83 Squadron's W/C "Joe" Northrop as Deputy, and the latter made four passes over the target, at 00.30 at 8,000 feet, 00.41 at 10,000 feet, and at 00.54 and 01.00 at 11,000 feet, dropping clusters of flares on the first two, green TIs on the third and red TIs on the fourth. The 49 Squadron crews bombed the above-mentioned TIs from 6,600 to 10,000 feet between 00.35 and 00.59, observing what appeared to be a concentrated attack that produced explosions, numerous fires and much black smoke. On return, F/L Matheson described it as one of the best-managed raids he had participated in.

S/L Bazin was promoted to wing commander rank and posted on the 15th to command 9 Squadron at Bardney, a post he would retain to the end of hostilities and beyond. A force of 297 aircraft from

1, 4, 5, 6 and 8 Groups was assembled on that day to try to do to Boulogne what had been done to Le Havre twenty-four hours earlier. It was again left to 617 Squadron to represent 5 Group, and the operation was concluded with equal success. While this was in progress, 5 Group dispatched 110 Lancasters and four Mosquitos to deal with a fuel dump at Châtellerault, situated between Tours and Poitiers in western France. The 52 Base squadrons were not involved in the operation, which took place under clear skies and in good visibility, after which, post-raid reconnaissance confirmed that eight out of thirty-five individual fuel storage sites within the target had been destroyed.

Plans were put in hand on the 16th, to launch 829 sorties that night against a number of targets. Just three days earlier, the first V-1 flying bombs had landed on London, and this prompted a response in the form of a second new campaign to open during the month, this one against the revolutionary weapon's launching and storage sites in the Pas-de-Calais. Four targets were earmarked for attention, the one handed to 5 Group a storage site at Beauvoir, located some twenty miles inland from Berck-sur-Mer. The large storage sites, many in various stages of construction, were referred to in Bomber Command parlance as "constructional works", while others, called "ski sites", were small buildings in the shape of a hockey stick and were attached to launching ramps. 112 Lancasters were detailed, twenty of them representing 49 Squadron, which departed Fiskerton between 22.42 and 23.05 with S/L Cox the senior pilot on duty for the first time. They all reached the target area to find nine to ten-tenths cloud with tops at 6,000 to 8,000 feet and bombed on the faint glow of red Oboe markers from 10,000 to 13,000 feet between 00.40 and 00.46. It was impossible to assess the outcome, which left crews with little to pass on to the intelligence section at debriefing.

The oil campaign continued on this night in the hands of 1, 4, 6 and 8 Groups at Sterkrade-Holten, a district of Oberhausen in the Ruhr, but cloudy conditions caused the bombing to be scattered, and there was little impact on production. With the exception of 617 Squadron, 5 Group remained inactive for the ensuing four nights, leaving the "specialists" to attack constructional works at Watten and Wizernes with Tallboys in daylight on the 19th and 20th. Cloudy conditions affected accuracy at the former and caused the latter to be aborted so as not to waste the precious, highly-engineered and inordinately expensive Tallboys.

5 Group had to wait until Mid-Summer's Night, the 21st, before becoming involved in the oil offensive, and was handed two targets to attack simultaneously. A force of 120 Lancasters and six Mosquitos was assembled for the Union Rheinische Braunkohlen-Treibstoff refinery at Wesseling, south of Cologne, and 120 Lancasters and four Mosquitos for the Hydrierwerke Scholven plant in the Buer district of Gelsenkirchen, both with a sprinkling of ABC Lancasters of 101 Squadron for RCM duties and the latter including a number of Oboe Mosquitos. 49 Squadron made ready twenty Lancasters for Wesseling and they departed Fiskerton between 23.05 and 23.24 with W/C Crocker and S/L Cox the senior pilots on duty, before heading into the greatest disaster to befall 5 Group in the war. They made landfall on the enemy coast in the Western Schelde and straddled the Belgian/Dutch frontier as they headed east into the clutches of a strong Luftwaffe night-fighter force, which proceeded to hack down Lancasters in an orgy of destruction. It is difficult to establish a sequence of the 49 Squadron casualties, but it seems that three were lost on the way to the target, beginning with S/L Cox and crew in ME808, which crashed without survivors at Loenhout on the Belgian side of the border within a minute or so of making landfall. F/L Hill and crew were some

twenty miles further east when ME675 came down at Lage-Mierde on the Dutch side, also without survivors. W/C Crocker DFC & Bar and his highly decorated crew had been joined by the BBC war correspondent, Kent Stevenson, and were further south in LL900, having crossed into Germany near Aachen. They were in the area of the town of Jülich, some twenty miles west of the target, when brought down without survivors, and between them they wore the ribbons of five DFCs and two DFMs.

It is believed that the others arrived in the target area, having observed many combats since the coast and expecting to find clear skies. Instead of this, they encountered up to ten-tenths low cloud at 2,500 to 4,000 feet, which was the Achilles heel in the otherwise highly-effective 5 Group low-level marking method. It meant that it was impossible for the Mosquito crews to do their job, and faced with this situation, the Master Bomber, W/C James "Willie" Tait, ordered a blind attack, which required the Lancaster crews to bomb on their own H2S or on the red and green TIs dropped by 83 Squadron also on H2S. The 49 Squadron crews complied from 16,500 to 19,900 feet between 01.40 and 01.49 in the face of heavy predicted flak, some observing a large explosion at 01.46, which caused an extensive red glow in the cloud, and another was witnessed at 01.51. P/O Green and crew were attacked twice by a night-fighter, the first pass putting the rear turret out of action, but it was only after the second attack had knocked out the port-inner engine that they jettisoned the bombs "live" and turned for home, where they would report watching many bombers fall from the sky. ND695 disappeared without trace with the crew of P/O Ross, and ND683 also went into the sea off the Dutch coast, taking with it the crew of P/O Shinn DFC. NE128 crashed in the general area of the Ruhr and was the only loss to produce survivors, although F/O Simpkin and his rear gunner were not among them. After the war, a secret German report would suggest a 40% loss of production at the site, but this was probably of very short duration as the limited number of casualties on the ground pointed to a scattered and largely ineffective raid. Whatever the degree of success, it was gained at the high cost of thirty-seven Lancasters, a massive 28%, and all but two of them belonged to 5 Group Squadrons. 44, 49, 57 and 619 Squadrons each lost six Lancasters, although one from 57 Squadron ditched off the English coast and the crew was rescued, while 207 and 630 Squadrons each had five empty dispersal pans to contemplate in the cold light of dawn.

An analysis concluded that the Wesseling force had been undone by night-fighters benefitting from the excellent visibility above the cloud, and it was 49 Squadron's heaviest loss of the war. Similar conditions had thwarted any chance of low-level marking at Scholven-Buer, but the preliminary Mosquito-borne Oboe markers had been backed up by red and green TIs from 97 (Straits Settlement) Squadron Lancasters, and the glow from these was observed dimly through the cloud. The crews aimed for these, but it was impossible to assess the outcome and the operation cost eight 5 Group aircraft, most falling to the same night-fighters waiting to greet them as they crossed Holland outbound. A secret German report would suggest a 20% loss of production for a limited period. The above-mentioned W/C Tait had been a 4 Group man to the core until joining the 5 Group Master Bomber fraternity at Coningsby. He had fluctuated between wing commander and squadron leader ranks since 1940, had commanded three 4 Group squadrons for brief periods and was among the most experienced bomber pilots in the Command. Within a matter of weeks, he would succeed W/C Cheshire as commanding officer of 617 Squadron. S/L Botting was elevated to acting wing commander status to enable him to succeed W/C Crocker, and he would remain in post until after the end of hostilities.

While more than four hundred aircraft of 3, 4, 6 and 8 Groups targeted four flying-bomb sites on the 23rd, 1 and 5 Groups were sent respectively against railway yards at Saintes and Limoges in western France. Ninety-seven Lancasters and four Mosquitos were detailed for the latter, and they found clear skies and good visibility in the target area, in which ground features like the River Vienne and the railway sidings stood out prominently. Red spotfires and green TIs marked out the aiming point and a number of large explosions were observed with much smoke. Another very large explosion was witnessed by some crews when one hundred miles into the return flight at 02.46, and post-raid reconnaissance would confirm a highly accurate and concentrated attack.

617 Squadron had attempted to continue the Tallboy assault on the constructional works at Wizernes in daylight on the 22nd, but the attack had been abandoned in the face of ten-tenths low cloud. The squadron returned the bombs to store and brought them back to France on the 24th to score a number of direct hits. Thirteen 49 Squadron crews were called to briefing on that day to learn of their part in a busy night of operations involving more than seven hundred aircraft targeting seven flying-bomb sites. 5 Group was assigned to Pommeréval and Prouville, situated respectively some fifteen miles south-east of Dieppe and east of Abbeville, and detailed 103 Lancasters and four Mosquitos for each. The 52 Base squadrons from Dunholme Lodge and Fiskerton were among those assigned to the former, and the latter's participants took off between 21.56 and 22.11 with F/Ls Edwards and Powell the senior pilots on duty. All reached the target area to be greeted by the favourable conditions of clear skies and twenty-mile visibility, and W/C Tait was again on hand in the role of Master Bomber to watch the Oboe marker go down on time at 23.50. He assessed that it was five hundred yards south of the aiming point and directed the flare force to illuminate another one that was much closer, before sending in the low-level Mosquitos. The main force Lancasters followed close on their heels and delivered concentrated bombing around the aiming point, which the 49 Squadron crews identified by green TIs. They delivered their bombs from 6,000 to 9,000 feet between 00.02 and 00.11, observing the bursts to be concentrated within a few hundred yards of them. There was little defence from the ground, but night-fighters were evident and four Lancasters failed to return, one of them, 49 Squadron's LM572, crashing twenty-five miles east of the target, killing three members of the crew and delivering F/O Taylor and three others into captivity.

At Prouville, the preliminary Oboe Mosquito was punctual, but the subsequent marking was hampered by intense searchlight activity working in co-operation with flak and night-fighters, and bombing was delayed while the aiming point was positively identified and marked. It took until all of the illuminator flares had been expended before the low-level Mosquitos dropped red spotfires and the heavy brigade from 97 (Straits Settlement) Squadron backed up with red and green TIs. The bombing was controlled by the Master Bomber, but the impression was of a somewhat haphazard attack that lacked concentration and cost thirteen Lancasters, possibly as a result of the delay in opening the attack.

More than seven hundred aircraft were detailed for operations against six flying-bomb sites on the 27th, while two railway yards would occupy the attention of other elements. There were two targets for 5 Group, a flying-bomb site at Marquise, situated some five miles inland from Cap Gris-Nez, and railway yards at Vitry-le-Francois south-east of Reims. 49 Squadron contributed a dozen Lancasters to the force of eighty-six assigned to the former and they departed Fiskerton between 22.47 and 23.00 with the recently arrived S/L Twiggs and F/L Powell the senior pilots on duty.

There were no early returns, and the outward flight was completed within seventy-five minutes under clear skies and in good visibility. The marking was punctual and accurate, and the 49 Squadron crews delivered their eleven 1,000 and four 500 pounders each onto red TIs from 15,000 to 18,000 feet between 00.50 and 00.55, before returning to report a successful operation. The 103 Lancasters and four Mosquitos assigned to the Vitry marshalling yards were greeted at the target by varying amounts of cloud, reported as between zero and seven-tenths at around 7,000 feet, but the visibility was good, and the aiming point was clearly marked by red spot fires and green TIs. Not all had bombed when the Master Bomber called a halt and ordered crews with bombs still aboard to take them home, after smoke obscured the aiming point.

There were no further operations for the 52 Base squadrons in a month that had brought eleven operations generating 199 sorties for the loss of nine Lancasters and their crews.

## July 1944

The new month began as June had ended, with flying-bomb sites providing employment for over three hundred aircraft on both the 1st and 2nd. It was the 4th before the Independent Air Force was invited to re-enter the fray, when it was called upon to attack a V-Weapon storage site in caves at St-Leu-d'Esserent, some thirty miles north of Paris. The caves had originally been used for growing mushrooms, and they were protected by some twenty-five feet of clay and soft limestone, to say nothing of the anti-aircraft defences brought in by the Germans. There is some confusion concerning the timing of the operation, which involved not only seventeen Lancasters, a Mustang and a Mosquito from 617 Squadron, but also 211 other Lancasters and eleven Mosquitos from 5 Group, with three ABC Lancasters to provide RCM cover and three Path Finder Oboe Mosquitos to carry out the marking of an initial reference-point. Some accounts suggest that 617 Squadron attacked early in the evening, and was followed by the group later on, when, in fact, both elements took off at the same time. There were actually two aiming points, the road and railway communications to the area dump for the main force, and the tunnel complex at Creil, a settlement located three miles north-east of St Leu, for 617 Squadron and forty-nine Lancasters from 52 Base, seventeen of which departed Fiskerton between 23.00 and 23.20 with S/L Twiggs the senior pilot on duty. All reached the target area under clear skies and in good visibility, which was of equal assistance to the night-fighters and despite the absence of searchlights, the expected volume of flak was thrown up as the two elements ran across their respective aiming points, the 49 Squadron crews carrying out their attacks with 1,000 and 500 pounders from 8,500 to 17,500 feet between 01.36 and 01.41. Night-fighters pounced on the bombers over the target and on the route home and the crews of P/O Buchanan, F/Os Pederson and Brady and F/L Edwards were all involved in a fight for life. They survived but observed others that failed to do so and thirteen Lancasters were missing from their stations, one of them belonging to 49 Squadron. PB195 crashed at 01.45 near Gourchelles, some twenty-five miles short of the French coast at Dieppe and there were no survivors from the crew of F/O Dod. Post-raid reconnaissance revealed that a large area of subsidence had blocked the side entrance to the caves at St-Leu and that the road and railway links had been cut over a distance of four hundred yards.

On the 6th, over five hundred aircraft were engaged on operations against V-Weapons targets, and 617 Squadron was assigned to a V-3 super-gun site at Mimoyecques. Originally planned as one of two sites near Cap Gris Nez containing twenty-five barrels each, test failures and delays meant that a single three-barrel shaft stretching a hundred metres into the limestone hill, five miles from the coast and 103 miles from its target, was all that existed at the time. Each fifteen-metre-long smooth-bore barrel, which was angled at 50 degrees and aimed at London, was designed on the multiple-charge principle to progressively boost the acceleration of the one-ton projectile as it travelled towards the muzzle. Once completed, the site would be capable of pounding London at the rate of hundreds of rounds per day without let-up. It was protected by a concrete slab thirty meters wide and five-and-a-half meters thick, which was correctly believed by the designers to be impregnable to conventional bombs. It had been attacked on a number of occasions without success, but 617 Squadron scored direct hits with Tallboys, and provisional reconnaissance revealed four deep craters in the immediate target area, one causing a large corner of the concrete slab to collapse. The extent of the damage underground would not be apparent to the planners at Bomber Command, but the shafts and tunnels had collapsed, and the site had been abandoned. Although Cheshire did not know it, this was to be his final operation, not only with 617 Squadron, but also of the war in Europe.

The authorities were not convinced that the site at St-Leu-d'Esserent had received terminal damage and scheduled another attack on it for the late evening of the 7th. Before the operation got under way, more than 450 aircraft from 1, 4, 6 and 8 Groups had carried out the first major operation in support of the Canadian 1st and British 2nd Armies, which were trying to break out of Caen. The target had been changed from German-fortified villages to an area of open ground north of Caen, where almost 2,300 tons of bombs were dropped somewhat ineffectively, and ultimately, that decision proved to be counter-productive by causing damage to the northern suburbs of the city rather than to German forces.

5 Group detailed 208 Lancasters and fifteen Mosquitos for St-Leu, the 49 Squadron element of sixteen departing Fiskerton between 22.12 and 22.27 with S/Ls Lace and Twiggs the senior pilots on duty. They arrived in the target area to find medium-level cloud, which prevented the moonlight from providing illumination, although the visibility was good below the cloud level. The Master Bomber was the former 207 Squadron pilot, W/C Ed Porter, and he oversaw the delivery of the Oboe yellow TI at 01.06, which was followed by the first stick of flares four minutes later. The first red spot fire went down at 01.08, a hundred yards south of the aiming point but in line with the direction of the bombing run and backing-up by red and green TIs continued until 01.13. The marking was assessed as sufficiently accurate to call in the main force at 01.15, and the 49 Squadron crews dropped their loads of eleven 1,000 and four 500 pounders each from 11,000 to 15,000 feet between 01.15 and 01.22. The Master Bomber's VHF was indistinct, so 83 Squadron's S/L Eggins assumed control and sent the force home at 01.25. Twenty-nine Lancasters and two Mosquitos failed to return after night-fighters got amongst them, and this represented 14% of the force. It was another sobering night for 5 Group and there was dismay at Fiskerton at the absence of two of its crews. LL976 crashed at around 01.30 at Beauvoir-en-Lyons, some twenty-five miles south-east of Dieppe and there were no survivors from the crew of F/O Baker. LM541 is believed to have been the victim of friendly fire from another Lancaster and crashed near the village of Le Chesne located midway between Paris and Caen, which suggests it might have been outbound at the time. There were no survivors from the crew of F/L Ball DFC, who were on their twenty-ninth sortie together, the thirtieth for the pilot, and both gunners were holders of the DFM which they

had earned during an action described earlier in the narrative. F/O McCracken and crew brought a badly damaged PB207 home after surviving an attack by a night-fighter, and following an inspection, the Lancaster was declared a write-off. Photo-reconnaissance revealed that both ends of the tunnel complex had collapsed, as had a section in the middle, and the approach road and rail links had been heavily cratered and blocked.

There was no immediate opportunity for the afflicted squadrons, particularly 106 and 207, which had lost five crews each, to "get back on the horse", and there must have been a sombre air, while the populations of RAF Metheringham and Spilsby each came to terms with the loss of thirty-five familiar faces in one night. A special congratulatory message arrived on the participating stations from A-O-C, AVM Sir Ralph Cochrane, who considered it the finest effort by the group to successfully press home the attack in the face of the fiercest opposition. Operations were posted on 5 Group stations on the 10th and 11th, and then cancelled, before the 12th, when fourteen 49 Squadron crews were called to briefing to be given the details about that night's operation against railway installations at Culmont-Chalindrey in eastern France. Two aiming points were planned, at the western and eastern ends, for which a force of 157 Lancasters and four Mosquitos was made ready. While this operation was in progress, another by elements of 1 Group would take place further south at a railway junction at Revigny. The Fiskerton crews took off between 21.38 and 21.54 with S/L Lace the senior pilot on duty and headed for Bridport to begin the Channel crossing as far as the Channel Islands, before turning east-south-east to pass south of Paris to reach the target. P/O Rowley and crew turned back after both port engines began to malfunction, leaving the others to fly out over eight-tenths low cloud until shortly before reaching the target area, where the conditions improved to provide clear skies, and promisingly, no sign of defensive activity from the ground. The controller at the eastern aiming point experienced VHF communications problems, which delayed that part of the attack, and eventually the entire force was directed to the western aiming point. The 49 Squadron crews delivered their eight 1,000 and two or three 500 pounders each onto two red spotfires from 5,200 to 8,000 feet between 01.51 and 02.10, and explosions were observed, followed by fires that remained visible for fifty miles into the return flight. The high proportion of delayed action fuses in use prevented an immediate assessment of results, but post-raid reconnaissance would confirm an effective operation.

Fiskerton was not called into action on the 14th, when a force of 111 Lancasters, six Mosquitos and an American twin-engine P38 Lightning for the Master Bomber, W/C Jeudwine, was made ready to attack the huge marshalling yards at Villeneuve-St-Georges, situated on the southern rim of Paris. In the event, W/C Jeudwine experienced compass trouble and would arrive on target twelve minutes late, so contacted his Deputy, 83 Squadron's W/C Joe Northrop, to take matters in hand and oversee a largely successful operation. Meanwhile, 1 Group had returned to Revigny, but had been thwarted by ground haze, which forced the Master Bomber to abandon the attack before any bombing could take place. Seven Lancasters were lost for no gain, and it would fall to 5 Group to finish the job a few nights hence at great expense.

Flying-bomb sites and railways dominated the target list on the 15th, and 5 Group was handed a railway junction at Nevers, a city on the North Bank of the Loire in central France. 49 Squadron contributed thirteen Lancasters to the force of 104 with four Mosquitos to carry out the low-level marking and they departed Fiskerton between 21.43 and 22.15 with S/L Lace the senior pilot on duty. All reached the target after an outward flight of more than three-and-a-half hours and found clear skies with a little haze and favourable conditions, which the marker force exploited to mark promptly and accurately. The 49 Squadron crews delivered their nine 1,000 and four 500 pounders each onto a red spotfire and green TIs from 3,500 to 5,000 feet between 01.55 and 02.14, but as the entire force was carrying delayed-action ordnance, no immediate assessment could be made. A large explosion suggested, perhaps, that an ammunition train or dump had been hit and photographic reconnaissance later in the day revealed that the Nevers site had been all but obliterated and much rolling stock damaged.

Sixteen 49 Squadron crews were called to briefing at midnight on the 17/18th to learn of their part in a tactical support operation to be carried out at dawn by a force of 942 aircraft, of which 201 of the Lancasters were to be provided by 5 Group. It was the start of the ground forces' Operation Goodwood, which was Montgomery's plan for a decisive breakout into wider France as a prelude to the march towards the German frontier. The aiming points were five enemy-held villages to the east of Caen, Colombelles, Mondeville, Sannerville, Cagny and Manneville, all of which stood in the path of the advancing British 2nd Army. The Fiskerton element took off between 03.30 and 03.55 with F/Ls Edwards and Matheson the senior pilots on duty, the latter accompanied by S/L Schofield as second pilot. All reached the target area to find their aiming point, the Mondeville steel works, which the Germans had converted into a strongly defended fortress, already marked by red and yellow TIs but about to be swallowed up and obscured by drifting smoke. Bombing took place from 6,000 to 10,000 feet between 05.41 and 05.59, either overshooting the yellow TIs or undershooting the reds in accordance with instructions from the Master Bomber, and as far as could be determined, most of the hardware fell accurately where intended. The RAF dropped five thousand tons of bombs to good effect onto the two German divisions in just half an hour, and the Americans followed up with a further two thousand tons.

Operations were not done for the day, and that night, following two failed attempts by 1 Group to cut a railway junction at Revigny at a combined cost of seventeen Lancasters, the job was handed to a 5 Group element of 109 Lancasters, four Mosquitos and a P38 Lightning containing the Master Bomber, W/C Jeudwine. It was to be a busy night of operations, which included another railway and two oil targets, along with support and diversionary activities involving a total of 972 sorties. 49 Squadron launched fifteen Lancasters from Fiskerton between 22.38 and 22.52 with S/L Twiggs the senior pilot on duty and they crossed the French coast near Dieppe, passing through an intense searchlight belt some twenty miles inland, while being harried all the way into eastern France by night-fighters, which had been fed into the stream shortly after it entered enemy airspace. In just forty-five minutes, sixteen Lancasters fell victim to night-fighters and one to flak, the first eleven falling during the long, straight leg to the final turning point at Aube. It was at Herbisse, near Aube, that JB178 came to grief after crossing paths with a night-fighter and there were no survivors from the crew of F/O Green DFC RNZAF. Some ten miles to the west-south-west, ND684 crashed at Granges-sur-Aube, killing P/O Appleyard RAAF and his entire crew. The twelfth to fall was 49 Squadron's PB231, which crashed at St-Ouen-en-Domprot with fatal consequences for F/O Lacey DFC and four of his crew, while the two gunners survived and were eventually captured and sent to Stalag Luft 7. The rest of the force reached the target to find clear skies but haze obscuring ground detail. This target continued to present problems, beginning with the first wave of flares delivered at about 01.30, which were too far to the east. More flares were ordered, and the bombing was put back by five minutes, while Wanganui markers were dropped by Mosquito and the situation was assessed. The Fiskerton crews attacked from 6,800 to 9,800 feet between 01.46 and

01.55, aiming at red spotfires in accordance with instructions from the Master Bomber, but the whole attack seemed chaotic and the use of many delayed-action bombs meant that it was difficult to see what was happening on the ground. JB473 was homebound and retracing the outward route when crashing at 02.30 at Vassimont-et-Chapelain after six of the crew had taken to their parachutes. F/O Deacon RCAF ended up in hospital at Châlons-sur-Marne, from where he would be liberated by Americans in late August, and the other survivors managed to retain their freedom. Photo-reconnaissance revealed that the operation had been successful in cutting the railway link to the battle front, but had cost twenty-four Lancasters, almost 22% of those dispatched. *(For a full and highly detailed account of the three Revigny raids and the fate of those reaching the ground alive, read the amazing book, Massacre over the Marne, by Oliver Clutton-Brock.)*

5 Group crews stood-by on the 19th for a possible daylight operation, and it was evening before orders came through to prepare for an attack on a flying-bomb storage site at Thiverny, situated just to the north of St-Leu-d'Esserent. A force of 103 Lancasters and two Mosquitos was detailed in the absence of a contribution from Fiskerton for what was to be a daylight attack under the protection of a Spitfire escort, with which the bombers rendezvoused at the south coast, before making their way to the target. They arrived to find fine weather conditions but the presence of ground haze to create challenging conditions in which to identify the aiming-point. Late preliminary marking by the Path Finder element and communications problems between the Master Bomber and his Deputy added to the frustrations and led to most crews having to orbit for five minutes before bombing visually in the face of moderate to intense heavy flak bursting as high as 18,000 feet. A sufficient number of aiming point photographs were brought back to suggest a successful outcome achieved without loss, although post-raid reconnaissance did reveal some loose bombing.

Railway yards and a triangle junction at Courtrai (Kortrijk) in Belgium provided the targets for a joint effort by 1, 5 and 8 Groups on the 20th, for which 49 Squadron contributed a dozen of its own to the 5 Group force of 190 Lancasters and five Mosquitos. They departed Fiskerton between 22.55 and 23.07 with F/Ls Edwards and Matheson the senior pilots on duty, and all reached the target area to find it free of cloud and slightly obscured by ground haze. The Oboe marking was well-placed in the marshalling yards and backed up by green TIs, onto which the squadron participants delivered their eleven 1,000 and four 500 pounders each from 10,000 to 13,700 feet between 00.56 and 01.05. They returned home safely to report a large orange explosion at 00.57 and a successful outcome, which was confirmed by post-raid reconnaissance that revealed both aiming-points to have been obliterated in return for the loss of nine Lancasters.

Following two nights at home for 5 Group and a two-month break from city-busting, Harris sanctioned a major raid on the naval and shipbuilding port of Kiel on the 23rd, for which a force of 629 aircraft was made ready. 49 Squadron dispatched a dozen Lancasters between 22.57 and 23.08 as part of a 5 Group force of ninety-nine Lancasters. S/L Lace was the senior pilot on duty as they headed for the rendezvous point to form up behind an elaborate "Mandrel" jamming screen laid on by 100 Group, before setting course for Denmark's western coast. *(In November 1943, 100 Group had been formed to take over the Radio Countermeasures (RCM) role, which had been the preserve of 101 Squadron since its introduction a number of months earlier. 101 Squadron, however, would remain in 1 Group and continue to provide RCM for the remainder of the war.)* When they arrived unexpectedly and with complete surprise in Kiel airspace, they rendered the enemy night-fighter controller confused and unable to bring his night-fighter resources to bear. Kiel was covered by a nine to ten-tenths veil of thin cloud with tops at 4,000 feet and a skymarking plan was put into action, which enabled the main force crews to bomb on the glow, first of the flares, and then of fires. The 49 Squadron contingent carried out their attacks from 16,000 to 19,700 feet between 01.28 and 01.32, and although the glow of fires remained visible for a hundred miles into the return journey to suggest an effective raid, it was not possible to determine the outcome. However, local sources conceded that this had been the town's most destructive raid of the war and had inflicted heavy damage on the port and shipyards, cutting off water supplies for three days and gas for three weeks. Many delayed-action bombs had been dropped, and these continued to cause problems for some time.

5 Group divided its forces on the 24th to enable it to support the first of a three-raid series in five nights on the city of Stuttgart and an oil refinery and fuel dump at Donges. Situated on the North Bank of the Loire to the east of St Nazaire, the latter target had been attacked successfully by elements of 6 and 8 Groups on the previous night but clearly required further attention. 5 Group detailed ninety-nine Lancasters for southern Germany in an overall force of 614, while 104 Lancasters and four Mosquitos were made ready for western France with five 8 Group Mosquitos in attendance. 49 Squadron supported the Donges operation with fourteen Lancasters and dispatched them from Fiskerton between 21.59 and 22.16 with F/Ls Edwards and Millington the senior pilots on duty. They arrived in the target area to find clear skies and excellent visibility, which the marker element exploited to leave the aiming point accurately marked with green TIs. The Fiskerton crews carried out their attacks from 8,000 to 11,000 feet between 01.41 and 01.54 in accordance with the instructions of the Master Bomber and set course for home fairly satisfied with the outcome, although it was impossible to make an accurate assessment after smoke drifted across the site. Meanwhile, some five hundred miles to the east, the main event had progressed more or less according to plan and returning crews reported a glow of fires covering an area of perhaps five square miles, which remained visible for eighty miles into the return journey. No local report came out of Stuttgart for this night, but it had been a successful and destructive raid, although gained at a cost of seventeen Lancasters and four Halifaxes.

5 Group split its forces again on the 25th to support the second of the raids on Stuttgart with eighty-three Lancasters and a daylight attack on an aerodrome and signals depot at Saint-Cyr involving ninety-four Lancasters and six Mosquitos. *(There are at least four locations called Saint-Cyr, and it is believed that the one targeted on this night was in the Ile-de-France to the west of Paris.)* 49 Squadron briefed fourteen crews for Stuttgart, which departed Fiskerton between 21.30 and 21.47 with S/Ls Lace and Twiggs the senior pilots on duty and headed for landfall on the French coast between Fecamp and Dieppe. They entered Germany north of Strasbourg accompanied by layers of cloud, which over the target was at five to ten-tenths with tops in places as high as 20,000 feet. There was haze below the cloud level to create further challenges for the marker force, and the red and green TIs appeared to the main force crews to be somewhat scattered. Bombing by the 49 Squadron crews took place from 16,000 to 20,600 feet between 01.56 and 02.07 in the absence of F/O Pederson and crew, who had become lost after evading searchlights and could not locate the target. They bombed a searchlight concentration in a built-up area close enough to the primary to become the objective for flak batteries and brought home a collection of holes in the fuselage and tailplane. F/O Sullings and crew were homebound over France at 21,000 feet when attacked by a night-fighter, with which they collided head-on, losing the starboard-outer propeller in the process.

The inboard power plant was also damaged and vibrated violently but was kept running. They ran into searchlight cones at Etampes and were down to 2,500 feet by the time that they broke free. The starboard-inner propeller fell away at 04.30, at which point the vibration ceased, and by the time the coast hove into view near Caen, the Lancaster was more comfortable to handle. The Channel crossing was begun with a degree of confidence that they would reach the other side and a SOS message brought out a Spitfire to shepherd the struggling bomber to a safe landing at Manston. Returning crews expressed little optimism at debriefings that a successful operation had taken place, when, in fact, it had been probably the most destructive of the three raids in this current series. It had cost eight Lancasters and four Halifaxes, and among the former was 49 Squadron's PB250, which crashed ten miles west-south-west of Versailles, almost certainly while homebound, and there were no survivors from the crew of F/O Buchanan. Post-raid reconnaissance confirmed a successful attack at the Saint-Cyr site, which had left all of the buildings severely damaged.

The hectic round of operations continued for 5 Group on the 26th with preparations for an attack on two aiming-points in the marshalling yards at Givors, situated on the west bank of the River Rhône in south-east-central France. 178 Lancasters and nine Mosquitos were made ready, nine of the former by 49 Squadron, and they departed Fiskerton between 21.22 and 21.32 with W/C Botting leading his troops for the first time and supported by S/L Lace. Ahead of them lay a round-trip of eleven hundred miles, and while the "Met" men had predicted bad weather, the conditions during the outward leg over France were even worse than forecast, with icing and electrical storms that were complicit in the early return of fourteen aircraft. There were no "boomerangs" from Fiskerton as the bomber stream covered the almost five-hour outward flight to reach the target to be greeted by severe weather conditions in the form of rain, thunderstorms and lightning. The cloud was down to around 7,000 feet with poor visibility below, and the flare force made a number of runs across the target between 01.42 and 02.07, orbiting in between awaiting instructions. There were occasional glimpses of the ground, but the Master Bomber was experiencing great difficulty in getting Mosquito TIs onto the two aiming points. Eventually, one of the Deputies managed to put a green TI onto the southern aiming-point and the main force began to bomb at around 02.00. The 49 Squadron crews carried out their attacks from 3,500 to 7,400 feet between 02.12 and 02.20, using the light from flares and aiming at green TIs, all in accordance with instructions. They could offer little to the intelligence section at debriefing, and it was left to post-raid reconnaissance to reveal that the attack at Givors had fulfilled its aims in closing the tracks to the north of the junction and damaging the locomotive depot in the yards.

The night of the 28/29th would prove to be busy, eventful and expensive as the Command prepared for major operations against Stuttgart and Hamburg and a number of smaller undertakings involving a total of 1,126 aircraft. The final raid of the series on Stuttgart was to be an all-Lancaster affair of 494 aircraft drawn from 1, 3, 5 and 8 Groups, while 307 Lancasters and Halifaxes of 1, 6 and 8 Groups carried out the annual last-week-of-July attack on Hamburg, a year and a day after the devastating firestorm of Operation Gomorrah. 5 Group put up 176 Lancasters, a dozen of them made ready by 49 Squadron, which departed Fiskerton between 21.51 and 22.30 with F/Ls Millington and Powell the senior pilots on duty. They joined other elements of the force over Reading and made landfall on the French coast south of Fécamp, before flying on across France in bright moonlight above the cloud layer. However, the forecast medium cloud at 18,000 feet was absent, which left them exposed to the night-fighter hordes that had infiltrated the bomber stream as it closed on the target. It was the Luftwaffe's Nachtjagd that would gain the upper hand on this night, and 49 Squadron's veteran Lancaster, JB701, was probably one of its victims outbound when crashing at St-Martin-sur-Oreuse without survivors from the crew of F/L Powell. There was a layer of up to ten-tenths thin cloud over the city, with tops in places at around 10,000 feet, and the Path Finders initially employed skymarker flares (Wanganui) and then green TIs, at which the 49 Squadron crews aimed their bombs from 14,000 to 18,000 feet between 01.53 and 02.04. Thirty-nine Lancasters failed to return, fourteen of them from 5 Group, and night-fighters also caught the Hamburg force on its way home, bringing down a further twenty-two aircraft to raise the night's casualty figure to sixty-one aircraft. Although it was difficult to make an accurate assessment of this final Stuttgart raid, the series had severely damaged the city, leaving its central districts devastated with most of its public and cultural buildings in ruins and 1,171 of its inhabitants dead.

A dozen 49 Squadron crews were briefed and put on stand-by at Fiskerton late on the 29th in anticipation of an early-morning tactical support operation in the Villers Bocage-Caumont region of the Normandy battle area south-west of Caen, in which they were to be part of an overall force of 692 aircraft to attack six enemy positions facing predominantly American forces. The 49 Squadron element took off for their aiming-point at Cahagnes between 05.53 and 06.06 with W/C Botting leading from the front and supported by S/L Lace. They approached the target over ten-tenths cloud with tops at 5,000 feet and a base at 3,500 feet and were five minutes from the bombing run at 07.59, when the Master Bomber sent them home with their bombs.

5 Group prepared for two daylight operations on the 31st, one of them an evening attack on a flying bomb storage tunnel at Rilly-la-Montagne, some five miles south of Reims, for which a force of ninety-seven Lancasters and three Mosquitos was assembled that included sixteen Lancasters of 617 Squadron, led by its recently appointed successor to Cheshire, the previously mentioned W/C Tait. A second operation was to be directed at locomotive facilities and marshalling yards at Joigny-la-Roche, situated north of Auxerre and some ninety miles south-east of Paris, for which a force of 127 Lancasters and four Mosquitos was drawn from 1 and 5 Groups. 49 Squadron briefed sixteen crews for Rilly and sent them on their way from Fiskerton between 17.22 and 17.41 with W/C Jessie Walker AFC DFM the senior pilot on duty, supported by S/L Lace. W/C Walker was returning to operations after a lengthy time away since a tour on Wellingtons with 99 Squadron as far back as 1940. He would be gaining experience with 49 Squadron before a posting to 83 Squadron to assume the role of flight commander. They made their way south to rendezvous with the rest of the two forces, 83 Squadron forming into two vics, one at 15,000 and the other at 18,000 feet, to lead the Rilly force to the target under a fighter escort. They arrived to find clear skies and the 49 Squadron crews bombed the northern tunnel entrance from 15,000 to 18,000 feet between 20.18 and 20.20, a number of them commenting on a Lancaster observed to break in two before crashing to the ground at 20.20. Two to five parachutes were reported and there was speculation as to the cause of the incident, whether flak or a friendly bomb from above. The description matched the loss of a 617 Squadron Lancaster carrying the crew of F/L Bill Reid VC, which had, indeed, fallen victim to friendly bombs and only he and one other survived.

Meanwhile, the Joigny-la-Roche force had arrived in the target area, also with a fighter escort, to find no more than three-tenths cloud with tops at 7,000 feet and good enough visibility to enable a visual identification of the aiming-point. The marking was concentrated and post-raid reconnaissance confirmed both operations to have been successful for the loss of a single Lancaster from Joigny and two from Rilly.

During the course of the month, the squadron carried out fourteen operations and dispatched 192 sorties for the loss of ten Lancasters and nine crews.

## August 1944

August would bring an end to the flying bomb offensive and also see a return to major night operations against industrial Germany. Flying bomb sites were to dominate the first half of the month, however, and would be targeted in daylight on each of the first six days. It began with the commitment of 777 aircraft to operations against numerous flying bomb-related sites on the afternoon of the 1st, although there were serious doubts about the weather conditions, which were poor over England. 5 Group's targets were at La Breteque, situated in Normandy some ten miles east-south-east of Rouen, Mont Candon, a mile or two south-west of Dieppe, and Siracourt, located some thirty miles east of the coastal town of Berck-sur-Mer. Forces of fifty-three Lancasters, fifty-nine Lancasters and a Lightning and Mosquito and sixty-seven Lancasters and four Mosquitos respectively were made ready, the first mentioned supported by 49 Squadron with nineteen Lancasters. They departed Fiskerton between 15.56 and 16.22 with W/C Walker the senior pilot on duty and joined forces with the others of their respective formations as they made their way towards the south. They lost the cloud as they began the Channel crossing, only for it to build again to nine to ten-tenths stratocumulus with tops at between 2,000 and 5,000 feet over the Pas-de-Calais region. One Lancaster bombed at La Breteque, before the Master Bomber called a halt to proceedings at 18.35, and the other two attacks were abandoned before any bombing took place. It was a similar story for the other groups, and, in total, only seventy-nine aircraft bombed.

On the following afternoon, 5 Group contributed 194 Lancasters, two Mosquitos and a P38 Lightning to operations by 394 aircraft against one flying bomb launching and three supply sites. Ninety-four Lancasters and two Mosquitos were assigned to a storage site at Trossy-St-Maximin, situated north of Paris and close to St-Leu d'Esserent, and a hundred Lancasters and the P38 to the Bois-de-Cassan facility. 49 Squadron loaded nineteen Lancasters with a mix of 1,000 and 500 pounders destined for the former, some with a delay fuse of up to thirty-six hours and dispatched them from Fiskerton between 14.19 and 14.39 with W/C Walker the senior pilot on duty. Some crews from other squadrons complained that the leaders flew too fast, and there were comments about excessive weaving, but all reached the target area to find three to five-tenths patchy cloud. The Oboe proximity markers went down on time, and were backed up with TIs, and once the bombing started, the defences opened up with accurate flak that caused damage to twenty-seven aircraft. Despite that, most of the formation passed over the aiming point and plastered it, the 49 Squadron crews from 15,000 to 18,000 feet between 17.01 and 17.04. Post-raid reconnaissance revealed many new craters, a large rectangular building stripped of its roof and sides and the southern end of two road-over-rail bridges demolished. At Bois-de-Cassan, there was three to five-tenths patchy cloud over the target, but few saw the Oboe proximity markers go down and most bombed on visual reference. The lead aircraft turned suddenly at the last moment and caused a number of those following to overshoot the aiming point, resulting in their bombs falling wide of the mark. Post-raid reconnaissance revealed fresh damage with many new craters.

Despite the effectiveness of the operation, the Trossy-St-Maximin site was included among targets for more than eleven hundred aircraft on the following day. The 1 and 5 Group crews were told at briefing, that the importance of the site to the Third Reich demanded that no building be left intact, and one or two may have escaped damage during the previous day's attack. 187 Lancasters, one Mosquito and the P38 Lightning were made ready as 5 Group's contribution to the operation, the eighteen 49 Squadron participants departing Fiskerton between 11.48 and 12.08 with F/L Millington the senior pilot on duty. Each Lancaster was loaded with a dozen 1,000 pounders and four of 500lbs, all of which reached the target area, where the 5 Group element was scheduled to attack about fifteen minutes after 1 Group. As they reached the start of the bombing run, smoke could be seen rising to 8,000 feet, and this combined with a fierce flak defence to present the crews with challenging conditions. The 49 Squadron element bombed on a visual reference from 15,000 and 16,000 feet almost in unison between 14.32 and 14.33 in accordance with instruction from the Master Bomber, having been prevented by the smoke from seeing the markers. LM648 was hit by flak from the Creil/St-Leu defence area and F/L Millington was forced to order the bombs to be jettisoned over open country after a severed hydraulics line caused a fire. Many aircraft returned to their respective stations bearing flak damage, although the 52 Base crews were more concerned about the dense concentration of aircraft over the aiming-point, which put them in danger of being hit from above and caused them to spread out with a consequent scattering of bombs. Photo-reconnaissance was unable to confirm that the site had been obliterated, and it would need to be attacked again on the following day, a job that would be handed to 6 Group, while most of 5 Group stayed at home.

The 5th dawned bright and clear and brilliant sunshine glinted off the Perspex of seventeen 49 Squadron Lancasters as they took off from Fiskerton between 10.29 and 10.48 bound for familiar airspace over St-Leu-d'Esserent with W/C Botting and S/L Lace the senior pilots on duty. They were part of a 5 Group force of 189 Lancasters and one Mosquito, which in turn, represented about 25% of the effort by 4, 5, 6 and 8 Groups against two flying-bomb sites, the other in the Forét-de-Nieppe, close to the Belgian frontier. It was an almost intact force that homed in on the target to find it partially protected by up to six-tenths patchy cloud with tops at about 12,000 feet. This prevented the Master Bomber from picking up the aiming-point until thirty seconds from it, which meant a very late course change to bring the bombers into position. This was achieved, however, although smoke and cloud hid the markers from view and most crews picked up the aiming-point by means of ground features. They ran through a spirited flak defence to the point of bomb release, and F/L Millington and crew were again badly shot up, although sustained no casualties. The 49 Squadron element bombed from a uniform 15,000 to 16,000 feet between 13.32 and 13.34 and returning crews reported a fairly concentrated attack, which PRU photos seemed to confirm with views of fresh damage and heavily cratered approaches. F/L Millington and crew were escorted by S/L Lace to a safe landing at Ford on the south coast.

Fiskerton was not called into action on the morning of the 6th, when a 5 Group force of ninety-nine Lancasters and the P38 Lightning were detailed for another swipe at the flying-bomb launching site at Bois-de-Cassan in the L'Isle-Adam, a few miles to the south-west of St-Leu. Heavy cloud over France broke up the formation, which could not be reformed and, ultimately, only thirty-eight aircraft carried out an attack in the face of fierce flak and fighter activity. Photo-reconnaissance revealed some fresh damage to the eastern side of the target, but two large buildings on the main roadway immediately south of the aiming point remained intact and further operations would be required.

Other than night flying tests (NFTs), there was little activity during the day on the 7th, the first time during the month that no daylight operations had been mounted. It was from teatime onwards that the feverish activity began with the preparation of 1,019 aircraft for attacks on five enemy positions facing Allied ground forces in the Normandy battle area. The aiming-point for 179 Lancasters and one Mosquito from 5 Group was the fortified village of Secqueville, situated some fifteen miles east of Le Havre. Seventeen 49 Squadron Lancasters departed Fiskerton between 21.07 and 21.34 with W/C Walker and S/L Twiggs the senior pilots on duty and joined up with the others as they travelled south. The target could be seen by the approaching bombers to be under clear skies, although haze shrouded ground detail to an extent, and star shells were fired from the ground to illuminate the aiming-point. This enabled the Path Finder aircraft to drop red TIs onto it for the main force crews to aim at, and the first phase of bombing proceeded according to plan in concentrated fashion, lasting fifteen minutes. Fourteen of the 49 Squadron crews carried out their attacks from 6,000 to 9,000 feet between 23.22 and 23.25, and it was then that smoke began to obscure the markers, persuading the Master Bomber to call a halt to proceedings at 23.24 before the remaining three had bombed. LM190 was hit by falling bombs but F/O Poole and crew were able to bring it home.

The 8th provided 52 Base crews with a day off, while just four 44 (Rhodesia) Squadron crew were sent mining in the Gironde estuary that night. The 9th was also operation-free until late afternoon, when briefings took place for that night's operation against an oil storage dump in the Forét-de-Châtellerault, situated south of Tours in western France. It was to be predominantly a 5 Group show involving 171 Lancasters and fourteen Mosquitos, but with five 101 Squadron Lancasters to provide RCM cover. 49 Squadron dispatched seventeen Lancasters between 20.26 and 20.50 with S/L Twiggs the senior pilot on duty and all arrived in the target area under clear skies, but with the presence of considerable ground haze. This created poor visibility for the marker crews, who attempted to identify the two aiming-points, while scattered flares dropped by the first two waves of the marker force prompted the Mosquito marker leader to deliver a Wanganui flare as a guide to the third flare-force crews. This meant that some main force crews had to orbit for up to twenty minutes before the Master Bomber was satisfied that the green TIs were in the right spot and called them in to bomb. They produced an accurate attack that resulted in three large explosions and volumes of black smoke, which, within five minutes, completely obscured the aiming-point. A pause in the bombing was called, before it recommenced, until the lack of a verifiable marker compelled the Master Bomber to end proceedings. All but three of the 49 Squadron crews carried out an attack from 4,500 to 7,600 feet between 00.03 and 00.23, and all returned home safely to make their reports.

The mighty Gironde estuary, situated on France's Biscay coast, narrows as it leads inland towards the south-east, before dividing to become the Garonne River to the west and the Dordogne to the east. Its banks and islands were home to a number of important oil production and storage sites at Pauillac, Blaye, Bec-d'Ambe and Bordeaux, and the region was a frequent destination for gardening activities. Bordeaux itself was a vitally important port to the enemy as a gateway to the Atlantic and contained U-Boot pens, which required it to be heavily defended along the entire length of the waterway. Orders were received on 52, 54 and 55 Base stations at teatime on the 10th to prepare sixty-two Lancasters and five Mosquitos to bomb oil storage facilities at Bordeaux, and 49 Squadron responded with eight of its own, which departed Fiskerton between 18.39 and 18.58 with F/Ls Arnold and Brady the senior pilots on duty. They headed towards the south, joining up with the other elements, which included nine Lancasters from 83 Squadron to act as the flare and marker force. The flight out was in daylight, which enabled the Deputy Master Bomber to recognise that the formation had become somewhat disorganized. There were about twenty main force aircraft ahead of the flare force, and the remainder behind it to starboard, but they were catching up and veering further and further to starboard until they were some ten to twenty miles off track. Fortunately, the situation rectified itself and the force arrived in the target area to find clear skies with a little ground haze. As they ran in on the aiming-point, a limited amount of heavy flak began to burst at 16,000 to 18,000 feet, while the considerable light flak fell short, and neither proved to be troublesome. Within thirty seconds of the flares illuminating the ground, the TIs were burning close to the aiming-point and the 49 Squadron crews bombed from 16,000 to 18,800 feet between 22.23 and 22.41. Returning crews were confident of a successful attack, but as few explosions were observed, it was difficult to accurately assess the outcome.

On the 11th, while 617 Squadron took care of the U-Boot pens at La Pallice, thirty-nine other Lancasters and two Mosquitos from 5 Group attacked a similar target at Bordeaux under the protection of six "Serrate" Mosquitos of 100 Group. *(Serrate was a highly effective and successful radar device that enabled 100 Group Mosquito night-fighters to home in on enemy night-fighters and turn the hunters into prey).* For the evening operation, 5 Group was switched to communications targets at Givors, located about twenty miles to the south of Lyon in south-east-central France. There were to be two aiming-points, the town's marshalling yards to the north and a railway junction to the south, and 49 Squadron's sixteen-strong element was assigned to the former in an overall force of 175 Lancasters and ten Mosquitos. They departed Fiskerton between 20.21 and 20.45 with S/L Twiggs the senior pilot on duty and arrived in the target area to find favourable conditions in the form of clear skies and a little haze, which the seemingly usual organized chaos of contradictory or confusing instruction via VHF and W/T threatened to waste. Unaccountably, and contrary to the opinions of the crews, the 5 Group ORB described the W/T control as excellent and the VHF R/T as good. Permission to bomb was not received until 01.12, by which time some crews had been forced to spend fifteen minutes orbiting three times while the Master Bomber and his Deputy discussed the accuracy of the markers. Despite the wrinkles, both aiming-points were well-illuminated and marked and the bombing was concentrated in the correct place. The 49 Squadron crews confirmed their positions by Gee and H2S-fix before carrying out their attacks on red TIs in accordance with the Master Bomber's instructions from 5,800 to 9,000 feet between 01.06 and 01.23. They all returned to home airspace critical of some aspects of the raid, but confident that it had been concluded successfully. Photo-reconnaissance revealed heavy damage to both aiming-points, with the ground badly-cratered and many tracks severed and the middle span of the railway bridge over the River Rhône had received a direct hit.

The main operation on the 12th was an experiment to gauge the ability of main force crews to locate and attack an urban target on the strength of their own H2S equipment in the absence of a Path Finder element. This resulted from the huge volume of operations generated by the four concurrent campaigns, each of which called upon the finite resources of 8 Group, compelling it, in the short term at least, to spread itself more and more thinly. The conclusion of the flying-bomb campaign at the end of the month together with the end of tactical support for the ground forces would remove the pressure and the planned independence of 3 Group through the G-H bombing system from the autumn would solve the problem altogether. In the meantime, however, no one knew what demands might be made of the Command, and it would be useful to see what main force crews could do when left to their own devices. The target was to be Braunschweig, for which a force of 379 aircraft was assembled, seventy-two of the Lancasters provided by 5 Group. It was a night of heavy Bomber Command activity at numerous locations involving more than eleven hundred sorties, of which 297 were assigned to a second large operation over Germany against the Opel tank works at Rüsselsheim, two hundred miles to the south. 49 Squadron's contribution amounted to eight Lancasters, which departed Fiskerton between 21.00 and 21.12 and headed east over the North Sea to cross the German coast with the bomber stream at 18,000 feet. Night-fighter flares were in evidence from then until the coast was crossed again on the way home, and it would prove to be an expensive night for the Command as a whole. P/O Poole and crew turned back after their starboard-outer engine failed, leaving the rest of the force to make its way eastwards under clear skies until nearing the target, when thin cloud built to nine to ten-tenths with tops at 7,000 feet. This was not a problem, as the whole purpose of the operation was to locate and bomb the target blind by H2S and the 49 Squadron participants fulfilled their brief from 19,200 and 21,500 feet between 00.04 and 00.08 and observed the glow of fires beneath the cloud. Some of the bombing did, indeed, hit Braunschweig, but there was no concentration and many outlying towns also reported bombs falling. Twenty-seven aircraft failed to return from this operation and a further twenty from a disappointing tilt at the Opel factory, demonstrating that the Nachtjagd still had sufficient resources to effectively divide its strength.

While the above operation was in progress, a "rush job" called upon the services of 144 crews to attack German troop concentrations and a road junction north of Falaise. 5 Group supported the attack with twenty-five Lancasters, three of them provided by 49 Squadron. The crews of S/L Lace and F/Os Barrie and Carlyle departed Fiskerton between 00.33 and 00.43 and arrived at the target to find a blanket of ten-tenths stratus cloud with tops at 2,000 feet, through which the green TIs were clearly visible. They bombed from 6,000 to 7,000 feet between 02.18 and 02.26 and observed a large explosion at 02.22 and a column of smoke breaking through the cloud tops. Post-raid reconnaissance confirmed that the area around the junction had been heavily cratered and the roads leading from it were mostly blocked.

5 Group began the 13th with an attack by elements of 617 and 9 Squadrons on the derelict French cruiser Gueydon at berth at Brest, which, it was believed, the enemy might sink strategically along with other ships in the harbour to render it unusable if liberated. In the early evening, fifteen Lancasters from 53 Base took off to target an oil storage depot at Bordeaux, while others mined the estuary in what was the Deodar garden.

The main activity during the afternoon of the 14th was an operation in support of Canadian divisions in the Falaise area, which involved 805 aircraft targeting seven enemy troop positions. 5 Group took part and detailed sixty-one Lancasters to target the village of Quesnay, for which fifteen 49 Squadron Lancasters took off between 12.07 and 12.25 with W/C Botting and S/L Twiggs the senior pilots on duty. Master Bombers were on hand to control the bombing at each aiming-point because of the close proximity of the opposing armies, and the Fiskerton gaggle was a little spread out as it attacked in accordance with instructions from 7,000 to 8,000 feet between 14.21 and 14.26 to leave the village in ruins. In the early stages, yellow TIs had been visible, but smoke soon obscured the area and crews were ordered to bomb the northern edge of the smoke, which was rising through 3,000 feet by the time the turned away. Despite the most stringent efforts to avoid friendly fire incidents, some bombs at another aiming point did fall into a quarry occupied by Canadian troops, killing thirteen men, injuring fifty-three others and destroying a large number of vehicles.

In the evening, 128 Lancasters and two Mosquitos were made ready to send back to Brest for another go at the Gueydon, a tanker and a hulk. A number of direct hits were observed on both vessels and smoke could be seen issuing out of the tanker, which, according to photo-reconnaissance, had settled on the bottom, and the cruiser had suffered a similar fate with its decks now awash.

In preparation for his new night offensive against Germany, Harris called for operations against enemy night-fighter airfields in Holland and Belgium, in response to which, a list of eight such targets was prepared for attention. Those at Eindhoven, Soesterberg, Volkel, Melsbroek, St-Trond, Tirlemont-Gossancourt and Le Culot were to be targeted in daylight during the course of the morning and early afternoon of the 15th, and Venlo that night, involving, in all, 1004 aircraft. 5 Group was handed Deelen in central Holland and Gilze-Rijen in the south and prepared forces of ninety-four Lancasters and five Mosquitos for the former and 103 Lancasters, four Mosquitos and the P38 Lightning for the latter. The P38 must have been a two-seat variant as it allegedly contained S/L "Count" Ciano and W/C Guy Gibson, the latter desperate to get back onto operations. 52 Base was assigned to Deelen, and 49 Squadron dispatched sixteen Lancasters between 09.32 and 09.47 with S/Ls Lace and Twiggs the senior pilots on duty. F/O Lee and crew turned back within the hour after a hydraulics leak rendered the rear turret inoperable, while the others found the target under clear skies in excellent visibility and were able to identify the aiming point visually. The Lancasters were each loaded with eleven 1,000 and four 500 pounders, which the 49 Squadron crews dropped onto yellow TIs almost as one from 14,500 to 16,200 feet between 12.11 and 12.13 in accordance with instructions from the Master Bomber. Many bomb bursts were observed on the aerodrome, and post-raid reconnaissance confirmed 230 craters on the runways and damage to hangars and other buildings.

The new offensive began with simultaneous attacks on Stettin and Kiel on the night of the 16/17th, 5 Group contributing 145 aircraft to the overall all-Lancaster force of 461 assigned to the former. 49 Squadron made ready thirteen Lancasters, which departed Fiskerton between 21.13 and 21.29 with S/L Twiggs the senior pilot on duty, but two hours into the outward flight, his rear gunner reported a hydraulics leak that rendered his turret unserviceable and they had to turn back. The others completed the three-and-a-half-hour outward flight and were greeted at the target by up to nine-tenths high cloud with a base at 18,000 to 20,000 feet and sufficient breaks to register clear visibility below. Concentrated red and green TIs could be seen marking out the aiming-point, and the 49 Squadron crews bombed these from 16,600 to 22,000 feet between 01.04 and 01.20 and reported fires taking hold. Smoke had reached 20,000 feet by the end of the raid but not all returning crews were confident about the outcome, some suggesting it to have been scattered, when, in fact, it had been highly successful, destroying fifteen hundred houses, numerous industrial premises, and sinking five ships in the harbour, while seriously damaging eight more. The attack on Kiel had been less effective but had caused extensive damage in the docks area and among the shipbuilding yards, while wasting much of the effort outside of the town to the north-west.

Ten 49 Squadron crews were called to briefing early on the 18th to be told of that morning's operation against two flying-bomb dumps in the Forét-de-L'Isle Adam, north of Paris. 158 Lancasters, six Mosquitos and the P38 Lightning were to be involved, with 83 Squadron leading and providing the back-up marking on the heels of the low-level Mosquitos at the two aiming-points in the east and west. The Fiskerton element took off between 11.37 and 11.47 with F/Ls Arnold, Blair and Gorton the senior pilots on duty and each Lancaster carrying ten 1,000 and four 500 pounders. They headed south in squadron formation to rendezvous with the rest of the force and pick up the fighter escort, and when over the mid-point of the Channel at 13.15, sixty or seventy American Liberators passed across the bows of the gaggle, heading east a thousand feet higher, prompting the lead Lancaster to change course. This may have been the cause of comments by some crews on return, that not all had observed station keeping as set out at briefing, a situation that would result in aircraft bombing out of the planned sequence and on incorrect headings. On arrival in the target area, they encountered five to seven-tenths cloud with tops at around 8,000 feet, which hampered identification of both aiming-points and instructions were issued by the Master Bomber to not bomb unless a clear view of the target had been established. Some were able to pick out the aiming-points assisted by smoke markers, and the 49 Squadron crews bombed from 11,000 feet between 14.08 and 14.11, observing a number of bursts. Five returned with flak damage picked up either over the target or to the north of Rouen and the suggestion at debriefing was that the bombing had been a little scattered. Bombing photos offered a similar conclusion that the attack had overshot to the north and this was confirmed later by PRU photos.

53 Base was called into action on the 19th to provide fifty-two Lancasters for an attack on La Pallice on what was the first day of a spell of wet, cloudy and sometimes windy weather, which would last for the next week, and apart from a number of small-scale operations, 5 Group would remained largely on the ground.

Major operations resumed on the 25th, when preparations were put in hand to make ready more than nine hundred aircraft to launch against three main targets, the Opel tank works at Rüsselsheim and the nearby city of Darmstadt in southern Germany, and the port of Brest, while a further four hundred would be engaged in a variety of smaller endeavours. The largest operation was to be the all-Lancaster affair involving 461 aircraft from 1, 3, 6 and 8 Groups in a return to the Opel works, while 334 others attended to eight coastal batteries around Brest. 5 Group was assigned to Darmstadt, a university city and centre of scientific research and development and one of a few almost virgin targets considered to be worthy of attention. 5 Group assembled a force of 191 Lancasters and six Mosquitos, seven of the former made ready by 49 Squadron, which departed Fiskerton between 20.43 and 20.57 with F/L Arnold the senior pilot on duty accompanied in the cockpit by F/L Blair. The Master Bomber was one of five crews to return early, leaving his two Deputies from 83 Squadron, F/L Meggeson DFC and S/L Williams DFC to step into the breach. The target area was found to be free of cloud, and some ground haze was present, but this was not responsible for matters going awry early on. VHF communication proved to be weak, which made it difficult for the Deputy Master Bombers to pass on instructions, and when five aircraft dropped flares at 01.05, they turned out to be too far to the west and the low-level Mosquitos reported at 01.07 that they were unable to find the aiming point. H-hour was pushed back to 01.22, although bombing actually began at 01.19, and soon afterwards, someone left their VHF on transmit, creating a noise that drowned out all voice communications at the same time that W/T became jammed. One of the Deputies was heard indistinctly instructing the crews to "bomb on the box" (H2S), and then he and the other Deputy were shot down. The main force crews did their best to comply, among them the 49 Squadron element, which was over the target at 7,600 to 9,800 feet between 01.23 and 01.41 and described a widely scattered attack. The lack of marking persuaded some of the force to seek alternative targets and some joined in at Rüsselsheim, while other chose targets of opportunity.

The German port of Königsberg, now Kaliningrad in Lithuania, is located on the eastern side of the Bay of Danzig and was being used by the enemy to supply its eastern front. It lay some 860 miles in a straight line from the bomber stations surrounding Lincoln, which increased to a round trip of 1,900 miles when the routing across Denmark was taken into account. This made it the most distant location ever targeted by the Command and was exceeded only by SOE flights to Poland. Such a distance required sacrificing bombs for fuel, and it was a reduced load of a single 2,000 pounder and twelve 500lb J cluster bombs that was loaded into each of 49 Squadron's eight Lancasters, which were part of an overall heavy force of 174. Having been briefed for this target twice before without going, there was some doubt as to whether or not this one would take place, but it did, and the first 49 Squadron Lancaster began to roll at Fiskerton at 20.20 to be followed by the others over the ensuing ten minutes. The senior pilots on duty were F/Ls Arnold, Blair and Sullings, who together with the rest of the force had a ten-hour marathon ahead of them and all from 49 Squadron would complete the outward flight to arrive at the target after flying through electrical storms and icing conditions over Denmark. In contrast, the skies in the target area were clear and the visibility good, and the force was greeted by around a hundred searchlights and an intense flak defence. The flare force went in at 14,000 to 15,000 feet between 01.05 and 01.12, to be followed minutes later by the heavy markers at a lower level. The 49 Squadron crews identified the aiming-point by red TIs and bombed them from 7,000 and 8,000 feet between 01.17 and 01.30, the latter time six minutes after the Master Bomber had issued the order to cease bombing. Returning crews were fairly enthusiastic about the outcome, reporting punctual marking, concentrated bombing and fires that could be seen, according to some, from 250 miles into the return journey. Photo-reconnaissance revealed that the main weight of the attack had fallen into the town's north-eastern districts, where fire had ripped through many building blocks at a cost of just four Lancasters. However, the job was not yet done, and a second operation would have to be mounted.

The final operations in the long-running flying-bomb campaign were conducted by small Oboe-led forces against twelve sites on the 28th, and Allied ground forces took control of the Pas-de-Calais a few days later. It was clear, that a decisive blow had not been delivered on Königsberg, and at 17.30 on the 29th, briefings took place on the participating 5 Group stations for the return. Six 49 Squadron crews learned that they were to be part of a 5 Group force of 189 Lancasters, while F/Ls Arnold and Sullings were among ten crews briefed to lay mines in the Tangerine garden in the approaches to the port. They departed Fiskerton together between 20.25 and 20.38 with F/L Blair the senior pilot on duty among the bombing brigade and because of the extreme range, they again carried between them only 480 tons of bombs to deliver onto four aiming-points. The bomber stream made its way across the North Sea and Denmark and reached the target to encounter eight to ten-tenths cloud with a base at around 10,000 feet. The Master Bomber, W/C Woodroffe, formerly of 49 Squadron and one of 5 Group's most experienced raid controllers, had decided upon a visual attack and instructed the first flare force wave to drop below the cloud, while keeping the spearhead of the main force circling for twenty minutes before the marking began. The later arrivals could see the markers going down as they approached for what was a complex plan of attack that proceeded with the first flares going down at around 01.05 and continuing at regular intervals thereafter. At 01.24, the third flare force wave was instructed to illuminate the red spot fire, and a minute later an instruction was given to overshoot by 400 yards to the east of the aiming-point. At 01.26, a marker aircraft was told to run over the red marker and overshoot by 300 yards, while, at 01.27, another was ordered to overshoot by 600 yards east of the aiming-point, before the visual backers-up were sent to track over the reds and greens and overshoot by 300 yards. The flare force was invited to go home at 01.30, and, at 01.34, the visual marker crews were instructed first to back up the greens by 600 yards on a westerly heading, and, two minutes later, the concentrations of reds and greens. The 49 Squadron crews identified the target by the red and green TIs and searchlight concentrations and confirmed their positions by H2S before bombing from 9,700 to 11,000 feet between 01.23 and 01.51, the early time that of F/O Dickson and crew who assumed that the marking was late and took matters into their own hands. The Master Bomber called a halt to bombing at 01.52 and sent the crews home, where the absence of four 50 Squadron Lancasters at Skellingthorpe prompted a scathing review of W/C Woodroffe's performance, blaming his stubbornness for the high casualty rate of fifteen Lancasters, 7.9% of those dispatched. They maintained that the backers-up had confirmed the marking to be on the aiming point, despite which, he kept some crews orbiting for up to forty minutes. Post-raid reconnaissance confirmed that the operation had been an outstanding success, which destroyed over 40% of the town's residential and 20% of its industrial buildings. The gardeners sneaked in under cover of the main event and were largely untroubled by the defences and the only hitch was the failure of F/L Arnold's H2S at the last minute. The bomb-aimer and navigator managed to establish their position visually and all mines were delivered into the briefed locations.

The flying-bomb campaign may now have ended, but a new one against V-2 rocket storage and launching sites began on the 31st with raids on nine suspected locations in northern France. 5 Group sent three forces of forty-nine, forty-six and fifty-two Lancasters with two Mosquitos each to respectively target sites at Auchy-les-Hesdin, Rollancourt and Bergueneuse, all situated some twenty miles inland from the coast at Berck-sur-Mer. Dunholme Lodge represented 52 Base at the first-mentioned, where five to eight-tenths cloud was met with a base at 6,000 feet and tops as high as 18,000 feet, out of which issued occasional heavy rain showers. After a delay caused by smoke markers failing to ignite, the Master Bomber directed the bombing to be carried out visually, and although it appeared to be a little scattered, the raid was largely successful, as were those at the other sites.

This concluded a month of feverish and record activity for most heavy squadrons, during which 49 Squadron carried out eighteen operations and dispatched 219 sorties without loss.

## September 1944

The destructive power of the Command was now almost beyond belief, each of its heavy bomber groups now capable of laying waste to a German town and city at one go, and from this point until the end of the war, this would be demonstrated in awesome and horrific fashion. Much of the

Command's effort during the new month would be directed towards the liberation of the three French ports remaining in enemy hands, but operations began for 5 Group with an attack on shipping at Brest on the 2nd, for which sixty-seven Lancasters were detailed from 52 and 55 Bases, although none from Fiskerton. In fact, there would be a gentle start to the new month for 49 Squadron as crews were stood-down to allow them the opportunity to get to grips with the new Village Inn night-fighter defence system. The squadron sat out the following morning's attacks on six Luftwaffe-occupied aerodromes in southern Holland involving a total of 675 aircraft, including 103 Lancasters and two Mosquitos of 5 Group. They were assigned to Deelen, on the way to which they met challenging conditions for formation-keeping in the form of varying amounts of cloud up to nine-tenths with tops at 7,000 feet. Once at the target they were instructed to orbit to await gaps through which to identify the aiming-point visually, and the bombing took place in the face of a spirited flak defence from the airfield only to be halted by the Master Bomber before all aircraft had attacked. There were no losses, but almost every Lancaster from Dunholme Lodge returned with flak damage to some degree. It was the 6th before photo-reconnaissance provided a partial cover of the target area and revealed at least sixty craters around runway intersections and taxiways.

Most of 5 Group remained at home over the ensuing five days, while enemy strong-points in and around Le Havre received daylight visitations from other elements of the Command on the 5th, 6th, 8th and 9th. These operations took place during a spell of unhelpful weather conditions and the attacks of the 8th and 9th were not fully pressed home. Mönchengladbach was posted as the target for 113 Lancasters and fourteen Mosquitos on the 9th, for which briefings took place on the participating stations at 13.30. With Operation Market Garden looming, the town was expected soon to be within striking distance of the advancing Allied forces. The operation took place under clear skies and in good visibility, and a number of large explosions were followed by a heavy pall of smoke rising to meet the crews as they turned away to find the glow of fires still visible from the Dutch coast up to eighty miles away. There were no losses, and photo-reconnaissance confirmed the positive claims of the crews to reveal a highly successful raid, which had left the town centre in ruins.

A further attack on German positions around Le Havre was carried out on the 10th and involved almost a thousand aircraft, 5 Group supporting the effort with 108 Lancasters and two Mosquitos. This was the opportunity for 49 Squadron to open its account for the month and contributed eight Lancasters, which departed Fiskerton between 15.31 and 15.37 with F/Ls Burns and Lee the senior pilots on duty. There were no early returns, and the crews were greeted at the French coast by clear skies and just a little ground haze, which enabled them to identify the target visually. They released their bombs almost as one and entirely unopposed onto red TIs from 10,000 and 11,000 feet between 17.26 and 17.28, and by the time that they turned for home, the area had become enveloped in smoke. The 11th would bring the final attacks on the environs of the port, and would involve 218 aircraft drawn from 4, 5, 6 and 8 Groups. 5 Group contributed ninety-three Lancasters from 53, 54 and 55 Bases, which arrived in the target area under clear skies with slight haze, and, just after dawn, located their respective aiming points to the north and south of the outer defences, each named after a car manufacturer, like Cadillac and Alvis. Initially, there were no markers on the northern aiming-point, and nothing was heard from the Master Bomber, which left the crews to their own devices. Photo-reconnaissance confirmed accurate and concentrated bombing, and, within hours of this operation, the German garrison surrendered to British forces.

Many of the crews involved in the morning activity found themselves on the order of battle and back in the briefing room later in the day to learn of their part in 5 Group's return to Darmstadt, which had escaped serious damage at its hands during the last week of August. A force of 221 Lancasters and fourteen Mosquitos was made ready, and the 49 Squadron element of nine departed Fiskerton between 20.59 and 21.03 with S/L Lace the senior pilot on duty. They began the Channel crossing at Beachy Head, aiming for the French coast near Berck-sur-Mer, before traversing France to enter Germany in the Strasbourg area and turning north towards the target. They arrived to find the skies over southern Germany clear of cloud, and, despite some ground haze, good visibility prevailing as the flare force went in at 17,000 feet at 23.52, homing in on a green TI delivered by a Mosquito. The Master bomber seemed satisfied with the illumination and required no further flares, leaving the backers-up to drop their TIs over the ensuing four minutes, before sending them home at 23.59. The main force crews followed up with extreme accuracy and concentration, those from 49 Squadron bombing on red and green TIs from 15,500 to 16,500 feet between 23.59 and 00.07. The city centre became engulfed in flames, which spread outwards to consume large parts of the built-up area and the glow, according to some, could be seen from the French coast 250 miles away. The operation cost the group twelve Lancasters, among which was the 83 Squadron aircraft containing W/C Walker and his crew, who had recently operated a few times with 49 Squadron. W/C Walker was among four to lose their lives, while the three survivors were taken into captivity. The conditions had been ideal for the 5 Group marking method, and photo-reconnaissance confirmed the main weight of the attack to have fallen in the central and surrounding districts to the south and east. It was learned after the war that the attack had resulted in a genuine firestorm, only the third to be recorded after Hamburg and Kassel in 1943, although a number of local ones may have occurred in other cities like Berlin and Stuttgart. More than twelve thousand people died in the inferno, and a further seventy thousand, 60% of a total population of 120,000, were made homeless.

Orders were received on 5 Group stations on the 12th to prepare for a return to southern Germany that night, this time to target Stuttgart. Nine 49 Squadron crews attended the briefing at Fiskerton and learned that they were to be part of a force of 195 Lancasters and fourteen Mosquitos, which would be accompanied by nine ABC Lancasters from 1 Group's 101 Squadron. A simultaneous operation by 378 Lancasters and nine Mosquitos of 1, 3 and 8 Groups would take place at Frankfurt, a hundred miles to the north. The 49 Squadron element took off between 18.45 and 18.58 with the station commander, G/C Weir, the senior pilot on duty, an officer with an extensive operational career behind him, which had culminated with the command of 61 Squadron. They joined the bomber stream as they headed south to adopt a course similar to that of twenty-four hours earlier and eventually lost the services of F/L Walker and crew to the failure of their H2S. The others mostly enjoyed an uneventful flight across France to Stuttgart, which was found to be under clear skies with moderate visibility and ground haze, and therefore, ideal conditions for the low-level markers. The marking and backing up was very accurate, and the main force bombing concentrated upon the city centre with a slight tendency to creep back towards the north-eastern district of Bad Canstatt and beyond into Feuerbach. Seven of the 49 Squadron crews bombed on red TIs from 17,000 to 18,800 feet between 23.11 and 23.20, but W/C Weir arrived at H+6, just as the Master Bomber called a halt and he retained his load. All returned safely to report a successful operation and a huge explosion at 23.25, which lasted for about five seconds, and when a PRU aircraft photographed the city on the following morning, the entire centre was obscured by the smoke from numerous and widespread fires. Local reports from Stuttgart described the central districts as "erased", and it seems that a firestorm erupted in northern and west-central districts, wiping them from the map. Almost twelve hundred people lost their lives, the highest death toll ever in this much-bombed city, in exchange for which, only four Lancasters were missing.

Other than the first of 617 Squadron's three attacks on Tirpitz on the 15th, launched from Yagodnik in Russia, 5 Group undertook no further operations until the morning of the 17th, when contributing to a total of 762 aircraft assembled to attack troop positions at seven locations around the port of Boulogne. The raids would be staggered over a four-hour period and benefit from a 5 Group effort of 195 Lancasters and four Mosquitos, thirteen of the former representing 49 Squadron and departing Fiskerton between 06.52 and 07.05 with W/C Botting the senior pilot on duty. The 52 Base squadrons were part of the first wave of aircraft to attack one of two aiming-points assigned to 5 Group and were an hour ahead of the second wave. They found clear skies with good visibility, no opposition and saw red TIs marking out the aiming-point, and although the Master Bomber's instructions were a little indistinct, they were sufficient to direct the bombing. All but one of the 49 Squadron crews delivered their eleven 1,000 and four 500 pounders each from 7,300 to 8,200 feet between 08.34 and 08.44, while F/O Alty and crew and others were either orbiting or on their bombing run when the Master Bomber halted the attack at 08.45. The following waves completed the job, although some crews were hampered by drifting smoke and a total of three thousand tons of bombs was sufficient to pave the way for Allied ground forces to move in shortly afterwards to accept the surrender of the German garrison. This left only Calais of the major French ports still under enemy occupation.

5 Group stations received orders on the 18th to prepared for an operation that night against the port of Bremerhaven, located on the east bank at the mouth of the River Weser, some thirty miles north of Bremen. It was to be a classic 5 Group-style attack, employing the low-level visual marking method and involved 206 Lancasters and seven Mosquitos. At Fiskerton, 49 Squadron loaded thirteen Lancasters with a mix of 2,000 pounders and 500lb J-Cluster bombs plus incendiaries and sent them on their way between 18.19 and 18.28 with S/Ls Gorton and Lace the senior pilots on duty. There were no early returns, and the 49 Squadron element arrived intact to find favourable weather conditions and good visibility as they ran in on the aiming-point at medium level to release their loads onto red TIs from 15,000 to 16,700 feet between 21.01 and 21.07, mostly in accordance with the Master Bomber's instructions. A number of huge explosions were witnessed at 21.02 and 21.07, and as they headed out of the target area, they could see many large fires spreading throughout the built-up area, the glow from which remained visible for at least 150 miles. Post-raid reconnaissance revealed that this first major attack on the port, carried out by what, at the time, could be considered to be a modest force, had devasted the built-up areas north and south of the harbour entrance, wiping out installations and warehousing, and only the most northerly and southerly suburbs had escaped complete destruction. Local reports produced a figure of 2,670 buildings reduced to rubble and thirty-thousand people bombed out of their homes, all at the modest cost to 5 Group of a single Lancaster and a Mosquito.

A dozen 49 Squadron crews assembled for briefing at Fiskerton on the 19th and learned that they were to be part of a predominantly 5 Group attack on the twin towns of Mönchengladbach and Rheydt. This represented a shallow penetration into Germany, just ten minutes from the Dutch border, and therefore, a short round trip of four-and-a-half to five hours followed by a night in bed.

217 Lancasters and ten Mosquitos were made ready, along with ten ABC Lancasters from 101 Squadron, and the 49 Squadron participants took off between 18.36 and 19.20 with S/L Gorton the senior 49 Squadron pilot on duty and G/C Weir once more on the order of battle, each Lancaster carrying a 2,000 pounder and eleven 500lb J-Cluster bombs. The Master Bomber for the operation was W/C Guy Gibson VC, DSO, DFC, who had been agitating to get back into the war before it was over and didn't want his service to end in a backwater, while others gained the glory by being in at the death. Gibson was a warrior, and the war had brought out of him qualities, which in peacetime, may have lain dormant. War had also given him a direction, and he revelled in the company of fellow operational types, particularly those of the officer class. Having been torn away from the operational scene following the success of the Dams operation, his purpose had gone and he had become listless, frustrated and discontented. His time in the operational wilderness had not, however, deprived him of his arrogance and self-belief, and when the opportunity to fly as Master Bomber on the coming raid presented itself, he grabbed it. He was driven the three miles from Coningsby to Woodhall Spa to collect his 627 Squadron Mosquito, which, for whatever reason, he rejected and swapped with F/L Mallender, causing a degree of resentment. Gibson had already set the tone for the evening by rejecting the advice of W/C Charles Owen, who had been Master Bomber at this target ten nights earlier. Owen had advised him to leave the target by a south-westerly route and cross north-eastern France to the coast, and also to observe orders to remain above 10,000 feet. Gibson insisted that he would fly home via a direct route across Holland at low level and would not be dissuaded. He took off ahead of the 627 Squadron element at 19.51 to meet up with the main force over the target, where two aiming-points were to be marked.

Some crews reported icing clouds at around 9,000 feet as they made their way to the target over Belgium at around 9,000 feet, and chose to keep below, before climbing fast to 15,000 feet as the cloud dispersed. The marking was complex, with a green marker to be dropped on a factory in a western district of Mönchengladbach and a yellow marker on railway yards in the north, while a red marker was to be placed on railway yards in Rheydt, two miles to the south. It would have been a demanding plan even for an experienced Master Bomber, which Gibson was not, but even so, his instructions were heard clearly. All seemed to be going to plan, with accurate and punctual marking for the green and yellow forces, but late, though accurate marking for the red force, and some of the red force crews were diverted to the green aiming-point. The 49 Squadron crews were assigned to the green force and identified it by flares and TIs before bombing from 14,000 to 15,200 feet between 21.46 and 21.55, observing the target to be well ablaze with the glow visible for at least a hundred miles into the return flight. Four Lancasters and a Mosquito failed to return from what post-raid reconnaissance confirmed to have been a highly destructive attack on both towns. Gibson had returned low over Holland, just as he said he would, and crashed on the outskirts of Steenbergen in south-western Holland, with fatal consequences for him and Coningsby's recently appointed station navigation officer, S/L James Warwick. The cause of the crash is unresolved, but the general belief is that Gibson's lack of familiarity with the Mosquito led to his failure to locate fuel transfer taps and the engines became starved of petrol.

It was now time to turn attention upon Calais as the final port still under enemy occupation. Only one 5 Group Lancaster was involved in the first round of attacks on enemy positions on the 20th, after which, the group remained inactive until the 23rd. Orders came through on that morning to prepare 136 Lancasters and five Mosquitos for an attack that night on the aqueduct section of the Dortmund-Ems Canal south of Ladbergen. It was the scene of a disaster for 617 Squadron in

September 1943, when five of eight crews had failed to return. An element from 617 Squadron would be on scene also on this night to open the attack with Tallboys, to which the raised banks containing the waterway were particularly vulnerable. Germany's canal system was a vital component in the transport network and facilitated the import of raw materials and the export of finished goods to support the war effort. Its wide thoroughfares allowed the passage of large barges, and as the slack in Germany's war production was taken up during 1944, traffic was being pushed through at increasing levels. While this operation was in progress, a second 5 Group force of 108 Lancasters, four Mosquitos and the P38 Lightning would hit the Handorf night-fighter airfield some ten miles to the south to prevent it from interfering. The main operation on this night, however, would be conducted by 549 aircraft from 1, 3, 4 and 8 Groups seventy miles to the south-west at Neuss, situated across the Rhine opposite Düsseldorf, and this, hopefully, might help to split the enemy defences.

49 Squadron prepared thirteen Lancasters to attack Handorf aerodrome, and they departed Fiskerton between 18.43 and 18.53 with S/Ls Gorton and Lace the senior pilots on duty. All reached the target area to encounter a layer of ten-tenths cloud between 8,000 and 9,500 feet but good visibility beneath. The Master Bomber found himself unable to direct the attack and experienced great difficulty in communicating the fact to his Deputy because of intense interference on VHF. Identification and marking of the aiming-points proved to be difficult, and only two green TIs could be seen by a few crews. There would be complaints later that there was no control, and some crews orbited and remained in the target area for up to thirty-five minutes before bombing either on green TIs at Handorf or on yellows at Münster, which had been selected as the last-resort target. Only the crews of F/L Walker and F/Os Cannon and Parkin carried out their attacks on Handorf from 15,700 to 19,000 feet between 21.51 and 22.04, while S/L Lace and crew were thwarted by the failure of their bomb-release system. The other Fiskerton crews attacked Münster from 18,000 to 19,000 feet between 21.39 and 22.07, while some from other squadrons still had their bombs on board when the Bomber called a halt. Fourteen Lancasters failed to return after the Canal-Busters were badly mauled by night-fighters on the way home, but post-raid reconnaissance revealed that breaches in both branches of the canal, probably caused by Tallboys, had left a six-mile stretch drained and unnavigable. It also revealed no new damage at Handorf, where only twenty-two aircraft had bombed.

The second of the series of raids on enemy positions around Calais was mounted by 188 aircraft on the 24th, for which 5 Group detailed thirty Lancasters from the 53 Base stations of Skellingthorpe and Waddington. In the event, only 126 aircraft bombed, eight of them from 5 Group, and they attacked either on a reference provided by Oboe skymarkers or came below the cloud base to bomb visually. At such a height, they were sitting ducks for the heavy and light flak batteries, which accounted for seven Lancasters and a Halifax. It was a similar story on the following day, when only a third of more than eight hundred aircraft were able to deliver their bombs, before the Master Bomber called a halt to proceedings in the face of low cloud. The campaign continued on the 26th, with two separate raids against seven enemy positions around Cap Gris Nez and nearer Calais involving more than seven hundred aircraft. This time the conditions were favourable, and bombing was observed to be concentrated around the aiming points.

On the afternoon of the 26th, fourteen 49 Squadron crews attended briefing and learned that the night's operation was to be against the city of Karlsruhe in southern Germany, for which 216

Lancasters of 5 Group were made ready along with ten of the ABC variety from 101 Squadron and eleven Mosquitos. It was to be a two-phase attack with a two-hour gap between, and the 52, 53 and 55 Base elements assigned to the second phase. This meant a late take-off and it was between 00.23 and 00.46 when the 49 Squadron crews departed Fiskerton with S/L Gorton the senior pilot on duty. They flew out over France with ten-tenths cloud beneath them, which persisted all the way to the target but thinned to a narrow band with the base estimated to be at between 6,000 and 7,000 feet. The plan was to bomb through the cloud on H2S, guided by Wanganui flares, and some approaching crews observed a red TI cascade above the cloud at 03.54. The 49 Squadron crews focused on the glow of red and green TIs and bombed them from 12,750 and 18,500 feet between 04.00 and 04.08 in accordance with the instructions of the Master Bomber. All returned safely to report what appeared to be a city in flames and the glow of fires visible for up to 150 miles into the return journey. There were no plottable bombing photos, but reconnaissance confirmed that the attack had been spread throughout the city and had left a large part of it devastated at a cost to the Command of two Lancasters.

As the crews returned to their stations after 07.00, elements of 1, 3, 4 and 8 Groups were preparing to leave theirs for a further attack on the Calais area. On arrival, the Master Bomber ordered the 340-strong force to come below the cloud base to bomb visually and another successful operation ensued. Later that day, an advance party from 619 Squadron headed east by road to establish a squadron presence at Strubby, a station located three miles north of Alford, west of Sutton-on-Sea, which had opened in April as a sub-station of 55 Base at East Kirkby. It had been occupied first by Coastal Command as a base for its Warwick air-sea rescue operations, and then elements of the 2$^{nd}$ Tactical Air Force, but was now to be home for the remainder of the war to 619 Squadron. Meanwhile, at Fiskerton, fifteen 49 Squadron crews attended briefing for an operation that night against Kaiserslautern, an historic city on the edge of the Palatinate Forest, some thirty miles west of Mannheim. It would be the first major attack of the war on this location, for which a heavy force of 217 Lancasters was assembled, which including ten from 101 Squadron, while ten Mosquitos were prepared for the low-level marking role. The 49 Squadron Lancasters were loaded with 2,000 pounders, 500lb J-Cluster bombs and 4lb incendiaries, which they lifted into the air between 21.39 and 22.03 with S/Ls Gorton and Lace the senior pilots on duty. Clear skies over England gave way to a build-up of cloud over the Channel, and from the French coast to near the target they encountered ten-tenths cumulus with a base at 2,800 feet. The target was partially covered by a thin layer of five to eight-tenths cloud with tops at 3,000 feet, with a further layer at 6,000 to 7,000 feet. The marking with red and green TIs was punctual and accurate, and a green TI visible in the centre of the town became the objective for the main force crews in accordance with the Master Bomber's instructions at 00.58. The 49 Squadron crews attacked from 3,000 to 5,500 feet between 01.01 and 01.07 and observed the bombing to be concentrated. Two yellow explosions were seen at 01.02 and fires were beginning to take hold as the force retreated towards the west. Reconnaissance revealed massive damage within the city, caused by more than nine hundred tons of bombs, which left an estimated 36% of the built-up area in ruins.

The final raids on German positions around Calais were carried out by 490 aircraft of 1, 3, 6 and 8 Groups on the 28$^{th}$ and the garrison surrendered to Canadian forces shortly thereafter. 619 Squadron completed its move to Strubby on this day, while 44 (Rhodesia) Squadron joined 207 Squadron at Spilsby, and, together with East Kirkby, this constituted the new 55 Base, while 52 Base was about to be disbanded. Dunholme Lodge, like nearby Scampton, was transferred to 1

Group and welcomed the recently reformed 170 Squadron with its Lancasters. However, because of its close proximity to Scampton, Faldingworth, Wickenby and Fiskerton with overlapping circuits, it was decided to take Dunholme Lodge out of the front line and 170 Squadron would move out at the end of November.

During the course of the month the squadron participated in nine operations and dispatched 106 sorties, for the second month in succession, without loss.

## October 1944

Having now discharged his primary obligation to SHAEF, Harris would turn his attention once more fully towards industrial Germany with a particular emphasis on oil production. A theme running throughout October was a campaign against the island of Walcheren in the Scheldt estuary, where heavy gun emplacements were barring the approaches to the much-needed port of Antwerp some forty miles upstream. Attempts to bomb these positions in September had proved unsuccessful, and it was decided to flood the land to inundate the batteries and render the terrain difficult to defend when the ground forces moved in. 252 Lancasters were drawn from 1, 5 and 8 Groups and made ready on the 3rd to attack the seawalls at Westkapelle, the most westerly point of the island. 5 Group contributed 128 Lancasters, allotted to four of eight waves of thirty aircraft each, with the Tallboy-carrying 617 Squadron Lancasters standing off to be called in only if required. A breach was opened by the fifth wave, which was extended by those following behind and the flood waters had reached the town by the time the last Lancasters turned for home.

49 Squadron had not been invited to take part in the above operation and it was the 5th before orders were received at Fiskerton to prepare sixteen Lancasters for 5 Group's first major outing of the month, a daylight attempt to bomb the port of Wilhelmshaven through ten-tenths cloud on H2S. A force of 227 Lancasters, one Mosquito and the P38 Lightning was assembled, and those representing 49 Squadron took to the air between 07.33 and 08.04 with W/C Botting the senior pilot on duty. Whether or not it was part of the plan, the controller led the force around the northern side of Heligoland before heading for Jade Bay, where the forecast layer of ten-tenths cloud was encountered between 3,000 and 5,000 feet with good visibility above. The 49 Squadron crews established their positions by H2S-fix or by observing others and delivered their ten 1,000 pounders and four 500lb J-Cluster bombs each from 15,000 to 17,000 feet between 11.04 and 11.09. No results were observed, and there was no possibility of making an assessment, but the impression of a scattered attack was confirmed later when photo-reconnaissance became possible.

From this point until the end of the war, German towns and cities were to be subjected to a new and terrible bomber offensive, beginning with a second Ruhr campaign, which was to open at Dortmund and for which a 3, 6 and 8 Group force of 523 aircraft was made ready on the 6th. 5 Group, meanwhile, had its own target and prepared 237 Lancasters and seven Mosquitos for what would prove to be the thirty-second and final raid of the war on the city of Bremen. 49 Squadron loaded seventeen Lancasters with a mixture of high explosives and incendiaries and dispatched them from Fiskerton between 17.03 and 17.24 with S/L Gorton the senior pilot on duty. Having climbed out and set course, they left the cloud behind and headed into crystal clear skies over the

North Sea with a three-quarter moon to light the way. They found the target area to be free of cloud, which was ideal for the 5 Group low-level marking method and the conditions handed the hapless city on a plate to the bombers. The 49 Squadron crews carried out their attacks in the face of many searchlights and the usual flak response, aiming for the red and green TIs from 16,500 to 19,500 feet between 20.17 and 20.52, before turning away from a city in flames, the glow from which remained visible for a hundred miles and more. The success of the operation was confirmed by post-raid reconnaissance and local reports, which described a huge area of fire and catalogued the destruction of more than 4,800 houses and apartment blocks, along with severe damage to war industry factories, all achieved at the modest cost of five aircraft. For the first time in more than two months, the squadron suffered loss and had to post missing two of its crews. PB353 disappeared into the sea with the crew of F/O Harrop, whose fate only became known when the remains of the bomb-aimer washed up on the coast of Norway two months hence. PB429 crashed at 20.11 at Leuchtenburg, some ten miles north-west of Bremen city centre and there were no survivors from the crew of F/O Beatson. Now that the focus of operations had moved from France to Germany, the number of sorties to complete a tour had been reduced from thirty-five to thirty-three, and this represented an unexpected bonus to some.

Following the failure of Operation Market Garden, the German frontier towns of Cleves (Kleve) and Emmerich were earmarked for attention by daylight on the 7th. Five miles apart and separated by the Rhine, both suffered massive damage at the hands of large forces from 1, 3, 4 and 8 Groups. 5 Group, meanwhile, returned to Walcheren to target the seawalls near Flushing with 121 Lancasters and three Mosquitos. Many of the bombs contained a thirty-minute delay fuse, while others detonated on impact, and the dyke was already beginning to crumble as the bombers headed home, where confirmation of a successful outcome would catch up with them. Focus remained on the Scheldt defences, and the gun battery at Fort Frederik Hendrik near Breskens on the East Scheldt was targeted by elements of 1 and 8 Groups on the 11th, while 115 Lancasters from 5 Group were assigned to others near Flushing on the north bank of the West Scheldt. At the same time, sixty-one Lancasters from Fiskerton and 55 Base and two Mosquitos were to attempt to breach the seawalls at Veere, situated on the eastern side of Walcheren opposite Westkapelle. 49 Squadron contributed a dozen Lancasters, which took off between 13.05 and 13.14 with W/C Botting and S/L Gorton the senior pilot on duty. On arrival at the target, crews encountered varying amounts of cloud between two and seven-tenths with tops at 4,000 to 5,000 feet, through which the 49 Squadron crews carried out their attacks from 4,000 to 7,800 feet between 14.47 and 14.54. Post-raid reconnaissance revealed an area of flooding of 800 x 250 yards at Veere, but no new damage to the gun positions.

The 14th was the day on which were fired the opening salvoes of Operation Hurricane, a terrifying demonstration to the enemy of the overwhelming superiority of the Allied air forces ranged against it. Bomber Command ordered a maximum effort from all but 5 Group to attack Duisburg, for which 1,013 Lancasters, Halifaxes and Mosquitos answered the call. The American 8th Air Force would also be in business on this day, targeting the Cologne area further south with 1,250 bombers escorted by 749 fighters. The RAF force took off at first light, picked up its own fighter escort, and delivered 4,500 tons of high-explosives and incendiaries into Duisburg shortly after breakfast time, causing unimaginable destruction. That night, similar numbers returned to press home the point about superiority, bringing the total weight of bombs over the two raids to 9,000 tons from 2,018 sorties in fewer than twenty-four hours. The only involvement by 5 Group were single sorties by a Lancaster and a Mosquito to conduct a photo-reconnaissance of the operation.

However, 5 Group took advantage of the evening activity over the Ruhr to return to Braunschweig, the scene of quite a number of unsatisfactory previous attempts to land a really telling blow. A force of 232 Lancasters and eight Mosquitos was made ready, of which eighteen of the former were provided by 49 Squadron and departed Fiskerton for the final time between 22.33 and 22.49 with W/C Botting and S/L Gorton the senior pilots on duty. They reached the target area to find conditions ideal for low-level marking but had to approach the aiming-point at 18,000 feet from the south-west, passing over Hallendorf and Salzgitter, the latter the home to the Reichswerke Hermann Göring steelworks. This forced them to run the gauntlet of searchlight cones and heavy flak for the three minutes it took to pass through, but once on the other side they were greeted by clear skies and good visibility, which facilitated accurate marking with red and green TIs. Although the early stages of bombing tended to undershoot, the Master Bomber quickly brought the attack back on track, calling for crews to overshoot by up to nineteen seconds. The 49 Squadron contingent passed over the aiming-point at 17,250 to 19,000 feet between 02.31 and 02.37 and delivered their loads accurately to contribute to a highly effective raid. 83 Squadron's F/O Price complained that main force crews were jettisoning incendiaries all the way back as far as the Rhine, and thereby illuminating the track for any stalking night-fighters. In the event, only a single Lancaster failed to return from what was, indeed, confirmed to be an outstanding result, which had wiped out the entire centre of this historic city, and visited damage on almost every district.

Earlier in the day, an advance party had arrived at Fulbeck to prepare the way for the main party's move on the 16th. Located some six miles to the east of Newark, the station had opened in 1940 and had been home to both RAF and USAAF units engaged predominantly in troop-carrying activities. Along with Syerston and Balderton, it would now form 56 Base under the command of G/C Pope, and in time would include 49, 189 and 227 Squadrons. The main operation on the 15th was the fourteenth and final major raid on the important shipbuilding and naval port of Wilhelmshaven, for which a force of 506 aircraft was drawn from all but 5 Group. What may have been spoof green TIs were reported some five miles to the west and north-west of the target, and these attracted a number of bomb loads, while the rest of the bombing appeared to be scattered, a fact largely confirmed by local sources, which named only the Rathaus (Town Council HQ) as completely destroyed. Stubborn resistance by the occupiers on Walcheren demanded further operations against the seawalls at Westkapelle, for which 5 Group detailed forty-seven Lancasters and three Mosquitos on the 17th. Once developed, the bombing photos brought back by most crews revealed no extension to the breach in the dyke.

An operation of significance on the morning of the 18th represented a major step forward in Bomber Command's evolution and brought with it for 3 Group the same level of independence enjoyed by 5 Group. The G-H bombing system had been under development for around two years and mirrored to an extent the American method of releasing bombs on observing the leader's fall away. While the American system was exclusively for daylight operations, the RAF system was equally effective at night and in 3 Group hands would prove to be particularly effective against precision targets like oil refineries and railways. As one of a few relatively intact German cities, Bonn, situated some twenty miles to the south-east of Cologne, was selected as the target for the first massed live trial on the assumption that fresh damage would be easily identified to assess the performance of G-H. The operation was not entirely successful, but time and practice would iron out the wrinkles.

49 Squadron had been allowed a number of days to settle into its new home and for the crews to familiarise themselves with the circuit, before orders came through on the 19th for the next operation. Nuremberg was posted as the target for a new record 5 Group force of 263 Lancasters and seven Mosquitos, in preparation for which, nineteen crews filed into the briefing room to learn of their part in the plan and to be told that the night's largest operation was to be conducted against Stuttgart by a force of 565 aircraft drawn from 1, 3, 6 and 8 Groups. The 49 Squadron contingent departed Fulbeck for the first time in anger between 17.15 and 17.39 with F/Ls Blair, Burns, Furber and Lee the senior pilots on duty. They crossed the French coast near Abbeville and enjoyed an uneventful flight across France to find the target covered by a wedge of eight to ten-tenths cloud at between 3,000 and 10,000 feet, with poor visibility below. The marker force laid down flares and backed them up with others along with red and green TIs, which were observed to be somewhat scattered, and bombing had to take place on their glow seen through the cloud. The 49 Squadron crews carried out their attacks from 18,300 to 19,300 feet between 20.55 and 21.07 in accordance with the Master Bomber's instructions, before returning home uncertain as to the outcome. The impression given by the glow of fires was of an effective attack, but post-raid reconnaissance revealed the bombing to have fallen not on the intended city centre aiming-point, but predominantly into the more industrial southern districts, where almost four hundred houses were destroyed along with forty-one industrial buildings.

It was back to Walcheren on the 23rd for 112 Lancasters of 5 Group, this time to target the coastal battery at Flushing. They were greeted at the target by eight to ten-tenths cloud with a base at between 3,000 and 5,000 feet and poor visibility below caused by haze and rain. The force was led in on what appeared to be a decent approach but was ordered to "orbit port" as the lead crews experienced great difficulty in identifying their respective aiming-points. A second run was no more revealing, even for those crews who ventured down as low as 2,000 feet, and twenty would still have their bombs on board when ordered to go home. Post-raid reconnaissance revealed evidence of seventy bomb bursts, including four near-misses and the destruction of a number of buildings on the site.

That evening, a new record force of 1,055 aircraft was sent against Essen as part of the Hurricane "message" and dropped 4,538 tons of bombs, more than 90% of which was high explosive. This number was achieved without 5 Group, which took the night off and committed only twenty-five Lancasters to gardening duties in northern waters on the following night. Essen was pounded again by more than seven hundred aircraft in daylight on the 25th, by which time it had ceased to be an important source of war production. Operation Hurricane moved on to Cologne on the 28th, when two districts east of the centre were totally devastated by more than seven hundred aircraft.

5 Group occupied the day with the preparation of a force of 237 Lancasters and seven Mosquitos for an operation that night against the U-Boot pens at Bergen in Norway. 49 Squadron made ready eighteen Lancasters, which departed Fulbeck between 22.30 and 23.09 with S/L Lace the senior pilot on duty. The bomber stream had to battle its way through electrical storms and lost only two of its number to early returns during the three-and-a-half-hour outward flight. The crews had been told at briefing to expect clear conditions, although some doubts had been expressed about the forecast and these were confirmed when the force was met by eight-to ten-tenths cloud between

4,000 and 14,000 feet, which obscured the aiming-point. This would not have been a problem over Germany, but the risk to Norwegian civilians was uppermost in the mind of the Master Bomber as he pondered his options, before calling for the main force to descend. Even then, most were unable to pick out any markers and the situation was exacerbated by intermittent VHF reception, which persuaded 83 Squadron's F/L Cornish to fly up and down the coast acting as a communications link between the Master Bomber and the main force. The flare force element did what it could from between 12,500 and 15,000 feet and some main force crews flew as low as 4,500 feet without being able to identify the target. The operation was abandoned after only forty-seven aircraft had bombed and the crews of F/O Nowrie and F/L Carlyle were the only ones from 49 Squadron to carry out an attack, from 5,000 at 02.07 and 4,300 at 02.26 respectively. On return, PB519 was diverted to Marston Moor, where it landed too far down the runway to be able to stop, went straight off the end and finished up on a main road minus its undercarriage. The Lancaster would never fly again but F/O Lee and his crew emerged unscathed to continue their operational career.

The final operations against Walcheren were undertaken by 5 Group on the 30th, when two forces of fifty-one Lancasters and four Mosquitos each were sent against coastal batteries at Westkapelle and Flushing two hours apart. The 49 Squadron element had been assigned to Flushing and its thirteen Lancasters were each loaded with fourteen 1,000 pounders before being sent on their way from Fulbeck between 12.59 and 13.22 with W/C Botting the senior 49 Squadron pilot on duty and G/C Weir also on the order of battle having been involved in the move from Fiskerton. F/O Nowrie led six aircraft to the target thirty minutes ahead of the main element to act as wind-finders, before joining the others to bomb. They ran into seven to ten-tenths cloud with a base at 4,000 feet over the target and visibility was no more than five miles as the attack began. The target area could be seen to be flooded already with buildings standing out of the water and some of the wind-finders were hit by flak while orbiting. Having lost their starboard-inner engine, F/O Mallinson and crew were among a number not to bomb, while F/O Nowrie and crew were forced to jettison their load. The others had to establish the aiming point visually in the absence of markers and only seven 49 Squadron crews were able to deliver their loads from 3,100 to 4,000 feet between 15.08 and 15.31. Ground forces went in on the following day, and a week of heavy fighting preceded the island's capture. Even then, the clearing of mines from the approaches to Antwerp kept the port out of commission for a further three weeks. On the evening of the 30th, nine hundred aircraft returned to Cologne, and almost five hundred went back again twenty-four hours later to complete the destruction of the Rhineland capital.

During the course of the month, the squadron operated on seven occasions and dispatched 113 sorties for the loss of two Lancasters and crews.

# November 1944

The new month began with a daylight operation on the afternoon of the 1st, against the Meerbeck synthetic oil refinery at Moers/Homberg, or, to give it its full title, the Gewerkschaft Rheinpreussen A G plant, located on the west bank of the Rhine opposite Duisburg on the western edge of the Ruhr. The name of this target would strike fear into the hearts of 3 Group crews, who had suffered heavy casualties while attacking the plant during the summer, but it meant nothing to 5 group crews, who were less familiar with it and would have found the name of Wesseling far more unsettling. 49 Squadron briefed fifteen crews as part of an overall 5 Group force of 226 Lancasters and two Mosquitos, which were to be joined by fourteen 8 Group Mosquitos to provide the Oboe marking. They took off from Fulbeck between 13.30 and 13.55 with S/L Lace the senior pilot on duty and reached the target to find it completely obscured by cloud with tops at between 6,000 and 9,000 feet. Wanganui flares from earlier arrivals were well-scattered over a circle with a ten-mile radius, prompting a backer-up from 83 Squadron to drop a yellow TI over the built-up area in the hope of attracting some bombing. The problem seemed to be, that crews at the head of the stream had seen no markers or were past them by the time that they became evident and had taken their bombs home. Some 49 Squadron crews caught a glimpse of the target area through a chink in the cloud, while others carried out a time-and-distance run from the last visual pinpoint, before aiming at red skymarkers to deliver their fourteen 1,000 pounders each from 16,000 to 17,500 feet between 16.10 and 16.12. The attackers had faced an intense flak response, and 49 Squadron's PB374 was hit and lost its hydraulics, which prevented the bomb doors from opening and the undercarriage from lowering and the air bottle had to be employed so that F/O Essenhigh could land on the emergency strip at Woodbridge. At debriefing, many crews reported difficulty in hearing the Master Bomber, after his VHF transmissions became jammed by a transmit button left on in another aircraft. Ultimately, the conditions rendered the whole attack ineffective, and although 159 crews released their bombs, it is unlikely that any hit the intended target.

Düsseldorf's turn to face a massive force came on the 2$^{nd}$, when 992 aircraft were made ready for what would prove to be the final major raid of the war on this much-bombed city. The "Lincolnshire Poachers" put up 187 Lancasters for this rare experience to operate with the rest of the Command and 49 Squadron pitched in with thirteen, while 189 Squadron, which had moved into Fulbeck from Bardney earlier in the day, managed a creditable four. The 49 Squadron element took off between 16.11 and 17.05 with S/L Lace the senior pilot on duty and passed over Reading on its way to beachy head for a southern approach to the Ruhr and arrived at the target to find clear skies, moonlight and only ground haze to slightly mar the vertical visibility. The moonlight nullified the searchlights ringing the city, but of greater concern was the heavy flak bursting at 17,000 to 20,000 feet. The main force crews found the aiming-point to be well illuminated and marked with red and green TIs, onto which each of the 49 Squadron participants dropped a cookie, six 1,000 pounders and six 500 pounders from 17,000 to 22,000 feet between 19.15 and 19.34. Returning crews reported fires beginning to take hold and smoke rising to 2,000 feet as they turned away and were confident of a successful raid. Eleven Lancasters and eight Halifaxes failed to return, although four of them came down in Allied-held territory. 49 Squadron's PB385 was shot down by a night-fighter, almost certainly while outbound, and crashed at Golzheim, four miles north-east of Düren with no survivors from the crew of F/O Harford. The effectiveness of the operation was confirmed by post-raid reconnaissance, which revealed that the northern half of the city had received the main weight of bombs and that five thousand houses had been destroyed or seriously damaged.

The continuing campaign against Ruhr cities would be prosecuted by 749 aircraft at Bochum on the 4$^{th}$, while 5 Group renewed its acquaintance with the Dortmund-Ems Canal, which had been repaired following the successful breaching of its banks near Ladbergen in September. Now that Germany's railways were being pounded to destruction, the Dortmund-Ems and the nearby Mittelland Canal took on a greater significance as vital components in the transportation system, particularly with regard to the movement of raw materials to and from the Ruhr region. A force of 168 Lancasters and two Mosquitos contained a dozen 49 Squadron aircraft, which took off between 17.32 and 17.47 with S/L Gorton the senior pilot on duty. They were heading for the familiar aqueduct section of the canal south of Ladbergen and hoped to sneak in under cover of the main operation sixty miles to the south, hopefully thereby, to avoid the attentions of night-fighters. The first marker aircraft of 83 Squadron arrived at the target at 19.19 after making a GPI run (ground position indicated) by means of H2S from Münster and encountered clear skies with ground haze. A blind-dropped green TI burst on the canal bank four hundred yards short of the aiming-point, and the flare force went in between 19.20 and 19.28. Red TIs were observed to fall between the two aqueducts, after which, the Master Bomber cancelled the third wave of flare-carriers and sent them all home to leave the way clear for the main force crews. The first bombs tended to overshoot, but, thereafter, the crews produced an accurate and concentrated attack, those from 49 Squadron bombing from 10,000 to 13,000 feet between 19.31 and 19.33. Photo-reconnaissance confirmed that both branches of the canal had been breached and drained, leaving barges stranded and the waterway unnavigable, and the success had been achieved for the loss of just three Lancasters. Among these was 49 Squadron's PB370, in which the crew of F/O Talbot all lost their lives.

To capitalize on the success, an attack was planned for the 6th against the Mittelland Canal at Gravenhorst, a point about a mile north of Das Nasse Dreieck, the "Wet Triangle" at Bergeshövede. As previously mentioned, this is a triangular basin into which the Dortmund-Ems and Mittelland Canals flow about ten miles north of Ladbergen, before the Dortmund-Ems continues on to the west and the Mittelland to the north and then east. It was a 5 Group show involving 239 Lancasters and seven Mosquitos, a dozen of the former representing 49 Squadron. They departed Fulbeck between 16.32 and 16.52 with F/Ls Furber, Hay and Walker the senior pilots on duty and all reached the target area to find clear skies but haze up to around 4,000 feet that affected the visibility. The Master Bomber called in the flare force, despite which, the low-level Mosquito markers experienced great difficulty in identifying the aiming-point. A single Mosquito eventually did deliver its target indicator accurately onto the aiming-point, where it fell into the water and was extinguished. The Master Bomber called a halt to proceedings at 19.38 after thirty-one aircraft had bombed, and the 49 Squadron participants jettisoned the delayed-action 1,000 pounders before setting course for home and encountering not only night-fighter activity, but also very challenging weather conditions of electrical storms and low cloud. Ten Lancasters failed to return, four of them from 467 Squadron RAAF alone.

Earlier on the 6th, a series of raids on Ruhr oil refineries had begun with a heavy area attack at Gelsenkirchen, and this was followed by smaller-scale operations at Homberg on the 8th, the Krupp Treibstoffwerke at Wanne-Eickel on the 9th and the Klöckner Werke A G refinery at Castrop-Rauxel on the morning of the 11th. Thirteen 49 Squadron crews attended briefing at Fulbeck later in the day to learn that they would shortly be attacking the Rhenania-Ossag synthetic oil refinery at Harburg, situated on the South Bank of the Elbe opposite Hamburg. 237 Lancasters and eight Mosquitos were to take part in another all-5 Group show, while elements of 1 and 8 Groups targeted the Hoesch-Benzin plant 170 miles to the south in the Wambel district of Dortmund. Most of the Lancasters were loaded with a cookie, six 1,000 and five 500 pounders, while a few would carry fourteen N°14 cluster bombs with their cookie. Another early evening take-off had the 49 Squadron element airborne between 16.22 and 16.47 with S/L Gorton the senior pilot on duty and all reached the target area to find largely clear conditions, with only a thin layer of stratus at 8,000 feet and another at 17,000 to 18,000 feet between them and the aiming-point. This they identified either by H2S or red and green TIs, before delivering their loads from 16,000 to 19,000 feet between 19.19 and 19.25. The defenders threw up a heavy flak barrage, which reached as high as 23,000 feet and this is almost certainly what accounted for 49 Squadron's PB369, which crashed in the target area with no survivors from the eight-man crew of B Flight commander, S/L Gorton. At debriefing, crews reported a large explosion at 19.28 followed by an oil fire, and local reports would confirm that heavy damage had been inflicted upon the town's residential and industrial districts.

The 16th was devoted to the destruction of the three small towns of Heinsberg, Jülich and Düren, located respectively in an arc from north to east of Aachen and close to the German lines upon which American ground forces were advancing. A total of 1,188 aircraft was involved, and 1, 5 and 8 Groups provided the heavy bombing and marking force of 485 Lancasters for the last-mentioned. 49 Squadron contributed eleven aircraft to the 5 Group effort of 214, and they took off from Fulbeck between 12.34 and 12.47 with F/L Carlyle the senior pilot on duty and each carrying eleven 1,000 and four 500 pounders. They flew to the target over ten-tenths cloud, which cleared to three-tenths stratus above 6,000 feet as they approached the aiming-point in the final wave of the attack. They bombed in accordance with the instructions of the Master Bomber from 10,000 to 13,200 feet between 15.31 and 15.42 and observed smoke rising through 9,000 feet as they turned for home, confident in the success of the attack. All of the Fulbeck crews believed that they had hit the target, but most of the photos were unplottable because of the smoke covering the area. Post-raid reconnaissance confirmed that the operation had been a complete success at a cost of just three aircraft and revealed that the town had been all-but erased from the map, local sources claiming a death toll in excess of three thousand inhabitants. In the event, unfavourable ground conditions prevented the American advance from succeeding.

Ten 49 Squadron crews attended briefing at Fulbeck on the 21st to be told that they were going back to the Mittelland Canal on a night of multiple operations involving 1,345 sorties. Three operations, each by 270 aircraft, were to be directed at railway yards at Aschaffenburg, situated about twenty miles south-east of Frankfurt, and oil plants at Castrop-Rauxel and Sterkrade in the Ruhr. 5 Group prepared two forces of 137 and 123 Lancasters respectively, with Mosquito support, for the Mittelland and Dortmund-Ems Canals, while a whole host of minor operations would complete the order of battle. 56 Base was one of those assigned to the former at Gravenhorst, for which the 49 Squadron element took off between 17.34 and 17.48 with F/Ls Carlyle and Hay the senior 49 Squadron pilots on duty and G/C Weir guesting. Those reaching the target area encountered a layer of six to ten-tenths cloud at between 4,000 and 8,000 feet, which did not inhibit the accuracy of the marking, but the instructions of the Master Bomber caused some confusion, a situation exacerbated by a week VHF signal. At first, he ordered the crews to come below the cloud base, to which some responded, before he changed his mind and told them to return to the briefed bombing height. This led to bombing heights among the 49 Squadron participants ranging from 3,200 to 8,200 feet as he issued further instructions to aim for the more southerly of two red TIs, and they complied as best they could between 21.03 to 21.09, observing what appeared to be a good concentration of bomb bursts. Just two Lancasters were lost, and both had taken off from Fulbeck. G/C Weir was the sole survivor from PB300, which exploded over the target during the bombing run, catapulting him into space attached to his seat parachute. He came to in the drained and muddy canal with no memory of his miraculous deliverance and was taken into captivity.

Among those losing their lives was the navigator, S/L "Pat" Kelly DFC & Bar, who had a long and distinguished career behind him, including a spell with 617 Squadron as a member of Cheshire's crew. Like some of the others on board the Lancaster, he did not need to put his life at risk but found it hard to resist the lure of operations. PB354 contained the crew of F/O Maul, and none survived the crash somewhere between the target and the Ruhr. Post-raid reconnaissance revealed that the Mittelland Canal had been breached over a distance of fifty feet on the western bank, south of the road bridge, and this had left a thirty-mile stretch of the waterway drained with fifty-nine barges stranded in one small section.

Reconnaissance at Ladbergen revealed success also, showing the left-hand channel, which was the only one repaired since the last attack, to have been breached again where it crossed the River Glane. The river had been unable to cope with the volume of water released and extensive flooding occurred on both sides of the canal. The Germans recognized that repairing the canals was an open invitation to Bomber Command to return, but so vital were they to the transportation system, that they could not be abandoned. The answer was to complete repairs, but to leave the sections drained and apparently still under repair until sufficient traffic had built up to push through in one night. They would then be flooded and re-emptied to dupe RAF reconnaissance flights and maintain the deception.

On the following night, 5 Group dispatched 171 Lancasters and seven Mosquitos to attack the U-Boot pens at Trondheim in Norway, a distance of more than eight hundred miles. 49 Squadron launched nine Lancasters into the air between 15.30 and 16.02 with S/L Lace the senior pilot on duty and all arrived in the target area to find clear skies and excellent visibility. Unfortunately, they were thwarted by an effective smoke screen that prevented the marker force from finding the aiming-point, and the Master Bomber had no option but to send the force home at 21.04.

The weather was mainly responsible for curtailing operations over the next few days until the 26th, when briefings took place on 5 Group stations at 20.00. The ten attending 49 Squadron crews learned that Munich was to be their target for an all-5 Group affair involving 270 Lancasters and eight Mosquitos, which represented a maximum effort. After the take-off time was pushed back, they departed Fulbeck between 23.30 and 23.46 with F/Ls Hay and Winter the senior pilots on duty and each carrying a 1,000 pounder and thirteen Nº4 J-Cluster bombs. PB432 was airborne for three minutes before crashing at Dry Doddington to the south-west of the aerodrome, killing the wireless operator and mid-upper gunner, while F/O Le Marquand and the others sustained injuries of varying degrees of severity. Forming up and climbing to operational altitude was a time-consuming business and it would be five hours before the target was reached. F/O Cannon and crew lost an engine after some ninety minutes and landed at Ford on the south coast, leaving the rest to find the target area under clear skies with good visibility, having been assisted by the use of Loran, a new navigation device based on Gee with a longer range. They confirmed their positions by means of H2S while the low-level marking was being carried out, and aside from one errant red TI, it was accurate and the Master Bomber ensured that the crews focused upon the reds and greens on and close to the planned aiming-point. The 49 Squadron crews bombed from 20,000 to 20,500 feet between 05.03 and 05.11 and returned safely to praise the quality of the route and target marking and the concentration of the attack. The last-mentioned was confirmed by post-raid reconnaissance and a local report that singled out railway installations as being particularly hard-hit.

This was the final operation of the month for 5 Group, but among others taking place before the end was an attack by 1 and 8 Groups on Freiburg in southern Germany. It was a minor railway centre within thirty-five miles of advancing American and French ground forces and was thought to be harbouring large numbers of enemy soldiers. The force of over 330 Lancasters delivered 1,900 tons of bombs, missing the railway yards, but destroying two thousand houses and killing over two thousand inhabitants. During the course of the month, the squadron took part in nine operations and dispatched 105 sorties for the loss of six Lancasters and five crews and two additional crew members.

# December 1944

There were no operations for 5 Group for the first three nights of the new month, largely because of the weather, and in the meantime, 1, 4, 6 and 8 Groups pounded the Ruhr town of Hagen on the night of the 2/3rd. Worthwhile targets were becoming more and more scarce at a time when the Command was at its most powerful, and this final period of the war would bring the most devastating attacks to date on the German homeland. When the 56 Base squadrons returned to action in the early evening of the 4th, it was to contribute towards a 5 Group force of 282 Lancasters and ten Mosquitos. Their target was the city of Heilbronn, situated thirty miles due north of Stuttgart, which had the River Neckar and a north-south rail link running through it, but otherwise, had no genuine strategic importance and its populace would not have been expecting to be attacked. The main operation on this night was actually by 535 aircraft of 1, 6 and 8 Groups at Karlsruhe, some fifty-six miles west-south-west of Heilbronn, and the concentration of aircraft in this area would be certain to bring out the night-fighters. The 49 Squadron element of a dozen Lancasters departed Fulbeck between 16.28 and 16.46 with F/Ls Carlyle, Galloway, Lee and Winter the senior pilots on duty and each Lancaster carrying a cookie and either five 1,000 pounders or twelve SBCs of 4lb incendiaries. They flew out across France in good conditions to find three to five-tenths thin stratus over the target at around 12,000 feet, through which some crews were able to pick out the Neckar and the aiming-points. The marshalling yards and the built-up area were illuminated by the flare force ahead of the low-level Mosquitos' run to drop red TIs for the visual marker crews to back up. The marshalling yards were marked with yellows, which the main force element was unable to distinguish in the burgeoning fires, and this persuaded them to focus on the red and green TIs in the city itself instead. The 49 Squadron crews attacked from 13,000 to 15,300 feet between 19.30 and 19.44, adding to the general destruction, and as the force retreated westwards into electrical storms, 82% of the city's built-up area was in the process of being destroyed by what probably amounted to a firestorm. The post-war British Bombing Survey estimated 351 acres of destruction and a death toll of at least seven thousand people. It cost 5 Group a relatively high twelve aircraft, the single Fulbeck casualty representing 189 Squadron. The operation against Karlsruhe had also been an outstanding success, which left southern and western districts, in particular, severely damaged.

On a night of heavy Bomber Command activity on the 6th, 475 Lancasters of 1, 3 and 8 Groups were to target the I G Farbenindustrie A G Merseburg-Leuna oil refinery near Liepzig in the east, while 450 aircraft from predominantly 4 and 6 Groups attacked railway installations at Osnabrück in the north. 5 Group's target was the town of Giessen, situated some eighty-five miles south-east of Cologne in west-central Germany and thirty-five miles north of Frankfurt. A force of 255 Lancasters was assembled, a dozen of them by 49 Squadron at Fulbeck, where the armourers loaded each of them with a cookie and thirteen SBCs of 4lb incendiaries. The main force crews had been assigned to two aiming-points, two-thirds of them to the town and the remainder to the marshalling yards, and it was for the latter that the 49 Squadron element took off between 16.59 and 17.14 with the newly promoted S/L Walker the senior pilot on duty. Those arriving in the target area found up to eight-tenths thin cloud and good visibility, by which time the flare force had begun illuminating, three minutes early and to the west of the target as events were to prove. However, the Mosquito-laid red TIs fell close to the aiming-point and the Master Bomber ensured that they were backed up by greens. The 49 Squadron crews bombed from 9,000 to 10,800 feet between 20.18 and 20.27 and all returned safely to report another successful raid, which would be confirmed by reconnaissance photographs.

The Urft Dam was one of a number of similar structures in the beautiful Eifel region of western Germany, close to the Belgian frontier. There was a fear that the enemy might strategically release flood water to hamper the American advance into Germany, and it was decided to attempt to breach the dam, to allow any excess water to drain away. The first of a number of attacks on the region took place on the 3rd at Heimbach, the small town nestling against the northern reaches of the reservoir, but the 1 and 8 Group force failed to identify it and no bombs fell. On the following day, a small 8 Group effort against the dam was unsuccessful, as was a 3 Group attack on the nearby Schwammenauel Dam on the 5th. The job was handed to 5 Group on the 8th, for which a force of 205 Lancasters was made ready, fourteen of them by 49 Squadron, while nineteen from 617 Squadron would be carrying Tallboys. They departed Fulbeck between 08.38 and 09.15 with F/Ls Galloway and Winter the senior pilots on duty and arrived at the target to be greeted by six to nine-tenths cloud at between 6,000 and 8,000 feet and moderate visibility, and most crews made multiple runs across the target area seeking out the dam. The 49 Squadron crews carried out their attacks from 8,000 to 9,650 feet between 11.11 and 11.16 and were among 129 to bomb before the Master Bomber called a halt and sent the force home. Poor weather conditions over Lincolnshire demanded a diversion, and all from Fulbeck landed at Lasham in Hampshire, from where they straggled back up to the north on the following day.

The conditions had prevented any assessment of results, which meant that another attempt on the dam would be necessary, and preparations were put in hand on the 9th to return with a force of 217 Lancasters early on the morning of the 10th. 49 Squadron detailed fourteen Lancasters, which took to the air between 04.15 and 04.39 on a cold and frosty morning only to be recalled with the rest of the force before it reached the English coast. The operation was rescheduled for early on the following morning, when 233 Lancasters and a Mosquito were to join five 8 Group Mosquitos at the target, but take-off was postponed until midday. The sixteen 49 Squadron participants departed Fulbeck between 12.27 and 12.41 with F/Ls Carlyle, Galloway and Lee the senior pilots on duty and encountered icing conditions at the French coast, before discovering that the weather in the target area was hardly an improvement on that of the previous day. Up to nine-tenths cloud with tops at 8,000 feet made life difficult for the Master Bomber, who tried to bring the crews down below the cloud base, some complying, while others were able to identify the aiming-point through a four-mile-long gap. The 49 Squadron crews attacked from 4,900 to 9,800 feet between 15.00 and 15.13 before the Master Bomber's "Dewdrop" instruction to cease bombing and go home. Post-raid reconnaissance revealed a number of hits on the stepped apron of the dam and cratering all around, but no actual breach had occurred. *(The cratering in the surrounding woodland remains visible to this day.)*

The crew of F/L Green took off for a night navigation exercise at 19.55 on the 11th and was never seen again. The belief was that they had flown into a towering bank of cumulonimbus cloud and had strayed over the Irish Sea, where icing conditions claimed them. The main operation on the night of the 15/16th was directed at Ludwigshafen in southern Germany, home to a number of I G Farben factories, which were among the most blatant exploiters of slave workers in the production of synthetic oil. The attack by 327 Lancasters and fourteen Mosquitos of 1, 6 and 8 Groups landed 450 high explosive bombs and incendiaries in the plant, causing massive damage and fires and was the greatest setback to production during the war. Further north, the Oppau factory ceased production completely for an extended period and five other industrial concerns also sustained severe damage, as did some residential areas. It was on the 16th that German ground forces began a new offensive in the Ardennes, in an attempt to break through the American lines and reach the port of Antwerp in what would become known as the Battle of the Bulge.

Munich had become something of a 5 Group preserve during the year, and a further operation against it was planned for the night of the 17/18th, which would turn out to be another night of heavy Bomber Command activity. The main raid was to be by more than five hundred aircraft, predominantly of 4 and 6 Groups on Duisburg, while 1 Group targeted Ulm with over three hundred Lancasters, leaving 5 Group to send 280 Lancasters some seventy miles beyond to the Bavarian capital city. 49 Squadron briefed seventeen crews, whose Lancasters were prepared for the 1,300-mile round-trip before departing Fulbeck between 16.11 and 16.41 with S/L Lace the senior pilot on duty. With him was a highly experienced all-officer crew containing no fewer than four flight lieutenants, one flying as second pilot. F/O Essenhigh and crew turned back at the Sussex coast after experiencing some kind of catastrophic failure that prevented them from jettisoning their bombs and forced the pilot to attempt an emergency landing on the beach at Worthing. PB355 exploded on impact at 17.55, vaporising all but one of the occupants and it would not be until well after the others had landed that the sad news reached Fulbeck. The others crossed the French coast near Berck-sur-Mer and reached the target to find generally clear skies and good visibility. They bombed on red and green TIs from 10,000 to 13,000 feet between 22.00 and 22.15 in accordance with the instructions of the Master Bomber, who declared himself satisfied with the results. They confirmed that the attack appeared to be effective with smoke rising through 7,000 feet and the resultant fires visible from a hundred miles into the return journey. As usual at this target, however, no local report emerged but Bomber Command claimed severe and widespread damage to the city.

On the following night, it was the turn of the distant Baltic port of Gdynia to play host to 5 Group, for which 49 Squadron put up sixteen Lancasters in an overall force of 236 of the type. The intention was to catch elements of the German fleet at anchor, in particular, the Lützow, and also to destroy harbour installations, as well as cause damage within the town. *(The original Lützow was actually never completed and had been sold to the Russian navy in 1940 as a hull minus superstructure. The pocket battleship, Deutschland, was renamed Lützow, to avoid humiliation for the nation should she be lost in battle.)* While this operation was in progress, fourteen other Lancasters of the group were to sneak in under cover of the main activity to deliver mines to the

Privet and Spinach gardens in Danzig (Gdansk) Bay. The 49 Squadron element departed Fulbeck between 16.42 and 17.15 with F/Ls Carlyle, Galloway, Milburn and Wright the senior pilots on duty. They reached the target area after an outward flight of almost five hours and found clear skies and good visibility in which the harbour and town could be picked out visually until a smoke screen was activated. In keeping with standard practice, the initial identification was by H2S before the illumination and marking proceeded according to plan and the 49 Squadron crews delivered their eight 1,000 pounders on red and green TIs from 11,000 to 15,400 feet between 21.54 and 22.18 in accordance with the Master Bomber's instructions and in the face of intense light flak. The smoke screen eventually obscured the Lützow, and crews with bombs still to deliver turned their attention upon the port area and town. It was not possible to make an accurate assessment of results, but bomb bursts were seen across the docks and quaysides. Reconnaissance photos confirmed that damage had been inflicted upon shipping, port installations and residential property in the waterfront districts, at a cost of four Lancasters.

Thick fog kept the crews on the ground on the 20th, and threatened to do so also on the 21st, but an operation was called on the basis that the weather over Scotland after midnight would be clear for returning aircraft, even if Lincolnshire remained fogbound. Sixteen 49 Squadron Lancasters were detailed for the 5 Group operation that night, and briefings took place while the ground crews did their best to get the aircraft ready in time. In briefing rooms across southern and south-eastern Lincolnshire, crews learned that their target would require them to retrace their recent steps to Germany's eastern Baltic region, although the I G Farben-owned Wintershall oil refinery at Politz, situated less than ten miles north of the port of Stettin, was some two hundred miles short of their trip to Gdynia. *(This location is often wrongly spelled Pölitz, which is a town in Germany's Schleswig-Holstein region at the western end of the Baltic. Politz is now Police in Poland.)* A force of 207 Lancasters and a single Mosquito was assembled, and, unusually, it included an element from 617 Squadron carrying Tallboys. The 49 Squadron element departed Fulbeck between 16.14 and 16.54 with no fewer than six pilots of flight lieutenant rank leading the way and each Lancaster carrying a cookie and twelve 500 pounders. F/O McRae and crew were well into the outward flight when PB349 was badly damaged by flak and returned to land at Milltown after being airborne for almost seven hours. F/L Wright and crew had been airborne for more than nine hours when they returned after severe icing had slowed their progress and left them with insufficient time to reach the target. Many of the others cut corners to keep up with the stream and found clear skies with ground haze over the refinery, which may have been a smoke screen. This important war-industry asset was protected by around fifty searchlights, and heavy flak accompanied the Lancasters as they ran in on the aiming-point. The markers fell some two thousand yards north-north-west of the plant, a situation recognized by the Master Bomber, but he was unable to persuade the backers-up to shift the point of aim accordingly and most of the bombing would miss the mark. The 49 Squadron element bombed on red and green TIs from 15,500 to 19,500 feet between 22.02 and 22.15 and observed most of the bomb bursts to be around the markers. Fires remained visible for almost a hundred miles into the return journey, the 49 Squadron crews landing at Dyce near Aberdeen. Photo-reconnaissance revealed that the plant had not been destroyed and it would be necessary to mount further raids.

The final wartime Christmas period was celebrated on 5 Group stations in traditional style and undisturbed by operational activity between the 22nd and Boxing Day, which was not the case for some other groups. The peace came to an end on the 26th, when crews from all groups were roused from any resulting stupor to attend briefings for operations against enemy troop positions at St Vith in Belgium. The German advance towards Antwerp had run out of steam after its earlier successes, and starved of fuel and ammunition, it was now attempting to withdraw back into Germany. 5 Group contributed twenty-six Lancasters to the force of 296 aircraft for the first joint operation since October. The target was situated within five miles of the German frontier and was found to be under clear skies with good visibility, which enabled crews to identify the aiming-point visually and by a red TI. When this became obscured by smoke, the Master Bomber ordered the crews to descend to 10,000 feet and bomb the upwind edge of the smoke.

On the 28th, the 49 Squadron crews of F/Ls Milburn and Nowrie and F/Os Lee, McPhee and Mallinson were told that they would be part of a 5 Group force of sixty-seven Lancasters targeting shipping, specifically the cruiser Köln, at Horten in Oslo Fjord. They departed Fulbeck between 19.26 and 19.43 and reached the target area after an outward flight of four-and-a-half hours. The skies were relatively clear and the visibility good, but a thin layer of alto-cumulus cloud at between 15,000 and 20,000 feet reduced the brightness of the moonlight and cast deceptive shadows on the water to prevent a clear identification of the target. The aiming-point was marked by Wanganui flares, but most crews followed the Master Bomber's instructions after establishing their own reference point. A patch of light flak to the north-east of the harbour mole was thought to be concealing a large naval unit, and this area was marked and bombed. Some crews would claim to have attacked a large vessel moving from this area in a southerly direction and other shipping in the harbour, all in the face of intense shipboard and shore-based light flak. The 49 Squadron quintet bombed from 4,500 to 8,000 feet between 23.48 and midnight, F/O Lee after making two passes, but claimed no direct hits and the operation produced inconclusive results.

The 29th dawned fine and frosty, and shortly after lunch, 5 Group sent eleven crews on daylight mining sorties in the Onions garden in Oslo harbour. 49 Squadron was not involved and would conduct its final operations of the year during the early hours of the New Year's Eve, when a dozen crews were briefed as part of a 5 Group force of 154 Lancasters to attack an enemy supply line at Houffalize in the Ardennes region of Belgium. They departed Fulbeck between 02.03 and 02.41 and found the target area under five to seven-tenths stratus cloud at 5,000 to 6,000 feet, with another layer of eight-tenths with tops at 9,000 feet. This rendered identification something of a challenge, despite which, the marking was punctual and accurate, although the red TIs were observed only by a proportion of the crews who chanced upon a gap in the clouds directly over the aiming-point. The 49 Squadron crews attacked from 6,500 to 12,000 feet between 05.03 and 05.12, the low height that of F/O Lee and crew, who were among a number to descend to below the cloud base, where they were able to confirm that the bombing was concentrated around the markers. Nevertheless, it would be deemed necessary to revisit this objective within a short time.

During the course of the month, the squadron carried out ten operations and dispatched 134 sorties for the loss of two Lancasters and crews. It had been another uncompromising year for the crews of 49 Squadron, which had seen the Command rise phoenix-like from the ashes of the dark days of the winter campaign to a point when the scent of victory was wafting in from the Continent. Much remained to be done, however, before the proud and tenacious enemy finally laid down his arms and further crews would be sacrificed in the remaining months of the war.

# January 1945

The final year of the war began with a flourish, as the Luftwaffe launched its ill-conceived and, ultimately, ill-fated Operation Bodenplatte (Baseplate) at first light on New Year's Day. The intention to destroy the Allied air forces on the ground at the recently liberated airfields in France, Holland and Belgium was only modestly realized, and it cost the German day fighter force around 250 aircraft. Many of the pilots were killed, wounded or fell into Allied hands, and it was a setback from which the Tagjagd would never fully recover, while the Allies could make good their losses within hours from their enormous stockpiles.

5 Group was also active that morning, having roused the crews early from their beds to attend briefings for an attack on the recently repaired Dortmund-Ems Canal near Ladbergen, for which 102 Lancasters and two Mosquitos were made ready. The 54 Base squadrons from Coningsby and Metheringham fell in line behind 83 Squadron, with the 55 Base squadrons from East Kirkby and Spilsby about three miles further back, and a third section, made up of 53 Base units from Waddington, Skellingthorpe and Bardney some twenty miles to the rear. They were allowed to catch up, putting the force two minutes behind schedule at point C, over the North Sea. It was between points C and D that the fighter escort was expected to join them, and, although it was not immediately apparent, it did eventually put in an appearance. The gaggles held together fairly well, although the controller would complain later that the legs were too short to keep them tight, and some aircraft were seen to break formation. When about eight minutes from the target, smoke from a Mosquito-laid red TI could be seen, which was assessed as being on the southern tip of the island between the two branches of the canal. It was clearly visible to all crews, who were able to home in on it without difficulty. A six-gun flak battery greeted their arrival with accurate salvoes, but this did not inhibit the bombing runs, and the impression was of an effective operation. On return, a number of 55 Base crews complained that the gaggle was too tight and put crews at risk from "friendly" bombs. The use of delay fuses prevented an immediate assessment of the results, but photo-reconnaissance revealed later that the canal had been breached again and the surrounding fields were flooded.

Operations for the day were not yet done for 5 Group, which now had an appointment with the Mittelland Canal at Gravenhorst, for which 152 Lancasters and five Mosquitos were made ready. 49 Squadron had not been required for the morning operation and had fourteen fully laden Lancasters lined up to depart Fulbeck between 16.28 and 16.56 with F/Ls Galloway, Milburn, Nowrie and Wright the senior pilots on duty. As they began their climb through fog, F/L Nowrie's a.s.i. failed and once at a safe height he headed for the jettison area before landing at Woodbridge. The others reached the target area to find that the clear conditions enjoyed during the morning raid nearby had persisted, and so accurate were the initial TIs and illumination, delivered visually or by H2S, that the third flare force was not required and was sent home. The main force was called in ahead of H-Hour at around 19.10, and the 49 Squadron element bombed on red TIs from 9,000 to 12,000 feet between 19.12 and 19.21. One of the perils of operating on New Year's Day was the risk of falling victim to trigger-happy American flak gunners, who had been spooked by the German raids at dawn and now fired at anything that moved, as a result of which, a number of RAF aircraft and crews would be lost to "friendly fire" incidents. The employment of predominantly delayed-action bombs again prevented an immediate assessment of results, but a highly successful operation was confirmed later by photo-reconnaissance. The 49 Squadron participants landed at Peterhead in Scotland and made their way home on the following morning.

The old enemy of Nuremberg was posted on the 2nd as the first major urban target of the New Year and would face a main force of 445 Lancasters drawn from 1, 3 and 6 Groups with a further sixty-nine Lancasters representing 8 Group to provide the marking and bombing support. 8 Group also contributed twenty-two Lancasters to a simultaneous attack by 351 Halifaxes of 4 and 6 Groups on two I G Farben chemicals plants, one in Ludwigshafen and the other close by in Oppau. Now that mobile Oboe stations had been set up on the Continent, both operations would also benefit from a Mosquito presence, seven for Nuremberg and twenty-two for Ludwigshafen. The two forces were to follow a similar route until dividing shortly before reaching Ludwigshafen, where the Nuremberg force would continue on towards the east for a further 140 miles. The success of the Ludwigshafen operation was confirmed by local reports that five hundred high-explosive bombs had fallen within the confines of the two production plants, along with many thousands of incendiaries. This had put an end to all production of synthetic oil, and adjacent industrial buildings, residential property and railway installations had also been destroyed. Nuremberg was left devastated by the loss of 4,640 houses, a large proportion of them apartment blocks, and more than four hundred industrial units were destroyed, and eighteen hundred people killed.

5 Group had remained on the ground during the above and many of its crews were called to briefing on the evening of the 4th to learn of a controversial attack planned against the small French town of Royan in the early hours of the 5th. The raid was in response to requests from Free French forces, which were laying siege to the town because of its location on the eastern bank at the mouth of the Gironde Estuary and in the way of an advance towards the port of Bordeaux. It was occupied by a German garrison, the commander of which had offered the inhabitants an opportunity to evacuate the area, but around two thousand had declined and would suffer the consequences. 1, 5 and 8 Groups put together a force of 347 Lancasters and seven Mosquitos, of which fourteen of the former represented 49 Squadron. They departed Fulbeck between 00.35 and 01.35 with F/Ls Nowrie and Winter the senior pilots on duty, each carrying a cookie and sixteen 500 pounders and were in the first of two waves heading for the unsuspecting target, separated by one hour. It was approaching 04.00 as they lined up for the bombing run in cloudless skies and excellent visibility, but the start of the attack was delayed for two minutes to allow misplaced markers to be corrected. A red TI went down at 04.01 very close to the aiming point, and another fell in the middle of the town near the beach, at which point, the Master Bomber called in the main force. The 49 Squadron crews carried out their attacks from 6,000 to 8,000 feet between 04.01 and 04.07 and witnessed a yellow oil fire at 04.08, which began to emit volumes of black smoke. This was just one of a number of large explosions created by the first phase of bombing, and the resultant fires would act as a beacon to the 1 Group force following behind. The attack destroyed about 85% of the town, and between five and eight hundred people lost their lives. In the event, the town was not taken, and it would be mid-April before the garrison surrendered.

5 Group was not involved in a major attack on Hannover by more than 650 aircraft on the night of the 5/6th, the first on this northern city since the series in the autumn of 1943. However, a rushed battle order came through to 5 Group stations at 18.30, which would lead to another late briefing and take-off for 131 crews, and it was actually between 00.20 and 00.59 on the 6th that nine 49 Squadron crews departed Fulbeck bound for a German supply column trapped at Houffalize in the

Belgian Ardennes. There were no senior pilots on duty as they made their way south on a clear night above low cloud, which, over the target, formed thin layers of eight to ten-tenths cover between 4,000 and 10,000 feet. The marker force crews were able to identify the aiming-point visually, and the first red Mosquito-laid TIs were seen to go down close together, followed by greens at H-3. They were backed up to leave a compact group of reds and greens visible by their glow through the clouds, and the Master Bomber, who was circling at 10,000 feet, called in the main force to bomb. Five of the 49 Squadron crews complied from 9,000 to 11,400 feet between 03.03 and 03.08, while the remainder were among around a third of the force to retain their bombs in accordance with instructions at briefing if they failed to identify the aiming-point. Afterwards, one of the marker crews descended to 3,500 feet between the cloud layers, where they saw two large columns of smoke, the source of which could not be identified. Post-raid reconnaissance confirmed that the target had been bombed with great accuracy, and the success had been gained for the loss of just two Lancasters.

A major operation against Munich was planned for the 7th, for which a two-wave force of 645 aircraft was drawn from all five of the Lancaster-equipped groups. 5 Group, which was unused to sharing this target, would lead the way with 213 Lancasters and three Mosquitos, leaving the second wave to follow on two hours later, the tanks of the heavy brigade containing sufficient fuel for a nine-hour round-trip. The 49 Squadron element of twelve Lancasters departed Fulbeck as dusk was descending between 16.27 and 17.01 with F/Ls Carlyle, Hay, Mellor and Milburn the senior pilots on duty and set course for Gravesend to make landfall on the French coast near Berck-sur-Mer. They entered Germany south of Strasbourg and encountered broken medium-level cloud at 14,000 feet above the target, with haze or thin cloud below, by which time the Master Bomber had made a visual identification of the aiming-point and sent the first two primary blind markers in to deliver their TIs at the same time, thirty seconds ahead of the planned opening of the attack. The flare force went in immediately afterwards and illuminated the city very effectively, allowing ground detail to be identified. Red TIs went down west and east of the River Isar, bracketing the aiming-point, and the Master Bomber ordered the backers up to drop their TIs between the reds, after which, the next batch of flares formed a circle around the aiming-point. The main force was then called in and the 49 Squadron participants delivered their loads accurately within the specified area from 18,000 to 20,000 feet between 20.23 and 20.42. F/L Hay and crew suffered a hang-up, and while completing a circuit to come round again, the bombs fell away and took the bomb doors with them. F/O Fricker and crew had made their first pass over the aiming point as supporters of the marker force and were preparing for their own bombing run as the Master Bomber called a halt at 20.49. To their credit, they brought their bomb load home. The city was seen to be burning well as the force withdrew, and the glow of fires could be seen from up to 130 miles away. Two hours after the 5 Group attack, in what would become an established pattern, the 1, 3, 6 and 8 Group force arrived to complete the destruction of the central and some industrial districts, and this proved to be the final large-scale attack of the war on Munich. Fourteen Lancasters failed to return, and among them was 49 Squadron's PB586, which was one of a number of Lancasters to fall on the south-eastern outskirts of Paris. There were no survivors from the crew of F/O Bolter who were on their fourth operation together.

With the exception of 617 Squadron, 5 Group remained on the ground for the ensuing six days, with snow-clearing providing exercise for all capable of wielding a shovel. The crews were, therefore, no doubt relieved to be called to briefing on the 13th, when they learned that 5 Group would be operating alone against the Wintershall oil refinery at Politz near Stettin. The plant had sustained damage in the previous attack in December, but production had not been halted, and a force of 218 Lancasters and seven Mosquitos was assembled for the return, of which a dozen of the Lancasters were provided by 49 Squadron. Another dusk departure saw them taking off between 16.15 and 16.42 with F/Ls Carlyle, Hay, Mellor and Nowrie the senior pilots on duty. They crossed the North Sea at 1,500 feet in accordance with instructions to not climb until approaching the Danish coast at 19.30. They arrived in the target area on time to find clear skies with slight haze, by which time the blind marker crews had identified the target by means of H2S and had delivered their green TIs in a line approaching the target shortly after 22.00. The illuminators then dropped their flares, which caused ground detail to stand out, highlighted by the snow on the ground. A blind-bombing attack had been planned, but because of the excellence of the conditions, Mosquitos were able to go in at low level, after which the main force was called in and the 49 Squadron crews bombed from 14,000 to 16,500 feet between 22.17 and 22.33 to help seal the fate of the plant. Photographic reconnaissance confirmed that the site had been severely damaged, and Bomber Command claimed it to be in ruins.

Oil targets would continue to dominate during the remainder of the month, and a two-phase attack was planned for the following night against the I G Farbenindustrie A G Merseburg-Leuna refinery, which lay some 250 miles from the Dutch frontier and five hundred miles from the bomber bases of eastern England. As previously mentioned, it was one of many similar sites situated in an arc on the western side of Leipzig from north to south. The first phase would be carried out by 5 Group, which detailed 210 Lancasters and nine Mosquitos, ten of the former contributed by 49 Squadron. They took off from Fulbeck between 16.27 and 16.37 with F/Ls Milburn and Winter the senior pilots on duty and headed for the Sussex coast near Brighton to begin the Channel crossing for the southern approach to eastern Germany. They reached the target area to find clear skies but poor vertical visibility due to a layer of haze, which, in the event, was no hindrance to the primary blind markers, whose job was to establish their position over the aiming-point by means of H2S. They delivered their TIs from 18,000 feet, after which, the first element of the flare force went in. The Master Bomber called for ground marking only, which was carried out by the low-level Mosquito element, and by 20.50, he was satisfied and sent the marker aircraft home. The main force crews produced what appeared to be concentrated bombing, those from 49 Squadron dropping their loads of a cookie and nine 500 pounders each onto red and green TIs from 14,000 to 16,750 feet between 21.00 and 21.11 with a fourteen-second overshoot in accordance with the Master Bomber's instructions. Returning crews reported explosions and smoke rising upwards as they turned for home, leaving behind them a beacon for the second wave of 363 Lancasters and five Mosquitos of 1, 6 and 8 Groups following three hours behind. They would add to the massive destruction, which effectively put the plant out of action for the remainder of the war.

Feverish activity across the Command on the 16th prepared more than twelve hundred aircraft for action, the majority to participate in four major operations that night, three to target oil refineries and the largest to deliver an area attack on the eastern city of Magdeburg, which also contained the Braunkohle A G Bergius process oil (hydrogenation) plant located in the Rothensee district to the north of the city centre. The independent 3 and 5 Groups were handed the refineries at Wanne-Eickel in the Ruhr and Brüx in north-western Czechoslovakia respectively, leaving 320 Halifaxes of 4 and 6 Groups to take care of Magdeburg and 283 Lancasters of 1 and 6 Groups to ply their trade at Zeitz-Tröglitz, the location of another Braunkohle-Benzin A G plant, situated some twenty miles south-west of Leipzig. Brüx, now known as Most in the Czech Republic, lay some 140 miles due south of Berlin and it was for this destination that thirteen 49 Squadron crews were briefed as part of a 5 Group force of 224 Lancasters and six Mosquitos, which would be accompanied by seven 101 Squadron ABC Lancasters for RCM duties. They were each carrying a cookie and nine 500 pounders for what would be a nine-hour round-trip and departed Fulbeck between 17.37 and 17.56 with F/Ls Carlyle, Mellor and Winter the senior pilots on duty. There were ten early returns from the force, but none from among the 49 Squadron contingent, which reached the target area over nine to ten-tenths low cloud with tops at 3,000 feet. This interfered with the low-level marking system, which began with four primary blind markers identifying the target by means of H2S and dropping green TIs, and they were followed by the first illuminators, who also relied on H2S to deliver their flares. It seems that a number of Mosquitos managed to get below the cloud base to put red TIs onto the aiming-point and reported that the greens were among the oil tanks. However, the reds were not generally visible through the clouds and the Master Bomber called for skymarking, while informing flare force 3 that it would not be required. The 49 Squadron participants bombed either on the glow of the red TIs or on the cascading greens from 14,000 to 16,700 feet between 22.30 and 22.42 and observed many explosions and large columns of thick, black smoke emerging through the cloud tops. Photo-reconnaissance would confirm that massive damage had been inflicted upon the plant, and a severe setback delivered to the enemy's oil production.

There would be no further operations for 5 Group during the month, although a number would be posted before being cancelled. The squadron spent the period inducting new crews, attending lectures, training, and during the last few days, clearing snow from the runways. A major operation on the 28th involved 602 aircraft from 1, 4, 6 and 8 Groups divided into two forces separated by three hours, each with its own specific target. The first phase, by 226 aircraft, was to be directed at the marshalling yards in the town of Kornwestheim, situated just beyond the northern boundary of Stuttgart, while the second phase would target the Hirth aero-engine factory at Zuffenhausen, some two miles to the south. The attacks were not entirely successful and scattered bombs across much of the city and in open country while causing some useful industrial damage.

During the course of the month the squadron operated on seven occasions and dispatched eighty-four sorties for the loss of a single Lancaster and its crew.

# February 1945

The weather at the start of February provided difficult conditions for marking and bombing, particularly for 5 Group, and a number of operations would struggle to achieve their aims in the face of thick, low cloud and strong winds. 5 Group was back in harness immediately at the start of the new month following the long lay-off, and 271 Lancaster and eleven Mosquito crews were called to briefings on all 5 Group stations on the 1st to learn that their target was to be the marshalling yards in the town of Siegen, situated some fifty miles east of Cologne. This was a 5 Group show, and was one of three major operations planned for the night, the others, by larger forces, taking place at Ludwigshafen and Mainz further into southern Germany. A high wind during the night had helped to clear some of the snow, and the sixteen 49 Squadron Lancasters took off without incident between 16.04 and 16.29 with F/Ls Carlyle, Galloway, McPhee and Winter the senior pilots on duty and each Lancaster carrying either twelve 1,000 pounders or a cookie and sixteen 500 pounders. They all reached the target area shortly after 19.00 and encountered ten-tenths cloud at between 3,000 and 7,000 feet, which caused problems for the flare and marker force, some of which were finding it difficult to obtain a clear H2S image on their screens. Eventually, one of the primary blind markers ran in and dropped green TIs at 19.05 from 15,000 feet, and their glow was visible through the clouds. This prompted the first flares, followed by an attempt to mark at low-level with red TIs, which were not visible through the clouds, and when the Master Bomber called for skymarking at 19.10, the remaining illuminators were superfluous to requirements and were sent home. The bombing phase was put back by four minutes until 19.20, forcing crews to either orbit or dogleg to waste time if they were still on approach, and then instructions were issued to aim at the skymarkers, which were being driven by the strong wind across the intended aiming-point and beyond the target. The glow of red target indicators was faintly visible through the clouds, but this was most likely a decoy fire site prepared by the Germans. It attracted many bomb loads, perhaps some from the 49 Squadron participants, who bombed from 8,000 to 11,750 feet between 19.20 and 19.27, contributing to what became a widely scattered raid. Much of the bombing fell into open and wooded country, and although the railway station sustained damage, the marshalling yards escaped.

The next briefing revealed the bad news that a tour of operations was to be increased again to thirty-six sorties. Thirteen 49 Squadron crews were in attendance at 15.00 on a drizzly afternoon on the 2nd, to be told further that the night's operation was to be against Karlsruhe in southern Germany. This was to be another 5 Group effort involving 250 Lancasters and eleven Mosquitos and was again only one of three major operations taking place. Wiesbaden was to receive its one and only major raid of the war at the hands of almost five hundred aircraft, while a 320-strong predominantly Halifax force dealt with an oil plant at Wanne-Eickel in the Ruhr. The 49 Squadron element departed Fulbeck between 19.39 and 20.38, the latter time that of F/O Watson and crew, whose take-off had been delayed by another aircraft bogging down. F/Ls Carlyle, McPhee, Milburn and Winter were the senior pilots on duty as the 49 Squadron contingent headed for the assembly point over Reading, before setting course for the French coast. F/O McCrae and crew ran into severe icing conditions at 4,000 feet as they climbed over the Channel and abandoned their sortie. The winds turned out to be lighter than forecast, and this caused a change in route, which now took the force directly from Reading to the target, straddling the Franco-Belgian frontier all the way to Germany, where they encountered heavy cloud between 3,000 and 15,000 feet. The flare force arrived over the target at 17,500 to 18,500 feet between 23.03 and 23.28 and tried to perform their assigned tasks in difficult conditions, some with malfunctioning H2S equipment. The Mosquito crews attempted to establish an aiming-point, but the illumination was not getting through to the ground, and even had they dropped red TIs, it is unlikely that they would have been visible. At 23.11 the Master Bomber called for skymarking and sent the Mosquitos and remaining illuminators home as the 49 Squadron crews began their bombing runs to attack the glow of markers from 14,000 to 16,250 feet between 23.17 and 23.27 in accordance with instructions. F/O Watson and crew were still forty miles short of the target when the Master Bomber called a halt, but their efforts would count as a completed sortie. This final raid of the war on Karlsruhe was a complete failure and cost fourteen Lancasters, four of them from Fulbeck's 189 Squadron.

While the frontier towns of Goch and Cleves were being pounded by the other groups ahead of the advancing British XXX Corps on the night of the 7/8th, 5 Group returned to the Dortmund-Ems Canal at Ladbergen with 177 Lancasters and eleven Mosquitos, the heavy brigade carrying delayed action bombs. 49 Squadron made ready a dozen Lancasters, which departed Fulbeck between 20.36 and 21.30 with S/L Wright the senior pilot on duty. They reached the target area to find seven to ten-tenths cloud at between 6,000 and 9,000 feet and delivered their fourteen 1,000 pounders each from 11,500 to 12,000 feet between 23.59 and 00.10 onto what were believed to be accurate TIs observed through gaps in the cloud and in accordance with the Master Bomber's instructions. It turned out to be a rare unsuccessful attack on this target, photographic reconnaissance revealing that the bombs had fallen into fields and had failed to cause any breach.

Fifteen 49 Squadron crews found themselves at briefing on the following day for another long round-trip to the Wintershall oil refinery at Politz, as part of a 5 Group force of 227 Lancasters and seven Mosquitos. They were to act as the first wave in a two-phase attack, which would be completed two hours later by 248 Lancasters from 1 and 8 Groups. The 49 Squadron element departed Fulbeck between 16.30 and 17.06 with F/Ls Carlyle, Galloway, McPhee and Milburn the senior pilots on duty. The blind markers and the flare force crews went in at 13,000 to 14,500 feet between 21.03 and 21.15 to carry out their assigned tasks in the face of an ineffective smoke screen, and fierce night-fighter activity was evident to the main force crews as they reached the target area to find clear skies and excellent visibility. The 49 Squadron crews identified ground detail in the light of the illuminating flares before delivering their loads onto red TIs from 9,000 to 12,000 feet between 21.16 and 21.33 with a thirteen second overshoot in accordance with the Master Bomber's instructions. SW274 was flipped onto its back by the detonation of a flak shell but W/O Cluer regained control and during a check of the crew, the mid-upper gunner, Sgt Wiggins, was found to be lifeless, possibly asphyxiated by his communications cord. A number of crews from other squadrons reported up to six explosions and smoke rising through 3,000 feet as they turned away to the west, confident in the quality of their work. Ten Lancasters failed to arrive back to home airspace, and among them was 49 Squadron's ME353, which came down in the target area killing F/L Galloway and all but his mid-upper gunner, who was taken prisoner. The Galloway crew had established themselves as one of the mainstays of the squadron and were lost on their twenty-sixth operation together.

Briefings took place on the 13th for the first round of Operation Thunderclap, the Churchill-inspired offensive against Germany's eastern cities, which was devised partly to act in support of the advancing Russians, and also as a demonstration to Stalin of RAF air power, should he turn against the Allies after the war. The historic and culturally significant city of Dresden was selected to open the offensive in another two-phase affair, with a 5 Group force of 246 Lancasters and nine Mosquitos leading the way, to be followed three hours later by 529 Lancasters of 1, 3, 6 and 8 Groups. It had proved to be a successful policy thus far, with the 5 Group low-level marking system and main force attacks providing a beacon for the second force, and should it be required on this night, 8 Group would provide any necessary marking for phase two from high level. The 49 Squadron contingent of seventeen Lancasters took off between 18.10 and 18.25 with S/L Wright the senior pilot on duty, and the crews had absolutely no concept of the ramifications of the operation, both in terms of its outcome on the ground and its hysterical aftermath. Dresden was Germany's seventh largest city and its largest remaining largely un-bombed built-up area, which, according to American sources, contained more than a hundred factories and fifty thousand workers contributing to the war effort. It was also an important railway hub, to the extent that the marshalling yards had been attacked twice in late 1944 by the USAAF.

The heavy force was two hours out when W/C Maurice Smith of 54 Base, the Master Bomber for the 5 Group attack, lifted off the Woodhall Spa runway at a few minutes before 20.00 hours in Mosquito KB401 AZ-E, a 627 Squadron aircraft, and he was followed away by eight others from 627 Squadron. The heavy brigade and the Mosquitos arrived in the target area at the same time to encounter three layers of cloud between 3,000 and 5,000 feet, 6,000 to 8,000 feet and 15,000 to 16,000 feet, but otherwise good visibility. The first primary blind marker crew delivered green TIs from 15,000 feet at 22.03 and was followed in by the flare force, which lit the way for the low-level Mosquitos. The main force Lancasters were carrying eight hundred tons of bombs, mostly in the form either of a cookie and twelve 500 pounders or one 2,000 pounder and fourteen cluster bombs, which the 49 Squadron crews delivered from 12,000 to 13,800 feet between 22.12 and 22.22 onto the glow of red TIs in accordance with the Master Bomber's instructions. As far as the crews were concerned, this was no different from any other attack, and the fires visible for more than a hundred miles into the return journey nothing out of the ordinary.

By the time that the second force of 1, 3, 6 and 8 Group Lancasters arrived over Dresden three hours after 5 Group, the skies had cleared, and the fires created by the earlier attack provided the expected reference point. A further eighteen hundred tons of bombs rained down onto the historic and beautiful old city, setting off the same chain of events that had devastated parts of Hamburg in July 1943 and a number of other cities since. Dresden's population had been swelled by masses of refugees fleeing from the eastern front, and many were engulfed in the ensuing firestorm, which was still burning on the following morning, when three hundred American bombers carried out a separate attack under the umbrella of a fighter escort and completed the destruction. There were claims that RAF aircraft had strafed the streets and open spaces to increase the level of terror, and such accusations abound in the city to this day. In fact, American fighters were responsible, and were trying to add to the general confusion and chaos. Initial propaganda-inspired reports from the Office of the Propaganda Minister, Joseph Goebbels, falsely claimed a death toll of 250,000 people, but an accurate figure of twenty-five thousand has been settled upon since.

The destruction of Dresden has been used by some in this country also as a weapon with which to denigrate Bomber Command and Harris, and label them as war criminals. Curiously, no accusations have been levelled at the Americans. It should also be understood that Harris had no interest in attacking Dresden and had to be nagged by Chief-of-the-Air-Staff Portal to fulfil Churchill's wishes. The aircrew simply did the job asked of them, and the Dresden raid was no different from any other attack on a city. The death toll at Hamburg was much higher, and yet, there has been no similar outcry. The legacy of this operation served to deny Harris and the men under his Command their due recognition for the massive part they played in the ultimate victory, and only in recent times has a monument been erected in Green Park in London and a campaign clasp awarded, sadly, far too little and far too late for the majority. Churchill, with his eyes set on a peacetime election, betrayed Harris and the Command in a typical politically motivated U-turn, in which he accused Harris of bombing solely for the purpose of inflicting terror. In the post-war honours, Harris was the only commander in the field to be omitted.

Round two of Thunderclap was planned for the following night, when Chemnitz was posted as the target for 717 aircraft drawn from 1, 3, 4, 6 and 8 Groups, while 224 Lancasters and eight Mosquitos of 5 Group targeted an oil refinery in the small town of Rositz, situated twenty-five miles due south of Leipzig and thirty miles north-west of Chemnitz. Eighteen 49 Squadron Lancasters were made ready, and they all departed Fulbeck safely between 16.30 and 17.07 with F/Ls McPhee, Milburn and Williams the senior pilots on duty. They pushed on across Germany to be greeted by six to ten-tenths thin cloud in the target area in two layers, one at 6,000 to 8,000 feet, and the other at 10,000 to 12,000 feet, but the primary blind marker made a good run on H2S at 15,000 feet at 20.48 to drop green TIs, and the illuminators followed up between 20.51 and 20.58 from a similar height. The main force crews arriving on time carried out support runs with the marker element, before being called in to bomb at 21.07, those from 49 Squadron crews carrying out their attacks on red and green TIs or on their glow from 7,500 to 12,000 feet between 21.00 and 21.20. Three or four large fires were evident in the oil plant and black smoke was rising through 5,000 feet as the force turned away. It was established afterwards, that the southern part of the site had been damaged but it would be necessary to return to finish the job. The Chemnitz raid had been compromised by adverse weather conditions and it would be March before success was achieved against this target.

An oil refinery at Böhlen was posted as the target on the 19th for a 5 Group force of 264 Lancasters and six Mosquitos. It was another of the collection of similar plants in the Leipzig area and some ten miles north of Rositz, for which 49 Squadron dispatched nineteen Lancasters in a late take-off between 23.31 and 00.12 with S/L Wright the senior pilot on duty. They all completed the three-and-a-half-hour flight out and would meet up with the later-departing Mosquito element at the target, which included the Master Bomber for the occasion, 54 Base's W/C Benjamin, who was flying the same Mosquito used by W/C Smith at Dresden six nights earlier. They encountered ten-tenths cloud over the target in two layers at 5,000 to 8,000 feet and 10,000 to 14,000 feet, and this would introduce a challenging element to the operation. The illuminators went in at around 15,000 feet between 04.05 and 04.13, and the VHF chatter suggested that a Mosquito had been able to mark a factory building with a red TI, and that that had been backed up. The main force was called in, before W/C Benjamin's VHF was suddenly cut off and his Deputy took over. It would be established later, that the Master Bomber's Mosquito had been shot down by flak and that W/C Benjamin DFC & Bar had died alongside his navigator. The 49 Squadron crews carried out their attacks in accordance with confusing instructions, doing so from 8,000 to 18,000 feet between 04.16 and 04.27, aiming mostly at the glow in the cloud of red and green TIs. Post-raid reconnaissance revealed only superficial damage to the site, which would have to be attacked again.

The following night, the 20th, proved to be a busy one, with more than five hundred Lancasters targeting Dortmund, while 268 Halifaxes from 4 and 6 Groups provided the heavy elements for raids on Rhenania-Ossag oil refineries in Düsseldorf and Monheim. 5 Group, meanwhile, prepared itself for a further attempt on the Mittelland Canal at Gravenhorst, for which ten 49 Squadron crews were briefed as part of an overall force of 154 Lancasters and eleven Mosquitos. They departed Fulbeck between 21.46 and 22.07 with W/C Botting and S/L Walker the senior pilots on duty, and all reached the target area to find ten-tenths cloud between them and the aiming-point. The primary blind marker crew succeeded in delivering two green TIs by H2S from 12,000 feet at 00.53, and they fell on the starboard side of the canal. After the flare force went in, the Mosquito element descended to 400 feet but could not identify the aiming-point, and just before H-Hour, the Master Bomber sent the markers home, to be followed almost immediately by the main force as he abandoned the operation.

The operation was rescheduled for twenty-four hours later, when Duisburg and Worms were also to be attacked by heavy forces of 362 and 349 aircraft respectively. 5 Group detailed 165 Lancasters and twelve Mosquitos, and among those attending the briefing at Coningsby was G/C Evans-Evans, the station commander, who would be taking the bulk of the 83 Squadron commanding officer's highly experienced crew with him. Evans-Evans was 43 and a larger-than-life character, who had commanded 115 Squadron for a spell earlier in the war during its Wellington era and had never lost the enthusiasm to be "one of the boys" and take part in operations. A number of years of good living had widened his girth, and it must have been a struggle to fit into the cramped confines of a Lancaster cockpit. The eleven 49 Squadron participants took off between 17.01 and 17.25 with F/L Milburn the senior pilot on duty and soon lost the services of F/O Eltis, whose Gee box caught fire as they climbed out. While extinguishing the blaze the navigator was splashed by fluid, and uncertain what the effects of that might be, it was decided to return to base. The others reached the target area to find moonlight beaming down from clear skies with some ground haze. One of the primary blind markers was able to deliver his green TIs two minutes late because of a change in the wind, and they fell about a mile south of the aiming-point, quite close to the Wet Triangle meeting point of the Mittelland and Dortmund-Ems Canals. After the flare force had done its job, the Mosquitos delivered their red TIs, which were backed up successfully, before the main force was called in at 20.25. The 49 Squadron crews released their loads of thirteen 1,000 pounders each from 8,200 to 9,800 feet between 20.33 and 20.40 but could not assess the outcome because of the use of long-delay fuses. The presence of night-fighters was clearly evident by the number of combats taking place, and among nine missing Lancasters were two belonging to 49 Squadron. NG327 was shot down by a night-fighter and crashed north-west of Mehr, eight miles north-west of Wesel, killing F/O Smith RNZAF and four of his crew. The flight engineer and bomb-aimer were taken into captivity, and the latter lost his life when hit during an Allied strafing attack on the 4th of April. PB568 came down in the German/Dutch border region and all but the rear gunner from F/O Mallinson's crew survived, four to be taken into captivity, while the navigator and wireless operator retained their freedom. They were almost at the end of their tour and had completed thirty-five sorties together. Among the other missing Lancasters was the one belonging to 83 Squadron containing G/C Evans-Evans and seven others. Only the rear gunner survived, and, among those killed was the twenty-two-year-old navigator, S/L Wishart DSO, DFC & Bar, who had completed sixty-one operations in Lancasters with 97 (Straits Settlement) Squadron and eighteen in Mosquitos as navigator to Master Bombers. G/C Ingham was left deeply saddened by the loss of his crew.

The 5 Group operation called on the 23rd was to involve seventy-three Lancasters and ten Mosquitos in an attack on what was believed to be a U-Boot base at Horten in Oslo Fjord, although whether or not a U-Boot base actually existed is uncertain. 49 Squadron made ready sixteen Lancasters and dispatched them from Fulbeck between 17.15 and 17.55 with S/L Walker the senior pilot on duty. The low-level Mosquito force had to negotiate intense light flak, but that was the only defensive activity, and the heavy brigade faced no searchlights, heavy flak or night-fighters as it failed to locate any shipping and aimed instead at the port and harbour installations. The 49 Squadron crews bombed from 8,000 to 10,500 feet between 20.30 and 21.00, and the last was ten minutes into the return flight when observing black smoke rising through 10,000 feet. A local report described heavy damage in the port area and a shipyard, and the sinking of a tanker and floating crane. While that was in progress, ten Lancasters from 5 Group sneaked in under cover of the main event to mine the waters of the Onions garden in Oslo harbour, a little further north.

Meanwhile, some 770 miles to the south, a force of 366 Lancasters, plus one from the Film Unit, and thirteen Mosquitos drawn from 1, 6 and 8 Groups had been sent against the city of Pforzheim, situated in southern Germany between Karlsruhe to the north-west and Stuttgart to the south-east. This would be the first area raid on the city, which was known as a centre for jewellery and watch manufacture but was believed by the Allies to be involved in the production of precision instruments in support of Germany's war effort. They were greeted by clear skies and bright moonlight in the target area, and the thin veil of ground haze proved to be no impediment as the first red Oboe TIs went down at 19.52, to be followed quickly by illuminator flares and salvoes of concentrated reds and greens. Fires rapidly took hold until the whole town north of the river looked like a sea of flames, and by 20.06, the fires were too dazzling for the TIs to be visible and the Master Bomber ordered the smoke to be bombed. The raid lasted twenty-two minutes, during which 1,825 tons of bombs fell into the built-up area, reducing 83% of it to ruins and setting off a firestorm in which 17,600 people lost their lives. This was the highest death toll to result from a single attack on a German city after Hamburg (40,000) and Dresden (25,000). It was during this operation that the final Victoria Cross was earned by a member of RAF Bomber Command. It went posthumously to the Master Bomber from 582 Squadron, Captain Ed Swales of the South African Air Force, who continued to control the attack in a Lancaster severely damaged by a night-fighter, before sacrificing his life to allow his crew to abandon the stricken aircraft.

A daylight attack on the Dortmund-Ems Canal was planned for the afternoon of the 24th, and would involve 166 Lancasters and five Mosquitos, eighteen of the former provided by 617 Squadron with Tallboys on board, while Fulbeck remained inactive. The force formed into gaggles and reached the target with an 11 Group fighter escort to encounter ten-tenths cloud with tops at between 4,000 and 9,000 feet, at which point the Master Bomber abandoned the operation and sent the force home with its bombs. Once back home at their respective stations, crews complained about the unsatisfactory forming up of Base gaggles, which had been generally chaotic. During the course of the month, 49 Squadron took part in ten operations and dispatched 147 sorties for the loss of three Lancasters and their crews and one additional crew member.

# March 1945

The new month would see the Command bludgeon its way across Germany, concentrating on oil, rail and road targets, along with the few towns still boasting a built-up area. Mannheim was raided for the last time in numbers by a large force from 1, 6 and 8 Groups on the 1st, while 5 Group remained at home. On the 2nd, Cologne was pounded for the final time, first by a force of seven hundred aircraft, which inflicted huge destruction across the city, particularly west of the Rhine, and later by a 3 Group force, of which only fifteen bombed because of a faulty G-H station in England. The city ceased to function, thereafter, and was still paralyzed when American forces marched in four days later. Just when it seemed that German resistance to air attack might end,

March would prove that the defenders were still capable of mounting a challenge, even though they were stretched beyond their capacity to protect every corner of the Reich.

5 Group opened its March account with a return to the Ladbergen aqueduct section of the Dortmund-Ems Canal on the evening of the 3rd, for which 212 Lancasters and ten Mosquitos were made ready. A dozen 49 Squadron crews attended briefing to learn of their part in the main event and departed Fulbeck between 18.19 and 18.37 with W/C Botting and S/L Wright the senior pilots on duty and each crew sitting on thirteen 1,000 pounders. F/O Mersey and crew had just crossed the Dutch/German frontier west of Duisburg and were taking evasive action to escape the clutches of searchlight cones when the pilot fainted. The bomb-aimer took over the controls and flew the Lancaster back to England, by which time the pilot had recovered sufficiently to complete the landing at Tilstock in Shropshire. The others encountered eight to ten-tenths cloud in the target area at between 3,500 and 6,000 feet, and it was noted that the defences had been strengthened since the last attack and were throwing up a curtain of intense light flak as high as 15,000 feet. H2S allowed the two 83 Squadron primary blind marker crews to locate the canal and deliver their green TIs from 14,000 feet at 21.47 and 21.49, and the first illuminators went in a minute later to light the way for the Mosquitos, after which, a large red glow could be seen through the clouds. At 21.59, the Master Bomber called in the main force to bomb on the glow or on sight of the TIs through gaps in the thin cloud, and the 49 Squadron crews complied from 8,200 to 10,000 feet between 22.01 and 22.07. They contributed to the breaching of both branches, which rendered the waterway unnavigable and out of action for the remainder of the war.

The Luftwaffe mounted Operation Gisella on this night, sending some two hundred intruders to catch the bombers as they prepared to land, and they succeeded in shooting down twenty for the loss of three of their own. The Fulbeck crews were warned of the danger and a 189 Squadron Lancaster was one of two 5 Group Lancasters to fall victim.

Nineteen 49 Squadron crews attended briefing on the 5th, to learn that 5 Group would be sending 248 Lancasters and ten Mosquitos back to Böhlen for another crack at the synthetic oil refinery. A simultaneous operation by a Thunderclap force of 760 aircraft would attempt to redress the recent failure at Chemnitz, some thirty-five miles to the south. Take-off from Fulbeck was accomplished without incident between 16.49 and 17.36 with a whole host of flight lieutenants representing the senior pilots on duty and all reached the target area, some after climbing above 15,000 feet to escape icing conditions. Ten-tenths cloud lay over the target in layers between 2,000 and 11,000 feet but the uncertainty of prevailing conditions on arrival had been anticipated and two marking plans prepared, low-level and skymarking. The lead primary blind marker made his first run at 14,000 feet to drop green TIs at 21.40 and although he did not see them burst because of the cloud, he thought that the illuminator flares were well-placed. Some of the marker crews experienced H2S difficulties and not all were able to pinpoint on Leipzig for the run-in. This meant that they were unsure of their position, and when the Master Bomber called for Wanganui flares at 21.45, they withheld them rather than risk dropping them inaccurately and attracting some of the bombing. A large explosion was witnessed at 21.50, and three minutes later, Wanganui flares were observed by the approaching main force crews. Eighteen of the 49 Squadron participants delivered their cookie and eleven 500 pounders each from 9,000 to 13,300 feet between 21.53 and 22.10, observing another large explosion at 21.57. The Master Bomber called a halt at 22.01 and sent everyone home before F/O Elkington and crew had bombed, and they left evidence of fires and smoke behind them. Post-raid reconnaissance revealed extensive damage to the coal-drying plant and some hits in other areas of the site, but it was still not a knockout blow. Meanwhile, the Thunderclap force had succeeded in inflicting severe fire damage in central and southern districts of Chemnitz.

The target posted on 5 Group stations on the 6th was the town and port area of Sassnitz, located on the Baltic Island of Rügen, about thirty miles north of Peenemünde, a region with memories of heavy casualties sustained by 5 Group in August 1943. The two-fold purpose of the operation was to destroy the port installations and facilities and sink shipping to render it unusable as a refuge for escaping Kriegsmarine units. 150 Lancasters and seven Mosquitos were made ready, thirteen of the former by 49 Squadron, which departed Fulbeck between 18.00 and 18.22 with F/Ls Babb, Bromfield and Carlyle the senior pilots on duty. F/O Hammond and crew became aware of a serious fuel leak and decided to turn back, leaving the others to reach the target area and find five to nine-tenths drifting cloud with tops in places at 8,000 feet. An 83 Squadron blind marker made a run at 22.50 to drop green TIs over the port from 12,000 feet, and the flare force maintained illumination of the town and outer harbour for the next twenty-five minutes. Apart from a short break, when cloud slid across the aiming-point, the markers remained visible to the main force crews, and those from 49 Squadron bombed on red TIs from 8,000 to 10,500 feet between 23.01 and 23.14. Bombing activity ceased at H+18, and those with bombs still aboard took them home. Three large ships identified in the harbour were attacked, and, according to post-raid reconnaissance, sunk, and there was also extensive damage in the northern part of the town.

It was back to the oil campaign for 5 Group on the following night, for an attack on a refinery at Harburg, south of Hamburg, for which a force of 234 Lancasters and seven Mosquitos was made ready. They would not be alone over Germany, however, as more than a thousand other aircraft would be engaged against similar targets at Dessau and Hemmingstedt and in minor and support operations. 49 Squadron provided eighteen Lancasters, which took off between 17.40 and 18.29 with F/Ls Carlyle, Mellor, Milburn and Winter the senior pilots on duty and arrived over the target to find eight-tenths thin cloud and red and yellow target indicators clearly visible, which they bombed in accordance with the Master Bomber's instructions with a seven-second overshoot from 10,750 to 12,200 feet between 21.58 and 22.09. F/O Elkington and crew were still approaching the target at 22.09 when the call came from the Master Bomber to cease the attack and having turned about, they were heading westwards in ME471 about to cross Jade Bight at 1,000 feet when they were sprayed by light flak, which killed the flight engineer and wounded the pilot. A check of crew positions revealed that the bomb-aimer had left the aircraft either by design or accident and it was learned later that he had failed to survive. Returning crews reported bomb bursts along with explosions and black smoke rising through 10,000 feet, and all but one from 49 Squadron returned safely to Fulbeck, confident in the success of the operation. PB537 was homebound when shot down at 22.15 to crash at Sandbostel, some thirty miles west of Hamburg, killing F/O Stark RAAF and three of his crew, two of whom were also Australians. The fourth member of the RAAF was one of three to survive to spend a short time in captivity. 5 Group crews distinguished themselves on this night by claiming the destruction of seven enemy fighters. Post-raid reconnaissance confirmed further damage to this previously attacked target, with oil storage tanks taking the most hits, and revealed that a rubber factory had also been severely damaged.

An all-time record was set on the 11th, when 1,079 aircraft, the largest Bomber Command force ever for a single target, was assembled to attack Essen for the last time. 5 Group contributed 199 Lancasters and a single Mosquito, 49 Squadron loading fourteen Lancasters with a cookie and sixteen 500 pounders each and dispatching them from Fulbeck between 11.54 and 12.05 with S/L Wright the senior pilot on duty. They found the target city covered by ten-tenths cloud with tops at 6,000 feet, which required the Path Finder element to employ skymarkers in the form of red and blue smoke puffs, and these were bombed by the 49 Squadron crews from 16,000 to 18,600 feet between 15.20 and 15.25. More than 4,600 tons of bombs were dropped into the already ravaged city and former industrial powerhouse and left it with a huge pall of smoke rising through 10,000 feet as the force turned away. It would still be in a state of paralysis when the American ground forces captured it unopposed on the 10th of April. Operations were not yet over for the 11th, as 5 Group sent eleven Lancasters that night to mine the approaches to Oslo harbour in the Onions III garden.

A little over twenty-four hours later, the short-lived record was surpassed by the departure from their stations in the early afternoon of 1,108 aircraft, which had Dortmund as their destination. This time 5 Group provided 211 Lancasters, fourteen of them from 49 Squadron, which departed Fulbeck between 13.29 and 13.41 with S/L Walker the senior pilot on duty and the station commander, G/C Spencer, fulfilling the role of his second pilot. Each Lancaster was carrying a cookie and sixteen 500 pounders, which arrived over the eastern Ruhr to find it still under a blanket of ten-tenths cloud, this time with tops at 6,000 feet. The Path Finders marked the target with green and blue smoke puffs and the main force was directed by the Master Bomber to aim for the blues, which the 49 Squadron crews strived to do from 15,100 to 17,600 feet between 16.46 and 16.59. F/L Babb and crew failed to carry out an attack but were able to describe the scene over the target so had possibly run out of time. Returning crews spoke of brown smoke climbing through the clouds to 8,000 feet from the northern end of the city, and also a ring of smoke encircling the entire area. In fact, the smoke was so dense that it remained visible for 120 miles into the return flight. A new record of 4,800 tons of bombs was delivered, and photo-reconnaissance revealed that the central and southern districts of the city had received the greatest weight and had been left in chaos with all industry silenced permanently and railway tracks torn up.

The Group's next objective was the Wintershall oil refinery at Lützkendorf, another site to the west of Leipzig and south-west of Leuna in the Geiseltal. *(Lützkendorf no longer exists on a map of Germany and is now known as either Mücheln or Krumpa)*. The briefing of 244 Lancaster and eleven Mosquito crews took place on the 14th, twenty of the former representing 49 Squadron, and they departed Fulbeck between 16.41 and 17.17 with S/L Walker the senior pilot on duty. They headed out over the Wash and the bulge of East Anglia en-route to the Scheldt Estuary, and crossed Belgium to swing south of Cologne, before pointing their snouts to the east for the long leg to the target. They were met on arrival by conditions described variously as ten-tenths cloud, no cloud, thin layer of cloud, thin banks of stratus with tops at 12,000 feet, a little medium cloud, poor visibility and good visibility, but there was unanimity with regard to the haze. Ahead, the primary blind marker aircraft could be seen delivering their green TIs at 21.49, followed by the illuminators immediately afterwards between 21.51 and 22.00 to drop flares and bombs. Finally, the low-level Mosquitos did their job to accurately mark the aiming-point before the main force crews were called in and the 49 Squadron participants bombed on red and green TIs in accordance with the Master Bomber's instructions from 8,200 to 11000 feet between 22.01 and 22.08. Returning crews claimed an accurate attack, reporting explosions and fires and thick black smoke drifting across the plant and ascending through 7,000 feet, which rendered impossible a detailed assessment. Night-fighters were very much in evidence over the target and during the return flight, and 49 Squadron's RF153 became a victim somewhere over eastern Germany, taking with it all but one member of the predominantly Canadian crew of F/L McPhee. Somehow, rear gunner, F/Sgt Corrigan RCAF managed to evade capture, a remarkable achievement from so deep in enemy territory, and turned up at Fulbeck a few weeks later. A hefty eighteen Lancasters failed to return, 7.4% of those dispatched, and post-raid reconnaissance revealed a partially successful operation, which meant that a further visit would be required.

Seventeen 49 Squadron crews assembled in the briefing room at 14.00 on the 16th, to learn that they were to attack the virgin target of Würzburg, a small city on the River Main, situated some sixty miles south-east of Frankfurt in southern Germany. While this operation was in progress, a similar-sized force drawn from 1 and 8 Groups would be delivering the final attack of the war on Nuremberg, fifty miles to the south-east. A 5 Group force of 225 Lancasters and eleven Mosquitos was made ready for an early-evening take-off, and the 49 Squadron element got away between 17.53 and 18.06 with F/Ls Babb and Williams the senior pilots on duty and F/O Le Marquand returned to duties following his recovery from injury. They reached the target area to find clear skies with ground haze from which the marking and flare forces carried out their assigned tasks between 21.25 and 21.34, leaving the way clear for the main force crews to exploit the favourable bombing conditions. The 49 Squadron crews found red and yellow target indicators marking the aiming-point and complied with the Master Bomber's call for a sixteen-second overshoot on delivery of their loads of a cookie and incendiaries each from 8,000 to 12,000 feet between 21.35 and 21.55. Returning crews reported a successful operation but had to wait for the reconnaissance photos to discover the extent of the destruction. The bombing had officially lasted just seventeen minutes, during which period 1,127 tons of bombs had fallen into the historic old cathedral city, destroying an estimated 89% of the built-up area and killing four to five thousand people. Among six missing Lancasters were 49 Squadron's NG352 and ME454, although it seems that the latter came down in Allied-held territory killing three of the crew, while F/O Whent and three others sustained injuries to some extent. The former crashed in Germany delivering F/O Gibson and four of his crew into captivity. Wireless operator, Sgt Hughes, had the misfortune to fall into the hands of the SS, a member of which murdered him on the 18th. Such atrocities increased as the desperate military and civilian personnel who owed their power to Nazism faced the inevitability of defeat. Joseph Axt would be tried after the war and sentenced to death for his war crime. The Nuremberg operation had also been highly destructive, but had cost 1 Group twenty-four Lancasters, thus proving that the enemy defences were not yet spent and could still give the Command a bloody nose.

There was still business to attend to at the Böhlen oil refinery, and 5 Group prepared a force of 236 Lancasters and eleven Mosquitos on the 20th to deal what was hoped to be the knockout blow. Briefings began at 20.00 and was attended at Fulbeck by sixteen 49 Squadron crews with F/Ls Carlyle, Mellor, Williams and Winter the most senior pilots present. They took off between 23.16 and 23.39, each carrying a cookie and eleven 500 pounders, and set out on the now familiar path to eastern Germany. The bomber stream arrived early because of stronger-than-forecast winds, and encountered fairly favourable conditions, with three to six-tenths cloud topping out at 6,000 to 8,000 feet. The main force element had to orbit while the first primary blind marker crew delivered green TIs at 03.33, which fell 750 yards south of the plant and were followed at H-16 by a yellow

TI bursting two miles short. A cluster of illuminator flares ignited ahead, revealing that a smoke screen had been activated and was generating much smoke to create difficulties for the Mosquito low-level markers. Despite the challenges, they deposited red TIs on the button and the main force was called in. A few dummy TIs attracted a number of bomb loads, but the 49 Squadron crews complied with the instructions of the Master Bomber to bomb on specific reds and yellows from 15,000 to 16,200 feet between 03.46 and 03.51. The main weight of the attack was concentrated around the target and numerous explosions were witnessed, as was smoke rising through 5,000 feet as they turned away. The operation put the oil plant out of action, and it was still idle when American forces moved in a few weeks later. The success cost nine Lancasters and their crews, including one belonging to 189 Squadron at Fulbeck.

It was after 22.00 on the 21st when 151 Lancaster and eight Mosquito crews of 5 Group were informed that the Deutsche Erdölwerke synthetic oil refinery at Hamburg was to be their target that night. 49 Squadron loaded fifteen Lancasters with a cookie and sixteen 500 pounders each and sent them into the air between 01.04 and 01.29 with W/C Botting the senior pilot on duty supported by the usual bevvy of flight lieutenants. They pinpointed on the Danish coast to approach the target from the north and found thin stratus cloud at around 2,000 feet, through which the primary blind marker crew dropped green TIs on H2S from 14,000 feet at 03.55. The first illuminators went in thirty seconds later and continued to light up the aiming-point until 04.01, by which time the Mosquitos had marked to allow the main force to be called in at 04.05. The 49 Squadron crews bombed from 14,900 to 15,500 feet between 04.00 and 04.13, observing many fires and a large explosion at 04.11 that produced red flame and black smoke. Another was reported at 04.16, and it was clear to the homebound crews that the attack had been successful, a fact confirmed by post-raid reconnaissance, which revealed that twenty storage tanks had been destroyed in exchange for the loss of just four Lancasters.

The 55 and 56 Base squadrons were not involved in 5 Group's operations against railway bridges at Nienburg and Bremen on the 22nd and 23rd, but they were called to briefing on the afternoon of the 23rd to learn of their part in a raid that night on the town of Wesel. This had the misfortune to lie close to the Rhine and directly in the path of the advancing British 21st Army Group, which, since the 16th of February, had caused it to be systematically reduced to rubble by repeated air attacks and now had one final onslaught to face, having already endured one by 3 Group earlier in the day. 195 Lancasters and eleven Mosquitos were made ready, the sixteen representing 49 Squadron departing Fulbeck between 19.11 and 19.23 with F/L Williams the senior pilot on duty. They found the target under clear skies with slight ground haze and were able to identify it visually, observing the aiming point to be well-marked by red and green TIs, which were bombed from 8,000 to 12,000 feet between 22.30 and 22.40 in accordance with the Master Bomber's instructions. F/O Fricker and crew were a minute from bomb-release when three other Lancasters five hundred feet above on the starboard beam began to converge and would have been directly overhead had F/O Fricker not edged away to port, a manoeuvre which wrecked his bombing run. It was noticed, that, despite the Master Bomber ending the attack at H+8, bombing had continued. Post-raid reconnaissance confirmed the effectiveness of the raid, which left only 3% of Wesel's buildings standing, and after the war it would claim justifiably to be the most completely destroyed town in Germany.

During the course of the month the squadron took part in eleven operations and dispatched 174 sorties for the loss of four Lancasters and their crews and two other crew members. Although the crews could not know, fewer than four weeks of operations remained ahead of them before the bombing war finally came to an end.

# April 1945

There would be a gentle introduction to April for 5 Group, with no operations until the 4th, when briefings were held to inform crews about that day's operation against what was believed to be a military barracks at Nordhausen, situated in the Harz Mountains between Hannover to the north-west and Leipzig to the south-east. The site was actually a pair of enormous parallel tunnels under the Kohnstein Hill, which had been developed originally by the BASF Company to mine gypsum between 1917 and 1934. Following the destruction of Peenemünde, smaller tunnels had been created as a link between them to form a horizontal ladder effect, and the site turned over to the Mittelwerk GmbH (Gesellschaft mit beschrenkter Haftung, or Limited Company) for the manufacture of V-2 rockets and other secret projects. The "barracks" were part of the Mittelwerk-Dora forced workers camp, where inmates existed under the most horrendous conditions and brutal treatment, while they were starved, worked to death or simply executed by an increasingly desperate regime seeking to change the course of the war. The site had been attacked with only modest success on the previous day by 1 Group, but the 5 Group operation by 243 Lancasters was to be divided between the barracks and the town, ninety-three to the former and 150 to the latter. The 56 Base squadrons were assigned to the latter and had been given the marshalling yards as the aiming point for their loads of a cookie and sixteen 500 pounders. The 49 Squadron element of nineteen departed Fulbeck between 06.07 and 06.34 with W/C Botting and S/L Wright the senior pilots on duty and headed south-east towards the Dutch coast to swing round the south-eastern corner of the Ruhr and then head north to the target. They arrived to encounter five-to-seven-tenths cloud with tops as high as 7,000 feet, through which they were able to establish a visual reference. The 49 Squadron crews carried out their attacks from 13,000 to 16,000 feet between 09.10 and 09.24 and although some of the early bombing of the town was seen to undershoot, the Master Bomber corrected this by calling for a five-second overshoot. Thereafter, the markers became obscured by smoke, which was a problem also for those assigned to the barracks and some redirected their attention upon the town. Only one aircraft failed to return, 49 Squadron's ME308, which came down somewhere in northern Germany on the way home and there were no survivors from the crew of F/O Fischer RAAF. At debriefing, the crews were able to report what appeared to be a concentrated attack on both aiming-points, claiming severe damage, but it would the 8th before photo-reconnaissance confirmed that a large part of the town had been left devastated and there was evidence also that the Mittelwerk site had sustained substantial damage. Tragically and inevitably, there would have been casualties among any unfortunate slave workers not working inside the tunnels.

The only sizeable effort on the night of the 7/8th was by 175 Lancasters and eleven Mosquitos of 5 Group, which had a benzol plant at Molbis, near Leipzig, as their target. Situated south of the city, and less than two miles east of Böhlen, it had become a familiar destination for 5 Group via a well-trodden route across Belgium to pass south of Cologne. 49 Squadron made ready thirteen Lancasters, which departed Fulbeck between 18.28 and 18.39 with S/L Walker the senior pilot on duty. They found themselves delayed by wrongly forecast head winds, and although they would reach the target area, not all would do so in time to participate in the attack. Two 83 Squadron primary blind markers formed the tip of the spear and identified Zeitz on H2S, before making the ten-mile north-easterly run from there to the target. Green TIs were released from 15,000 feet at 22.48 and the flare force followed up between 22.50 and 22.57 to enable the low-level Mosquitos to drop red and green TIs among the chimneys of the plant. The approaching main force crews were greeted by clear skies with ground haze, or perhaps, a smoke screen in operation, but the highly accurate and visible marking was an invitation for them to plaster the aiming-point with high explosives. In the event, only the 49 Squadron crews of F/O Cluer and F/L Abbott arrived too late to bomb with the others on red and green TIs from 11,800 to 13,600 feet between 23.01 and 23.14, while F/O Perkins and crew suffered the frustration of a complete hang-up. Photo-reconnaissance confirmed the operation to have been a complete success, which ended all production at the plant. Later in the day, the length of a tour would be reduced from thirty-six to thirty-three sorties and hand an unexpected bonus to a lucky few.

Two major operations were scheduled for the 8th, the larger one involving 440 aircraft from 4, 6 and 8 Groups to be directed against Hamburg's shipyards, where the new Type XXI U-Boots were under construction. 5 Group, meanwhile, would take on the Lützkendorf refinery, following a failed attempt on the 4th by 1 and 8 Groups to conclusively end production at the site. A force of 231 Lancasters and eleven Mosquitos was put together, of which the nineteen 49 Squadron participants departed Fulbeck between 18.11 and 18.26 with S/L Wright the senior pilot on duty. They set course for Berck-sur-Mer on the French coast and crossed northern Luxembourg before swinging to the north-east on track for the target, where conditions were as they had been twenty-four hours earlier, with clear skies and either ground haze or generated smoke. The primary blind markers ran in at 14,000 feet at 22.33 to deliver green TIs, and the illuminators followed between 22.35 and 22.42, after which, the main force was called in. The 49 Squadron crews attacked in accordance with the Master Bomber's instructions to bomb the northerly red and yellow TIs and ran in at 11,000 to 14,000 feet between 22.44 and 22.52. All but two of the 49 squadron crews returned safely, confident that it would not be necessary to return to that particular target. They described their experiences to the intelligence section at debriefing, reporting many explosions, including a large one at 22.47, which was surpassed in size by another one two minutes later from which flames were said to have reached up to 3,000 feet. RA531 crashed in northern Germany on the way home with no survivors from the crew of F/O Perkins and PB374 disappeared without trace with the crew of F/O Cluer. The complete destruction of the site was confirmed by photo-reconnaissance, and the plant would remain out of action for what remained of the war.

55 and 56 Bases sat out a modest 5 Group raid on oil storage tanks and U-Boot pens at Hamburg in daylight on the 9th, and 56 Base was also not included on the following night, when the target for 5 Group was a stretch of railway track linked to the Wahren marshalling yards, situated to the north-west of Leipzig. A force of seventy-six Lancasters and eleven Mosquitos was to be accompanied by a further eight Oboe Mosquitos, which would benefit from the mobile Oboe stations that had been set up on the Continent enabling them to operate over the whole of Germany. It would be the third raid in succession in the Leipzig area, while a larger operation on this night involved more than three hundred aircraft from 1 and 8 Groups in an attack on the Plauen marshalling yards to the south-west of Dresden. Photographic-reconnaissance of the 5 Group raid would confirm serious damage to the eastern half of the targeted stretch of track.

A major attack on Kiel by elements of 3, 6 and 8 Groups was planned for the night of the 13/14th, while 5 Group took advantage of that activity to send eighteen Lancasters to lay mines in the Forget-me-not garden in Kiel harbour. 5 Group was used to being handed the most distant targets, and as the final days of the bombing war approached, it found itself facing three long-range trips on consecutive nights, all to railway targets. The first of these was at Pilsen in Czechoslovakia, for which a force of 222 Lancasters and eleven Mosquitos was made ready. The fourteen 49 Squadron crews departed Fulbeck for what would be the last time in anger between 23.38 and 23.56 and F/L Mellor and crew were within fifty-five miles of their destination when the loss of an engine prevented them from maintaining height above 7,000 feet and forced them to turn back. The others found clear skies in the target area with only slight haze, and ahead, watched the first primary blind marker crew deliver green TIs at 03.38, before the flare forces followed between 03.51 and 03.56. The main force was called in at 03.58, and the 49 Squadron participants bombed from 11,900 to 14,000 feet between 04.00 and 04.06, aiming at the north-westerly red and yellow TIs with an eight-second overshoot in accordance with the Master Bomber's instructions. Returning crews reported a large explosion at 04.00, followed by oily smoke, and it was concluded that the raid had been successful.

There was good news to celebrate on the 17th, when the length of a tour was reduced yet again to thirty sorties, releasing many crews to contemplate a long future. The target posted for ninety 5 Group Lancasters and eleven Mosquitos that night was the marshalling yards at Cham, on Germany's border with Czechoslovakia, while 56 Base remained at home. 5 Group was not involved when a force of over nine hundred aircraft reduced the island of Heligoland to the appearance of a cratered moonscape on the 18th, and the 55 and 56 Base squadrons also sat out a raid that night by 113 Lancasters and ten Mosquitos that put out of action the railway yards at Komotau (now Chomutov), also in Czechoslovakia. This proved to be the last raid in the communications offensive, which had begun more than a year earlier in preparation for D-Day.

F/O Hytch and crew climbed into ME357 on the 19th and took off at 11.27 for bombing practice at the Epperstone Range in Nottinghamshire and air-firing over the North Sea. Reducing height to drop a flame float, the pilot briefly lost consciousness and came to just in time to level the Lancaster out but could not prevent it from ditching five miles off Skegness at 13.20. The crew managed to deploy the dinghy and scramble in before the Lancaster slipped below the surface after just three minutes, and they were spotted by an American crew, who alerted the rescue services. They were picked up by a coaster, MV Northgate, after being adrift for ninety minutes, and were landed at Hull. On the 22nd, the squadron moved to the 56 Base main station at Syerston, during the course of which, F/O Elkington decided upon a low-level fly-past, a regular farewell gesture. Tragically, at 09.57, PB463 smashed into buildings near the M/T section killing all six on board and the debris cut down members of the 5015 Airfield Construction Unit, who were on parade nearby. Ten were killed instantly and five others succumbed to their injuries over the ensuing days, the last on the 8th of May, the day on which the war ended.

Syerston was not called into action when 5 Group sent 148 Lancasters to attack the railway yards and port area of Flensburg on the eastern coast of the Schleswig-Holstein peninsula on the 23rd. They reached the target area to encounter ten-tenths cloud with tops at 4,500 feet, which persuaded the Master Bomber to send the force home with their bomb loads intact. 5 Group operated for the final time on the 25th, with an operation in the morning against the SS barracks at Hitler's Eaglesnest retreat at Berchtesgaden in the Bavarian mountains, and later that night against an oil refinery at Tonsberg in Norway. 5 Group supported the former with eighty-eight Lancasters and a single Mosquito in an overall 1, 5 and 8 Group force of 359 Lancasters and sixteen Mosquitos. The twelve 49 Squadron participants departed Syerston between 04.20 and 04.32 with F/Ls Abbott, Babb, Winter and Wright the senior pilots on duty, and all arrived in the target area to find clear skies. Despite the favourable conditions, it proved difficult to identify the barracks in the absence of visible markers and the Master Bomber's instructions were not getting through. However, a nearby lake and the town stood out clearly, and all but two of the 49 Squadron crews were able to establish their position before carrying out their attacks from 14,000 to 15,000 feet between 09.00 and 09.03. When F/O Hawkins and crew touched down in PB559 at 13.20, they brought to an end the illustrious offensive career of 49 Squadron. It had been difficult to assess the accuracy of this final operation, but it appeared to be effective, and no local report emerged to provide clarity.

During the afternoon, 482 aircraft from 4, 6 and 8 Groups targeted heavy gun batteries on the Island of Wangerooge, which controlled the approaches to Wilhelmshaven and Bremen, and tragically six aircraft and their crews were lost to collisions while outbound over the North Sea. That night, 5 Group conducted its and Bomber Command's final offensive operation of the war involving heavy bombers, when sending 107 Lancasters and seven Mosquitos to attack an oil-related target at Tonsberg, situated close to the western shore of Oslo Fjord, a dozen or so miles south of the recently attacked Horten. At the same time, fourteen 5 Group Lancasters carried out the final gardening sorties of the war nearby in Oslo Fjord. Operations were posted over the ensuing days, but cancelled, and meanwhile, the humanitarian Operations Manna and Exodus were launched, the former to feed the starving Dutch people still under German occupation and the latter to repatriate prisoners of war, a process which would continue into the summer. During the course of the month, the squadron took part in five operations and dispatched seventy-seven sorties for the loss of five Lancasters and four crews.

## May 1945

49 Squadron was not involved in Operation Manna, but ten of its Lancasters departed Syerston between 14.32 and 14.45 on the 1st, bound for Juvincourt in north-eastern France to play their part in Operation Exodus. They were led by W/C Botting and S/L Walker, having been briefed to bring home 236 former prisoners of war and deliver them to Westcott in Surrey. The operation was repeated on the 4th, when S/L Walker led a dozen of the squadron's Lancasters to Melsbroek and returned to Wing in Bedfordshire with 288 passengers. It had been a long and exacting war for those squadrons like 49, which had been involved from the start. Many of the finest men to serve in Bomber Command passed through the squadron during the course of the war, and many, many more had sacrificed their lives or their freedom in serving it. As one of the mainstays of 5 Group and the Command, there can be few squadrons to parallel its excellence and certainly none to surpass it. It ended the war with the fifth highest number of sorties in Bomber Command to its credit, the third highest number of overall operations in 5 Group, the second highest number of sorties in 5 Group and the fourth highest number of aircraft operational losses in 5 Group.

# Roll of Honour

| | | | | | |
|---|---|---|---|---|---|
| ADAMS | Daniel Gilbert | F/Sgt | 27 | BA | 25.04.44 |
| ALDRIDGE | Horace | Sgt | 23 | Wop/AG | 06.07.41. |
| ALEXANDER | Leopold Gordon | Sgt | 30 | AG | 02.02.43. |
| ALLEN | Francis Harry | Sgt | 21 | AG | 14.02.43. |
| ALLEN | Keith | Sgt | 31 | A/Obs | 20.06.42. |
| ALLIN | Ronald | F/O | 32 | Nav/B | 14.02.43 |
| ANCELL | Robert Hasting | Sgt | 39 | AG | 24.05.43. |
| ANDERSON | Adam | Sgt | 20 | Pilot | 21.04.43. |
| ANDERSON | Arthur Leslie | P/O | 22 | Pilot | 08.05.44. |
| ANDERSON | Cyril Thorpe | P/O | 28 | Pilot | 23.09.43. |
| ANDERSON | Hector Hugh Watson | F/Sgt | 31 | BA | 31.03.44 |
| ANDERSON | Kenneth | F/Sgt | 20 | Nav | 22.03.44 |
| ANDREWS | William Henry Thomson | P/O | 32 | Pilot | 10.03.42 |
| ANSELL | Allan Alfred | Sgt | 20 | AG | 19.07.44 |
| APPLETON | George Edward | F/Sgt | 20 | Wop/AG | 27.07.41 |
| APPLEYARD | William David | F/O | 22 | Pilot | 19.07.44 |
| ARCHER | Kenneth Arthur | Sgt | 19 | AG | 20.02.44 |
| ARMSTRONG | Arthur | Sgt | 20 | AG | 22.06.44 |
| ARMSTRONG | Robert Gow | F/L | 22 | Pilot | 27.04.44 |
| ASH | Maurice Samuel | Sgt | 29 | AG | 31.05.42 |
| ASHBY | Arthur | Sgt | 21 | FE | 26.07.44 |
| ASHCROFT | Albert Henry | Sgt | 19 | FE | 27.10.44 |
| ASHMAN | Frederick Edward | Sgt | 19 | Nav | 26.11.43 |
| ASHWORTH | William Storey | P/O | 36 | BA | 09.07.43 |
| ATKINS | Clarence Leslie | Sgt | 35 | AG | 08.01.45 |
| ATKINS | George Thomas | Sgt | 21 | W/Op | 06.01.42 |
| ATKINSON | Ernest Charles | F/Sgt | 21 | Wop/AG | 28.12.41 |
| BACON | Donovan John | F/L | 29 | Pilot | 12.04.44 |
| BAILES | Richard | F/O | 28 | Nav | 30.04.44 |
| BAILEY | Clifford | Sgt | 23 | W/Op | 26.03.44 |
| BAILEY | George Cooley | F/L | 21 | Pilot | 22.11.43 |
| BAILY | George Hadley | F/O | 21 | Nav | 04.11.44 |
| BAIRNSFATHER | Ralph McPherson | W/O | 23 | BA | 07.03.45 |
| BAKER | Cyril | F/O | 21 | Pilot | 08.07.44 |
| BAKER | John | Sgt | 20 | W/Op | 25.08.40 |
| BAKER | Terence Charles | Sgt | 22 | BA | 31.03.44 |
| BALL | George Edward | F/L | 24 | Pilot | 08.07.44 |
| BALL | Leslie | Sgt | 23 | Pilot | 20.11.40 |
| BALLAS- ANDERSEN | Konstantine | P/O | 26 | Pilot | 28.10.40 |

| | | | | | |
|---|---|---|---|---|---|
| BAMFORD | Charles Glendinning | Sgt | 19 | FE | 17.04.43 |
| BARCLAY | Douglas McLeod | Sgt | 22 | Pilot | 27.03.41 |
| BARNARD | Henry Walter | S/L | 26 | Pilot | 17.09.42 |
| BARNES | Keith Ormond | P/O | 20 | Pilot | 28.01.44 |
| BARNETT | Conrad Alfred Stanley | Sgt | 19 | Nav | 15.06.43 |
| BARRETT | Duncan Henry | Sgt | 23 | Nav | 29.08.41 |
| BARRETT | Martin | F/Sgt | 19 | AG | 09.07.43 |
| BATCHELOR | Harold Ockenden | F/O | 22 | Nav | 18.08.43 |
| BATHO | Reginald Frank | Sgt | 24 | Nav | 06.08.40 |
| BATTY | William James | Sgt | 20 | AG | 06.09.43 |
| BATTYE | Edmund | Sgt | 19 | AG | 21.11.44 |
| BENSON | Arthur Herbert | P/O | 29 | Pilot | 25.04.40 |
| BENSON | Leslie Bernard | P/O | 24 | Nav | 22.06.44 |
| BERESFORD | Ronald William | Sgt | 24 | FE | 26.03.44 |
| BERRETT | Eric Albert | Sgt | 22 | W/Op | 28.08.42 |
| BERRY | Robert William | Sgt | 19 | AG | 22.05.44 |
| BERRY | Royston Willett | F/O | 28 | AG | 04.11.44 |
| BETTINSON | Donald William | Sgt | 20 | Wop/AG | 13.07.43 |
| BICHARD | Frederick James William | Sgt | 22 | Wop/AG | 28.10.40 |
| BICKLE | William Douglas | F/Sgt | 21 | Wop/AG | 23.09.43 |
| BICKNELL | George Alfred | Sgt | 21 | AG | 23.09.43 |
| BIGGIN | Harry | Sgt | 20 | Nav | 15.06.43 |
| BIGNELL | Roy Arthur Frank | Sgt | 19 | AG | 20.12.42 |
| BIRBECK | Douglas Brigg | Sgt | 21 | AG | 16.03.44 |
| BIRD | Sydney Dennis | F/Sgt | 23 | Nav/B | 15.06.43 |
| BISHOP | Alfred William | P/O | 24 | W/Op | 21.11.44 |
| BLACK | Stuart Corliss | F/Sgt | 27 | Pilot | 12.12.41 |
| BLACKMORE | Alfred Henry | P/O | 21 | Pilot | 20.12.43 |
| BLAIKIE | Donald Victor | Sgt | 22 | AG | 09.06.44 |
| BLAKE | Edward George | Sgt | 19 | AG | 26.11.44 |
| BLANCHARD | Arthur | Sgt | 21 | Nav | 11.12.44 |
| BLOCK | David | F/Sgt | 30 | Pilot | 31.05.42 |
| BLUMFIELD | Dennis William | F/Sgt | 21 | Nav | 19.07.44 |
| BLYTHE | Ronald Charles | F/O | 20 | Nav | 17.06.43 |
| BOARDMAN | Frederick | Sgt | 20 | FE | 30.04.44 |
| BOLTER | Alec John | F/O | 30 | Pilot | 08.01.45 |
| BOLTON | Kenneth | F/Sgt | 23 | Wop/AG | 06.03.43 |
| BOLTON | Sidney David | Sgt | 20 | Nav | 21.11.44 |
| BOLTON | Thomas Owen | P/O | 21 | Nav | 08.02.45 |
| BONE | Alexander Victor | F/O | 31 | Pilot | 17.04.43 |
| BONNETT | Dorian Dick | F/L | 23 | Pilot | 24.10.42 |
| BOOTH | Peter Waring | Sgt | 31 | AG | 20.12.43 |
| BOSWELL | Herbert Geoffrey | Sgt | 21 | FE | 27.11.43 |

| | | | | | |
|---|---|---|---|---|---|
| BOUFFLER | Keith Arnold | Sgt | 21 | FE | 17.09.42 |
| BOURNE | Leonard Bertie | Sgt | 28 | Nav | 17.12.44 |
| BOURTON | Eric | F/O | 21 | Nav | 06.10.44 |
| BOXER | George Ernest | Sgt | 21 | AG | 03.11.43 |
| BOYCE | Robert James | Sgt | 20 | FE | 27.04.44 |
| BRAMES | Ronald | Sgt | 22 | Wop/AG | 21.03.41 |
| BRATT | Douglas Stuart | Sgt | 20 | AG | 06.03.43 |
| BREIVIS | John | Sgt | 19 | AG | 29.08.42 |
| BROAD | Leslie Henry | Sgt | 19 | AG | 31.03.44 |
| BROCKLEHURST | Thomas | Sgt | 29 | AG | 18.08.43 |
| BROMHAM | John William Thomas | P/O | 22 | Pilot | 07.09.41 |
| BRONSKY | Harold | Sgt | 24 | FE | 26.11.43 |
| BROOKES | Eric | Sgt | 28 | AG | 30.10.42 |
| BROOKES | Reginald | Sgt | 22 | FE | 28.02.43 |
| BROOKS | Alfred Bryan | F/Sgt | 20 | Wop/AG | 17.09.42 |
| BROWN | Horace Stanley | Sgt | 30 | Wop/AG | 15.04.42 |
| BROWN | James | Sgt | 28 | W/Op | 17.10.40 |
| BROWN | Reginald William | Sgt | 22 | BA | 30.03.43 |
| BROWN | Robert William Burdon | Sgt | 22 | A/Obs | 06.04.42 |
| BROWNE | James Arthur Gerald | Sgt | 25 | Wop/AG | 31.01.43 |
| BROWNLIE | Archibald Halliday | Sgt | 20 | FE | 07.10.43 |
| BRUNT | Ronald | W/O | 21 | Pilot | 26.11.43 |
| BRYAN-SMITH | Anthony | P/O | 28 | AG | 15.04.40 |
| BRYANT | Keith | Sgt | 21 | Pilot | 11.11.41 |
| BUCHANAN | Norman William | F/Sgt | 22 | AG | 18.08.43 |
| BUCHANAN | Walter John Fergus | F/O | 28 | Pilot | 26.07.44 |
| BUCK | Arthur William | Sgt | 28 | AG | 23.09.43 |
| BUFTON | John Raymond | F/O | 25 | Pilot | 28.10.40 |
| BULMER | Alan | F/O | 21 | Pilot | 11.11.40 |
| BUNN | Myrl Ellwood | F/Sgt | 21 | AG | 17.06.43 |
| BURDETT | Donald William | Sgt | 22 | AG | 06.09.43 |
| BURNETT | Reginald | Sgt | 25 | AG | 13.07.43 |
| BURNSIDE | John | Sgt | 23 | Pilot | 17.06.43 |
| BURRIDGE | Colin Frederick Peter | Sgt | 19 | AG | 21.02.45 |
| BURTON | Edward George | F/Sgt | 22 | Pilot | 29.08.42 |
| BUTCHER | Alfred Frank | Sgt | 36 | AG | 08.01.45 |
| BUTLER | John Ronald | Sgt | 21 | W/Op | 28.05.41 |
| BUTLER | Peter Saumarez | F/O | 23 | Pilot | 25.05.40 |
| BUTTEL | Albert Francois | Sgt | 22 | Pilot | 07.06.42 |
| BUTTERWORTH | John | Sgt | 24 | A/Obs | 11.02.41 |
| BUTTREY | Harold | Sgt | 28 | AG | 17.06.43 |
| BYERS | Colin Edward | F/Sgt | 20 | AG | 22.11.43 |
| CALDWELL | David Alexander | Sgt | 20 | Wop/AG | 11.02.41 |

| | | | | | |
|---|---|---|---|---|---|
| CALLON | Gordon Frederick | F/Sgt | 20 | AG | 17.12.44 |
| CAMM | Philip Otley | Sgt | 23 | FE | 03.01.44 |
| CAPTON | Leslie James | F/Sgt | 20 | AG | 29.08.42 |
| CARFOOT | Norman Henry | F/L | 21 | Pilot | 03.11.43 |
| CARON | Aime Leon | Sgt | 24 | AG | 17.09.42 |
| CARR | David Hounsell | P/O | 21 | AG | 22.06.44 |
| CARR | Harry | Sgt | 21 | Nav/B | 27.11.43 |
| CARR | Walter | Sgt | 29 | Nav | 30.03.43 |
| CARRINGTON | Henry Joseph | P/O | 32 | Pilot | 22.05.44 |
| CARTER | John Philip | P/O | 20 | Pilot | 31.05.42 |
| CARTWRIGHT | Leslie Henry | Sgt | 22 | Wop/AG | 27.11.43 |
| CASTLE | Frederick John | Sgt | 23 | AG | 25.04.44 |
| CATLEY | Frederick Norman Colin | Sgt | 21 | Pilot | 29.09.40 |
| CHAMBERLAIN | Thomas Henry | Sgt | 22 | AG | 06.01.41 |
| CHARLES | Edward Christopher | Sgt | 24 | FE | 11.12.44 |
| CHATFIELD | Walter Lawrence | F/Sgt | 22 | AG | 15.06.43 |
| CHATTERTON | Haigh | Sgt | 22 | AG | 08.04.43 |
| CHEETHAM | William Harris | P/O | 29 | A/Obs | 02.11.41 |
| CHESNUTT | Cyril | F/Sgt | 25 | FE | 08.03.45 |
| CHRISTY | Robert | P/O | 21 | Wop/AG | 24.05.43 |
| CHUTE | George Edward | P/O | 20 | BA | 26.03.44 |
| CLARK | Frank | P/O | 29 | Pilot | 25.04.44 |
| CLARK | Hilary Daniel | F/O | 28 | AG | 10.06.44 |
| CLARKE | James Cunningham | Sgt | 30 | Nav | 25.08.40 |
| CLIFTON | Frederic Allan Newell | F/O | 36 | AG | 23.05.44 |
| CLOSE | Peter Thrale | P/O | 31 | A/Obs | 10.01.42 |
| CLOUGH | James Thomas Bartle | P/O | 24 | Nav | 16.02.42 |
| CLOVER | Arthur James | Sgt | 19 | AG | 02.02.43 |
| CLUER | Roger | F/O | 28 | Pilot | 09.04.45 |
| CLUFF | Robert Fraser | P/O | 21 | BA | 27.04.44 |
| CLUTTERBUCK | William George | P/O | 33 | Nav | 03.11.43 |
| COATES | Harold Kenneth | F/O | 25 | Pilot | 04.09.43 |
| COLE | Albert Stanley | F/O | 21 | BA | 29.07.44 |
| COLE | Elliot Livesey | F/Sgt | 23 | Pilot | 31.01.43 |
| COLE | George Stanley | Sgt | 20 | Pilot | 15.06.43 |
| COLEMAN | Ronald F | Sgt | 21 | FE | 22.05.44 |
| COLHOUN | William Andrew Lawrence | F/O | 25 | Pilot | 31.03.44 |
| COLLINS | William Alfred | Sgt | 26 | Wop/AG | 10.04.42 |
| COLLINS | William Stewart | Sgt | 20 | AG | 03.09.42 |
| COMPTON | William Walter Stanley | Sgt | 21 | Nav | 20.02.44 |
| CONEY | Kenneth | F/Sgt | 20 | W/Op | 06.07.41 |
| CONNATTY | Terence Robert | F/Sgt | 23 | Wop/AG | 25.04.44 |
| CONRAD | Henry | Sgt | 20 | W/Op | 03.01.44 |

| | | | | | |
|---|---|---|---|---|---|
| CONSIDINE | Anthony Talbot Percy | Sgt | 20 | A/Obs | 10.04.42 |
| COOK | Derek Alfred | P/O | 21 | Pilot | 17.03.42 |
| COOK | William Alexander | Sgt | 21 | BA | 21.04.43 |
| COOPER | Dennis John | Sgt | 19 | AG | 27.04.44 |
| COOPER | William | Sgt | 22 | FE | 21.11.44 |
| COPE | Ronald | Sgt | 23 | AG | 17.04.43 |
| CORBETT | Frank | Sgt | 22 | Wop/AG | 16.10.40 |
| COTTINGHAM | Cyril Morgan | F/O | 25 | Pilot | 22.11.43 |
| COULSEY | John Robert | Sgt | 23 | Wop/AG | 15.06.43 |
| COURT | Jack | Sgt | 19 | FE | 08.01.45 |
| COWAN | Hamilton | Sgt | 22 | AG | 17.01.43 |
| COWARD | Clifford William | P/O | 23 | Nav | 11.04.44 |
| COX | James Lawford | F/Sgt | 28 | BA | 05.07.44 |
| COX | Leonard Edgar | S/L | 30 | Pilot | 22.06.44 |
| CRANE | Clifford John | Sgt | 20 | AG | 26.07.44 |
| CRAWSHAW | Stanley Raynor | Sgt | 18 | FE | 04.11.44 |
| CREIGHTON | Allan David | P/O | 26 | AG | 22.06.44 |
| CRIDGE | Robert John | Sgt | 22 | W/Op | 12.02.42 |
| CRIPPS | Basil Robert | Sgt | 20 | Wop/AG | 13.06.43 |
| CROCKER | Malcolm | W/C | 27 | Pilot | 22.06.44 |
| CROSS | James Arthur | Sgt | 33 | FE | 30.03.43 |
| CRUICKSHANK | David Alexander | Sgt | 21 | A/Obs | 11.02.41 |
| CULLEN | John Kennedy | F/Sgt | 32 | BA | 13.10.42 |
| CULLY | Victor Charles | P/O | 29 | BA | 22.06.44 |
| DALLAWAY | Douglas Demas Russell | Sgt | 20 | AG | 03.01.44 |
| DANGERFIELD | Edwin | Sgt | 25 | Wop/AG | 15.06.43 |
| DANGERFIELD | Richard Desmond | F/Sgt | 20 | Nav | 24.10.42 |
| DANIEL | Thomas Steadman | Sgt | 22 | FE | 20.12.43 |
| DARBYSHIRE | Herbert | Sgt | 22 | AG | 16.03.45 |
| D'ARCY | James Marcus | Sgt | 26 | Nav | 08.11.41 |
| DAVENPORT-JONES | Garton Vincent | Sgt | 19 | W/Op | 07.12.40 |
| DAVIES | James Owen | Sgt | 22 | Wop/AG | 06.09.43 |
| DAVIES | Malcolm Haydn | Sgt | 19 | W/Op | 07.12.40 |
| DAVIES | William Arthur | F/Sgt | 23 | BA | 18.08.43 |
| DAVIS | Leslie | F/Sgt | 24 | Pilot | 07.04.42 |
| DAVISON | Colin | F/Sgt | 23 | Wop/AG | 19.07.44 |
| DAY | Wilfred Robert | Sgt | 20 | BA | 16.12.43 |
| DAY | William Edward | F/O | 25 | AG | 22.06.44 |
| DEACON | John William | Sgt | 20 | BA | 15.06.43 |
| DE MESTRE | Peter Morrice | S/L | 24 | Pilot | 07.06.42 |
| DEW | Thomas George William | F/Sgt | 20 | W/Op | 15.03.45 |
| DICKEN | Albert Edward | Sgt | 19 | AG | 22.06.44 |
| DICKIE | Alexander McKeen | W/OII | 25 | BA | 28.02.43 |

| | | | | | |
|---|---|---|---|---|---|
| DICKINSON | John Russell | P/O | 21 | Pilot | 27.04.44 |
| DIXON | Alan Norris | F/Sgt | 22 | Nav | 17.04.43 |
| DOBSON | Reginald Patrick | Sgt | 26 | Nav/B | 28.08.42 |
| DOD | Harold Frederick | F/O | 26 | Pilot | 05.07.44 |
| DOMLEO | Stanley Victor | Sgt | 24 | W/Op | 20.12.43 |
| DOWNES | Thomas Kenneth | Sgt | 22 | Pilot | 12.02.42 |
| DOWNING | Dennis | Sgt | 20 | FE | 28.02.43 |
| DRAKES | David Baron | S/L | 22 | Pilot | 02.11.41 |
| DREAVER | Bruce Colin | P/O | 22 | AG | 13.08.43 |
| DREW | Sydney Trevor | Sgt | 20 | Wop/AG | 10.03.42 |
| DRON | William | F/O | 23 | Pilot/RG | 08.02.45 |
| DUDLEY | Charles William | Sgt | 20 | FE | 13.06.43 |
| DUFFY | Patrick James | Sgt | 19 | Wop/AG | 08.09.41 |
| DUNAND | Emile Joseph Francis | F/O | 25 | Wop/AG | 02.02.43 |
| DUNCAN | Frederick Colin | W/OII | 26 | Pilot | 28.02.43 |
| DUNNE | James Bernard | P/O | 26 | Obs | 10.03.42 |
| DUNNET | Charles William | F/L | 24 | Pilot | 17.06.43 |
| DURHAM | Eric Victor | Sgt | 28 | Pilot | 08.09.41 |
| DURRELL | Donald | Sgt | 22 | AG | 22.10.43 |
| DUTTON | Kenneth | F/O | 22 | BA | 22.06.44 |
| DUTTON | Ronald Leslie James | Sgt | 19 | Wop/AG | 27.06.40 |
| DUTTON | William Arthur | Sgt | 22 | BA | 17.06.43 |
| EDWARDS | Charles Arthur | P/O | 20 | AG | 17.06.43 |
| EDWARDS | William Frank | Sgt | 20 | FE | 22.03.44 |
| ELKINGTON | George Frank | F/O | 30 | Pilot | 22.04.45 |
| ELLAM | Kenneth | Sgt | 22 | W/Op | 31.03.44 |
| ELLENOR | John | Sgt | 33 | AG | 27.04.44 |
| ELLIOTT | Richard Frederick | F/O | 21 | Pilot | 12.10.42 |
| ELLIS | Derek Atkinson | F/O | 21 | W/Op | 12.11.44 |
| ELLIS | James Edwin | Sgt | 22 | W/Op | 20.02.44 |
| ELLIS | Richard Leonard Ashburton | Sgt | 23 | Pilot | 21.03.41 |
| ENDEAN | Douglas Edgar | Sgt | 23 | FE | 27.04.44 |
| ESSENHIGH | Edward Gordon | F/O | 24 | Pilot | 17.12.44 |
| EVANS | Brian Herbert | F/L | 24 | Pilot/Nav | 31.03.44 |
| EVANS | Gordon Joseph | Sgt | 20 | Wop/AG | 21.04.43 |
| EVANS | Gwilyn Richard | Sgt | 23 | AG | 24.05.43 |
| EVANS | Harold Thomas | F/Sgt | 23 | BA | 20.12.43 |
| EVANS | Leonard William | F/Sgt | 22 | Nav | 22.04.45 |
| EVERETT | Edwin William | Sgt | 27 | AG | 08.07.44 |
| EWAN | Eric | F/Sgt | 21 | AG | 23.09.43 |
| EYLES | Stanley Clarence | P/O | 20 | Pilot | 09.07.43 |
| FAIRLIE | David Gow | Sgt | 21 | FE | 06.03.43 |
| FALCK | John | Sgt | 29 | AG | 22.11.43 |

| | | | | | |
|---|---|---|---|---|---|
| FAWCETT | Nicoll B | P/O | 20 | Pilot | 25.08.40 |
| FAZAKERLEY | Thomas | Sgt | 23 | AG | 30.03.43 |
| FINDLAY | Alexander | F/Sgt | 22 | BA | 02.11.44 |
| FINNERTY | Austin | Sgt | 23 | AG | 16.03.45 |
| FISCHER | Arthur Benjamin | F/O | 21 | Pilot | 04.04.45 |
| FISHER | Arthur George | Sgt | 25 | Nav | 22.10.43 |
| FISHER | Ian Malcolm Temple | F/Sgt | 25 | Nav | 06.07.41 |
| FITCH | John Dennis | Sgt | 24 | Wop/AG | 07.07.41 |
| FLANAGAN | Peter | Sgt | 20 | Wop/AG | 17.10.40 |
| FLEMING | Norman | Sgt | 22 | AG | 23.09.43 |
| FLETCHER | James Frederick | Sgt | 20 | AG | 17.04.43 |
| FLOYD | Philip Nevil | P/O | 21 | Pilot | 31.05.42 |
| FOLEY | John | F/Sgt | 29 | Wop/AG | 22.10.43 |
| FORD | Roy Arthur | Sgt | 22 | BA | 22.10.43 |
| FOSTER | Raymond Norman Percy | Sgt | 22 | FE | 17.04.43 |
| FOSTER | Sidney Frederick | Sgt | 21 | W/Op | 27.04.44 |
| FOULKES | Lawrence | Sgt | 19 | AG | 22.05.44 |
| FOURNIER | Bernard Maurice | P/O | 21 | Pilot | 29.08.41 |
| FOWLER | Frederick Robert | Sgt | 19 | AG | 15.06.43 |
| FOWLS | Robert Leslie | Sgt | 24 | FE | 08.05.44 |
| FOWLSTON | Reginald | Sgt | 29 | Wop/AG | 18.08.43 |
| FRANCIS | Leonard Thomas | P/O | 22 | BA | 12.11.44 |
| FRANKLIN | Geoffrey Edward | F/O | 31 | Nav | 29.07.44 |
| FRASER | Hugh Scott | WOI | 22 | AG | 18.11.43 |
| FRECKLETON | James McGregor | F/O | 23 | Nav | 22.06.44 |
| FREEMAN | Leslie Frank | Sgt | 31 | Nav | 18.08.43 |
| FRIEND | Kenneth Charles | Sgt | 19 | Wop/AG | 16.10.40 |
| FULLAGER | Dennis Raymond | P/O | 21 | Nav | 09.07.43 |
| FULTON | Basil Terence Macy | Sgt | 21 | Pilot | 21.11.40 |
| FYFE | Norman Watt | Sgt | 21 | BA | 15.06.43 |
| GALLAGHER | Vincent | F/Sgt | 24 | BA | 19.07.44 |
| GALLOWAY | Somerville Russell | F/L | 24 | Pilot | 08.02.45 |
| GAROS | Alexander | Sgt | 19 | AG | 20.06.42 |
| GARRATT | Reginald Henry Hobson | F/Sgt | 21 | Pilot | 02.06.42 |
| GARRETT | Maurice John Clive | F/Sgt | 20 | Pilot | 22.04.45 |
| GASCOYNE | John Patrick | F/Sgt | 23 | AG | 21.02.45 |
| GAULD | Albert Alexander | Sgt | 27 | Wop/AG | 10.03.42 |
| GILBERT | Robert Cecil | Sgt | 22 | AG | 07.03.45 |
| GILLIN | James William | WOII | 38 | Nav | 13.07.43 |
| GOLDBERG | Norman Myer | Sgt | 22 | W/Op | 23.05.44 |
| GOLDIE | Thomas | Sgt | 19 | Wop/AG | 07.12.40 |
| GOLDRING | Charles E | Sgt | 22 | Pilot | 20.06.42 |
| GOODYEAR | Paul Arnold Urquhart | Sgt | 26 | FE | 13.07.43 |

| | | | | | |
|---|---|---|---|---|---|
| GORDON | Norman | F/Sgt | 25 | Nav | 05.07.44 |
| GORTON | Harold | S/L | 30 | Pilot | 12.11.44 |
| GOSPEL | Leslie Warren | P/O | 23 | Pilot | 16.08.43 |
| GOWER | Richard Francis | P/O | 24 | Pilot | 11.08.40 |
| GRAVES-HOOK | Philip Rodney | P/O | 24 | Pilot | 23.05.44 |
| GRAY | William Arthur Bill | Sgt | 24 | A/Obs | 20.01.42 |
| GREEN | Edwin George | Sgt | 32 | Pilot | 12.02.42 |
| GREEN | Gerald Wilson | F/L | 30 | Pilot | 11.12.44 |
| GREEN | Gilbert John | F/Sgt | 21 | BA | 23.09.43 |
| GREEN | William Raeburn | F/L | 28 | Pilot | 19.07.44 |
| GREENHALGH | Reginald Ernest | Sgt | 25 | AG | 29.09.41 |
| GREENSTREET | Irvine Stewart | Sgt | 20 | A/Obs | 12.02.42 |
| GREENWOOD | Ernest | Sgt | 23 | AG | 26.07.44 |
| GREENWOOD | George Edward | Sgt | 22 | FE | 28.01.44 |
| GREEVES | Stuart Gordon | Sgt | 22 | Pilot | 07.12.40 |
| GREGORY-COLEMAN | William Patrick Joseph | Sgt | 21 | Pilot | 07.09.42 |
| GREIG | Ronald | F/Sgt | 22 | Pilot | 22.03.44 |
| GREMS | Arthur Charles | Sgt | 23 | AG | 20.02.44 |
| GREY | Llewellyn | F/Sgt | 26 | BA | 31.01.43 |
| GRIFFIN | Arthur Desmond | Sgt | 24 | AG | 22.06.44 |
| GRIFFITHS | Myrddin | Sgt | 24 | Wop/AG | 07.04.42 |
| GWYER | Herbert Harry Stephen | F/O | 23 | BA | 11.12.44 |
| HADAWAY | Gordon Alfred | Sgt | 28 | AG | 28.05.41 |
| HAINSWORTH | Richard Beetham | Sgt | 23 | FE | 27.04.44 |
| HALES | Joseph Harold England | Sgt | 31 | Nav | 22.05.44 |
| HALEY | Michael Frederick | Sgt | 21 | Wop/AG | 17.06.43 |
| HALL | Thomas Albert | Sgt | 23 | AG | 22.06.44 |
| HALLAM | John William | Sgt | 30 | Wop/AG | 20.01.42 |
| HALLIDAY | Douglas Stephen | Sgt | 22 | Wop/AG | 06.06.42 |
| HALSALL | William | Sgt | 32 | AG | 14.02.43 |
| HAMBLY | Alfred | F/O | 30 | AG | 22.06.44 |
| HANCOCK | Charles William | Sgt | 23 | Wop/AG | 26.06.41 |
| HANDS | Gordon Ernest Deryck | Sgt | 19 | AG | 19.07.44 |
| HANDS | Kenneth | Sgt | 22 | AG | 14.02.43 |
| HANNON | William Gerrard | F/Sgt | 24 | Nav | 12.11.44 |
| HARDISTY | Thomas Hollas | Sgt | 21 | W/Op | 08.12.41 |
| HARDY | Douglas William Edward | Sgt | 22 | AG | 22.06.44 |
| HARDY | Hubert William John | Sgt | 20 | FE | 08.02.45 |
| HARDY | William Edgar | Sgt | 22 | W/Op | 16.03.44 |
| HARFORD | Peter Edward George | F/O | 22 | Pilot | 02.11.44 |
| HARKER | Brian Leslie Gordon | P/O | 22 | Pilot | 04.10.39 |
| HARNETT | Ronald Edward | Sgt | 21 | FE | 22.10.43 |

| | | | | | |
|---|---|---|---|---|---|
| HARPER | John Perryer | Sgt | 21 | FE | 15.06.43 |
| HARRIS | Edwin Arthur | P/O | 29 | Nav | 11.08.40 |
| HARRISON | Denis | Sgt | 21 | FE | 06.10.44 |
| HARRISON | John | Sgt | 20 | BA | 25.05.40 |
| HARROP | Kenneth | F/O | 22 | Pilot | 06.10.44 |
| HARTLEY | Clement Arthur Victor | Sgt | 29 | Wop/AG | 07.04.42 |
| HARVEY | Alexander Muir | F/O | 21 | Pilot | 20.01.42 |
| HASTIE | Bertram Victor | Sgt | 21 | Wop/AG | 29.09.40 |
| HAWES | Stanley | F/Sgt | 22 | Wop/AG | 22.06.44 |
| HAYLOCK | Frank Robert | Sgt | 20 | FE | 16.03.45 |
| HAYNES | George Charles | Sgt | 22 | Nav | 31.05.42 |
| HAYWARD | Hugh Walter | F/O | 22 | BA | 21.11.44 |
| HEALEY | Wilbert Arley | F/L | 30 | Pilot | 30.04.44 |
| HEARD | Kenneth William | Sgt | 20 | Pilot | 12.02.42 |
| HEDGE | Herbert | Sgt | 21 | Wop/AG | 16.08.43 |
| HEMMENS | Philip Derek | F/O | 20 | BA | 18.10.44 |
| HENDERSON | Andrew James | F/O | 27 | Pilot | 06.07.41 |
| HENDRIE | Alexander Rae | Sgt | 22 | FE | 12.10.42 |
| HENLEY | Leslie James | Sgt | 43 | FE | 18.08.43 |
| HENNESSEY | John Patrick | Sgt | 27 | FE | 11.04.44 |
| HENSON | Rex William | Sgt | 19 | AG | 11.12.44 |
| HEPBURN | Elmer James | F/O | 32 | BA | 07.10.43 |
| HERD | Mervyn J | F/Sgt | 23 | W/Op | 26.03.44 |
| HERDMAN | George | Sgt | 19 | W/Op | 11.11.40 |
| HEWITT | Herbert Henry | F/Sgt | 31 | BA | 08.07.44 |
| HIBBITT | Albert | Sgt | 21 | Wop/AG | 25.01.42 |
| HIGGINS | Wilfred | Sgt | 34 | W/Op | 08.07.44 |
| HILL | John Rowland | F/L | 29 | Pilot | 22.06.44 |
| HILL | John Travers | W/O | 23 | AG | 28.01.44 |
| HILL | Ronald Charles | Sgt | 20 | Wop/AG | 22.05.44 |
| HINCH | Lawrence Alexander | F/Sgt | 23 | BA | 09.06.44 |
| HOBAN | Walter John | Sgt | 26 | Wop/AG | 17.09.42 |
| HOBBY | Geoffrey | F/Sgt | 27 | Wop/AG | 20.02.44 |
| HODGE | Gordon | Sgt | 25 | AG | 12.10.42 |
| HODGKINSON | Alan | F/Sgt | 21 | Pilot | 22.10.43 |
| HODGKINSON | Sidney | Sgt | 36 | AG | 06.10.44 |
| HODGSON | Harold Seth | P/O | 22 | Pilot | 27.03.44 |
| HODKINSON | Charles | Sgt | 29 | Wop/AG | 29.08.41 |
| HOGARTH | Thomson | LAC | 22 | Wop/AG | 25.04.40 |
| HOLDEN | Clifford Charles | Sgt | 31 | Wop/AG | 22.06.44 |
| HOLDEN | John | Sgt | 21 | Wop/AG | 10.06.44 |
| HOLLARD | Mervyn Charles | P/O | 21 | BA | 19.07.44 |
| HOLLOWAY | Edward | Sgt | 25 | Nav | 16.12.43 |

| | | | | | |
|---|---|---|---|---|---|
| HOLMES | Lester Bertram | W/O | 29 | Nav | 19.07.44 |
| HOLMES | Sydney Charles | Sgt | 28 | FE | 10.06.44 |
| HOLT | Mervyn Harry | Sgt | 22 | Pilot | 12.02.42 |
| HOOD | Hugh Charles | Sgt | 33 | Wop/AG | 06.06.42 |
| HOOK | Edwin Frank | F/O | 24 | BA | 04.04.45 |
| HOOLE | Ronald | Sgt | 20 | FE | 16.03.44 |
| HORDERN | Alfred Peter Burdett | P/O | 22 | Pilot | 25.04.40 |
| HORNE | Alexander Manson | WOII | 33 | BA | 06.03.43 |
| HORNE | John William Beresford | F/O | 31 | AG | 12.10.42 |
| HORNER | Leon | Sgt | 22 | Wop/AG | 05.07.44 |
| HORNSBY | Norman | LAC | 19 | W/Op | 26.04.40 |
| HORSLEY | Victor | Sgt | 24 | BA | 15.06.43 |
| HOUGH | Ronald Foxley | Sgt | 20 | Pilot | 25.11.41 |
| HOUGHTON | John | Sgt | 19 | AG | 21.11.44 |
| HOWELL | Edward William | Sgt | 20 | Wop/AG | 23.09.43 |
| HOWISON | Arnold | Sgt | 22 | Wop/AG | 20.12.42 |
| HUBBARD | Frank William | F/Sgt | 35 | AG | 25.04.44 |
| HUDSON | Robert Hall | Sgt | 22 | AG | 27.04.44 |
| HUGHES | Donald John | F/Sgt | 20 | Wop/AG | 18.03.45 |
| HULL | Dennis Frank | F/Sgt | 18 | AG | 09.04.45 |
| HUMBLE | George | Sgt | 19 | AG | 18.08.43 |
| HUMPHRY | Edward Henry | AC1 | 20 | W/Op | 21.12.39 |
| HUNTER | Brian | Sgt | 27 | Wop/AG | 12.02.42 |
| HUNTINGFORD | Archie Edwin | Sgt | 22 | AG | 16.08.43 |
| HURST | Percy Joseph | Sgt | 27 | OBS | 26.04.40 |
| HUTCHISON | John | P/O | 24 | Pilot | 13.06.43 |
| IBBOTSON | Ernest Claude | Sgt | 22 | Wop/AG | 29.08.42 |
| ILLINGWORTH | George Ernest | F/O | 24 | Pilot | 12.11.44 |
| IMBER | Dennis Sydney | Sgt | 21 | Pilot | 16.10.40 |
| INGRAM | John Herbert | F/O | 29 | FE | 22.06.44 |
| IRVING | Henry | Sgt | 22 | Nav | 12.01.41 |
| IVETT | Philip Frederick | Sgt | 22 | FE | 15.03.45 |
| JACK | Henry | Sgt | 26 | Nav | 04.09.43 |
| JACKSON | Alexander | Sgt | 20 | W/Op | 12.02.42 |
| JACKSON | Arthur Leslie | F/Sgt | 22 | BA | 21.11.44 |
| JACKSON | Ernest William | F/Sgt | 21 | Wop/AG | 19.04.42 |
| JACKSON | Leonard | Sgt | 19 | AG | 12.01.41 |
| JACKSON | Peter Frederick Chester | Sgt | 20 | Nav | 09.04.45 |
| JACKSON | Robert Arthur | F/L | 27 | Pilot | 02.02.43 |
| JACOBS | Thomas Frederick | P/O | 21 | Pilot | 10.01.42 |
| JAMES | Arthur Francis | Sgt | 19 | OBS | 25.04.40 |
| JAMES | Brynley | F/O | 22 | Wop/AG | 18.08.43 |
| JAMES | Charles | Sgt | 26 | BA | 17.04.43 |

| | | | | | |
|---|---|---|---|---|---|
| JAMES | Mervyn | F/O | 34 | BA | 22.06.44 |
| JAMES | Ronald | Sgt | 23 | FE | 16.08.43 |
| JAMESON | George Walter | F/Sgt | 31 | BA | 19.07.44 |
| JARDINE | Leonard Arthur | Sgt | 20 | Wop/AG | 25.01.42 |
| JEFFREYS | Gordon Sidney | F/O | 21 | Pilot | 17.01.43 |
| JELLEY | Percy William Norman | Sgt | 20 | Wop/AG | 11.08.40 |
| JENKINS | Gordon Ralph | F/O | 32 | Pilot | 16.02.42 |
| JENNINGS | Robert James | Sgt | 24 | Pilot | 06.08.40 |
| JEWELL | John Gillian | Sgt | 31 | AG | 30.03.43 |
| JOHN | Frederick Edwin | P/O | 31 | AG | 12.11.44 |
| JOHNSON | Ernest Walter Haynes | Sgt | 19 | BA | 13.06.43 |
| JOHNSON | William George Wesley | F/O | 20 | Nav | 23.05.44 |
| JOHNSTON | Edward Irvine | F/Sgt | 21 | Pilot | 20.12.42 |
| JONES | David George Charles | F/Sgt | 22 | Nav | 10.08.43 |
| JONES | Ernest George | Sgt | 22 | FE | 23.05.44 |
| JONES | Frederick Edward | Sgt | 37 | FE | 12.11.44 |
| JONES | John | Sgt | 19 | AG | 06.08.40 |
| JONES | John Cuthbert | Sgt | | FE | 20.09.45 |
| JONES | Joseph | Sgt | 24 | W/Op | 30.04.44 |
| JONES | Kenneth Walton | F/O | 27 | Nav | 22.06.44 |
| JONES | Lewis James | Sgt | 20 | Wop/AG | 07.06.42 |
| JONES | Ninian Lewis | Sgt | 24 | Pilot | 26.04.40 |
| JUDD | James Frederick | F/O | 39 | Wop/AG | 25.06.44 |
| KAY | Herbert | Sgt | 20 | Wop/AG | 28.02.43 |
| KEEN | Victor Albert | Sgt | 25 | FE | 05.07.44 |
| KEHOE | John Edward | Sgt | 20 | Wop/AG | 08.11.41 |
| KELLOW | Leslie George | P/O | 25 | Pilot | 31.03.44 |
| KELLY | James Andrew | Sgt | 22 | AG | 28.02.43 |
| KELLY | Phillip | S/L | 34 | Nav | 21.11.44 |
| KENDREW | Clarence | Sgt | 20 | Wop/AG | 04.09.43 |
| KENNEDY | Leonard Thomas | W/OII | 25 | BA | 27.04.44 |
| KERNAHAN | John | P/O | 21 | W/Op | 08.07.44 |
| KETTLEWELL | Arthur | Sgt | 25 | Wop/AG | 07.09.41 |
| KIDD | George William Adriaan | F/O | 24 | BA | 08.02.45 |
| KING | Bede James Veitch | F/Sgt | 19 | AG | 16.12.43 |
| KING | James Charles | F/O | 23 | BA | 06.10.44 |
| KIRKPATRICK | George Edward | Sgt | 30 | AG | 29.07.44 |
| KIRWAN | John Anthony | Sgt | 25 | AG | 08.07.44 |
| KITTO | Philip Malcolm | F/Sgt | 23 | Nav | 26.07.44 |
| KNAPMAN | Richard Mannering | Sgt | 25 | AG | 20.01.42 |
| KNOWLES | John Joseph | F/O | 23 | BA | 16.03.44 |
| LABRIE | Reginald Edmund | F/Sgt | 20 | AG | 09.07.43 |
| LACY | Clifford | F/O | 26 | Pilot | 19.07.44 |

| | | | | | |
|---|---|---|---|---|---|
| LAIDLAW | Graeme Lonarch | P/O | 26 | Nav | 12.10.42 |
| LANE | Albert William | P/O | 28 | BA | 02.02.43 |
| LANGLEY | Norman Isaac | Sgt | 22 | Wop/AG | 26.11.44 |
| LAPPING | James Balam | F/O | 21 | Nav | 08.04.43 |
| LARVIN | William Patrick | Sgt | 19 | AG | 26.03.44 |
| LATHAM | Jim | P/O | 19 | AG | 31.03.44 |
| LAWN | George Stanley | Sgt | 31 | AG | 20.12.43 |
| LAWRENCE | Raymond George | F/Sgt | 20 | Wop/AG | 24.10.42 |
| LAWSON-TANCRED | Andrew Thomas | F/L | 29 | Pilot | 14.01.44 |
| LEE | Clifford Lawson | Sgt | 24 | A/Obs | 12.02.42 |
| LEE | Eric | Sgt | 19 | FE | 22.03.44 |
| LEEKE | George Charles | Sgt | 24 | AG | 16.03.45 |
| LESLIE | James Guthrie | F/Sgt | 32 | AG | 28.05.41 |
| LEWIS | Ronald George | P/O | 21 | Pilot | 03.09.42 |
| LEWIS | Thomas Glendenning Harries | P/O | 31 | BA | 24.05.43 |
| LINDSAY | James Fenton | Sgt | 20 | W/Op | 06.08.40 |
| LIPP | Peter | Sgt | 39 | FE | 09.04.45 |
| LIST | Stephen McCarthy | F/Sgt | 22 | AG | 03.11.43 |
| LITTLE | George Henry | F/Sgt | 21 | AG | 23.05.44 |
| LOCHHEAD | Clifford Molyneux | P/O | 20 | Nav | 19.09.40 |
| LOCKIE | George | F/O | 32 | BA | 13.07.43 |
| LOGIE | Alexander | Sgt | 21 | Wop/AG | 06.06.42 |
| LONG | Robert William | W/O | 34 | W/Op | 08.05.44 |
| LOSA | Ricardo | F/Sgt | 27 | AG | 16.12.43 |
| LOVELAND | John Thomas | Sgt | 22 | BA | 20.02.44 |
| LOVETT | Angus Thomas Jellicoe | F/Sgt | 28 | Wop/AG | 07.03.45 |
| LOWE | Harry | P/O | 22 | BA | 27.11.43 |
| LOWRIE | John | F/O | 21 | Pilot | 28.08.42 |
| LYON | Charles John | Sgt | 23 | AG | 21.03.41 |
| MABEE | George Floyd | F/O | 26 | Pilot | 30.03.43 |
| MACAULAY | Hugh | F/O | 28 | BA | 22.04.45 |
| MacFADYEN | Duncan | F/O | 28 | Nav | 10.06.44 |
| MacGREGOR | Gordon Fraser | P/O | 24 | BA | 22.06.44 |
| MacKENZIE | Norman Alexander Freeman | W/OII | 20 | BA | 27.04.44 |
| MacKENZIE | Robert Ian Leonard | Sgt | 23 | A/Obs | 25.04.40 |
| MACKEW | Gerald Victor | F/Sgt | 21 | BA | 23.04.44 |
| MacKINNON | Ian Donald | Sgt | 21 | AG | 25.08.41 |
| MACLELLAN | Malcolm | Sgt | 21 | AG | 20.12.42 |
| MacLENNAN | George Alexander | Sgt | 28 | AG | 09.04.45 |
| MAGDER | Hiam Murray | F/Sgt | 20 | A/Obs | 02.02.43 |
| MANDERS | Robert Emmett | P/O | 21 | A/Obs | 17.03.42 |
| MANNING | Bernard Charles | Sgt | 19 | AG | 09.04.45 |
| MARSHALL | William John | Sgt | 21 | A/Obs | 13.04.42 |

| MARSLAND | Albert Edgar Arthur | Sgt | 22 | FE | 16.12.43 |
| MARSON | Wilfred Henry | Sgt | 21 | AG | 03.11.43 |
| MATHER | William | F/O | 24 | Wop/AG | 22.06.44 |
| MATHESON | Everett Morley | P/O | 21 | AG | 19.07.44 |
| MATHIESON | Alexander James | Sgt | 20 | FE | 22.11.43 |
| MATHISON | William Thomas | P/O | 30 | BA | 06.09.43 |
| MATON | James Alfred Thomas | Sgt | 20 | AG | 22.06.44 |
| MATTHEWS | Albert Edward Anderson | F/L | 30 | FE | 22.06.44 |
| MAUL | Edwin Charles | F/O | 22 | Pilot | 21.11.44 |
| McCARTHY | Eric Joseph Frank | P/O | 25 | Wop/AG | 21.02.45 |
| McCLENAHAN | James Stark | Sgt | 21 | W/Op | 06.10.44 |
| McCRACKEN | Ronald George | F/O | 20 | Nav | 28.02.43 |
| McENEANEY | Terence Conlon | F/Sgt | 22 | Nav | 16.03.44 |
| McGRENERY | Thomas Hill | Sgt | 23 | Wop/AG | 10.04.42 |
| McGUFFIE | Hugh Martin | F/O | 23 | Pilot | 23.03.42 |
| MCGUIGAN | John Harrie | F/Sgt | 20 | Wop/AG | 08.04.45 |
| McGURK | Francis Leo | AC2 | 22 | W/Op | 04.10.39 |
| McKAY | Murray Roy | F/O | 20 | BA | 09.04.45 |
| McKENNA | Terence Francis Breen | Sgt | 21 | A/Obs | 20.06.42 |
| McKENZIE | John Gilmour | Sgt | 21 | FE | 06.10.44 |
| McLAREN | Alexander Stewart | Sgt | 21 | Wop/AG | 30.03.43 |
| McLAREN | Ian | Sgt | 26 | A/Obs | 19.04.42 |
| McLEOD | Benjamin | Sgt | 20 | AG | 08.05.44 |
| McMAHON | Owen Bernard | Sgt | 24 | Pilot | 25.08.41 |
| McMONAGLE | Lance Raymond | F/O | 24 | W/Op | 06.10.44 |
| McNUTT | Frank Arthur | W/OII | 23 | Wop/AG | 30.03.43 |
| McPHEE | Joseph Noel | F/L | 23 | Pilot | 15.03.45 |
| MELLON | Tom Henry | Sgt | 22 | W/Op | 21.11.40 |
| MELNICK | Nicholas | F/O | 30 | BA | 11.04.44 |
| MICHIE | Kenneth William | F/O | 24 | Pilot | 07.12.40 |
| MIDDLEBROOK | Reginald Frank | Sgt | 37 | FE | 17.06.43 |
| MILES | George John Arscott | Sgt | 29 | AG | 02.06.42 |
| MILLAR | George | P/O | 22 | Nav | 08.07.44 |
| MILLAR | John Guy | F/O | 32 | Pilot | 13.07.43 |
| MILLER | Frederick Charles | W/O | 20 | Wop/AG | 07.01.45 |
| MILLER | Gifford Benjamin Coles | F/Sgt | 31 | Pilot | 14.02.43 |
| MILLNS | Reginald | Sgt | 19 | AG | 26.03.44 |
| MINNS | Herbert | Sgt | 25 | AG | 03.11.43 |
| MITCHELL | James Baird | Sgt | 38 | FE | 02.11.44 |
| MITCHELL | Norman Rae | F/Sgt | 20 | Wop/AG | 28.08.42 |
| MONCK | Peter | Sgt | 20 | Wop/AG | 11.04.44 |
| MONTGOMERY | Robert | P/O | 22 | Pilot | 27.04.44 |
| MOODY | Donald Beverley | P/O | 22 | Wop/AG | 17.09.42 |

| | | | | | |
|---|---|---|---|---|---|
| MOORE | James Worrall | Sgt | 39 | AG | 17.12.44 |
| MOORE | Ronald Thomas | Sgt | 20 | Wop/AG | 15.06.43 |
| MOORE | Thomas | Sgt | 30 | AG | 29.07.44 |
| MOORE | Trevor Bryn | F/Sgt | 21 | AG | 04.04.45 |
| MORONEY | William John | F/O | - | AG | 04.11.44 |
| MORRIS | Frederick William | Sgt | 31 | FE | 20.12.42 |
| MORRIS | Thomas Harrison | P/O | 20 | AG | 27.04.44 |
| MORTON | Charles Gregory | F/Sgt | 21 | Nav | 22.06.44 |
| MOSS | John Morris | Sgt | 19 | FE | 08.07.44 |
| MOTTERAM | Harry Lawrence | F/O | 29 | BA | 04.11.44 |
| MUIR | Robert Kennedy Buchanan | Sgt | 32 | AG | 15.06.43 |
| MULLENGER | Stanley Gordon | Sgt | 21 | Wop/AG | 08.11.41 |
| MUNRO | Alexander Lyon | F/O | 23 | Wop/AG | 08.04.43 |
| MURRAY | John William | F/O | 27 | AG | 06.10.44 |
| MUSSON | Charles Ronald | Sgt | 24 | AG | 10.08.43 |
| MYERS | William Henry Ingham | P/O | 26 | BA | 24.10.42 |
| NEAL | Dennis William | Sgt | 25 | FE | 09.07.43 |
| NEAL | Herbert Reginald | F/Sgt | 32 | Nav | 19.07.44 |
| NEWBERRY | Kent | Sgt | 24 | Pilot | 29.08.42 |
| NEWBY | Joseph | F/Sgt | 22 | Nav | 21.02.45 |
| NEWHOUSE | Hugh Francis Perceval | P/O | 27 | Pilot | 12.01.41 |
| NICOL | William | Sgt | 26 | Pilot | 29.09.40 |
| NIGHTINGALE | Linton Henry | Sgt | 22 | Wop/AG | 22.03.44 |
| NINEHAM | Ronald Eric | Sgt | 19 | AG | 08.07.44 |
| NIXON | Norman | W/O | 20 | Pilot | 15.06.43 |
| NOBLE | William | Sgt | 30 | BA | 14.02.43 |
| NORLEY | Ronald William | Sgt | 23 | Wop/AG | 26.11.43 |
| NORTHROP | Kenneth Edward | Sgt | 22 | Obs | 25.01.42 |
| NUGENT | John Percival | F/Sgt | 29 | Nav | 23.09.43 |
| O'BRIEN | John Ormond | Sgt | 23 | Pilot | 20.06.42 |
| O'DEA | Ronald Patrick | F/Sgt | 21 | AG | 26.11.43 |
| O'KEEFE | Daniel Patrick | Sgt | 20 | BA | 08.03.45 |
| O'LEARY | Timothy Thomas | Sgt | 20 | Nav | 07.10.43 |
| OLSON | Charles Stanley | P/O | 30 | Nav | 13.06.43 |
| OPENSHAW | John Derek | LAC | 19 | W/Op | 25.04.40 |
| OSBALDESTON | James Duckett | Sgt | 22 | AG | 29.08.42 |
| OSBORNE | Raymond George | F/Sgt | 21 | Nav | 27.04.44 |
| PALMER | Cecil John Edward | F/L | 21 | Pilot | 03.01.44 |
| PALMER | Dennis William | Sgt | 23 | FE | 22.06.44 |
| PALMER | Ernest Richard | F/Sgt | 21 | Wop/AG | 29.08.41 |
| PARAMORE | Roger Edward Rawle | F/L | 23 | Pilot | 06.06.42 |
| PARBERY | Donald George | Sgt | 22 | FE | 04.04.45 |
| PARISH | Edward Francis | Sgt | 20 | W/Op | 07.12.40 |

| | | | | | |
|---|---|---|---|---|---|
| PARKER | Edwin Earle | F/Sgt | 20 | AG | 22.10.43 |
| PARKER | Richard Cecil | F/O | 21 | Pilot | 17.10.40 |
| PARKIN | Dennis | Sgt | 20 | AG | 18.08.43 |
| PARKIN | Terence | Sgt | 23 | Wop/AG | 27.04.44 |
| PARKINSON | Gordon James William | F/Sgt | 20 | AG | 08.07.44 |
| PARSONS | George Rene Joseph | LAC | 19 | W/Op | 25.05.40 |
| PARTINGTON | Ralph | Sgt | 22 | AG | 23.04.44 |
| PATERSON | Robert Campbell | Sgt | 36 | FE | 23.09.43 |
| PATEY | Ernest Albert | Sgt | 21 | AG | 02.06.42 |
| PAWSON | George Stanley | Sgt | 19 | AG | 04.09.43 |
| PEACOCK | Clarence | F/Sgt | 24 | W/Op | 22.03.44 |
| PEARCE | Wilfred | F/O | 25 | BA | 22.03.44 |
| PEARSON | Edward Henry | Sgt | 19 | AG | 13.06.43 |
| PEIRCE | William Dudley | Sgt | 20 | Wop/AG | 28.08.42 |
| PENRY | David Trevor | Sgt | 25 | Pilot | 17.04.43 |
| PERKINS | Robert George | F/O | 22 | Pilot | 09.04.45 |
| PERRY | Geoffrey John | F/Sgt | 21 | Wop/AG | 19.07.44 |
| PETCH | John William | F/Sgt | 24 | W/Op | 22.04.45 |
| PETTIT | Norman George Valentine | Sgt | 20 | FE | 22.06.44 |
| PHILLIPS | Edward Walter | Sgt | 21 | Pilot | 12.02.42 |
| PHILLIPS | Leslie John | F/Sgt | 22 | BA | 22.03.44 |
| PHIPPS | Roger | Sgt | 21 | AG | 14.01.44 |
| PICKER | George William | Sgt | 21 | W/Op | 26.07.44 |
| PINCH | Francis James | F/Sgt | 20 | BA | 08.05.44 |
| PITMAN | Charles Derek | F/O | 30 | Pilot | 17.10.40 |
| PITTARD | Frederick Stanley Tristram | Sgt | 23 | FE | 31.01.43 |
| PLANT | Fred | F/O | 22 | BA | 18.08.43 |
| POLLITT | David Charles | F/Sgt | 20 | Pilot | 12.02.42 |
| POLLOCK | John Howie | Sgt | 22 | AG | 06.06.42 |
| POTTER | Robert | Sgt | 20 | Wop/AG | 17.10.40 |
| POTTS | Samuel Hainey | Sgt | 23 | Obs | 21.12.39 |
| POWELL | William Leonard | F/L | 22 | Pilot | 29.07.44 |
| POXON | Douglas Guy Frank | Sgt | 28 | AG | 12.02.42 |
| PRATT | Thomas Pinckney | P/O | 25 | Pilot | 29.08.41 |
| PRICE | Gordon Ernest | P/O | 33 | Pilot | 06.01.41 |
| PRICE | Harrington Warren | Sgt | 27 | Wop/AG | 20.06.42 |
| PRING | George Stanley | Sgt | 29 | BA | 08.04.43 |
| PRIOR | John Henry | F/Sgt | 27 | Nav/B | 06.03.43 |
| PROSSER | Peter Charles | Sgt | 19 | W/Op | 12.01.41 |
| PRUSHER | Derek Francis | Sgt | 18 | AG | 03.01.44 |
| PRUST | Harold | Sgt | 22 | FE | 09.04.45 |
| PURDIE | William Smith | Sgt | 20 | FE | 20.02.44 |
| PURRINGTON | Arthur | Sgt | 22 | FE | 18.08.43 |

| | | | | | |
|---|---|---|---|---|---|
| RAE | George Arthur | P/O | 23 | BA | 08.07.44 |
| RAINBOW | Leslie John Clifford | Sgt | 20 | W/Op | 09.06.44 |
| RAINE | Albert | Sgt | 28 | Wop/AG | 29.09.41 |
| RAMMAGE | Albert John | P/O | 20 | AG | 20.07.44 |
| RAMSEY | John Cook | Sgt | 27 | AG | 31.05.42 |
| RANDALL | Harry John | F/O | 33 | Pilot | 18.08.43 |
| RANDALL | Leslie | F/Sgt | 22 | W/Op | 08.02.45 |
| RATCLIFFE | Gordon Lennox | P/O | 23 | Pilot | 16.12.43 |
| RAY | Charles Lawrence | Sgt | 25 | Pilot | 26.06.41 |
| READ | Harry George John Heaps | Sgt | 21 | Wop/AG | 13.07.43 |
| REAY | Gordon | AC1 | 19 | AG | 25.08.40 |
| REED | Joseph John | Sgt | 23 | AG | 10.06.44 |
| REES | Frederick Bernard | F/Sgt | 22 | W/Op | 17.12.44 |
| REES | Terence | F/Sgt | 24 | AG | 06.10.44 |
| REES | William Thomas | Sgt | 23 | Wop/AG | 16.12.43 |
| REYNOLDS | Robert George | Sgt | 26 | Wop/AG | 03.09.42 |
| RHODES | Harry Robert | Sgt | 22 | AG | 15.06.43 |
| RICHARD | Clarence Edwin | F/Sgt | 24 | AG | 11.04.44 |
| RICHARD | Russell Bernard | F/O | 24 | Nav | 22.11.43 |
| RICHARDS | Edward Gordon Coke | F/Sgt | 28 | AG | 15.03.45 |
| RICHARDSON | Roy Joseph | P/O | 25 | Pilot | 27.11.43 |
| RICKETTS | Richard Frank | Sgt | 23 | AG | 22.10.43 |
| RIDLEY | Frank | F/O | 21 | Nav | 31.01.43 |
| RIMES | Edwin Samuel | Sgt | 25 | W/Op | 17.12.40 |
| RIX | John Albert | Sgt | 21 | AG | 02.11.44 |
| ROACH | Joseph Charles | P/O | 24 | Nav | 08.05.44 |
| ROBERTS | Roly Frederick | Sgt | 23 | Pilot | 31.08.40 |
| ROBERTSON | James | Sgt | 22 | AG | 30.03.43 |
| ROBERTSON | Robert Forrest | Sgt | 21 | Wop/AG | 28.10.40 |
| ROBERTSON | Thomas Charles | Sgt | 23 | Wop/AG | 17.04.43 |
| ROBERTSON | William Burns | Sgt | 21 | Wop/AG | 10.01.42 |
| ROBINSON | Graeme Alastair | F/O | 20 | Nav | 15.03.45 |
| RODEN | Ernest Howard | Sgt | 32 | FE | 10.08.43 |
| ROGERS | Neville John | Sgt | 19 | AG | 20.06.42 |
| ROGERS | Ormond Roy | P/O | 21 | AG | 22.03.44 |
| ROLFE | Douglas | Sgt | 21 | Nav | 25.04.44 |
| ROLLINS | James Leslie | P/O | 27 | AG | 08.04.43 |
| ROOKE | William James | P/O | 26 | Nav | 18.08.43 |
| ROONEY | Raymond Joseph | Sgt | 19 | BA | 17.04.43 |
| ROSE | Robert Frederick | Sgt | 25 | Pilot | 16.10.40 |
| ROSS | Alexander Robert | P/O | 23 | Pilot | 22.06.44 |
| ROSS | Colin Patrick | F/O | 26 | BA | 03.11.43 |
| ROSS | William Charles Henry | F/Sgt | 25 | W/Op | 12.10.42 |

| | | | | | |
|---|---|---|---|---|---|
| ROWAN-ROBINSON | Derrick Paul Woodrow | F/O | 22 | Pilot | 25.04.40 |
| ROWCLIFFE | David | Sgt | 21 | Nav | 01.04.44 |
| ROXBY | Henry | Sgt | 23 | AG | 02.11.44 |
| RUDD | John Alan | Sgt | 20 | W/Op | 11.12.44 |
| RUSHTON | Edward William | Sgt | 25 | AG | 08.05.44 |
| RUSSELL | Ernest Albert | P/O | 26 | BA | 06.10.44 |
| RYAN | Douglas James | F/Sgt | 22 | W/Op | 19.07.44 |
| SACRE | John George | Sgt | 30 | FE | 04.09.43 |
| SANDERSON | Douglas Albert | Sgt | 20 | Wop/AG | 09.06.44 |
| SANDERSON | John Thomas | Sgt | 21 | BA | 07.01.45 |
| SAUNDERS | Christopher Arthur | W/O | 28 | Pilot | 08.11.41 |
| SAVILLE | Bernard John | P/O | 34 | Nav | 20.12.43 |
| SAWDY | Edward George | Sgt | 26 | Pilot | 28.12.41 |
| SCOLTOCK | Anthony Terence Nicholas | F/L | 22 | Pilot | 17.12.40 |
| SCOTT | Bruce Robert | Sgt | 21 | AG | 05.07.44 |
| SCOTT | Raymond David | P/O | 31 | Nav | 06.10.44 |
| SEATON | Robert Harold | Sgt | 29 | AG | 06.06.42 |
| SELBY-LOWNDES | Richard Montacute William | Sgt | 20 | AG | 17.06.43 |
| SEYMOUR | Francis Stanley | Sgt | 22 | FE | 19.07.44 |
| SHACKLETON | Ernest | F/Sgt | 22 | BA | 26.07.44 |
| SHACKLETON | William Clifford | P/O | 21 | Pilot | 02.06.42 |
| SHAW | Deryck Harold | Sgt | 22 | BA | 14.01.44 |
| SHAW | Frank | Sgt | 22 | FE | 25.04.44 |
| SHAW | John Cecil | Sgt | 23 | Pilot | 04.01.42 |
| SHAW | William Oliver | F/Sgt | 20 | W/Op | 02.11.44 |
| SHEPHERD | Gordon George | Sgt | 22 | Wop/AG | 09.07.43 |
| SHINGLES | Ivan | Sgt | 23 | FE | 19.07.44 |
| SHINN | Albert William | P/O | 30 | Pilot | 22.06.44 |
| SILVER | Sydney Gordon | Sgt | 19 | FE | 31.03.44 |
| SILVESTER | George Bernard | F/Sgt | 26 | AG | 18.08.43 |
| SIMMONDS | George Herbert | Sgt | 21 | BA | 04.04.45 |
| SIMMONS | William Albert | Sgt | 19 | AG | 31.03.44 |
| SIMONSON | Percy Hardy | F/Sgt | 32 | Nav | 27.03.44 |
| SIMPKIN | Leslie Norman | F/O | 24 | Pilot | 22.06.44 |
| SIMPSON | Robert John | P/O | 20 | AG | 21.02.45 |
| SINCLAIR | Francis Frederick | Sgt | 21 | Wop/AG | 04.04.45 |
| SINDEN | Francis Edward | F/O | 22 | BA | 23.05.44 |
| SIZER | Claude William Frank | Sgt | 20 | W/Op | 27.04.44 |
| SLAUGHTER | Robert William | Sgt | 26 | AG | 18.08.43 |
| SLINGO | Francis William | Sgt | 26 | Pilot | 19.04.42 |
| SMALL | Cyril Alexander | Sgt | 20 | W/Op | 06.01.41 |
| SMALL | Ronald John | Sgt | 21 | Wop/AG | 10.08.43 |
| SMILEY | Thomas Stamper | P/O | 26 | Pilot | 09.06.44 |

| | | | | | |
|---|---|---|---|---|---|
| SMITH | David Arthur | S/L | 23 | Pilot | 28.05.41 |
| SMITH | Edward | Sgt | 20 | AG | 02.12.43 |
| SMITH | Edward Percival | F/O | 27 | Pilot | 21.02.45 |
| SMITH | George Edward | Sgt | 27 | Wop/AG | 25.11.41 |
| SMITH | James Thompson John | Sgt | 20 | AG | 13.04.42 |
| SMITH | John | Sgt | 18 | Wop/AG | 31.05.42 |
| SMITH | Robert Gordon | Sgt | 21 | Nav | 17.06.43 |
| SMITH | Stanley | F/Sgt | 24 | Nav | 27.04.44 |
| SMITH | Thomas Haydon | Sgt | 21 | A/Obs | 29.09.41 |
| SMITH | Thomas James | Sgt | 23 | Wop/AG | 14.01.44 |
| SMITH | William | Sgt | 27 | AG | 12.02.42 |
| SOUTHERN | Derek John Nigel | F/O | 22 | Pilot | 08.04.43 |
| SPEAK | Leslie George | F/Sgt | 25 | W/Op | 04.11.44 |
| SPICKETT | William Alfred | Sgt | 26 | AG | 27.06.40 |
| SPIERS | Joseph | Sgt | 21 | BA | 23.09.43 |
| SPROSTON | Hugh Raymond | F/Sgt | 20 | Nav | 04.04.45 |
| STANCLIFFE | Cecil | Sgt | 23 | Wop/AG | 18.08.43 |
| STANLEY | John Bottomley | F/O | 26 | Nav | 22.06.44 |
| STANTON | David | F/Sgt | 23 | Pilot | 23.09.43 |
| STARK | Roussel William Galloway | F/Sgt | 23 | Pilot | 07.03.45 |
| STEELE | John Anthony | Sgt | 19 | Wop/AG | 16.02.42 |
| STEELL | Douglas George Buchan | Sgt | 19 | Wop/AG | 20.11.40 |
| STEPHEN | Andrew | Sgt | 26 | AG | 06.10.44 |
| STEPHENS | Donald Carl | F/Sgt | 20 | W/Op | 29.07.44 |
| STEVENS | Donald Nabe | Sgt | 19 | AG | 20.02.44 |
| STEVENSON | Kent | Mr | 36 | BBC | 22.06.44 |
| STEWART | Charles Duncan Stuart | Sgt | 23 | Pilot | 25.01.42 |
| STIBBARD | John Hamilton | W/O | 23 | Nav | 08.07.44 |
| STILES | William John | Sgt | 31 | BA | 18.08.43 |
| STOBART | Hanley | Sgt | 21 | AG | 11.12.44 |
| STOBO | Ronald | F/O | 21 | BA | 03.01.44 |
| STOREY | George Gerard | S/L | 32 | Pilot | 17.06.43 |
| STUART | Ian Douglas | F/Sgt | 20 | Nav | 09.06.44 |
| SULLIVAN | Edward Thomas Ebenezer | Sgt | 28 | AG | 14.01.44 |
| SWAN | Gilbert Aitken | Sgt | 25 | Nav/B | 29.08.42 |
| TABENOR | Geoffrey | Sgt | 20 | Wop/AG | 22.11.43 |
| TALBOT | Derrick | F/O | 22 | Pilot | 04.11.44 |
| TALBOT | Frank Leslie | AC2 | 18 | W/Op | 23.11.39 |
| TAVERNER | Philip Ackroyd | P/O | 21 | Pilot | 22.10.43 |
| TAYLOR | Colin William | F/Sgt | 21 | AG | 16.08.43 |
| TAYLOR | Harold | Sgt | 24 | Wop/AG | 13.04.42 |
| TAYLOR | Stanley | AC1 | 18 | AG | 23.11.39 |
| TELFER | Adam | Sgt | 22 | FE | 21.04.43 |

| | | | | | |
|---|---|---|---|---|---|
| TELFORD | Phillip | F/Sgt | 19 | AG | 21.11.44 |
| THOM | James Myles | Sgt | 29 | Pilot | 06.03.43 |
| THOMAS | Cecil George | F/L | 33 | Pilot | 03.11.43 |
| THOMAS | Harry | Sgt | 19 | AG | 20.02.44 |
| THOMAS | Owen Dixon | F/O | 29 | Pilot | 17.09.42 |
| THOMPSON | Raymond Franklin | F/O | 30 | BA | 15.03.45 |
| THOMPSON | Robert | Sgt | 21 | AG | 25.06.44 |
| THOMSON | James Andrew | F/O | 25 | BA | 17.12.44 |
| THORNDYKE | Ronald Henry James | P/O | 21 | A/Obs | 07.06.42 |
| TIEDEMAN | James Henry | Sgt | 25 | A/Obs | 17.12.40 |
| TILEY | Charles John | Sgt | 19 | FE | 08.04.43 |
| TINGLE | Frank | P/O | 22 | AG | 12.11.44 |
| TODD-WHITE | Richard Nevil | S/L | 27 | Pilot | 18.08.43 |
| TOGHILL | Leslie Cyril | Sgt | 23 | AG | 12.02.42 |
| TOMLIN | Thomas Edwin | P/O | 22 | Pilot | 18.08.43 |
| TOMS | Peter Alfred | Sgt | 20 | AG | 15.06.43 |
| TONGE | Harry Clifford | P/O | 29 | Nav | 29.08.41 |
| TONKIN | Thomas | P/O | 23 | AG | 18.08.43 |
| TRUSCOTT | James Robert | P/O | 20 | AG | 05.07.44 |
| TUNLEY | James | Sgt | 32 | FE | 23.09.43 |
| TURNER | Donald George | F/O | 28 | Pilot | 22.03.44 |
| TURNER | Howard Ernest | P/O | 24 | FE | 19.07.44 |
| UNDERLIN | George Samuel | Sgt | 22 | FE | 17.06.43 |
| UPTON | Gathorne Field | Sgt | 23 | Pilot | 25.08.41 |
| UPTON | Stanley James | F/Sgt | 22 | Nav | 22.03.44 |
| VAREY | Harry | Sgt | 24 | FE | 17.12.44 |
| VERRIER | Alfred Reginald | F/O | 22 | AG | 21.11.44 |
| VINCENT | Harold Jessie | P/O | 29 | A/Obs | 06.06.42 |
| VINES | Frank Harry Liddon | Sgt | 21 | AG | 06.03.43 |
| VIOLLET | Robert Frederick Henry | Sgt | 24 | AG | 19.07.44 |
| WADDELL | James | Sgt | 22 | Wop/AG | 06.04.42 |
| WAINWRIGHT | George Albert | Sgt | 28 | A/Obs | 20.12.42 |
| WAKEFORD | Donald William | P/O | 23 | Pilot | 11.11.40 |
| WALE | Frederick William | F/Sgt | 21 | Nav | 27.04.44 |
| WALFORD | Leonard Ernest | Sgt | 23 | Wop/AG | 31.03.44 |
| WALKE | William Arthur | F/Sgt | 22 | BA | 02.12.43 |
| WALKER | Alfred Cole | Sgt | 23 | Pilot | 29.09.41 |
| WALKER | Cyril Ivan | F/Sgt | 20 | FE | 22.04.45 |
| WALKER | Thomas Ellwood | Sgt | 27 | Nav | 08.01.45 |
| WALL | Guy Reginald | F/Sgt | 23 | Wop/AG | 09.04.45 |
| WALLIS | Robert Joseph | Sgt | 27 | FE | 24.10.42 |
| WALLNER | John Isidore | F/Sgt | 23 | AG | 18.08.43 |
| WALMSLEY | Donald Parker | Sgt | 30 | A/Obs | 07.04.42 |

| | | | | | |
|---|---|---|---|---|---|
| WALTON | Charles Frederick | F/Sgt | 26 | Nav | 23.09.43 |
| WARD | John Richard | Sgt | 20 | FE | 20.02.44 |
| WARDMAN | Eric | Sgt | 21 | FE | 08.07.44 |
| WARING | William Henry | Sgt | 33 | BA | 17.06.43 |
| WARREN | John | Sgt | 20 | Wop/AG | 10.01.42 |
| WARRINGTON | Peter John | F/Sgt | 22 | Nav | 09.04.45 |
| WATSON | Dennis | Sgt | 21 | W/Op | 29.08.41 |
| WATSON | Kenneth Ernest | Sgt | 33 | FE | 18.08.43 |
| WATSON | William Anderson | F/Sgt | 21 | Wop/AG | 01.11.41 |
| WATT | Archibald Campbell | Sgt | 28 | Pilot | 28.12.41 |
| WATT | Bruce Emmott | P/O | 22 | AG | 17.04.43 |
| WATT | David Walter | Sgt | 20 | AG | 11.11.40 |
| WATT | P McGregor | S/L | 32 | Pilot | 23.11.39 |
| WATTS | Christopher Anthony | F/O | 26 | Nav/B | 17.01.43 |
| WAUGH | Thomas William | P/O | 23 | Pilot | 16.03.44 |
| WAY | Stanley William Alfred | P/O | 21 | Wop/AG | 12.02.42 |
| WEBB | Bernard Frank | Sgt | 20 | FE | 09.06.44 |
| WEBBE | Leslie William | Sgt | 25 | A/Obs | 15.04.42 |
| WEBLEY | Raymond John | Sgt | 22 | Wop/AG | 19.04.42 |
| WEEDON | Stanley William | Sgt | 20 | AG | 11.04.44 |
| WEEKS | Courtenay Arthur | P/O | 21 | Pilot/Nav | 25.04.40 |
| WELBOURN | Ernest | Sgt | 25 | Wop/AG | 25.08.41 |
| WELCH | Arnold Gregory | Sgt | 27 | AG | 31.05.42 |
| WEST | Geoffrey Llewellyn | Sgt | 21 | Pilot | 06.01.42 |
| WEST | John Frederick | Sgt | 29 | FE | 29.07.44 |
| WHEWELL | Thomas Birtwistle | Sgt | 21 | Wop/AG | 22.06.44 |
| WHITE | David | F/O | 23 | Pilot | 26.04.40 |
| WHITE | Edward | F/Sgt | 20 | Pilot | 20.02.44 |
| WHITE | Raymond Charles | Sgt | 21 | Wop/AG | 17.04.43 |
| WHITEHILL | Maxwell Elliot | F/Sgt | 29 | AG | 07.06.42 |
| WHITELEY | Herbert | F/Sgt | 32 | AG | 22.03.44 |
| WHITFIELD | George Clive | Sgt | 32 | Wop/AG | 06.06.42 |
| WHITING | Philip Edward | Sgt | 23 | AG | 26.06.41 |
| WHITTAKER | Alan Ewart | F/O | 29 | Nav | 15.06.43 |
| WHITTEMORE | Harold | Sgt | 29 | Pilot | 06.06.42 |
| WICK | Sidney John | Sgt | 19 | AG | 20.12.42 |
| WIGGINS | Ronald Rodney | Sgt | 28 | AG | 08.02.45 |
| WILBY | Frank Paul | Sgt | 21 | FE | 06.09.43 |
| WILDE | Colin | Sgt | 21 | FE | 15.06.43 |
| WILKINS | Ronald Ernest | F/Sgt | 23 | AG | 09.04.45 |
| WILKINSON | John Ernest | F/Sgt | 26 | BA | 09.04.45 |
| WILKINSON | John William | Sgt | 20 | AG | 10.04.42 |
| WILLIAMS | Ivor Gordon | P/O | 22 | Wop/AG | 21.11.44 |

| | | | | | |
|---|---|---|---|---|---|
| WILLIS | Arthur Charles | Sgt | 22 | Wop/AG | 29.08.41 |
| WILSON | Dennis Alfred | Sgt | 20 | AG | 25.06.44 |
| WILSON | Edward D | Sgt | 20 | AG | 26.11.43 |
| WILSON | Frank William Moles | Sgt | 20 | A/Obs | 02.06.42 |
| WILSON | The Hon. Robert David | P/O | 25 | Pilot | 22.03.41 |
| WINNING | William Burton Cecil | Sgt | 26 | Pilot | 06.01.41 |
| WISDOM | Henry William | Sgt | 22 | W/Op | 28.12.41 |
| WISE | John Grenfell | Sgt | 19 | AG | 16.03.44 |
| WITTY | George Frederica | Sgt | 34 | FE | 22.06.44 |
| WOOD | Alexander Milne | Sgt | 26 | Wop/AG | 17.12.40 |
| WOOD | George Frederick | F/Sgt | 19 | AG | 22.06.44 |
| WOOD | Henry Leonard | Sgt | 20 | Wop/AG | 03.11.43 |
| WOOD | Terence Albert | F/Sgt | 20 | AG | 10.08.43 |
| WOOD | Thomas Henry Forrest | Sgt | 24 | Pilot | 12.02.42 |
| WOOD | William Charles | Sgt | 22 | AG | 31.01.43 |
| WOODHEAD | Stuart | Sgt | 28 | A/Obs | 10.04.42 |
| WOODING | Frederick Arthur | F/O | 24 | FE | 21.11.44 |
| WOODROFFE | John Arthur | Sgt | 22 | Wop/AG | 16.02.42 |
| WORKMAN | Leslie Edmund | F/Sgt | 29 | AG | 13.06.43 |
| WORTHINGTON | James Robert | F/O | 30 | W/Op | 22.06.44 |
| WORTHY | Reginald Percy | F/O | 27 | Pilot | 10.04.42 |
| WRIGHT | Frank | Sgt | 32 | AG | 04.04.45 |
| WRIGHT | Maurice Winter | F/O | 20 | BA | 22.11.43 |
| YEATES | Lawrence John | Sgt | 26 | Wop/AG | 31.05.42 |
| YELLAND | Cyril William | Sgt | 23 | Nav/B | 17.04.43 |
| YOUNG | George Thomas | F/O | 31 | Nav | 03.01.44 |
| YOUNG | Leslie | Sgt | 28 | A/Obs | 07.12.40 |
| YOUNG | Stanley | Sgt | 20 | FE | 14.02.43 |

# 49 Squadron

MOTTO **CAVE CANEM** (Beware of the dog)  Code **EA**

## STATIONS

| | |
|---|---|
| **SCAMPTON** | 14.03.38. to 02.01.43. |
| **KINLOSS** (Detachment to Coastal Command). | 26.01.40. to 20.03.40. |
| **FISKERTON** | 02.01.43. to 16.10.44. |
| **FULBECK** | 16.10.44. to 22.04.45. |
| **SYERSTON** | 22.04.45. to 28.09.45. |

## COMMANDING OFFICERS

| | |
|---|---|
| **WING COMMANDER** J S CHICK MC AFC | 27.02.39. to 01.12.39. |
| **WING COMMANDER** W C SHEEN | 01.12.39. to 08.04.40. |
| **WING COMMANDER** J W GILLAN DFC AFC | 08.04.40. to 22.12.40. |
| **WING COMMANDER** J N JEFFERSON | 22.12.40. to 17.07.41. |
| **WING COMMANDER** R D STUBBS DFC | 17.07.41. to 14.05.42. |
| **WING COMMANDER** L C SLEE DSO DFC | 14.05.42. to 05.04.43. |
| **WING COMMANDER** P W JOHNSON DFC AFC | 05.04.43. to 15.09.43. |
| **WING COMMANDER** A A ADAMS | 15.09.43. to 01.05.44. |
| **WING COMMANDER** M CROCKER DFC | 01.05.44. to 22.06.44. |
| **WING COMMANDER** L E BOTTING | 23.06.44. to 12.06.45. |

## AIRCRAFT

| | | |
|---|---|---|
| **HAMPDEN** | 09.38. to | 04.42. |
| **MANCHESTER** | 04.42. to | 07.42. |
| **LANCASTER I/III** | 07.42. to | 10.49. |

# OPERATIONAL RECORD

| OPERATIONS | SORTIES | AIRCRAFT LOSSES | % LOSSES |
|---|---|---|---|
| 674 | 6501 | 163 | 2.5 |

## CATEGORY OF OPERATIONS

| BOMBING | MINING | LEAFLET |
|---|---|---|
| 543 | 105 | 26 |

## HAMPDENS

| OPERATIONS | SORTIES | AIRCRAFT LOSSES | % LOSSES |
|---|---|---|---|
| 342 | 2636 | 55 | 2.1 |

### CATEGORY OF OPERATIONS

| BOMBING | MINING | LEAFLET |
|---|---|---|
| 241 | 82 | 19 |

## MANCHESTERS

| OPERATIONS | SORTIES | AIRCRAFT LOSSES | % LOSSES |
|---|---|---|---|
| 10 | 47 | 6 | 12.8 |

### CATEGORY OF OPERATIONS

| BOMBING | MINING | LEAFLET |
|---|---|---|
| 4 | 2 | 4 |

## LANCASTERS

| OPERATIONS | SORTIES | AIRCRAFT LOSSES | % LOSSES |
|---|---|---|---|
| 323 | 3818 | 102 | 2.7 |

### CATEGORY OF OPERATIONS

| BOMBING | MINING | LEAFLET |
|---|---|---|
| 298 | 21 | 3 |

# Aircraft Histories

| | |
|---|---|
| **HAMPDEN** | **To April 1942.** |
| **L4034** | From CFS. Crashed at Waddington during training 23.11.39. |
| **L4036** EA-R | FTR Dortmund 11/12.8.40. |
| **L4038** | To 106 Squadron. |
| **L4040** | FTR from a mining sortie 25/26.4.40. |
| **L4041** | To 7 Squadron. |
| **L4042** | To 44 Squadron via 7 Squadron and 16 Operational Training Unit. |
| **L4043** | Crashed on a Northumberland beach on return from a mining sortie 15.4.40. |
| **L4044** EA-R | Crashed soon after take-off from Scampton when bound for Amiens 8.6.40. |
| **L4045** EA-Q | Crashed in Lincolnshire on return from Wilhelmshaven 12.1.41. |
| **L4046** | To 44 Squadron. |
| **L4053** | To 83 Squadron. |
| **L4060** EA-H | To 5 Bombing and Gunnery School. |
| **L4066** | To 83 Squadron. |
| **L4067** | To 144 Squadron. |
| **L4068** | FTR Mönchengladbach 11/12.5.40. Crew got home. |
| **L4072** | Crashed in Northumberland on return from reconnaissance sweep off Norway 21.12.39. |
| **L4077** EA-S | From 50 Squadron. Crashed in Norfolk on return from a mining sortie 21.7.40. |
| **L4086** | From 44 Squadron via 14 OTU. To 420 (Snowy Owl) Squadron RCAF. |
| **L4092** | FTR from mining sortie 25/26.4.40. |
| **L4125** | From 144 Squadron. Crashed on take-off from Scampton when bound for a mining sortie 7.2.42. |
| **L4129** EA-P | From 144 Squadron. FTR from a mining sortie 16/17.10.40. |
| **L4195** EA-H | From 185 Squadron. Crashed in Kent on return from a mining sortie 17.10.40. |
| **P1153** | To 455 Squadron RAAF. |
| **P1174** | To 16 OTU. |
| **P1175** | Crashed on landing at Scampton on return from a mining sortie 21/22.4.40. |
| **P1176** | To 14 OTU. |
| **P1177** | To 25 OTU. |
| **P1206** EA-Z/K | FTR from an intruder sortie to Bocholt 8/9.11.41. |
| **P1226** | Crashed in Devon during a transit flight 17.3.42. |
| **P1310** | From 14 OTU. To 415 (Swordfish) Squadron RCAF after conversion for use as torpedo bomber. |
| **P1314** | From Central Gunnery School. To 420 (Snowy Owl) Squadron RCAF. |
| **P1318** EA-B | FTR from a communications target in the Krefeld/Aachen area 25/26.5.40. |
| **P1319** | FTR from a mining sortie 25/26.4.40. |

| | |
|---|---|
| **P1323** | From 61 Squadron. To 16 OTU. |
| **P1333** EA-F | FTR Merseburg 16/17.8.40. |
| **P1347** EA-D | FTR Stettin 4/5.9.40. |
| **P2063** | To 144 Squadron. |
| **P2068** EA-A/F | Crashed soon after take-off from Scampton while training 19.6.41. |
| **P2095** | To 25 OTU. |
| **P2111** | To 25 OTU. |
| **P2112** EA-V | To 14 OTU. |
| **P2134** EA-W | Crashed in Lancashire during training 29.9.40. |
| **P2135** | Crashed soon after take-off from Scampton on a ferry flight 31.8.40. |
| **P2143** EA-A | Crashed in Hampshire on return from Bordeaux 17.10.40. |
| **P2145** | To 16 OTU. |
| **P4299** | FTR Düsseldorf 4/5.2.41 |
| **P4304** EA-O | To 489 Squadron RNZAF after conversion for use as torpedo bomber. |
| **P4305** EA-U | FTR from a mining sortie 26/27.6.40. |
| **P4321** EA-T | To 1 AAS. |
| **P4322** EA-N | FTR from a mining sortie 5/6.1.41. |
| **P4350** EA-L | FTR Stettin 5/6.9.40. |
| **P4351** EA-R | Ditched off Lincolnshire coast on return from Kiel 3/4.8.40. |
| **P4377** EA-K | From 106 Squadron. FTR from a mining sortie 6/7.8.40. |
| **P4384** | Crashed in Berkshire during an operation to Bordeaux 27/28.12.40. |
| **P4403** EA-M | Crashed on landing at St Eval on return from a mining sortie 4.4.41. |
| **P4404** EA-R | FTR from attack on airfields in France 6/7.12.40. |
| **P4409** | To 50 Squadron. |
| **P4416** EA-L | FTR Berlin 25/26.8.40. |
| **P5324** EA-T | From 83 Squadron. FTR from shipping strike (Channel Dash) 12.2.42. |
| **X2900** EA-S | Crashed while landing at Abingdon after recall from a mining sortie 16/17.10.40. |
| **X2912** | From 61 Squadron. To 455 Squadron RAAF after conversion for use as torpedo bomber. |
| **X2959** | To 25 OTU. |
| **X2962** EA-D | Force-landed in Cornwall on return from Berlin 20/21.10.40. |
| **X2985** EA-W | FTR Danzig 10/11.11.40. |
| **X3001** EA-H | FTR Hanover 10/11.2.41. |
| **X3021** | To 106 Squadron. |
| **X3024** EA-H | FTR Lützkendorf 19/20.11.40. |
| **X3027** EA-A | Shot down by an intruder off Skegness on return from Hamburg 27/28.10.40. |
| **X3028** EA-S | Crashed near Dunholme Lodge on return from an operation to French aerodromes 7.12.40. |
| **X3029** EA-D | Crashed near Scampton soon after take-off when bound for Kiel 4.11.40. |
| **X3050** EA-N | FTR from operation against aerodromes in France 6/7.12.40. |
| **X3052** EA-C | FTR Hamburg 24/25.11.40. |
| **X3054** EA-S | Crashed in Devon on return from Lorient 21/22.3.41. |
| **X3057** EA-J | From 44 Squadron. To 420 (Snowy Owl) Squadron RCAF. |

| | |
|---|---|
| **X3060** | Crashed on landing at Scampton on return from mining sortie 26.6.41. |
| **X3063** | Crashed off Isle-of-Wight on return from Mannheim 16/17.12.40. |
| **X3134** EA-C | FTR Düsseldorf 30.6/1.7.41. |
| **X3135** | Crashed near Scampton during training 11.11.41. |
| **X3136** EA-K | Crash-landed in Norfolk on return from Berlin 3.9.41. |
| **X3151** EA-T | Crash-landed near Scampton on return from Hannover 26.7.41. |
| **AD719** EA-C | Shot down near Lincoln by intruder on return from Hannover 11.2.41. |
| **AD729** EA-N | FTR from mining sortie 27/28.5.41. |
| **AD733** EA-B | FTR Frankfurt 28/29.9.41. |
| **AD739** EA-A | FTR Brest 6/7.7.41. |
| **AD744** EA-Q | From 83 Squadron. Crashed in Scotland on return from a mining sortie 7.9.41. |
| **AD759** | Crashed in Lincolnshire while training 25.11.41. |
| **AD788** EA-V | FTR Kiel 25/26.6.41. |
| **AD792** | To 14 OTU. |
| **AD799** | From 106 Squadron. To 144 Squadron. |
| **AD805** EA-R | Crash-landed in Lincolnshire on return from Kassel 9.9.41. |
| **AD824** | From 50 Squadron. To 144 Squadron. |
| **AD842** | To 408 (Goose) Squadron RCAF. |
| **AD845** | To 14 OTU. |
| **AD856** EA-P | Shot down by intruder off Cromer on return from Osnabrück 6.7.41. |
| **AD865** | From 83 Squadron. To 455 Squadron RAAF after conversion for use as torpedo bomber. |
| **AD896** EA-M | Crashed on approach to Scampton during training flight 6.1.42. |
| **AD909** EA-G/H | FTR from mining sortie 9/10.1.42. |
| **AD910** EA-Y | Force-landed near Pocklington on return from Bremen 13.7.41. |
| **AD931** EA-X | FTR Dortmund 14/15.4.42. |
| **AD960** EA-L | To 420 (Snowy Owl) Squadron RCAF. |
| **AD964** | From 83 Squadron. To 144 Squadron. |
| **AD967** EA-H | Collided with X3121 (83 Squadron) over Lincolnshire on return from Düsseldorf 25.8.41. |
| **AD968** | From 420 (Snowy Owl) Squadron RCAF. To 408 (Goose) Squadron RCAF. |
| **AD971** EA-O | FTR Duisburg 28/29.8.41. |
| **AD973** | To 144 Squadron. |
| **AD974** | From 61Squadron. To 455Squadron. |
| **AD976** EA-D | To 455 Squadron RAAF after conversion for use as torpedo bomber. |
| **AD979** EA-W | To 144 Squadron. |
| **AD980** EA-V | To 408 (Goose) Squadron RCAF. |
| **AE123** | To 106 Squadron. |
| **AE126** EA-N | FTR Duisburg 28/29.8.41. |
| **AE132** EA-U | FTR from shipping strike (Channel Dash) 12.2.42. |
| **AE145** EA-I | To 455 Squadron RAAF after conversion for use as torpedo bomber. |
| **AE194** EA-T | To 455 Squadron RAAF after conversion for use as torpedo bomber. |
| **AE203** EA-F | Crash-landed in Suffolk on return from Berlin 3.9.41. |
| **AE224** EA-Z | FTR from Shipping strike off the Frisians 1/2.11.41. |
| **AE227** EA-O | To 408 (Goose) Squadron RCAF. |

| | |
|---|---|
| **AE236** EA-P | FTR Kiel 7/8.9.41. |
| **AE237** | To 83 Squadron. |
| **AE240** EA-P | FTR from shipping strike (Channel Dash) 12.2.42. |
| **AE241** | To 5 OTU after conversion for use as torpedo bomber. |
| **AE261** | From 106 Squadron. To 489 Squadron RNZAF after conversion for us as torpedo bomber. |
| **AE262** EA-Y | Crashed on landing at Scampton on return from Braunschweig 15.8.41. |
| **AE354** EA-S | Crashed on landing at Scampton during training 18.12.41. |
| **AE357** | Converted for use as torpedo bomber. |
| **AE368** | To 144 Squadron. |
| **AE372** | To 408 (Goose) Squadron RCAF. |
| **AE376** EA-E | Crashed in Lincolnshire soon after take-off for Frankfurt 29.9.41. |
| **AE396** EA-W | FTR from shipping strike (Channel Dash) 12.2.42. |
| **AE397** EA-G | Ditched off Isle of Wight on return from Mannheim 14/15.2.42. |
| **AE419** EA-T | FTR Hüls 28/29.12.41. |
| **AE421** EA-P | From 83 Squadron. FTR Essen 10/11.4.42. |
| **AT111** | To 489 Squadron RNZAF after conversion for use as torpedo bomber. |
| **AT112** EA-M | From 83 Squadron. Crashed near Upwood on return from Mannheim 15.2.42. |
| **AT118** | To 50 Squadron. |
| **AT124** EA-C | FTR from a mining sortie 16/17.2.42. |
| **AT126** EA-Z | FTR Essen 6/7.4.42. |
| **AT129** EA-O | From 83 Squadron. Crashed on take-off from Scampton when bound For Brest 25.1.42. |
| **AT148** EA-S | FTR Emden 20/21.1.42. |
| **AT150** | To 455 Squadron RAAF after conversion for use as torpedo bomber. |
| **AT156** EA-C | FTR Cologne 5/6.4.42. |
| **AT174** EA-E | FTR Essen 10/11.3.42. |
| **AT178** | From 106 Squadron. To 408 (Goose) Squadron RCAF. |
| **AT179** | To 408 (Goose) Squadron RCAF. |
| **AT180** | To 408 (Goose) Squadron RCAF. |
| **AT185** | To 420 (Snowy Owl) Squadron RCAF. |
| **AT190** EA-A | From 106 Squadron. FTR Essen 10/11.4.42. |
| **AT191** | From 106 Squadron. To 408 (Goose) Squadron RCAF. |
| **AT196** | Abandoned over Yorkshire on return from Essen 13.4.42. |
| **AT217** EA-S | FTR from a mining sortie 19/20.4.42. |
| **AT227** | To 408 (Goose) Squadron RCAF. |
| **AT228** | To 420 (Snowy Owl) Squadron RCAF. |

**MANCHESTER.** **From April 1942 to July 1942.**

| | |
|---|---|
| **L7281** | From 1654 Conversion Unit. No operations. To 1661 Conversion Unit. |
| **L7287** EA-G | FTR Emden 6/7.6.42. |
| **L7290** EA-K | From 97 (Straits Settlement) Squadron. FTR Cologne 30/31.5.42. |
| **L7293** | From 83 Squadron. To 61 Squadron. |
| **L7296** | Conversion Flight only. To 1661 Conversion Unit. |

| | |
|---|---|
| **L7325** | From 97 (Straits Settlement) Squadron via 25 OTU. No operations. Became ground instruction machine. |
| **L7386** | Crash-landed at Scampton during training 5.10.42. (May have been on 57 Squadron charge.) |
| **L7387** | From 83 Squadron. FTR from sea search 20.6.42. |
| **L7389** EA-L | From 83 Squadron. To 1660 Conversion Unit. |
| **L7397** | From 83 Squadron. Training only. To 207 Squadron. |
| **L7398** EA-W | From 106 Squadron. To 1661 Conversion Unit. |
| **L7420** | From 25 OTU. Training only. To 1660 Conversion Unit. |
| **L7421** EA-O | To 1660 Conversion Unit. |
| **L7429** EA-R | Conversion Flight only. FTR Cologne 30/31.5.42. |
| **L7453** EA-T | From 61 Squadron. To 1661 Conversion Unit . |
| **L7469** EA-I | To 50 Squadron and back. FTR Emden 6/7.6.42. |
| **L7479** EA-A | Ultimate fate unknown. |
| **L7484** | From 83 Squadron. Became ground instruction machine. |
| **L7493** EA-F | From 25 OTU. To 1661 Conversion Unit. |
| **L7515** | From 106 Squadron. To 1656 Conversion Unit after 22 operations. |
| **L7524** EA-X | From 25 OTU. To 1485 Flight. |
| **L7526** EA-V | From 25 OTU. To 207 Squadron. |
| **R5771** EA-E | From 25 OTU. To 420 (Snowy Owl) Squadron RCAF. |
| **R5772** EA-Z | From 25 OTU. Flew the last operation by a Manchester, to Bremen, 25/26.6.42. To 83 Squadron Conversion Flight. |
| **R5775** EA-N | To 83 Squadron. |
| **R5780** | From 83 Squadron. To 57 Squadron. |
| **R5788** EA-K | From 83 Squadron. Training only. To 1660 Conversion Unit. |
| **R5793** | From 25 OTU. Training only. To 83 Squadron. |
| **R5794** EA-S | From 25 OTU. FTR Essen 1/2.6.42. |
| **R5835** | From 83 Squadron. To 50 Squadron. |
| **R5836** | From 83 Squadron. To 1661 Conversion Unit. |
| **LANCASTER** | **From July 1942.** |
| **L7567** | From 44 (Rhodesia) Squadron. FTR Nuremberg 28/29.8.42. |
| **R5658** | To 1654 Conversion Unit. |
| **R5698** | Training only. To 1654 Conversion Unit. |
| **R5751** EA-E | To 57 Squadron after 21 operations. |
| **R5752** EA-D | Crash-landed at Martlesham Heath on return from Duisburg 7.9.42. |
| **R5757** | To 156 Squadron. |
| **R5762** EA-G | FTR Duisburg 20/21.12.42. |
| **R5763** EA-S | FTR Karlsruhe 2/3.9.42. |
| **R5842** | From 49 Conversion Flight. To 1661 Conversion Unit. |
| **R5850** | From 83 Squadron. Conversion flight only. To 1661 Conversion Unit. |
| **R5855** | From 83 Squadron. Conversion flight only. To 1661 Conversion Unit. |
| **R5889** | To 97 (Straits Settlement) Squadron. |
| **R5890** | FTR Essen 16/17.9.42. |
| **R5892** | To 1661 Conversion Unit. |

| | |
|---|---|
| **R5894** | To 9 Squadron. |
| **R5896** | To 97 (Straits Settlement) Squadron. |
| **R5897** | FTR Nuremberg 28/29.8.42. |
| **R5898** | 22 operations. To 44 (Rhodesia) Squadron. |
| **R5912** | 17 operations. To 156 Squadron. |
| **R5916** | To 9 Squadron and back. To 9 Squadron. |
| **W4104** | No operations. To 83 Squadron. |
| **W4107** EA-P | FTR Stuttgart 22/23.11.42. |
| **W4108** | To 1654 Conversion Unit. |
| **W4113** | 24 operations. To 156 Squadron. |
| **W4116** EA-I | FTR Wismar 12/13.10.42. |
| **W4129** | No operations. To 207 Squadron. |
| **W4140** | Conversion flight only. To 156 Squadron. |
| **W4181** | 19 operations. To 15 Squadron via 1660 Conversion Unit. |
| **W4183** | To 1661 Conversion Unit. |
| **W4196** | To 156 Squadron. |
| **W4235** | To 156 Squadron. |
| **W4245** | To 156 Squadron. |
| **W4258** | Conversion flight only. To 1661 Conversion Unit. |
| **W4306** | Crashed at Ford on return from Milan 24.10.42. |
| **W4314** | 11 operations. To 156 Squadron. |
| **W4761** | 18 operations. To 9 Squadron. |
| **W4773** EA-F | 16 operations. To 156 Squadron. |
| **W4822** | From 467 Squadron. To 57 Squadron. |
| **W4835** | To 97 (Straits Settlement) Squadron. |
| **W5010** | From Bombing Development Unit. To 9 Squadron. |
| **DV166** EA-F | To 44 (Rhodesia) Squadron. |
| **DV178** EA-N | To 617 Squadron on loan. Returned to 49 Squadron. To 50 Squadron. |
| **DV238** EA-D/O | From 619 Squadron. To 44 (Rhodesia) Squadron. |
| **ED310** EA-P | To 97 (Straits Settlement) Squadron. |
| **ED348** | To 57 Squadron. |
| **ED352** | To 57 Squadron. |
| **ED387** | To 50 Squadron. |
| **ED416** EA-J | FTR Mannheim 5/6.9.43. |
| **ED426** EA-P | FTR Stuttgart 7/8.10.43. |
| **ED427** EA-O | FTR Pilsen 16/17.4.43. |
| **ED428** EA-Q | Crashed on approach to Fiskerton on return from Hamburg 31.1.43. |
| **ED431** EA-M | FTR Essen 5/6.3.43. |
| **ED432** EA-R/N | FTR Oberhausen 14/15.6.43. |
| **ED434** EA-T | FTR Oberhausen 14/15.6.43. |
| **ED435** EA-G/K | FTR Berlin 29/30.3.43. |
| **ED438** EA-P/R | FTR Düsseldorf 3/4.11.43. |
| **ED440** EA-L | FTR Cologne 2/3.2.43. |
| **ED441** EA-D/E | FTR Pilsen 16/17.4.43. |
| **ED444** EA-B/C | FTR Berlin 17/18.1.43. |
| **ED445** EA-H | To 50 Squadron. |

| | | |
|---|---|---|
| **ED448** EA-M | Crash-landed at Dunholme Lodge after ferry flight 15.9.43. | |
| **ED450** EA-G | Hit balloon cables on return from Lorient 13/14.2.43 and crashed in the sea off Plymouth. | |
| **ED452** EA-F | Crashed on landing at Fiskerton following early return from Pilsen 14.5.43. | |
| **ED453** EA-G | FTR Oberhausen 14/15.6.43. | |
| **ED467** EA-E | FTR St Nazaire 28.2/1.3.43. | |
| **ED469** EA-A | FTR Berlin 29/30.3.43. | |
| **ED497** EA-C | FTR Cologne 16/17.6.43. | |
| **ED584** EA-U | FTR Bochum 12/13.6.43. | |
| **ED590** EA-L | FTR Duisburg 8/9.4.43. | |
| **ED597** EA-B | To 619 Squadron. | |
| **ED602** EA-B | From 83 Squadron. To 619 Squadron. | |
| **ED620** EA-K | FTR Stettin 20/21.4.43. | |
| **ED625** EA-R | FTR Nuremberg 10/11.8.43. | |
| **ED663** EA-O | FTR Cologne 8/9.7.43. | |
| **ED719** EA-K | FTR Mannheim 9/10.8.43. | |
| **ED721** EA-T | To 9 Squadron. | |
| **ED726** EA-V | FTR Turin 12/13.7.43. | |
| **ED756** | To 617 Squadron. | |
| **ED785** | FTR Cologne 16/17.6.43. | |
| **ED805** EA-S | FTR Peenemünde 17/18.8.43. | |
| **ED813** EA-W | FTR Dortmund 23/24.5.43. | |
| **ED999** EA-A | To 617 Squadron on loan. Returned to 49 Squadron. To 44 (Rhodesia) Squadron. | |
| **EE134** EA-B/Y | To 619 Squadron. | |
| **EE186** EA-U | To 106 Squadron. | |
| **JA690** EA-G | To 9 Squadron. | |
| **JA691** EA-L | FTR Peenemünde 17/18.8.43. | |
| **JA851** EA-P | FTR Peenemünde 17/18.8.43. | |
| **JA892** EA-O | FTR Peenemünde 17/18.8.43. | |
| **JA894** EA-C | To 617Squadron. | |
| **JA959** EA-C | From Bombing Development Unit. Became ground instruction machine. | |
| **JB126** EA-S | Ditched in North Sea on return from Berlin 3/4.9.43. | |
| **JB139** EA-U | To 617 Squadron. | |
| **JB144** | To 617 Squadron. | |
| **JB178** EA-V/U | FTR Revigny 18/19.7.44. | |
| **JB229** EA-S | Crashed on the beach at Chapel-St-Leonards on return from Berlin 24.11.43. | |
| **JB231** EA-N | FTR Berlin 2/3.1.44. | |
| **JB235** EA-B/C | Crashed on approach to Fiskerton on return from Berlin 27.11.43. | |
| **JB295** EA-R | FTR Brunswick 14/15.1.44. | |
| **JB301** | FTR Mannheim 23/24.9.43. | |
| **JB305** EA-E | FTR Düsseldorf 3/4.11.43. | |
| **JB314** EA-Q | FTR Nuremberg 30/31.3.44. | |
| **JB360** EA-M | FTR Berlin 27/28.1.44. | |

| | | |
|---|---|---|
| **JB362** EA-D | FTR Berlin 26/27.11.43. | |
| **JB368** EA-G | FTR Berlin 22/23.11.43. | |
| **JB371** EA-J | FTR Berlin 2/3.12.43. | |
| **JB399** EA-A/H | To 1653 Conversion Unit. | |
| **JB411** EA-L | Crashed on take-off from Fiskerton while training 18.10.43. | |
| **JB413** EA-P | FTR Kassel 22/23.10.43. | |
| **JB416** | FTR Kassel 22/23.10.43. | |
| **JB421** EA-K | FTR Salbris 7/8.5.44. | |
| **JB466** EA-A | FTR Nuremberg 30/31.3.44. | |
| **JB467** EA-T | FTR Frankfurt 20/21.12.43. | |
| **JB469** EA-B | FTR Leipzig 19/20.2.44. | |
| **JB473** EA-Q/U/W | FTR Revigny 18/19.7.44. | |
| **JB533** EA-P | Crashed on take-off from Fiskerton when bound for Modane 10.11.43. | |
| **JB545** EA-O | FTR Berlin 16/17.12.43. | |
| **JB679** EA-D | FTR Schweinfurt 26/27.4.44. | |
| **JB680** EA-P | FTR Essen 26/27.3.44. | |
| **JB701** EA-G | FTR Stuttgart 28/29.7.44. | |
| **JB710** EA-G | To 630 Squadron. | |
| **JB714** EA-J/K | FTR Etampes 9/10.6.44. | |
| **JB727** EA-S | FTR Berlin 2/3.1.44. | |
| **LL899** EA-P | FTR Aachen 11/12.4.44. | |
| **LL900** EA-T | FTR Wesseling 21/22.6.44. | |
| **LL908** EA-H | FTR Schweinfurt 26/27.4.44. | |
| **LL912** | Damaged in taxying accident at Fiskerton while training 8.5.44. | |
| **LL976** EA-A | FTR St Leu d'Esserent 7/8.7.44. | |
| **LM190** EA-R | To 1656 Conversion Unit. | |
| **LM191** | To 619 Squadron. | |
| **LM207** | To 619 Squadron. | |
| **LM306** EA-FE | To 44 (Rhodesia) Squadron. | |
| **LM337** EA-V | FTR Milan 15/16.8.43. | |
| **LM539** EA-D | FTR Duisburg 21/22.5.44. | |
| **LM541** EA-N | FTR St Leu d'Esserent 7/8.7.44. | |
| **LM572** EA-P | FTR Pommeréval 24/25.6.44. | |
| **LM648** EA-P | To 44 (Rhodesia) Squadron. | |
| **LM649** EA-T | To 630 Squadron. | |
| **LM653** EA-J | To 57 Squadron. | |
| **ME308** EA-F | FTR Nordhausen 4.4.45. | |
| **ME322** EA-A | | |
| **ME353** EA-Q | FTR Politz 8/9.2.45. | |
| **ME357** EA-U/C | From 460 Squadron RAAF. Crashed off Lincolnshire coast while training 19.4.45. | |
| **ME454** EA-E | From 227 Squadron. FTR Würzburg 16/17.3.45. | |
| **ME471** EA-K | | |
| **ME491** EA-P | | |
| **ME675** EA-R | FTR Wesseling 21/22.6.44. | |
| **ME787** | To 619 Squadron. | |

| | |
|---|---|
| **ME808** EA-D | FTR Wesseling 21/22.6.44. |
| **ND383** EA-E | To 1668 Conversion Unit. |
| **ND473** EA-O | To 467 Squadron RAAF. |
| **ND474** EA-T | FTR Stuttgart 15/16.3.44. |
| **ND498** EA-R | Crashed on take-off from Fiskerton when bound for Stuttgart 21.2.44. |
| **ND512** EA-C | To 1653 Conversion Unit. |
| **ND516** EA-N | FTR Leipzig 19/20.2.44. |
| **ND533** EA-M | FTR Etampes 9/10.6.44. |
| **ND536** EA-U/F | FTR Frankfurt 22/23.3.44. |
| **ND537** EA-S | FTR Munich 24/25.4.44. |
| **ND647** EA-N | To 1653 Conversion Unit. |
| **ND672** EA-F/U | FTR Frankfurt 22/23.3.44. |
| **ND676** EA-M | Crash-landed at Coltishall on return from Essen 26/27.3.44. |
| **ND677/G** | From 460 Squadron RAAF. To 115 Squadron. No operations. |
| **ND683** EA-K | Detached to 617 Squadron. Returned to 49 Squadron. FTR Wesseling 21/22.6.44. |
| **ND684** EA-V | FTR Revigny 18/19.7.44. |
| **ND687** EA-P | FTR Schweinfurt 26/27.4.44. |
| **ND695** EA-B | FTR Wesseling 21/22.6.44. |
| **ND713** | From 460 Squadron. One operation. |
| **ND787** EA-F | To 1668 Conversion Unit. |
| **ND791** | From 460 Squadron RAAF. |
| **ND792** EA-A | To 619 Squadron. |
| **ND957** EA-Q | To 619 Squadron. |
| **NE125** EA-K | FTR Brunswick 22/23.5.44. |
| **NE128** EA-J | FTR Wesseling 21/22.6.44. |
| **NE142** | From 460 Squadron RAAF. |
| **NE176** EA-V | From 460 Squadron RAAF via 1LFS. |
| **NG327** EA-E/K | FTR Mittelland Canal at Gravenhorst 21/22.2.45. |
| **NG352** EA-J | FTR Würzburg 16/17.3.45. |
| **NX581** EA-X | |
| **PB195** EA-P | FTR Creil (St Leu d'Esserent) 4/5.7.44. |
| **PB207** | Damaged beyond repair at St Leu d'Esserent 7/8.7.44. |
| **PB226** EA-F | From 460 Squadron RAAF. |
| **PB231** EA-H | FTR Revigny 18/19.7.44. |
| **PB250** EA-J | FTR Stuttgart 25/26.7.44. |
| **PB295** | To 207 Squadron. |
| **PB299** EA-K | To 467 Squadron RAAF. |
| **PB300** EA-K | FTR Mittelland Canal at Gravenhorst 21/22.11.44. |
| **PB306** EA-N | To 467 Squadron RAAF. |
| **PB347** EA-W | To 106 Squadron. |
| **PB348** | To 227 Squadron. |
| **PB349** EA-H | To 35 (Madras Presidency) Squadron. |
| **PB353** EA-E | FTR Bremen 6/7.10.44. |
| **PB354** EA-G | FTR Mittelland Canal at Gravenhorst 21/22.11.44. |
| **PB355** EA-B | Crashed on Worthing beach on early return from Munich 17.12.44. |

| | |
|---|---|
| **PB359** | To 106 Squadron. |
| **PB360** | To 44 (Rhodesia) Squadron. |
| **PB361** EA-R | From 35 (Madras presidency) Squadron. |
| **PB369** EA-A | FTR Harburg 11/12.11.44. |
| **PB370** EA-F | FTR Dortmund-Ems Canal at Ladbergen 4/5.11.44. |
| **PB373** EA-O | To 115 Squadron. |
| **PB374** EA-N | FTR Lützkendorf 8/9.4.45. |
| **PB383** EA-E | From 460 Squadron RAAF. |
| **PB385** EA-V | FTR Düsseldorf 2/3.11.44. |
| **PB406** EA-X/L | From 460 Squadron RAAF. |
| **PB429** EA-S | FTR Bremen 6/7.10.44. |
| **PB432** EA-O | Crashed in Lincolnshire soon after take-off from Fulbeck when bound for Munich 26.11.44. |
| **PB433** EA-L | To 115 Squadron. |
| **PB455** EA-W/V | To 115 Squadron. |
| **PB460** EA-R | |
| **PB463** EA-Y | From 460 Squadron RAAF. Crashed at Fulbeck during transit flight 22.4.45. |
| **PB479** EA-D | From 460 Squadron RAAF. |
| **PB484** EA-T | |
| **PB504** EA-U | |
| **PB519** EA-Q | Crashed on landing at Marston Moor on return from Bergen 29.10.44. |
| **PB522** | From 460 Squadron RAAF. No operations. |
| **PB537** EA-X | FTR Harburg 7/8.3.45. |
| **PB559** EA-B | From 460 Squadron RAAF. |
| **PB568** EA-Y | FTR Mittelland Canal at Gravenhorst 21/22.2.45. |
| **PB571** EA-Z | To 115 Squadron. |
| **PB586** EA-E/V | FTR Munich 7/8.1.45. |
| **PB791** EA-V | |
| **PB797** EA-K | |
| **PB799** EA-G | FTR from night flying training 11.12.44. |
| **PB844** EA-D | To 57 Squadron. |
| **PB873** EA-N | From 460 Squadron RAAF. |
| **PB875** EA-G | From 460 Squadron RAAF. |
| **PB907** EA-Q | To 115 Squadron. |
| **RA531** EA-R/S | FTR Lützkendorf 8/9.4.45. |
| **RF153** EA-K | From 50 Squadron. FTR Lützkendorf 14/15.3.45. |
| **RF179** EA-Y | |
| **RF215** EA-E | |
| **RF216** EA-J | |
| **SW256** EA-C | From 1661 Conversion Unit. To 57 Squadron. |
| **SW265** EA-B | To 106 Squadron. |
| **SW274** EA-G | |

**HEAVIEST SINGLE LOSS.** 21/22.06.44. Wesseling. 6 Lancasters FTR.

# Key to Abbreviations

| | |
|---|---|
| **A&AEE** | Aeroplane and Armaments Experimental Establishment. |
| **AA** | Anti-Aircraft fire. |
| **AACU** | Anti-Aircraft Cooperation Unit. |
| **AAS** | Air Armament School. |
| **AASF** | Advance Air Striking Force. |
| **AAU** | Aircraft Assembly Unit. |
| **ACM** | Air Chief Marshal. |
| **ACSEA** | Air Command South-East Asia. |
| **AFDU** | Air Fighting Development Unit. |
| **AFEE** | Airborne Forces Experimental Unit. |
| **AFTDU** | Airborne Forces Tactical Development Unit. |
| **AGS** | Air Gunners School. |
| **AMDP** | Air Members for Development and Production. |
| **AOC** | Air Officer Commanding. |
| **AOS** | Air Observers School. |
| **ASRTU** | Air-Sea Rescue Training Unit. |
| **ATTDU** | Air Transport Tactical Development Unit. |
| **AVM** | Air Vice-Marshal. |
| **BAT** | Beam Approach Training. |
| **BCBS** | Bomber Command Bombing School. |
| **BCDU** | Bomber Command Development Unit. |
| **BCFU** | Bomber Command Film Unit. |
| **BCIS** | Bomber Command Instructors School. |
| **BDU** | Bombing Development Unit. |
| **BSTU** | Bomber Support Training Unit. |
| **CF** | Conversion Flight. |
| **CFS** | Central Flying School. |
| **CGS** | Central Gunnery School. |
| **C-in-C** | Commander in Chief. |
| **CNS** | Central Navigation School. |
| **CO** | Commanding Officer. |
| **CRD** | Controller of Research and Development. |
| **CU** | Conversion Unit. |
| **DGRD** | Director General for Research and Development. |
| **EAAS** | Empire Air Armament School. |
| **EANS** | Empire Air Navigation School. |
| **ECDU** | Electronic Countermeasures Development Unit. |
| **ECFS** | Empire Central Flying School. |
| **ETPS** | Empire Test Pilots School. |
| **F/L** | Flight Lieutenant. |
| **Flt** | Flight. |
| **F/O** | Flying Officer. |
| **FPP** | Ferry Pilots School. |

| | |
|---|---|
| **F/S** | Flight Sergeant. |
| **FTR** | Failed to Return. |
| **FTU** | Ferry Training Unit. |
| **G/C** | Group Captain. |
| **Gp** | Group. |
| **HCU** | Heavy Conversion Unit. |
| **HGCU** | Heavy Glider Conversion Unit. |
| **LFS** | Lancaster Finishing School. |
| **MAC** | Mediterranean Air Command. |
| **MTU** | Mosquito Training Unit. |
| **MU** | Maintenance Unit. |
| **NTU** | Navigation Training Unit. |
| **OADU** | Overseas Aircraft Delivery Unit. |
| **OAPU** | Overseas Aircraft Preparation Unit. |
| **OTU** | Operational Training Unit. |
| **P/O** | Pilot Officer. |
| **PTS** | Parachute Training School. |
| **RAE** | Royal Aircraft Establishment. |
| **SGR** | School of General Reconnaissance. |
| **Sgt** | Sergeant. |
| **SHAEF** | Supreme Headquarters Allied Expeditionary Force. |
| **SIU** | Signals Intelligence Unit. |
| **S/L** | Squadron Leader. |
| **SOC** | Struck off Charge. |
| **SOE** | Special Operations Executive. |
| **Sqn** | Squadron. |
| **TF** | Training Flight. |
| **TFU** | Telecommunications Flying Unit. |
| **W/C** | Wing Commander. |
| **Wg** | Wing. |
| **WIDU** | Wireless Intelligence Development Unit. |
| **W/O** | Warrant Officer. |

www.ingramcontent.com/pod-product-compliance
Lightning Source LLC
Chambersburg PA
CBHW081207230426
43666CB00015B/2670